PRINCIPLES OF PROGRAMMING LANGUAGES: Design, Evaluation, and Implementation

SECOND EDITION

Bruce J. MacLennan
NAVAL POSTGRADUATE SCHOOL

HOLT, RINEHART AND WINSTON
New York Chicago San Francisco Philadelphia
Montreal Toronto London Sydney
Tokyo Mexico City Rio de Janeiro Madrid

To Gail

Publisher: Ted Buchholz
Senior Acquisitions Editor: Myles Thompson
Production Manager: Paul Nardi
Project Editor: Melinda Wirkus
Composition: Meridian

Library of Congress Cataloging in Publication Data

MacLennan, Bruce J.
Principles of programming languages (second edition).

Includes bibliography p. 549. Includes index.
1. Programming languages (Electronic computers)
I. Title.
QA76.7.M33 1986 005.13 86-22942
ISBN 0-03-005163-0

Address correspondence to:
383 Madison Avenue
New York, New York 10017

Printed in the United States of America
Published simultaneously in Canada

7 8 9 039 9 8 7 6 5 4 3 2

CBS COLLEGE PUBLISHING
Holt, Rinehart & Winston
The Dryden Press
Saunders College Publishing

CONTENTS

PREFACE TO THE SECOND EDITION

Another damned, thick, square book! Always scribble, scribble, scribble! Eh! Mr. Gibbon?

—Duke of Gloucester (1743–1805)

There is virtue in small books. There is also a disconcerting tendency for books to get longer with each succeeding edition. I have attempted to combat that tendency in the second edition of *Principles of Programming Languages.*

In particular, I have resisted the temptation to discuss additional programming languages. The reason is that the languages are the means rather than the end. Every language I've included, in addition to being well-known or important in its own right, is intended to illustrate a number of important language design principles. In the interests of economy I've attempted to use the minimum number of languages that cover the relevant topics. Any more would be superfluous.

On the other hand, I have expanded the discussion on several topics included in the first edition, specifically functional programming, Smalltalk, and Prolog, to reflect the increasing importance of these fifth-generation programming languages.

Another way in which the text has been expanded is by the inclusion of over 140 new exercises, especially ones that are not open-ended "thought questions." Although I prefer essay-like thought questions, I realize that they may be inappropriate in an environment characterized by large class size, for which short-answer and mathematical exercises are more appropriate.

Finally, I have attempted to make it apparent that the book's structure is a series of *case studies* illustrating the five principal programming language generations. To this end I have added to the chapters for each generation a summary of its salient characteristics.

I am grateful to a host of reviewers, colleagues, and students who suggested many of the changes incorporated in this second edition. Such customer feedback is very valuable. I am especially grateful to my wife Gail, who spent many long evenings proofreading and indexing. She has contributed to the completion of this second edition in these and many other ways.

PREFACE

PURPOSE

The purpose of this book is to teach the skills required to design and implement programming languages. *Design* is an important topic for all computer science students regardless of whether or not they will ever have to create a programming language. The user who understands the motivation for various language facilities will be able to use them more intelligently. The compiler writer who understands the motivation for these facilities will be able to implement them more reasonably. *Implementation* is also an important topic since the language designer must be aware of the costs of the facilities provided. Both topics are important to all computer scientists because all computer scientists use languages and because there is an increasing number of language-like human interfaces (word processors, command languages, etc.) that require these skills in their development. Thus, this book treats the design and implementation of programming languages as fundamental skills that all computer scientists should possess.

All designers, whether architects, aeronautical engineers, electrical engineers, and so on, require *descriptive skills*, techniques, and notations for communicating their ideas to their clients, to other designers, and to implementers. The ability of descriptive tools to abstract important characteristics of a design and omit irrelevant details makes these tools valuable for *comparing* and *evaluating* designs. Thus, this book aims to teach the descriptive tools important to programming language design and implementation.

History is an important aspect of any design discipline. Often the designs used in the past can only be understood in their historical context. Also, it is important that the student be aware of the designs tried in the past and why they succeeded or failed. Thus, this book presents language facilities and styles in their historical context.

SCOPE

In a rapidly moving field such as computer science, there is a danger that any book will be out of date in a few years. Worse, there is the danger that a computer scientist's knowledge will soon be out of date. It is therefore imperative that we teach principles of enduring value rather than technical details that are soon obsolete. As a result, the implementation techniques discussed in this book are seminal; they form the basis of techniques that are likely to be useful for a long time to come and that can be varied to achieve a wide range of goals. *Principles are emphasized more than details.*

However, this alone is not sufficient to prevent the explosion of knowledge. Rather than trying to present all of the important language styles, language facilities, descriptive tools, and implementation techniques, this book instructs the student in the creation of these things. In the long run this will be much more valuable, since most of the specific techniques we teach will become obsolete. The techniques become obsolete in part because of the activity of those who can create new techniques. *Methods are emphasized more than results.*

Experience with programming languages has shown that although the syntactic form of a language is important, the real effectiveness of a language is determined by its semantics. In other words, what we say is more important than exactly the way we say it. For this reason, this book compares and evaluates languages on the basis of what can be said in the language rather than the details of their syntax. By the same token, the implementation of semantics (i.e., the run-time organization) is stressed at the expense of the implementation of syntax (i.e., parsing). *Semantics is emphasized more than syntax.*

ORGANIZATION

There are two basic ways a programming language text can present the characteristics of a number of languages: horizontally and vertically. In a vertical organization, various language topics are treated one by one, tracing each through several languages. For example, one chapter may treat procedures, discussing their characteristics in FORTRAN, Algol, and Pascal. Another chapter may discuss scope in FORTRAN, Algol, and LISP, and so forth, for all the various facilities. One danger of a vertical organization is that it is apt to degenerate into a catalog of features.

A horizontal organization treats languages as wholes. For example, one chapter would discuss FORTRAN, covering procedures, scope, and other important characteristics. Another chapter would discuss Algol, another Pascal, and so on. A horizontal organization is used in this book because it facilitates discussing the interrelationships between the parts of a programming language. This often overlooked aspect of language design is the cause of many unforeseen complications. The horizontal approach is also necessary if languages are to be considered in their historical context.

The importance of historical context leads to another organizing principle, summarized as: *ontogeny recapitulates phylogeny.* This principle means that if in the learning process, the student repeats in summary form the historical learning process in the computer science field, he or she will have a firmer grasp of the subject. This does not mean that the student must be exposed to every mistake and explore every dead end in the field of programming languages; ontogeny *recapitulates* phylogeny, it does not duplicate it. Therefore this book is organized around a stripped down, or pruned, history of programming languages that allows the student to see issues in their historical context and to appreciate the way languages evolve.

Each technical field has its own set of peculiar concepts and terminology; programming language design is no exception. Some of these concepts are of utmost importance; others are details of transient value. It is crucial that the language designer understand the important concepts fully, in all of their ramifications. For this to be the case, each concept must be seen and investigated several times in a number of different contexts. When students finally see a formal definition of a concept in its full generality they will understand its implications; it will not seem arbitrary, as definitions so often do. Thus, an inductive, or bottom-up, approach is used for presenting concepts and abstractions.

Conversely, a top-down approach is used for presenting the structures and facilities that are found in programming languages. The reason is that a programming language facility or feature is best understood in context, that is, in terms of its function with respect to the rest of the language and the goals of the language. Thus, structures and facilities are presented in their functional context. This will help the student to understand the language as a unified whole.

The result of these considerations is that the book as a whole is organized horizontally, and each chapter is organized vertically. That is, each language is analyzed into its major structural subsystems.

In all cases the goal has been to give the student a comprehensive understanding of the most important aspects of programming language design and implementation.

This book is intended for a one-semester course; for shorter courses some of the later chapters (such as Chapters 12 or 13) can be omitted if necessary. It is suggested that, no matter what else is skipped, time be reserved at the end of the course for discussing the content of Chapter 14, "Principles of Language Design."

Most of the problems are practical exercises in language design. They could form the basis for a separate language-design laboratory or for classroom discussion. In a few cases they are potential thesis topics.

In accord with the book's goal of emphasizing broad principles rather than details, no language is presented in full. The student will not find syntax charts for FORTRAN, Pascal, or Ada. Further, it is unlikely that students will be able to program in any of these languages solely on the basis of their description here. Instead, students will learn the fundamental concepts of programming languages, which will simplify their learning the details of whatever languages they may have to use.

To make this book more versatile, a concept directory has been included in addition to the more conventional index and table of contents. This is a vertically organized outline of topics in language design. With it students can find, for example, all of the sections describing parameter passing modes.

ACKNOWLEDGMENTS

Several generations of students in my introductory programming languages course at the Naval Postgraduate School have lived through early drafts of this book. Their comments, criticisms, and tolerance are gratefully acknowledged.

R. W. Hamming has contributed substantially to the completion of this book through his encouragement, insightful reviews of early drafts, and many discussions of the philosophy of book writing. I take this opportunity to thank him publicly. Any errors or inadequacies are, of course, my own responsibility.

Most important, I thank my wife, Gail, without whose constant support this book might not have been completed.

CONCEPT DIRECTORY

I. HISTORY, MOTIVATION, AND EVALUATION

Note: Page numbers denote the entire subsection that begins on the specified page.

II. DESIGN AND IMPLEMENTATION

III. PRINCIPLES

IV. IMPLEMENTATION

INTRODUCTION

WHAT IS A PROGRAMMING LANGUAGE?

The subject of this book is programming languages, specifically, the principles for their design, evaluation, and implementation. Thus, we must begin by saying what a programming language is.

A programming language is a language intended for the description of programs. Often a program is expressed in a programming language so that it can be executed on a computer. This is not the only use of programming languages, however. They may also be used by people to describe programs to other people. Indeed, since much of a programmer's time is spent reading programs, the understandability of a programming language to people is often more important than its understandability to computers.

There are many languages that people use to control and interact with computers. These can all be referred to as *computer languages*. Many of these languages are used for special purposes, for example, for reserving seats on airplanes, conducting transactions with a bank, or generating reports. These special-purpose languages are not *programming* languages because they cannot be used for general programming. We reserve the term *programming language* for a computer language that can be used, at least in principle, to express any computer program.[1] Thus, our final definition is:

A programming language is a language that is intended for the expression of computer programs and that is capable of expressing any computer program.

THE DIFFERENCES AMONG PROGRAMMING LANGUAGES

Since, by definition, any programming language can be used to express any program, it follows that all programming languages are equally powerful—any program that can be written in one can also be written in another. Why, then, are there so many programming languages? And why should one study their differences, when in this very fundamental sense they are all the same? The reason is that, although it's possible to write any program in any programming language, it's not equally *easy* to do so. Thus, in this book, we will not be very concerned with the *theoretical* power of programming languages (they're all the same). Rather, we concentrate on their *practical* power, as real tools used by real people. In this regard they will be seen to differ in many important respects. But why devote so much time to just one kind of tool?

IMPORTANCE OF THE STUDY OF PROGRAMMING LANGUAGES

Programming languages are important for students in all disciplines of computer science because they are the primary tools of the central activity of computer science: programming. As a result, the progress of computer science can be traced in the progress of programming languages, and many issues of computer science manifest themselves as programming language issues. This is particularly true in programming methodology, where advances in languages and programming techniques have gone hand in hand. The reason is simple: Programming languages remain the focal point of the problem-solving process of computer science.

1 This is not a vague notion. There is a precise theoretical way of determining whether a computer language can be used to express any program, namely, by showing that it is equivalent to a universal Turing machine. This topic is beyond the scope of this book.

INFLUENCE OF LANGUAGES ON PROBLEM SOLVING

The Sapir–Whorf hypothesis is a (still controversial) linguistic theory that states that the structure of language defines the boundaries of thought. While there is no evidence that the use of a particular language will prevent us from thinking certain thoughts, it is the case that a given language can facilitate or impede certain modes of thought. When applied to programming languages, the analogous statement is that while no programming language can prevent us from finding certain solutions to a problem, a given language can influence the class of solutions we are likely to see. This topic is discussed in more depth later when unconventional languages, such as LISP, are studied.

BENEFITS FOR ALL COMPUTER SCIENTISTS

The study of programming languages is important to anyone who uses them, that is, anyone who programs. The reason is that from this study you will learn the motivation for and the use of the most important facilities found in modern programming languages. You will learn the benefits of these facilities, as well as their costs, by studying the techniques used to implement them. This will provide you with a basis for evaluating languages, which will aid you in choosing the best language for your application. The understanding acquired of the motivations for the facilities in a language will enable you to use those facilities to their fullest potential. The repertoire of language mechanisms with which you are familiar will have been increased so that even if the language you must use does not provide the facilities you need, you will be able to simulate them through your knowledge of their implementation.

There are many programming languages now in widespread use—many more than can be taught to you as part of your computer science education. This means that from time to time in your computer science career you will be required to learn a new programming language and to put it to effective use. Your speed in learning new languages is one aspect of your versatility as a computer scientist. Now it is a fact that underneath the surface details most languages are very similar. Therefore, the study of programming languages, by increasing the range of facilities in which you are fluent, will enable you to see more that is familiar in any new language that you encounter. This will speed your learning of new languages.

BENEFITS FOR LANGUAGE DESIGNERS

Although, as indicated above, the study of programming languages is important to all students of computer science, it is especially important to certain disciplines. Obviously, it is important if you are a student of language design. All engineering design is a cumulative process; we learn from the successes and failures of the designs of the past. To this end it is necessary to be familiar with the history of programming languages. As George Santayana said, "Those who cannot remember the past are condemned to repeat it." An understanding of the reasons why certain designs have been tried in the past and later abandoned will help you to develop a sense of good language design and to become skillful in making design trade-offs. To help you remember the lessons of the past, we have formulated and illustrated a number of *maxims* or *principles* of good programming language design. The central role these play has dictated the book's title: *Principles of Programming Languages.*

BENEFITS FOR LANGUAGE IMPLEMENTERS

If you are interested in language implementation, you will gain insight into the motivations for various language facilities, thus allowing you to make reasonable implementation trade-offs. You will also learn the most useful and important techniques for implementing a number of common programming language facilities. These will be seminal techniques that can be elaborated to satisfy more stringent requirements or varied to solve related problems.

BENEFITS FOR HARDWARE ARCHITECTS

By understanding the requirements of programming language implementation, hardware architects will gain insight into the ways machines may better support languages. More important, you will learn to design a semantically coherent machine—a machine with complete and coherent sets of data types and operations on those data types. The reason for this is simple. Just as a programming language can be considered a *virtual computer,* that is, a computer implemented in software, so a computer can be considered a programming language implemented in hardware. This view suggests that many of the principles of programming language design can be equally well applied to computer architecture, and indeed they can.

BENEFITS FOR SYSTEM DESIGNERS

Designers of all sorts of systems (e.g., operating systems and database systems) will learn principles and techniques applicable to all human interfaces. Many systems, including job control languages, database systems, editors, text formatters, and debuggers, have many of the characteristics of a programming language. The study of both language design and implementation is obviously valuable here. Knowledge of programming languages is more directly necessary for designers of file systems, linkage editors, and other software that must interface with programming languages.

BENEFITS FOR SOFTWARE MANAGERS

Finally, if you manage software development efforts, then you will benefit in several ways from the study of programming languages. The project manager often makes decisions regarding the language to be used on a given project, or whether an existing language should be used or extended, or whether a completely new language should be designed. You will be better able to do this if you know what common languages can and cannot do, and if you know the current direction and state of the art of programming language research. You will be better able to make these decisions if you know the costs of designing or extending a language, the costs of implementing a language, and the benefits of various language facilities.

PLAN OF THE BOOK

In 1965 an American Mathematical Association Prospectus estimated that 1700 programming languages were then in use.[2] In the intervening years, many more have been invented. Clearly, it is impossible to discuss every language, or even a sizable fraction of them. How have we chosen the languages to present in this book?

2 Quoted in P. J. Landin, "The Next 700 Programming Languages," *Comm. ACM* 9, 3 (March 1966), p. 157.

Certainly, we have chosen languages of actual or potential importance. All other things being equal, we have chosen languages that you are likely to encounter in your career as a computer scientist. But there are other, more important factors in our selection.

An understanding of these factors is implicit in the purpose of this book—which is not to teach you to program in half a dozen programming languages. As noted before, there is little chance that we could teach you just those languages you will later need to know. Rather, our goal is to present the most important principles for the design, evaluation, and implementation of programming languages. To this end, we have chosen languages that will serve as good *case studies* to illustrate these principles.

These principles have developed in a series of historical stages, each being a reaction to the perceived problems of the previous stage. For this reason, we have chosen programming languages that are illustrative of the major generations of programming language evolution. Thus, FORTRAN, Algol-60, Pascal, and Ada are representatives of the first, second, third, and fourth programming language generations.[3] We have picked these particular languages because they form a single evolutionary line in the family tree of programming languages.

Since language development is just entering the fifth generation, it is too early to predict what the next stage in programming language evolution will be. Therefore, we have illustrated the fifth generation with representatives of three important new programming paradigms: function-oriented programming (LISP), object-oriented programming (Smalltalk), and logic-oriented programming (PROLOG). It is likely that all three of these paradigms will be important in the years to come.

3 Note that some authors use the term *fourth-generation language* to refer to various application generation packages. These are not *programming* languages in the sense referred to previously; we are discussing fourth-generation *programming* languages.

1

THE BEGINNING: PSEUDO-CODE INTERPRETERS

1.1 HISTORY AND MOTIVATION

Programming Is Difficult

Almost as soon as the first computers were built, it became obvious that programming was very difficult; this fact has not changed. Indeed, the tasks we have attempted to accomplish with computers have grown rapidly in ambitiousness and size. Much of the difficulty of programming stems from *complexity,* the necessity of dealing with many different details at one time. Programs may contain hundreds of thousands, or even millions, of lines of code. Considering these lines (together with the operators and operands that make them up) as parts that must be assembled individually to make a program work correctly leads to the conclusion that programs are some of the most complicated artifacts ever built. One of the primary tasks of programming languages is the conquest of this complexity.

Programming Early Computers Was Especially Difficult

Although the problems addressed on early computers were smaller than many of those now addressed, programming was still very difficult. Part of the reason was that early computers had very little storage; a few thousand words were considered a large memory. Thus, compact code was a necessity. Also, by modern standards the early computers were very slow, so it was important that programs be coded very efficiently. Finally, early computers were more complicated to program than the ones with which we are now familiar.

As an example of this complexity, some of the drum computers (which stored both the data and the program on a rotating drum) had a *four-address* instruction code, which means that each instruction contained the address of the next instruction to execute. This permitted a process called *optimal coding.* This means that when programmers coded, for example, an ADD instruction, they would determine how far the drum had rotated while that ADD instruction was being executed. They would then use that drum location for the next instruction after the ADD, placing its address in the ADD instruction. In this way the next instruction was always under the drum head when it was ready to be executed, thus saving wasted drum revolutions and greatly increasing the speed of the program. Aside from the difficulty of doing the calculations, there were always complications. For example, the optimal location for the next instruction might already be occupied, in which case the next available location in that track had to be used. Figure 1.1 shows a small part of a program written in the mid-1950s for the IBM 650. Notice that each instruction contains in its rightmost field (INST) the address of the next instruction (LOC).

Needless to say, programming these machines was a tedious and error-prone process. Much of it was done without the aid of any software tools, including assemblers. There were other complications in programming these machines. For example, since the bits of an instruction often directly controlled the opening and closing of gates in the central processor, the codes used for various operations appeared to the programmer to follow no simple rule. This apparent irregularity made them very difficult to remember.

Many Program Design Notations Were Developed

The complexity of programming led to the development of *program design notations,* the precursors of programming languages. One of the earliest of these was von Neumann and Goldstine's *flow diagrams,* which developed into the flowcharts that are still often used during program design. Throughout the world, many different notations and languages were developed to try to conquer the

LOC	OP	DATA	INST	COMMENTS
1107	46	1112	1061	Shall the loop box be used?
1061	30	0003	1019	
1019	20	1023	1026	Store C.
1026	60	8003	1033	
1033	30	0003	1041	
1041	20	1045	1048	Store B.
1048	60	8003	1105	
1105	30	0003	1063	
1063	44	1067	1076	Is an 02-operation called for?
1067	10	1020	8003	
8003	69	8002	1061	Go to an 01-subroutine.

Figure 1.1 Part of an IBM 650 Program

complexity of programming. Some of these helped the programmer to design the memory layout and control flow of the program without being concerned with details (such as optimal coding). Others provided mnemonics for the machine operations, much like an assembly language. Konrad Zuse, in Germany, developed a sophisticated programming notation that included a data structure definition facility. He even outlined methods for compiling this notation in 1945! By and large, however, these languages and notations were intended for use by people during the design process, not for direct processing by the computer. The actual coding process was still done in numeric codes or with the aid of simple "assembly programs" (assemblers).

Floating Point and Indexing Were Simulated

The earliest computers did not have built-in floating-point operations; these did not appear until the IBM 704 in 1953. On the other hand, the primary application of many of these machines was in scientific and numerical computations, which require numbers of a wide range of magnitudes. This necessitated *manual scaling,* a technique in which numbers were multiplied by scale factors in order to keep them within the range of the integer arithmetic facilities of the computer. This was a very complicated process, which required a detailed analysis of the algorithm. The difficulty of manual scaling led to the development of floating-point subroutines, that is, of subroutines for performing basic floating-point operations (addition, subtraction, multiplication, division, square root, etc.).

Although these often slowed down a program by at least an order of magnitude, they so simplified the programming of numerical problems that they were widely used.

Another facility missing from many early computers was *indexing*, the ability to add a variable index quantity to a fixed address in order to address an element of an array. You are probably aware from your own programming experience that the array is one of the most common data structures; it was even more common in the scientific and numerical problems that dominated the use of early computers. Now, one of the important ideas of von Neumann, and one of the distinguishing characteristics of a *von Neumann machine* (which includes most computers), is that the program and data are stored in the same memory. Therefore, it is possible for a program to modify itself or another program as though it were data. Since most early computers did not have index registers or indexed addressing modes as do modern computers, it was necessary to accomplish indexing through *address modification*. That is, the program would add the index to the address part of a data accessing instruction. Needless to say, this was an error-prone process. It also consumed much of the scarce memory with this address modification code. For this reason, it was also common to use subroutines to perform indexing. You can probably imagine that since floating-point operations and indexing account for much of what is done in numerical algorithms, most of the actual execution time was spent inside the floating-point and indexing subroutines. This justified the use of pseudo-code interpreters, which we will discuss next.

Pseudo-Code Interpreters Were Invented

It was quickly recognized that consistent use of the floating-point and indexing subroutines simplified the programming process; it allowed one to program as though these facilities were provided by the hardware of the computer. This led to the idea of a *pseudo-code*, that is, an instruction code that is different from that provided by the machine—and presumably better. Since the program was going to spend most of its time in the floating-point and indexing subroutines anyway, why not simplify programming by providing an entire new instruction code that was easier to use than the machine's own? This idea was first described in the famous Appendix D of the first programming book, *The Preparation of Programs for an Electronic Digital Computer*, written by Wilkes, Wheeler, and Gill in 1951. This appendix described the design of a simple pseudo-code and the design of an "interpretive subroutine" for executing that pseudo-code—what we now call an *interpreter*. There is some indication that the authors did not realize the full significance of what they were describing, otherwise they wouldn't have buried it in Appendix D. They present interpreters primarily as a means of saving memory since the pseudo-code is more compact than the machine's real instruction code. Other programmers soon grasped the importance of this idea and many pseudo-code interpreters sprang into existence. Later in this chapter, we will investigate the design and implementation of one of these.

The significance of these pseudo-code interpreters is that they implemented a *virtual computer* with its own set of data types (e.g., floating point) and operations (e.g., indexing) in terms of the *real computer* with its own data types and operations. One advantage of the virtual computer over the real computer was that it was *higher level;* that is, it provided facilities more suitable to the applications and it eliminated many details from programming. This is an example of the Automation Principle.

The Automation Principle

Automate mechanical, tedious, or error-prone activities.

The virtual computer was also more *regular,* that is, simpler to understand through the absence of special cases. We will see that all programming languages can be viewed as defining a virtual computer that is better in some respects than the real computer. Although the interpreter usually ran at least a factor of 10 slower than the real computer, most of this time was spent in the floating-point and indexing routines that were considered necessary anyway. Thus, pseudo-code interpreters were a valuable programming aid that imposed little additional cost.

Compiling Routines Were Also Used

At this same time, another approach was being used for implementing pseudo-codes—*compiling routines.* G. M. Hopper and others began to use programs to extract subroutines from libraries and combine them (a process called compiling) under the direction of a pseudo-code. Since this process was done once at compiling time, it did not involve the overhead that resulted from interpretation. Therefore, the compiled program would run considerably faster than an interpreted program. Perhaps because this approach did not encourage programmers to look at a pseudo-code as a virtual computer, it did not produce pseudo-codes that were as regular. For this reason we will concentrate on interpreters in this chapter. We will return to compiling routines when we discuss FORTRAN, since they developed into what we now call *compilers.*

1.2 DESIGN OF A PSEUDO-CODE

A Linear, Card-Oriented, Fixed-Format Syntax Is Used

In this section we design a pseudo-code. It is similar to real pseudo-codes, the language L_1 and L_2 designed by Bell Labs for the IBM 650 in 1955 and 1956. In Section 1.3 we discuss the design of an interpreter for this pseudo-code.

For the sake of the example, we will assume that we are designing this pseudo-code for a computer with 2000 words of 10-digit memory; this was the capacity of the 650 and is a reasonable assumption for machines of that vintage. Of course, we will want our virtual computer to provide the facilities found in any computer, such as arithmetic, control of execution flow, and input-output, but in a more regular fashion than real computers. So let's begin by making a list of some of the functions our pseudo-code should accommodate:

- Floating-point arithmetic ($+$, $-$, $\times$, $\div$, square root)
- Floating-point comparisons ($=$, $\neq$, $<$, $>$, $\leqslant$, $\geqslant$)
- Indexing
- Transfer of control
- Input-output

What syntax should be used for this pseudo-code? Since many early computers did not have facilities for alphabetic input-output, we will have to use a numeric code for the statements of the language. Furthermore, since the most common input devices were card readers, we will adopt the convention of writing one number (representing an operation) on each card. Next, if we suppose that each operation will be represented by one word, we will have 10 digits with which to represent each operation. How large will the addresses be? Two digits are clearly insufficient; they would only allow 100 locations to be addressed. Four digits are too much since they would permit addressing 10,000 locations and there are only 2000 in the machine. So three digits seems the right choice; it permits addressing 1000 locations, which is adequate (at least it was considered adequate at that time), and leaves the other 1000 locations for the interpreter and program. If the first 1000 locations are used for data, then three digits will not allow addressing out of the data area. This is an example of *security.* In this case we have made it impossible for the user to commit a particular class of errors: overwriting the program or the interpreter. Thus, it is an example of the Security Principle, which was first proposed by C. A. R. Hoare:

> ***The Security Principle***
>
> No program that violates the definition of the language, or its own intended structure, should escape detection.

Instruction Format

Let's consider the form of the arithmetic operations since they will be the most common. The instructions could have two, three, or four addresses:

- Two addresses: $x + y \rightarrow x$
- Three addresses: $x + y \rightarrow z$
- Four addresses: $x + y - z \rightarrow w$

Each of these addresses must be represented in an instruction. Therefore, four-address instructions require 12 digits for the operand addresses, too much to fit in a 10-digit word. Two-address instructions will work since they only require six digits for the operand addresses, although this leaves four digits for the operation, which is excessive. This would allow 10,000 operations, and we only have 13 in our list. Three-address instructions will consume nine digits for the operands, leaving one for the operations. This one digit, together with the sign, will allow the encoding of 20 operations, which is adequate for our purposes. This leads to the following format for our arithmetic instructions:

s op opn1 opn2 dest

where *s* is the sign, *op* is the operation, *opn1* and *opn2* are the operands (x and y), and *dest* is the destination (z). For instance, if $+1$ means addition, then

```
+1 010 150 200
```

would add the contents of location 010 to the contents of location 150 and store the result in location 200 (we have added blanks to the code to make it more readable).

Orthogonal Design

Since we are coding operations by numbers, we can expect that it will be difficult for programmers to remember them, and so any help we can give them will be valuable. To put it another way, there isn't much point to our pseudo-code if it isn't simpler and more regular than the real code. Since some of the arithmetic operations come in pairs (e.g., + and −, × and ÷), we can use the sign to distinguish these pairs. A preliminary encoding of operations is

	+	−
1	+	−
2	×	÷
3	square	square root

Notice that we have added the square function; it is useful, and since we already had its inverse, the square root, it is *symmetric* to include square.[1]

This is an example of *orthogonal* language design; that is, there are two orthogonal, or independent, mechanisms: (1) the digit (1, 2, 3), which selects the class of operation (additive, multiplicative, quadratic), and (2) the sign, which selects the direct operation or its inverse. Here we have applied the Orthogonality Principle.

> ***The Orthogonality Principle***
>
> Independent functions should be controlled by independent mechanisms.

This principle is a corollary of the Regularity Principle.

> ***The Regularity Principle***
>
> Regular rules, without exceptions, are easier to learn, use, describe, and implement.

In this case, the regularity will help the programmer to remember the operation codes.

Why does orthogonality simplify a language? If we assigned an arbitrary number to each pseudo-code operation, it would be necessary for the programmer to remember 20 independent facts for the 20 pseudo-code operations. Instead, we reflect in the coding the distinction between the direct and inverse

1 You may have noticed that square and square root are different from the other operations in that they are *unary*, that is, they only have one operand. The extra operand position in the instruction will be unused.

operations. Therefore, structure in the operations is reflected in structure in the coding. The result is that the programmer only has to remember 12 independent facts: the plus and minus signs associated with the direct and inverse forms of the operations and the group that is associated with each of the digits. Another way to express this is the well-known architectural principle: *form follows function.*

Orthogonal means right angled. What do right angles have to do with language design? If we have two independently meaningful axes, one with m positions and another with n positions, then we can describe mn different possibilities even though we only have to memorize $m+n$ independent facts:

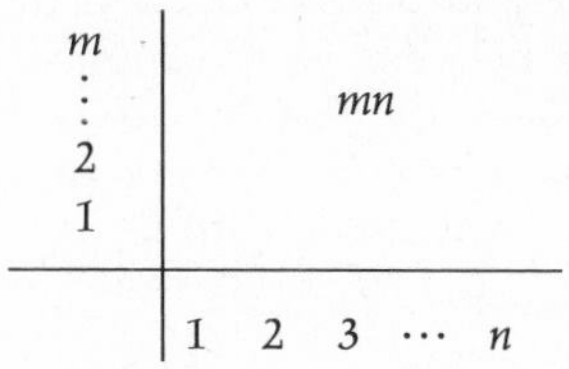

```
 m |
 : |      mn
 2 |
 1 |
---+-----------------
   | 1  2  3  ...  n
```

As m and n increase, mn grows much faster than $m+n$. Thus, orthogonal design becomes more important as more possibilities must be described. When there are many possibilities, it may be advantageous to have more than two orthogonal axes.

Too much orthogonality can harm a language since the language may become cluttered with facilities that have been included for symmetry but are of little use. That is, some of the mn possibilities may be useless or difficult to implement. Some of them may even be illegal; in this case, the programmer must remember them as exceptions (thus violating the Regularity Principle). If e is the number of exceptions, then orthogonalization is advantageous only if $m+n+e < mn-e$.

EXERCISE 1-1: Explain in detail the justification for the formula $m+n+e < mn-e$.

EXERCISE 1-2: Code an operation to add the contents of location 125 to the contents of 206 and store the result in 803.

EXERCISE 1-3: Code an operation to divide the contents of location 401 by the contents of location 623 and store the quotient in location 107.

EXERCISE 1-4: Let the contents of locations 402 and 761 be x and y. Code instructions to compute $(x+y)^2$ into location 100. Assume that the first 10 locations of data memory are available for temporary storage.

EXERCISE 1-5: How can the $+3$ and -3 operations be altered to be more regular (i.e., more like the other operations), while still accomplishing the square and square-root functions?

Comparisons

We have said that we want our virtual computer to be regular so that it will be easier to use than the real computer. Achieving regularity will be easier if we use the same format for our other operations that we've used for the arithmetic operations. Let's see how this applies to the comparison operations. In some sense *equal* is the inverse of *not equal,* and *greater than or equal* is the inverse of *less than,* so we can use signs to distinguish between each operation and its inverse. We extend the operation table as follows:

	+	−
1	+	−
2	×	÷
3	square	square root
4	if = goto	if ≠ goto
5	if ⩾ goto	if < goto

For example, the instruction

```
+4 200 201 035
```

means: If the contents of (data) location 200 equal the contents of (data) location 201, then goto the instruction in (program) location 035. Notice that it is not necessary to include the *greater* and *less than or equal* comparisons since they can be coded by reversing their operands (e.g., $x>y$ is coded as $y<x$, operation −5). We have also omitted positive, negative, and zero tests since these can be coded using the comparisons. For instance, if we adopt the convention that location 000 always contains the number zero, then we can jump to location 100 if location 702 is negative by

```
-5 702 000 100
```

Of course, any location that we know to be zero could be used, but it is always valuable to adopt standard *coding conventions.*

EXERCISE 1-6: Code an instruction to jump to program location 103 if the value of data location 732 is greater than or equal to that of location 500.

EXERCISE 1-7: Suppose data location 000 contains zero. Code an instruction to jump to program location 803 if data location 465 is zero.

EXERCISE 1-8: Code instructions to compute the absolute value of the contents of location 231 and store the result in location 505. Assume that the instructions you write will go into program location 102 and the succeeding program locations. State any other assumptions that you make.

EXERCISE 1-9: This pseudo-code does not include an unconditional jump. How could you do an unconditional jump using the facilities provided?

Moving

What other operations do we need for programming? Certainly, one of the most common operations is simply to move the contents of one location to another without doing any operation. Strictly speaking, it is not necessary to have a separate operation for this; it could be accomplished by adding zero. For example,

```
+1 150 000 280
```

effectively moves the contents of location 150 to location 280. Since a premise of this design is that floating-point arithmetic is quite slow, you can see that this would be a very inefficient way to move values between locations. Therefore, we will use the +0 operation to move one location to another.

Why did we choose +0 rather than +6? By picking +0 for the move, the series of codes 0, 1, 2, 3, 4 stand for an easy-to-remember series of operations of increasing complexity:

move, add, multiply, square

This application of the Regularity Principle will make the codes easier to remember.

EXERCISE 1-10: Code an instruction to move the contents of data location 100 into data location 101.

EXERCISE 1-11[*2]:* What should be the function of the −0 operation? Our symmetric design leads us to expect it to be related to a simple move. It should

2 Exercises marked by an asterisk require more thought and time than those not so marked. Exercises with two asterisks are major projects.

be a useful operation that is not easily or efficiently accomplished with the other operations.

Indexing

One of the justifications for our pseudo-code was that it provided built-in indexing, so we will turn to the design of this facility next. To perform indexing we will need the address of the array and the address of the index variable, thus consuming two of the three address fields in the instruction. Therefore, the only operations we can perform directly on array elements are to move them to or from other locations. We can use the codes +6 and −6 to move from or to an array: $x_i \leftarrow z$ and $x \rightarrow y_i$. The formats of these operations are:

+6 *xxx iii zzz*
−6 *xxx yyy iii*

For example, if there is a 100-element array beginning at location 250 in data memory, and location 050 contains 17, then

```
+6 250 050 803
```

will move the contents of location 267 (= 250 + 17) to location 803. Similarly,

```
-6 722 250 050
```

will move the contents of location 722 to location 267.

Of course, one of the main reasons for using arrays is that we can write a loop to perform the same operation on each element of the array. To do this requires us to be able to initialize, increment, and test index variables. We may expect that we can use the arithmetic and comparison facilities already defined in our pseudo-code for this. But this is not so because these are floating-point operations, and indices are represented by integers. Even if this were not so, it would be useful to abstract out the code common to all loops. By building this into a pseudo-code operation, we eliminate another source of error. This is an example of the Automation Principle and its corollary, the Abstraction Principle.

> ***The Abstraction Principle***
>
> Avoid requiring something to be stated more than once; factor out the recurring pattern.

Since we can use the move instruction ($+0$) to initialize indices, the new operation ($+7$) will only have to increment and test indices. To perform this operation, we need to know the location of the index, the location of the upper bound for the loop, and the location where the loop begins. The following format is analogous to the format of the comparisons:

$+7$ *iii nnn ddd*

Here *iii* is the address of the index, *nnn* is the address of the upper bound, and *ddd* is the location of the beginning of the loop. The operation increments location *iii* and loops to instruction *ddd* if the result is less than the contents of *nnn*. What is the meaning of the -7 operation? There are several possibilities—for instance, a *decrement* and test operation—so we will leave it undefined for the time being.

EXERCISE 1-12: Suppose that there is an array stored in data memory beginning at location 401. Code an instruction that moves the contents of 207 into the array element indexed by location 950.

EXERCISE 1-13: Suppose that an array begins at location 100 in data memory. Code instructions that add to location 020 the array element indexed by location 010.

EXERCISE 1-14: Code an instruction that increments location 010, and loops to code location 005 if the contents of 010 are less than the contents of 030.

EXERCISE 1-15: Suppose that an array begins at location 100 in data memory, and that location 030 contains the number of elements in the array. Code instructions that sum the elements of the array into location 005. State any additional assumptions that you make.

Input-Output

The only functions in our list that we have not yet addressed are the input and output operations. A program is not usually useful if it can't read data or print a result. Therefore, we will use the $+8$ operation to read a card containing one 10-digit number into a specified memory location and the -8 operation to print the contents of a memory location. (In a real pseudo-code, a punch operation would be more common than a print operation since this would allow the output of one program to be used as the input to another.) The complete list of operations is summarized in Figure 1.2. Notice that we have added a stop instruction to terminate program execution.

EXERCISE 1-16: Code an instruction to read a number into location 044.

EXERCISE 1-17: Suppose that an array begins at location 650 in data memory, and that location 907 contains the number of elements in the array. Code instructions to print out all the elements of the array. State any assumptions you make.

EXERCISE 1-18: Suppose an array begins at location 100 in data memory. Code instructions to read numbers into consecutive array elements until a card containing +9 999 999 999 is read. State any assumptions you make.

Program Structure

We now know how to write individual instructions, but we have not designed a means of constructing the program as a whole. For example, how do we arrange to get the program loaded into memory? How do we initialize locations in the data memory? How do we provide input data for the program? The simplest solution to this problem is to have the interpreter read initialization cards and store their content in consecutive memory locations. Thus, the structure of a program is:

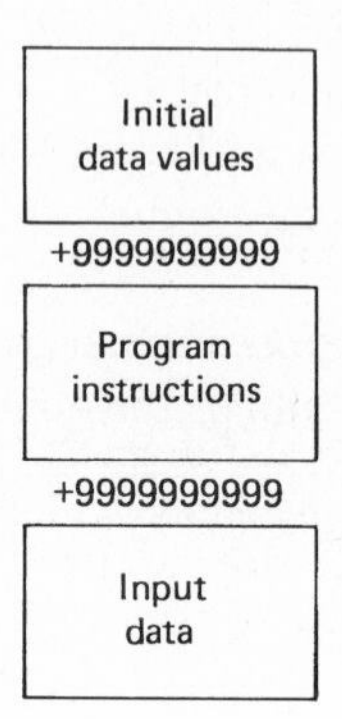

We have used a card containing the "flag value" +9999999999 to separate the initial values from the program and the program from the input data. The loader reads in the initial data values and stores them in consecutive locations (starting with 000) in the data memory. Then the loader reads in the program instructions and stores them in consecutive locations (starting with 000) in the program memory. The loader does *not* read the input data; this is read by the user's program whenever it executes a +8 instruction.

Therefore, the general structure of a program is (1) declarations, (2) executable statements, and (3) input data. This is not unlike the structure of a Pascal or FORTRAN program.

s	f	xxx	yyy	ddd

s = sign, f = function, xxx = operand1,
yyy = operand2, ddd = destination

	+	−
0	move	(exercise)
1	+	−
2	×	÷
3	square	square root
4	=	≠
5	⩾	<
6	$x(y) \rightarrow z$	$x \rightarrow y(z)$
7	incr. and test	(unused)
8	read	print
9	stop	(unused)

Figure 1.2 Pseudo-Code Operations

EXAMPLE: Absolute Mean of an Array As an example of the use of this pseudo-code, we show a program to compute the mean of the absolute values of an array. That is, if A is the array and it has n elements, we compute

$$\frac{1}{n}\sum_{i=1}^{n}|A_i|$$

The first problem is to determine the variables that will be needed and to lay out the data memory. We have used location 000 for a constant zero. The array to be averaged occupies locations 006 through the end of the data memory. The complete program appears in Figure 1.3; annotations on the right explain the steps.

EXERCISE 1-19: Write a complete pseudo-code program to read in data cards (until a +9 999 999 999 flag card), add up the numbers on the cards, and print out the sum.

EXERCISE 1-20: Write a complete pseudo-code program to print out the squares of the numbers from 1 to 100.

EXERCISE 1-21: Write a complete pseudo-code program to print out the first 100 Fibonacci numbers.

```
+0 000 000 000  (loc  0)     constant 0
+0 000 000 000  (loc  1)     index, i
+0 000 000 000  (loc  2)     sum of array
+0 000 000 000  (loc  3)     average of array
+0 000 000 000  (loc  4)     number of elements in array
+0 000 000 000  (loc  5)     temporary location
+0 000 000 000  (loc  6-999) the array
+9 999 999 999               end of initial data
+8 000 000 004  (loc  0)     read number of elements
+8 000 000 005  (loc  1)     read data into temp
+5 005 000 004  (loc  2)     if positive, skip
-1 000 005 005  (loc  3)     else negate
-6 005 006 001  (loc  4)     move temp into array sub i
+7 001 004 001  (loc  5)     incr. i, test with n, loop to loc. 1
+0 000 000 001  (loc  6)     reinitialize i to zero
+6 006 001 005  (loc  7)     add array sub i
+1 005 002 002  (loc  8)       to sum
+7 001 004 007  (loc  9)     incr. i, test with n, loop to loc. 7
-2 002 004 003  (loc 10)     sum / number of elements → avg.
-8 003 000 000  (loc 11)     print average
+9 000 000 000  (loc 12)     stop
+9 999 999 999               end of program
+0 000 000 010               number of input values
   input data
```

Figure 1.3 Pseudo-Code Program Example

EXERCISE 1-22: Write a pseudo-code program to read in the coefficients of a quadratic equation and print both roots (if they exist). In solving this exercise, you will probably find that it is valuable to make a *variable map* that shows the location in which various variables are stored. It will also be useful to use symbolic labels until enough of the program is written to determine the actual location of the instructions.

1.3 IMPLEMENTATION

Automatic Execution Is Patterned after Manual Execution

In this section we will see how to construct an interpreter for our pseudo-code. This will be an example of an *iterative interpreter,* one of the two important kinds (the other is a *recursive interpreter,* which is discussed in Chapter 11). How do we go about designing an interpreter? We can frequently get the insight necessary to design an interpreter by investigating how we would execute the language by hand. If we are to execute pseudo-code programs by hand, we will need some way to record the *state* of the computation, that is, the contents of the data memory. We will also need a listing of the program memory with the instruction at each location, together with a record of our place in the program (the latter is also part of the state). The major data structures required by our interpreter are those shown in Figure 1.4. Notice that we are using two arrays (each indexed from 0 to 999) to represent the areas of memory used for data and program storage. The data and program arrays are called 'Data' and 'Program' and the *instruction pointer* (which records our location in the program) is called 'IP'.[3] For example, 'Program[IP]' represents the instruction in the Program array designated

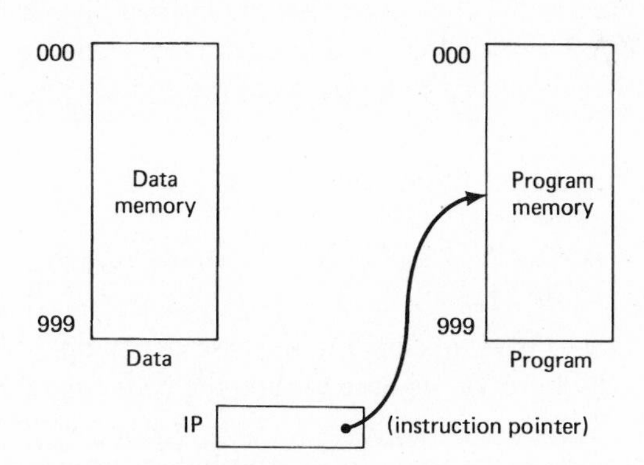

Figure 1.4 Interpreter Data Structures

3 Throughout this book we use single quotes (' ') around program text. The text being discussed is exactly that between the quotes (i.e., we don't include punctuation within the quotes). Double quotes (" ") will be used for all other purposes, such as direct quotations and titles. No quotation marks are used around displayed program text.

by IP. We may find that we need some other minor data structures as we continue with the design.

The Read-Execute Cycle Is the Heart of an Iterative Interpreter

We can now consider how a program is actually interpreted. Roughly, what we will do is read the next instruction to be executed (as indicated by the instruction pointer), determine the operation encoded by the instruction, and then perform that operation. When execution of the operation is completed, we will begin this process again with the next instruction to be executed. This process is called the *read-execute cycle,* and can be summarized as follows:

1. Read the next instruction.
2. Decode the instruction.
3. Execute the operation.
4. Continue from step 1 with the next instruction.

Have you noticed that we have omitted a small but crucial detail? When is the instruction pointer advanced? The natural place to do this would seem to be step 4, since this is just prior to reading the next instruction. While this works fine as long as the program continues to execute sequentially, it will be difficult to handle jumps since they must alter the instruction pointer (in step 3). A better solution, and the one that is adopted in most computers (both real and virtual), is to advance the instruction pointer at the end of step 1. Typical code for step 1 is:

```
instruction := Program[IP];
IP := IP+1;
```

The IP either is ready for the next cycle if sequential execution is to continue, or it can be altered in step 3 in the case of a jump.

Notice that we have written the code for step 1 in a Pascal-like descriptive notation (a *program design language).* Why would we want to write a pseudo-code interpreter if we have Pascal available for programming? We wouldn't. If we wanted to be realistic, we would write the pseudo-code interpreter in machine language. The result would look like Figure 1.1, which is actually a small part of a pseudo-code interpreter. This would be carrying things too far; our goal is to understand iterative interpreters, not to relive the 1950s. Therefore, we will use a more convenient, Pascal-like notation for describing the interpreter. This will allow us to see the algorithm without getting bogged down in the details of machine-language programming.

Instructions Are Decoded by Extracting Their Parts

We will discuss each of the other steps in the read-execute cycle. Since our pseudo-code has been designed with a regular structure, decoding is simple; we simply extract the sign, operation code, and three address fields. For example, the destination address could be extracted by

```
dest := abs (instruction) mod 1000
```

(where 'x mod y' gives the remainder of dividing x by y). We will assume that the names of these extracted parts are 'sign', 'op', 'opnd1', 'opnd2', and 'dest'.

EXERCISE 1-23: Write the code to extract the other fields in an instruction.

The next step in instruction decoding is to determine what kind of operation has to be performed. This is specified by a combination of the 'sign' and the 'op' fields. We can break down the execution into cases, depending on the value of these fields. The operation to be performed by each case is just read from Figure 1.2. The result is shown in Figure 1.5.

EXERCISE 1-24: Fill in the rest of the second case-statement in Figure 1.5.

EXERCISE 1-25:* Estimate the overhead of this pseudo-code interpreter. That is, estimate the number of memory references made in the read-execute cycle beyond those actually required for computing the result (e.g., the floating-point operation). What percentage of the execution time will be overhead if the average software-implemented floating-point operation requires 100 memory references? What percentage is overhead if the floating-point operations are implemented in the hardware and take just three memory references.

Computational Instructions

Most of the computational instructions are simple to interpret. For example, to interpret a multiplication, the two operands (Data[opnd1] and Data[opnd2]) must be fetched, multiplied by the floating-point multiplication routine, and stored at the destination location (Data[dest]). We can express this as:

```
Multiply:
Data[dest] := floating product (Data[opnd1], Data[opnd2]).
```

The other computational instructions are analogous.

EXERCISE 1-26: Write in a program design language the implementation of the other computational instructions of the pseudo-code (all the codes except ± 4 through 7).

Control-Flow Instructions

The control-flow instructions are implemented in an analogous manner; the only difference is that the IP must be altered if the test is satisfied. For example,

```
Test equality:
if floating equality (Data[opnd1], Data[opnd2]) then
    IP := dest.
```

EXERCISE 1-27: Write in a program design language the implementation of the comparison operations of the interpreter.

EXERCISE 1-28: We now have a complete design for the "main loop" of a pseudo-code interpreter. In order to have a complete interpreter, it is necessary to write a *loader* that will read in the initialization and program cards and load

```
if sign is '+' then
    do case op of:
        0:    move;
        1:    add;
        2:    multiply;
        3:    square;
        4:    test equality;
        5:    test greater or equal;
        6:    fetch from array;
        7:    increment and test;
        8:    read;
        9:    stop.
if sign is '−' then
    do case op of
        0:    do operation from exercise;
        1:    subtract;
        ⋮
```

Figure 1.5 Instruction Decoding

them into the Data and Program arrays. Design this part of the interpreter and write it in a program design language.

EXERCISE 1-29:* Translate the entire interpreter into your favorite programming language and test it on the example program in Figure 1.3. You do not have to implement your own floating-point arithmetic; just use the floating-point operations provided in your chosen programming language.

Interpreters Simplify Debugging

Next, we will investigate some improvements that can be made to this interpreter. In the beginning of this chapter, we said that one of the motivations for pseudo-codes was the difficulty of programming; you probably know from your own experience that much of this is a result of the difficulty of debugging. Since debugging can often be expedited by a better understanding of what the program is doing, programmers have often resorted to "playing computer," that is, to interpreting their programs by hand to see what they do. Clearly, this is a process that can be profitably automated. What we would like is the ability to get a *trace* of the execution of the program, that is, a record of the instructions it has executed. This can be done by adding code to step 1, Read Next Instruction, to print out the location and code for the current instruction:

```
Read Next Instruction:
    instruction := Program[IP];
    if trace is enabled then
        print IP, instruction;
    IP := IP + 1.
```

A trace of the program in Figure 1.3 would begin

```
000  +8000000004
001  +8000000005
002  -6005006001
003  +7001004001
001  +8000000005
         ⋮
```

EXERCISE 1-30: Show the next 10 steps in the trace of the program in Figure 1.3.

EXERCISE 1-31: The above modification prints out the instruction as a 10-digit number. It would be preferable to print it out in interpreted form, that is, with its fields separated. For example, the trace may begin:

LOC	OP	OPND1	OPND2	DEST
000	+8	000	000	004
001	+8	000	000	005
002	−6	005	006	001
003	+7	001	004	001
001	+8	000	000	005
		⋮		

(Of course, this assumes the availability of a printer that can print letters.) Alter the interpreter to produce an interpreted trace.

EXERCISE 1-32:* The trace can be made even more valuable by printing out the operation name in English, the values of the source operands, and the value to be placed in the destination operand. Alter the interpreter to do this. Note, however, that not all fields are used in all of the instructions.

EXERCISE 1-33:* For a large program, the trace could be very long, even though the programmer was interested in only a very small region of the program. Design an interpreter operation (−9 perhaps) that will allow the programmer to enable and disable tracing at different points in the program.

EXERCISE 1-34:* Another useful debugging tool is breakpoints. This feature allows the programmer to specify certain instruction addresses as *breakpoint addresses*; whenever execution reaches one of these addresses, interpretation of the program stops until the programmer restarts it. This allows the programmer to investigate the state of the data memory at selected points during execution. Design a breakpoint facility for the pseudo-code interpreter.

EXERCISE 1-35:* Design a *data trap* facility. This is like a breakpoint except that interpretation is interrupted whenever specified locations in the *data* memory are referenced.

Statement Labels Simplify Coding

We will now consider an aid to the coding of a program. One of the major goals of programming languages is the elimination of the tedious, error-prone tasks in programming (the Automation Principle). One of these tasks results from the use of absolute locations in pseudo-code instructions. Consider what would happen if we wanted to insert a new instruction (e.g., a trace instruction) after the instruction in location 000 in Figure 1.3. This would shift down all of the remaining instructions and require us to correct the destination addresses in locations 003 and 007. We can see that maintenance would be almost impossible for a large program, since we would have to find all the addresses that could be altered by a change.

One solution adopted by several early pseudo-codes was the provision of *symbolic labels* for statements. Let's see how this would work. When we describe an algorithm in English, such as the read-execute cycle described earlier, we often number the steps so that they can be referred to from other steps, for example, "Continue from step 1." This is an example of the Labeling Principle.

> ***The Labeling Principle***
>
> Do not require the user to know the absolute position of an item in a list. Instead, associate labels with any position that must be referenced elsewhere.

We can modify the pseudo-code to do this by introducing a label definition operator. The instruction

```
−7 0LL 000 000
```

defines the statement number, or *label*, *LL*. (We will only allow labels in the range 00–99 so that we can use a 100-element label table.) Notice that this is not an *executable statement*; it merely marks the place in the program to be labeled *LL*. We call such statements *declarations* and say that they *bind* a symbolic label to an absolute location. We will also alter the jump instructions to refer to symbolic labels in their destination field rather than *absolute* labels. Thus, the format of the equality test is

```
+4 xxx yyy 0LL
```

In the following illustration, the executable part of our example program has been rewritten making use of labels.

```
+8 000 000 004        read number of elements
−7 020 000 000     20:
+8 000 000 005        read into temp
+5 005 000 040        if positive, skip to label 40
−1 000 005 005        negate temp
−7 040 000 000     40:
−6 005 006 001        move temp to array sub i
+7 001 004 020        incr. i, test with n, loop to label 20
+0 000 000 001        reinitialize i to zero
```

```
-7 050 000 000     50:
+6 006 001 005        add array sub i
+1 005 002 002           to sum
+7 001 004 050        incr. i, test with n, loop to label 50
         etc.
```

How can we interpret symbolic labels? Again, we can begin by observing how people do it. If we were interpreting the above program and came to a jump to location 50, we would very likely find its location by looking through the program until we found a −7 instruction with a 050 in the destination field. This is, in fact, the way some interpreters work, such as those found in some programmable hand-held calculators. We can see, though, that if the program were very large, we would be spending a lot of time scanning the program to find labels. We would probably save ourselves this trouble by making a *label table* that listed the labels and their absolute locations, for example,

Label	Location
20	001
40	005
50	009

This table could be constructed exactly the way we do it by hand: The first time we search for a label, we put it in the table so that we will have the absolute location for later uses of the label. It would be better, however, to build the label table as the program is read into Program memory. This simplifies the interpretation of jumps since we know all labels are defined before execution begins. More important, it allows us to increase *security* by ensuring that all the labels that are referenced are defined once and only once. This is in accord with the Security Principle.

This checking can be done by initializing the label table to some value that we will interpret to mean "undefined," say −1. During loading, whenever we encounter a −7 instruction defining a label, before we enter its absolute location into the label table, we will ensure that it has not already been defined by seeing if its entry is negative. Conversely, whenever we encounter an instruction *referencing* a label (e.g., +7), we will check to see if it has been defined, as indicated by a nonnegative value. If it has been defined, then all is well; if it hasn't, then we will store the value −2 indicating a label that has been referenced but not defined. If the label is later defined, this −2 will be changed to a positive value reflecting the absolute location of the label. At the end of loading, a final scan of the label table for any remaining −2 values will enable us to report the undefined labels. The label table we have described is a rudimentary form of a *symbol table;* this data structure is used in all programming language implementations for keeping track of labels, variables, and other symbolically named objects. Symbol tables will be discussed periodically throughout this book.

EXERCISE 1-36:* Modify your pseudo-code interpreter to use symbolic statement labels of the type we have described. Test it on the modified Mean program (p. 23).

EXERCISE 1-37:* We have only allowed statement labels in the range 0–99 so that only a 100-element label table will be required. Even so, for small programs many of the entries will be unused. Design a scheme for storing the absolute locations (and "undefined" codes) for labels in the range 0–999.

EXERCISE 1-38:* Label declarations provide new opportunities for debugging aids. For example, the interpreter can print a message every time the program jumps to a label or the interpreter can pause for programmer interaction whenever a label is encountered. Design and implement one or more of these debugging facilities for your interpreter.

Variables Can Be Processed Like Labels

Since we have eliminated the error-prone use of absolute statement labels, we will probably want to know if we can also eliminate absolute data addresses. The answer is "yes"; we can do this by constructing a *symbol table* that holds the absolute location of every variable. We can then use fixed *symbolic* labels (still in the form of three-digit numbers) in the pseudo-code instructions. In the initial-data section of the program, pairs of cards could be used to declare simple variables and arrays. Thus,

+0 *sss* *nnn* 000
±*d* *ddd* *ddd* *ddd*

will declare a storage area with the symbolic name *sss*, *nnn* locations long, initialized to all ±*d ddd ddd ddd*. For instance,

```
+0 666 150 000
+3 141 592 654
```

could be used to declare a 150-element array to be identified by the label '666' and initialized to all +3141592654. Two simple variables, labeled '111' and '222', could be declared and initialized to zero by

```
+0 111 001 000
+0 000 000 000
```

```
+0 222 001 000
+0 000 000 000
```

We know they are simple variables because the amount of memory allocated to each is one word.

For each declaration the loader keeps track of the next available memory location and *binds* the symbolic variable number to that location. Therefore, we say that the *binding time* of this declaration is load time. We will see in later chapters that other binding times are possible. Also, notice that the loader has taken over another job for the programmer: *storage allocation*.

EXERCISE 1-39: What principle does the loader illustrate?

After the above declarations, we could use 111 to index 666 and store the result in 222 by

```
+6 666 111 222
```

This is analogous to the Pascal statement

```
V222 := V666 [V111]
```

where the variable names 'V222', 'V666', and 'V111' correspond to the symbolic storage labels '222', '666', and '111'.

Clearly, these symbolic data names can be implemented in exactly the same way we implemented symbolic statement labels. We can also perform the same checking for undefined names, as well as additional checking, such as for out-of-bounds array references. That is, the interpreter can record in the symbol table the size of the array and then on each array reference instruction (± 6) ensure that the index is less than this bound. This is in accord with the Security Principle since it detects a violation of the program's intended structure.

EXERCISE 1-40: Rewrite the Mean program using the variable declarations we have described.

EXERCISE 1-41:* Modify the loader to build a symbol table for the variables and to initialize the Data array. Modify the interpreter to use these symbolic variable numbers. Include the error-checking facilities described above.

EXERCISE 1-42:* Propose a debugging aid based on symbolic variable numbers and describe its implementation in detail.

The Ideas Presented Above Are Easily Extended to a Symbolic Pseudo-Code

The provision of symbolic numbers for variables and statement labels has gone a long way toward making our pseudo-code easier to use. It is still necessary for users to remember the relationship between their variables and the numeric tags they invent. This is an error-prone process since the programmer has to remember whether −2 or −3 is divide, whether 111 is the index or the temporary, and so on. The programmer will probably keep lists of the correspondence between these codes and the abstractions they represent, such as the list of operation codes in Figure 1.2. Therefore, we can eliminate this source of errors by maintaining this correspondence for the user. This was done in many of the early pseudo-codes when input-output equipment that could handle alphabetic characters became available.

EXERCISE 1-43: What principle is illustrated by making the computer keep track of the correspondence described above?

How will we go about designing a symbolic pseudo-code? First, let's consider the *syntax* of (way to write) the variables. Currently, the interpreter looks up a three-digit symbolic variable number in the symbol table in order to find the absolute location of that variable in the Data array. If we replace this three-digit number with a three-character alphanumeric name, then we will be able to use the same lookup process while allowing the programmer to pick more mnemonic variable names. The programmer will be able to use a name like AVG instead of an absolute location (003) or an arbitrary numeric tag (123). The same can be done for the operation codes, using mnemonic words like ADD and READ instead of codes like +1 and +8. The loader will have to look these up in a symbol table and replace them by their codes. Therefore, a typical statement in this symbolic pseudo-code would look like

```
ADD TMP SUM SUM
```

As has been said, the primary input medium for early computers was punched cards. Since there was a long tradition (dating from the use of office punched card equipment in the first half of the 20th century) of assigning particular fixed columns to the *fields* of data records, the same kind of *fixed format* convention was adopted for the pseudo-codes. If the operation names are limited to four characters and the variable names and statement labels to three characters, then we can use a format such as the following:

Columns 1-4:	operation	10-12:	operand 2
6-8:	operand 1	14-16:	destination

Only uppercase letters will be used since these were all that were available on key punches at that time. In Figure 1.6 the Mean program is shown translated into this symbolic pseudo-code. We have not included a list of all the mnemonics since they should be clear from context.

We can see that the general structure of a program is

```
declarations
END
statements
END
```

This format, declarations followed by statements, has been preserved in most programming languages. For instance, in the language Ada it takes the form:

```
declare
  declarations
begin
  statements
end;
```

Also, variable declarations have the syntax (form)

```
VAR variable-name type
initial-value
```

where 'type' means the number of locations the variable occupies. This format is also preserved in many modern languages. In Ada we write

```
variable-name : type := initial-value;
```

although the idea of a type in Ada (and most modern languages) involves much more than just the amount of storage to be allocated. There is one more thing to notice about the syntax of this pseudo-code: The operation comes first in the statements:

```
operation   operand1   operand2   destination
```

This is called a *prefix* format (pre = before), and is still used for statements in most programming languages, for example, in FORTRAN

```
DO 20 I=1, 100
PRINT 30, AVG
```

```
OPER  OP1   OP2   DST   COMMENTS

VAR   ZRO   1           CONSTANT ZERO
+0000000000
VAR   I     1           INDEX
+0000000000
VAR   SUM   1           SUM OF ARRAY
+0000000000
VAR   AVG   1           AVERAGE OF ARRAY
+0000000000
VAR   N     1           NUMBER OF ELEMENTS IN ARRAY
+0000000000
VAR   TMP   1           TEMPORARY LOCATION
+0000000000
VAR   DTA   990         THE DATA ARRAY
+0000000000
END
READ  N                 READ NUMBER OF ELEMENTS
LABL  20
READ  TMP               READ INTO TEMP
GE    TMP   ZRO   40    IF POSITIVE, SKIP TO 40
SUB   ZRO   TMP   TMP   NEGATE TEMP
LABL  40
PUTA  TMP   DTA   I     MOVE TEMP INTO THE I-TH ELEMENT
LOOP  I     N     20    LOOP FOR ALL ARRAY ELEMENTS
MOVE  ZRO         I     REINITIALIZE INDEX TO ZERO
LABL  50
GETA  DTA   I     TMP   ADD I-TH ELEMENT
ADD   TMP   SUM   SUM     TO SUM
LOOP  I     N     50    LOOP FOR ALL ARRAY ELEMENTS
DIV   SUM   N     AVG   COMPUTE AVERAGE
PRNT  AVG               AND PRINT IT
STOP
END
```

Figure 1.6 Absolute Mean of Array in Symbolic Pseudo-Code

There is no reason why we had to pick a prefix form (there are others such as postfix and infix), although it does agree with English grammar in putting the verb first in an imperative sentence.

To implement the symbolic pseudo-code, all that is required is that as the loader reads in each instruction, it look up the operation and the operands in the symbol table and replace them with the proper codes. The encoded form of the instruction is then stored in the Program array. Thus, we can see that the loader is performing a *translation* function since it is translating the *source form* of the program (the symbolic pseudo-code) into an *intermediate form* (the numeric pseudo-code) that is more suitable for the interpreter. This two-stage process, translation followed by interpretation, is very common and will be discussed at length in the following chapters. In fact, the translator, with its name lookup and storage allocation functions, is a rudimentary form of a *compiler*. The function of a compiler is to translate a program in some source language into a form that is more convenient for execution. This form is often machine language, which can be directly executed, but it may also be an intermediate language suitable for interpretation.

EXERCISE 1-44:* Modify your interpreter to implement this symbolic pseudo-code and test it on the Mean program. Translate your quadratic roots program into this pseudo-code and execute it with this interpreter.

EXERCISE 1-45:* Describe how you would make the pseudo-code *free format*, that is, independent of the columns in which the fields appear (of course, they must be in the correct order). How would you implement this?

1.4 EVALUATION AND EPILOG

Pseudo-Code Interpreters Simplified Programming

We have seen that pseudo-codes simplified programming in many ways. Most important, they provided a *virtual computer* that was more *regular* and *higher level* than the real computers that were available at first. Also, they decreased the chances of error while taking over from the programmer many of the tedious and error-prone aspects of coding. Pseudo-codes increased *security* by allowing error checking, for example, for undeclared variables and out-of-bounds array references. Finally, they simplified debugging by providing facilities such as execution traces. We will see in later chapters that all of these remain important advantages of newer programming languages.

Floating-Point Hardware Made Interpreters Unattractive

Decoding pseudo-code instructions adds a great deal of overhead to program execution. In the beginning of this chapter, we pointed out that most of this overhead was swamped by the time necessary to simulate floating-point arithmetic. That is, since programs were doing mostly floating-point arithmetic, which was slow, they were spending most of their time in the floating-point subroutines. The little additional time they spent in the interpreter was well worth the advantages of the pseudo-code. This changed when floating-point hardware was introduced on the IBM 704 in 1953. Experience with floating-point arithmetic and indexing facilities in the pseudo-codes led IBM and the other manufacturers to include these in the newer computers. Since programs were no longer spending most of their time in floating-point subroutines, the factor of 10 (or more) slower execution of interpreters became intolerable. Since at this time computer time was still more expensive than programmer time, interpreters became unpopular because the total cost of running a machine-language program was less than that of a pseudo-code program.

Pseudo-codes are still used for special purposes such as intermediate languages. For example, Pascal is often translated into a pseudo-code called P-code. The P-code program is then either translated into machine language or interpreted. Programmers no longer write directly in pseudo-codes, except when programming hand-held calculators.

Libraries Led to the Idea of "Compiling Routines"

An alternative to the use of interpreters was the "compilation" of programs from libraries of subroutines. The idea was that a programmer would write pseudo-code instructions that would, at load time, call for subroutines to be copied from a library and assembled into a program. Since the translation and decoding were done once, at compilation time, compiled programs ran more quickly than interpreted programs. This was so because an interpreter, for example, must decode the instructions in a loop every time through the loop.

However, since the subroutines assembled by a compiler could not be made to fit together perfectly in all combinations, there was an *interface overhead* that made compiled programs less efficient than hand-coded ones. The result was that programmers considered these "automatic coding" techniques inherently inefficient and only suitable for short programs that would be run only a few times. Thus, the prevailing attitude in the early to mid-1950s was that important programming had to be done in assembly language. Although, as we will see in the next chapter, FORTRAN proved the viability of "automatic coding," this attitude was to continue for many years.

EXERCISES*

1. Compare and contrast the numeric pseudo-code interpreter, the symbolic pseudo-code interpreter, and an assembler.

2. Study the manual of an assembly language and critique that language with respect to the language design principles you have learned. Pay particular attention to the regularity and orthogonality of the language.
3. Pick some programmable calculator and evaluate its instruction set as a pseudo-code.
4. Make the following specification more precise, that is, make reasonable assumptions and justify them: *Free format* pseudo-code instructions allow the operator and operands of instructions to be separated by any number of blanks, and allow any number of instructions to be put on one line.
5. Alter the symbolic pseudo-code loader to accept the free format instructions specified in the previous exercise.
6. Suppose we wanted to add the three trigonometric functions (sin, cos, tan) and their inverses to our pseudo-code interpreter. Design this extension to the language. (Note that this extension will increase the number of operators to more than 20.)
7. As languages evolve, they often must be extended. Discuss how to design a pseudo-code to accommodate the later addition of new operations. Discuss a policy for limiting extensions to those that are necessary.
8. In this chapter we designed a pseudo-code for numerical and scientific applications. Design a pseudo-code for commercial (business data-processing) applications. Discuss your rationale for including or omitting various features.
9. Implement the pseudo-code designed in the previous exercise.
10. Pick an application area that interests you (e.g., stock portfolio management, poker betting, dates/appointments, checkbook management, grading). Design a pseudo-code appropriate to a hand-held computer that would be helpful in this application area. You will be graded on your adherence to the principles you've learned and on the wisdom of engineering trade-offs.
11. Implement the pseudo-code designed in the previous exercise.

2

EMPHASIS ON EFFICIENCY: FORTRAN

2.1 HISTORY AND MOTIVATION

Automatic Coding Was Considered Unfeasible

In the early 1950s, there was little sympathy for the idea of a high-level programming language.[1] Indeed, many programmers were even opposed to the use of decimal numbers in programming! An elegant algebraic language developed by Laning and Zierler of MIT was compiling code as early as 1952, but it was largely ignored. Simple assemblers and libraries of subroutines were the accepted tools of the day. Simple interpreters continued to be used since the overhead of simulating floating-point arithmetic masked the overhead of interpretation. John

1 Historical information in this chapter comes mostly from the "History of Programming Languages Conference Proceedings," *SIGPLAN Notices 13*, 8 (August 1978). See Backus (1978).

Backus of IBM had designed one such system, called Speedcoding, which was very popular among IBM 701 installations. Backus's recognition that it already was more expensive to design and debug a program than to run it led to his development of Speedcoding and to his suggestions to include floating-point arithmetic and indexing in the IBM 704. When the 704 with its floating-point hardware was released, it exposed the inherent overhead of the interpretive routines and made them much less attractive. These factors led Backus to conclude that programming costs could be decreased only by a system that allowed the programmer to write in conventional mathematical notation and that generated code whose efficiency was comparable to that produced by a good programmer. In late 1953 Backus proposed these ideas to his management at IBM, and in January of 1954, with one assistant, he began work on what was to become FORTRAN.

Preliminary FORTRAN Was Designed

In the 1950s Grace Murray Hopper, another pioneer language developer, organized a number of symposia under the auspices of the Office of Naval Research (ONR). At the ONR symposium of May 1954, Backus and a colleague presented a paper on Speedcoding in which they discussed some of their ideas for a programming language based on mathematical notation. They were given a copy of a report describing the Laning and Zierler system, which was demonstrated for them in June 1954. By November 1954 Backus and three associates had produced a preliminary external specification for "the IBM Mathematical FORmula TRANslating System, FORTRAN." At a 1978 conference on the history of programming languages, Backus stated, "As far as we were aware, we simply made up the language as we went along. We did not regard language design as a difficult problem, merely as a simple prelude to the real problem: designing a compiler which could produce efficient programs." According to Backus, the preliminary specification of FORTRAN was met with "indifference and skepticism."

The FORTRAN Compiler Was Successful

Backus and his team, which eventually included nine others, began the design and programming of FORTRAN in early 1955 and released the system in April 1957 after 18 man-years of work. By most accounts the system didn't really work at this time, although by April 1958 it had been enthusiastically accepted. At the 60 IBM 704 installations in existence in late 1958, more than half of the instructions were being generated by FORTRAN. In part this can be attributed to the exceptionally clear documentation that accompanied the FORTRAN system. It was also because of some very sophisticated optimization techniques, which Backus claims were not surpassed until the late 1960s. These optimizations allowed the FORTRAN system to deliver the efficiency that had been promised.

FORTRAN Has Been Revised Several Times

The experience gained with this FORTRAN system led Backus and his colleagues to propose FORTRAN II in September 1957. The compiler was available in the spring of 1958, and the language remains in use to this day. A dialect called FORTRAN III was designed and implemented in late 1958, but it never achieved widespread use because of its many dependencies on the IBM 704. In 1962 the FORTRAN IV language was designed; it is still an important FORTRAN dialect. In *Programming Languages: History and Fundamentals,* Jean Sammet said, "By 1963 virtually all manufacturers had either delivered or committed themselves to producing some version of FORTRAN." Reflecting FORTRAN's popularity, the American National Standards Institute (ANSI) began development of standard FORTRAN IV (ANS FORTRAN) in 1962; this was completed in 1966. Unfortunately, dialects of FORTRAN are very common and few compilers implement exactly the ANSI standard. In 1977 a new ANS FORTRAN was developed that is sometimes known as FORTRAN 77. This language incorporates many ideas from later languages, which gives it a very different appearance. It may be that it has gone too far, in that it is so different from previous FORTRAN versions that it will not benefit from their popularity, and it has not gone far enough, in that it is still a 1950s language in its capabilities. In any case, we will concentrate on the 1966 ANS FORTRAN since our intent is to illustrate the characteristics of first-generation languages, and these are more apparent in FORTRAN IV. Unless otherwise specified, in this chapter the name FORTRAN refers to ANS FORTRAN IV.

2.2 DESIGN: STRUCTURAL ORGANIZATION

Figure 2.1 displays a small FORTRAN I program to compute the average of the absolute value of an array. (Since we are trying to illustrate a number of FORTRAN's features, we have not written the best program possible to do this job.) Although we have used FORTRAN I for the example so that the similarity to pseudo-codes is more apparent, with just minor alterations this example would be legal in any version of FORTRAN.

```
      DIMENSION DTA(900)
      SUM = 0.0
      READ 10, N
10    FORMAT(I3)
      DO 20 I = 1, N
      READ 30, DTA(I)
30    FORMAT(F10.6)
      IF (DTA(I)) 25, 20, 20
25    DTA(I) = -DTA(I)
20    CONTINUE
      DO 40 I = 1, N
      SUM = SUM + DTA(I)
40    CONTINUE
      AVG = SUM/FLOAT(N)
      PRINT 50, AVG
50    FORMAT(1H , F10.6)
      STOP
```

Figure 2.1 A FORTRAN I Program

Programs Are Divided into Disjoint Subprograms

The pseudo-code we discussed in Chapter 1 and the preliminary FORTRAN specification both lacked what is now considered to be a crucial part of programming languages: subprograms (e.g., procedures, functions, and subroutines). By the time the FORTRAN I system was released, a subprogram facility had been included. The overall structure of a FORTRAN program is a *main program* and zero or more *subprograms*, for example,

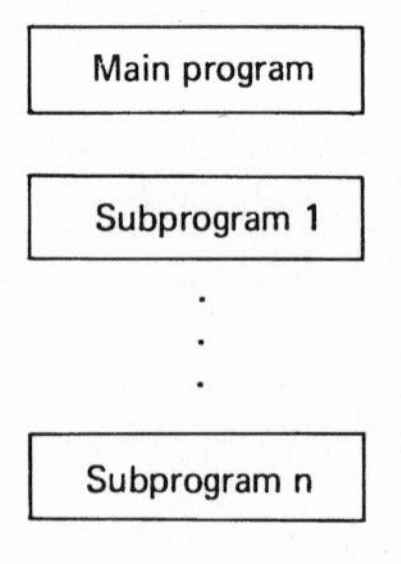

Subprograms will be discussed in detail in Section 2.3; suffice it to say that they can communicate using *parameters* or through shared data areas called *COMMON blocks.*

Constructs Are Either Declarative or Imperative

We saw in Chapter 1 that pseudo-code programs were divided into two parts: first, a *declarative* part, which described the data areas, their lengths, and their initial values; second, an *imperative* part, which contained the commands to be executed during the running of the program. Declarative and imperative constructs occur in almost all programming languages, although they may be called by different names. For example, in FORTRAN the declarative constructs are often called *nonexecutable statements* and the imperative constructs are often called *executable statements.*

Declaratives are like declarative statements in natural languages: They state facts about the program, which are used at *compile-time.* Imperatives are like imperative statements in natural languages: They give a command, which the program obeys at *run-time.* Next, we briefly survey the FORTRAN constructs of each of these types.

Declarations Include Bindings and Initializations

In our pseudo-code we saw that the declarations performed three functions:

1. They *allocated* an area of memory of a specified size.
2. They attached a symbolic name to that area of memory. This is called *binding* a name to an area of memory.
3. They *initialized* the contents of that memory area.

These are three important functions of declarations in most languages, including FORTRAN. For example, the declaration

```
DIMENSION DTA (900)
```

causes the loader to allocate 900 words and to bind the name "DTA" to this area. A separate kind of declaration, called a DATA declaration, can be used for initialization. For example,

```
DATA DTA, SUM / 900*0.0, 0.0
```

would initialize the array DTA to 900 zeroes and the variable SUM to zero. FORTRAN does not require the programmer to initialize storage; this lack of initialization is a frequent cause of errors. Declarations and initializations are discussed in Section 2.3.

Imperatives Are Either Computational, Control-Flow, or Input-Output

In our pseudo-code we saw that there were three different kinds of imperative statements:

1. Computational statements, such as the arithmetic and the move operations.
2. Control-flow statements, such as the comparisons and the looping statements.
3. Input-output statements, namely, READ and PRINT.

FORTRAN provides imperatives of exactly the same three types. The primary computational statement is the *assignment* statement, for example,

```
AVG = SUM / FLOAT(N)
```

The assignment statement is also one of the contexts in which *algebraic expressions* can appear. Recall that the ability to use conventional algebraic notation was one of the important contributions of FORTRAN.

Corresponding to the comparisons in the pseudo-code, there are *conditionals,* which are called IF-statements in FORTRAN. Similarly, corresponding to the looping instruction of the pseudo-code, FORTRAN has a DO-loop. Finally, FORTRAN provides an unconditional transfer instruction, the GOTO-statement, which we did not put in the pseudo-code (because it was so easily expressed by the equality test). We can see that FORTRAN does not go too far beyond the pseudo-code in its control-flow statements.

FORTRAN has a much more elaborate set of input-output instructions than did our pseudo-code. In fact, even FORTRAN I had, out of a total of only 26 statements, 12 statements for performing or controlling input-output. Some of these were for handling a wider variety of devices, such as tapes and drums, and some of these were for providing more explicit control over the format of data on the input-output media. FORTRAN's imperative statements will be discussed in Section 2.3.

A Program Goes Through Several Stages to Be Run

As we have seen, one of the most important goals for FORTRAN was efficient execution; therefore, the overhead for interpretation was completely intolerable. The approach adopted, and still used in most FORTRAN systems, is that the program progresses through a series of stages:

1. Compilation
2. Linking
3. Loading
4. Execution

The first step, compilation, translates individual FORTRAN subprograms into *relocatable object code.* That means that by a process similar to the pseudo-code translator, the FORTRAN statements are translated into the instructions, or *object code,* of a real computer. Since each subprogram must reside in memory with other subprograms that may not have yet been compiled, it is impossible to determine at compile-time the exact location in memory where each subprogram will go. Therefore, the exact addresses of variables and statements are not yet known; we say that they have a later *binding time* because they are bound to addresses at load-time rather than at compile-time. It is for these reasons that the object program is represented in a special *relocatable* format that allows the addresses to be assigned at load-time. Relocatable format is similar to the symbolic statement and variable labels in our pseudo-code.

The second step, linking, addresses the need for incorporating *libraries* of already programmed, debugged, and compiled subprograms. Needless to say, the presence of a good library can greatly simplify the programming process, as we saw with floating-point libraries in Chapter 1. The use of libraries means that programs contain *external references* to subprograms in these libraries. Furthermore, these library subprograms may themselves contain external references to other library subprograms. To obtain a complete program, all of these external references must be resolved or *satisfied* by finding the corresponding subprograms in the library. This is the goal of the linking process; its result is usually a file containing all of the parts of the program, still in relocatable format, but with their external references satisfied.

The third step, loading, is the process in which the program is placed in computer memory. This requires converting it from relocatable to *absolute* format, that is, it requires binding all code and data references to the addresses of the locations that the code and data will occupy in memory.

The final step, execution, is the one in which control of the computer is turned over to the program in memory. Since the program is executed directly rather than interpreted, it has the potential of running much faster.

Compilation Involves Three Phases

The compilation process is obviously one of the most important steps in the processing of a FORTRAN program since it is this step that determines the efficiency of the final program. For a language such as FORTRAN, compilation usually involves three tasks. These may be performed one after the other or interleaved in various ways.

1. **Syntactic analysis**: The compiler must classify the statements and constructs of FORTRAN and extract their parts.
2. **Optimization**: As we have said, efficiency was a prime goal of the original FORTRAN system. For this reason the original FORTRAN system included

a sophisticated optimizer whose goal was to produce as good a code as could be produced by an experienced programmer. Most FORTRAN compilers perform at least a moderate amount of optimization.

3. **Code synthesis**: The final task of compilation is to put together the parts of the object code instructions in relocatable format.

2.3 DESIGN: CONTROL STRUCTURES

Control Structures Govern Primitive Statements

In Section 2.3 we discuss FORTRAN's *control structures,* that is, those constructs in the language that govern the flow of control of the program. We will see that these control structures are elaborations of the control structures found in the pseudo-code of Chapter 1. In the pseudo-code we saw that the purpose of control structures was to direct control to various *primitive* computational and input-output instructions such as ADD and READ. (By a *primitive* operation we mean one that is not expressed in terms of more fundamental ideas in the language.) The situation is similar in FORTRAN; the computational and input-output instructions do the actual data processing work of the program, while the control structures act as "schedulers" or "traffic managers" by directing control to these primitive statements. We will see in later chapters that this organization is common to all *imperative* programming languages.

As we have said (Section 2.1), the ability to write more or less familiar looking algebraic equations was one of the major contributions of FORTRAN. Without doubt, the assignment statement is the most important statement in FORTRAN. In fact, a FORTRAN program can be considered as a collection of assignment statements with provision for directing control (i.e., the control structures) to one or the other of these assignment statements.

Control Structures Were Based on IBM 704 Branch Instructions

FORTRAN was originally designed as a programming language for the IBM 704 computer; it was thought that there would be similar, but different, languages for other computers. Backus has said that he never imagined that FORTRAN would be used on the computers of other manufacturers. It is thus not surprising that the first FORTRAN had many similarities to the 704 instruction set; designers have a tendency to include in a language the features they have previously found useful. This *machine dependence* is a characteristic of first-generation languages.

We can see this machine dependence in FORTRAN's control structures in Figure 2.2, which displays the similarities between FORTRAN II's control structures and the branch instructions of the IBM 704. It is not important that you understand the 704 instructions or even the FORTRAN statements at this point; what is important is the correspondence. It is one reason that FORTRAN has sometimes been called an "assembly language for the IBM 704," although some of the more blatantly machine-dependent statements (e.g., IF QUOTIENT OVERFLOW) were removed from FORTRAN IV and later versions. This correspondence also explains some of FORTRAN's more unusual control structures, for example, the *arithmetic IF-statement*

IF (e) n_1, n_2, n_3

evaluates the expression e and then branches to n_1, n_2, or n_3 depending on whether the result of the evaluation is negative, zero, or positive, respectively. This is exactly the function of the 704's CAS instruction, which compares the accumulator with a value in storage and then branches to one of three locations. The arithmetic IF was not very satisfactory for a number of reasons, including the difficulty of keeping the meaning of the three labels straight and the fact that two of the labels were usually identical (because two-way branches are more common than three-way branches). In later versions of FORTRAN, a more conventional *logical IF-statement* was added, for example,

```
IF (X .EQ. A(I)) K = I-1
```

(FORTRAN uses '.EQ.' for the equality relation.)

FORTRAN II Statement	704 Branch	
GOTO n	TRA k	(transfer direct)
GOTO n, (n1, n2, ..., nm)	TRA i	(transfer indirect)
GOTO (n1, n2, ..., nm), n	TRA i,k	(transfer indexed)
IF (a) n1, n2, n3	CAS k	(compare AC with storage)
IF ACCUMULATOR OVERFLOW n1, n2	TOV k	(transfer on AC overflow)
IF QUOTIENT OVERFLOW n1, n2	TQO k	(transfer on MQ overflow)
DO n i = m1, m2, m3	TIX d,i,k	(transfer on index)
CALL name (args)	TSX i,k	(transfer and set index)
RETURN	TRA i	(transfer indirect)

Figure 2.2 Similarity of FORTRAN and IBM 704 Branches

The GOTO Is the Workhorse of Control Flow

Just as in most computers, the transfer (i.e., branch or jump) instruction is the primary means for controlling the flow of execution, so in FORTRAN the GOTO-statement and its variants are the fundamental control structures. We will now investigate the implications of this fact on program readability.

In FORTRAN, the GOTO-statement is the raw material from which control structures are built. For example, a two-way branch is often implemented with a logical IF-statement and a GOTO:

```
      IF (condition) GOTO 100
      ... case for condition false ...
      GOTO 200
100   ... case for condition true ...
200   ...
```

We can see that this corresponds to the **if-then-else**, or *conditional* statement of newer programming languages. This is an example of dividing the control flow into two cases. For dividing it into more than two cases, a *computed GOTO* is provided, for example,

```
      GOTO (10, 20, 30, 40), I
10    ... handle case 1 ...
      GOTO 100
20    ... handle case 2 ...
      GOTO 100
30    ... handle case 3 ...
      GOTO 100
40    ... handle case 4 ...
100   ...
```

The meaning of this is branch to statement 10, 20, 30, or 40 if I is 1, 2, 3, or 4, respectively. We can recognize this as the equivalent of the **case**-statement that is included in many contemporary languages.[2]

Both the IF-statement and the computed GOTO are examples of *selection* statements, so called because they select between two or more possible control paths.

Loops can be implemented by various combinations of IF-statements and GOTOs (the DO-loop is discussed later). For example, a *trailing-decision loop* could be written:

2 The labels in a computed GOTO need not be unique.

```
100     ... body of loop ...
        IF (loop not done) GOTO 100
```

and a *leading-decision loop* could be written:

```
100     IF (loop done) GOTO 200
        ... body of loop ...
        GOTO 100
200     ...
```

We can recognize these as the **while-do** and **repeat-until** constructs of languages such as Pascal. These constructs are called *indefinite iterations* because the exact number of iterations is not known in advance (i.e., not definite).

One problem with using one statement to build all control structures is that we never know what control structure is intended. For example, in Pascal, when we see **while** we know that a leading-decision loop is intended; when we see **repeat** a trailing-decision loop is intended; and when we see **if** a conditional statement is intended. In FORTRAN, when we see an IF-statement, we don't know (without looking closely) whether it's the beginning of a leading-decision loop, the end of a trailing-decision loop, a conditional selection, or part of a more complicated control structure (such as the mid-decision loop, discussed below). This difficulty in identifying structures makes it much harder for a reader to determine the programmer's intent.

EXERCISE 2-1: Use arithmetic IF's and assignment statements to accomplish the following: store $+1$ in S if $X>0$, store -1 in S if $X<0$, and store 0 in S if $X=0$. Do the same with logical IF's. (Note that in FORTRAN '<' and '>' are written '.LT.' and '.GT.', respectively.)

EXERCISE 2-2: Write in FORTRAN IV a leading-decision loop that doubles N until it is greater than 100.

EXERCISE 2-3: Write FORTRAN IV code to compute the first Fibonacci number greater than 1000.

EXERCISE 2-4: Translate 'GOTO (10, 20, 30, 40), I' into IF-statements.

EXERCISE 2-5: Write a computed GOTO that, on the basis of a number M representing a month, branches to label 100 if the month is February, to label 200 if the month has 30 days, and to label 300 if the month has 31 days.

It Is Difficult to Correlate Static and Dynamic Structures

Of course, the patterns shown above are not the only ways of combining IF and GOTO statements in FORTRAN. It is possible to write *mid-decision loops,*

```
100     ... first half of loop ...
        IF (loop done) GOTO 200
        ... second half of loop ...
        GOTO 100
200     ...
```

and much more complicated control structures. The GOTO-statement is a very primitive and powerful control structure. It is a two-edged sword because it is possible to implement almost any control regime with it—those that are good, but also those that are bad.

What makes a control regime good or bad? Mainly it is understandability; in a good control structure the static form of the structure (i.e., its appearance to the reader) corresponds in a simple way to its dynamic behavior. Therefore, it is easy for a reader to visualize the effect of a control structure from its written form. The undisciplined use of the GOTO-statement permits the construction of very intricate control structures, which are correspondingly hard to understand. We will see in Chapters 3–5 that newer languages depend much less on the GOTO-statement.

The idea of a good control structure is embodied in the Structure Principle first proposed by E. W. Dijkstra[3]:

> ***The Structure Principle***
>
> The static structure of a program should correspond in a simple way to the dynamic structure of the corresponding computations.

What this principle means is that it should be possible to visualize the behavior of the program easily from its written form. For example, when the execution of one segment of code precedes another in time, the statements of the first segment should precede those of the second in the program. Similarly, the statements whose execution is repeated by a loop should be easy to identify.

3 See Dijkstra (1968).

This is simplified if they are a contiguous, indented block of text. We will see many other examples of the Structure Principle in this book.

EXERCISE 2-6: Suggest a practical use for mid-decision loops.

The Computed and Assigned GOTOs Are Easily Confused

Two statements in FORTRAN, the *computed* GOTO and the *assigned* GOTO, illustrate the pitfalls that await the language designer. We have seen the computed GOTO:

GOTO (L_1, L_2, ..., L_n), I

where the L_i are statement numbers and I is any integer variable. The computed GOTO transfers to statement number L_k if I contains k. Computed GOTOs are usually implemented by a jump table: The compiler stores addresses (of the statements numbered L_i) in an array in memory and then compiles code to use I as an index into this array.

FORTRAN also provides another control structure for branching to a number of different statements, the assigned GOTO:

GOTO N, (L_1, L_2, ..., L_n)

where N is also an integer variable. This statement transfers to the statement whose *address* is in the variable N; in other words, this is an indirect GOTO. The list of statement labels is not actually necessary since all the information necessary to perform the jump is in N. The list is provided as documentation since otherwise the reader would have no way of knowing where the GOTO goes. Most compilers don't check whether the statement whose address is in N has its label included in the list.

The assigned GOTO must be used in conjunction with another statement, the ASSIGN statement. The effect of

```
ASSIGN 20 TO N
```

is to put the address of statement number 20 in the integer variable N. Note that this is completely different from the assignment statement 'N = 20', which stores the integer 20 into N. In general, the address of statement number 20 will not be 20 (recall that the symbolic labels in our pseudo-code had no relation to the addresses to which they were bound). Thus, the effect of 'ASSIGN 20 TO N' will be to put some other number (the address of statement 20, say 347) into N.

The computed and assigned GOTOs are easily confused; they look almost identical. Therefore, it is not uncommon for a programmer to write one where the other is expected. Let's consider the consequences of writing a computed GOTO where an assigned GOTO is intended:

```
ASSIGN 20 TO N
    ⋮
GOTO (20, 30, 40, 50), N
```

The ASSIGN-statement will assign the address of statement number 20 (say, 347) to N. The computed GOTO will then attempt to use this as an index into the jump table (20, 30, 40, 50). In this case, the index (347) will be well out of range, but most systems don't check this so we will fetch some value out of memory to use as the destination of the jump. The result is that the program will transfer to an unpredictable location in memory, thus leading to a very-difficult-to-find bug.

Now let's consider the opposite error: using an assigned GOTO where a computed GOTO is intended.

```
I = 3
  ⋮
GOTO I, (20, 30, 40, 50)
```

Since the assigned GOTO expects the variable I to contain the address of a statement, it will transfer to that address. In this case, it will transfer to address 3, which is almost certainly not the address of one of the statements in the list and is very likely not the address of a statement at all (low-addressed locations are often dedicated to use by the system). Again, a difficult bug results.

What are the causes of these problems? The most obvious cause is the easily confused syntax of the two constructs:

GOTO (L_1, ..., L_n), I
GOTO I, (L_1, ..., L_n)

This is a violation of the Syntactic Consistency Principle.

> ***Syntactic Consistency Principle***
>
> Things which look similar should be similar and things which look different should be different.

Generally speaking, it is best to avoid syntactic forms that can be converted into other legal forms by a simple error. (FORTRAN's use of '**' for exponentiation has been criticized on this basis, since leaving out one of the asterisks converts it into a legal FORTRAN multiplication sign '*'.)

A more fundamental cause for the GOTO problem is FORTRAN's *weak typing*, which results from using integer variables to hold a number of things besides integers, such as the addresses of statements, and character strings (discussed in Section 2.4, under "The Integer Type Is Overworked"). If FORTRAN had variables of type LABEL for holding the addresses of statements, and if a LABEL variable were required in an assigned GOTO, then confusing the two GOTO statements would lead to an easy-to-find compile-time error not to an obscure run-time error. Thus, FORTRAN violates the principle of Defense in Depth.

Defense in Depth Principle

If an error gets through one line of defense (syntactic checking, in this case), then it should be caught by the next line of defense (type checking, in this case).

This example also illustrates one of the hardest problems of language design: identifying the *interaction* of features. (In this case, the interaction is between the syntax of the GOTOs and the decision to use integer variables to hold the addresses of statements.)

EXERCISE 2-7:* Propose and defend a solution to the problem of assigned and computed GOTOs in FORTRAN. If you decide to introduce a type LABEL, keep in mind that you must analyze the interaction of this feature with others already in the language. For example, will you allow LABEL arrays? Will you allow parameters of type LABEL or allow functions to return LABELs?

The DO-Loop Is More Structured than the GOTO

We have seen that the GOTO- and IF-statements provide *primitive*, or *low-level*, control structuring mechanisms. That is, they are simple components from which higher-level control structures can be built. FORTRAN contains only one built-in, higher-level control structure, the DO-loop, which we discuss next. Much like the LOOP instruction in our pseudo-code, the DO-loop provides a simple method of constructing a counted loop (sometimes called a *definite iteration*). For example,

```
      DO 100 I = 1, N
      A(I) = A(I)*2
100   CONTINUE
```

is a command to execute the statements between the DO and the corresponding CONTINUE with I taking on the values 1 through N. The variable that changes values (I in this case) is called the *controlled variable,* and the statements that are repeated, which extend from the DO to the CONTINUE with a matching label, are called the *extent* or *body* of the loop.

EXERCISE 2-8: Write the above example using only IF and GOTO (i.e., without the DO-loop).

EXERCISE 2-9: Write a DO-loop that computes into SUM the sum of the array elements A(1) + A(2) + ··· + A(100).

The DO-Loop Is Higher Level

The DO-loop is called *higher level* because it allows programmers to state what they *want* (namely, for the commands in the loop to be executed N times), rather than how to do it (e.g., initialize I, increment it, test it). Higher-level constructs such as this are safer to use because they remove from the programmer the opportunity to make certain errors, such as incorrect testing for loop termination. Thus, the DO-loop illustrates the Automation Principle because we have made the computer take over a routine, tedious, error-prone task.

The DO-Loop Can Be Nested

One of the important characteristics of the DO-loop is that it can be nested; that is, DO-loops are constructed *hierarchically.* More complicated loops can be built up from simpler ones by nesting DO-loops one within another, for example,

```
      DO 100 I = 1, M  ─────────┐
      :                         │
         DO 200 J = 1, N  ──┐   │
         :                  │   │
200      CONTINUE  ─────────┘   │
      :                         │
100   CONTINUE  ────────────────┘
```

Hierarchical structures such as these are very common in programming languages and in other contexts where complicated systems must be built or described. An important requirement of hierarchical structure is that the structures must be properly nested. For example,

```
        DO 100 I = 1, M  ──┐
            :              │
        DO 200 J = 1, N  ──┤──┐
            :              │  │
100     CONTINUE ──────────┘  │
            :                 │
200     CONTINUE ─────────────┘
```

is incorrectly nested, as shown by the brackets to the right. Insisting on a hierarchical structure ensures that there is a *regular* flow of control whose dynamic structure corresponds to the static structure of the program (the Structure Principle). Unfortunately, this regularity is compromised by the fact that FORTRAN permits the programmer to jump into and out of DO-loops under certain circumstances.

Overall, FORTRAN has a linear rather than a hierarchical structure, which reflects the pseudo-codes and machine language from which it is derived. The statements are listed one after another and numbered in a way reminiscent of memory addresses rather than being nested like the statements in more modern languages. Other than the DO-loop, the only nesting permitted in FORTRAN statements is in the logical IF, although the statement controlled by the IF is only allowed to be a simple unconditional statement (e.g., an assignment or GOTO, not an IF or DO).[4]

The DO-Loop Is Highly Optimized

In Section 2.1 we discussed the resistance that the first FORTRAN system faced; programmers were convinced that a compiler could not produce as good code as they could produce. It was therefore imperative that the FORTRAN system produce excellent code. The most troublesome area in this regard was the use of index registers for array subscripting. Programmers were able to see what variables would be used for indexing in a loop and thereby were able to keep their values in index registers; this allowed faster indexing than could be obtained by fetching their values from memory. Similarly, the index registers would be

4 FORTRAN 77 makes more consistent use of hierarchical structure, which is a characteristic of second-generation languages. We restrict our attention to FORTRAN IV because it is more consistently first generation.

incremented and tested directly without being stored in memory. Producing code of comparable quality posed a significant challenge for the designers of the first FORTRAN compiler. However, by using sophisticated optimization techniques they were able to produce code better than most assembly language programmers. Some of these techniques are discussed in Section 2.4 under "FORTRAN Arrays Allow Many Optimizations."

The ability to optimize the DO-loop can be partly attributed to its *structure*, the fact that the *controlled variable* and its initial and final values are all stated explicitly along with the extent of the loop. All this useful information, which is provided explicitly by the DO-loop, must be discovered by the compiler if the more primitive IF and GOTO are used. Although this can be done, it is difficult to program and expensive to execute. It is often the case that higher-level programming language constructs are easier to optimize than the lower-level ones. This is an example of the Preservation of Information Principle.

> ***Preservation of Information Principle***
>
> The language should allow the representation of information that the user might know and that the compiler might need.

Subprograms Were an Important, Late Addition

It is surprising to realize that the preliminary description of FORTRAN I omitted what is now considered one of the most important programming language facilities—subprograms. Of course, FORTRAN programs made use of library procedures, such as those for input-output, and the mathematical functions (SIN, COS, etc.) just as our pseudo-code did. What FORTRAN I did *not* provide was the capability for programmers to define their own subprograms. This deficiency was remedied in FORTRAN II with the addition of the SUBROUTINE and FUNCTION declarations. In the rest of Section 2.3 we will discuss subprograms and their implementation.

Subprograms Define Procedural Abstractions

To see the need for subprograms, we will work through a very simple example. Suppose we have a program, which in outline form is

```
  ⋮
DIST1 = X1 - Y1
IF (DIST1 .LT. 0) DIST1 = -DIST1
  ⋮
DIFFER = POSX - POSY
IF (DIFFER .LT. 0) DIFFER = -DIFFER
  ⋮
```

(In FORTRAN, '.LT.' means "less than.") We can see that essentially the same program fragment has been repeated twice, although with different variables. When we *abstract* out this fragment from the particular variables it mentions, we have

$d = x - y$
IF (d .LT. 0) $d = -d$

In the first occurrence, d, x, and y are DIST1, X1, and Y1; in the second they are DIFFER, POSX, and POSY.

Instead of repeating this sequence every time it is needed, we can define this *procedural abstraction* (or *control abstraction*) once, and then call for it to be used every time we need it. This definition is done with a subprogram declaration. In this case, the kind of subprogram we need is a *subroutine*, which is declared by:

```
SUBROUTINE name (formals)
... body of subroutine ...
RETURN
END
```

where 'name' is the name to be bound to the subroutine and 'formals' is a list of the names of the *formal parameters* (or dummy variables); these are the variables that will stand for different variables each time the subroutine is used. (Although the RETURN-statement normally occurs at the end of the subprogram, it is allowed anywhere a statement is allowed.)

A subroutine that embodies the procedural abstraction in our example is

```
SUBROUTINE DIST (D, X, Y)
D = X - Y
IF (D .LT. 0) D = -D
RETURN
END
```

This subroutine can then be *invoked* by a CALL-statement; for example, the program fragment with which we started can now be written:

```
      ⋮
CALL DIST (DIST1, X1, Y1)
      ⋮
CALL DIST (DIFFER, POSX, POSY)
      ⋮
```

When such a procedure is invoked, we say that the formals are *bound* to the actuals; that is, in the first case, we bind D to DIST1, X to X1, and Y to Y1. In the second we bind D to DIFFER, X to POSX, and Y to POSY. By this means variables in the *caller's* environment can be accessed by referring to the formal parameters in the *callee's* environment (the callee is the subprogram being called).

Executing the CALL-statement passes control from the caller to the callee. Executing a RETURN-statement in the callee passes control back to the caller, which resumes execution at the statement following the CALL.

The advantages of procedural abstraction are discussed next.

EXERCISE 2-10: Define a subroutine 'PUTABS (X, Y)' that computes the absolute value of X and stores it in Y.

Subprograms Allow Large Programs to Be Modularized

One obvious advantage of procedural abstraction is that it saves writing, as we saw in the example above. We can save ourselves from writing the same or a similar code sequence over and over again by defining it as a subprogram and calling it when needed. There is a much more important reason for defining procedural abstractions that derives from the nature of human perception. Humans seem to be able to keep only a few distinct things (about seven) in their minds at one time. One result of this is that the complexity of understanding a system's design (whether software or not) increases rapidly with the size of the system. One of the most common approaches used to solve large problems is to break them into smaller problems. This is basically the function of procedural abstraction. By defining a program as a set of relatively small subprograms, the total difficulty of the design process can be decreased since each subprogram can be written, debugged, and read as an independent unit. We have seen this idea before; it is called *modularizing* a program because the program (and the programming task) is divided up into a number of manageable *modules*. *Abstraction*, one of the most common methods of modularization, is the process in which we *abstract out* the common parts of a system. This is familiar from elementary algebra, where, for example, an expression can be simplified by factoring:

$$ax - bx = (a - b)x$$

These ideas are embodied in a very important principle:

> ***The Abstraction Principle***
>
> Avoid requiring something to be stated more than once; factor out the recurring pattern.

Subprograms Encourage Libraries

There are other advantages to subprograms, such as *separate compilation.* Since subprograms are largely independent of one another, they can be separately translated to relocatable object code by the compiler and later combined by the linker. Hence, when one module of a program is modified, only that module has to be recompiled because it can later be linked with the already compiled versions of the other modules. In a large program this can mean a great saving of computer time.

A natural adjunct to this separate compilation is the idea of maintaining a *library* of already debugged and compiled useful subprograms. This allows a programmer to build upon the work of others. A well-designed library is an enormous aid in program development; indeed, many programs are written as no more than a series of calls on library procedures. This sort of modular, or "prefab," program construction is called *programming in the large* to contrast it with the usual *programming in the small,* wherein many small components, the statements of a language, are assembled to make the program.[5]

EXERCISE 2-11:* Investigate the contents of the libraries on your local computer system. Which application areas are best supported by libraries? Which are least supported?

Parameters Are Usually Passed by Reference

In our discussion of the DIST subroutine example on page 51, we described the action of CALL as though the actual parameters were substituted textually for the formal parameters. This is called the *copy rule* for subprogram invocation; that is, the body of the subprogram is copied into the place from which it was

5 These terms were introduced in DeRemer and Kron (1976).

called, with the actual parameters substituted for the formals. While this is a handy way to think about the meaning of parameters, it is not the way they are in fact implemented. The copies would occupy too much space and it would take too much time to substitute the parameters. Next, we discuss the *parameter passing modes*, or ways in which parameters are actually passed, in FORTRAN.

FORTRAN permits subprogram parameters to be used for input or output or both. In the DIST example, the X and Y parameters were used as input values and the D parameter was used as an output value. If the values of X and Y had been altered by the subroutine, then these would have been both input and output parameters. How can these parameters be implemented? First, consider an output parameter: If a subprogram is to be able to write into a variable passed as an actual parameter (e.g., DIFFER in our example), then it must be passed the address of this variable's location in memory. In other words, the formal parameter D is bound to the *address* of the actual parameter DIFFER. Therefore, when the assignment 'D = X−Y' is executed, it is DIFFER that is modified. Thus, the formal parameter gives the callee read-write access to the actual parameter in the caller. The technical term used in programming languages for an address of a location in memory is a *reference* because it *refers* to a memory location. For this reason the parameter passing mode we have just described is called *pass by reference.* Since FORTRAN does not permit programmers to specify whether they intend to use a parameter for input or output or both, all parameters are passed by reference just on the chance they may be output parameters. The consequences of this decision are discussed next.

Pass by Reference Is Always Efficient

One of the advantages of pass by reference is that it is always efficient. To show this we investigate how several different kinds of actual parameters are passed. The key point is that pass by reference always passes just the reference to (address of) the actual parameter. Since references are usually small (one word or less), this means that very little information is passed from the *caller* to the *callee.* In the case of actuals that are simple variables, as in 'CALL DIST (DIFFER, POSX, POSY)', the addresses of the three actuals (DIFFER, POSX, and POSY) are passed.

Suppose that the actual parameters were array elements, for example,

```
CALL DIST (D(I), POS(I), POS(J))
```

The address of POS(I) is easily computed from the address of the first element of POS and the value of the index I (this process is described in the section on data structures, page 70). Therefore, all the caller has to do is compute the addresses of the array elements, D(I), POS(I), and POS(J), and pass these to the caller, just as it did for simple variables.

We have seen how array elements are passed to subprograms; how about the entire array, which is often useful? For a simple example, consider the following FUNCTION that computes the mean (average) of an array. (A FUNCTION is a subprogram that computes a value and hence may be called from an expression.)

```
      FUNCTION AVG (ARR, N)
      DIMENSION ARR(N)
      SUM = 0.0
      DO 100 I = 1, N
        SUM = SUM + ARR(I)
100   CONTINUE
      AVG = SUM / FLOAT(N)
      RETURN
      END
```

A simple program that uses this function is

```
      DIMENSION VALUES (100)
          ⋮
      AVGVAL = AVG (VALUES, 100)
          ⋮
```

It is necessary to pass the size of the array to the subprogram because it is needed to control the DO-loop (among other uses). Unfortunately, having to pass the array size means that the programmer has the opportunity to pass the wrong size. This may introduce a bug into the program if the size passed is too small, or it may compromise the security of the FORTRAN run-time system if it is too big. This is so because FORTRAN permits programmers to oversubscript arrays, that is, to use array subscripts that are *out of bounds* (the reason this is permitted is discussed later). Thus, the programmer may inadvertently store into tables or other data structures that the compiler has placed in memory for the use of the run-time system. This causes the program either to abort or to behave in mysterious ways.

Clearly, the array must be passed in such a manner that all of its elements are accessible to the callee. This is accomplished by passing the address of the first element of the array; that is, the formal ARR is bound to the first element of the array actual, VALUES(1). The callee can then compute the address of an array element ARR(I) in the usual way. This is a very efficient way of passing arrays since only a single address is passed from the caller to the callee. Unfortunately, this efficiency has bad consequences, some of which are discussed in the next section.

We must note that there is an efficiency *cost* associated with reference parameters: the cost of *indirection.* Instead of the subprogram having the value of the actual parameter directly available, it only has the address of the actual. Therefore, an extra memory reference is required to fetch or store the value of a parameter passed by reference. This is discussed further in Chapter 8 (Section 8.1).

Pass by Reference Has Dangerous Consequences

The most serious problems with passing all parameters by reference result from the assumption that all parameters can potentially be used for both input and output. This can be dangerous if the actual parameter is a variable since it means that an input variable may be inadvertently updated by a subprogram. This is called a *side effect* of the subprogram call. Although this may introduce a bug into the program that is difficult to find, it does not undermine the security of the FORTRAN system (i.e., it is not possible to corrupt the FORTRAN system's own data structures). This is not the case if a literal constant or expression is the actual parameter to the subprogram. Consider the following subroutine definition:

```
SUBROUTINE SWITCH (N)
N = 3
RETURN
END
```

SWITCH simply writes 3 into its parameter. Therefore, the invocation 'CALL SWITCH(I)' would result in 3 being stored in I. Now consider the invocation 'CALL SWITCH(2)'. What will be the effect of this? Recall that in our pseudo-code program (Chapter 1) we stored the constants to be used by the program in memory locations; for example, we stored the constant zero in location 000. This is a very common practice, and compilers frequently allocate an area of memory, called a *literal table,* to contain the values of all of the literal constants used in a program. To return to our example, the literal 2 would be assigned a location in the literal table, and it is the address of this location that is passed to the subroutine. Therefore, when the subroutine assigns 3 to its parameter it will overwrite the value 2 in the literal table. The problem with this is that the compiler will compile a program so that it loads the contents of this location whenever it needs a constant 2, even though that location now contains a 3. Therefore, if the program now executed the assignment 'I = 2+2', the value stored in I would be 6. We have used the SWITCH procedure to change a "constant." You can imagine the debugging difficulties this could cause as the programmer tries to discover how the variable I has become set to 6 when the program clearly states 'I = 2+2'.

You might object that this would never happen in practice, that a programmer would never write a subroutine like SWITCH. Unfortunately, there is a legend that a programmer once used exactly this device because he had uniformly used an incorrect constant throughout his program. Needless to say, this kind of practice results in unmaintainable programs. Even if this story is not true, there is a much more common cause of this situation. Both subroutines and functions often have output parameters, for example, to reflect the manner in which the subprogram completed its task. Programmers frequently are unaware that these parameters are used for output, either because the subprograms are poorly documented, or because the programmers have read the documentation and forgotten this detail. Thus, it is quite possible that the programmer could inadvertently pass a constant as an output parameter. This is an example of a lack of *security* in the language implementation, since the compiler allows its own runtime data structures (e.g., the literal table) to be corrupted.

You might object that the compiler should not permit this; that since the actual parameter is a *constant* it cannot be stored into, that storing is only allowed for *variables*. You might also point out that when a constant or expression is used as an actual parameter, the programmer intends for the *value* of that actual parameter to be passed, not some address that the compiler happens to have stored that value into. These are both correct observations, and we will see that newer languages allow the programmer to distinguish between parameters that are intended to be used for input or output. The compiler can then ensure that a constant or expression is not used where an output parameter is expected. This also has an efficiency benefit, since it avoids needless indirect reference to input parameters.

Pass by Value-Result Is Preferable

Although the best solution to this problem is to allow the programmer to specify whether a parameter is to be used for input or output, there is another way of implementing FORTRAN's parameters that does not present a security loophole; this is pass by *value-result*. The idea of this approach is that the *value* of the actual parameter is copied into the formal parameter at subprogram entry, and the *result*, or final value of the formal, is copied into the actual parameter at subprogram exit. Since both of these operations are done *by the caller*, the compiler can know to omit the second operation (copying out the result) if the actual was a constant or expression. Thus, the caller takes the result value only if the actual is something that can be meaningfully stored into, that is, a variable or array element in FORTRAN. The callee never has direct access to the caller's variables; it only has access to its formals. The caller is responsible for moving values to and from the formals. Note that pass by value-result does not prevent the programmer from accidently having one of the variables altered, but at least it preserves the security of the implementation.

EXERCISE 2-12:* Determine how the FORTRAN compilers available to you implement parameters. Check the manuals and try some experiments (such as the SWITCH subroutine) to determine the parameter passing mode used. What do the ANS FORTRAN standards say about the way parameters are to be passed?

EXERCISE 2-13: Consider the following FORTRAN SUBROUTINE:

```
SUBROUTINE TEST (X, Y, Z)
X = 1
Z = X + Y
RETURN
END
```

and consider the following code fragment:

```
N = 2
CALL TEST (N, N, M)
```

What will be the final value of M if the parameters are passed by reference? What will it be if they're passed by value-result?

EXERCISE 2-14:* There are several different varieties of pass by value-result: The address of the actual can be computed once, at subprogram entry time, or twice, once on entry and once on exit. Describe the output of this program under each of these two varieties of value-result:

```
DIMENSION A(2)
I = 1
A(1) = 10
A(2) = 11
CALL SUB (I, A(I))
PRINT, A(1), A(2)
END

SUBROUTINE SUB (K, X)
PRINT, X
K = 2
X = 20
RETURN
END
```

Does the outcome depend on the order in which the results are copied from the formals back into the actuals?

Subprograms Are Implemented Using Activation Records

In this section we investigate the way subprograms (subroutines and functions) are implemented. What happens when a subprogram is invoked? Clearly, we must transmit the parameters to the subprogram, which is the first step. This may be done by reference or by value (the first half of the value-result process).

It may seem that the next step is to enter the subprogram, but we must do something else first. If we entered now, there would be no way to get back to the caller because a subprogram can be called from many different callers and from many different places within one caller (as we saw in the DIST example). Therefore, there is not a unique place to which the callee should return when it has finished. To put it another way, it is necessary to tell the callee who its caller is; then, when the callee executes its RETURN statement it will know to whom to return.

There is one other issue we must address: saving the state of the caller. As you probably know, most computers have a number of *registers* that can be used for high-speed temporary storage. Since subprograms may be separately compiled, it is not usually possible to know the registers that another subprogram uses. Therefore, when one subprogram calls another, it is necessary for one or the other to preserve the content of the registers in a private area of memory. The content of the registers can then be restored when the caller gets control back from the callee.

We summarize these ideas as follows: When one subprogram calls another, the *state* of the caller must be preserved before the callee is entered and must be restored after the callee returns. By the state of the caller, we mean all of the information that characterizes the state of the computation in progress. This includes the contents of all of the variables, the contents of any registers in use, and the current point of execution (as indicated by the IP, or instruction pointer register). Of course, any information that is already stored in memory locations private to the caller is already saved and need not be saved again. All of the other information must be stored in a caller-private data area before the callee is entered. This data area is often called an *activation record* because it holds all the information relevant to one *activation* of a subprogram. A subprogram is *active* if it's been called but hasn't yet returned. In a nonrecursive language such as FORTRAN, there is one activation record for each subprogram (activation records for recursive subprograms are discussed in Chapter 3). The concept of an activation record is very important and will be discussed repeatedly in the following chapters.

The activation record serves a number of useful functions. For example, we have said that the caller must *transmit* the actual parameters to the callee. This means that the actual parameters (either their values or their references) must be placed in a location where the callee knows to find them. Where should this be? The callee's activation record is often a good choice (although there are others, such as registers). Thus, a subprogram's state includes its current parameters.

Since the activation record contains all of the information needed to restart a subprogram (its IP, register values, etc.), it is convenient to think of the activation record as a repository for all information relevent to the subprogram. We said earlier that the callee must be passed some sort of reference to the caller so that it will know which caller to resume when it returns. A very convenient way to do this is to transmit to the callee a pointer to the caller's activation record. The callee then has all of the information required to resume its caller. For example, the return address for the return jump to the caller can be obtained by the callee from the caller's activation record.

How are we to transmit to the callee the pointer to the caller's activation record? The simplest method is to store the pointer in the callee's activation record. This pointer from a callee's activation record to its caller's activation record is called a *dynamic link*. The *dynamic chain* is the sequence of dynamic links that reach back from each callee to its caller. The dynamic chain begins at the currently active subprogram (i.e., the one now in control) and terminates at the main program. See Figure 2.3 for an example. We show the situation in which the main program has called *S*, *S* has called *T*, *T* has called *F*, and *F* is still active.

Let's summarize the tasks that must be completed to perform a subprogram invocation.

1. Place the parameters in the callee's activation record.
2. Save the state of the caller in the caller's activation record (including the point at which the caller is to resume execution).
3. Place a pointer to the caller's activation record in the callee's activation record.

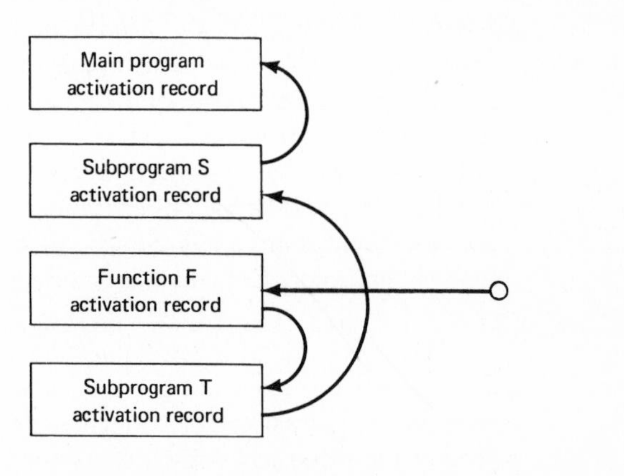

Figure 2.3 The Dynamic Chain of Activation Records

4. Enter the callee at its first instruction.

The steps required to return from the callee to the caller are as follows:

1. Get the address at which the caller is to resume execution and transfer to that location.
2. When the caller regains control, it will have to restore the rest of the state of its execution (registers, etc.) from its activation record.

In addition, if the callee were a function (as opposed to a subroutine), then the value it returns must be made accessible to the caller. This can be accomplished by leaving it in a machine register or by placing it in a location in the caller's activation record.

From this discussion, we can see that an activation record must contain space for the following information:

1. The parameters passed to this subprogram when it was last called (we call this part PAR, for parameters)
2. The IP, or resumption address, of this subprogram when it is not executing
3. The dynamic link, or pointer to the activation record of the caller of this subprogram (we call this DL)
4. Temporary areas for storing register contents and other volatile information (we call this TMP)

It is not particularly important what format is used for this information, although certain layouts may be particularly efficient on certain machines (Figure 2.4).

We can make these ideas a little more specific by looking at the code for each of the steps in a CALL and a RETURN. In order to do this, we have to introduce some notation. Rather than introduce the assembly language for either a real or made-up machine, we use a conventional high-level language syntax. We must be careful to use statements that are very simple so that they can be implemented with one or two instructions on most machines. First, we use the notation 'M[*k*]' to represent the memory location with the address *k*. For example,

---

- PAR parameters
- IP resumption address
- DL dynamic link
- TMP temporary storage

Figure 2.4 Components of Nonrecursive Activation Record

```
M[R1] := IP;
```

could be an instruction to store the contents of the IP register in the memory location whose address is in the R1 register.

We also need a notation for denoting activation records and their parts. If *S* is a subprogram, then 'AR(*S*)' is the address of its activation record. We also use a dot to select the *fields* of the activation record; for example,

```
M[AR(S)].DL
```

denotes the dynamic link field of *S*'s activation record.

We now look at the code in the caller for each part of a subprogram invocation. We assume that the caller, *S*, is going to invoke the function '*F* (*P*, *Q*)'. The first step is to save the state of the caller, including the address at which it is to be resumed, in the caller's activation record. The resumption address is the address of the instruction after that which enters the callee; we call it 'resume':

```
save registers etc. in M[AR(S)].TMP;
M[AR(S)].IP := resume;
```

The second step is to compute the actual parameters *P* and *Q* and store their references in the PAR part of *F*'s activation record:

```
M[AR(F)].PAR[1] := reference to P;
M[AR(F)].PAR[2] := reference to Q;
```

The third step is to store a pointer to the caller's activation record, AR(*S*), into the DL field of the callee's activation record:

```
M[AR(F)].DL := AR(S);
```

The final step in calling the function is to start execution at its entry address, which we will denote by 'entry(*F*)':

```
goto entry(F);
```

When the callee returns, the caller begins executing at the next instruction, which we have called 'resume'. When the caller regains control, it will have to restore its registers from its activation record and, if the subprogram was a function, fetch the answer from wherever the callee left it (a register or the caller's activation record):

```
resume:
restore registers etc. from M[AR(S)].TMP;
get value returned by F;
```

What code must the callee execute to return from a subprogram? As we saw before, the first step is to place the value to be returned in a place accessible to the caller. In FORTRAN the value returned is the last value assigned to a variable with the same name as the function, '*F*' in this case. Therefore, the answer is transmitted to the caller by placing the value of this variable in a machine register or in a field in the caller's activation record.

The pointer to the caller's activation record is just the dynamic link, that is, M[AR(*F*)].DL. The last step in a return is to transfer to the caller's resumption address; this is in the IP field of the caller's activation record:

```
goto M[M[AR(F)].DL].IP;
```

The code to invoke and return from a subprogram is summarized in the *translation rules* in Figures 2.5 and 2.6. Figure 2.5 shows the code produced in the caller for a CALL-statement; Figure 2.6 shows the code produced in a subroutine for a RETURN-statement.

EXERCISE 2-15: The above implementation works for parameters passed by

---

Code in Caller *S*:

$F(P_1, \ldots, P_n) \Rightarrow$

```
    save registers etc. in M[AR(S)].TMP;
    M[AR(S)].IP := resume;

    M[AR(F)].PAR[1] := reference to P1;

      ⋮

    M[AR(F)].PAR[n] := reference to Pn;

    M[AR(F)].DL := AR(S);
    goto entry(F);
resume:
    restore registers etc. from M[AR(S)].TMP;
    get value returned by F, if it's a function;
```

Figure 2.5 Implementation of Nonrecursive Call

```
            Code in Callee F:
RETURN  ⇒
    place returned value where accessible to caller, if F a function;
    goto M[M[AR(F)].DL].IP;
```

Figure 2.6 Implementation of Nonrecursive Return

reference. What modifications would have to be made to accommodate pass by value-result?

EXERCISE 2-16:* Design an activation record format appropriate for some machine with which you are familiar. Implement the code sequences in Figures 2.5 and 2.6 in the assembly language of that machine.

EXERCISE 2-17:* The particular code sequences discussed above were chosen because they will generalize to other languages, for example, ones with recursive procedures. There are several improvements that can be made to the above code sequence, if we know that procedures are nonrecursive, as in FORTRAN. Find these improvements and estimate the savings (in terms of memory references per invocation) that would result.

2.4 DESIGN: DATA STRUCTURES

Data Structures Were Suggested by Mathematics

FORTRAN is a scientific programming language. Therefore, the data structuring methods included in FORTRAN were those most familiar to scientific and engineering applications of mathematics: scalars and arrays. Languages from this period (ca. 1960) that were intended for commercial applications, such as COBOL and its predecessors (e.g., FLOW-MATIC, 1957), included data structuring methods appropriate to these applications, for example, character strings and records. As we will see, the data structuring methods provided by all these programming languages were also largely determined by the computer architectures and programming techniques of that time.

The Primitives Are Scalars

Since scientific programming makes heavy use of numbers, it follows that numeric scalars are the primary data structure *primitives* provided in FORTRAN.

Most computers designed after the IBM 704 included both integer and floating-point arithmetic. As we saw in the pseudo-code of Chapter 1, integers are most commonly used for indexing and counting, and floating-point numbers are used for evaluating mathematical and physical formulas. In the early 1960s, a number of computers began to appear that supported *double-precision* arithmetic, that is, floating-point arithmetic with numbers twice as large as the normal floating-point numbers. To provide access to this, the FORTRAN II language included a *type* DOUBLE PRECISION and arithmetic operation on numbers of this type. FORTRAN II included several other important additions, including COMPLEX numbers, which are very important for scientific applications, and LOGICAL (or Boolean[6]) values. Next, we will discuss the primitive data types and the operations defined on them.

The Scalar Types Are Represented in Different Ways

Computers of the early 1960s were mostly *word-oriented,* that is, the basic addressable unit of storage was a *word,* which was also the basic unit in which most information was manipulated. For example, integer, floating-point, and logical values all normally occupied one word. Even characters were normally manipulated in groups that corresponded to the number of characters that could fit in one word (typically about six).

Each of the primitive data types was *represented* in a manner appropriate to the operations defined on that data type. For example, integers were usually represented as a binary number with a sign bit:

s	b_{30}	b_{29}	$\cdots$	b_2	b_1	b_0

For the sake of this and the following examples, we will presume a computer with a 32-bit word. The number represented by this bit pattern is:

$$(-1)^s \sum_{i=0}^{30} b_i 2^i$$

Of course, there are many possible ways to represent integers; for example, the sign bit could be at the other end of the word or a 1-bit could be used to represent positive numbers rather than negative numbers, as we have done. The operations provided by most computers for manipulating integers include the four

6 George Boole, 1815–1864, was a British mathematician and logician whose work on formalized logic is widely used in computer science and electrical engineering.

arithmetic operations (addition, subtraction, multiplication, and division), tests for zero, and tests of the sign bit. The last can be used for greater-than and less-than comparisons by subtracting and testing the sign of the result. The primitive integer operations provided by FORTRAN were just those operations that could be implemented in one or two machine instructions; namely, the arithmetic operations, the comparisons, absolute value, and exponentiation to an integer power.

As you know, floating-point numbers are related to scientific notation, that is, to the convention of representing a number by a coefficient and a power of 10, for example, -1.5×10^3. A typical representation for a floating-point number is:

sm	sc	c_7	...	c_0	m_{21}	m_{20}	...	m_1	m_0

The value represented by this number is $m \times 2^c$, where m is the *mantissa,*

$$m = (-1)^{sm} \sum_{i=0}^{21} m_i 2^{i-22}$$

and c is the *characteristic,*

$$c = (-1)^{sc} \sum_{i=0}^{7} c_i 2^i$$

Notice that the mantissa is always less than one. Again, there are many ways of representing floating-point numbers; the general idea is important here, not the details. The floating-point operations of FORTRAN follow closely those typically implemented on a computer: the four arithmetic operations, the comparisons, and absolute value. Exponentiation is also provided, although this is implemented through calls on library routines.

Notice that all of the numeric operations in FORTRAN are *representation independent*; that is, they depend on the logical, or *abstract,* properties of the data values and not on the details of their representation on a particular machine. A set of data values, together with a set of operations on those values that is defined without reference to the representation of the data values, is called an *abstract data type.* This is a very important concept that you will encounter many times in this book.

EXERCISE 2-18:* A commonly cited advantage of FORTRAN is *portability,* that is, the ability to transport FORTRAN programs from one computer to another with few or no changes to the program. Discuss the relevance of abstract data types to portability.

The Arithmetic Operators Are Overloaded

In mathematics, the integers are taken to be a subset of the real numbers, and the real numbers are taken to be a subset of the complex numbers. The arithmetic operations (i.e., addition, subtraction, multiplication, and division) are so defined that the operations on reals are extensions of the operations on integers and the operations on complex numbers are extensions of the operations on reals. The result is that it is meaningful to write $x+y$, $x-y$, etc., regardless of whether x and y are integers, reals, or complex numbers. We can also see that it is perfectly reasonable to write $x+1$, where x is a real number, since the integer 1 is also a real number. We have said that a primary goal of FORTRAN was to allow the programmer to write in the conventional algebraic notation; therefore, it was necessary for FORTRAN to support mixed expressions involving integer, floating-point, and complex numbers. This leads to a problem because computer numbers are not related in the same way as mathematical numbers; integers are not special kinds of floating-point numbers and floating-point numbers are not special kinds of complex numbers (we saw this in the last section). Indeed, the machine operations for performing integer arithmetic are completely different from those for performing floating-point arithmetic (this is necessary because the numbers are represented completely differently). Therefore, it is necessary to *overload* several meanings onto each arithmetic operation. For example, '+' can denote either integer, floating-point, or complex addition depending on its context, that is, depending on the type of the operands with which it is used. The compiler must look at this context in order to determine the machine instructions it must generate. This process can be expressed in rules such as these:

- Integer + integer ⇒ integer addition
- Real + real ⇒ floating-point addition
- Double precision + double precision ⇒ double floating addition
- Complex + complex ⇒ complex addition

There are several other terms you will hear in connection with overloaded operators. You will sometimes hear them called *generic* operators because they apply to a whole class of related data types (generic = relating to an entire group or class). The operations are also sometimes called *polymorphic* (poly = many, morphe = form) because they have many code sequences corresponding to them.

As we said, it is common to mix operations on integers, reals, and complex numbers in mathematical formulas. Early FORTRAN systems did not permit this; for example, if a programmer wanted to add the real variable X to the integer variable I, it would have been necessary to *convert* I to floating-point, 'X + FLOAT(I)'. Similarly, to assign X to I the programmer would write 'I = IFIX(X)'. Later versions of FORTRAN allowed *mixed-mode expressions*, that is, expressions of more than one *mode*, or type. Such an expression is 'I = X + I', which is interpreted to mean

```
I = IFIX (X + FLOAT(I))
```

We say that I has been *coerced* from integer to real and that X+I has been coerced from real to integer. A *coercion* is an implicit, context-dependent type conversion. In this case, when an integer (e.g., I) appears in a context where a real is expected (e.g., addition to a real number), the integer is implicitly converted to a real. Most programming languages coerce integers to reals (this is required for a conventional algebraic notation), and some languages provide a much more extensive set of coercions (e.g., PL/I and Algol-68). The coercion rules of a programming language can be expressed in transformation rules that reflect the automatic insertion of the type conversion. For example, if we let X be a real variable or expression and I be an integer variable or expression, then the FORTRAN coercion rules are:

```
X + I  ⇒  X + FLOAT(I)
I + X  ⇒  FLOAT(I) + X

X − I  ⇒  X − FLOAT(I)
etc.

X = I  ⇒  X = FLOAT(I)
I = X  ⇒  I = IFIX(X)
```

Notice that although reals can be coerced to integers on assignment, in expressions integers can be coerced to reals but reals cannot be coerced to integers; reals are said to *dominate* integers. This results from the fact that, mathematically, integers are a subset of the reals. It should be noted that the 1966 ANS FORTRAN Standard does *not* permit integers and floating-point numbers to be mixed in one expression although it does permit mixed assignments and mixed expressions involving real, double-precision, and complex numbers.

The Integer Type Is Overworked

In FORTRAN the integer type is required to do double duty: It represents both integers and character strings. This results from the fact that a *Hollerith*[7] *constant*

7 This is named for Herman Hollerith who developed the 80-column punched card in the 19th century.

is considered to be of type integer. A Hollerith constant was an early form of what is now called a *character string*; for example, the Hollerith constant 6HCARMEL represents the six-character string 'CARMEL'. The syntax of a Hollerith constant is (1) a literal integer (e.g., '6'), followed by (2) the letter 'H' (for "Hollerith"), followed by (3) the number of characters specified by the literal integer (e.g., the six characters 'CARMEL').

Character strings are not *first-class citizens* in FORTRAN; this means that it is not possible to use them in all the ways we would normally expect to use data values. This violates the Regularity Principle. For example, there is no such thing as a Hollerith variable and there are no Hollerith comparison operations. Instead, FORTRAN permits character strings to be read into integer or real variables and permits Hollerith constants to be used as parameters where integers are expected. For example, given the function definition

```
FUNCTION ISUCC (N)
ISUCC = N+1
RETURN
END
```

FORTRAN permits us to write

```
N = ISUCC (6HCARMEL)
```

even though this makes absolutely no sense. This is an example of *weak typing* since FORTRAN allows (in some circumstances) something of one type (e.g., Hollerith) to be used where another type (e.g., integer) is expected solely because they are represented the same way (a one-word bit-string). This is a *security* loophole because it allows meaningless operations to be performed without any warning, for example, adding 1 to a character string. This is a violation of the Security Principle since it allows a program that violates the definition of the language to escape detection.

FORTRAN's traditional lack of facilities for dealing with character strings has forced many programmers to write *machine-dependent* (and hence *nonportable*) programs that use integer and logical operations to manipulate characters. The FORTRAN 77 Standard has alleviated this problem by defining a CHARACTER data type with some character manipulation operations; characters are no longer second-class citizens.

The Data Constructor Is the Array

As we said before, the data structuring methods of FORTRAN are those of science and engineering—scalars and arrays. We have seen in the previous sections the various scalars provided by FORTRAN. We call these the *primitive* data structures because they are the basic data from which more complex data structures are built. The linguistic methods used to build complex data structures from the primitives are called the *constructors* for data structures. This terminology is used throughout this book to denote the two aspects of a structuring mechanism. In FORTRAN the only data structure constructor is the array. The remainder of this section is devoted to a discussion of arrays.

Arrays Are Static and Limited to Three Dimensions

In FORTRAN arrays are declared by means of a DIMENSION statement. For example,

```
DIMENSION DTA(100), COORD(10,10)
```

declares DTA to be a 100-element array (with subscripts in the range 1–100) and COORD to be a 10 × 10 array (with subscripts in the range 1–10). We can see that with the exception of a little "syntactic sugar," the first of these is really the same as the array declaration in our pseudo-code:

```
VAR DTA 100
+0000000000
```

Note that FORTRAN does not require arrays to be initialized. FORTRAN is like the pseudo-code (and, incidentally, unlike most assembly languages) in requiring the dimensions of the array to be *integer denotations,* that is, literal integer constants (e.g., '100'), that are fixed for all time. This permits the FORTRAN system to allocate storage in the same simple way that our pseudo-code did.

FORTRAN limits arrays to at most three dimensions (seven in FORTRAN 77) for efficiency reasons that are discussed later. In Chapter 3 we will see that this violates an important Regularity Principle (called the Zero-One-Infinity Principle) that tells us to avoid numbers like three and seven when we design languages.

Array Implementation Is Simple and Efficient

We saw in Chapter 1 that one-dimensional arrays are implemented as contiguous regions of memory; this permits indexing to be accomplished by adding the index value to the base address of the array. In this section we investigate the implementation of arrays in more detail. Consider first a one-dimensional array A declared by

DIMENSION $A(n)$

where n represents an integer denotation. The layout of A in memory is:

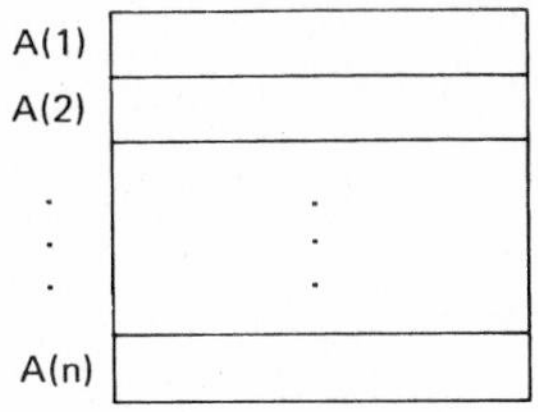

A(1)	
A(2)	
⋮	⋮
A(n)	

If we let $\alpha\,\{A(1)\}$ mean the address in memory of $A(1)$, then we can see that the address of $A(2)$ is $\alpha\,\{A(1)\}+1$, the address of $A(3)$ is $\alpha\,\{A(1)\}+2$, and so on, to the address of $A(n)$, which is $\alpha\,\{A(1)\}+n-1$. In general, we have

$$\alpha\,\{A(i)\} = \alpha\,\{A(1)\}-1+i$$

This is called the *addressing equation* for the array A. (It assumes that each array element is stored in one addressable storage unit.)

Next, we derive the addressing equation for a two-dimensional array. Suppose A is declared by

DIMENSION $A(m, n)$

FORTRAN arranges arrays in memory in *column-major* order, that is, with the columns occupying adjacent memory locations as shown in Figure 2.7. (Most programming languages either use *row-major* order or, more frequently, preserve machine independence by not specifying the layout at all.) If we look at Figure 2.7 for a pattern, we can see that the address of $A(I, J)$ is $\alpha + (J - 1)m + I - 1$; therefore, the addressing equation for two-dimensional column-major arrays is:

$$\alpha\,\{A(I,J)\} = \alpha\,\{A(1,1)\}+(J-1)m+I-1$$

EXERCISE 2-19: Test the above equation by computing the address of A(1,1), A(m,1), A(1,2), A(m,2), A(1,3), and A(m,n) and comparing the results with Figure 2.7.

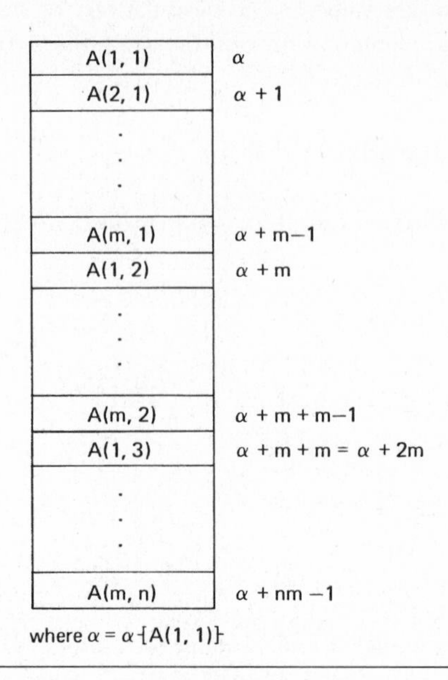

Figure 2.7 Column-Major Layout of Two-Dimensional Array

EXERCISE 2-20: Derive the addressing equation for two-dimensional arrays stored in row-major order.

EXERCISE 2-21: Derive the addressing equation for three-dimensional arrays stored in column-major order; do the same for row-major order.

EXERCISE 2-22: Double-precision and complex numbers both occupy two words each rather than just one. Derive the addressing equation for one-, two-, and three-dimensional arrays of double-precision or complex numbers.

FORTRAN Arrays Allow Many Optimizations

We said in the beginning of this chapter that efficiency was the primary goal of the FORTRAN system. We also saw that the FORTRAN system was introduced simultaneously with the inclusion of index registers in computer hardware. It was thus crucial that FORTRAN make optimum use of the index registers. Let's look at a concrete case, a simple DO-loop.

```
      DO 20 I = 1, 100
      SUM = SUM + A(I)
20    CONTINUE
```

The obvious implementation of this loop is to initialize to 1 an index register (corresponding to I) at the beginning of the loop and to increment the index register on each successive iteration. The reference to A(I) in the body of the loop would be implemented in the straightforward way: computing the address of the array element according to the addressing equation $\alpha\{A(1)\}-1+\mathrm{IR}$ (we have used IR to represent the contents of the index register). Thus, on each iteration of the loop an addition must be performed adding the constant $\alpha\{A(1)\}-1$ to the contents of the index register IR. The loop can be summarized by this code:

```
        initialize IR to 1;
loop:   compute the address α {A(1)} − 1 + IR;
        fetch the contents of this and add to SUM;
        increment IR;
        if IR is less than or equal to 100, goto loop.
```

The problem is that this addition is unnecessary and a smart assembly language programmer could avoid it. It could be avoided by initializing the index register to the address of the first element of the array and then using the index register as an indirect address for the array element. That is, the loop would be implemented:

```
        initialize IR to α {A(1)};
loop:   fetch the contents of the location whose address
            is in IR and add to SUM;
        increment IR;
        if IR is less than or equal to α {A(100)}, goto loop.
```

We can see that this saves an addition on each iteration; it was optimizations such as this that sold the first FORTRAN compiler.

You are probably aware that most languages allow subscripts that are more complicated than simple variables, for example, 'A(I+1)', 'A(3*I-6)', and 'A(1+A(J))'. You can probably also see that elaborate expressions such as these could so complicate analysis that it would make optimizations of the type described above impossible. For this reason early versions of FORTRAN restricted subscript expressions to one of the following forms:

c
v
$v+c$ or $v-c$
$c*v$
$c*v+c'$ or $c*v-c'$

where c and c' are integer denotations, and v is an integer variable. Therefore, A(2), A(I), A(I−1), and A(2*I−1) are all legal array references, but A(1+I), A(I−J), A(100−1), and A(I*J) are not. Of course, this seemingly arbitrary restriction is very confusing for programmers. Why was it adopted? The reason is that it allows just the sort of optimizations we have been discussing. Consider the most complicated case, an array reference of the form 'A(c*I+f)', where c and f are integer denotations and I is the controlled variable of a DO-loop. To perform the optimization shown above, we want to factor out all of the addressing equation that doesn't vary from one iteration to the next. This is called removing invariant code from the body of a loop. To see what the variant part is, let's compute the difference between the I-th and (I+1)-st iterations:

$$\alpha\,\{A(c*(I+1)+f)\} - \alpha\,\{A(c*I+f)\}$$
$$= \Big[\alpha\{A(1)\} + c(I+1) + f-1\Big] - \Big[\alpha\{A(1)\} + cI+f-1\Big]$$
$$= c(I+1) - cI = c$$

Therefore, the address changes by c on each iteration, so if the address of the current array element is kept in an index register, all that is necessary is to add c to that index register on each iteration. To what value should the index register be initialized? If we suppose the loop begins with I = 1, we can compute

$$\alpha\,\{A(c*I+f)\} = \alpha\{A(c+f)\} = \alpha\,\{A(1)\} + c + f-1$$

which, since c and f are constants, is itself a constant.

EXERCISE 2-23: Show that the same optimizations will not work for array subscripts of the form '$u*v$', where u and v are variables.

We now investigate two-dimensional arrays; that is, we will optimize the use of index registers for two nested loops. We take as an example:

```
      DO 20 I = 1, 100
        DO 30 J = 1, 64
          SUM = SUM + A(I,J)
30      CONTINUE
20    CONTINUE
```

The analysis will be performed for simple variable subscripts; you will extend it in an exercise. What is the difference in array element addresses for each iteration of the inner loop? Since this increments J, it is (assuming A is dimensioned m by n):

$$\alpha\{A(I, J+1)\} - \alpha\{A(I, J)\}$$

$$= \left[\alpha\{A(1,1)\} + (J+1-1)m + I - 1\right] - \left[\alpha\{A(1,1)\} + (J-1)m + I - 1\right]$$

$$= Jm - (J-1)m = m$$

Thus, the index register must be incremented by m on each of the inner iterations. On each of the outer iterations, I is advanced so the index register must be incremented by

$$\alpha\{A(I+1, J)\} - \alpha\{A(I, J)\}$$

$$= \left[\alpha\{A(1,1)\} + (J-1)m + (I+1) - 1\right] - \left[\alpha\{A(1,1)\} + (J-1)m + I - 1\right]$$

$$= 1$$

Therefore, in the outer loop the index register is incremented by 1 on each iteration.

EXERCISE 2-24: Perform an analysis analogous to that above, but assume that the loops are nested so that the first subscript varies more rapidly than the second.

EXERCISE 2-25: Perform the above index register optimization analysis for the general two-dimensional subscript case, '$A(c*I+f, d*J+g)$'. Assume A is dimensioned m by n.

EXERCISE 2-26:* Perform the above analysis for three-dimensional arrays.

We can see from this last exercise why FORTRAN limited arrays to three dimensions. Backus has said that the number of special cases they had to consider increased exponentially with the number of subscripts, therefore, they chose three as a limit.

2.5 DESIGN: NAME STRUCTURES

The Primitives Bind Names to Objects

We pointed out in Section 2.4 that composite structures are built up by applying a set of *constructors* to the *primitive* structures. We will see that this is also the case with name structures, which are discussed in this section. One of the goals of this section is to make the notion of *name structure* clear. We can get a handle on name structures by considering the structures that we've already seen. What does a data structure structure? The data, of course. In other words, the purpose of a *data structure* is to organize the primitive data in order to simplify its manipulation by the program. What about a control structure? It's easy to see that the purpose of a *control structure* is to organize the control-flow of a program. Now, what can we say about name structures? By analogy we would expect them to organize the names that appear in a program, and this is correct. The subject of the remainder of this section (and of many other sections in this book) is the meaning of organizing names and what this organization accomplishes.

What are the primitive name structures of FORTRAN? These are simply those constructs that give meanings to names, that is, declarations or *binding constructs* (sometimes abbreviated *bindings*). In Chapter 1 we discussed the very simple means provided by the pseudo-code for binding symbolic names to addresses of memory locations. For example,

```
VAR SUM 1
+0000000000
```

bound the *identifier* SUM to a location in data memory (it happened to be location 002 in the example in Chapter 1) and initialized that location to zero. The pseudo-code's bindings have three functions: allocating a region of memory (one word long in this case), initializing that region (to zero in this case), and binding the identifier (SUM in this case) to the address of that region. These functions are performed by FORTRAN declarations, although in a slightly different form. For example,

```
INTEGER I, J, K
```

declares I, J, and K to be integer variables. This means that storage must be allocated for these variables (one word each), and the names I, J, and K must be bound to the addresses of these locations. Notice that this declaration does not perform the initialization function; this is accomplished with a separate DATA-statement in FORTRAN. The other important function fulfilled by this declaration is to specify the *type* of the variables, namely, INTEGER. Therefore, when these variables appear in an expression, the compiler will be able to determine which kind of operations to perform (e.g., integer addition or floating-point addition) and whether any coercions are necessary.

Declarations Are Nonexecutable

FORTRAN declarations are often called *nonexecutable* statements to differentiate them from *executable* statements such as assignment statements, GOTOs, IF-statements, and subroutine calls. Nonexecutable statements provide information for the compiler and other preexecution processors of the program (such as the linker and loader). For example, the type in the declaration (e.g., INTEGER) is used to determine the amount of storage that must be allocated for the variables. The compiler keeps track of the locations that have been allocated just as our pseudo-code loader did. Since this allocation is done once, before the program is executed, and never changes, it is called *static allocation.* As we will see in the following chapters, most programming languages now do *dynamic allocation,* that is, storage is allocated and recycled dynamically (i.e., at run-time) during program execution. Dynamic allocation is discussed at length in later chapters.

The pseudo-code interpreter kept track of the location of variables by placing them in a *symbol table;* compilers do exactly the same thing. For example, after a FORTRAN compiler has decoded the declaration 'INTEGER I, J, K', it will make entries in the symbol table for each of I, J, and K. These entries will contain the location of these variables in memory and their types, in other words, everything the compiler needs to know about these variables in order to generate correct code. We can visualize a symbol table like this:

Name	Type	Location
⋮	⋮	⋮
I	INTEGER	0245
J	INTEGER	0246
K	INTEGER	0247
⋮	⋮	⋮

Optional Variable Declarations Are Dangerous

FORTRAN has an unusual convention that has been abandoned in almost all newer programming languages: automatic declaration of variables. In other words, if a programmer uses a variable but never declares it, the declaration will be automatically supplied by the compiler. This was originally conceived as a convenience for programmers since it saved them the effort of declaring all of their variables. As we will see below, it is a false economy since it undermines security.

You may ask, "If FORTRAN automatically declares undeclared variables, then how does it know what type the variable should be declared to be?" In other words, if the statement 'I=I+1' appears in a program, and I has not been declared, then does the compiler declare it INTEGER, REAL, COMPLEX, or what? FORTRAN solves this problem with the "I Through N Rule," which states that any variables whose names begin with I through N are declared integers and all others are declared reals. This tends to correspond to mathematical convention since the variables *i, j, k, l, m,* and *n* are usually used for indexes and counts (i.e., integers), and the variables *x, y, z, a, b, c,* and so forth, are usually used for other things. This rule has the unfortunate consequence that it leads programmers to pick obscure names for variables (e.g., KOUNT, ISUM, XLENGTH) so that they don't have to declare them.

There is a much more serious problem with this automatic declaration convention, however. Suppose a programmer intended to type the statement 'COUNT = COUNT + 1' but accidently typed 'COUNT = COUMT + 1' (i.e., an 'M' instead of an 'N'). What would be its effect? Since the variable COUMT has not been declared, the compiler will automatically declare it, as a real in this case. Since there is no DATA-statement to initialize it, it will probably contain whatever was left over in that memory location. The result will be that a strange and inexplicable value will be stored into COUNT and that the programmer will have a difficult debugging problem. If FORTRAN did not automatically declare variables, this error would have been caught at compile-time, since COUMT would have been reported as an undeclared variable. This is one example of how a small design error, such as a misplaced concern for writing convenience, can seriously undermine the security of a language and cause debugging nightmares for the programmer. We will see in a later section that this particular error also interacts with other small errors in the FORTRAN design to create some other serious problems.

Environments Determine Meanings

As you are aware, the meaning of a sentence often depends on the *context* in which it is stated; words can have different meanings, depending on their context. The same is true in programming languages; a statement such as 'X = COUNT(I)' may have many meanings, depending on the definitions of its constituent names. For example, X may be either an integer or a real and COUNT may be either an array or a function. The *context* of this statement, or any programming language construct, is thus the set of definitions that are *visible* to that statement or construct. Since the context of a construct can be thought of as surrounding that construct, a context is often called an *environment.* Thus, we can say that an environment determines the visibility of bindings. The concept of context or environment is very important in programming languages and is discussed many times in this book. In fact, name structures can be defined as the means of organizing the environment.

Variable Names Are Local in Scope

Context is a very important issue in understanding English, and it is likewise important in programming languages. Therefore, we will investigate contexts (environments) in FORTRAN.

We saw earlier that FORTRAN programs are divided into a number of disjoint *subprograms* and that this division allows subprograms to be developed independently and stored in libraries. Suppose someone has defined a FORTRAN function SUM that sums the elements of an array. It really makes no difference to a user of this function whether the formal parameters are called A and N, or X and SIZE, or whatever. All a user of this function needs to know is that the first parameter is the array and the second parameter is its size. Similarly, the user does not care whether the programmer of the function used I for the controlled variable of the DO-loop, or J, or whatever. These are details of the implementation that are of no concern to the user of the function and, in fact, that may be changed at some point by the implementor of the function. Therefore, information such as this (e.g., the variable names used by the implementation of the function) should be hidden from the user, a principle called *Information Hiding,* which is discussed later. Suffice it to say now that observing this principle makes programs much more maintainable.

How does information hiding relate to environments? It relates in a very straightforward way: We have said that the caller of a subprogram should not be able to see the names of any variables declared in that subprogram (including the formal parameters). This means that these names are not *visible* to the caller, that is, they are not in the caller's environment. Therefore, since a FORTRAN program is made up of a number of disjoint subprograms, we can see that each of these subprograms must have a *disjoint environment* containing just the variables (and formal parameters) declared in that subprogram. This avoids cluttering the name space with a lot of variables that do not have to be accessible.

Subprogram Names Are Global in Scope

Clearly, the above argument cannot apply to the names of the subprograms themselves; if the name of a subprogram were only visible within that subprogram, then it would be impossible for anyone else to call that subprogram.

Instead, FORTRAN specifies that subprogram names are visible throughout the program; they are thus said to be *global.* In contrast we say that variable names are *local* to the subprograms in which they are declared. Thus, the names fall into two broad classes, depending on their visibility. This property is called the *scope* of a name; that is, subprogram names have global scope and variable names have local scope. The *scope* of a binding of a name is defined as that region of the program over which that binding is visible. Consider Figure 2.8. In this program the scope of the binding of X marked (*) is the main program and the scope of the binding of X marked (**) is the subroutine R. Similarly, the scope of the binding of Y (**) is R and the scope of the binding (***) is S. The scopes of the two uses of N as formal parameters are the bodies of the corresponding subroutines. Finally, the scope of the declarations of the subroutines R and S is the entire program.

These relationships can be depicted in a *contour diagram,* such as that in Figure 2.9. These diagrams (which were invented by John B. Johnston[8]) should be interpreted as though the boxes were made of one-way mirrors that allow us

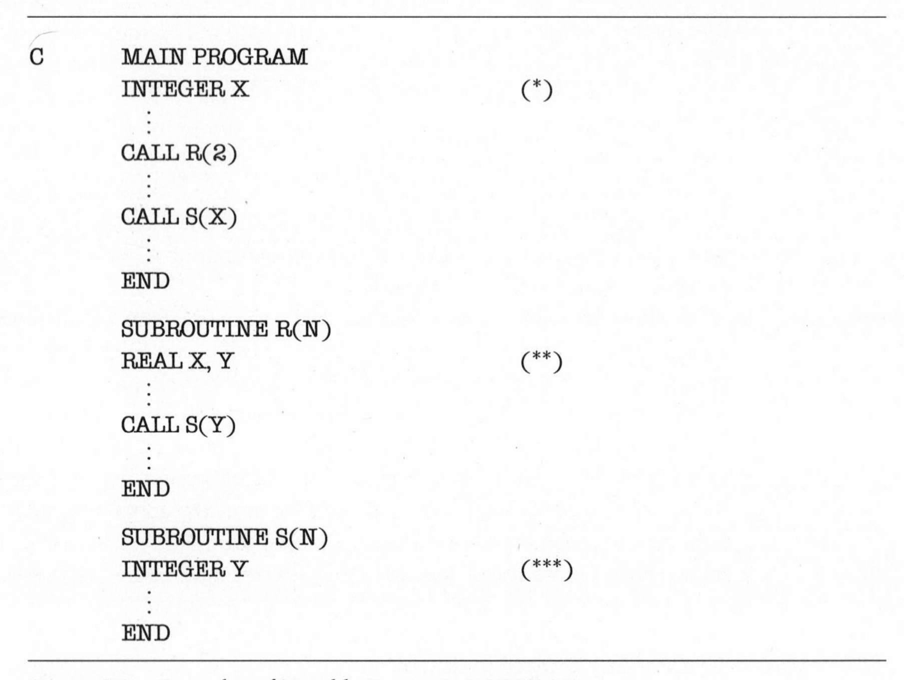

```
C         MAIN PROGRAM
          INTEGER X                       (*)
            :
          CALL R(2)
            :
          CALL S(X)
            :
          END
          SUBROUTINE R(N)
          REAL X, Y                       (**)
            :
          CALL S(Y)
            :
          END
          SUBROUTINE S(N)
          INTEGER Y                       (***)
            :
          END
```

Figure 2.8 Examples of Variable Scopes in FORTRAN

8 See Johnston (1971).

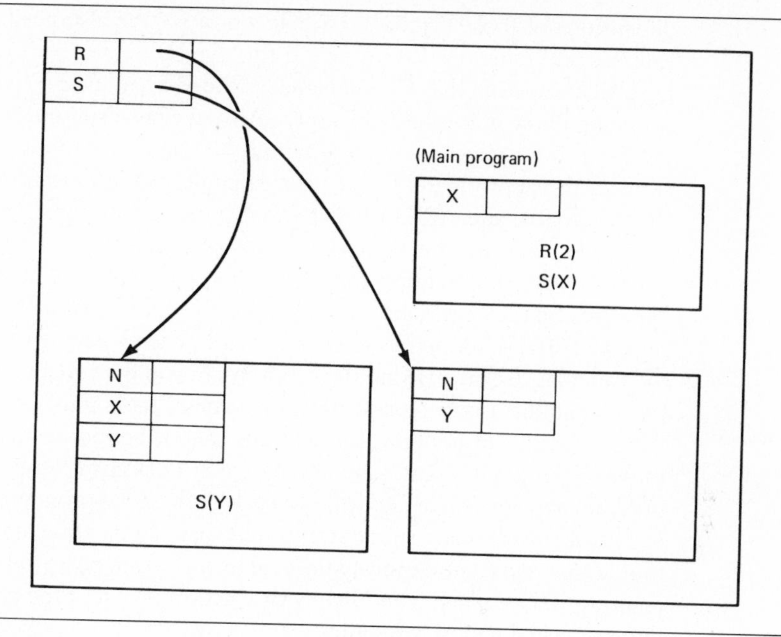

Figure 2.9 Contour Diagram Showing Scopes of Variables

to look out of a box but not into one. The arrows on the diagram show, for example, that R can see the bindings of S and its own Y, but that it cannot see the Y in S or the X in the main program. Contour diagrams are a valuable aid to visualizing scopes, particularly in languages with more complicated scope rules than FORTRAN. We will use them again in later chapters.

EXERCISE 2-27: Write in skeleton form a FORTRAN program involving at least three subprograms. Draw a contour diagram that shows the visibility relations between the bindings and uses of names.

It Is Difficult to Share Data with Just Parameters

Since all variables are subprogram local, it would seem that the only way to pass information from one subprogram to another is through parameters. Let's see what the consequences of this would be. Suppose that we need to implement a symbol table in FORTRAN; the simplest way to do this is to represent the symbol table as four parallel arrays. That is, each element of the array NAMES contains the name of a symbol, the corresponding element of the array LOC contains the location of the name, the array TYPE contains an integer code specifying the type of the name (integer, real, etc.), and the array DIMS contains the dimensions of those symbols that name arrays. We also need a number of subroutines and functions for managing this symbol table. For example, we need a LOOKUP function that takes a name (encoded as an integer) and finds the corresponding entry in the NAMES array. Also, we need subroutines that create new entries in the symbol table by entering the names, locations, types, and dimensions in the appropriate arrays. For example, we may want VAR that enters a simple variable and ARRAY1 that enters a one-dimensional array.

Let's consider the organization of the name space of this program. The various arrays representing the symbol table constitute a database that is managed by the *accessing* subprograms, LOOKUP, VAR, ARRAY1, etc. The scope rules of FORTRAN permit a subprogram to access data from only two sources: the variables declared within the subprogram and the variables passed as parameters. Since the arrays representing the symbol table must be accessible to all of the accessing subprograms, these arrays cannot be local variables of any one of these subprograms. The only alternative is to declare these arrays in the main program and pass them explicitly to each of these subprograms. This means that each of these accessing subprograms must have four extra parameters that are the four arrays representing the symbol table. For example, to enter a declaration for an array whose name is in NM, with location AVAIL, type code INTCOD, and dimensions M and N, we write:

```
CALL ARRAY2 (NM, AVAIL, INTCOD, M, N, NAMES, LOC, TYPE, DIMS)
```

This is not very readable; the four extra parameters clutter up the CALL. In fact, the user of these symbol table subprograms really doesn't care whether the symbol table is represented by four arrays, or one array, or 20. On the contrary, requiring the user to supply this information causes a serious maintenance problem. Since the user of this symbol table package is required to declare the four arrays in the main program and pass them on each call of the accessing subprograms, it means that it will be very difficult for the implementor of these routines to change the organization of the symbol table. For example, if we wanted to modify it so that five arrays were required, we would have to track down every subroutine using these routines so that the appropriate changes could be made in the user's program. This could be very complicated since, if the user has subprograms that call the symbol table routines, these subprograms will have to have these same four array parameters. In other words, the details of the organization of the symbol table are scattered throughout the user's program. This means that even the slightest change in the symbol table's organization will have a devastating effect. The practical result will probably be that the symbol table package is never altered.

These observations are summarized in the Information Hiding Principle of D. L. Parnas.

> ***Information Hiding Principle***
>
> Modules should be designed so that: (1) The user has all the information needed to use the module correctly, *and nothing more.* (2) The implementor has all the information needed to implement the module correctly, *and nothing more.*

This principle is discussed at length in Chapter 7.

COMMON Blocks Allow Sharing Between Subprograms

For the reasons discussed above, using parameters to share data is unsatisfactory, so it is fortunate that FORTRAN provides a mechanism to avoid it. Let's be clear about the problem. What we are trying to do is provide a set of subprograms that collectively manage a shared database; this is a very common situation. The Information Hiding Principle suggests that the problems result from the fact that information about the representation of the database, which is relevant only to the accessing subprograms, has been spread to other parts of the program. This was necessitated by the scope rules of FORTRAN. What is needed is a mechanism that allows this information to be accessible to just the symbol table subprograms without being passed as explicit parameters. This mechanism is found in the FORTRAN COMMON block.

As suggested by their name, COMMON blocks permit subprograms to have common variables, that is, to share data areas (Figure 2.10). This can most easily be explained by seeing its application to our symbol table example. Since we want the accessing subprograms to share the four arrays representing the

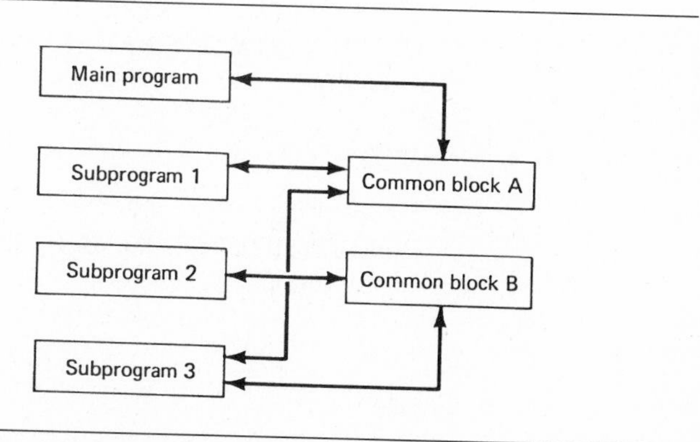

Figure 2.10 Subprogram Communication Through COMMON Blocks

symbol table, we can place them in a COMMON block called SYMTAB that is declared in each of these subprograms. This is shown in outline form in Figure 2.11.

Only the subprograms that include a declaration of the COMMON block SYMTAB will have access to this data area. Other subprograms can share other data areas through COMMON blocks with different names.

COMMON Permits Aliasing, Which Is Dangerous

In the above example, we can see that each subprogram includes an identical specification of the SYMTAB COMMON block. This should lead us to ask the question, "What if all the specifications don't agree?" You might expect the compiler to diagnose this as an error, but this is not the case; indeed, FORTRAN does not require the programmer to use the same names in different specifications of the same COMMON block. For example, the VAR subroutine could specify this COMMON block by

```
COMMON /SYMTAB/ NM(100), WHERE(100), MODE(100), SIZE(100)
```

Then, VAR's use of WHERE(I) would be equivalent to ARRAY2's use of LOC(I).

```
C      MAIN PROGRAM
         :
       CALL ARRAY2 (NM, AVAIL, INTCOD, M, N)
         :
       END

       SUBROUTINE ARRAY2 (N, L, C, D1, D2)
       COMMON /SYMTAB/ NAMES(100), LOC(100), TYPE(100),
       DIMS(100)
         :
       END

       SUBROUTINE VAR (N, L, C)
       COMMON /SYMTAB/ NAMES(100), LOC(100), TYPE(100),
       DIMS(100)
         :
       END

       etc.
```

Figure 2.11 Example of the Use of COMMON Blocks

There's little point in doing this. Unfortunately, this could occur accidently; for instance, a programmer might reverse the LOC and TYPE arrays in one of the subprograms:

```
COMMON /SYMTAB/ NAMES(100), TYPE(100), LOC(100), DIMS(100)
```

Whenever this subprogram makes a change to what seems to be the LOC array, it will in fact be changing the TYPE array. Needless to say, bugs like this can be very difficult to find.

The problem is even more serious, however, because FORTRAN does not even require separate specifications of the same COMMON block to agree in *structure*. For example, one subprogram may contain the specification

```
COMMON /B/ M, A(100)
```

and another may contain

```
COMMON /B/ X, K, C(50), D(50)
```

The names included in each COMMON specification are made to correspond to locations in the block according to their position in the specification; this is shown in Figure 2.12.

We see that the location called M in the first subprogram is called X in the second program. These two variables don't even have the same type! If the programmer stores an integer in M and then uses X as a floating-point number, the result will be gibberish since integers and floating-point numbers are represented completely differently. This is a security loophole since it violates FORTRAN's type

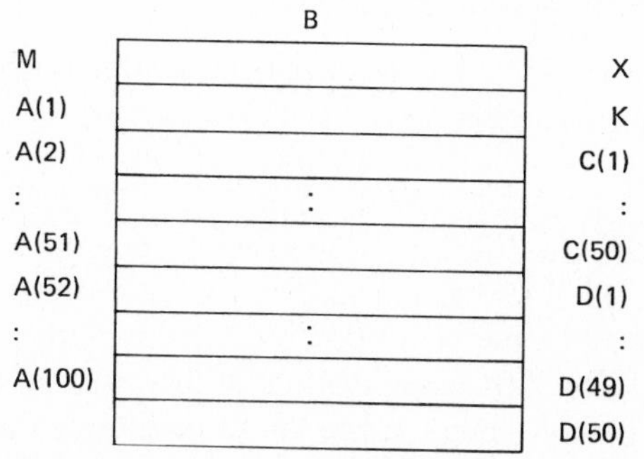

	B	
M		X
A(1)		K
A(2)		C(1)
:	:	:
A(51)		C(50)
A(52)		D(1)
:	:	:
A(100)		D(49)
		D(50)

Figure 2.12 Aliasing in COMMON Blocks

system; that is, it allows meaningless operations to be performed (floating-point operations on integer data). We also see that the array A partially overlaps the arrays C and D so that A(2) is the same location as C(1) and A(52) is the same location as D(1). Location D(50) is not even accessible from the first subprogram.

You might argue that this is a willfully pathological example and that no programmer would ever do this. In fact, programmers sometimes do exactly this to conserve storage (by making several arrays occupy the same storage locations) or purposefully to circumvent the type system.

They may also do these things accidently; for example, the specification of SYMTAB could be easily mistyped as

```
COMMON /SYMTAB/ NAMES(10), LOC(100), TYPE(100), DIMS(100)
```

This situation can also arise when a programmer updates a COMMON specification in one subprogram but forgets to update it in another.

In all of these cases, the problem is that FORTRAN COMMON blocks permit *aliasing,* the ability to have more than one name for the same memory location. Aliasing makes programs difficult to understand and difficult to maintain. We will discuss aliasing and means for avoiding it repeatedly in this book. We will see in later chapters that other languages have provided better solutions than COMMON blocks to the problem of shared data.

EXERCISE 2-28: Show the correspondence of the two declarations of SYMTAB in the case mentioned above, in which 'NAMES(100)' was mistyped as 'NAMES(10)'.

EXERCISE 2-29:* Suggest some alterations to the FORTRAN COMMON facility that would make it more secure and safer to use.

EQUIVALENCE Allows Sharing Within Subprograms

Recall that FORTRAN was developed at a time when computer memories were extremely small, often only a few thousand words. It, therefore, was mandatory that programs make optimum use of memory, for example, by sharing. In most large programs, each data structure will go through periods when it's being used and periods when it's not. For example, a large array may be used for holding data when it's first read in and for its initial processing. After this first stage, that array may no longer be needed, but a different array may be needed, for example, for the results of the computation. If the program is finished with the first array before it needs to begin using the second array, then memory will be better utilized if the two arrays can occupy the same area in memory. In FORTRAN this can be accomplished with an EQUIVALENCE declaration such as:

```
DIMENSION INDATA(10000), RESULT(8000)
EQUIVALENCE (INDATA(1), RESULT(1))
```

This states that the first element of INDATA is to occupy the same memory location as the first element of RESULT. In other words, we have *explicitly aliased* the two arrays so that they will share storage. Needless to say, this has all of the problems of aliasing that we discussed in connection with COMMON. Although it was introduced as a method for economizing storage, it can be used for many purposes, including subversion of the type system. For example, a logical variable may be equivalenced to a real variable so that the programmer can use logical operations ('.AND.', '.OR.', '.NOT.') to access the parts of the floating-point representation of the number. This kind of programming leads to very machine-dependent, and hence nonportable, programs and is usually unnecessary anyway since there are better solutions to these problems. In many cases, these problems result from trying to use FORTRAN for applications for which it was not intended, such as string manipulation and systems programming.

The EQUIVALENCE statement has outlived its usefulness for a number of reasons. First, computer memories are now much larger so that economization of storage is no longer the problem that it was in the 1950s. Second, many computers now have *virtual memory* systems that automatically and safely manage the sharing of real memory. Finally, as we will see in later chapters, modern programming languages provide dynamic storage management facilities that also automatically and safely manage the allocation of memory.

EXERCISE 2-30: Suppose we have three arrays dimensioned A(1000), B(700), and C(700). Further suppose that A is never in use at the same time as B or C, but that B and C may be in use at the same time. Write an EQUIVALENCE statement to share storage as much as possible. How would you change your solution if B and C were never in use at the same time?

EXERCISE 2-31:* Most FORTRAN systems allow the same variables to appear in both COMMON and EQUIVALENCE statements. For example,

```
COMMON /B/ U(100), V(100)
DIMENSION W(100)
EQUIVALENCE (U(60), W(1)), (W(80), V(10))
```

What do you suppose the effects of these declarations are? You can consult a FORTRAN manual or try to figure it out on your own. What *should* be the effects of these statements?

2.6 DESIGN: SYNTACTIC STRUCTURES

Languages Are Defined by Lexics and Syntax

The *syntax* of a language is the way that words and symbols are combined to form the statements and expressions. In the previous sections, we indirectly discussed the syntax of many FORTRAN constructs. For example, we saw that a DO-loop has the word 'DO', followed by a statement number, followed by an integer variable, followed by the symbol '=', followed by an integer expression, followed by a comma symbol, followed by another integer expression, and optionally followed by another comma symbol and another integer expression. You have probably seen the syntax of programming languages described with a formal grammatical notation, for example,

```
<DO-loop> ::= DO <label> <var> = <exp>, <exp> [, <exp>]
```

We will discuss these notations in Chapter 4.

The *lexics* of a language is the way in which characters (i.e., letters, digits, and other signs) are combined to form words and symbols. For example, the lexical rules of FORTRAN state that an identifier must begin with a letter and be followed by no more than five letters and digits. Lexical rules are also frequently expressed in formal grammatical notations; in fact, the term *syntax* is often used to refer to both the lexical and syntactic rules of a language. The *syntactic analysis* phase of a compiler is often broken down into two parts: the *lexical analyzer* (also called a *scanner*) and the *syntactic analyzer proper* (also called a *parser*). In the following sections, we will discuss the lexics and syntax of FORTRAN.

A Fixed Format Lexics Was Inherited from the Pseudo-Codes

The pseudo-code we developed in Chapter 1 was typical of these languages in its *fixed format* lexical conventions. It was card-oriented, that is, there was one instruction per card and particular columns of these cards were dedicated to particular purposes, for example, columns 1–4 for the operation. FORTRAN has similar lexical conventions, namely, one statement per card and columns dedicated to particular purposes:

Columns	Purpose
1–5	statement number
6	continuation
7–72	statement
73–80	sequence number

Since a statement may not entirely fit on one card, it can be continued onto following cards, if these continuation cards have a character punched in column 6. The bulk of the card, columns 7–72, was devoted to the actual statement, which was *free format*; that is, it did not have to be punched in specific columns. This general lexical style was common in languages of the late 1950s and early 1960s such as COBOL. Although it is adequate for use with punched card equipment, it is quite awkward for use with the interactive program preparation methods now generally in use. It also has other limitations that we will discuss later.

Ignoring Blanks Everywhere Is a Mistake

FORTRAN adopted the unfortunate lexical convention that blanks are ignored everywhere in the body of the statement. While this was certainly an improvement over the fixed fields of the pseudo-code interpreters, it was a significant deviation from natural languages, in which blanks are significant.

Itisveryhardtoreadasentencewithnoblanks,

yet this is exactly what FORTRAN compilers were required to do. In FORTRAN, the statement

```
DIMENSION IN DATA (10000), RESULT (8000)
```

is exactly equivalent to

```
DIMENSIONINDATA(10000),RESULT(8000)
```

and, for that matter,

```
D I M E N S I O N  IN DATA (10 000), RESULT (8 000)
```

While this may seem to be a harmless convenience, in fact it can cause serious problems for both compilers and human readers. Consider this legal FORTRAN statement:

```
DO 20 I = 1. 100
```

which looks remarkably like the DO-statement:

```
DO 20 I = 1, 100
```

In fact, it is an assignment statement of the number 1.100 to a variable called 'DO20I', which we can see by rearranging the blanks:

```
DO20I = 1.100
```

You will probably say that no programmer would ever call a variable 'DO20I', and that is correct. But suppose the programmer *intended* to type the DO-statement above but accidently types a period instead of a comma (they are next to each other on the keyboard). The statement will have been transformed into an assignment to 'DO20I'. The programmer will probably not notice the error because ',' and '.' look so much alike. In fact, there will be no clue that an error has been made because, conveniently, the variable DO20I will be automatically declared. If you think that things like this can't happen, you will be surprised to learn that an American Viking Venus probe was lost because of precisely this error.

You should also notice that the real seriousness of this problem results from the *interaction* of two language features. If it weren't for FORTRAN's implicit declaration convention, the mistake would have been diagnosed as a missing declaration of DO20I. This is an example of a violation of the Principle of Defense in Depth, which states that if an error can get through the first line of defense without detection, then it should be caught by the next line of defense, and so forth. FORTRAN throws out what in most languages is the most significant lexical feature: the breaks between the words. Modern programming languages have lexical conventions very much like natural languages: Blanks can be (and in some cases must be) used to separate the *tokens* (words and symbols). This is both more secure and more readable.

EXERCISE 2-32: Define a new set of lexical conventions for FORTRAN. They should permit blanks to be inserted for readability but avoid the problems we have discussed above.

EXERCISE 2-33: Suggest a new syntax for the DO-loop that is less prone to the mistake illustrated above.

The Lack of Reserved Words Is a Mistake

FORTRAN granted programmers the dubious privilege of using as variables words with meaning in FORTRAN. For example, FORTRAN permits a programmer to have an array called IF:

```
DIMENSION IF(100)
```

Uses of this array

```
IF(I-1) = 123
```

are likely to be confused with IF-statements:

```
IF (I-1) 1,2,3
```

Again, a programmer is not likely willfully to write such a deceptive statement. The point is that when a compiler has seen 'IF (I − 1)', it still doesn't know whether it is processing an assignment statement or an IF-statement. The combination of ignoring all blanks and allowing keywords to be used as variables makes the syntactic analysis of FORTRAN programs a nightmare. Consider what is required to classify something as a DO-statement. The instruction may begin with the letters 'DO', a sequence of digits, a legal variable name, and an '=' sign and still not be a DO-statement; the assignment to 'DO20I' is an example. Furthermore, it is not even enough to see if there is a comma to the right of the equals sign since

```
DO 20 I = A(I,J)
```

is not a DO-statement.

EXERCISE 2-34: Classify the statement on line 5:

```
        DIMENSION FORMAT(100)
5       FORMAT(11H) = 10*(I-J)
```

EXERCISE 2-35:* Describe a procedure for distinguishing between a DO-statement and an assignment statement.

Algebraic Notation Was an Important Contribution

We will now turn from lexics to syntax. Recall that one of the goals of FORTRAN was to permit programmers to use a conventional algebraic notation. This goal was partially met; for example, the expression

$$\frac{-b+\sqrt{b^2-4ac}}{2a}$$

would have to be written

```
(-B + SQRT (B**2 - 4*A*C)) / (2*A)
```

This is probably about the best that could be expected considering the commonly available input-output equipment at the time FORTRAN was developed. It is interesting to note that the Laning and Zierler system, which the FORTRAN designers had seen, provided a much more natural, interactive programming notation than FORTRAN or most other programming languages, even to this day. In any case, the provision of a quasi-algebraic notation was without doubt one of the major selling points of FORTRAN.

Arithmetic Operators Have Precedence

An important idea is the *precedence*, or priority, of an operator. This was developed so that quasi-algebraic notations would be unambiguous and have the expected meaning. For example, in mathematical notation the arithmetic expression '$b^2 - 4ac$' is equivalent to '$(b^2) - (4ac)$', that is, exponentiation and multiplication are done before addition. Also, ab^2 means $a(b^2)$, so exponentiation is done before multiplication. Considerations such as these have led to the following precedences among arithmetic operators:

1. Exponentiation
2. Multiplication and division
3. Addition and subtraction

This means that in the absence of parentheses, exponentiation is done before multiplication and division, and multiplication and division are done before addition and subtraction. Operators of the same precedence (e.g., addition and subtraction) are done in order from left to right, i.e., they associate to the left:

$$a - b + c - d = ((a - b) + c) - d$$

Languages differ on the precedence of unary operators (e.g., $-b$ and $+b$); some give them a higher priority than exponentiation, others the same priority as addition. Neither is entirely consistent with mathematical convention.

EXERCISE 2-36: Fill in the parentheses in the following expressions:

```
A+B * C-D / E
A-B-C-D
A/B/C
A / B*C
A ** B * C
I+1 / J-1
```

EXERCISE 2-37: Compare the precedence conventions of at least three programming languages for which you can find descriptions.

A Linear Syntactic Organization Is Used

We saw in Chapter 1 that pseudo-codes were patterned after machine languages; the instructions were listed in order in exactly the same way they were stored in memory. Numeric statement labels were used that were reminiscent of the addresses of machine instructions. For the most part, FORTRAN follows this same pattern. Statements are strung together, one after another, just like the instructions in memory; they are addressed with numeric labels. This is what we mean when we say that FORTRAN has a *linear* syntactic organization; the statements are arranged in a simple sequence ('linear' = line). You may be familiar with what are often called *structured* programming languages in which some statements can be nested within others, but this was a later development. The only nesting that occurs in most FORTRAN dialects is in the arithmetic expressions and in the DO-loop, although the FORTRAN 77 Standard has incorporated more modern structures. We will see in later chapters that *hierarchical structure* and *nesting* are important methods for conquering the complexity of large structures.

2.7 EVALUATION AND EPILOG

FORTRAN Evolved Into PL/I

In this chapter we mainly concentrated on FORTRAN IV, the dialect designed in 1962 and most characteristic of first-generation languages. This should not be taken to mean that work on FORTRAN ceased in 1962; rather, it has continued to the present. For this reason we will pick up the history of FORTRAN just after the design of FORTRAN IV in 1962.

The success of FORTRAN led to its use in many applications that were not strictly scientific. This led to the recognition of a serious deficiency in FORTRAN—its lack of any character manipulation facilities—and to a short-lived project within IBM to design a FORTRAN V with these facilities. Later (1963) a committee was set up by SHARE (the IBM users' group) to study extending FORTRAN so that it would be useful for both commercial and scientific applications. Although the language designed by this committee was originally known as FORTRAN VI, it soon became clear that it would be impossible to satisfy all of the goals and maintain compatibility with FORTRAN. In a preliminary specification of the language released in 1964, the language was called NPL (New Programming Language), although its name was changed to PL/I in 1965 because of protests from the National Physics Laboratory in England.

As may be expected of a language that tries to be a tool for all applications,

PL/I is a very large language. The number of features in PL/I and the intricacy of some of their interactions have led to a lot of criticism. For example, Dijkstra has said,[9] "If FORTRAN has been called an infantile disorder, then PL/I must be classified as a fatal disease." You may be surprised to hear such virulent remarks made about a programming language, although they can be understood in the context of the developments in programming methodology taking place at that time. Specifically, the late 1960s and early 1970s saw the development of *structured programming,* a body of programming methods intended to foster easier and more reliable programming. A complex, unpredictable, large programming language was seen as more of a hindrance than a help. For this, among other reasons, PL/I's popularity has waned in recent years, although it remains a reasonably popular programming language.

FORTRAN 77 Is the Newest Standard Dialect

Although structured programming is discussed in more detail in later chapters, we must understand a few things about it to appreciate the later development of FORTRAN. We have seen that FORTRAN depended heavily on the GOTO-statement as a control-structuring mechanism. Unfortunately, the undisciplined use of GOTOs can lead to "rat's nest" control structures that are hard to understand, debug, and maintain. For this reason language designers proposed higher-level control structures that obey the Structure Principle, such as the **if-then-else** and **while-do**. Although newer programming languages included these facilities, FORTRAN remained the most widely used language. For this reason many *preprocessors* (such as RATFOR) were designed that accepted these structured control structures and translated them into legal FORTRAN. These preprocessors were quite popular because they allowed programmers to take advantage of the wide availability of FORTRAN without giving up the use of the new control structures. Ultimately this led to a new FORTRAN dialect, called FORTRAN 77, which has now become an American National Standard. This language includes the new structured control structures along with some rudimentary character manipulation facilities. Like PL/I, however, it is sufficiently different from earlier FORTRANs that it may be unable to supplant FORTRAN IV. The FORTRAN committee of ANSI (the American National Standards Institute) plans to develop on a periodic basis additional dialects of FORTRAN. Thus, FORTRAN will continue to evolve.

FORTRAN Has Been Very Successful

By any standard, FORTRAN has been very successful. It accomplished its goal of demonstrating that a high-level language could be efficient enough to be used

9 *A Short Introduction to the Art of Programming.*

in production programs. FORTRAN is still the most heavily optimized programming language.

FORTRAN has been used effectively in almost every application area; it has shown itself to be quite amenable to extension and alteration. The awkwardness of its use in certain areas, particularly commercial data processing, led to attempts to incorporate these ideas into FORTRAN; PL/I is an example of this. The lack of more elaborate data structuring methods, such as COBOL's records, and recursive subprograms has prevented FORTRAN's effective application to nonnumerical problems. For its time, FORTRAN was a triumph of design; it still holds many lessons for us.

Characteristics of First-Generation Programming Languages

In this chapter we have used FORTRAN (specifically, FORTRAN IV) to illustrate the characteristics of *first-generation* programming languages. We now pause to summarize those characteristics.

In general, we've seen that the structures of first-generation languages are based on the structures of the computers of the early 1960s. This is natural, since the only experience people had in programming was in programming these machines.

This machine orientation is especially apparent in first-generation *control structures.* For example, FORTRAN's control structures correspond almost one for one with the branch instructions of the IBM 704. First-generation conditional instructions are nonnested (unlike those in later languages), and first-generation languages depend heavily on the GOTO for building any but the simplest control structures. One exception to this rule is the definite iteration statement (e.g., FORTRAN's DO-loop), which is hierarchical in first-generation languages. Recursive procedures are not permitted in most first-generation languages (BASIC is an exception), and there is generally only one parameter passing mode (typically, pass by reference).

The machine orientation of first-generation languages can also be seen in the types of *data structures* provided, which are patterned after the layout of memory on the computers available around 1960. Thus, the data structure *primitives* found in first-generation languages are fixed and floating-point numbers of various precisions, characters, and logical values—just the kinds of values manipulated by the instructions on these computers. The data structure *constructors* are arrays and, in business-oriented languages, records, which are the ways storage was commonly organized. As with control structures, first-generation languages provide little facility for hierarchical data organization (an exception is COBOL's record structure). That is, data structures cannot be nested. Finally, many first-generation languages are characterized by a relatively weak type system; that is,it is easy to subvert the type system or do representation-dependent programming.

Hierarchical structure is also absent from first-generation *name structures*, with disjoint scopes being the rule. Furthermore, variable names are bound directly and statically to memory locations since there is no dynamic memory management.

Finally, the *syntactic structures* of first-generation languages are characterized by a card-oriented, linear arrangement of statements patterned after assembly languages. Further, most of these languages had numeric statement labels that are suggestive of machine addresses. First-generation languages go significantly beyond assembly languages, however, in their provision of algebraic notation. Their usual lexical conventions are to ignore blanks and to recognize keywords in context.

In summary, the salient characteristics of the first generation are machine orientation and linear structures. We will see in the next chapter that the second generation makes important moves in the directions of application orientation and hierarchical structure.

EXERCISES*

1. Study the 1966 ANS FORTRAN IV Standard and compare it with the dialect accepted by a particular compiler. Document the ways in which the implemented language differs from the standard.
2. Critique the FORTRAN 77 Standard with respect to the language design principles we've discussed.
3. Compare FORTRAN 77 with one or more structured FORTRAN processors (e.g., RATFOR, WATFIV).
4. Study the FORTRAN FORMAT-statement. Critique the FORMAT-statement sublanguage of FORTRAN with respect to regularity, orthogonality, structure, etc.
5. Suppose that eight decimal-digits (4 bits each) will fit in one computer word. Design a decimal arithmetic facility for FORTRAN. This must include a DECIMAL data type and appropriate arithmetic operations and relations. Discuss the dominance rules and coercions that will be provided.
6. Study the COBOL programming language and discuss its similarities to and differences from FORTRAN. Propose a list of properties characterizing first-generation languages.
7. Some languages (e.g., BASIC) allow matrix arithmetic. Design a matrix arithmetic facility for FORTRAN, or present detailed arguments why such a facility should not be provided.

8. Find descriptions of FORTRAN II, FORTRAN IV, and FORTRAN 77. Make a chart showing the statements and constructs in each of these. This chart should simplify seeing the evolution of FORTRAN through the features that have been added and deleted.
9. Write to the American National Standards Institute (Committee X3J3) and find out what its current FORTRAN standardization efforts are. Critique the latest proposed standard.
10. Defend or attack the following statement: Instead of developing new FORTRAN standards that attempt to incorporate new ideas in an obsolete framework, we should freeze FORTRAN in its current state and concentrate on standardizing newer languages.
11. It has been said that FORTRAN is like the cockroach: It has survived essentially unchanged from prehistoric times, and nobody is sure why. Write an essay discussing the longevity of FORTRAN.

3

ELEGANCE AND GENERALITY: ALGOL-60

3.1 HISTORY AND MOTIVATION

An International Language Was Needed

Already in the mid-1950s it was becoming apparent to some computer scientists that a single, universal, machine-independent programming language would be valuable. The problem, of course, was portability; since each machine had its own instruction sets, assemblers, and pseudo-code interpreters, it was very difficult to transport programs from one machine to another. As early as 1955,[1] GAMM, a European association for applied mathematics and mechanics, had set up a committee to study the development of such a language. The problem was serious enough that at a conference in Los Angeles in May 1957, representatives of ACM (The Association for Computing Machinery) and three manufacturer's

1 Most of the historical information in this section comes from the "History of Programming Languages Conference Proceedings," *SIGPLAN Notices 13*, 8 (Aug. 1978).

users' groups suggested that ACM form a committee to study and recommend action for the creation of a universal programming language. In June ACM appointed representatives of the computer industry, users, universities, and the federal government to such a committee. In October GAMM proposed to ACM that a joint effort be undertaken, to which ACM agreed. In this proposal GAMM made several points; for example, that no existing language was so popular that it should be chosen as the standard and that another "nonideal" language would not solve the problem of the proliferation of languages. GAMM also stressed that the passing of time aggravated the problem since each month brought more programming languages and more programs written in those languages. A joint meeting of four members of each of the ACM and GAMM subcommittees was scheduled for May and June 1958 in Zurich.

The Algol-58 Language Was Developed

The language now known as Algol-58 was designed by the eight representatives who met in Zurich. The European members brought several years of work on algebraic language design and the Americans brought their experience in implementing pseudo-codes and other programming systems. For example, John Backus was one member of the American group. This combination of talents proved very productive, and in eight days the language was essentially completed. In December 1958 Perlis and Samelson, writing for the committee, published the "Preliminary Report—International Algebraic Language," in the *Communications of the ACM.* At that time the official name of the new language was IAL, although the acronym Algol (Algorithmic Language) had already been proposed. It is for this reason that the 1958 document is often known as the "Algol-58 Report."

It is instructive to see the objectives of the new language as stated in the Algol-58 Report:

I. The new language should be as close as possible to standard mathematical notation and be readable with little further explanation.

II. It should be possible to use it for the description of computing processes in publications.

III. The new language should be mechanically translatable into machine programs.

As our description in this book progresses, you should try to decide how well Algol met these goals.

Algol-58 created a great stir when it was announced; implementations were begun at many universities and laboratories. Indeed, many of IBM's users even suggested that IBM abandon FORTRAN and throw all of its support behind

Algol; IBM, however, decided against that course. Many dialects of Algol-58 appeared, including NELIAC, the Navy Electronic Laboratories International Algol Compiler, and JOVIAL, which is still widely used by the Air Force. JOVIAL is an acronym for "Jules' Own Version of the International Algebraic Language," reflecting the alterations made to IAL (Algol-58) by Jules Schwartz. By jumping too soon on the Algol bandwagon, these efforts diminished Algol's value as a universal language since they committed their users to an obsolete version of Algol.

A Formal Grammar Was Used for Syntactic Description

The Algol-58 Report was only a preliminary specification; it was intended that critiques and suggested improvements would be collected until November 1959, when the final language would be designed. One of the media for exchange of Algol information was the International Conference on Information Processing held by UNESCO in Paris in June 1959. At this conference John Backus presented a description of Algol using a formal syntactic notation he had developed. Peter Naur, then the editor of the *Algol Bulletin*, was surprised because Backus's definition of Algol-58 did not agree with his interpretation of the Algol-58 Report. He took this as an indication that a more precise method of describing syntax was required and prepared some samples of a variant of the Backus notation. As a result, this notation was adopted for the Algol-60 Report and is now known as BNF, Backus–Naur Form, reflecting the contributions of both men. This important method for describing programming languages is discussed in the next chapter.

Algol-60 Was Designed

Thirteen members of ACM and GAMM met in Paris for six days in January 1960 in order to prepare a final report on the language incorporating the various suggestions that had been received. The language that resulted, Algol-60, was very different from Algol-58 and was described in a report published in May 1960. The resulting language was remarkable for its generality and elegance, particularly considering that it was designed by a committee. Alan Perlis has described it as "more of a racehorse than a camel." A few remaining errors and ambiguities were corrected at a meeting in Rome in 1962, and the "Revised Report on the Algorithmic Language ALGOL-60" was published in the *Communications* in January 1963. Algol has continued to evolve, a process that we discuss at the end of this chapter.

The Report Is a Paradigm of Brevity and Clarity

At a time when programming language descriptions often stretch to hundreds or thousands of pages, it is remarkable to realize that the original Algol-60 Report was 15 pages long. The brevity and clarity of this report contributed significantly to Algol's reputation as a simple, elegant language. How was it possible to produce so short a report? One reason was the use of the BNF notation; this provided a simple, concise, easy-to-read, precise method of describing Algol's syntax. We discuss it in the next chapter.

BNF is only useful for describing the *syntax* of a language. How was the *semantics*, or meaning, of Algol's constructs described? The committee decided to use clear, precise, unambiguous English-language descriptions, which resulted in a report that was readable by potential users, implementers, and language designers. The clarity and brevity of the Algol-60 Report have rarely been achieved since; it remains a standard against which all programming language descriptions can be compared.

3.2 DESIGN: STRUCTURAL ORGANIZATION

Figure 3.1 displays a small Algol-60 program to compute the mean (average) of the absolute value of an array. In Algol, the reserved words of the language (e.g., '**if**') are distinct from the identifiers (e.g., 'if'), therefore, it is common to print the reserved words in boldface or to underline them, as can be seen in this example. These lexical conventions are discussed in Chapter 4, Section 4.1.

Algol Programs Are Hierarchically Structured

One of the primary characteristics and important contributions of Algol is its use of *hierarchical structure*, or nesting, throughout its design. For example, an Algol program is composed of a number of nested environments, as we can see in the contour diagram in Figure 3.2, which corresponds to the program in Figure 3.1. The nesting of environments is discussed in Section 3.3, on name structures.

Algol-60 also allows control structures to be nested. For instance, a **for**-loop, such as,

```
for i := 1 step 1 until N do
  sum := sum + Data[i]
```

can be made the object of an **if**-statement. For example,

```
if N > 0 then
  for i := 1 step 1 until N do
    sum := sum + Data[i]
```

```
begin
  integer N;
  Read Int (N);

  begin
    real array Data[1:N];
    real sum, avg;
    integer i;
    sum := 0;

    for i := 1 step 1 until N do
      begin real val;
        Read Real (val);
        Data[i] := if val < 0 then -val else val
      end;
    for i := 1 step 1 until N do
      sum := sum + Data[i];
    avg := sum/N;
    Print Real (avg)
  end
end
```

Figure 3.1 An Algol-60 Program

This nesting greatly decreases the number of **goto**-statements required in a program. Some of its implications are discussed in Section 3.5 on control structures.

Constructs Are Either Declarative or Imperative

As in FORTRAN, the constructs of Algol-60 can be divided into two categories —*declarative* and *imperative.* The declarative constructs bind names to objects (variables and procedures in Algol's case) and the imperatives do the work of computation.

There are three kinds of declarations in Algol-60—variable declarations, procedure declarations, and **switch**-declarations. Variable declarations are similar to FORTRAN's, except that the only data types allowed are **integer**, **real**, and **Boolean**; for example,

```
integer i, j, k
```

The array declarations are analogous, although the lower bound is allowed to be numbers other than 1:

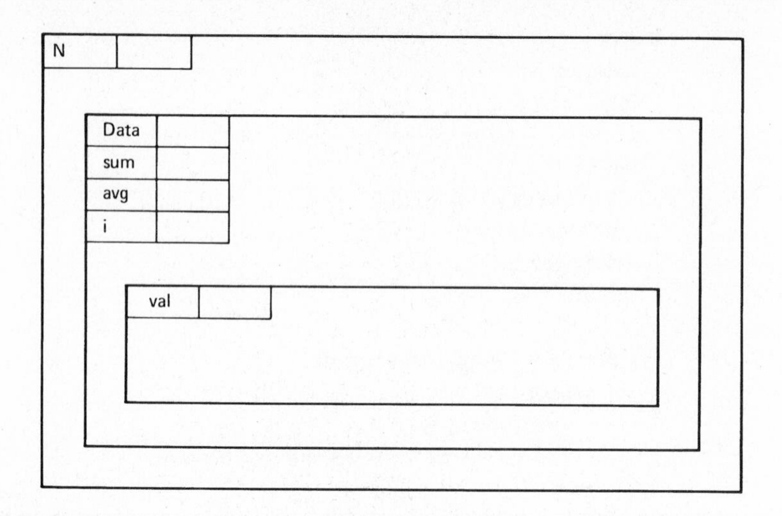

Figure 3.2 Contour Diagram of an Algol Program

```
real array Data[-50:50]
```

Algol has *dynamic arrays,* that is, their bounds can be computed at run-time; this will be discussed in Section 3.4 on data structures.

Algol uses the term *procedure* to refer to a subprogram and distinguishes between *typed* procedures (Algol's name for a *function)* and *untyped* procedures, which are like FORTRAN subroutines. Since there are no implicit declarations in Algol, procedure declarations are required to specify the types of their formal parameters; for example,

```
real procedure dist (x1, y1, x2, y2);
  real x1, y1, x2, y2;
  dist := sqrt ((x1-x2)↑2 + (y1-y2)↑2)
```

In Section 3.5 on control structures, we will take an in-depth look at procedures.

Finally, the **switch**-*declaration* serves the same function as the FORTRAN computed GOTO, namely, breaking a problem down into cases; it is discussed in Section 3.5 on control structures.

Imperatives Are Computational and Control-Flow

There are two classes of imperative constructs in Algol-60—the computational and the control-flow. There are no input-output constructs in Algol-60; it was intended that input-output be handled by library procedures. As in FORTRAN the only computational statement is the *assignment*, which has the form 'variable := expression', where 'variable' is a simple variable or an array reference and 'expression' is an integer, real, or Boolean expression constructed from variables, constants, and operators. Algol provides the standard arithmetic operators (+, −, etc.), relational operators, which return a Boolean result (=, >, ≤, etc.), and Boolean operators (∧, ∨, ¬, etc.). All of these are organized by precedence to give a natural appearance to the notation.

The assignment operation, ':=', deserves some comment. FORTRAN had used an equal sign for assignments by the analogy with mathematical definition, for example, 'let $C = 2\pi r$'. It was widely recognized that this notation was really not very accurate, since assignment and definition are really two different things. For example, 'I = I+1' makes no sense as a definition, although it is a very useful assignment operation. Early programming notations (and indeed other engineering notations) commonly used a rightward pointing arrow to indicate assignment. For instance, 'I+1 → I' indicates that the value I+1 is to be put into I. A number of notations had been used for the assignment arrow in early programming languages, including '=>' and '⪰', but the limitations of input devices led the Algol designers to compromise on '=:' as an arrow symbol. Later, on the basis of experience with FORTRAN, this was turned around into a leftward assignment: 'i := i+1'. Almost all programming languages now use this notation.

Algol Has the Familiar Control Structures

All other Algol imperatives alter the flow of control in the program. The most obvious of these is the **goto**-*statement*, which transfers to a labeled statement. Algol has a conditional statement, the **if-then-else** and an iterative statement, the **for**-*loop*, which is an elaboration of FORTRAN's DO-loop. Finally, it has a procedure invocation, as we have seen. Control structures are the subject of Section 3.5.

The Compile-Time, Run-Time Distinction Is Important

Algol-60 programs typically go through a compilation process very much like that of FORTRAN programs. There are a few important differences, however. FORTRAN is completely static, that is, all of the data areas are allocated and arranged by the compiler. By the time the program is loaded into memory, it is ready to run, with only the contents of the memory locations being altered by the program. We will see in Sections 3.3–3.5 of this chapter that various features in Algol (e.g., dynamic arrays and recursive procedures) preclude a static, compile-time layout of memory. Rather, various data areas are allocated and deallocated at run-time by the program. In other words, Algol data structures have a later *binding time* than FORTRAN data structures. More specifically, the name is bound to a memory location at run-time rather than compile-time. As in FORTRAN, it is bound to its type at compile-time.

The Stack Is the Central Run-Time Data Structure

There are many disciplines for organizing the dynamic allocation and deallocation of memory. The one used by Algol (and most other programming languages) is the *stack*. We will see in Sections 3.3–3.5 that Algol programs have one stack that they use for holding activation records for procedures and blocks. Dynamic allocation and deallocation are achieved by pushing and popping these activation records on the stack. Nonstack-oriented run-time structures are discussed in Chapter 12 (Section 12.5).

3.3 DESIGN: NAME STRUCTURES

The Primitives Bind Names to Objects

We saw in Chapter 2 that the purpose of name structures was to organize the name space, that is, the collection of names used in the program. We also saw that in FORTRAN the primitive name structures are the declarations that define names by binding them to objects; the same is the case in Algol. There is one major difference; in FORTRAN a variable name is statically bound to a memory location, whereas in Algol we will find that a single variable may be bound to a number of different memory locations and that these bindings can change during run-time. To see why this is the case, we have to investigate the *constructors* of name structures.

The Constructor Is the Block

One of the important contributions of Algol-58 was the idea of a *compound statement*. This allows a sequence of statements to be used wherever one was permitted. For instance, although one statement would normally form the body of a **for**-loop, such as,

```
for i := 1 step 1 until N do
  sum := sum + Data[i]
```

several statements can form the body if they were surrounded by **begin-end** brackets:

```
for i := 1 step 1 until N do
  begin
    if Data[i] > 1000000 then Data[i] := 1000000;
    sum := sum + Data[i];
    Print Real (sum)
  end
```

Similarly, in Algol (as opposed to Pascal and many other languages), the body of a procedure is taken to be a single statement. For example, in the following definition of 'cosh' the body is a single assignment statement:

```
real procedure cosh (x); real x;
  cosh := (exp(x) + exp(-x))/2;
```

The fact that a group of statements can be used anywhere that one statement is expected is an example of *regularity* in language design. As we saw in Chapter 1, a regular language is generally easier to learn and understand (other things being equal) than an irregular one. The compound statement idea had important consequences for control structures, which are discussed in Section 3.5.

Between the publication of the Algol-58 and the Algol-60 reports, a lot of research and discussion were devoted to name structures. This included some of the problems we investigated in Chapter 2, such as the sharing of data among subprograms. The issue of name structure also interacted with other issues, such as parameter passing modes and dynamic arrays. The eventual outcome of all this work was a very important idea, *block structure.*

Blocks Define Nested Scopes

In FORTRAN we saw that environments are composed of scopes nested in two levels. All subprograms are bound in the outer (global) scope and all (subprogram-local) variables are bound in inner scopes, one for each subprogram (see Figure 2.9). Although COMMON blocks are effectively bound at the global level (since they are visible to all subprograms), in fact they must be redeclared in each subprogram. Algol-60 avoids this redeclaration by allowing the programmer to define any number of scopes nested to any depth; this is accomplished with a *block*:

```
begin declarations; statements end
```

This defines a scope that extends from the **begin** to the **end**. This is the scope of the names bound in the declarations immediately following the **begin**; therefore, these names are visible to all of the statements in the block. Since these statements may themselves be blocks, we can see that the scopes can be nested.

Contour diagrams are often helpful in visualizing name structures. Let's compare the program in Figure 3.1 with the contour diagram in Figure 3.2 to be sure that we understand it. Remember that the rule for contour diagrams is that we can look out of a box but we can't look into one. Figure 3.3 shows an outline of a more complicated Algol program; its contour diagram is in Figure 3.4.

Notice that the contours are suggested by the *scoping lines* we have drawn to the left of the program in Figure 3.3. Contour diagrams originated by completing scoping lines into boxes. We can see that in addition to blocks, procedure declarations also introduce a level of nesting since the formal parameters are local to the procedure. We can also see where the name "contour diagram" came from; the diagrams are suggestive of contour maps.

We have said that the purpose of name structures is to organize the name space. Why is this important? Virtually everything a programmer deals with in a program is named. Therefore, as programs become larger and larger, there will be more and more names for the programmer to keep track of, which can make understanding and maintaining the program very difficult. Another way to say this is that the *context* that programmers must keep in their heads is too large; too many names are visible. Therefore, the goal of name structures is to limit the context with which the programmer must deal at any given time. Name structures do this by restricting the visibility of names to particular parts of a program, in the case of block structure, to the block in which the name is declared. For example, in the program in Figure 3.3, the variable 'val' is only needed for the

```
┌ begin
│   real x, y;
│ ┌ real procedure cosh(x); real x;
│ └   cosh := (exp(x)+exp(-x))/2;
│
│ ┌ procedure f(y,z);
│ │   integer y, z;
│ │ ┌ begin real array A[1:y];
│ │ │     :
│ └ └ end
│   :
│ ┌ begin integer array Count [0:99];
│ │   :
│ └ end
│   :
└ end
```

Figure 3.3 Nested Environments

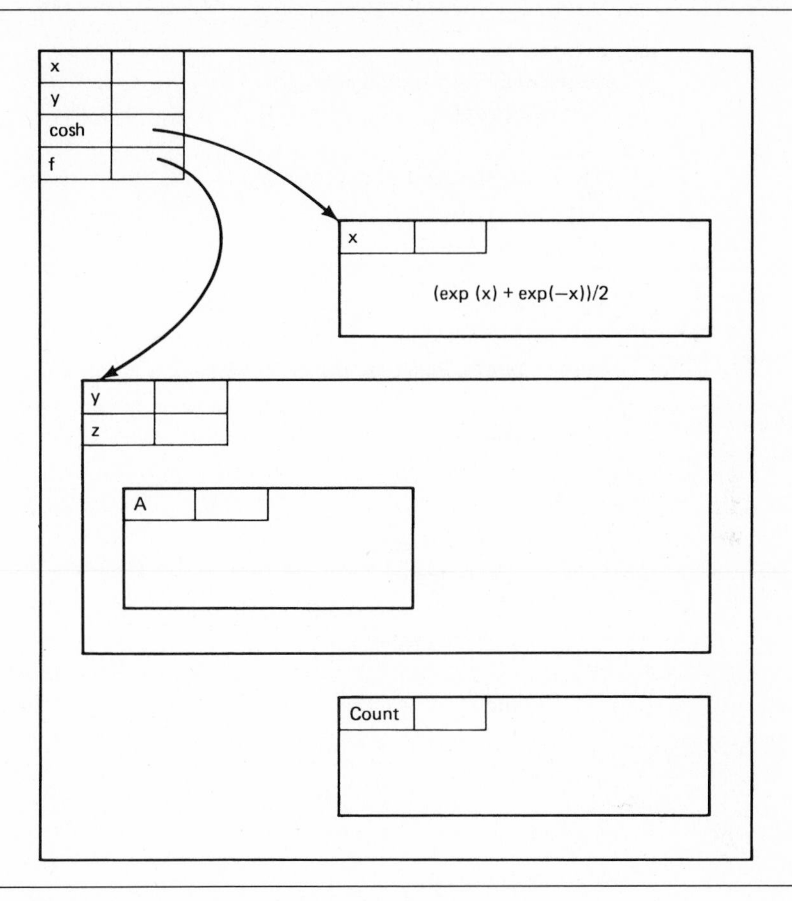

Figure 3.4 Contour Diagram of Nested Scopes

two statements in the body of the first **for**-loop. Therefore, it is declared in the block that forms the body. We can see from this example that it would be very inconvenient if the variables declared in the outer blocks (N, Data, sum, avg, and i) were not visible in the inner block. For this reason, an inner block *implicitly inherits* access to all of the variables accessible in its immediately surrounding block; this is what's shown by the contour diagrams. The names declared in a block are called *local* to that block; those declared in surrounding blocks are called *nonlocal*. The names declared in the outermost block are called *global* because they are visible to the entire program.

EXERCISE 3-1: Draw a contour diagram for a program whose outline is shown in Figure 3.5. *Hint:* Recall that the body of a procedure is a single statement, which may be a compound statement or block.

```
begin integer i, j;
    procedure P(x,y); integer x, y;
        begin real z;
            :
            begin real array A[1:x];
                :
                A[i] := j;
                :
            end
            :
            begin Boolean array B[1:y];
                :
            end
            :
        end
    procedure Q(x); real x;
        begin integer n;
        procedure R(a,b); integer a, b;
            begin integer x;
                :
            end
        :
        P(n,i);
        :
        end
    begin integer j, k;
        Q(0.0);
    end
end
```

Figure 3.5 Algol Program for Exercise

EXERCISE 3-2:* Before the designers of Algol decided on block structure, they considered the possibility of *explicit inheritance,* that is, having each block explicitly declare the names from the surrounding environment to which it needed access. Compare and contrast implicit and explicit inheritance and discuss some advantages and disadvantages of each. Design name structuring facilities for explicit inheritance in Algol-60.

Blocks Simplify Constructing Large Programs

You will recall that FORTRAN COMMON was designed to allow sharing data structures among a group of subprograms. One of the problems with COMMON is that the COMMON declaration must be repeated in each subprogram, which is wasteful and a potential source of errors. Now, a general guideline in language design is the *Abstraction Principle.* Whenever the programmer must restate the same thing, or almost the same thing, over and over again, we should find a way to *abstract* the common parts.

To see how Algol-60 blocks apply the Abstraction Principle to shared data structures, we look again at the symbol table example from Chapter 2. Recall that we represented a symbol table as four parallel arrays called NAMES, LOC, TYPE, and DIMS. These were managed by subprograms such as LOOKUP, VAR, and ARRAY1. The problem is that these subprograms needed access to the symbol table arrays but that it is undesirable to pass the arrays to them explicitly. The solution in FORTRAN was to put the arrays into a COMMON block, but this scattered about the program the information about the structure of the symbol table.

Algol block structure solves this problem since the symbol table arrays can be factored out into a block that surrounds the symbol table management procedures. This is shown in Figures 3.6 and 3.7.

```
begin
  integer array NAME, LOC, TYPE, DIMS [1:100];

  procedure LOOKUP (n);
    ... LOOKUP procedure ...

  procedure VAR (n, l, t);
    ... Enter variable procedure ...

  procedure ARRAY1 (n, l, t, dim1);
    ... Enter 1-dimensional Array procedure ...

   ... other symbol table procedures ...

   ... uses of the symbol table procedures, e.g.,
  ARRAY2 (nm, avail, intcode, m, n);
   ...
end
```

Figure 3.6 Shared Data and Block Structure

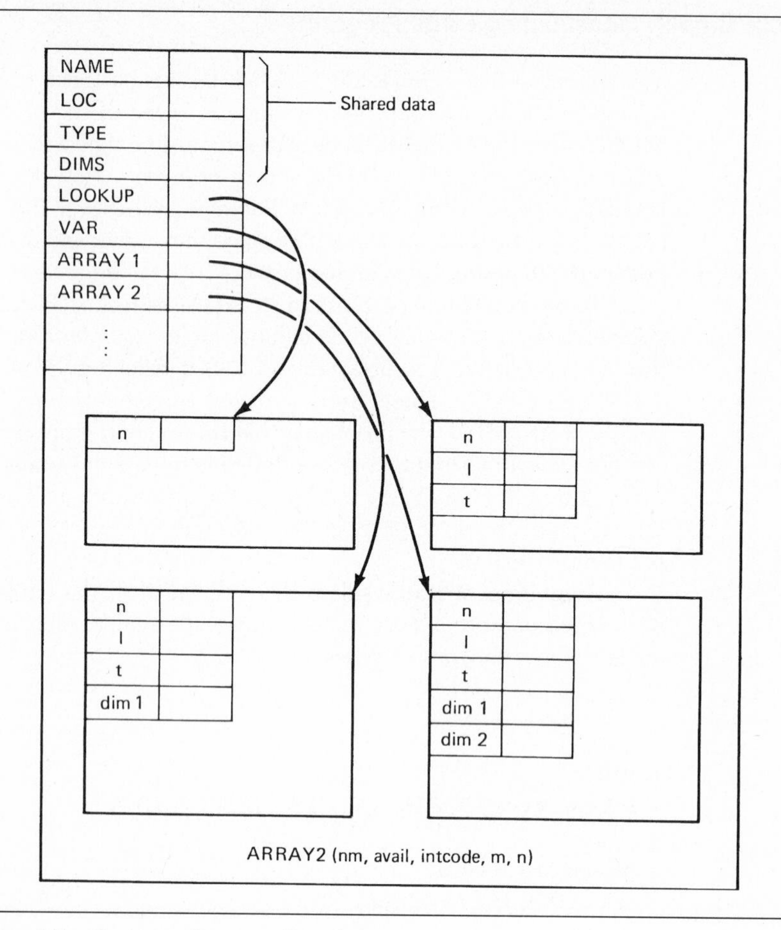

Figure 3.7 Contours Showing Shared Data

Notice that the block that includes the declarations of the symbol table arrays must also include all the invocations (users) of the symbol table managers. Since the managers must be visible to the users, and the data structures must be visible to the managers, we can see that the data structures must be visible to the users; this is a necessary effect of Algol block structure. This means that users of the symbol table can directly access the symbol table without going through the symbol table managers. This creates a maintenance problem since the users' code will be dependent on the structure of the symbol table and will have to be modified whenever the structure of the symbol table is altered. Notice that the FORTRAN solution did not have this problem; the structure of the symbol table was confined to the COMMON block declarations, which were confined to the symbol table managers. This problem in Algol block structure is called *indiscriminate access* and was not solved for many years; its solution is discussed in Chapter 7. It is a violation of the Information Hiding Principle described in Chapter 2.

EXERCISE 3-3: What algebraic property of the visibility relation have we appealed to in showing that the data structures must be visible to the users?

Dynamic Scoping Allows the Context to Vary

There are two scoping rules that can be used in block-structured languages—static scoping and dynamic scoping. In static scoping a procedure is called in the environment of its *definition;* in dynamic scoping a procedure is called in the environment of its *caller.* Although Algol uses static scoping exclusively, we take this opportunity to investigate each of these scoping strategies and their consequences.

Some languages use dynamic scoping and some use static scoping. Which is better? Debate on this question dates back to at least 1960 when the advocates of Algol's static scoping confronted the advocates of LISP's dynamic scoping. To see some of the issues involved, look at this program:

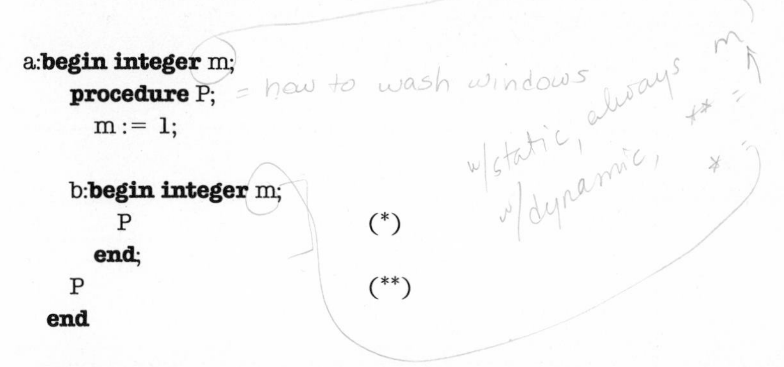

```
a:begin integer m;
    procedure P;
      m := 1;

    b:begin integer m;
        P                    (*)
      end;
    P                        (**)
  end
```

With *dynamic scoping* the assignment 'm := 1' refers to the outer declaration of 'm' when P is called from the outer block (**) and the inner declaration of 'm' when P is called from the inner block (*). Look at this contour diagram for the call (**):

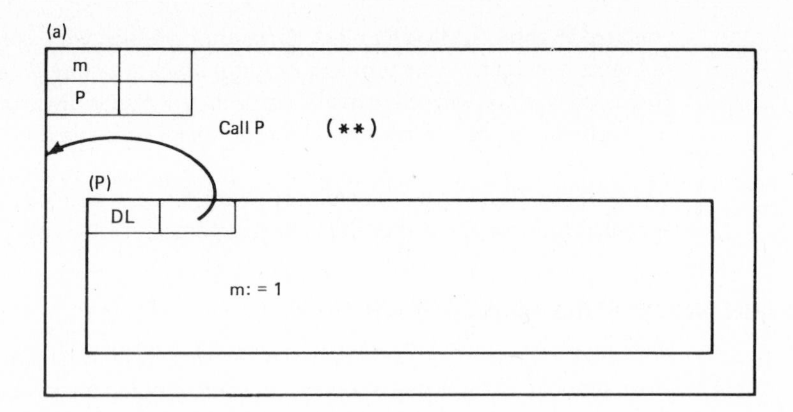

(In this diagram we have used 'DL' to refer to the dynamic link, that is, to a pointer from the callee to the caller.) Since P is called in the environment of its caller, block (a), the contour for P is nested in the contour of block (a). Hence, 'm := 1' refers to the 'm' declared in block (a).

The invocation (*) is represented by the contour diagram below, since P is called from block (b), which is nested in block (a):

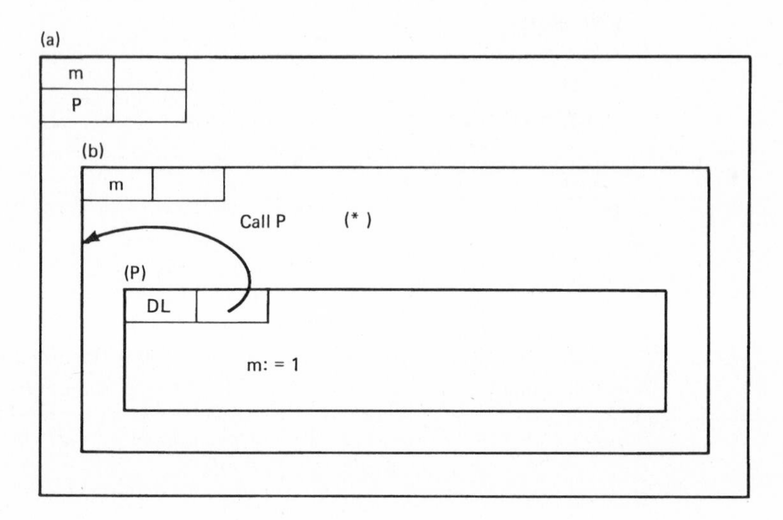

We can see that the identifier 'm' in 'm := 1' refers to the variable declared in block (b). What we mean when we say that P is *called in the environment of the*

caller is that the contour for P is nested (dynamically) inside the contour of its caller. This is also why this scope rule is called *dynamic* nesting or *dynamic* scoping; the scope structure is determined dynamically, that is, at run-time. Thus, the context in which P is executed is the context from which it was called.

With *static scoping* the assignment 'm := 1' always refers to the variable 'm' in the outer block. This is so because P is always *called in the environment of its definition*; i.e., the context in which P is executed is always the context in which it was originally defined. This means that the contour for P must be nested in the contour in which it was defined *regardless of where it's called from.* Therefore, the contour for the call (*) is:

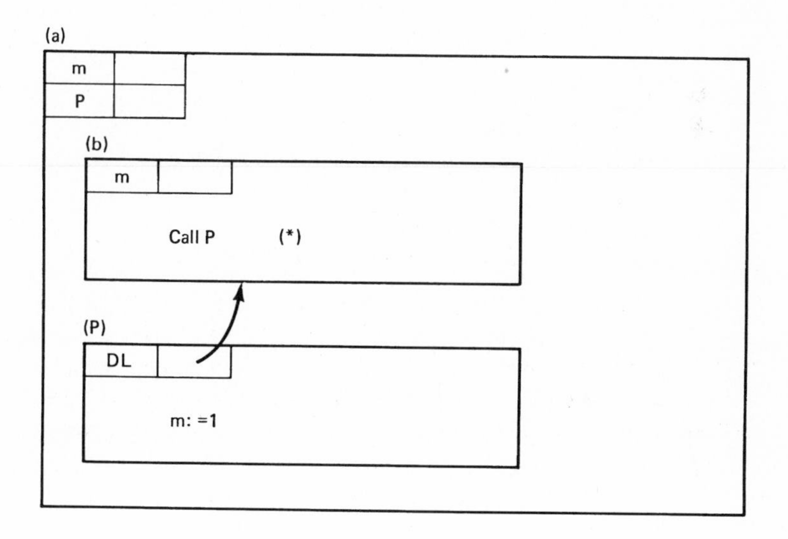

Observe that the contour for P is nested in the contour for block (a) even though P was called from block (b); the context in which P executes will always be block (a) regardless of P's caller. The contour diagram shows that the 'm' visible from the body of 'P' is the 'm' declared in block (a).

Since scope rules apply uniformly to all names (not just variable names), the differences between dynamic and static scoping can also be seen in the scope of procedure names. This affords a good example of the advantages and disadvantages of each.

Suppose we wished to define a function 'sum' which summed the values of a function 'f' from 0 to 1. This is easily accomplished with dynamic scoping:

```
begin
  real procedure sum;
    begin real S, x; S:=0; x:=0;
      for x := x+0.01 while x≤1 do
        S := S + f(x);
      sum := S/100
    end;
    ...
end
```

To use the 'sum' function, it is only necessary to name the function to be summed 'f'. For example, the function $x^2 + 1$ could be summed by embedding the following block in the scope of 'sum' (indicated by '..., above):

```
begin
  real procedure f(x);
    value x; real x;
    f:= x↑2 + 1;
  sumf := sum
end
```

Since 'sum' is called in the environment of the *caller*, it will be called in an environment in which 'f' is the function $x^2 + 1$. This is one of the advantages of dynamic scoping: We can write a general procedure that makes use of variables and procedures supplied by the caller's environment. This can also be accomplished by passing these variables and procedures as explicit parameters to the procedure, which can be conveniently done in Algol with Jensen's device (described in Section 3.5).

EXERCISE 3-4: Show that the above definition of 'sum' works by drawing a contour diagram for the above program when it is executing in 'sum'.

EXERCISE 3-5: Write the 'sum' procedure using Jensen's device and static scoping (see Section 3.5).

EXERCISE 3-6: Describe how 'sum' would be implemented in Pascal, FORTRAN, or some other language with which you are familiar.

We have seen above how we can use to advantage the fact that in a dynamically scoped language a procedure is executed in the environment of its caller. Next, we investigate the problems to which this can lead. Suppose we wished to define a procedure 'roots' to compute the roots of a quadratic equation, $ax^2 + bx$

$+ c = 0$. To do this it is useful to have an auxiliary function 'discr (a,b,c)' that computes the *discriminant*, $b^2 - 4ac$. Our program could be structured like this:

```
begin
  real procedure discr (a, b, c);
    value a, b, c; real a, b, c;
    discr := b↑2 - 4 × a × c;

  procedure roots (a, b, c, r1, r2);
    value a, b, c; real a, b, c, r1, r2;
    begin
      ... d := discr (a, b, c); ...
    end
  ⋮
  roots (c1, c2, c3, root1, root2 );
  ⋮
end
```

Now, suppose someone happened to call our 'roots' procedure from a block in which a different procedure named 'discr' had been defined:

```
begin
  real procedure discr (x, y, z);
    value x, y, z; real x, y, z;
    discr := sqrt (x↑2 + y↑2 + z↑2);
  ⋮
  roots (acoe, bcoe, ccoe, rt1, rt2);
  ⋮
end
```

Our 'discr' procedure has been inadvertently replaced by another! Needless to say, our 'roots' procedure will not give the right results. In fact, if this imposter 'discr' had not happened to have the right number of parameters of the right type, it would have caused our 'roots' to produce an error.

EXERCISE 3-7: One way to decrease the probability of these errors happening is to pick "unlikely" names for our auxiliary procedures, for example, 'QdiscrQ057'. Discuss the implications of this practice for program readability.

EXERCISE 3-8: Draw the contour diagram that illustrates the 'roots' example.

The problem described above is an example of *vulnerability*, so called because the 'roots' procedure is *vulnerable* to being called from an environment in which its auxiliary procedure is not accessible. To put it another way, there is no way 'roots' can preserve its access to its 'discr'. Vulnerability and a means of eliminating it are discussed in Chapter 7.

EXERCISE 3-9: Show that the above problem can be solved, even in the presence of dynamic scoping, by a proper arrangement of the nesting of 'roots' and 'discr'. Show, on the other hand, that if 'discr' is shared by two or more procedures, then there is no way to prevent vulnerability in the presence of dynamic scoping; that is, there is no way these procedures can ensure their access to 'discr'.

Static and Dynamic Scoping Summarized

Let's try to summarize what we've seen about static and dynamic scoping. In all languages the meaning of a statement or expression is determined by the context in which the statement or expression is interpreted. The context, in turn, is determined by the scope rules of the language. Since in a dynamically scoped language the scopes of names are determined dynamically, that is, at run-time, we can see that in such a language the meanings of statements and expressions may vary at run-time.

Conversely, in a statically scoped language, the scopes of names are determined statically by the structure of the program so the meanings of statements and expressions are fixed. To put this another way, the meanings of all statements and expressions can be determined by inspecting the *static structure* of the program without having to understand its *dynamic behavior.* To summarize:

- In *dynamic scoping* the meanings of statements and expressions are determined by the *dynamic structure* of the computations evolving in time.
- In *static scoping* the meanings of statements and expressions are determined by the *static structure* of the program.

Static Scoping Aids Reliable Programming

The emphasis on reliable programming in recent years has led to the general rejection of dynamic scoping. It is not hard to understand why. We know how confusing it can be if someone uses the same word in the same conversation in two different ways, if the context is switched without warning. This practice can be so detrimental to clear thought that it is classified as a logical fallacy, *equivocation.* The same holds for programs. Programmers will be more likely to write reliable programs if, when they write a statement or expression, they know what it means. A scoping discipline that allows the meaning of procedures to shift and slide depending on their context of use is not conducive to reliable programming. This is the reason that Algol and almost all new programming languages (including newer dialects of traditionally dynamically scoped languages such as LISP) have adopted static scoping.

In summary, we have seen that static scoping causes the static structure of a program to agree more closely with its dynamic behavior than does dynamic scoping. But this is just the Structure Principle, which states that the dynamic behavior of a program should correspond in a simple way to its static structure. Therefore, we can say that static scoping is in accord with the Structure Principle, but dynamic scoping is not.

EXERCISE 3-10:* Discuss static and dynamic scoping. Do you agree that static scoping is better? Can you think of any ways in which dynamic scoping could be improved without losing its good points?

Blocks Permit Efficient Storage Management on a Stack

In Chapter 2 we saw that the FORTRAN EQUIVALENCE-statement was intended to permit a programmer to conserve memory by using it for multiple purposes. We also discussed some of the pitfalls in this mechanism and hinted that newer languages provide a better solution. To understand this better solution, consider this Algol program outline:

```
a:begin integer m, n;
    b:begin real array X[1:100]; real y;
          :
      end
  :
    c:begin integer k; integer array M[0:50];
          :
      end
end
```

The contour diagram of the above program outline is shown in Figure 3.8. We can see that the two blocks labeled (b) and (c) are *disjoint,* that is, neither is nested in the other. What are the consequences of this? Whenever the program is executing in (b), the local variables of (c), namely k and M, are not visible since the site of execution is not in their scope. Conversely, whenever the program is executing in (c), the local variables of (b) are not visible. To put it another way, the variables X and y are never visible at the same time as the variables k and M because the two sets of variables have disjoint scopes.

It is only necessary to make one assumption in order to turn this fact about disjoint scopes into a solution of the storage-sharing problem. This assumption is that the value of a variable is retained only so long as the program is executing in the scope of that variable or in a block or procedure that will eventually return

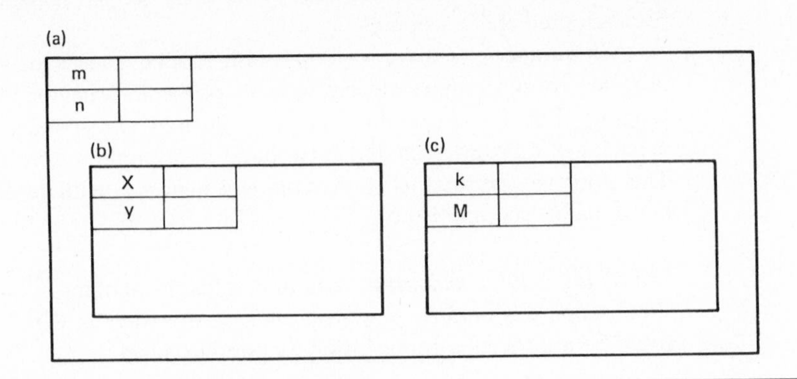

Figure 3.8 Contours of Disjoint Scopes

to the scope of that variable. In other words, if the flow of control leaves the scope of a variable (i.e., leaves the block in which the variable is declared), then the contents of that variable are discarded.[2] That is, when the flow of control enters a block, all of the variables declared in that block become visible but with undefined content—that is, they are uninitialized.

Why does this solve the shared array problem? Consider the previous example (Figure 3.8): The array X only exists when the program is executing in block (b) or a block or procedure that can return to (b). Whenever the program leaves this block, the array becomes invisible and its contents are discarded. In other words, for all intents and purposes, when the program is not in block (b), the array X does not exist. The same applies to the array M; it only exists when the program is within, or can return to, the (c) contour. Since these contours are disjoint, the program can never be in both of them at the same time so the arrays X and M never exist at the same time. This is the solution to our problem: Since these two arrays can never coexist, they can occupy the same storage locations when they do exist.

Notice that this is much more *secure* than FORTRAN EQUIVALENCE. Recall that with EQUIVALENCE there was the danger that a program might store into one array (say M) while the other (say X) was still needed. In Algol this can never happen since the arrays are never visible at the same time. By sharing storage only between disjoint environments, Algol prevents arrays from

2 For situations where this is not desirable, that is, where the value of a variable must be retained from one activation of a block to its next, Algol provides a mechanism called an **own** variable. We will not discuss this further in this book.

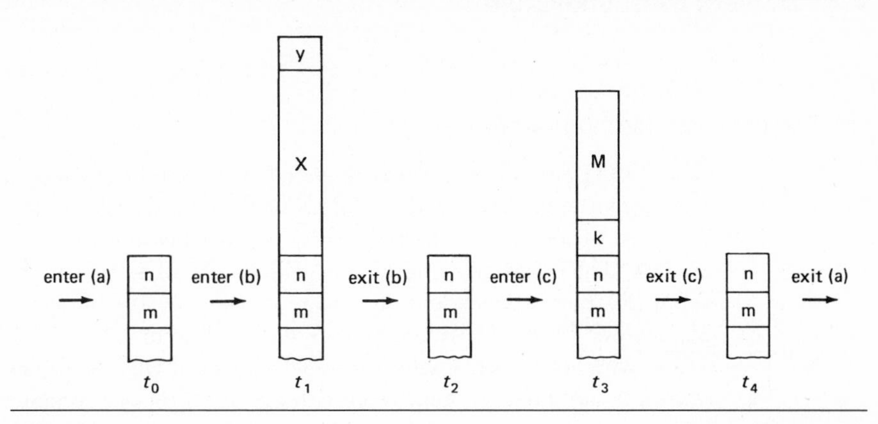

Figure 3.9 Storage Reallocation on a Stack

being corrupted and ensures (at least in this situation) the security of the system.

We have seen that Algol block structure *permits* memory to be used for multiple purposes, but we have not discussed how this is *implemented.* Notice that Algol blocks obey a last-in, first-out discipline. That is, the block that was last entered is the first to be exited, and the block that was first entered (i.e., the outermost) is the last to be exited. This is a simple consequence of the fact that blocks are nested, that is, they are structured hierarchically. Whenever we encounter a last-in, first-out discipline, the data structure that should come to mind is a *stack.* In fact, stacks are often called LIFOs (pronounced "lie-foe"), an acronym for "last-in, first-out." Stacks are used for storage allocation in the following way. Whenever a block is entered, an *activation record* for that block is pushed onto the top of the run-time stack. This activation record contains space for all the variables local to that block. Conversely, whenever the block is exited, its activation record will be popped off of the stack, thus freeing its storage for use by other blocks. This process is pictured in Figure 3.9.

We can see that the arrays X and M share the same memory locations; storage for them is *dynamically* (i.e., at run-time) allocated and deallocated, and the block structure of Algol ensures that this is done in a secure way. Before we leave this subject, we must mention that it was not an accident that the storage area associated with a block was called an *activation record;* we will see in Section 3.5 that this use of the term is completely consistent with its use in Chapter 2 to denote the state of a subprogram.

3.4 DESIGN: DATA STRUCTURES

The Primitives Are Mathematical Scalars

Like FORTRAN, Algol-60 was intended to be used for scientific applications. Therefore, the primitive data types are mathematical scalars—**integer**, **real**, and **Boolean**. There are no double-precision types because their use is necessarily machine dependent and one of the goals of Algol was to be a universal, and hence machine-independent, language. Why is double precision machine dependent? Suppose we wanted six digits of accuracy in a computation. To decide whether to use single or double precision, we would have to know the word size and floating-point representation used on our computer. If we then transported the program to another computer with a different word size, we would have to look at every declaration to decide whether it should be single or double precision on the new computer. The solution adopted by the Algol designers was to have only one precision in the language; if the *implementation* provided more than one precision, this would be selected by non-Algol constructs (e.g., specially interpreted comments). An alternate approach, which some languages have adopted, is to let the programmer specify the precision desired (e.g., six digits), and have the compiler pick the appropriate representation (e.g., single or double). This adds to the complexity of the language since there must be means for the programmer to specify this information. Algol took the simpler approach, a single type **real**.

EXERCISE 3-11:* Do you agree with the designers of Algol on the issue of precision? Design a mechanism for Algol that allows the programmer to specify the precision of floating-point numbers in a machine-independent way. Discuss the trade-offs involved in each of the two methods.

Algol also did not provide a **complex** data type (recall that FORTRAN provided COMPLEX numbers). Although complex numbers are useful in scientific computation, they were omitted from Algol because they are not *primitive*, that is, it is not very difficult or inefficient to define them in terms of the other primitives, namely, **real**s. Although this can be done, it is not very convenient. Consider the following fragment of a FORTRAN program that uses COMPLEX numbers:

```
COMPLEX X, Y, Z
X = (Y+Z)/X
```

To manipulate complex numbers in Algol, it would be necessary to write procedures to perform the complex arithmetic operations (e.g., ComplexAdd,

ComplexDivide). Complex numbers themselves would have to be represented either as pairs of real variables or as two-element real arrays. If we chose the latter representation, the FORTRAN fragment shown above would look like this in Algol-60:

```
real array x,y,z,t [1:2];
ComplexAdd (t,y,z);
ComplexDivide (x,t,x);
```

Notice that it is necessary to introduce a new temporary array, t. We can see that the Algol-60 solution is much less convenient and considerably less readable. This is a classic trade-off in programming language design: Are the convenience, readability, and efficiency of an additional data type (**complex**, in this case) worth the complexity of adding it to the language? Notice that there is substantial complexity associated with adding the **complex** type. If we wish to maintain the regularity of the language (thus following the Regularity Principle), we will want complex numbers to be first-class citizens. This means that there must be complex variables, complex arrays, complex parameters, complex operations, and complex relational tests. There must also be a syntax for writing complex numbers and input-output formats for reading and printing them. Finally, it will be necessary to decide whether there are meaningful *coercions* between complex numbers and other values. For instance, we will certainly want to be able to add complex and real numbers. But how about complex numbers and integers? How will we extract the real and imaginary parts of a complex number? We can see that the addition of a data type to a programming language is not a simple decision and should not be made lightly.

EXERCISE 3-12:* Do you think complex numbers should have been included in Algol-60? Take a position and defend it.

EXERCISE 3-13: Program ComplexAdd, etc., in Algol-60 or another language without a built-in **complex** data type.

Sometimes designers do decide to have second-class citizens in a programming language. An example of this is the **string** data type in Algol-60. We mentioned earlier that Algol-60 does not contain any input-output statements such as the FORTRAN READ-, WRITE-, and FORMAT-statements. Rather, it was intended that each Algol implementation would provide a set of library procedures for input-output. The Algol designers saw that this implied a facility for passing *strings* to procedures since otherwise there would be no way of printing headings or other alphanumeric information on listings. Rather than introduce a full-fledged **string** data type with all its associated variable declarations, operators, relations, and so on, the Algol designers decided to allow strings in only a few limited contexts. Specifically, string denotations (i.e., string literals such as 'Carmel') are only allowed as actual parameters, and the **string** type is only allowed in the specifications of formal parameters. There are no operators, relations, coercions, or variable declarations for strings. The effect of these restrictions is that the only thing that can be done with strings is to pass them as arguments to procedures. All those procedures can do is pass them as arguments to other procedures, and so forth. What good is this? There's no point in just passing strings around; sooner or later someone must *do* something with them. That is correct, but it can't be done in Algol. Ultimately, the string must be passed to a procedure coded in some other language, probably assembly language. This would be typical of, for example, input-output procedures.

We have seen that in both FORTRAN and Algol-60 character strings are second-class citizens, although in Algol, at least, this doesn't cause a loophole in the type system. The exclusion of strings was justified on the basis that these were scientific languages. Commercial programming languages such as COBOL, on the other hand, provided strings as bona-fide data types. We will see, however, the Algol was the last major programming language without strings; almost all newer languages, including PL/I, Algol-68, Pascal, and Ada, have some ability to deal with strings in the language.

EXERCISE 3-14:* Design a **string** data type for Algol-60. Address issues such as the operations, relations, and coercions to be provided.

Algol Follows the Zero-One-Infinity Principle

We have said that *regularity* was a goal of the Algol-60 design. Since a regular design has fewer special cases, it is generally easier to learn, remember, and master. There is a special application of the Regularity Principle called the Zero-One-Infinity Principle.

> ***Zero-One-Infinity Principle***
>
> The only reasonable numbers in a programming language design are zero, one, and infinity.

The easiest way to see what this means is to look at a couple of examples. The FORTRAN design is filled with numbers other than zero, one, or infinity; for example, identifiers are limited to six characters, there are at most 19 continuation cards, and arrays can have at most three dimensions. Six, 19, three, and so on, are all numbers that a FORTRAN programmer must remember, which will be difficult since the numbers seem completely arbitrary. Consider that in FORTRAN identifiers are limited to six characters. Why six? No one knows, but it probably has something to do with the representation of the symbol table in the original FORTRAN I implementation or the word size on the IBM 704. This number is small enough to be an annoyance to the programmer since a longer identifier will often make the program more readable. The Zero-One-Infinity Principle says that the number of characters allowed in a name should be zero, one, or infinity. Zero, of course, wouldn't make any sense in this case; a one-character limit would make sense, although we would consider it very limiting. Indeed, many early programming languages (including preliminary FORTRAN and BASIC) allowed only one-character names (as is common in mathematics). Algol and most newer languages have chosen the infinity option; that is, there is no limit on the length of an identifier. In reality there must be *some* limit, such as the memory capacity of the computer, but the limit is so large as to be effectively infinite. In summary, the Zero-One-Infinity Principle states that any limit in a programming language design should be none, one, or (effectively) infinite.

Arrays Are Generalized

Recall that FORTRAN arrays are limited to three dimensions; this was a result of efficiency considerations in the first FORTRAN system. This is clearly a violation of the Zero-One-Infinity Principle, so Algol arrays are generalized to allow any number of dimensions. This is not a pointless generalization; arrays of more than three dimensions are not uncommon in scientific computation.

Algol also generalizes FORTRAN arrays by allowing lower bounds to be numbers other than 1. That is, FORTRAN arrays are always addressed as A(1) through A(n), where n is the dimension of the array. In Algol, if the array is declared 'A[m:n]', then the legal array references are A[m] through A[n]. We can see that this array has $n-m+1$ elements. It is often useful to have lower bounds other than 1. For example, to keep track of number of days according to temperature, from -100 to $+200$, we declare an array

```
integer array Number of days [−100:200]
```

and then use negative indexes for temperatures below zero. For example, 'Number of days [−25]' represents the number of days with a temperature of −25. Of course, the same can be accomplished with a fixed lower bound. 'Number of days [temperature]' could be written in FORTRAN as 'NUMDAY(TEMPER + 101)'. The latter is less readable and more error-prone since the programmer must always remember to include the *bias* of 101 in every array reference and to correct it if the program changes. Most programming languages designed since Algol-60 allow the programmer to specify both upper and lower bounds.

EXERCISE 3-15: Write the addressing equation for one-, two-, and three-dimensional arrays with arbitrary (i.e., user-specified) lower bounds.

EXERCISE 3-16: Generalize the above equation for an n-dimensional array with dimensions

$$[k_1{:}u_1,\ k_2{:}u_2,\ \ldots,\ k_n{:}u_n]$$

Stack Allocation Permits Dynamic Arrays

It is often the case that the size required for an array is not known when the program is written; often it depends on the data with which the program is run. Consider the example in Figure 3.1, the Absolute-Mean program; clearly, the array Data should be exactly N elements long, where N is the number of input values. In the FORTRAN program in Figure 2.3, we dimensioned the array to 900 elements. If there are fewer than 900 input values to be processed, then the rest of the array will be wasted (which means that the program is larger than was necessary). If more than 900 values are supplied, the program will try to oversubscript the array, which either will cause an error or cause the program to fail in some more mysterious way. This is a pervasive problem with languages that have *static* array dimensions; it is always necessary to pick *some* number to use as the dimension. Hence, the programmer must trade off wasting space by making the array large enough to handle almost all applications against not being able to handle some data sets because the array is too small. Static arrays force the programmer to violate the Zero-One-Infinity Principle in the *application* program since in its documentation it will be necessary to say something like, "The number of input values cannot exceed 900."

The Algol committee recognized this problem and devoted much discussion to dynamic arrays between the Algol-58 and Algol-60 reports. We can see from the example in Figure 3.1 that Algol-60 permits expressions to be used in array declarations, N in this case. This value N, representing the number of input values, is read in within the outer block. The result is that the array Data is exactly the right size; there are no unused array elements and there is no limit on the number of input values that can be processed (aside, of course, from the computer's memory capacity). Notice that Algol-60's arrays are dynamic in a limited fashion; the array's dimensions can be recomputed each time the block to which it is local is entered, but once the array is allocated, its bounds remain fixed until its scope is exited. Some other programming languages (including Algol-68) permit arrays that are even more dynamic. In these languages the arrays can grow or shrink at any time; these are sometimes called *flexible* arrays. The Algol-60 design is actually a good trade-off between flexibility and efficiency since, as we will see below, dynamic arrays are very simple to implement on a stack.

In Section 3.3 (Name Structures) we saw the way that a stack permits efficient storage allocation in a block-structured language. Every time a block is entered, an activation record for that block, containing all of the block's local storage, is pushed onto the run-time stack. When the block is exited, this activation record is deleted. This makes Algol's dynamic arrays particularly simple to implement; since the array is part of the activation record and its size is known at block-entry time, an appropriate size activation record can be allocated. This activation record is deleted at block-exit time so that on the next entry to that block a completely different size activation record can be created. We can also see some of the difficulty in implementing flexible arrays since, if an array grew, it would be necessary to move everything above it on the stack in order to make room. Algol's dynamic arrays are an excellent example of a programming language design trade-off. Newer languages (e.g., Pascal) have not always provided dynamic arrays; in Chapter 5 we will see some of the problems this has caused.

Algol Has Strong Typing

Algol-60 is an example of a programming language with *strong typing,* which means that the type abstractions of the language are enforced. A strong type system prevents the programmer from performing meaningless operations on data. A less formal way of saying this is that there are no typing "loopholes"; for instance, a programmer can't do an integer addition on floating-point numbers, or do a floating-point multiply on Boolean values.[3] In Chapter 2 we saw that FORTRAN is not a strongly typed language. In particular, by using COMMON and EQUIVALENCE it is possible to set up situations where two or more variables, with different types, are *aliases* for the same location. This is a security problem when done accidently and a maintenance problem when done intentionally. In Algol there is no way to trick the system into believing and acting as though an integer were a Boolean or anything similar.

We should carefully distinguish between illegitimate type violations of this sort and perfectly legitimate *conversions* and *coercions* between types. For instance, Algol, like most programming languages, coerces integers to reals and provides a conversion operator for converting reals to integers. These are machine-independent operations. The results of a type system violation, however, depend on the particular data representations used on a particular implementation; we say they are *implementation dependent.* Obviously, implementation dependencies defeat portability.

If you have done any system programming using a high-level language, you are probably saying right now, "That is all very well for application pro-

3 Algol does have a loophole in its typing caused by inadequate specification of procedural parameters. Since Pascal has the same problem, we defer its discussion to Section 5.5.

grammers, but systems programmers often *have* to violate the type system." That is correct. For example, if we are programming a memory management system, it is necessary to treat memory cells as raw storage without regard for the type of the values stored in them. As another example, the input-output conversion routines will probably have to be able to manipulate the characteristic and mantissa of floating-point numbers as integers. However, we must recognize that a programming language's type system is a *safety feature,* and as such, it must be circumvented with extreme care. You are probably aware of the interlock on most electrical equipment that disconnects the line cord when the back is removed; this is to prevent dangerous electrical shock. Since electrical technicians must be able to operate the equipment with its back off in order to repair it, they use "cheater cords" to supply power and "cheat" the interlock system. This requires extra precautions that are part of the training of an electrical technician. The same applies to the type system; it is true that it must be "cheated" in some situations, but this should only be done by "qualified service personnel" who know the proper precautions. One of the precautions is that it be done only when *really* necessary; another is that the violation be clearly documented. Since we all consider ourselves qualified, and we all think that our needs are *really* necessary, considerable self-discipline is required. In fact, most legitimate type system violations can be replaced by special conversion functions that provide access to the representation. Most of the violations that people think are necessary really aren't; there are usually better, safer ways to accomplish the task. Most programming languages that are intended for systems programming do provide some "loophole" through the type system, but the conscientious programmer is advised to avoid it if at all possible, since it will likely lead to unreliable, nonportable, unmaintainable programs. Intentional cheating of this safety system will not be discussed further in this book.

EXERCISE 3-17:* Do you agree with the above analysis of violations of the type system? List some of the situations in which a violation of the type system is justified. Describe safe programming language mechanisms that will handle these problems. How much additional complexity does this add to the programming language? (Keep in mind that these facilities will be rarely used.)

EXERCISE 3-18:* Most FORTRAN systems do not check that the types of actual and formal parameters agree. For example, an integer can be passed to a subprogram that is expecting a real. Discuss the security implications of this. How could this loophole be avoided? (Don't forget to take separately compiled subprograms into account.)

EXERCISE 3-19:* Identify some other safety features in the languages we have discussed and in any other languages with which you may be familiar. Propose at least two new safety features that will catch programmer errors without getting too much in the way.

3.5 DESIGN: CONTROL STRUCTURES

Primitive Computational Statements Have Changed Little

The primitives from which control structures are built are those computational statements that do not affect the flow of control. In Algol, this is the assignment statement, which is essentially the same as FORTRAN's (except that a different symbol is used, ':='). Recall that in FORTRAN the input-output statements are also control structure primitives; this is not the case in Algol. Input-output is performed by library procedures rather than specialized statements. Therefore, it is quite accurate in the case of Algol to say that the function of control structures is to direct and manage the flow of control from one assignment statement to another.

Control Structures Are Generalizations of FORTRAN's

We saw in Chapter 2 that FORTRAN's control structures are closely patterned on the branch instructions of 1950s computers.[4] Algol has provided essentially the same structures in a generalized and regularized form. For example, FORTRAN has a simple logical IF-statement:

```
IF (logical expression) simple statement
```

in which the *consequent*, or **then**-part, of the IF is required to be a single, simple, unconditional statement (such as an assignment, GOTO, or CALL). In Algol this apparently arbitrary restriction is removed, and the consequent is allowed to be any other statement, including another **if**-statement. Furthermore, the consequent is allowed to be a group of statements, as we will see.

The **if**-statement is also extended beyond FORTRAN by having an *alternate*, or **else**-part, which is executed if the condition is false, for example,

4 Throughout this section 'FORTRAN' refers to 'FORTRAN IV'. We concentrate on this dialect because our intention in to contrast second-generation languages (e.g., Algol-60) with first-generation languages (e.g., FORTRAN IV).

```
if T[middle] = sought then location := middle
else lower := middle + 1;
```

This allows a more *symmetric* analysis of a problem into two cases, one for which the condition is true and one for which it is false.

The Algol **for**-loop is also more general than FORTRAN's DO-loop. It includes the function of a simple DO-loop, for example,

```
for i := 1 step 2 until N × M do
  inner[i] := outer[N × M − i];
```

It also has a variant that is similar to the **while**-loops found in languages such as Pascal. For instance, the Algol-60 **for**-loop:

```
for NewGuess := Improve(OldGuess)
    while abs(NewGuess − OldGuess) > 0.0001
  do OldGuess := NewGuess;
```

This corresponds to the Pascal **while**-loop:

```
NewGuess := Improve(OldGuess);
while abs(NewGuess − OldGuess) > 0.0001 do
  begin
    OldGuess := NewGuess;
    NewGuess := Improve(OldGuess)
  end;
```

We will see later in this section that there are a number of other cases in which Algol-60's control structures are more regular, more symmetric, more powerful, and more general than FORTRAN's. There are a number of reasons for this. As we've seen, FORTRAN has many restrictions, such as the restrictions on the IF-statement mentioned above and the restrictions on array subscripts described in Chapter 2. These restrictions were made for many reasons, including efficiency (the array restrictions) and compiler simplicity (the IF restrictions). Whatever their reasons, these restrictions almost always seem inexplicable to the programmer; violations of the Zero-One-Infinity Principle and other instances of *irregularity* in a language's design make the language harder to learn and remember. The Algol designers attempted to eliminate all asymmetry and irregularity from Algol's design. Their attitude was, "Anything that you think you ought to be able to do, you will be able to do." As we will see, they got carried away in a few instances.

Nested Statements Are Very Important

As we've mentioned, there is an irregularity in FORTRAN's IF-statement. That is, if the consequent of the IF is a single statement it can be written directly, for example,

```
IF(X .GT. Y) X = X/2
```

But if it is more than one statement, it is necessary to negate the condition and jump over the consequent; for example,

```
      IF(X .LE. Y) GOTO 100
        X = X/2
        Y = Y+DELTA
100   ...
```

One of the most obvious problems with this is that it makes it difficult to modify a program; adding one statement to a consequent may require restructuring the entire IF-statement. Thus, the FORTRAN IF undermines *maintainability.* The other objection to FORTRAN's syntax is simply that it is irregular; conditionals are written in completely different ways solely on the basis of the number of statements in their consequents. This is a source of errors since programmers may forget to negate the condition with multistatement consequents.

Recall that FORTRAN's DO-loop doesn't have this problem because it can be nested. That is, its syntax is

```
      DO 20 I = 1, N
        statement 1
        statement 2
          ⋮
        statement m
20    CONTINUE
```

This allows any number of statements to be included in the body of the loop (including other DO-loops); this is clearly a much better solution. We can see that the DO and CONTINUE form *brackets,* like parentheses, that mark the beginning and end of the loop. Since FORTRAN allows CONTINUE statements to be placed anywhere in a program (they act as "do nothing" statements), matching statement labels ('20' in the example above) are used to decide which DO goes with which CONTINUE. We will see that this same approach is used in some newer programming languages.

There is another situation in which FORTRAN handles the single- and multiple-statement cases asymmetrically. As we saw, the usual way to define a function in FORTRAN is a declaration such as

```
FUNCTION F(X)
  statement 1
      ⋮
  statement m
END
```

This is the multiple-statement case; the body of the function is bracketed by a matching FUNCTION and END (although FORTRAN does not allow functions to be nested like DO-loops). However, if the body of the function is composed of a single statement, 'F = expr', then this declaration can be written in an abbreviated form[5]:

```
F(X) = expr
```

Again, we can see that the two cases are handled asymmetrically.

The Algol designers realized that all control structures should be allowed to govern an arbitrary number of statements, so in Algol-58 these statements were all made *bracketing*. That is, each control structure (such as **if-then**) was considered an opening bracket that had to be matched by a corresponding closing bracket (such as **end if**). Later, during the Algol-60 design, and largely as a result of seeing the BNF description of Algol-58, they realized that one bracketing construct could be used for all of these cases. The approach they used was that all control structures are defined to govern a single statement; for example, the body of a **for**-loop is a single statement and the consequent and alternative (**then**-part and **else**-part) of **if**-statements are both single statements. Even the body of a procedure is a single statement. However, the designers went on to define a special kind of statement, called a *compound statement*, that brackets any number of statements together and converts them to a single statement. That is, a group of statements surrounded by the brackets **begin** and **end**, for example,

```
begin
  statement 1;
  statement 2;
      ⋮
  statement n
end
```

is considered a single statement and can be used anywhere a single statement is allowed. Look again at Figure 3.1 and compare the two **for**-loops. The body of

5 In this case, however, the function F is local to the subprogram in which it is declared, a further instance of irregularity.

the first is a compound statement containing two simple statements, and the body of the second is a single assignment statement. In Figure 3.3 we can see several procedure declarations. In the definition of 'cosh' the body of the procedure is a single simple statement, similar to FORTRAN's abbreviated function definition. The declaration of 'f' is the more common case, in which the body of the procedure is a compound statement.

You have probably noticed by now that in Algol the **begin–end** brackets do double duty—they are used both to group statements into compound statements and to delimit *blocks,* which define nested scopes. This is a lack of *orthogonality* in Algol's design; there are two independent functions—the defining of a scope and the grouping of statements—that are accomplished by the same construct. This may seem like an economy, but it often leads to problems. For example, we saw in Section 3.2 that block entry requires the creation of an activation record to hold the local variables of the block. Since in a compound statement there are no local variables, no activation record is required. In fact, it would be quite inefficient and needless to create an activation record everywhere a compound statement is used since this is just a syntactic mechanism for grouping statements together, similar to parentheses in expressions. Therefore, it is necessary for compilers to determine whether any variables or procedures are declared in a block or procedure in order to determine whether or not to generate block entry-exit code. We will see in later chapters that newer languages have separated the two functions of statement grouping and scope definition.

We should point out that Algol's syntax does not entirely solve the problems with FORTRAN's syntax. In particular, there still is a minor maintenance problem since if a loop body (or procedure body, or consequent, or alternate) is changed from a single statement to several statements, the programmer must remember to insert the **begin** and **end**. Forgetting this is a common mistake, since their absence is not obvious in a well-indented program; for example,

```
for i := 1 step 1 until N do
    ReadReal(val);
    Data[i] := if val < 0 then -val else val;
for i := 1 step ...
```

For this reason many Algol programmers have adopted the *coding convention* of always using **begin** and **end**, even if they only surround a single statement. We will see in Chapter 8 that newer languages have solved this problem.

EXERCISE 3-20:* We have seen several problems with blocks and compound statements in Algol. Discuss some alternate approaches that have the advantages of blocks and compound statements but solve these problems.

EXERCISE 3-21:* In FORTRAN, a CONTINUE only matches a DO-loop with the same statement number, whereas in Algol an **end** matches the nearest preceding unmatched **begin**. Furthermore, the same brackets are used for all nested statements. Discuss the consequences of a missing **end** in the middle of a large, deeply nested Algol program. When is the compiler likely to notice the error? What sort of diagnostic would it produce? Suggest improvements.

Compound Statements Are Hierarchical Structures

Algol's compound statement is a good example of *hierarchical structure.* Starting with the simple statements, such as assignment, procedure invocation, and the **goto**-statement, complex structures are built up by *hierarchically* combining these statements into larger and larger compound statements. Hierarchical structure is one of the most important principles of language and program design.

Nesting Led to Structured Programming

We saw that in FORTRAN an IF-statement with a compound consequent had to be implemented with a GOTO-statement; specifically, the GOTO-statement was used to skip the statements of the consequent. Algol eliminated the need for the **goto**-statement by using compound statements. The same situation arises in an **if-then-else** statement. The Algol program

```
if condition then
  begin
    statement 1;
        :
    statement m
  end
else
  begin
    statement 1;
        :
    statement n
  end
```

can only be expressed in FORTRAN by a circumlocution:

```
      IF (.NOT.(condition)) GOTO 100
         statement 1
             :
         statement m
         GOTO 200
100      statement 1
```

```
            ⋮
        statement n
200     ...
```

As we said in Chapter 2, the GOTO is the workhorse of control-flow in FORTRAN.

Almost as soon as programmers began writing in Algol-60, they noticed that many fewer **goto**-statements were required than in other languages. They also noticed that their programs were, on the whole, much easier to read. This led several computer scientists, including Peter Naur, Edsger Dijkstra, and Peter Landin, to experiment with programming without the use of **goto**-statements. This is completely impossible in a language like FORTRAN, but it is quite possible in Algol. It prompted Edsger Dijkstra to write, in 1968, a now-famous letter to the editor of the *Communications of the ACM.* It was called "Go To Statement Considered Harmful" and stated that "the **go to** statement should be abolished from all 'higher level' programming languages." Dijkstra discovered that the difficulty in understanding programs that made heavy use of **goto**-statements was a result of the "conceptual gap" between the static structure of the program (spread out on the page) and the dynamic structure of the corresponding computations (spread out in time). We can call this the Structure Principle.

> ***The Structure Principle***
>
> The static structure of the program should correspond in a simple way to the dynamic structure of the corresponding computations.

Dijkstra's letter sparked immediate and vigorous debate and by 1972 led to an entire session of the ACM National Conference being devoted to the "go to controversy." Ultimately this led to a loose body of programming methods and techniques called *structured programming* and a greater awareness among computer programmers and scientists of the problems of reliable programming. Although most of the controversy has now died down and most programming languages still have a **goto**-statement, these statements are needed much less often. Most programming languages have a rich set of *structured* control structures and most programmers have a better understanding of when a **goto**-statement is appropriate. This is only one example of a situation in which a programming language issue has been the focal point of a wider issue in programming methodology.

Procedures Are Recursive

To illustrate the idea of a recursive procedure, we use a very simple example. In fact, this particular function could be as easily defined without recursion. The *factorial* $n!$ of an integer n is defined to be the product of the integers from 1 to n. That is,

$$n! = n(n-1)(n-2) \ldots (2)(1)$$

This is not an entirely precise definition since it is not clear about the meaning of $n!$ for $n < 3$. Rather, we can define 0! to be 1 and $n!$ to be $n \times (n-1)!$ for $n > 0$. This is a preferable definition since it clearly specifies the meaning of $n!$ for all $n \geqslant 0$. This can be summarized in a *recursive* definition such as

$$n! = \begin{cases} n \times (n-1)! & \text{if } n > 0 \\ 1 & \text{if } n = 0 \end{cases}$$

This is a recursive definition because the thing being defined is defined in terms of itself (recur = to happen again). Of course, this would not be a sensible thing to do if there weren't some *base* for the recursion, as is provided by the $n = 0$ case in the definition of factorial. Recursive definitions are very common in computer science and mathematics so it is important to get used to them.

Algol permits procedures to be defined recursively, as we can see by looking at an Algol factorial procedure:

```
integer procedure fac(n);
  value n; integer n;
  fac := if n=0 then 1 else n × fac(n - 1);
```

You may be surprised to see an **if** used on the right of an assignment statement; this is called a *conditional expression* (as opposed to the usual *conditional statement*). The condition is used to determine whether the consequent (**then**-part) or alternate (**else**-part) is to be evaluated. This is a common pattern for many recursive definitions: A *stopping condition* is used to break the evaluation into two cases, one that involves a recursive call of the procedure and one that doesn't. We will see many examples of recursive definitions in later chapters.

EXERCISE 3-22: The number of combinations of m things taken k at a time, $C(m,k)$, is defined by

$$C(m,k) = \frac{m!}{k!(m-k)!}$$

Devise a recursive definition of $C(m,k)$ in terms of $C(m-1,k)$ and write an Algol procedure to implement it.

Locals May Have Several Instantiations

We saw in Chapter 2 that the values of actual parameters are stored in memory locations in the activation record for the procedure. There is one of these locations for each formal parameter, and whenever a formal parameter is referenced, the corresponding location is accessed. Now consider the factorial procedure described above; there must be a memory location corresponding to 'n' to hold the value of that parameter. Therefore, when 'fac(3)' is invoked, this location will contain the number 3. Before this invocation of 'fac' is completed, the expression 'fac(2)' must be evaluated. We can see that if there were only one location for 'n', the value 2 would overwrite the value 3 before the evaluation of 'fac(3)' had been completed. The same would happen again as 'fac(1)' and 'fac(0)' were invoked. This is clearly wrong; it is necessary to set aside separate memory locations corresponding to 'n' for each invocation of 'fac'. Another way to say this is that each invocation of 'fac' must have its own *instance* of the formal parameter 'n', which will contain the actual parameter to that invocation. We will see in Chapter 6 that this is accomplished by creating a new activation record for 'fac' each time it is called. In general, each invocation (or *activation*) of a procedure results in the *instantiation* (i.e., creation) of a new activation record for that procedure. These activation records contain space for the parameters and local variables of the procedure. We have already seen (Section 3.4) how the creation of activation records at block-entry time permits efficient dynamic storage management. We will see in Chapter 6 how the instantiation of activation records is accomplished.

Parameters Can Be Passed by Value

Our definition of the 'fac' procedure contained the specification '**value** n'. This specifies that the parameter 'n' is to be *passed by value*, one of the two ways of passing parameters in Algol-60. As its name suggests, pass by value is the first half of pass by value-result; that is, the value of the actual parameter is copied into a variable corresponding to the formal parameter. Pass by value is quite secure. Since a local copy is made of the actual, there is no possibility of an assignment to the formal overwriting the actual; such an assignment will just modify the local copy. For example, a procedure that is similar to the one that allowed us to change the value of constants in FORTRAN:

```
procedure switch (n);
  value n; integer n;
  n := 3;
```

is perfectly harmless in Algol. An invocation such as 'switch (2)' will cause the value 2 to be copied into the location for the formal 'n'. The assignment 'n := 3' merely alters the value of this location; it has no effect on the actual, 2, and does not endanger the literal table. You probably have noticed that **value**-parameters are only useful for input parameters; they do not allow a value to be output from a procedure. For example, the call 'switch (k)' can have no effect on the variable 'k'. Later in this section, we investigate Algol's other parameter passing mode, which does allow output parameters.

Pass by Value Is Very Inefficient for Arrays

Consider the following skeleton for a procedure to compute the average of an array:

```
real procedure avg (A, n);
  value A, n;
  real array A; integer n;
  begin
     ⋮
  end;
```

Since both the array to be averaged (A) and the number of elements in the array (n) are input parameters, we have passed them both by value. Let's consider the consequences of this. When the procedure 'avg' is called, an activation record will be created containing space for the values of the actual parameters. This will include space for the entire array A! Not only is this wasteful of storage, but it also wastes time since the entire actual parameter corresponding to A must be copied into the activation record! For a large array, it could take almost as long to pass the array parameter as to compute its average. The conclusion we can draw is that pass by value is not a satisfactory way of passing arrays.

EXERCISE 3-23:* Suggest an alternative to Algol-60's pass by value that has the security advantages of pass by value (i.e., the value of input parameters cannot be changed) but is more efficient for arrays.

Pass by Name Is Based on Substitution

We have seen in Chapter 2 that the problem with FORTRAN's parameters results from the failure to distinguish parameters intended for input from those intended for output (or both input and output). Algol-60 attempted to solve this problem by providing two parameter passing modes: pass by value for input parameters and *pass by name* for all other kinds of parameters. Suppose we wanted to write a procedure to increment a variable; for example, 'Inc (i)' adds 1 to 'i'. We can pattern it after a FORTRAN procedure:

```
procedure Inc (n);
  integer n;
  n:= n+1;
```

If the parameter 'n' were passed by value, this would not work since the assignment 'n := n+1' would affect the local copy of the actual but not the actual 'i' itself. What we want is for the *name* 'i' to be substituted into the procedure rather than the *value* of 'i'. This is accomplished by pass by name, which is the mode we get if we don't specify pass by value. Thus, in the above example 'n' is passed by name.

In Chapter 2 (Section 2.3) we discussed the *Copy Rule* for procedure invocation. The rule states that a procedure can be replaced by its body with the actuals substituted for the formals. This is the effect of pass by name in Algol-60, so the call 'Inc (i)' has the same effect as if it were replaced by

```
i:= i+1;
```

that is, the body of 'Inc' with 'n' replaced by 'i'. Similarly, the invocation 'Inc (A[k])' acts as though it were replaced by

```
A[k]:= A[k]+1;
```

We can see that pass by name satisfies Algol's need for output parameters. Although name parameters *act* as though they were substituted for the corresponding formals, this is not the way they are actually implemented; it would be too inefficient. The implementation of name parameters is discussed later in this section.

Pass by Name Is Powerful

Consider the following FORTRAN subroutine:

```
SUBROUTINE S (EL, K)
K = 2
EL = 0
RETURN
END
```

and the program segment:

```
A(1) = A(2) = 1
I = 1
CALL S (A(I), I)
```

Further, suppose that parameters are passed by reference. When S is called, a reference must be passed for each of the actual parameters A(I) and I. Since I has the value 1 at the time of call, the reference passed for A(I) will be the address of A(1). The subroutine S has two effects. First, it assigns K = 2, which assigns 2 to I since the formal K is bound to the address of I. Second, it assigns EL = 0, which assigns 0 to A(1) since the formal EL is bound to the address of A(1). The fact that in the meantime I has been changed to 2 has no effect on EL since the reference of A(I) was computed at call time. When S exits, I will have the value 2 and A will have the values (0,1).

Next, consider an analogous Algol program. The procedure S is

```
procedure S (el, k);
  integer el, k;
  begin
    k := 2;
    el := 0
  end;
```

```
a[1] := a[2] := 1;
i := 1;
S (a[i], i);
```

Since the parameters are passed by name, the effect of S will be as though the actuals were substituted for the formals. That is, the effect of 'S(a[i], i)' will be

```
i := 2;
a[i] := 0;
```

Thus, S will assign 2 to 'i' and 0 to 'a[2]', so when S exits 'i' will have the value 2 and 'a' will have the value (1,0). Notice that the Algol result is different from the FORTRAN result. It is as though the formal parameter 'el' were bound to the string 'a[i]' rather than an address. Therefore, every time 'el' is referenced, the actual parameter is reevaluated. Hence, if 'i' has changed in the meantime, a different element of 'a' will be referenced.

Jensen's device makes explicit use of this property of name parameters. Suppose we wish to write a procedure to implement the mathematical sigma notation. That is, we want a procedure 'Sum' such that

$$x = \sum_{i=1}^{n} V_i$$

can be written

```
x := Sum (i, 1, n, V[i])
```

This is easy to do with name parameters; by altering the index variable 'i', the actual 'V[i]' can be made to refer to each element of the array. This is Jensen's device. For example,

```
real procedure Sum (k, l, u, ak);
  value l, u;
  integer k, l, u; real ak;
  begin real S; S := 0;
    for k := l step 1 until u do
      S := S+ak;
    Sum := S;
  end;
```

To determine the effect of

```
x := Sum (i, 1, n, V[i])
```

simply perform the substitutions into the body of Sum. The result is:

```
begin real S; S := 0;
  for i := 1 step 1 until n do
    S := S+V[i];
  x := S
end
```

We can see that it has the desired effect since the **for**-loop alters the values of 'i' from 1 to n and this causes 'V[i]' to refer to V[1] through V[n]. This Sum procedure is very general; for instance,

$$x = \sum_{i=1}^{m} \sum_{j=1}^{n} A_{ij}$$

can be computed by

```
x := Sum (i, 1, m, Sum (j, 1, n, A[i,j]))
```

There are few programming languages that provide this flexibility.

How is all this power implemented? It would be much too inefficient to follow the Copy Rule literally: This would involve passing the text of the actual parameter to the procedure. It would then be necessary to compile and execute this text every time the parameter was referenced. A better solution would be to compile the actual parameter into machine code and then copy this code into the callee everywhere the parameter is referenced. This would also be inefficient since the code for the actual parameter would be copied many times. It would be difficult to implement since different actual parameters would have different-length code sequences. These problems can be avoided by passing the address of the code sequence compiled for the actual parameter. Then, every time the parameter is referenced, the callee can execute the code for the parameter by jumping to this address. The result of executing the code, an address of a variable or array element, is then returned to the callee. This implementation technique has the proper effect of reevaluating the actual parameter every time it is referenced. It is also reasonably efficient.

One of the first Algol implementers, P. Z. Ingerman, used the name *thunk* to refer to these pieces of code that provide an address. The name has stuck.

Thunks are very similar to procedures. Like procedures, they are called from several different locations and must return a result to their callers. In fact, a simple way of implementing name parameters is to convert the actual parameters into procedures and to convert references to the formal parameters into indirect procedure calls. For example, in the call

```
x := Sum (i, 1, m, Sum (j, 1, n, A[i,j]))
```

the actual parameter 'Sum (j, 1, n, A[i,j])' would be converted into a parameterless function; the address of this function would then be passed to the outer activation of Sum. Within Sum, references to the formal parameter 'ak' would be interpreted as indirect invocations of this procedure. Thus, we formally define a *thunk* to be an invisible, parameterless, address-returning function used by a compiler to implement name parameters and similar constructs.

EXERCISE 3-24: Write an Algol statement to compute

$$x = \sum_{i=1}^{n} A_{ij}$$

EXERCISE 3-25: Write an Algol statement to compute

$$x = \sum_{i=1}^{m} \sum_{j=1}^{i} (j!\, A_{ji})$$

Pass by Name Is Dangerous and Expensive

You may think that pass by name is the ideal solution to the output parameter problem. The idea of substitution, on which it is based, is very simple and we get flexibility like the Sum procedure for free in the bargain. Unfortunately, pass by name has some dark corners and hidden inefficiencies. To show this, we will consider what should be a simple use of name parameters—an exchange procedure. The idea is to write a procedure 'Swap (x,y)' that exchanges the values of the variables x and y. This definition would seem to do it:

```
procedure Swap (x,y);
  integer x, y;
  begin integer t;
    t := x;
    x := y;
    y := t
  end
```

To see if this works, we can try 'Swap (i,j)' and use the Copy Rule:

```
begin integer t;
  t := i;
  i := j;
  j := t
end;
```

As we would expect from a swap procedure, 'Swap (j,i)' produces exactly the same effect as 'Swap (i,j)'. Now let's consider the effect of 'Swap (A[i],i)':

```
begin integer t;
  t := A[i];
  A[i] := i;
  i := t
end;
```

This is correct. Now consider 'Swap (i,A[i])', which should have the same effect:

```
begin integer t;
  t := i;
  i := A[i];
  A[i] := t
end;
```

This does something completely different! If you don't see this, then try executing it assuming that 'i' contains 1 and 'A[1]' contains 27. The effect will be to assign the value of 'A[1]' to 'i' and the value of 'i' to 'A[27]'; it doesn't do an exchange at all! It is a sign of a design mistake when a simple procedure, such as

Swap, has such surprising properties. We have programmed this procedure in the obvious way and found that it doesn't work. What is even worse is that computer scientists have shown that there is *no way* to define a Swap procedure in Algol-60 that works for all actual parameters! Lest you think that this reveals some hidden subtlety in the idea of a swap, we must hasten to say that it's trivial to write a correct Swap procedure in FORTRAN:

```
SUBROUTINE SWAP(X,Y)
INTEGER X, Y, T
T = X
X = Y
Y = T
RETURN
END
```

We can see why this is so: In the FORTRAN procedure 'X' and 'Y' are bound to fixed locations at call time; in the Algol procedure the parameters 'x' and 'y' are reevaluated every time they are used and, hence, may refer to different locations on each use. It is traps such as these that have led language designers to avoid pass by name in almost all languages designed after Algol-60. We will see in Chapter 6 that pass by name is also quite expensive to implement.

The three parameter passing modes that we have discussed can be distinguished by the times at which they inspect the value of the actual.

1. *Pass by value.* At the time of call, the formal is bound to the *value* of the actual. Since the value parameter takes a snapshot of the actual parameter, later changes in the actual's value will not be seen by the callee.
2. *Pass by reference.* At the time of call, the formal is bound to a reference to the actual. The reference cannot vary thereafter, although the value stored at that reference can.
3. *Pass by name.* At the time of call, the formal is bound to a thunk for the actual. Although this cannot vary, each time it is evaluated it may return a different reference and consequently a different value.

We can see that pass by value represents an early inspection time, while pass by name represents a very late inspection time (the latest found in most languages). A consequence of this is that there is less variability and flexibility in pass by value than in pass by name. One way to think of this is that a late inspection time, such as pass by name, puts off until later a commitment to the meaning of the formal parameter.

*EXERCISE 3-26**:* Propose an alternate to Algol's pass by name. It should allow values to be output through the parameters of a procedure. Try to make it powerful enough to define a Sum procedure without it also having the problems of pass by name.

EXERCISE 3-27: Algol makes pass by name the *default* mode for passing parameters; that is, it is what you get if you don't include a **value** specification. Given that both value and name parameters have their problems, discuss which should be the default parameter passing mode.

Out-of-Block gotos Can Be Expensive

We saw that FORTRAN has different scope rules for different kinds of names. For example, variables and statement labels are subprogram local while subprogram names are global. Algol has one scope rule for all identifiers: An identifier declaration is visible if we are nested within the block in which it occurs (and the same identifier hasn't been redeclared in an inner, surrounding block). This is reflected in the contour diagrams. A consequence of this is that we can jump to statement labels from any block nested in the block in which they are declared. Consider this program skeleton:

```
a: begin array X[1:100];
       ⋮
       b: begin array Y[1:100];
              ⋮
              goto exit;
              ⋮
          end;
exit: ⋮
   end
```

Since the label 'exit' is declared in the block (a), which encloses the block (b), this label is visible to the **goto**-statement in block (b). Consider the effect of executing the **goto**-statement. When this occurs there will be activation records for both blocks (a) and (b) on the stack. If we exited block (b) normally (i.e., through the **end**), the activation record for (b) would be deleted, leaving that for (a) on the top of the stack. The same must be done if block (b) is exited by a jump: The activation record for (b) must be deleted. Therefore, the process of executing an Algol **goto**-statement may be much more complicated than a simple machine jump since it may involve exiting through several levels of block structure.

The problem is more complicated than this since the number of levels to be exited (and hence the number of activation records to be popped) may not even be a constant. Consider this Algol program:

```
begin
  procedure P(n);
    value n;  integer n;
    if n=0 then goto out
    else P(n-1);

  P(25);
out:
end
```

We can see that 'P(25)' will cause P to be called recursively 25 times, at which point it will jump to the label 'out'. Each recursive call will require an activation record for P to be pushed onto the stack, all of which must be deleted when the procedure transfers to 'out'. Since the number of recursions, and hence the number of activation records to be discarded, are data dependent, the compiler cannot know beforehand how many activation records to delete. Instead, this **goto**-statement might be implemented as a call of a run-time routine that finds the appropriate activation record and deletes all the ones above it. Needless to say, this can be an expensive process.

Feature Interaction Is a Difficult Design Problem

Feature interaction is one of the most difficult problems in language design. In our example, two apparently simple features—the Algol visibility rules and the **goto**-statement—interact in a way that is complex and can lead to inefficient execution. This is a very common problem in language design since the number of possible interactions is so large. If there are 100 features in a language (a small number), then the designer must investigate $100^2 = 10{,}000$ interactions between pairs of features, $100^3 = 1{,}000{,}000$ interactions between triples of features, and so on. Since it is impossible to investigate *all* of these possible interactions, successful language designers must (through experience) develop a "nose" for spotting possible problem areas. This process is greatly aided if the language has a regular, orthogonal structure. Since the number of interactions between even pairs of features goes up with the square of the number of features in the language, we can see that a *simple* language is much less likely to have dangerous interactions. Other examples of feature interactions will be discussed later in this book.

The for-Loop Is Very General

Earlier in this chapter, we looked at the Algol **for**-loop, which is a generalization of FORTRAN's DO-loop. We saw the following two forms:

```
for var := exp step exp' until exp'' do stat
for var := exp while exp' do stat
```

In fact, the Algol **for**-loop is much more general than this. The idea behind it is that the **for**-loop generates a sequence of values to be assigned successively to the controlled variable. This sequence of values is described by a list of "for-list-elements." For example, the for-list-element

```
1 step 1 until 5
```

generates the sequence 1, 2, 3, 4, 5. Also, if the most recent value of 'i' were 16, the for-list-element

```
i/2 while i≥1
```

would generate the values 8, 4, 2, 1. Finally, values to be used in the for-list can be listed explicitly; for example,

```
for days :=  31, 28, 31, 30, 31, 30,
             31, 31, 30, 31, 30, 31 do ...
```

causes the controlled variable to take on the values of the days in the months. Algol even permits a conditional expression to be used, thus allowing leap years to be handled correctly[6]:

```
for days := 31,
  if mod (year, 4) = 0 then 29 else 28,
  31, 30, 31, 30, 31, 31, 30, 31, 30, 31 do ...
```

EXERCISE 3-28: Suppose Algol did not have the ability described above for listing arbitrary sequences of values in a for-list (most languages don't). How would you solve the problem of programming the above loop? Remember to handle leap years correctly.

The for-Loop Is Baroque

You may be surprised at the generality of the Algol **for**-loop, but it has even greater possibilities! The sequence of controlled variable values can be defined by a list of for-list-elements. For example, the **for**-loop

6 We have assumed a 'mod' function, which is not a built-in function in Algol-60.

```
for i :=  3, 7,
          11 step 1 until 16,
          i/2 while i ≥ 1,
          2 step i until 32
do print (i)
```

will print the sequence of values

```
3  7  11  12  13  14  15  16  8  4  2  1  2  4  8  16  32
```

Check this to be sure you understand it.

There is another aspect of Algol's **for**-loop that deserves mention—the binding time of the loop parameters. Algol specifies that any expressions in the current for-list-element are reevaluated on each iteration. For example, the body of a **for**-loop such as

```
for i := m step n until k do ...
```

may change the values of the loop parameters 'i', 'm', 'n', and 'k'. Of course, this means that the programmer really doesn't have a very clear idea of how many times the loop will iterate. This undermines the idea of a *definite iteration,* which is what the **for**-loop is supposed to be. Furthermore, these expressions must be reevaluated on each iteration even if they haven't changed. This means that the most common loops, which do not change their parameters during the loop, will bear the cost of providing for these more general loops. This violates a basic principle of language design.

> ***The Localized Cost Principle***
>
> Users should only pay for what they use; avoid distributed costs.

In other words, language designers should avoid features whose costs are distributed over all programs regardless of whether these features are used.

It is difficult to imagine why anyone would ever need this much generality in a **for**-loop. Computer scientists call constructs such as this, which are cluttered with features of extreme generality and doubtful utility, *baroque.* As you are probably aware, this term refers to a style of art characterized by elaborate and rich ornamentation and a certain irregularity in shape. Language designers call a language baroque when it is irregular in structure and has a surplus of features of questionable usefulness. Baroque became a pejorative term during the movement toward simplicity that characterized the third-generation languages (including Pascal). This is discussed in Chapter 5.

EXERCISE 3-29:* Define a simplified looping construct (or constructs) for Algol. How will you respond to those users that say they need some of the baroque features you have eliminated?

The switch Is for Handling Cases

In Chapter 2 we discussed FORTRAN's computed GOTO-statement, which was a mechanism for handling several different cases of a problem. Just as it did with FORTRAN's DO-loop, Algol has generalized FORTRAN's computed GOTO. The construct in question is called a **switch**-*declaration* and amounts to an array of statement labels. Let's consider an example. Suppose we are processing personnel records and must handle separately the cases of single, married, divorced, and widowed employees. Further, suppose that these cases are represented by the numbers 1, 2, 3, 4. The four cases can be handled by a **switch**-declaration such as:

```
begin
  switch status = single, married, divorced, widowed;
    ⋮
  goto status[i];

single:       ... handle single case ...
              goto done;
married:      ... handle married case ...
              goto done;
divorced:     ... handle divorced case ...
              goto done;
widowed:      ... handle widowed case ...

done:         ...
end
```

It is as though 'status' were an array initialized to the statement labels 'single', 'married', 'divorced', and 'widowed'. The **goto**-statement then transfers to the label given by 'status[i]'.

In the above example, the flow of control can go in one of four directions, depending on the value of 'i'. These four control paths rejoin at the label 'done', which is a good pattern for using a **switch** since it breaks the processing down into four distinct cases. This pattern is not required by the **switch**, however, and it is possible to use it to write programs that are very hard to understand. Earlier in this chapter we discussed some of the problems with the **goto**-statement, in particular, that it complicated correlating the dynamic and static structure of the program. We can see that the **switch** is even worse since it is not even obvious where it goes! There are several possible destinations; they may be almost anywhere in the program, and the list of them is in the switch-declaration, which may be very far away from the **goto**. These are some of the reasons the **switch** has been replaced in newer languages, such as Pascal and Ada, by the much more structured **case**-statement.

The switch Is Baroque

The **switch** is another example of a baroque feature. For instance, Algol permits the **switch** elements to be conditional expressions that are evaluated at the time of the **goto**. Consider the following example:

```
begin
  switch S = L, if i>0 then M else N, Q;
  goto S[j];
end
```

If j = 1, then the **goto** transfers to label L; if j = 3, then the **goto** transfers to label Q; and if j = 2, the **goto** transfers to label M or N, depending on the value of i. We can see this by the Copy Rule, that is, by substituting the value of S[2] into the **goto**-statement:

```
goto if i>0 then M else N;
```

This will transfer to M if i>0, and N otherwise. This textual substitution process may remind you of name parameters; in fact, they are essentially the same and they must be implemented in the same way, by thunks. They also have many of the same problems as name parameters, which does not help an already difficult-to-understand feature.

*EXERCISE 3-30**: The effect of an Algol statement such as '**goto** S[k]', where 'k' is out of range (i.e., either less than 1 or greater than the number of switch elements in S), is to go on to the following statement. In other words, an out-of-range **switch** is interpreted as a *fall-through*. Evaluate this behavior with respect to the Security Principle. Mention any situations in which this behavior would be desirable.

*EXERCISE 3-31**: What restrictions would you place on the **switch**-declaration to make it easier to understand and implement, without seriously diminishing its usefulness?

EXERCISES*

1**. Study the Algol-68 language and evaluate its control structures with respect to regularity, orthogonality, and structure.
2. Read about **own** variables in the Algol-60 Report (or an Algol text). Investigate whether they can be used to solve the information-hiding problems we encountered in the symbol table example in Section 3.3.
3**. In Algol-60 arrays as well as simple variables can be **own**. Arrays can also be dynamic. Discuss feature interaction in dynamic **own** arrays. What does it mean when an **own** array changes size? How are dynamic **own** arrays implemented?
4. Design a **complex** data type for Algol. Discuss operators, relations, coercions, declarations, etc.
5. Investigate the use of Algol-60 for systems programming. What problems would be encountered? Can they be avoided or should Algol be extended to solve them?
6. Describe how strings could be made first-class citizens in Algol-60. Describe in detail data types, operators, relations, coercions, etc.
7. Read, summarize, and critique Knuth's article, "Structured Programming with GOTO Statements" (*ACM Comp. Surveys 6*, 4, 1974).
8. Write a recursive procedure to compute the Fibonacci numbers. Recall that $F(0) = F(1) = 1$ and $F(n) = F(n-1) + F(n-2)$ for $n > 1$. Compute the asymptotical time complexity of this procedure and compare with the asymptotical complexity of the corresponding iterative procedure. If the recursive solution is much worse than the iterative one, then define a more efficient recursive procedure.
9. Prove that it is impossible to write in Algol-60 a Swap procedure that will work for all **integer** operands.
10. What values are printed by the following Algol program if:
    a. x is passed by value and y is passed by value;
    b. x is passed by value and y is passed by name;
    c. x is passed by name and y is passed by value; and
    d. x is passed by name and y is passed by name?

```
begin integer i, j; integer array A[1:3];

    procedure P(x,y); integer x, y;
      begin
        y := 2;
        Print(x);
        i := 3;
```

```
    Print(x);
    Print(y)
  end

 A[1] := 7;  A[2] := 11;  A[3] := 13;
 i := 1;
 P (A[i], i);
 P (i, A[i])
end
```

4

SYNTACTIC ISSUES: ALGOL-60

4.1 DESIGN: SYNTACTIC STRUCTURES

Machine Independence Led to a Free Format

In Chapter 3, Section 3.1, we saw that Algol resulted from an attempt to solve the problem of *software portability,* that is, the problem of making programs work on a wide variety of computers. In other words, Algol had to be *machine independent.* This goal affected all aspects of Algol's design, including its syntactic structures. For instance, many different input devices were then in use on computers; some machines used 80- or 90-column punched cards, others used teletypewriter-like devices and punched paper tape, and so forth. Hence, the goal of machine independence ruled out a *fixed format* such as that used in FORTRAN; instead, Algol adopted a *free format,* that is, a format independent of columns or other details of the layout of the program. This convention is familiar from natural languages, such as English, in which the meaning of sentences does not depend on the columns or the number of lines on which they're written. Almost all languages designed after Algol have used a free format.

Since Algol did not force a particular layout on programmers, for the first time programmers had to think about the problem of how a program *should* be formatted. For example, a program could be written in a FORTRAN-like style:

```
sum := 0;
for i := 1 step 1 until N do
begin
real val;
Read Real (val);
Data[i] := if val < 0 then -val else val
end;
for i := 1 step 1 until N do
sum := sum + Data[i];
avg := sum/N;
```

Or it could be written, English style, in a continuous stream:

```
sum := 0; for i := 1 step 1 until N do begin real val; Read real (val); Data[i]
:= if val < 0 then -val else val end; for i := 1 step 1 until N do sum := sum+
Data[i]; avg := sum/N;
```

Ultimately, this question led to the idea of formatting a program in a way that reflects the structure of the program. That is, the layout of the program should obey the *Structure Principle* by making the program's textual arrangement correspond to its dynamic behavior. For example, a better layout of the above program fragment is

```
sum := 0;

for i := 1 step 1 until N do
  begin real val;
    Read Real (val);
    Data[i] := if val < 0 then -val else val
  end;

for i := 1 step 1 until N do
  sum := sum + Data[i];
avg := sum/N;
```

This format is better because it helps the eye to identify portions of the program that are within the same control and name contexts. The hierarchical structure of the program is made manifest in its layout.

Three Levels of Representation Are Used

The attempt to have a machine-independent language in the face of differing computers and varying national conventions led to a unique specification of Algol's lexical structure. The differing input-output devices available on different computers meant that there was no universal character set that could be used by Algol. Certainly, all computers provided for uppercase letters, digits, and a few punctuation symbols (such as '.', ',', '+'). Beyond this, however, there was little uniformity; some provided lowercase letters, some provided special logical and mathematical symbols ($<$, $\wedge$, $\vee$, etc.), others had various commercial symbols (@, #, etc.), some had format controls (e.g., subscripts and superscripts), and some even had the ability to use two colors (e.g., red and black). Two solutions are apparent: We can either design our language to use just those symbols that are available in all character sets, which will severely restrict the lexics of the language, or we can make the design of our language independent of particular character sets.

The Algol committee took the latter approach. They were forced into this position by the inability to solve a seemingly simple problem. It is conventional in the United States to use a period to represent a decimal point, while in Europe it is conventional to use a comma. When the Algol committee came to the issue of how to write numbers, both sides refused to budge. It seemed that the prospects for an international programming language would be defeated by a decimal point! (It is a folk theorem of programming language design that the more trivial an issue is, the more vehemently people will fight over it!) The solution adopted by the committee was to define three levels of language: a *reference language*, a *publication language*, and several *hardware representations*. These languages differed in lexical conventions but had the same syntax.

The *reference language* is the language used in all examples in the Algol Report, as well as in this book. Here is an example of the reference language:

$$a[i+1] := (a[i] + pi \times r\uparrow 2)/6.02_{10}23;$$

The *publication language* was intended to be the language used for publishing algorithms in Algol. It was distinguished by allowing various lexical and printing conventions (e.g., subscripts and Greek letters) that would aid readability. For instance, the published form of the above statement could be:

$$a_{i+1} \leftarrow \{a_i + \pi \times r^2\}/6.02 \times 10^{23};$$

In practice, the publication language has usually been the same as the reference language.

Finally, the committee left it up to Algol implementors to define *hardware representations* of Algol that would be appropriate to the character sets and input-output devices of their computer systems. For instance, the above example may have to be written in any of these ways:

```
a(/i+1/) := ( a(/i/) + pi*r**2 ) / 6,02e23;

A(.I+1.) .= ( A(.I.) + PI * R 'POWER' 2 ) / 6.02'23 .,

a[i+1] := (a[i] + pi*r^2)/6.02E23;
```

The various representations were required to permit any program to be translated into any of the different forms.

Algol Solved Some Problems of FORTRAN Lexics

Algol's distinction among reference, publication, and hardware languages led to the idea that the keywords of the language are indivisible basic symbols. That is, boldface (or underlined) words such as '**if**' and '**procedure**' are considered single symbols, like '⩽' and ':=', and have no relation to similarly appearing identifiers such as 'if' or 'procedure'. This means that the confusion between keywords and identifiers that we saw in FORTRAN is not possible in Algol. For example, it is perfectly unambiguous (although somewhat confusing) to write:

if procedure **then** until := until + 1 **else** do := **false**;

There are many possible hardware representations for these compound symbols, including,

```
'if' procedure 'then' until := until + 1 'else' do := 'false';

IF procedure THEN until := until + 1 ELSE do := FALSE;

#IF PROCEDURE #THEN UNTIL := UNTIL + 1 #ELSE DO := #FALSE;

if Xprocedure then Xuntil := Xuntil + 1 else Xdo := false;
```

The last example illustrates the *reserved word* approach; the symbols used for keywords are not allowed as identifiers. Although this seems to be the most convenient convention, it really violates the spirit of Algol since the keywords can conflict with the identifiers.

It is useful to distinguish the following three lexical conventions for the words of a programming language:

1. *Reserved words.* The words used by the language ('if', 'procedure', etc.) are reserved by the language, that is, they cannot be used by the programmer for identifiers. This is quite readable and is essentially the convention used in natural languages. It may not be too readable to a novice in the language since it doesn't clearly distinguish those words that are and aren't part of the language.
2. *Keywords.* This is the strict Algol approach. The words used by the language are marked in some unambiguous way (e.g., preceding with a '#', surrounding with quotes, or typing in another case or type font). This is usually difficult to type and it is not very readable unless a different font can be used.
3. *Keywords in context.* This is the FORTRAN (and PL/I) approach. Words used by the language are keywords only in those contexts in which they are expected, otherwise they are treated as identifiers. For instance, the following is a legal PL/I statement:

```
IF IF THEN
  THEN = 0;
ELSE;
  ELSE = 0;
```

The first occurrences of IF, THEN, and ELSE are keywords, while the second occurrences are identifiers. Clearly, this convention can be confusing for both people and compilers. We saw in Chapter 2 how the keyword in context convention made it harder to catch errors in programs.

Most modern programming languages use the *reserved word* convention.

Arbitrary Restrictions Are Eliminated

Algol adheres to the Zero-One-Infinity Principle in many of its design decisions. For example, there is no limit on the number of characters in an identifier (FORTRAN allowed at most six). It also eliminates many other restrictions, for example, any expression is allowed as a subscript, including other array elements:

```
A[2 × B[i] − 1]
Count [if i > 100 then 100 else i]
```

Although these facilities are not often needed, they reduce the number of special cases the programmer must learn and they support the idea that "anything you think you ought to be able to do, you will be able to do." All of these features contribute to Algol's reputation as a general, regular, elegant, orthogonal language.

EXERCISE 4-1:* Do you agree that you can do anything you may want to be able to do in Algol? Can you do too much already? Either propose some restrictions that should be eliminated from Algol and show that they are cost effective (i.e., their benefits outweigh their costs) or list some restrictions that should be imposed and show that they are worthwhile.

The if-Statement Had Problems

Algol's syntactic conventions did have some problems. Consider this **if**-statement:

if *B* **then if** *C* **then** *S* **else** *T*

Does the **else** go with the first **if** or the second? That is, is this statement equivalent to

if *B* **then begin if** *C* **then** *S* **else** *T* **end**

or is it equivalent to

if *B* **then begin if** *C* **then** *S* **end else** *T*

This is called the *dangling 'else' problem.* Algol solved this problem by requiring that the consequent of an **if**-statement be an unconditional statement. Thus, the example, '**if** *B* **then if** *C* **then** *S* **else** *T*', is illegal and must be written in one of the two ways shown, depending on the programmer's intent. Other languages have adopted other solutions to this problem. For example, PL/I says that an **else** goes with the nearest preceding unmatched **if**. We will see in later chapters that newer languages have avoided this problem altogether.

EXERCISE 4-2:* What do you think is the best solution to the dangling **else** problem? Take and defend a position.

Algol Defined the Style of Almost All Successors

Algol's lexical and syntactic structures became so popular that virtually all languages designed since have been "Algol-like"; that is, they have been hierarchical in structure, with nesting of both environments and control structures. Even PL/I (which started out as FORTRAN VI) adopted these conventions and many other ideas from Algol.

EXERCISE 4-3:* Pick some language designed after Algol-60 (e.g., Pascal, Ada, PL/I, Algol-68, FORTRAN 77) and compare its syntax with Algol's. List the major differences and similarities in both lexical and syntactic structures. Are these improvements or not?

EXERCISE 4-4:* List at least two programming languages (designed after Algol-60) that are not Algol-like. Are their conventions better than Algol's? Why do you think their designers chose these conventions?

4.2 DESCRIPTIVE TOOLS: BNF

English Descriptions of Syntax Proved Inadequate

An important skill in any design discipline is the use of *descriptive tools* to formulate, record, and evaluate various aspects of the developing design. Although English and other natural languages can often be used for this purpose, most designers have developed specialized languages, diagrams, and notations for representing aspects of their work that would otherwise be difficult to express. Imagine how hard it would be for an architect to work without elevations and floor plans or for an electrical engineer to work without circuit diagrams. In this section we will discuss a very valuable *descriptive tool* for programming language design: BNF.

Recall (Section 3.1) that the decision to use the BNF notation in the Algol-60 Report resulted from Peter Naur's realization that his understanding of the Algol-58 description did not agree with that of John Backus. This is true because natural language prose is not sufficiently precise. So that we can see some of the problems inherent in using a natural language to describe syntax, we will work through a simple example.

Algol-60, like most programming languages, allows numeric denotations (i.e., numeric literals) to be written in three forms: integers such as '-273', fractions such as '3.14159', and numbers in scientific notation, such as '$6.02_{10}23$' (meaning 6.02×10^{23}). Here we have defined the format of numeric denotations by giving three representative examples; using examples gives the reader a clear idea of what numbers look like in Algol.

While examples are adequate for many purposes, they do leave a number of questions unanswered. For example: Are leading negative signs allowed on fractional and scientific numbers? Are negative exponents (e.g., '$3.1_{10}-50$') allowed? Is the coefficient of a scientific number required to contain a decimal point or are numbers like '$3_{10}8$' allowed?

One solution to this problem is to give more examples that cover these questionable cases. We could add that '$3.1_{10}-50$', '-3.14159', and '$3_{10}8$' are legal numbers, while '3.', '$3._{10}8$', '$--273$', '$+-273$', and so forth, are not. Unfortunately, this still does not specify precisely what a numeric denotation is. Are leading decimal points, such as '.5', allowed? How about scientific numbers without a leading coefficient (e.g., '$_{10}-6$' meaning 10^{-6})? Is a leading positive sign allowed (e.g., '+5')? Is it allowed on the exponent (e.g., '$3_{10}+8$')?

We can see that what seemed to be a simple problem, specifying the syntax of a number, actually has many hidden pitfalls. Couldn't we just be more careful in our English description? After all, legal documents, which must be very precise, are written in natural languages. Let's give it a try; here's a precise description of a number.

1. An *unsigned integer* is a sequence of one or more *digits.*[1]
2. An *integer* has one of the following three forms: It is either a positive sign ('+') followed by an *unsigned integer,* or a negative sign ('−') followed by an *unsigned integer,* or an *unsigned integer* preceded by no sign.
3. A *decimal fraction* is a decimal point ('.') immediately followed by an *unsigned integer.*
4. An *exponent part* is a subten symbol ('$_{10}$') immediately followed by an *integer.*
5. A *decimal number* has one of three forms: It is either an *unsigned integer,* or a *decimal fraction,* or an *unsigned integer* followed by a *decimal fraction.*
6. An *unsigned number* can take one of three forms: It is either a *decimal number,* or an *exponent part,* or a *decimal number* followed by an *exponent part.*
7. Finally, a *number* can have any one of these three forms: It can be a positive sign ('+') followed by an *unsigned number,* or a negative sign ('−') followed by an *unsigned number,* or an *unsigned number* preceded by no sign.

This is surely an exhaustive (and exhausting!) description of Algol numbers. We have the feeling that we have read a very precise specification of what a number is without having a very clear idea of what they look like. Indeed, we probably won't have a clear idea unless we make up some examples:

- unsigned integer — '273', '3', '02', '14159', '23'
- integer — '3', '+3', '−273'
- decimal fraction — '.02', '.14159'
- exponent part — '$_{10}23$', '$_{10}-6$'
- decimal number — '273', '3.1', '6.02', '3.14159'
- unsigned number — '273', '$6.02_{10}23$', '3.14159', '$3_{10}8$'
- number — '−273', '$6.02_{10}23$', '3.14159', '$+3_{10}8$'

In fact, if these examples were provided with the above description, most people would be inclined just to look at the examples and only refer to the legalistic

1 We are presuming that the class of *digits* has been precisely defined, probably by enumeration.

prose when they were in doubt. The prose, although precise, is so opaque that the language designer who wrote it is likely to have some misgivings about whether it accurately expresses the ideas intended.

Backus Developed a Formal Syntactic Notation

We noted above that examples often give a better idea of a thing than a precise definition of its form. This is the way we learn most concepts, including our native language. The problem with a description by examples is that it is always incomplete. We saw in the *number* example that there was a seemingly endless list of borderline cases and questionable instances that were not handled by our examples. On the other hand, the precise English description dealt with all these borderline cases (we think) but really didn't show us what a number is in a very digestible form. What we need is a way of combining the perceptual clarity of examples with the precision of formal prose.

In Chapter 2 we said that FORTRAN restricts subscript expressions to one of the following forms:

c

v

$v + c$ or $v - c$

$c*v$

$c*v + c'$ or $c*v - c'$

where c and c' are integer denotations (*unsigned integers*) and v is an integer variable. What does this have to do with BNF? It turns out that this is exactly the way Backus described subscript expressions in the original FORTRAN I manual. It combined the advantages of both examples and a formal specification since the formulas above *look like* example expressions (e.g., '25', 'I', 'I + 25', '2*I − 1'), while at the same time it precisely described subscript expressions. For example, the above formulas say that one form of a *subscript expression* is a c (i.e., integer denotation), followed by a star (*), followed by a v (i.e., integer variable), followed by a plus sign (+), followed by another c (i.e., integer denotation). The formulas make use of the *syntactic categories* c and v, which stand for integer denotations and integer variables.

This notation is just as precise as our prose but much clearer in its meaning. In fact, these formulas almost draw a picture of the legal subscript expressions. Backus formalized this notation and used it to describe Algol-58.

BNF Is Naur's Adaptation of the Backus Notation

Naur adapted the Backus notation to the Algol-60 Report by making a number of improvements. It is this modified notation that is most widely known; it is called BNF (for Backus–Naur Form) in recognition of Naur's contribution.

To see how BNF works, we will look again at the number problem. We can see that in our formal prose definition of *numbers* we made use of several names for various syntactic components of numbers. For example, *integer* represented strings like '3', '+3', and '−273'; and *decimal fraction* represented strings like '.02' and '.14159'. What we were really doing was defining certain *syntactic categories* of strings, like *decimal number*, in terms of other syntactic categories, like *unsigned integer*. BNF notation represents classes of strings (syntactic categories) by words or phrases in angle brackets such as <decimal fraction> and <unsigned integer>.

Let's look at part of a BNF description. In description 3 of the definition of *number*, we said that a *decimal fraction* is a decimal point ('.') followed by an *unsigned integer*. Following the principle that the description should look like the things it describes, BNF represents this as:

```
<decimal fraction> ::= .<unsigned integer>
```

The '::=' symbol can be read "is defined as"; it is reminiscent of Algol's assignment operator.

Notice that BNF preserves the descriptive advantages of examples by representing particular symbols (such as '.') by themselves, and the concatenation of strings by the juxtaposition of their descriptions. That is, the fact that the decimal point is followed by a member of the class <unsigned integer> is represented by writing

```
.<unsigned integer>
```

The symbols, such as '.', that represent themselves are called *terminal symbols* (*terminus* is the Latin word for limit or end), while those that represent syntactic categories, such as <unsigned integer>, are called *nonterminals*. A descriptive language like BNF is called a *metalanguage* (*meta* is Greek for after or beyond) because it is used to describe another language, the *object language* (Algol in this case). Metalanguages are very important tools for both the language designer and the language user.

BNF Describes Alternates

Most of the definitions in our description of *number* were not as simple as that of *decimal fraction*; most of them listed several *alternative forms* that the things being described can take. For example, an <integer> has three different possible forms:

```
+ <unsigned integer>
- <unsigned integer>
  <unsigned integer>
```

Clearly, *alternation* such as this is very common; BNF provides a means to express it. The symbol '|' is read as "or"; using it <integer> can be defined as follows:

```
<integer>    ::= + <unsigned integer>
               | − <unsigned integer>
               |   <unsigned integer>
```

We have written the alternatives on separate lines for readability; this is not necessary since BNF, like Algol, is free form.

Recursion Is Used for Repetition

Using the elements of BNF that we have described so far, all of the rules defining *numbers* can be expressed, except one. This is the very first rule, which defines an <unsigned integer> to be a sequence of one or more <digit>s. How can we express the idea "sequence of one or more of..."?

One way to solve a problem like this is to ask how we can generate a member of this syntactic category. In this case, the question is: How can we generate an <unsigned integer>? The definition says that any sequence of one or more <digit>s is an <unsigned integer>, so if we want an <unsigned integer>, we can start by picking any <digit>. For example, '2' is an <unsigned integer>. Now, what do we do if we want a longer <unsigned integer>? We can take our string of length one and pick another <digit>, say '7', and add it to the end giving the <unsigned integer> '27'. This process can be continued. We can pick another <digit>, say '3', and append it to the <unsigned integer> '27' to get the <unsigned integer> '273'.

Thus, we can get an <unsigned integer> in exactly two ways: either by taking a single <digit> or by adding a <digit> to an <unsigned integer> that we already have. It is now straightforward to write this in BNF:

```
<unsigned integer>    ::= <digit>
                        | <unsigned integer> <digit>
```

Notice that this is a *recursive* definition, that is, <unsigned integer> is defined in terms of itself. It is not a *circular* definition because the single <digit> provides a *base* or starting point for the recursion. That is, one of the alternatives in the definition of <unsigned integer> is not recursive. This is called a *well-founded* recursive definition.

Recursive definitions such as this are the usual way of specifying sequences of things in BNF. We will see shortly that some dialects of BNF have additional notations for expressing sequences in a more readable form.

Recursion is also used for describing nested syntax such as Algol's control structures. We will see an example of this later. Before we get to these things, make sure that you thoroughly understand the BNF definition of <number>, the syntactic category of numeric denotations, in Figure 4.1.

EXERCISE 4-5: Show that the following strings satisfy the definition of <number>: '−273', '6.02$_{10}$23', '3.14159', '+3$_{10}$8', '3.1$_{10}$−50', '$_{10}$−6', '.5', '−0'.

EXERCISE 4-6: Show that the following strings do not satisfy the definition of <number>: '−−273', '3.', '3.$_{10}$−8', '2$_{10}$0.5', '.$_{10}$2', '3.−14159'.

EXERCISE 4-7: Write a BNF description of identifiers that have the following syntax. An identifier is a string of letters, digits, and underscores ('__'), subject to the following restrictions: (1) an identifier must begin with a letter, (2) consecutive underscores are not permitted, and (3) an identifier may not end with an underscore. *Hint:* Start by writing out some examples of legal and illegal identifiers so that you can identify the pattern.

Extended BNF Is More Descriptive

Several extensions have been made to BNF to improve its readability. Often these directly reflect the words and phrases commonly used to describe syntax. For example, in the prose description of *number,* we defined an *unsigned integer* to be a "sequence of one or more *digits.*" This was expressed in BNF through a recursive definition. Although we can get used to recursive descriptions such as this, it would really be more convenient to have a notation that directly expresses the idea "sequence of one or more of . . . ." One such notation is the *Kleene cross,*[2] C^+, which means a sequence of one or more strings from the syntactic category C. Using this notation, the syntactic category <unsigned integer> can be defined:

<unsigned integer> ::= <digit>$^+$

A useful variant of this notation is the *Kleene star,* C^*, which stands for a sequence of *zero* or more elements of the class C. For example, an Algol identifier (name) is a <letter> followed by any number of <letter>s or <digit>s (i.e.,

2 Pronounced "klane-uh" and named after the mathematician and logician S. C. Kleene (1909–).

a sequence of zero or more <alphanumeric>s). This can be written as:

<alphanumeric> ::= <letter> | <digit>

<identifier> ::= <letter> <alphanumeric>*

If <alphanumeric> is used in only one place, namely, the definition of <identifier>, then it is pointless to give it a name. Rather, it would be better to be able to say directly a "sequence of <letter>s or <digit>s." Some dialects of BNF permit this by allowing us to substitute '{<letter> | <digit>}' for <alphanumeric>:

<identifier> ::= <letter> {<letter> | <digit>}*

This can be read, "An identifier is a letter followed by a sequence of zero or more letters or digits." It can be made even more pictorial by stacking the alternatives:

<identifier> ::= <letter> { <letter>
<digit> }*

<unsigned integer> ::= <digit>
| <unsigned integer> <digit>

<integer> ::= + <unsigned integer>
| − <unsigned integer>
| <unsigned integer>

<decimal fraction> ::= .<unsigned integer>

<exponent part> ::= $_{10}$<integer>

<decimal number> ::= <unsigned integer>
| <decimal fraction>
| <unsigned integer> <decimal fraction>

<unsigned number> ::= <decimal number>
| <exponent part>
| <decimal number> <exponent part>

<number> ::= + <unsigned number>
| − <unsigned number>
| <unsigned number>

Figure 4.1 BNF Definition of Numeric Denotations

Let's see if there are any other improvements that can be made to this notation. The rule for an <integer> is

```
<integer>   ::=  + <unsigned integer>
              |  − <unsigned integer>
              |    <unsigned integer>
```

One immediate simplification should be apparent; we can use our alternative notation

$$\langle\text{integer}\rangle ::= \left\{ \begin{array}{c} + \\ - \end{array} \right\} \langle\text{unsigned integer}\rangle$$

$$\quad | \quad \langle\text{unsigned integer}\rangle$$

This is better; but the idea that we really want to express is that the <unsigned integer> is *optionally* preceded by a '+' or '−'. The square bracket is often used for this purpose, that is, '[+ | −]' or

$$\langle\text{integer}\rangle ::= \left[\begin{array}{c} + \\ - \end{array} \right] \langle\text{unsigned integer}\rangle$$

This is a very graphic notation; it *shows* us what an integer looks like. A two-dimensional metalanguage like this was first used in the 1960s to describe the COBOL language. Figure 4.2 shows the definition of <number> using this extended BNF.

Why is this extended BNF preferable to pure BNF? It is because it adheres better to the Structure Principle, that is, the forms of the extended BNF defini-

$$\langle\text{unsigned integer}\rangle ::= \langle\text{digit}\rangle^{+}$$

$$\langle\text{integer}\rangle ::= \left[\begin{array}{c} + \\ - \end{array} \right] \langle\text{unsigned integer}\rangle$$

$$\langle\text{decimal number}\rangle ::= \left\{ \begin{array}{l} \langle\text{unsigned integer}\rangle \\ [\langle\text{unsigned integer}\rangle]\,.\,\langle\text{unsigned integer}\rangle \end{array} \right\}$$

$$\langle\text{number}\rangle ::= \left[\begin{array}{c} + \\ - \end{array} \right] \left\{ \begin{array}{l} \langle\text{decimal number}\rangle \\ [\langle\text{decimal number}\rangle]\ {}_{10}\ \langle\text{integer}\rangle \end{array} \right\}$$

Figure 4.2 Extended BNF Definition of Numeric Denotations

tions are closer (visually) to the strings they describe than are the pure BNF definitions. In other words, extended BNF has more of the advantages of examples.

EXERCISE 4-8: Show that the extended BNF definitions in Figure 4.2 are equivalent to (i.e., describe the same class of strings as) the pure BNF definitions in Figure 4.1.

EXERCISE 4-9: Write an extended BNF definition of the class of identifiers described in Exercise 4-7.

BNF Led to a Mathematical Theory of Programming Languages

In the late 1950s, Noam Chomsky, a linguist at MIT, was attempting to develop a mathematical theory of natural languages. He produced a mathematical description of four different classes of languages that are now known as:

- Chomsky type 0, or *recursively enumerable* languages
- Chomsky type 1, or *context-sensitive* languages
- Chomsky type 2, or *context-free* languages
- Chomsky type 3, or *regular* languages

Each of these classes includes the one below it; for example, all regular languages are context-free, and all context-free languages are context-sensitive.

Chomsky also defined a class of *grammars*, or language descriptions, corresponding to each of these language classes. For example, each *context-free grammar* describes a corresponding context-free language, and, conversely, each context-free language can be described by a context-free grammar. There may be several alternative ways of describing the same language so there may be several grammars corresponding to the same language.

It was quickly realized that Backus's notation is equivalent to Chomsky's context-free (or type 2) grammars, so that the class of languages describable by BNF is exactly the context-free languages. Since Chomsky had developed a mathematical theory of these classes of grammars and languages, the connection between BNF and the Chomsky hierarchy immediately enabled the mathematical analysis of the syntax and grammar of programming languages. This has had important practical benefits since it has permitted the development of automatic parser-generators, thus automating what had been one of the more difficult parts of compiler writing.

Context-Free and Regular Grammars Are the Most Useful

Although a full treatment of formal languages is beyond the scope of this book, we will discuss the significance of the two most important classes of languages and grammars: context-free and regular.

There are mathematical definitions of context-free and regular languages, but the simplest way to see the difference is by reference to the extended BNF notation. A *regular grammar* is one that is written in extended BNF without the use of any recursive rules. For example, the definition of <number> in Figure 4.2 is an example of a regular grammar. A language is formally defined as the set of strings described by a grammar. Therefore, a *regular language* is a language that can be described by a regular grammar. For example, the language defined by <number>, which is {'–273', '$6.02_{10}23$', '3.14159', '$+3_{10}8$',...} is a regular language. Notice that we said that a regular language is one that *can* be described by a regular grammar, not one that *must* be. The distinction is important since the grammar in Figure 4.1 uses recursion and defines the same language as that in Figure 4.2.

A *context-free* grammar is any grammar that can be expressed in extended BNF, possibly including recursively defined nonterminals. Analogously, a *context-free language* is a language that can be described by a context-free grammar. All regular grammars are also context-free grammars, and all regular languages are also context-free languages.

Thus, the difference between regular and context-free grammars is in the use of recursion in the definitions. What are the implications of this? Basically, recursion allows the definition of *nested* syntactic structures. We have already seen the importance of nesting in Algol. Nesting is easy to express in BNF, which probably encouraged the widespread use of nested constructs in Algol. Consider this simplified form of Algol's definition of a <statement>:

```
<unconditional statement> ::=

{ <assignment statement>                 }
{ for <for list> do <statement>          }

<statement> ::=

{ <unconditional statement>                                                    }
{ if <expression> then <unconditional statement>                               }
{ if <expression> then <unconditional statement> else <statement>              }
```

We can see that <statement> is defined recursively in terms of itself since part of an **if**-statement is itself a <statement>. Also, <statement> is defined in terms of <unconditional statement>, which is in turn defined in terms of <statement>; this is an example of *indirect recursion.* This recursive definition is not circular because the <assignment statement> alternative (which is not defined in terms of <statement>) provides a *base* for the recursion.

It is easy to see that these definitions allow the nesting of statements. For example, since 'x = x + 1' is an <assignment statement>, it is also an

<unconditional statement>. Therefore, it can be made part of an **if**-statement, for instance,

```
if x<0 then x := x+1
```

Since this **if**-statement is itself a <statement>, it can be made the part of a **for**-loop, for example,

```
for i := 1 step 1 until n do if x<0 then x := x+1
```

This process of embedding statements into yet larger statements can be continued indefinitely. Before the development of the BNF notation, it would have been much more complicated to describe these recursively nested structures.

Since regular grammars do not permit recursion, it is not possible to specify indefinitely deep nesting in a regular grammar. Thus, the major difference between regular and context-free languages is the possibility of indefinitely deep nesting in the latter. A simple example of this is the language of balanced parentheses. This is a make-believe language whose only strings are sequences of properly balanced parentheses. For example,

((()))()((()()))

is an expression in this language, while '(((()' is not. This language is easy to describe as a context-free grammar:

```
<expression> ::= <balanced>*

<balanced> ::= (<expression>)
```

(*N.B.* It may look as though there is no base to the recursive definitions above, but that is not the case since the Kleene star notation allows *no* repetitions of <balanced> to be an <expression>.)

EXERCISE 4-10: Show that the above grammar describes the balanced and only the balanced strings of parentheses.

EXERCISE 4-11: Show that *limited* nesting does not require context-free rules. *Hint:* Show that strings of parentheses nested at most three (or any fixed number) deep can be defined by a regular grammer.

4.3 EVALUATION AND EPILOG

Algol-60 Never Achieved Widespread Use

Algol-60 began with ambitious goals; it was to be a universal programming language for communicating algorithms to both people and machines. Unfortunately, it never achieved widespread use in the United States and was only moderately successful in Europe. What were the reasons for Algol's failure?

Algol Had No Input-Output

One widely cited reason for Algol's lack of success is its lack of input-output statements. This has even been a source of ridicule. For example, people have said, "Algol is the perfect programming language, except that you can't read in any data or print out any results!" Clearly, Algol's designers realized that a language without input-output was worthless, so why didn't they specify it?

To understand their reasoning, we must remember that Algol-60 was designed at a time when there was little uniformity among input-output conventions; there were few standards. We discussed this situation in Section 4.1, along with its effect on Algol's lexical conventions. Another result of this situation was the input-output statements of FORTRAN I, which were very dependent on the IBM 704. Only later versions of FORTRAN achieved a degree of machine independence.

Faced with this situation, and believing that input-output was not a major part of most scientific programs, Algol's designers decided to omit all input-output statements. They felt that input-output statements would make this intended universal language too machine dependent. Rather, they decided that input-output would be accomplished by calling library procedures. It was their intention that each implementation of Algol provide a set of procedures appropriate for the machine on which it was implemented.

Eventually several sets of standard input-output procedures were designed for Algol. Some of these were based on experience with later versions of FORTRAN and with COBOL. Since COBOL was a language for commercial programming, it could not avoid the issues of machine-independent input-output. Unfortunately, standardized input-output came too late to Algol to correct the damage done. The momentum of Algol's introduction had been lost and could not be recovered.

Algol Also Directly Competed with FORTRAN

Although there are many other reasons for Algol's failure, one that deserves mention is that it directly competed with FORTRAN. It *was* designed for the same application area—scientific computation. Furthermore, within this application area Algol's unique features (e.g., nested control structures, block structure, and recursion) were not considered very important. Instead, they were seen as causes for inefficiency, which was a very important issue in the early 1960s.

We should realize that four years passed from the initial excitement accompanying the Algol-58 Report to the Revised Report in 1962, and there was still no input-output. In the meantime, FORTRAN had gained considerable ground and acquired a large user community; standardization efforts were under way and most manufacturers were developing compilers. The coup de grace came when IBM, which had been considering supporting Algol, decided instead to reaffirm its commitment to FORTRAN. Most potential users of Algol saw that the costs of a switch were too great and the benefits too meager. Therefore, use of FORTRAN spread while Algol became an almost exclusively academic language.

Algol Was a Major Milestone in Programming Languages

It is remarkable that although Algol never achieved widespread use, it is one of the major milestones in programming language development. This is partly reflected in the terms it added to the programming language vocabulary, which include type, formal parameter, actual parameter, block, call by value, call by name, scope, dynamic arrays, and global and local variables.[3]

The development of Algol compilers led to a number of concepts that will be discussed in Chapter 6, including activation records, thunks, displays, and static and dynamic chains. Algol not only has introduced programming language terminology, but has motivated much of the work in programming language design and implementation that has occurred since the late 1950s. Perlis has said that Algol "was to become a universal tool with which to view, study and proffer solutions to almost every kind of problem in computation."[4] We will discuss some of the indirect accomplishments of Algol.

Naturally, Algol has influenced most succeeding programming languages. For example, there was Algol-68, which was a direct generalization of Algol-60. Since we have seen that in some respects Algol-60 was already *too* general, you will not be surprised to learn that Algol-68 has been even less successful than Algol-60. Nevertheless, Algol-68 has had a considerable impact of its own by introducing new terms and concepts into computer science.

Eventually almost all programming languages became "Algol-like," that is, block-structured, nested, recursive, and free form. Unfortunately, the overgenerality of Algol-68 and other later languages, such as PL/I, which included many ideas from Algol, has led some computer scientists to say, "Algol was

3 This list is adapted from Perlis (1978).
4 Ibid.

indeed an achievement; it was a significant advance on most of its successors."[5] As we will discuss in Chapter 5, this notion led to the quest for simplicity in language design and description that ultimately resulted in Pascal.

Algol has also formed the basis for several direct extensions, one of the most important of which is Simula. Simula is basically Algol-60 with a new feature added, called the *class*, that allows the grouping of related procedures and data declarations. The class is an example of an *encapsulation mechanism*, an important concept discussed in Chapter 7. Simula was also an early example of an *extensible language* (discussed in Chapter 5) and ultimately provided many of the ideas upon which the Smalltalk system and other object-oriented programming languages are based (Chapter 12).

As more and more languages became Algol-like, computer architects began to realize that the effective performance of their computers could be increased by building in mechanisms to support Algol implementation. In the 1960s the Burroughs B5500 was one of the first computers to do this. Now almost all computers, even microcomputers, provide some support for block-structured, recursive programming languages. Thus, Algol has had a direct effect on computer architecture.

Also, as we have discussed, the use of BNF in the Algol Report led to the development of the mathematical theory of formal languages and to automatic means for generating programming language parsers. To date, compilers remain the most successful domain of automatic software generation.

Finally, the imprecision in the English-language descriptions of semantics stimulated a tremendous amount of research into the formal specification of semantics. The goal, which is yet to be reached, is to be able to automate the semantic parts of compiler writing to the same extent as the syntactic parts.

Thus, Algol, although a commercial failure, was a scientific triumph. It has remained an inspiration to later language designers. Naur has said, "The language demonstrates what can be achieved if generality and economy of concept is pursued and combined with precision in description."[6]

Characteristic of Second-Generation Programming Languages

Algol-60 was the first *second-generation* programming language, and its characteristics are typical of the entire generation. Broadly, we can say the second-generation structures are elaborations and generalizations of the corresponding first-generation structures.

First, consider the *data structures*, which are very close to first-generation structures. There are some simple generalizations, such as arrays with lower

5 Ibid.
6 Naur (1978).

bounds other than 1, and dynamic arrays, but by and large the structures are still linear and closely patterned on machine addressing modes. However, second-generation languages do usually have strong typing of the built-in types (there aren't user-defined types).

The second generation makes one of its biggest contributions in its *name structures*, which are hierarchically nested. This permits both better control of the name space and efficient dynamic memory allocation. The introduction of block structure is perhaps the most characteristic attribute of this language generation.

Another characteristic of the second generation is its *structured control structures*, which, by hierarchically structuring the control flow, eliminate much of the need for confusing networks of **goto**s. The second generation also elaborated many of the first generation's control structures. Some of these elaborations are important contributions, such as recursive procedures and the idea of a choice of parameter passing modes. Others are more questionable, and the second generation is known for a proliferation of baroque and expensive constructs.

In its *syntactic structures* the second generation saw a shift away from fixed formats, toward free format languages with machine-independent lexical conventions. A number of languages shifted to keyword or reserved word policies, although the keyword-in-context rule was also used (e.g., PL/I).

In general, the second generation can be seen as the full flowering of the technology of language design and implementation. The many new techniques developed in this period encouraged unbridled generalization—with both desirable and undesirable consequences. We will see that the third generation tried to compensate for the excesses while retaining the accomplishments.

EXERCISES

1. Given the widespread use of the ASCII character set, do you think it is still wise to distinguish among reference, publication, and hardware languages? Discuss the pros and cons.
2. Name a part of the syntax of most programming languages that *cannot* be expressed as a regular grammar, that is, that requires a context-free grammar.
3. Write a BNF or extended BNF description of legal FORTRAN IV subscript expressions.
4. Write a BNF or extended BNF description of Algol-60's **for**-loop, including all the different kinds of for-list-elements. Assume that <variable>, <statement>, <Boolean expression>, and <arithmetic expression> are already defined.

5. (Difficult) Write a BNF or extended BNF grammar that describes the solution of the dangling **else** problem that matches an **else** with the nearest preceding unmatched **then**.
6. A very common syntactic pattern in programming language descriptions is "a sequence of one or more ... separated by ...." For example, an <actual parameter list> can be defined as a sequence of one or more <expression>s separated by commas. Also, a <compound statement> can be defined as a **begin**, followed by one or more <statement>s separated by semicolons, followed by an **end**. Show how to express these patterns in BNF and extended BNF. Design a new extension to these notations that simplifies expressing this pattern.
7. Some programming languages are not truly context-free. For example, some languages (such as Ada, Chapters 7 and 8) allow an identifier to be placed on the **end** at the end of a procedure declaration:

```
procedure <name> (<formals>) is
  <declarations>
begin
  <statements>
end <name>;
```

   This is not context-free because the <name> on the **end** is required to match the <name> of the procedure. Invent a syntactic notation for expressing these context-sensitive dependencies.
8. Do you think it is wise of the Algol committee to have omitted input-output from Algol-60? Defend your position and then do one of the following two exercises.
9. Design an extension to Algol-60 to handle input-output.
10. Specify a procedure library that Algol programs can invoke to perform input-output.
11. Suppose you had to write a numerical or scientific program and that both FORTRAN and Algol compilers were available. Describe how you would decide which to use.
12. Read, summarize, and critique Knuth's article, "The Remaining Trouble Spots in ALGOL 60" (*Comm. ACM 10*, 10, 1967).
13. Study and critique Algol-68 (van Wijngaarden et al., "Revised Report on the Algorithmic Language Algol 68," *Acta Inf. 5*, 1975, or *SIGPLAN Notices 12*, 5, 1977). Since orthogonality was a major design goal of Algol-68, you should pay particular attention to orthogonality in your critique.
14. Study the PL/I language (*Amer. Natl. Stand. Prog. Lang. PL/I*, ANS X3.53-1976, ANSI, New York, 1976). Identify features and ideas derived from FORTRAN and Algol-60.

5

RETURN TO SIMPLICITY: PASCAL

5.1 HISTORY AND MOTIVATION

There Were Many Attempts to Extend Algol's Applicability

Algol was so successful that there were immediate attempts to use its ideas in other application areas. These included Algol-like languages for list processing, string manipulation, systems programming, and artificial intelligence. There were several proposals to include the input-output facilities that Algol lacked and that might have made it feasible to use Algol for commercial programming.

PL/I Attempted To Be One Language for All Applications

PL/I, as we saw in Chapter 2, was IBM's 1964 effort to design FORTRAN VI. The resulting language, which incorporated ideas from FORTRAN, Algol, and COBOL, was so different from FORTRAN that it was renamed PL/I (programming language one). PL/I combined ideas from many sources, including the block structure of Algol, the record and file handling capabilities of COBOL, and the syntactic style of FORTRAN. The result was a very large language—perhaps the largest ever to achieve widespread use. It is more like the union of FORTRAN, COBOL, and Algol than their intersection. The promoters of PL/I argued that users could learn just the subset of the features that were relevant to their applications. This turned out not to be possible since the subtle and unpredictable interactions among the various features of PL/I meant that, practically, programmers had to be aware of the entire language. As a result, PL/I has become the classic example of a "Swiss army knife" approach to language design; that is, the attempt to provide in one language all the gadgets or features that anyone might ever want. The result is inevitably a language so large as to be unmanageable and too complicated to be mastered by most programmers. Dijkstra, Hoare, and several other computer scientists have severely criticized PL/I; in Chapter 2 we cited Dijkstra's characterization of PL/I as a fatal disease. In his Turing Award paper, he called PL/I "a programming language for which the defining documentation is of a frightening size and complexity. Using PL/I must be like flying a plane with 7000 buttons, switches, and handles to manipulate in the cockpit."

Extensible Languages Were Another Approach

Many programming language designers believed that it was futile to design a language that was all things to all programmers. After all, we don't try and make do with one camera that's suitable for everyone and everything—for professionals, amateurs, beginners; for science, art, astronomy, advertising, and so forth. Rather, these designers believed that a more effective approach was to have a closely knit family of application-oriented languages. Of course, the cost of implementing all of these languages would be prohibitive, so it was necessary to develop a new approach to language implementation. This was the *extensible language* approach; the idea that one is given a simple, application-independent *kernel*, or *base*, language and an *extension mechanism* that allows the kernel language to be extended into various application areas. Early examples of extensible languages are the MAD language and McIlroy's "syntax macros."

A Simple Kernel Language Was Necessary

The kernel language had to be simple and efficient since it would form the basis for all the application-oriented languages. Further, it had to be application independent so that it would be useful for implementing extended languages in a wide variety of application areas. The most common choices for kernel languages were simple subsets of Algol-60 (with somewhat more general data structuring capabilities). Since, as opposed to PL/I, the goal was to have as small a kernel language as possible, the extensible language effort produced useful experience about the minimal facilities required in a usable language.

There Were Many Kinds of Extension

Extensible languages varied greatly in the forms of extension they provided. A form common to almost all these languages was *operator extension*, the ability to define new, application-oriented operators. For example, if a programmer wanted to use 'x # y' for the symmetric difference between two real numbers, a typical operator definition would be:

```
operator 2 x # y; value x, y; real x, y;
  begin
    return abs(x-y)
  end;
```

We can see that this is a lot like an Algol procedure declaration, except that the template 'x # y' is used in place of a procedure heading like 'dif (x, y)'. The '2' following **operator** indicates the precedence of the new operator; for instance, '1' might be the precedence of the relational operators (=, <, >, etc.), and '3' might be the precedence of the additive operators (+, −).

Other languages went much further by providing *syntax macros* that allowed the programmer to introduce new syntax into the programming language. For example, a summation notation might be defined:

```
real syntax sum from i = lb to ub of elem;
  value lb, ub;
  integer i, lb, ub; real elem;
  begin real s; s := 0;
    for i := lb step 1 until ub do
      s := s+elem;
    return s
  end;
```

In this case, the syntactic template replaces the usual heading, such as 'sum (i, lb, ub, elem)'. This definition allows the programmer to write statements such as

```
Total := sum from k=1 to N of Wages[k];
```

instead of the usual

```
Total := sum (k, 1, N, Wages[k]);
```

The intention was that programmers could use the notation common to their application areas.

Extensible Languages Are Usually Inefficient

Unfortunately, extensibility usually resulted in very inefficient languages. First, the necessity of handling a variable syntax made extensible compilers large and unreliable. Second, the fact that all source constructs were ultimately reduced to kernel language constructs meant that minor inefficiencies in the kernel implementation became magnified at the application language level. Part of this inefficiency is unavoidable since there is always a small overhead associated with the concatenation of kernel language constructs that might have been avoided by implementing the extended facilities directly.

Extensible Languages Have Poor Diagnostics

Another problem with extensible languages was their poor diagnostics. Since most of the error checking (for instance, checking for type compatibility) was done by the kernel language compiler, most diagnostics were issued in terms of kernel language constructs. This was, of course, confusing for a user working at the application language level.

These problems, and others, ultimately defeated extensible languages. Although they were once the most active area of programming language research, they are now rarely discussed. This does not imply that all of their ideas have been abandoned; we will see that the idea of extensible data types has been incorporated into Pascal and its successors and that a limited form of operator extension is provided by Ada (Chapters 7 and 8).

Wirth Designed a Successor to Algol-60

After the release of the Revised Report on Algol-60, the Algol committee continued to meet in order to develop a successor to Algol-60. Wirth and Hoare, in their article "A Contribution to the Development of Algol" (in the *Communications of the ACM*), had already suggested several modest but important improvements to Algol-60. In 1965 these ideas were presented to the Algol committee, which rejected them in favor of the larger, more subtle, excessively complex language now known as Algol-68.

The language that Wirth presented was implemented at Stanford University and became known as Algol-W. It was used as an instructional language at Stanford and several other universities for many years. In the meantime, Wirth had designed and implemented two other programming languages—Euler and PL360—which, like Algol-W, were characterized by their extreme simplicity.

A Competitor to FORTRAN Must Have Clear Advantages

The experience with first- and second-generation languages (such as FORTRAN and Algol-60) had led to the belief that useful languages with powerful facilities were inefficient at both compile-time and execution time. Further, there was the long-standing belief that different languages were needed for commercial and scientific programming, a belief that was reinforced by the failure of PL/I. Wirth knew that if a new language were to be a significant competitor to FORTRAN, it would have to have clear advantages, such as the ability to handle nonnumeric data, and at the same time maintain the compile-time and run-time efficiency of FORTRAN. Wirth saw that it was Algol's data types that limited its applications to scientific applications, so his approach was to start with Algol-60, eliminate the ill-conceived or expensive features, and expand the data structuring capabilities while maintaining its efficiency.

Pascal Combines Simplicity and Generality

The Pascal design had explicitly stated goals:

1. The language should be suitable for teaching programming in a systematic way.
2. The implementation of the language should be reliable and efficient, at compile-time and run-time, on available computers.

The development of Pascal began in 1968 and resulted in a compiler written entirely in Pascal in 1970. The Pascal Report's brevity, 29 pages, emulates the Algol-60 Report's 16 pages. The language was slightly revised in 1972 and became an international standard in 1982.[1] It has become very popular as a language for teaching programming and is widely used on microcomputers.

5.2 DESIGN: STRUCTURAL ORGANIZATION

Pascal's Syntax Is Algol-Like

Figure 5.1 displays a small Pascal program to compute the mean of the absolute value of an array. Notice that the general style of Pascal is very similar to Algol; it is an *Algol-like* language. In this chapter we will show all of the reserved sym-

1 See the International Organization for Standards' *Specification for Computer Programming Language Pascal,* ISO 7185-1982, 1982.

bols of Pascal in boldface. This will simplify distinguishing built-in and user-defined constructs. Unlike Algol's keywords, Pascal's reserved words are not typed differently from identifiers.

There Are New Name, Data, and Control Structures

Pascal includes important additions to Algol's name, data, and control-structuring mechanisms. We can see examples of variable declarations in Figure 5.1; they are introduced by the word **var** and have the syntax

<names> : <type>;

Procedure and function declarations are quite similar to Algol's, except that the **begin** comes after the local declarations rather than before them:

```
program AbsMean (input, output);
  const Max = 900;
  type index = 1..Max;
  var
    N: 0..Max;
    Data: array [index] of real;
    sum, avg, val: real;
    i: index;
begin
  sum := 0;
  readln(N);

  for i := 1 to N do
    begin
      readln (val);
      if val < 0 then Data[i] := -val
      else Data[i] := val
    end;

  for i := 1 to N do
    sum := sum + Data[i];

  avg := sum/N;
  writeln (avg)
end.
```

Figure 5.1 A Pascal Program

```
procedure <name> (<formals>);
  <declarations>
begin
  <statements>
end;
```

In addition to variable and procedure declarations, Pascal has constant and type bindings. We can see this in Figure 5.1; 'Max' is declared to be a constant equal to 900, and 'index' is declared to be the type of integers in the range 1 to Max. This new data type is then used in the declarations of the array 'Data' and the variable 'i'. Type declarations are introduced by the word **type** and have the syntax

```
<name> = <type>
```

In Section 5.3 we will see that Pascal has added a character data type for nonnumeric programming and a variety of data type constructors for arrays, records, sets, pointers, and so forth. Programmers can use these, in conjunction with type declarations, to design data types specifically suited to their applications.

Pascal's control structures incorporate many of the ideas of structured programming. Of course the **if-then-else** and **for**-loop (in a very simplified form) are provided. Pascal also provides leading and trailing decision loops and a **case**-statement for handling the breakdown of a problem into many cases. The **goto** is also provided.

5.3 DESIGN: DATA STRUCTURES

The Primitives Are Like Algol-60's

Recall that Algol-60 has three primitive data types: reals, integers, and Booleans. These, in turn, were very similar to the primitive data types provided by FORTRAN. This reflects the fact that both of these languages are predominantly *scientific* programming languages, and numbers and logical values are the most useful objects for scientific programming. Pascal extends its applicability to commercial and systems programming by providing one additional primitive data type, *characters.* A variable of type **char** (character) can hold exactly one character; longer strings of characters are manipulated as arrays of characters.

Enumeration Types

Often programs must manipulate nonnumeric data; this is usually character data, but it can also be more abstract. For example, a commercial data-processing program may need to be able to deal with days of the week. In a language like FORTRAN or Algol, these would usually be encoded as integers, say in the range 0–6. This coding can make a program very hard to read unless it is carefully commented:

```
today := 2;                comment Tuesday;
tomorrow := today + 1;     comment advance to next day;
```

There is always the danger that the programmer will write the wrong code (do we start from Sunday or Monday?) or that the reader will misinterpret the code. This is not very good.

One approach that can be used in most languages is to initialize meaningfully named variables to the proper values. In Algol we could write

```
begin integer today, tomorrow;
  integer Sun, Mon, Tue, Wed, Thu, Fri, Sat;
  Sun := 0; Mon := 1; Tue := 2; Wed := 3;
  Thu := 4; Fri := 5; Sat := 6;
    :
  today := Tue;
  tomorrow := today + 1;
```

This is certainly more readable and less error-prone to write. It still has problems, however.

The major problem is that 'today' and 'tomorrow' are just integer variables and, as far as the compiler is concerned, it is meaningful to treat them as integers. For example, all of these statements are legal, although they make no sense on days of the week:

```
today := 355;
tomorrow := -3;
today := (tomorrow - 100)/today + 5280;
```

This is a lack of *security;* the compiler is allowing us to write statements that have no meaning (in our application domain).

The situation is even worse since we may have other logically different types that are represented as integers:

```
begin integer gender, ThisMonth;
  integer Jan, Feb, Mar, ... , Dec;
  integer male, female;
  Jan := 0; Feb := 1; ... ; Dec := 11;
  male := 0; female := 1;
    :
  today := male;
  gender := (female + Thu)/Dec;
  ThisMonth := 15;
```

Of course, errors as blatant as these are not likely to occur, but they do illustrate the problem.

To eliminate this lack of security, Pascal provides *enumeration types.* This is a mechanism for constructing types by *enumerating*, or listing, all their possible values. For example, we can declare the types for months, days of the week, and sexes like this:

```
type
  month =   (Jan, Feb, Mar, Apr, May, Jun
             Jul, Aug, Sep, Oct, Nov, Dec);
  DayOfWeek = (Sun, Mon, Tue, Wed, Thu, Fri, Sat);
  sex = (male, female);
```

(Notice that an enumeration type declaration is a *binding construct* since it binds the enumerated names, 'Sun', 'Mon', etc., to the values of the type.)

After these type declarations, it is possible to declare variables of these types and use them as usual:

```
var
  today, tomorrow: DayOfWeek;
  ThisMonth: month;
  gender: sex;
begin
    :
  today := Tue;
  today := tomorrow;
  ThisMonth := Apr;
  gender := female;
```

Pascal also preserves security by preventing the programmer from performing meaningless operations on enumeration values. Remember that there are two parts to an *abstract data type*: the set of data values and the primitive operations on those data values. For an enumeration type, the set of data values is specified in the enumeration. The operations don't have to be specified because they are the same for all enumeration types:

:=, **succ**, **pred**, =, < >, <, >, <=, >=

The *ordering relations* (<, >, etc.) are defined according to the order specified in the declaration of the enumeration type; for example, Mon < Wed and Dec > Jan. The **succ** and **pred** functions give the succeeding and preceding elements in the list; for example, **succ**(Mon) = Tue and **pred**(Mar) = Feb. These operations are also *secure*; for example, **succ**(Sat) and **pred**(Jan) are errors.

The implementation of enumeration types is very efficient. The compiler does essentially what programmers would have to do if they didn't have enumeration types: It assigns consecutive integer codes to the values. There is an important difference (aside from security), however. When the programmer declares a variable of type DayOfWeek, the compiler knows that the only possible values are Sun, Mon, ... , Fri. Therefore, the only values that can be assigned to this variable are integers in the range 0–6, seven different values. Since seven values can be represented in 3 bits, the compiler can use 3 bits to represent a DayOfWeek variable rather than the 16 or 32 that are usually required for an integer:

```
Sun   Mon   Tue   Wed   Thu   Fri
000   001   010   011   100   101
```

Operations such as **succ** and **pred** and the relations are very efficient since these are just implemented as simple integer operations.

We can summarize the benefits of enumeration types:

1. They are *high level* and *application oriented*; they allow programmers to say what they mean.
2. They are *efficient* since they allow the compiler to economize on storage, and the operations can be performed quickly.
3. They are *secure* since the compiler ensures that programmers can't do meaningless operations.

EXERCISE 5-1: Write an enumeration type declaration for automobile manufacturers, such as might be used in an automobile registration database system.

Subrange Types

We have seen that the enumeration type improves *security* since the compiler can check if the programmer is doing something meaningless, such as asking for the successor of the last element in the enumeration. The Pascal *subrange type constructor* extends this checking to integers and allows tighter checking on other types. Suppose the variable DayOfMonth is going to hold the number representing a day of the month; the meaningful values of this variable are the numbers 1–31. Although this could be declared as an integer variable, our program will be more secure if we use a subrange type:

```
var DayOfMonth: 1 .. 31;
```

This means that DayOfMonth can hold values in the range 1–31 (inclusive).

If we attempt to assign to this variable a value outside this range, we will get an error. It has been observed that if a programmer consistently uses subranges, then many program errors will manifest themselves as subrange violations. It is usually easier to find the cause of a subrange violation than the cause of the more subtle errors that often result if the violation is not caught.

Subrange declarations also allow the compiler to economize on storage utilization. For example, since DayOfMonth can only take on 31 different values, it can be stored in 5 bits (since $2^5 = 32$) rather than the 16 or 32 bits required for integers. This could make a big difference if we had a large array of such values.

Subrange types can be based on types other than integers. For example, we can declare a type WeekDay whose only possible values are the days Monday through Friday:

```
type WeekDay = Mon .. Fri;
```

(Note that we are assuming the previous definition of 'DayOfWeek' so that the names 'Mon' and 'Fri' are defined.) Then, if we accidently assigned Sat or Sun to a variable of type WeekDay, we would get an error.

Pascal permits the programmer to define subranges of any *discrete type*, that is, enumeration types, integers, and characters. It does not permit defining a subrange of the real numbers, which is a *continuous type*.

EXERCISE 5-2: Write a subrange type declaration for the type 'age' representing the age of a child in school.

Set Types

Pascal provides the ability to manipulate small finite sets using the standard operations of set theory. As we will see, the set type is almost an ideal data type; it is high level and application oriented and yet very efficient. First, let's investigate its capabilities.

The description of a set type has the form

set of <ordinal type>

where a <ordinal type> is an enumeration type (including **char** and **Boolean**), a subrange type, or a name of one of these. These restrictions on the *base type* of set types allow its efficient implementation.

For an example, suppose we have two variables of a set type:

var S, T: **set of** 1 .. 10;

This says that each of S and T is a variable that can hold a set of the numbers from 1 to 10. If we had declared S and T by

var S, T: 1 .. 10;

then we would have said that S and T can each hold exactly one number in the range from 1 to 10. With the set declaration, S and T can each hold any group (including zero) of numbers in this range.

How do we get a set into these variables? In mathematics, if we want to say that S is the set containing the numbers 1, 2, 3, 5, 7, we write

$$S = \{1, 2, 3, 5, 7\}$$

In Pascal, if we want to assign this set to the variable S, we write

```
S := [1, 2, 3, 5, 7]
```

We can see that Pascal has followed mathematical notation closely, although limited character sets have forced some deviations.

The sets in Pascal can be manipulated just like mathematical sets. For example, if we have assigned

```
T := [1 .. 6]
```

then T contains the set [1, 2, 3, 4, 5, 6]. If we then form the intersection $S \cap T$ and store it in T by

```
T := S * T
```

the result will be that T contains [1, 2, 3, 5]. Notice that the product notation '*' is used instead of the usual set notation '$\cap$'. After the above operation is performed, T has the value [1, 2, 3, 5], which we can test with the equality relation:

```
if T = [1, 2, 3, 5] then ...
```

Similarly, the union (+) and difference (−) operations can be performed on sets.

If x is an integer in the proper range (1–10 in this case), then we can ask if x is in a set by writing 'x **in** S'. This is just the set theory '$x \in S$'. For example, '3 **in** S' is true, but '6 **in** S' is false. Another common relation between sets is the *subset* relation. We say that $S \subseteq T$ if every member of S is also a member of T. In Pascal this is written 'S < = T'. For example, if

```
S = [1, 2, 3, 5, 7], and
T = [1, 2, 3, 5]
```

then 'T < = S' returns **true**. The relational operators '=', '< >' (not equal), '< =', and '> =' are provided among sets. Inexplicably, the proper set inclusion operations '<' and '>' are *not* provided. However, they are easy to implement; for example, 'S < T' is equivalent to 'S < = T **and** S < > T'.

EXERCISE 5-3: Show that the preceding definition of proper set inclusion (<) is correct.

The set-type constructor is very high level; it allows the programmer to present algorithms in a natural notation. For example, suppose that we are writing a compiler; it is necessary to categorize the characters in the program we are reading. This can be done by defining sets of characters that reflect the different categories, as is shown in Figure 5.2. Once the sets 'digits', 'letters', and 'punctuation' have been defined, any character can be classified by testing to see which set it is in. To find out if 'ch' is alphanumeric, we just write

```
ch in letters + digits
```

since the alphanumeric characters are just the union of the letters and the digits.

One of the best characteristics of the set-type constructor is its efficiency. Consider our example, S, which is of type '**set of** 1 . . 10'. This means that there are 10 potential members of any set stored in S, the numbers 1–10. To know what set is stored in S, it is only necessary to know, for each of these 10 numbers, whether that number is or isn't in the set. This means that the set S can be represented by 10 bits, with each bit being one if the corresponding value is in the set and zero if it's not. For example, the set [1, 2, 3, 5, 7] is represented by the bits

S	=	1	1	1	0	1	0	1	0	0	0
		↑	↑	↑	↑	↑	↑	↑	↑	↑	↑
		1	2	3	4	5	6	7	8	9	10

This means that 1 is in the set, 2 is in, 3 is in, 4 isn't, 5 is, and so on. This is certainly a compact representation: We have represented a set containing up to 10 numbers in only 10 bits! Other sets require different size bit strings. For example, a '**set of** WeekDay' will only require 5 bits (since there are only five weekdays). If there are 256 characters in the character set, then a '**set of char**' will require 256 bits.

We have seen that sets are represented very compactly. How efficient are the set operations? It turns out that the set operations are simple to implement and very fast. Consider set intersection: We want an element to be in the intersection only if it is in both of the operand sets. In other words, we want the elements bit to be set in the result set only if it is set in both of the operand sets. This is just an 'and' operation on the bit strings. This example shows how doing a bit-by-bit 'and' between S and T gives the bits for '$S * T$':

S	=	1	1	1	0	1	0	1	0	0	0
T	=	1	1	1	1	1	1	0	0	0	0
$S*T$	=	1	1	1	0	1	0	0	0	0	0

You are probably aware that most computers have instructions for performing a

```
var digits, letters, punctuation: set of char;
    ch: char;
begin
    digits := ['0', '1', '2', '3', '4', '5', '6', '7', '8', '9'];
    letters := ['a', 'b', 'c', ... , 'z', 'A', 'B', ... , 'Z'];
    punctuation := ['(', ')', '.', ',', ';', ':', '!'];
      ⋮
    read(ch);
    if ch in letters then ... handle letters ...
    else if ch in digits then ... handle digits ...
    else if ch in punctuation then ... handle punctuation ...
    else ... handle illegal characters ...
      ⋮
end
```

Figure 5.2 Using Sets to Classify Characters

logical 'and' between bit strings; in fact, these are often the fastest operations a computer can do, faster even than integer arithmetic. Of course, if the set takes more bits than will fit in a word, then several 'and's may be required. For example, with a 32-bit word size, it will take eight (256/32) 'and's to intersect two sets of characters. This is still quite efficient.

The other set operations are also simple: Union is a logical 'or', complementation is a logical 'not', and equality and inequality tests are simple comparisons of the bit strings. Testing whether a given value is a member of the set, '*x* **in** *S*', reduces to determining if the bit corresponding to *x* is set. On most machines this can be accomplished by shifting this bit into the most significant position and doing a sign test. Again, this is very efficient. A subset test is performed by an 'and' and equality test since

$$S <= T \text{ if and only if } S = S * T$$

The other relations are implemented similarly.

In summary, the set-type constructor is almost ideal: It is very high level, very readable, and efficiently implemented. It also enhances security because it does all the normal type checking and it saves programmers from having to do their own error-prone bit manipulation.

EXERCISE 5-4: Write a type declaration for sets of days of the week.

EXERCISE 5-5: Write a test, using set operations, for determining if 'ch' is *not* alphanumeric.

Array Types

Algol-60 generalizes FORTRAN arrays in two respects: It allows any number of dimensions and it allows lower bounds other than one. We will see that Pascal has generalized Algol's arrays in some respects and has restricted them in others.

One of the generalizations is in the allowable *index types*. In FORTRAN and Algol, arrays could only be subscripted by integers; in Pascal they can be subscripted by many other types, including characters, enumeration types, and subranges of these. This is simple to understand. Suppose we declare an array A, holding 100 reals, indexed by the integers 1–100:

```
var A: array [1..100] of real;
```

Notice that the dimensions of the array have been specified as a *subrange* of the integers.

Now, suppose we wanted an array to record the number of hours worked on each of the days Monday through Friday. We could declare an array with the dimensions '1 . . 5', but we have already discussed the disadvantages of manually encoding things as integers. A better approach is to use a subrange of DayOfWeek as the index type:

```
var HoursWorked: array [Mon .. Fri] of 0 .. 24;
```

Think of this as a table whose entries are labeled with Mon, Tue, ... , Fri:

Mon	Hours
Tue	
Wed	
Thu	
Fri	

Notice that we have also made the *base type* of the array '0 . . 24' since we know that it is impossible to work fewer than zero or more than 24 hours in a day. This adds security to our program.

Arrays subscripted by noninteger index types can be used in the usual way. For example, to find the total number of hours worked in the week:

```
var day: Mon .. Fri;
    TotalHours: 0 .. 120;
begin
  TotalHours := 0;
  for day := Mon to Fri do
    TotalHours := TotalHours + HoursWorked[day];
```

Notice that it is not necessary to check the bounds of HoursWorked at run-time; since 'day' is of type 'Mon. .Fri' it *cannot* hold an illegal subscript value. This is one of the advantages of using subranges: Much checking can be done at compile-time rather than run-time.

Actually, any *finite discrete type* (i.e., any type that can be represented as a finite contiguous subset of the integers) can be used as an index type. For example, if we wanted to count the number of occurrences of different characters, we could declare

```
var Occur: array [char] of integer;
```

Then, 'Occur[ch] := Occur[ch] + 1' would increment the number of occurrences of the character in 'ch'. We could test if there are more 'e's than 't's by

```
if Occur['e'] > Occur['t'] then ....
```

Another way in which Pascal generalizes Algol arrays is in the allowable element types. In Algol the programmer is allowed to have arrays of reals, integers, or Booleans (since these are the only data types in the language). In Pascal any other type can be the *base type* of an array type. That is, we can have arrays of integers, reals, characters, enumeration types, subranges, records, pointers, and so forth.

In general, a Pascal array-type constructor has the form

```
array [ <index type> ] of <base type>
```

where <index type> is any finite discrete type and <base type> is any type at all. Thus, Pascal arrays can be considered *finite mappings* from the index type to the base type.

So far we have discussed only one-dimensional arrays. Doesn't Pascal allow multidimensional arrays? In fact, it doesn't, although the other generalizations of Pascal more than compensate for their absence. Suppose we need a 20 × 100 array of reals M; this can be considered a 20-element array, each of whose elements is a 100-element array of reals. That is,

```
var M: array [1 .. 20] of array [1 .. 100] of real;
```

As we said, the base type of an array can be any type, including another array type.

Subscripts can be combined to access any element of the matrix. For example, since 'M[3]' is the third row of M, 'M[3][5]' is the fifth element of the third row of M; in other words, $M_{3,5}$. Pascal allows the programmer to use more standard notation by providing 'M[i,j]' as *syntactic sugar* for 'M[i][j]'. Similarly, the declaration of M can be written

```
var M: array [1 .. 20, 1 .. 100] of real;
```

although it is still interpreted as an array of arrays. Thus, although the programmer has lost neither power nor convenience, the language and the compiler have been simplified because they only have to deal with one-dimensional arrays.

Problems with Array Bounds

There are two significant ways in which Pascal's arrays are more restrictive than Algol's. Recall that Algol has dynamic arrays: The bounds of the array are computed at scope entry time and can vary from one activation of the scope to another. This is not the case in Pascal; all arrays are static just as in FORTRAN. Why has this useful facility been deleted? One reason is that dynamic arrays are a little less efficient than static arrays, but this doesn't seem to be the primary reason. Rather, static arrays are implied by two fundamental design decisions in Pascal:

1. All types must be determinable at compile-time.
2. The dimensions are part of an array type.

The first decision is required in order to be able to do type checking at compile-time. The result is that all Pascal objects have *static types*; they cannot change at run-time. The second decision means that two array types are considered the same if their index types match and their base types match. This is usually reasonable; it doesn't make much sense to assign a 1..100 array of reals to a -20..20 array of reals. Notice, however, that these two decisions *interact* to imply static arrays: Since the dimensions are part of the type and the type must be static, the dimensions also must be static. In this case, the *feature interaction* is not too serious; we can live without dynamic arrays, particularly in a language intended for teaching. Next we will discuss a more serious example of feature interaction.

Consider these two Pascal[2] design decisions (we have already discussed the first):

1. The dimensions are part of an array type.
2. Pascal enforces strong typing; therefore, types of actuals must agree with types of formals.

Generally, *strong typing* says that in any context in which a thing is used, the type of that thing must agree with the type expected in that context. In particular, the types of actual parameters must agree with the types of the corresponding formal parameters. Since the dimensions of an array are part of its type, this means that the dimensions of an actual array parameter must agree with the dimensions of the corresponding formal array parameter. Let's look at an example.

```
type vector = array [1 .. 100] of real;

var U, V: vector;

function sum (x: vector): real;
   ...
begin ... end {sum};
```

2 We mean the Pascal of the Revised Report (Jensen & Wirth, 1973). Although the problem has been corrected in the ISO Standard, it is still a good illustration of feature interaction.

Given these definitions, it is perfectly legal to write 'sum (U)' and 'sum (V)' since the types of 'U' and 'V' match the type of 'x'. Suppose we have another array 'W', of length 75:

```
var W: array [1 .. 75] of real;
```

It is not legal to write 'sum (W)' because the types of 'W' and 'x' don't agree. If we want to sum the elements of 'W', we will have to write another sum procedure that works on 75-element arrays! In fact, our sum procedure won't even work on 100-element arrays whose index type is 0..99! We will have to write a separate 'sum' procedure for every different length array that appears in our program (and that we want to sum).

This situation is a terrible state of affairs; it is a gross violation of the Abstraction Principle. Furthermore, it makes Pascal almost unusable for programs that perform similar manipulations on a large number of different size arrays, such as scientific programs. It's impossible to write a general array manipulation procedure in Pascal. We can see that this results from the *interaction* of two design decisions that separately seem quite reasonable. Anticipating undesirable feature interactions is one of the most difficult aspects of language design.

We will see in Chapter 7 that Ada has eliminated this problem, as well as restored dynamic arrays, by changing the decision on which both restrictions are predicated: Dimensions are not considered part of an array type in Ada. The Pascal standardization efforts have solved the array parameter problem by defining a *conformant array schema* that can be used to specify a formal parameter. Thus, if we write the header for 'sum' as follows:

```
procedure sum (x: array [lwb .. upb: integer] of real): real;
```

then real array indexed by integers can be passed to 'sum'. The calls 'sum (U)', 'sum (V)', and 'sum (W)' are all legal. On each call of 'sum' the identifiers 'lwb' and 'upb' are bound to the lower and upper bounds, respectively, of the index type of the actual corresponding to 'x'. A typical use of these identifiers would in the limits of a **for**-loop:

```
for i := lwb to upb do
  total := total + x[i];
```

The syntax of a simple conformant array schema is:

```
array [<identifier> .. <identifier>: <type identifier>] of <type identifier>
```

Although conformant array schemas solve the array parameter problem, they do so at the expense of extra language complexity.

EXERCISE 5-6:* Discuss conformant array schemas as a solution to the array parameter problem. Do you think the right decision was made? Can you suggest an alternative?

EXERCISE 5-7:* Suppose strings are represented as arrays of characters. What problems would you face upon implementing a string manipulation package in Revised Report Pascal (i.e., Pascal without conformant array schemas)? Discuss possible solutions.

EXERCISE 5-8:* Write the procedure headers for a string manipulation package for ISO Standard Pascal (i.e., Pascal with conformant array schemas).

EXERCISE 5-9:* The ISO Pascal Standard defines two "levels of compliance." A compiler complies at level 1 if it implements all of the standard *except* conformant array schemas; it complies at level 1 if it implements all of the standard *including* conformant array schemas. Why do you suppose there are these two levels of compliance? Discuss the pros and cons.

Record Types

One of the most important data structure constructors provided by Pascal is the *record-type constructor.* This is a data structure that allows arbitrary groupings of data. The idea first appeared in commercial data-processing languages such as COBOL; in the mid-1960s Hoare suggested adding the facility to scientific languages. Records appeared in both Algol-W and several extensible languages.

A typical example of a record, a personnel record, appears in Figure 5.3. Just like an array, a record has a number of *components.* Unlike an array, however, the components of a record can be of different types, as we can see in the definition of 'person'. Notice also that the components of records can themselves be complex data types. For example, the 'name' component is a 'string', which is a 30-element array of characters. Hence, records can contain arrays. Also, the 'birthdate' and 'hiredate' components have the type 'date', which is itself a record with three components. Hence, records can contain other records.

The components of arrays are selected by subscripting. How are the components of records selected? Suppose we have declared 'newhire' to be a variable of type 'person':

```
var newhire: person;
```

A component of a record is selected by placing a period between the name of the record and the name of the component. For example, to set newhire's age and sex we can write:

```
newhire.age := 25;
newhire.sex := female;
```

If 'today' is a variable of type 'date', then newhire's hiredate can be set to today by

```
newhire.hiredate := today;
```

Notice that this is an assignment of one record variable to another. This is legal since the record name denotes the entire record, which can be assigned and compared for equality—like variables of any other types.

Selectors for records and arrays can be combined as needed to access a particular component. For example, since 'newhire.hiredate' is itself the name of a record, we can use the dot notation to select its components. To set the date of hire to June 1, we can write:

```
newhire.hiredate.mon := Jun;
newhire.hiredate.day := 1;
```

```
type person =
  record
    name: string;
    age: 16 .. 100;
    salary: 10000 .. 100000;
    sex: (male, female);
    birthdate: date;
    hiredate: date;
  end;

string = packed array [1 .. 30] of char;

date = record
    mon: month;
    day: 1 .. 31;
    year: 1900 .. 2000;
  end;

month = (Jan, Feb, Mar, Apr, May, Jun, Jul, Aug, Sep, Oct, Nov, Dec);
```

Figure 5.3 Example of a Record Type—A Personnel Record

Similarly, we can test whether the first character of newhire's name is an 'A' by

```
if newhire.name[1] = 'A' then ....
```

As another example, we can use an array to hold the personnel records of all our employees:

```
type employeeNum = 1000 .. 9999;

var employees: array [employeeNum] of person;
    EN: employeeNum;
```

If we now wish to know the year of birth of the employee with number 'EN', we can write

```
employees[EN].birthdate.year
```

Notice that '[EN].birthdate.year' essentially defines an *access path* to a particular component of the 'employees' data structure.

Observe that a record type is a *scope-defining* structure in Pascal; it groups the field names together. The field names are not visible outside of the record declaration unless a record is "opened up" with the dot operator.

If a number of successive statements reference fields of one record, such as

```
newhire.age := 25;
newhire.sex := female;
newhire.salary := 30000;
```

then Pascal permits this record to be opened once for all of them. This is accomplished by the **with**-statement:

```
with newhire do
  begin
    age := 25;
    sex := female;
    salary := 30000
  end;
```

This ability to *enter* another environment and make its names visible becomes very important in the fourth-generation languages discussed in Chapter 7.

You may have wondered why Pascal includes both arrays and records since they are both methods of grouping data together. They differ in two important respects. Arrays are *homogeneous* (homo = same; gene = kind), that is, all of the components of an array are the same type; records are *heterogeneous* (hetero = different), that is, their components do not have to be the same type (consider 'person'). In this sense records are more general than arrays.

The other difference between arrays and records is in their manner of selecting components. We can select specific array elements with expressions like 'A[1]', 'A[2]' just as we can select specific record components with expressions like 'R.mon', 'R.day'. The difference is that we can *compute* the selector to be used with arrays; that is, we can write 'A[*E*]' where *E* is an expression whose value will only be known at run-time. This is an important feature since it allows, for example, writing a loop that processes all the elements of an array. This can't be done with records; we can't write an expression like 'R.*E*', where *E* may refer to any of the fields 'mon', 'day', or 'year'. Why? Recall that it is a basic design decision of Pascal that all types can be checked at compile-time (i.e., that Pascal is *statically* typed). Since all of an array's elements are the same type, the compiler knows the type of 'A[*E*]' even if it doesn't know which element will be selected. This is not the case with records: 'R.*E*' has different types, depending on whether *E* is 'mon', 'day', or 'year'. The differences between arrays and records are summarized in the following table:

Composite Data Structures

	Element types	Selectors
Array	homogeneous (less general)	dynamic (more general)
Record	heterogeneous (more general)	static (less general)

EXERCISE 5-10: Define a record type 'automobile', including all auxiliary declarations, for an application such as an automobile registration database. Automobiles should have attributes such as manufacturer, model, year, value, owner, and so forth.

Next, we discuss another kind of record: *variant records.* To see their motivation, suppose that we are writing a program to keep track of all of the airplanes of an airline company. What data structure should we use? A record is the natural choice since each plane will have a number of different attributes and these will surely be of different types. What are some of these attributes? For all planes we will want to know the flight number and the type of aircraft. If a plane is in the air, then it will have an *altitude, heading, arrival time,* and *destination.* If it is landing or taking off, then it will have an *airport* and *runway number.* If it is parked at a gate at the terminal, then it will have an *airport, gate number,* and *departure time.* Possible type declarations are shown in Figure 5.4.

There are at least two problems with this approach. First, it is inefficient. A *plane* record will have to contain space for all of these fields, even though some of them can't be in use at the same time. For example, since a plane can't be in the air and parked at a gate at the same time, it can't have an altitude and a gate number at the same time. It would be helpful if, like Algol blocks, there were some way to declare disjoint subrecords that could not be in use at the same time.

There is also a potential *security* problem in this record definition. It allows us to perform meaningless operations, such as to ask the altitude of a plane whose status is 'onGround'. What we need is some way of grouping the different fields according to the status with which they are associated. This is the function of a *variant record.*

The situation with which we are faced is the following: Certain attributes are possessed by all planes, regardless of their status (i.e., flight number and kind of aircraft). Other attributes have meaning only when the plane is in a certain status. What we need is a record type with a *variant* for each possible situation in which a plane can be. Such a *variant record* is illustrated in Figure 5.5.

The status of a plane at a given time is indicated by the value of the *tag field*, 'status'. Since the status of a plane can be only one of '(inAir, onGround, atTerminal)' at a time, the fields in different variants can't be in use at the same time. This means that, just like disjoint blocks in Algol, they can share the same

```
type plane = record
  flight:       0 .. 999;               {flight number}
  kind:         (B727, B737, B747);
  status:       (inAir, onGround, atTerminal);
  altitude:     0 .. 100000;            {feet}
  heading:      0 .. 359;               {degrees}
  arrival:      time;
  destination:  airport;
  location:     airport;
  runway:       runwayNumber;
  parked:       airport;
  gate:         1 .. 100;               {gate number}
  departure:    time
end {plane};

time = packed record hrs: 00 .. 23; min: 00 .. 59 end;
airport = packed array [1 .. 3] of char;
runwayNumber = packed record dir: (N,E,S,W); num: 00 .. 99 end;
```

Figure 5.4 Record Without Variants

```
type plane = record
  flight:        0 .. 999;
  kind:          (B727, B737, B747);

  case status:   (inAir, onGround, atTerminal) of

  inAir: (
    altitude:    0 .. 100000;
    heading:     0 .. 359;
    arrival:     time;
    destination: airport );

  onGround: (
    location:    airport;
    runway:      runwayNumber );

  atTerminal: (
    parked:      airport;
    gate:        1 .. 100;
    departure:   time )

end {plane};
```

Figure 5.5 Type Declaration for Record with Variants

storage locations.[3] This solves the efficiency problem: Since only one of the variants can exist at a time, the compiler need only set aside storage for the largest variant. This is illustrated in Figure 5.6. In this case, the 'inAir' variant requires the most space.

Variant records also solve the *security* problem that we discussed. Since the *altitude* field only has meaning when the plane's status is 'inAir', the compiler can generate code to check that the tag field has the correct value before permitting a field reference.

Unfortunately, variant records introduce a loophole into Pascal's type system. Pascal does not require the programmer to initialize the fields of a variant after changing the value of the tag field.[4] The values found in these locations will be whatever was left there from the previous variant and may be of a different

3 The analogy with blocks extends further, since variant parts can contain variant parts. That is, variant parts, like blocks, can be nested.

4 This is in reality an uninitialized storage problem. Pascal, like most block-structured languages, does not require variables to be initialized when their scope is entered. Access to uninitialized variables may yield the values left from the block previously using the same area of storage.

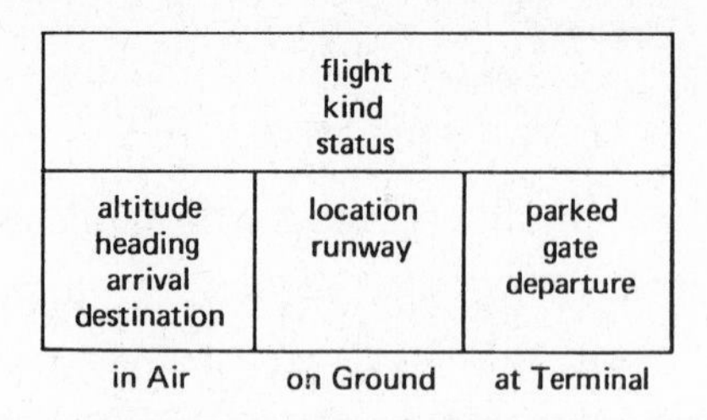

Figure 5.6 Memory Layout of a Variant Record

type. This has actually been used intentionally as a means of getting around the Pascal type system! We can see that the root cause of the problem is that variant records permit a form of *aliasing* since the fields in the different variants are aliases for the same memory locations. In Chapter 7 we will see the way that Ada has solved this problem.

Pointer Types

You are probably well aware of the value of linked lists, trees, graphs, and other linked data structures in many applications. These all make use of *pointers*, the ability to have one memory location contain the address of another location (or block of locations). For many years most programming languages did not provide any way for programmers to use pointers; programmers had to program in assembly language to make effective use of them. The reason is that the early high-level languages (e.g., FORTRAN and Algol) were designed for scientific programming, and linked structures were not often needed in this application area. Linked structures were most often needed in systems programming, which was almost always done in assembly language.

In the late 1960s and early 1970s, many programmers began to realize the advantages of doing *all* programming, including systems programming, in higher-level languages. This led to a demand for a pointer facility in these languages.

Some languages (e.g., PL/I) have satisfied this demand by introducing a single, new primitive type, called, for example, **pointer**. Here is an example using this feature (it's not in a real language):

```
var    p: pointer;
       x: integer;
begin
  new (p);
     :
```

```
  p↑ := 5;
     ⋮
  x := x + p↑;
     ⋮
end
```

This program allocates a memory location and puts its address in 'p', stores 5 in the memory location whose address is in 'p' (that is the meaning of 'p↑'), and then adds the contents of this location to 'x'.

Unfortunately, this approach is not compatible with *strong typing*. Consider this example:

```
var    p: pointer;
       x: real;
       c: char;
begin
  new (p);
  p↑ := 3.14159;
  c := p↑;
end
```

This stores a real number in the location pointed to by 'p' and then moves the contents of this location to the character variable 'c'. We have subverted the type system; we have managed to get a real number into a character variable by going through the (untyped) pointer 'p'. The problem is that the system has no way of knowing the type of the memory location whose pointer is in 'p'.

Although programmers do sometimes subvert the type system intentionally, this kind of error usually happens accidently. In programs that do a lot of pointer manipulation, it is not unusual for a programmer to think that a pointer points to something other than what it actually points to. This is the reason that Pascal provides *typed* pointers; these allow the compiler to enforce strong typing even when pointers are used. In Pascal a pointer is the address of an object of a particular type. Thus, there is not one pointer type but a constructor for creating many pointer types. This is written:

```
↑ <type name>
```

This is the type of all pointers to things of type <type name>. For instance, our previous example would be written this way in Pascal:

```
var    p: ↑real;
       x: real;
       c: char;
```

```
begin
  new(p);
  p↑ := 3.14159;
  c := p↑;          { Illegal! }
end
```

The assignment to 'c' is now illegal because: (1) The type of 'p' is pointer to **real**, (2) thus 'p↑' is the name of a **real** variable. (3) Since it violates strong typing to assign a **real** variable to a character variable, (4) it is thus illegal to assign 'p↑' to 'c'. Typed pointers eliminate the *possibility* of many of the bugs that plague programs in both assembly languages and high-level languages with untyped pointers.

The *base type* of a pointer type can be any other type, including records and arrays. This means that the pointer following operator (i.e., '↑') can form a part of an access path along with array and record selectors. For example, if we have declared

```
var p: ↑plane;
```

then we can access the first character of the airport at which the plane is parked by

```
p↑.parked[1]
```

The elements of records and arrays can be pointers, so almost any combination of pointer followers, array selectors, and record selectors can occur in an access path.

EXERCISE 5-11: Write an expression that returns the 'hrs' field of the departure time of the 'plane' recorded pointed to by 'p'.

Type Equivalence Was Not Clearly Specified

The Revised Pascal Report states that an expression can be assigned to a variable if the expression and variable have "identical type." Unfortunately, the report does not specify what it means for two types to be identical, and different implementers have interpreted this phrase in different ways. Although the ISO Pascal Standard clears up this ambiguity, it is instructive to consider the possible interpretations.

One such interpretation is called *structural equivalence*, because two types are considered equivalent if they have the same structure. Consider these two variable declarations:

```
var    x:   record id: integer; weight: real end;
       y:   record id: integer; weight: real end;
```

Is the assignment 'x := y' legal? The Structural Equivalence Rule says "yes" since the types associated with the two variables have the same structure (i.e., the same description). Next, consider these declarations:

```
type   person  = record id: integer; weight: real end;
       car     = record id: integer; weight: real end;

var    x: person;
       y: car;
```

The Structural Equivalence Rule would still allow 'x := y' since 'person' and 'car' are just two different names for what amounts to the same type. Structural equivalence can be defined as follows: Two objects are considered to have the same type if the *structural descriptions* of their types are the same (i.e., word for word).

This last example suggests the problem with structural equivalence: If programmers declare two types, called 'person' and 'car', then they probably intend them to represent different things, and it probably doesn't make any sense to assign one to the other. The fact that they happen to be defined by the same record structure may be a coincidence. This leads to another rule for type equivalence, called *name equivalence*. The Name Equivalence Rule says that two objects have the same type if the *names* of their types are the same. Therefore, in the last example, 'x := y' is illegal since the type of 'x' is 'person' and the type of 'y' is 'car', and these are two different names. What about the previous example?

```
var    x:   record id: integer; weight: real end;
       y:   record id: integer; weight: real end;
```

Different versions of the Name Equivalence Rule differ on whether 'x' and 'y' have the same type or not. One common interpretation says that they have different types since the compiler makes up different names for these *anonymous types*:

```
type   T00029 = record id: integer; weight: real end;
       T00030 = record id: integer; weight: real end;

var    x: T00029;
       y: T00030;
```

Name equivalence has some problems of its own. Consider this example:

```
type   age = 0 .. 150;
var    n: integer;
       a: age;
```

Is the assignment 'n := a' legal? Pure name equivalence says "no" since 'n' and 'a' have different **type** names (namely, 'integer' and 'age'). In this case the Revised Pascal Report explicitly allows this assignment since it says that two objects are considered to have the same type if the type of one is a subrange of the type of the other. This is an exception to the general Name Equivalence Rule and the programmer must remember this exception.

Which is better, structural equivalence or name equivalence? There has been a lot of debate on this among programming language designers. The general consensus seems to be that name equivalence is better. There are two reasons:

1. Name equivalence is generally safer since it is more restrictive. It is presumed that if programmers declare the type twice, then they probably have a reason for doing it—the two types probably represent different things. Therefore, considering these types different protects the *security* of the program (it prevents the programmer from doing something meaningless).
2. Name equivalence is simpler to implement; the compiler only has to compare the character strings representing the names of the types. For structural equivalence, it is necessary to write a recursive function that compares the data structures representing the types of the two objects. This also slows down the compiler.

It is for reasons such as these that the ISO Pascal Standard specifies that name equivalence be used, although it deviates from pure name equivalence in several ways. We will see in Chapter 7 that Ada has also adopted a modified form of name equivalence that attempts to provide the security of name equivalence with the flexibility of structural equivalence.

EXERCISE 5-12:* Can you think of any circumstances under which the Structural Equivalence Rule is preferable? Suppose you have a function that returned the sum of the elements of a '1 . . 100' array of reals. Wouldn't it be convenient if this function could be used on any such array type, no matter what it's called? Discuss.

5.4 DESIGN: NAME STRUCTURES

There Are Six Name-Binding Mechanisms

Pascal provides six kinds of primitive name structures, or methods of binding names to their meanings. They are

1. Constant bindings
2. Type bindings
3. Variable bindings
4. Procedure and function bindings
5. Implicit enumeration bindings
6. Label bindings

The fifth of these we discussed in Section 5.3, where we discussed enumeration types. There is little to say about label bindings, beyond the fact that all statement labels must be listed in the declaration part of the procedure containing the statement they label. The other binding mechanisms are discussed in this section.

Constants Aid Readability and Maintainability

Pascal includes the ability to name *constants* of discrete types (integers, enumerations, and characters). Constant declarations are introduced by the word **const** and have the syntax

```
<name> = <constant>;
```

What is the importance of constant declarations?

Consider a large program that manipulates arrays. In such a program, there will normally be many dependencies between the dimensions of these arrays and other parts of the program. For example, if the arrays have dimensions '[1 . . 100]', then there will normally be **for**-loops with bounds '1 **to** 100' or '100 **downto** 1'. Further, there may be other arrays that have dimensions '[1 . . 100]', '[0 . . 99]', and so forth, in order to be compatible with the first array. All of these interdependencies are *implicit*, although proper documentation can help to make them explicit.

Next, suppose that in the normal process of maintaining this program it is decided that the size of one of these arrays should be changed to '[1 . . 150]' (say, to accommodate larger data sets). This will imply that the dimensions of some of the other arrays also be changed and that the limits on some of the **for**-loops be changed. The programmer will have to find all numbers that *implicitly depend* on the changed dimension and make appropriate changes to these numbers. It is not as simple as using an editor to change all '100's to '150's since some '100's depend on the array's dimensions and some don't. Rather, each instance of '100' must be considered individually. This is a very error-prone and tedious process.

Pascal's constant declarations solve many of these problems since they allow implicit dependencies to be made explicit. They do this through the application of the Abstraction Principle since all the dependent constants are abstracted out of the program and are given a name. For example, given the declaration

```
const MaxData = 100;
```

the programmer can use the named constant 'MaxData' in all declarations, **for**-loops, and so on, that depend on this parameter. (Instances of '100' that do not depend on it would presumably have their own names.) Changing this parameter to 150 is then simple since only the constant declaration has to be changed; all other dependent changes are made automatically.

We must mention important limitations of Pascal's constant declarations: The constant cannot be described by an expression, and expressions cannot be used in variable and type declarations. For example, suppose that a dependent array 'A' had dimensions '[0..99]'; we should declare this as

```
var A: array [0 .. MaxData - 1] of real;
```

Unfortunately, this is not allowed since Pascal does not permit expressions (even constant expressions like 'MaxData − 1') to be used as array dimensions or subrange bounds. The best we can do is to declare two constants and document the dependency:

```
const  MaxData = 100;
       MaxDataMinus1 = 99; { = MaxData - 1 }

var    A: array [0 .. MaxDataMinus1] of real;
```

Some newer languages (e.g., Ada, Chapter 7) have eliminated this restriction.

The Constructor Is a Simplification of Algol's

There are two major name structure constructors in Pascal. One is the record-type constructor, which is discussed in Section 5.3. The other constructor is the procedure (or function), which is the major scope defining construct.

A procedure declaration has the form:

```
procedure <name> ( <formals> );
  <declarations>
begin
  <statements>
end;
```

This is very similar to the Algol procedure declaration:

```
procedure <name> ( <formals> ); <formal specifications>
begin
  <declarations>
  <statements>
end
```

We can see that the main difference is that the parts have been rearranged a little.

The scope rules of Algol and Pascal bindings are essentially the same. The scope of the <declarations> is the entire block, including all the <declarations> and the <statements>. The scope of the <formals> includes both the local <declarations> and the <statements> in the body of the procedure.

The ISO Pascal Standard places an additional restriction on the order of declarations to permit one-pass compilation. The scope of each of the <declarations> includes that declaration, all of the following declarations, and the <statements>. This means that names must be bound before (textually) they are used, whereas in Algol and Revised Report Pascal this is not the case. This restriction simplifies the compiler since it means that declarations can be processed in a single pass across the source. However, there are two problems.

First, structured programming methods encourage programmers to structure their programs in a *top-down* order. That is, the uppermost procedures are defined first, then the lower level ones that they call, and then the lower level ones that these call, and so on. This is *exactly the opposite* order from that required by ISO Standard Pascal, since it means that every procedure will be called before (textually) it is defined.

The second problem with this restriction is that mutually recursive procedures *cannot* be defined before they are called. For example, suppose that P calls Q and Q calls P. The following declarations are incorrect since Q is used before it's declared:

```
procedure P ( ... );
begin
    :
  Q ( ... );
```

```
      ⋮
end;

procedure Q ( ... );
begin
      ⋮
  P ( ... );
      ⋮
end;
```

To solve this problem, ISO Pascal provides a **forward** declaration, which gives the compiler the information it needs before the procedure is actually declared. For example,

```
procedure Q ( ... ); forward;

procedure P ( ... );
begin
      ⋮
  Q ( ... );
      ⋮
end;

procedure Q;
begin
      ⋮
  P ( ... );
      ⋮
end;
```

Most Pascal dialects (including the ISO Standard) require the declarations in a procedure or program to be in a particular order: labels, constants, types, variables, and subprograms:

```
procedure <name> (<formals>);
  <label declarations>
  <const declarations>
  <type declarations>
  <var declarations>
  <procedure and function declarations>
begin
  <statements>
end
```

This is not an unreasonable order for declarations to be in. As we can see in Figure 5.1, constant declarations are often used in succeeding type declarations; type declarations are used in succeeding variable declarations; and the variables are used in the subprograms. Requiring this order can be inconvenient in large programs, however, since it prevents the user from grouping together related constant, type, variable, and subprogram declarations. This problem is solved by the encapsulation mechanisms provided in fourth-generation languages (Chapter 7).

Pascal Eliminates the Block

Recall the distinction in Algol-60 between a *block* and a *compound statement*: A block contains local declarations and statements, whereas a compound statement contains only statements. Blocks facilitate the sharing of storage since arrays declared in disjoint blocks can occupy the same memory locations. This is not possible in Pascal since Pascal provides compound statements but no blocks. In Pascal, storage can be shared only between disjoint *procedures*. Although this simplifies Pascal's name structures, it complicates efficient use of memory.

EXERCISE 5-13: Recall the example on p. 119 of storage sharing in Algol-60. How would you program this in Pascal so that the arrays 'x' and 'M' share storage?

5.5 DESIGN: CONTROL STRUCTURES

Control Structures Reflect Structured Programming Ideas

Pascal has more control structures than Algol-60, although they are simpler than Algol-60's. As in Algol-60, the control-structure constructors route control among the basic computational primitives of the language: those operations that fetch, store, and operate on the values of variables.

In Chapter 3 (Section 3.5), we described how Algol's ability to nest control structures led to the ideas of structured programming. Pascal continues this development by providing several more structured control structures. Each of these is characterized by having one entry point from the previous statement and one exit point to the following statement. This is exemplified by Pascal's **if-then-else** statement, which is exactly like Algol's. This single entry–single exit property simplifies programs by satisfying the Structure Principle: The static structure of the program corresponds in a simple way to its dynamic structure.

Pascal does have a **goto**-statement, although the richness of the other control structures means it is rarely needed. As in Algol, nonlocal transfers are permitted.

Pascal, like almost all languages designed since Algol, has fully recursive procedures.

The for-Loop Is Very Austere

Recall the complexity of Algol's **for**-loop; it included stepping elements, **while**-conditions, and lists of arbitrary values. Furthermore, the expressions in the bounds were evaluated on every iteration, giving them the ability to change from one iteration to the next. This is exactly the kind of baroque, inefficient control structure that Pascal tries to avoid. As we will see, Pascal's **for**-loop is even simpler than FORTRAN's DO-loop!

The syntax for a Pascal **for**-loop is:

for <name> := <expression> { **to** / **downto** } <expression> **do** <statement>

The loop can step up by +1 increments or down by −1 increments, as indicated by the words **to** and **downto**; step sizes other than 1 are not allowed. Critics have maintained that this is carrying things too far because nonunit step sizes are very useful and don't add much to the complexity of the language. This is one case where Pascal may have overreacted to the complexity of the second-generation languages.

Pascal also specifies that the bounds of the loop are computed once, at loop entry, rather than on every iteration as is done in Algol. The result is that a Pascal **for**-loop always executes a definite number of times (provided, of course, the programmer does not jump out of it with a **goto**). For this reason the Pascal **for**-loop is both more efficient and easier to understand. It is an example of a *definite iterator,* that is, a structure that iterates a definite (predictable) number of times. We will see below that Pascal also provides indefinite iterators.

EXERCISE 5-14: Write a Pascal **for**-loop to sum into 'S' the elements of

```
var A: array [min .. max] of real;
```

EXERCISE 5-15:* Discuss Pascal's **for**-loop. Is it too simple? Should a variable step size be provided? Suggest a syntax and justify its inclusion. Should it be even simpler (e.g., not allow **downto**)? Justify this choice. Should it be eliminated altogether since **for**-loops can be implemented using the indefinite iterators?

EXERCISE 5-16:* The ISO Pascal Standard requires the controlled variable of a **for**-loop to be a *local variable* of the procedure or function containing the loop. Why have the language designers imposed this restriction? Discuss the trade-offs pro and con.

Leading- and Trailing-Decision Indefinite Iterators

Pascal provides two constructs for *indefinite iteration,* that is, for looping when the exact number of iterations is not known at loop entry. In these cases, a *condition* that's tested on each iteration determines whether or not the loop has completed.

In Chapter 2 (Section 2.3), we discussed two places in the loop where the decision can be placed—the beginning and the end of the loop. These two situations are handled by Pascal's **while**-loop and **repeat**-loop, respectively:

```
while <condition> do <statement>
repeat <statements> until <condition>
```

The **while**-loop is an example of a *leading-decision* iterator and the **repeat**-loop is an example of a *trailing-decision* iterator.

Although these two constructs handle most loops, there are other places the decision can be put. For example, a *mid-decision* iterator places the decision in the middle of the loop. For these Pascal must use a **goto**:

```
while true do
  begin
    ... first half of loop body ...
    if <done> then goto 99;
    ... second half of loop body ...
  end;
99:
```

Some newer languages (e.g., Ada, Chapter 8) have provided a mid-decision indefinite iterator.

EXERCISE 5-17: Suggest a situation in which a mid-decision loop would be useful. *Hint:* Recall the example of an Algol-60 **for-while** loop in Section 3.5.

EXERCISE 5-18:* Do you think Pascal should include a mid-decision loop? Discuss the relative merits of a **goto** and a mid-decision loop. Can the **goto** be eliminated if a mid-decision loop is included? Should it be eliminated? Can all of the indefinite iterators be handled by one loop statement? Suggest a possible syntax.

The case-Statement Is an Important Contribution

It is quite common in programming (and problem solving in general) to break a problem down into two or more subproblems. That is, a problem is often divided into several *cases* that are handled differently. For example, if we are processing 'plane' records (Section 5.3), then we may want to divide them into three cases, depending on whether their 'status' is 'inAir', 'onGround', or 'atTerminal'. This is handled by the Pascal **case**-statement.

Other languages also have mechanisms for handling cases; for example, FORTRAN provides the computed GOTO. If we want to do one group of statements (S_1) if I = 1, another (S_{23}) if I = 2 or 3, and a third (S_4) if I = 4, then we can write

```
      GOTO (100, 250, 250, 400), I
100   ... S1 ...
      GOTO 500
250   ... S23 ...
      GOTO 500
400   ... S4 ...
500   ... rest of program ...
```

This is quite efficient since the computed GOTO is compiled as a jump table; but it is not very readable since there is no way to tell from the GOTO where the labels are. They could be anywhere in the subprogram so the flow of control is not obvious. This violates the Structure Principle.

Several programming languages have attempted to provide more structured alternates to FORTRAN's computed GOTO and Algol's **switch**. These were patterned on the **if-then-else**, which breaks the problem into two cases depending on the condition. These constructs are called **case**-statements and usually look something like the following:

```
case <expression> of
  <statement>,
  <statement>,
        :
  <statement>
end case;
```

The meaning is as follows: If the value of <expression> is 1, the first <statement> is executed; if it's 2, the second is executed, and so forth. Like the **if-then-else**, the **case**-statement has a single entry from the preceding statement and a single exit to the following statement.

There are several problems with this construct. First, if there are many cases (and **case**-statements with 50 or 100 cases are not unusual), then it may be difficult for the reader to tell which statements correspond to which cases. Commenting on the statements with the case numbers helps, but there is still the problem of incorrect comments: programmers often change the code without bothering to change the comments.

Another problem is that this construct only works for cases that are indexed by integers beginning with 1. This kind of **case**-statement will not handle other data types, such as '(inAir, onGround, atTerminal)', as the basis for the case breakdown.

Another problem is that it is difficult to handle two or more cases with the same code. For our previous example, where both cases 2 and 3 were handled by the code S_{23}, we would have to write

```
case I of
  begin ... S1 ... end,
  begin ... S23 ... end,
  begin ... S23 ... end,
  begin ... S4 ... end
end case
```

Notice that we have repeated the statements S_{23} for each of the cases 2 and 3. This violates the Abstraction Principle and makes the program harder to read, harder to write, and harder to maintain. In particular, since it's not obvious that the code for cases 2 and 3 is the same, one might fix a bug in one without realizing that it also has to be fixed in the other. We could factor out the code S_{23} into a procedure P and call this procedure from each of cases 2 and 3, but this approach tends to clutter the program with procedures that are not very meaningful.

A solution to all of these problems can be found in Pascal's *labeled* **case**-*statement* designed by C. A. R. Hoare. Hoare has said that this is the most important of his many contributions to language design.

Like the unlabeled **case**-statement described above, the labeled **case**-statement contains one or more case clauses:

```
case <expression> of
  <case clause>;
  <case clause>;
        :
  <case clause>
end
```

Unlike in the unlabeled **case**-statement, however, each case clause begins with one or more constants that *label* that clause:

```
<constant>, <constant> , ... : <statement>
```

This solves the problem of handling cases 2 and 3 with the same code:

```
case I of
  1:    begin ... S1 ... end;
  2,3:  begin ... S23 ... end;
  4:    begin ... S4 ... end
end
```

Notice that this is more *secure* than the unlabeled **case**-statement; there is no possibility that the case label is incorrect as there was when they were just comments. The cases can even be out of order. The programmer can rest assured that the case labeled 1 will be executed when I is 1. Another way of looking at this is that the labeled **case**-statement is *self-documenting*; that is, it does not depend on the programmer properly documenting which case is which. The labeled **case**-statement illustrates the Labeling Principle.

> ***The Labeling Principle***
>
> Avoid arbitrary sequences more than a few items long; do not require the user to know the absolute position of an item in a list. Instead, associate a meaningful label with each item and allow the items to occur in any order.

The labeled **case**-statement is also more flexible than the unlabeled **case**-statement. In particular, values other than integers can be used to discriminate between the cases. Our 'plane' example can be written

```
case NextFlight.status of
  inAir:          ... handle plane in air ... ;
  onGround:       ... handle plane on runway ... ;
  atTerminal:     ... handle parked plane ...
end
```

This saves the programmer from the error-prone process of manually mapping plane 'status' into integers and provides clear documentation of the case breakdown.

The **case**-statement is also quite efficient. Since the compiler can determine the type of the case-selection expression, it knows the possible values that this expression can have. It can then construct a jump table of the appropriate size for the **case**-statements. Some compilers go even further and generate either a jump table, a hash table, a binary search of a sorted table, a sequential search of a linear table, or a series of **if**-tests, depending on the number of values, their range, and their clustering.

In summary, the labeled **case**-statement is just as efficient as the computed GOTO, but it is higher level, more secure, more readable, and more structured.

EXERCISE 5-19: Write a **case**-statement that assigns to a variable 'days' (of type '28 . . 31') the number of days in the month stored in 'ThisMonth' (of type 'month').

EXERCISE 5-20:* Consider at least three ways of implementing a **case**-statement (e.g., sequential test, jump table, and binary search). Assuming all the cases are equally likely, derive formulas for the average amount of time to execute a **case** given each of the implementation methods. State parameters by which a compiler could decide which implementation to use for any given **case**-statement.

EXERCISE 5-21:* Perform an analysis similar to that in the previous exercise, but compute the average amount of storage required for the **case**. Suggest ways of trading off space against time.

Parameters Are Passed by Value or Reference

The Revised Report on Pascal describes two parameter passing modes: pass by value and pass by reference. Pass by reference replaces the expensive and confusing *name* parameters of Algol-60 with the simpler mechanism provided by FORTRAN. The purpose of pass by reference is to allow a procedure to alter its actual parameters; in other words, reference parameters are output (or input-output) parameters. The problem with pass by reference in FORTRAN was that a procedure could alter actuals that it made no sense to alter, such as literal constants (see Chapter 2, Section 2.3). Pascal solves this problem since the programmer must specify in the procedure declaration whether a parameter is to be passed by value or reference. If a parameter is passed by reference, then the Pascal compiler will ensure that the corresponding actual is something that it is meaningful to store into, that is, a variable, array element, or record field. Therefore, in Pascal, reference parameters are *secure.*

Reference parameters are also *efficient* since only an address is passed, no matter how large the corresponding actual is. In contrast, name parameters are expensive since a *thunk* (Chapter 3, Section 3.5) must be invoked on each use of the parameter.

Pass by value in Pascal is exactly like pass by value in Algol; a copy of the actual parameter is made in a variable local to the procedure. This is intended for input parameters since it prevents modification of the actual. It has the same efficiency problems as Algol's pass by value since an array or other large data structure will have to be copied.

Pass as Constant Was Once Provided

The original Pascal Report did not specify pass by reference and *pass by value* as the parameter passing modes; rather, it specified pass by reference and *pass as constant.* Constant parameters are similar to value parameters in that they are intended for inputs, but they have an efficiency advantage that value parameters do not. We discuss this below.

A parameter passed by constant is considered a constant within the body of the procedure; therefore, it is not legal to use that parameter as the destination of an assignment. It is also illegal to use it in any other context where it is a destination, such as an actual parameter passed by reference. Thus, the compiler protects the security of constant parameters.

Since the compiler prevents a constant parameter from being altered, the compiler can either pass the value of the actual or pass its address, whichever is more efficient. For example, for small values, such as integers, characters, and elements of enumeration types, the compiler can copy the value of the actual parameter into local storage, as it would for pass by value. For large values, such as arrays and large records, the compiler can just pass the address of the actual. This saves the time and extra space required for a copy of the parameter with pass by value. There is no danger of the actual being inadvertently modified because the compiler prevents assignments to constant parameters. (In Chapter 8, Section 8.1, we analyze quantitatively the trade-offs between passing addresses or copies of parameters.)

We can see that constant parameters have the security advantages of value parameters and the efficiency advantages of reference parameters. So why were they eliminated from Pascal and replaced with value parameters in the Revised Report (and the ISO Standard)? One possibility is that the security is not airtight. Pascal permits limited forms of *aliasing*. For example, the same variable may be visible in two ways, as a nonlocal and as a parameter. Consider this program fragment

```
type vector = array [1 .. 100] of real;
var A: vector;

  procedure P (x: vector);
  begin
    writeln (x[1]);
    A[1] := 0;
    writeln (x[1])
  end;

begin
  P(A)
end.
```

Notice that within the procedure P the same area of storage has two names: 'x' and 'A'. Since 'x' is a constant parameter, the compiler may choose to pass the address of 'A' to P. Then, since the assignment to 'A' alters the value of the array, the two references to 'x[1]' may produce different values even though there is no assignment to 'x' between them.

Unfortunately, the alternative chosen—providing only value and reference parameters—encourages programmers to pass things by reference for the sake of efficiency, even though they have no intention of altering the actual from the procedure. This undermines the security of their programs and misleads the reader.

The problem is that two *orthogonal* issues are being confused: (1) the issue of whether a parameter is to be used for input or output and (2) the issue of whether to copy its value or pass the address of its value. Newer languages such as Ada (Chapter 8) have separated these decisions better by returning to a mode similar to constant parameters.

Procedural Parameters Are a Security Loophole

Pascal allows *procedural* and *functional* parameters, that is, procedures and functions passed as arguments to other procedures and functions; this restores some of the flexibility lost by omitting name parameters. For example, suppose we need to define the function 'difsq (f, x)', which computes $f(x^2) - f(-x^2)$ for any real function f and real number x. Thus,

$$\text{difsq}(\sin,\theta) = \sin(\theta^2) - \sin(-\theta^2)$$

In the Revised Report Pascal dialect, 'difsq' would be defined:

```
procedure difsq (function f: real; x: real): real;
  begin
    difsq  :=   f(x*x) - f(-x*x)
  end;
```

This seems straightforward enough.

Unfortunately, this method of specifying a functional parameter introduces a serious security loophole into Pascal. Notice that the procedure header for 'difsq' only specifies that 'f' is a **real** function; it says nothing about the number or types of the parameters of 'f'. This makes it almost impossible for the compiler to determine if a particular call of 'difsq' is legal or not (recall that 'difsq' could itself be passed to another procedure).

For this reason the ISO Pascal Standard requires the programmer to specify the arguments of a formal procedure parameter, for example,

```
procedure difsq (function f(y: real): real; x: real): real;
  begin .... end;
```

This allows the compiler to do complete type checking, thereby preserving Pascal's strong typing. The correct implementation of 'difsq' is shown in Figure 5.7.

```
var theta, phi: real;

function sin (x: real): real;
  begin .... end;

function exp (x: real): real;
  begin .... end;

function difsq (function f (y: real): real; x: real): real;
  begin
    difsq  :=  f(x*x) - f(-x*x)
  end;

begin
  readln (theta); readln (phi);
  writeln (difsq (sin, theta));
  writeln (difsq (exp, phi))
end.
```

Figure 5.7 Example of Function Passed as Parameter

There are several costs associated with the solution just discussed. One obvious cost is increased language complexity. A more subtle cost is the implication that procedures are first-class citizens. Since this solution allows procedure types to be used in formal parameter specifications, the user could also reasonably expect to use them in variable declarations. If this were allowed, then the language would have to define the meaning of procedure variables, arrays of procedures, procedure-valued functions, files of procedures, and so on. There are many complex language-design and implementation issues involved in these concepts (some of which are discussed in later chapters). On the other hand, if the language did not permit procedure types to be used in variable declarations, then procedure types would not be first-class citizens and the user would have to learn more exceptions. This also adds to the complexity of the language.

EXERCISE 5-22: Discuss the ISO Standard's way of providing secure procedural and functional parameters in Pascal. Defend the ISO solution to this problem or propose and defend your own solution.

5.6 EVALUATION AND EPILOG

Pascal Has Lived Up to Its Goals

Recall that Pascal's primary goal was to be a good language for *teaching* programming. This led to subsidiary goals of reliability, simplicity, and efficiency. Even in the face of some of the problems we have discussed, Pascal has been very successful in these areas. Many universities and colleges now teach Pascal as a first programming language. This use has been encouraged by the good Pascal implementations that exist on almost all computers, including microcomputers. The quality of these implementations must in part be attributed to the small size and careful design of the language.

Much of the criticism Pascal has received results from trying to use it for purposes for which it was not designed. For example, Pascal has been criticized for its lack of a separate compilation facility, even though such a facility is not especially important in teaching programming (the language's intended application). Indeed, it is to Pascal's credit that it has been so successfully applied in so many areas for which it was not intended.

Pascal Has Been Extended

Although Pascal was intended as a teaching language, many programmers have found that it is also suitable for "real" programming. Its strong typing simplifies debugging and helps catch latent errors in production programs; its rich set of efficient, high-level data types simplifies many nonnumerical programs; and its small size means that a programmer can acquire mastery of the language in a moderate amount of time.

These qualities have made Pascal an attractive vehicle for programming language research. Pascal has been extended for concurrent programming, to support verification, and for operating systems writing. Like Algol before it, Pascal has become a basis for almost all new language designs; most new languages are "Pascal-like." This includes the language Ada, which is the topic of Chapters 7 and 8.

Characteristics of Third-Generation Programming Languages

The third-generation languages, as typified by Pascal, show an emphasis on simplicity and efficiency, and more generally a reaction to the excesses of the second generation. We consider individually the domains of data, name, and control structure.[5]

The *data structures* of the third generation show a shift of emphasis from the machine to the application. This is clearest in the provision of user-defined data types, which permit programmers to create the data types needed for their applications. It is also exemplified by application-oriented type constructors, such as sets, subranges, and enumeration types. The third generation is also character-

5 The syntactic structures are essentially those of the second generation.

ized by the ability to nest data structures to any depth, that is, by the ability to organize data hierarchically.

The *name structures* of the third generation are generally some simplification of Algol-60 block structure. On the other hand, third-generation languages typically have new binding and scope-defining constructs, often associated with data type constructors, such as records and enumeration types.

Third-generation *control structures* are simplified, efficient versions of those found in the second generation. This is especially apparent in Pascal's **for**-loop, but it can also be seen in the rejection of name parameters and similar delayed-evaluation mechanisms. The third generation also has new control structures that are more application oriented, such as the **case**-statement.

In summary, the third generation combines practical engineering principles with the technical achievements of the second generation. The result, especially in the case of Pascal, is a simple, efficient, secure programming tool for many applications.

EXERCISES*

1**. Read about Euler (*Comm. ACM* 9, 1-2, 1966), Algol W (*Comm. ACM* 9, 6, 1966), and PL360 (*Jour. ACM* 15, 1, 1968). Trace the development of Wirth and Hoare's ideas from Algol-60, through Euler, Algol W, and PL360, to Pascal.

2**. Critique Wirth's new language, MODULA (*Softw. Prac. and Exper.* 7, 1977).

3**. Study the *Proceedings* of the 1969 and 1971 symposia on extensible languages (*SIGPLAN Notices* 4, 8, 1969 and *SIGPLAN Notices* 6, 12, 1971). Write a report surveying the entire field at this time, or pick out one or more particular languages and write a detailed critique of them.

4**. Read, summarize, and critique Wirth's article, "On the Design of Programming Languages" (*Inf. Proc.* 74, Amsterdam: North-Holland, 1975).

5**. Pascal does not have a formatted input-output system. Decide whether formatted input-output should be part of Pascal or be provided by a procedure library, and design a corresponding input-output system.

6. A deficiency of Pascal's input-output system is that it does not allow input-output of values that are elements of enumeration types. Identify the problem with input-output of these values and design an input-output system that accommodates enumerations.

7. Pascal does not allow constants to be defined by an expression, even if the value of that expression is constant (see Section 5.4). Discuss this restriction thoroughly. What would be the benefits of allowing expressions in constant declarations? What restrictions, if any, should be placed on the

allowable expressions? Are there other changes that could be made to the language to mitigate the absence of expressions in constant declarations?

8. All enumerations in Pascal are *ordered*. For example, with the enumeration declaration

```
type sex = (male, female);
```

we have male < female and **succ**(male) = female. These relationships really don't make any sense and the fact that Pascal permits them violates the Security Principle. One solution would be to add to Pascal another kind of enumeration type, an *unordered* enumeration. Discuss the trade-offs involved in deciding whether to add this feature to Pascal.

9. Suppose 'S' is a set variable. If we wanted to perform some operation on each element of 'S', we would like to be able to write a **for**-loop like this:

```
for x in S do ....
```

Unfortunately, this is not legal Pascal. Instead we have to write a loop over all the elements of the base type of 'S' and, for each element, test whether it is in 'S' and perform the operation if it is. That is,

```
for x := least to greatest do
  if x in S then ....
```

What set operations could be added to Pascal to solve this problem?

10. Derive the addressing equation for Pascal arrays.

11. Propose a solution to the security problem posed by variant records.

12. Show how a Pascal program would have to be structured so that two arrays share the same memory locations.

13. To write a **case**-statement that does one thing for digits and another for letters, we would have to write something like this:

```
case ch of
      '0',   '1',   '2',   '3',   '4',
      '5',   '6',   '7',   '8',   '9':   ... do digit case ...

      'a',   'b',   'c',   'd',   'e',
      'f',   'g',   'h',   'i',   'j',
      'k',   'l',   'm',   'n',   'o',
      'p',   'q',   'r',   's',   't',
      'u',   'v',   'w',   'x',   'y',
      'z':                                ... do letter case ...
end
```

Develop an extension to Pascal that avoids the error-prone and tedious process of listing all the digits and letters.

14. Some Pascal dialects permit an **otherwise** clause on **case**-statements. This clause is executed if the value of the case selector is not among the case labels. Write a BNF (or extended BNF) description of a **case**-statement with an **otherwise** clause.

6

IMPLEMENTATION OF BLOCK-STRUCTURED LANGUAGES

6.1 ACTIVATION RECORDS AND CONTEXT

Block-Structured Languages Required the Development of New Run-Time Techniques

We have seen in previous chapters that Algol and Pascal contain many features that prevent the use of the run-time structures that are used with FORTRAN. For example, since Algol and Pascal procedures can be recursive, there may be several instances of a procedure active at one time; hence, there must be some provision for the dynamic creation of activation records to hold the state of these instances. Therefore, the static "one activation record per procedure" techniques that we learned in Chapter 2 will not work. Also, we have seen that Pascal provides dynamic memory management by allocating space for the locals of a procedure on a stack. This storage is allocated on procedure entry and deallocated on procedure exit. This means that variables cannot be statically bound to memory locations as is common in FORTRAN and assembly languages. In this chapter we study in depth the implementation techniques required for Pascal since they are applicable to almost all modern languages.

An Activation Record Represents the State of a Procedure

Since the FORTRAN notion of an activation record is not adequate for block-structured languages like Algol and Pascal, it is worthwhile to reanalyze activation records by considering their purposes. Activation records record the state of an activation of a procedure. To know the state of a procedure activation, we need to know the following information:

1. The code, or algorithm, that makes up the body of the procedure
2. The place in that code where this activation of the procedure is now executing
3. The values of all of the variables visible to this activation

Since item 1, the code, does not vary between instances of execution of the procedure, it does not have to be part of the activation record; the other two items may vary between instances and so must be part of the activation record. The result is that we divide the representation of the state of a procedure into two parts:

1. A fixed *program* part
2. A variable *activation record* part

We will now analyze the parts of an activation record.

The Instruction Part Represents the Site of Control

In order to know the state of execution of a procedure, we must know both the current statement or expression and the context in which it is to be executed. The first of these is represented by the *ip* or *instruction part* (also, instruction pointer) of the activation record. Typically, this is just a pointer to the next instruction of the procedure to be executed; this is analogous to the IP of our interpreter and is usually contained in the IP register of the computer when the instance is executing.

The Environment Part Represents the Context

It is a familiar fact that the meanings of natural language sentences depend on their contexts. For example, the sentence "John shot a buck" means that John spent a dollar when interpreted in the context of John's trip to the store. Conversely, it means that he shot a male deer, when interpreted in the context of John's hunting trip.

The same is the case in programming languages. The FORTRAN statement

```
X = A(I)
```

denotes a subscripting operation in a context in which 'A' has been declared to be an array and a function invocation in a context in which 'A' has been declared to be a function. It is thus crucial that the interpreter (whether human or computer) interpret programming language constructs in the correct context.

What does this have to do with activation records? In Pascal, procedures are *scope defining* constructs; that is, the statements and expressions inside a procedure are interpreted in a different *context* from those outside. Therefore, to know the state of a procedure activation, it is not sufficient to know the statement it is currently executing; it is also necessary to know the context in which this statement must execute.

The context is defined by the *ep* or *environment part* (also, environment pointer) of an activation record. The result is that an activation record has these two parts:

1. The *ep* (environment part), which defines the context to be used for this activation of the procedure
2. The *ip* (instruction part), which designates the current instruction being (or to be) executed in this activation of the procedure

Activation Records Contain the Locals

The context of the statements contained in a procedure is simple: It is just the names declared in that procedure together with the names declared in the surrounding procedures. We must add the condition that if any name is declared in more than one of these procedures, then it is the innermost binding that is seen; This is the rule of the contour diagrams. We state this in a more procedural way: If we wish to look up a name, then we look to see if it is in the local environment. If it is, we take this binding; otherwise we look in the surrounding environment. This process continues, looking in outer and more outer surrounding environments until a binding for the name is found; if no binding is found, then the name is undeclared and the program is in error.

To implement recursive procedures and the dynamic storage allocation features of Algol and Pascal, we have seen (Section 3.3) that an activation record is used to hold the local variables and formal parameters of each procedure. These activation records are created and deleted when the corresponding procedures are entered and exited, thereby allocating and deallocating storage for the local variables. This provides immediate access to part of the context—the local variables—since they are stored directly in the activation record. The environment part of the activation record must also make some provision for gaining access to the nonlocal parts of the context. Thus, there are two components to the environment part:

1. The local context
2. The nonlocal context

Our analysis has yielded the following representation for procedure activations:

- I. Fixed program part
- II. Variable activation-record part
  - A. instruction part
  - B. environment part
    1. local context
    2. nonlocal context

We now develop one means for providing the nonlocal access.

A Static Link Points to the Outer Activation

Every variable is local to some procedure. Hence, every variable can be found in the activation record for some procedure. Therefore, to provide access to the nonlocal variables of a procedure, it is necessary to provide access to the activation records of the procedures to which these variables are local.

How can we provide access to the activation record for the surrounding procedure? The simplest approach is to keep a pointer to it, as we can see by looking at a contour diagram. Consider the program in Figure 6.1; the contour diagram shows the context when the procedures (a), (b), and (c) have all been entered. To look up a variable, such as N, we start in the current local context, indicated by EP (representing the processor), and begin looking outward through the contexts. Thus, we must provide a *link* from each contour to the surrounding one. Together these links form a *chain* leading from the currently active activation (containing EP) to the outermost (or global) activation. This link is called the *static* link (and the chain, the *static* chain), because it reflects the *static* structure of the program, that is, the way the procedures are nested. (Compare the *dynamic chain* discussed in Section 2.3.)

Figure 6.2 shows a typical implementation of the activation records of procedures. The state of execution is presumed to be inside of procedure (c). We can see that there is an activation record on the stack for each of procedures (a), (b), and (c) and that the static link points from each record to the one below it on the stack. Each activation record contains both an SL (static link) field containing the static link and space for the local variables (and other information not shown). The EP (environment pointer) register points to the activation record for the currently active context; we will call this the *current* activation record. The SP (stack pointer) register always points to the top of the stack. We call the IP-EP register pair the *locus of control*, because these two registers together define the instruction and context controlling the computer.

The formats we use for activation records here (or anywhere else in this book) are not sacred; the format chosen for a particular machine will often depend on the instruction set and other characteristics of that machine. For example, we have chosen to make the static links (including the EP register) point at the base of the activation records (specifically, at their static link fields); this

```
program a(...);
  var  N: integer;

  procedure b (sum: real);
    var  i: integer;
         avg: real;
         Data: array [1..10] of real;

    procedure c (val: real);
    begin
      :
        writeln (Data[i]);
      :
    end {c};

  begin
    :
  end {b};

begin
  :
end {a}.
```

Program

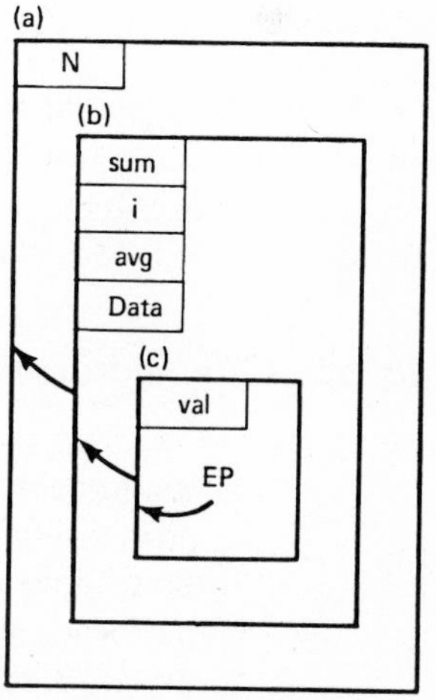

Dynamic structure

Figure 6.1 The State of a Program

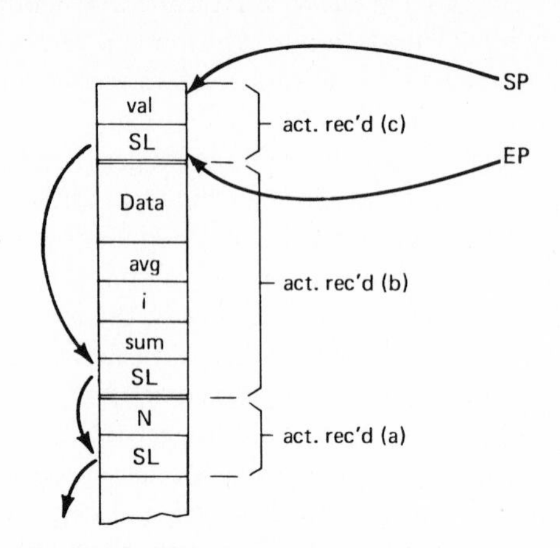

Figure 6.2 Activation Records for Procedures

makes it easy to chain from one activation record to another when accessing a variable (a process discussed below).

EXERCISE 6-1: Draw the stack and EP and SP registers when the assignment to 'val' is being executed in the program in Figure 6.14 (p. 253).

EXERCISE 6-2: Draw the stack and EP and SP registers just after the call 'Q(P)' is executed [i.e., before 'fp(5)' is executed] in the program skeleton in Figure 6.5 (p. 241).

Variables Are Addressed by Two Coordinates

It's probably apparent that it would be very inefficient to carry out this search process literally; it would require variable names to be looked up at run-time every time a variable is referenced. Thus, we must find some way to avoid this overhead. In Chapter 2 we saw that a FORTRAN compiler assigns fixed memory locations to each variable and then uses the addresses of these locations to access the variables at run-time. This binding of variables to locations is done by the compiler and is recorded in its *symbol table.* The symbol table is discarded at the end of the compilation process since all variable references have been replaced by absolute addresses. Here is an example of a FORTRAN symbol table.

Name	Type	Location
⋮	⋮	⋮
I	INTEGER	0245
J	INTEGER	0246
K	INTEGER	0247
⋮	⋮	⋮

Static binding will not work for Pascal since variables are allocated memory locations at run-time and since there may be several instances of the same variable in existence at the same time. To see how this can be implemented, look again at the contour diagram in Figure 6.1. The variable 'val' is local to the procedure (c), so it is contained in the currently active activation record; we don't have to follow the chain to get to it. The variable 'sum' is contained in procedure (b), which immediately surrounds (c); we have to follow the static chain a distance of one link to get to the activation record containing 'sum'. Finally, 'N' is declared in the procedure (a), so we have to follow the static chain a distance of two links to get to the activation record containing 'N'. Therefore, if we know the "distance" from the *use* of a variable to its *declaration,* then we can traverse that many links of the static chain to get to the environment of definition of the variable. Hence, we must investigate the determination of this distance.

It is clear that this distance depends on how deeply nested the use of the variable is within the procedure in which the variable is declared. That is, if the procedure of use is two levels deeper than the procedure of declaration, then the distance is two. Some terminology will help to clarify these ideas. We will call the number of levels of **procedure-end** containing a use or declaration of a name the *static nesting level* of that use or declaration. To put it another way, the static nesting level of a use or declaration of a name is the number of contour lines surrounding that use or declaration. For example, the static nesting level of the declaration of 'N' is one, of the declaration of 'sum' is two, and of the declaration of 'val' is three. The static nesting level of the use of 'Data' in procedure (c) is three.

The *static distance* between two constructs is the difference between their static nesting levels. For example, since the static nesting level of the use of 'Data' in procedure (c) is three and the static nesting level of the declaration of 'Data' is two, the static distance between this use of 'Data' and its declaration is one. We can see that the static distance between a use of a variable and its declaration tells us how many static links must be traversed to get to the activation record containing that variable.

It is quite easy for the compiler to keep track of this information: It must always know the static nesting level of the procedure it is compiling so it increments this number whenever it encounters a **procedure** and decrements it whenever it encounters a procedure **end**. Then, whenever the compiler processes a declaration, it must record in the symbol table entry for the declared variable the static nesting level (snl) of its declaration. For example, a symbol table for the program in Figure 6.1 might look like this (ignore the 'offset' field for now):

Name	Type	Snl	Offset
N	integer	1	1
sum	real	2	1
i	integer	2	2
avg	real	2	3
Data	real array	2	4
val	real	3	1

For any statement containing a variable, the difference between the static nesting level of that statement and the static nesting level given for that variable in the symbol table is the distance to the activation record containing the variable.

It is not sufficient to know the particular activation record in which a variable resides; it is also necessary to know its position within that activation record. This is the purpose of the *offset* field in the symbol table shown above; it gives the fixed offset, or distance, from the base of the activation record to the variable. Therefore, we can see that we are using a *two-coordinate* method of addressing variables: The first coordinate is the static nesting level of the variable's declaration, which allows us to get to the activation record in which the variable resides. The second coordinate is the 'offset', or position of the variable within that activation record. Notice that although the position of the activation record may vary at run-time, the position of the variable within that activation record is fixed. We will find that many objects in block-structured languages are addressed by these two coordinates:

1. An *environment pointer* (the static nesting level, in this case), which allows us to get to the activation record for the environment of definition of the object
2. A *relative offset* (the variable offset, in this case), which allows us to access the desired object within its activation record

EXERCISE 6-3: Compute the static nesting levels of all identifiers (i.e., variable and procedure names) in the programs in Figures 6.5 and 6.14. Compute the static nesting levels of each use of a name and the static distances between the uses and declarations of the names in these programs. Finally, compute the offsets of the variables in these programs.

Accessing a Variable Requires Two Steps

Since two coordinates are needed to locate a variable, it is natural that two steps are required to access a variable: (1) The activation record for the environment of definition must be located. (2) The variable must be located within this activation record. More specifically,

1. At run-time skip down the static chain the number of links given by the static distance to get to the activation record in which the variable resides. The static distance between the use and the declaration of the variable is a constant computed by the compiler.
2. The address of the variable is obtained by adding the fixed offset of the variable to the address obtained in step 1. This offset is also a constant computed by the compiler.

To see how this might actually be implemented on a computer, we will suppose the formats shown in Figure 6.2. Now, suppose that we wish to access a local variable, say 'val', from within procedure (c). Since it is local, the static distance to its activation record is zero so we don't have to follow the chain at all. Therefore, the address of 'val' is just EP + 1, where 1 is the fixed offset recorded in the symbol table entry for 'val'. The general case can be symbolized:

fetch M[EP + offset (v)]

where v is any local variable and 'offset (v)' is the constant offset recorded for v in the symbol table.

Next consider accessing 'sum', which is at a static distance of one. This means that one link of the static chain must be traversed to get the address of sum's activation record. We will hold this address in a temporary register AP (activation record pointer):

AP := M[EP];	traverse static link
fetch M[AP+1]	access the variable

since 1 is the offset of 'sum'.

Finally, let's consider the code to access 'N', which is at a static distance of two. In this case, two links of the static chain must be traversed:

AP := M[EP];	traverse first static link
AP := M[AP];	traverse second static link
fetch M[AP+1]	access the variable

since 1 is the offset of 'N'.

Let's summarize the steps to access a variable. If the variable is at a static distance of zero, then it can be accessed directly by 'M[EP + offset (v)]'. If it is at a static distance greater than zero ($sd > 0$), then the steps required are:

```
               AP := M[EP];                traverse first static link
(sd - 1) ×     AP := M[AP];                traverse remaining static links
               fetch M[AP+offset(v)]       access the variable
```

where sd is the static distance. The meaning of the second line above is $(sd - 1)$ duplicates of the instruction 'AP := M[AP]'. If $sd = 1$, this instruction is omitted and if $sd = 0$, the first two instructions are omitted and EP is used instead of AP.

We pause to analyze the performance of this method of accessing variables. Notice that each traversal of a static link requires one memory reference (ignoring any memory references required to decode the instructions themselves), so sd memory references are required to get to the activation record. An additional memory reference is required to read or write the variable once it is located so the total memory references required to access a variable by this method is $sd + 1$. (The exact count may vary from machine to machine.) Therefore, it can be quite expensive to access variables at a long static distance, although access to local variables is quite inexpensive. It has been observed that programs most frequently reference local variables and global variables (i.e., variables declared in the innermost and outermost procedures), therefore, in a deeply nested program, the average time to access a variable could become excessive. This is important because the time required to access the variables often dominates the running time of a program. Later in this chapter, we will discuss another way of implementing variable accesses that is better in this regard.

6.2 PROCEDURE CALL AND RETURN

Activation Records Represent the State of an Activation

In Chapter 2 (Section 2.3), we discussed the implementation of FORTRAN subprograms and we saw that the *state* of each subprogram was represented in an *activation record*, which held all of the information necessary to characterize the state of the computation in progress. This included the storage for the procedure's parameters, local variables, and temporaries; the resumption address of the subprogram; and a *dynamic link*, or pointer to the caller's activation record.

These activation records can be easily adapted to accommodate block-structured, recursive languages. Combining the needs of environmental access under block structure and recursive procedure call and return implies that a procedure activation record has these parts:

1. The *ep* (environment part), which defines the context to be used for this activation of the procedure and comprises the following:
   a. The *parameters* and *local variables*, which are the innermost (local) scope
   b. The *static link*, which provides access to the surrounding (nonlocal) scope
2. The *ip* (instruction part), which designates the current instruction being (or to be) executed in this activation of the procedure (essentially the *resumption address* of Chapter 2)
3. The *dynamic link*, which points to the activation record of the caller of this activation of this procedure (i.e., the *activator* of this activation) and allows us to restore the state of the caller upon procedure exit

Procedures Require Both Static and Dynamic Links

We have described above two links for a procedure—the static link and the dynamic link. Is it possible to combine these two links into one? Are they really the same thing? After all, they both point to activation records lower down on the stack. In fact, two separate links *are* required.

Recall that Algol and Pascal use *static scoping*; that is, a procedure executes in the environment of its definition rather than the environment of its caller (see Chapter 3, Section 3.3). The dynamic link field of a procedure's activation record, as we have described it in Chapter 2, points to the previous activation record on the stack, which is the activation record of the caller. Therefore, if we follow the dynamic chain, we won't get to the correct environment for the procedure; we will get the environment of the caller rather than the environment of definition.

Furthermore, the environment of definition is not at any fixed location down the dynamic chain. To see this, suppose that two procedures P and Q are defined in the same procedure B and that P calls itself recursively a number of times before it calls Q. When Q has been called, the stack looks like this (the arrows represent the dynamic chain):

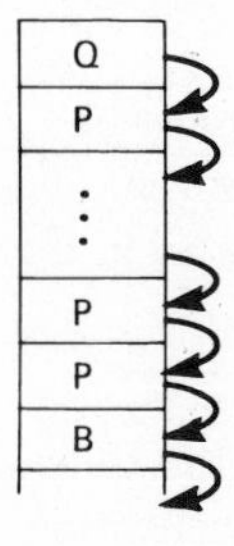

Notice that Q's environment of definition is B. There is no way that the compiler can know how many of P's activation records are between Q's and B's since this number depends on the dynamic behavior of P. In other words, there is no simple way that Q can get to its context, B, via the dynamic chain.

One straightforward solution to this problem is to provide an explicit pointer from Q to its environment of definition as illustrated below:

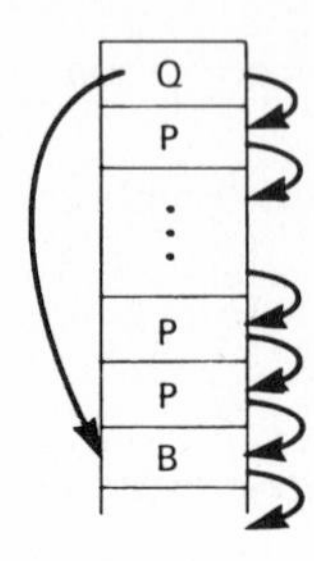

This pointer is the static link.

Procedure Activation Has Three Steps

In Chapter 2 (Section 2.3) we saw that four steps are required to invoke a FORTRAN subprogram:

1. Transmit the parameters to the callee.
2. Save the caller's state in the caller's activation record.
3. Establish the dynamic link from the callee to the caller.
4. Enter the callee at its first instruction.

These can be rearranged into the following basic functions that must be accomplished to activate a procedure:

1. The state of the caller must be saved (step 2 above).
2. An activation record for the callee must be created (steps 1 and 3 above).
3. The callee must be entered in the context of the new activation record (step 4 above).

That is, to *deactivate* the caller and *activate* the callee, it's necessary to (1) suspend the caller into its activation record, (2) initialize the callee's activation record, and (3) transfer the locus of control from the caller to the callee.

Saving the Caller's State

Let's consider the first of these steps, saving the state of the caller. The state of the caller has two major components—the instruction part *(ip)* and the environment part *(ep)*. The *ip* is the address at which the caller must resume execution after the callee exits so we must store this address in the IP part of the caller's activation record,[1] that is,

```
M[EP].IP := resume;          save resume location
```

The EP register always points to the activation record of the currently active procedure (i.e., the caller).

The second component of the caller's state is the environment part, which is in turn composed of the locals and the nonlocals. The access to the nonlocals is already saved in the static link of the caller's activation record so no further work is required on the nonlocals' account. The locals are contained in the caller's activation record so they are also safe.

Have we accounted for all of the caller's context? It would seem so since we've ensured that both the locals and the nonlocals are saved. Unfortunately, we've only taken care of the *programmer visible* environment; there are other variables, such as temporary locations and the machine's registers, that must really be considered part of the local context. After all, their contents affect the meaning of the machine code instructions in the procedure. We saw in the FORTRAN call sequence that a necessary step was saving these temporaries. Since the details are, of necessity, very machine dependent, we ignore saving and restoring the temporary locations and machine registers in the rest of this chapter.

Creating the Callee's Activation Record

The second of the steps in activating a procedure is to create a properly initialized activation record for the callee and to install this activation record as the new active context. What is required to accomplish this? We have seen that a procedure activation record has these parts:

- PAR parameters
- SL static link
- IP resumption address
- DL dynamic link

1 Note that there are IP and EP *registers*, which are related to, but not the same as, the IP and EP *fields* in the activation record.

Therefore, each of these parts must be properly initialized. Also, to install this activation record as the new active context, a pointer to the activation record must be placed in the EP register (which points to the beginning of the static chain, see Section 6.1).

Next, we will consider each of these steps in the order listed above, although they do not necessarily have to be performed in that order. In fact, the best order for the operations usually depends on the particular arrangement chosen for the activation record, which varies from machine to machine. There are a few *logical* dependencies among the above steps that we will note as they occur.

The Actuals Are Put in the Parameter Part

The parameter part of the activation record (PAR) contains the parameters to this activation: the parameter's value in the case of *value* parameters, its address in the case of *reference* parameters, and a pointer to a *thunk* (Chapter 3, Section 3.5) in the case of *name* parameters. Therefore, each actual parameter must be evaluated to yield either a value or an address, as appropriate, and this result must be stored in the appropriate place in PAR. Therefore, if 'callee' represents the address of the new activation record for the callee, then the parameter transmission process can be written:

```
M[callee].PAR[1]  :=  evaluation of parameter 1;
M[callee].PAR[2]  :=  evaluation of parameter 2;
                   ⋮
M[callee].PAR[n]  :=  evaluation of parameter n;
```

We will determine the value of 'callee' later.

Whenever we see that something is to be evaluated, as in the above code sequence, we must ask ourselves: "In what environment should this thing be evaluated"? Clearly, since the actual parameters are *written* in the context of the caller, they should also be *evaluated* in the context of the caller. This is the context that the programmer was assuming when the call was written, and we do not want to violate these assumptions. Since the parameters must be evaluated in the context of the caller, the parameter-part initialization must be done before the new activation record (callee) is installed as the new active context (i.e., before the EP register is altered). This is one of those constraints on the ordering of the steps that we mentioned above.

The Static Link Is Set to the Environment of Definition

The static link (SL) is the next part of a procedure activation record that must be initialized. By definition, the static link points to the *environment of definition* of the procedure. How do we get to this environment? We faced a similar problem in accessing a variable (Section 6.1) since it was necessary first to get to the *environment of definition* of the variable before its contents could be accessed. This was done by following (at run-time) the static chain for the number of links given by the *static distance* (computed at compile-time) between the use of the variable and its definition. This same technique works for procedures. At compile-time we must record in the symbol table entry for each procedure the static nesting level of that procedure's definition. Then, when a procedure call is being compiled, the compiler subtracts the static nesting level of the definition from the static nesting level of the call; this gives the static distance between the call and the definition and, hence, the distance down the static chain to the environment of definition.

We summarize the operations to initialize the static link in the following instructions. If the procedure is defined in the current context (i.e., the static distance from call to definition is zero), then this code suffices:

```
M[callee].SL := EP;          set the static link to this context
```

In this case the environment of definition is the environment of the caller.

If the distance from the call to the definition is $sd > 0$, then it is first necessary to traverse the static chain to get to the environment of definition:

```
            AP := M[EP];           traverse first static link
(sd - 1) × AP := M[AP];           traverse remaining static links
            M[callee].SL := AP;    set the static link
```

Notice the similarity between this and the code for accessing a nonlocal variable. This is so because the Pascal scope rules apply to both variables and procedures so the same process is required to get to the context in which either kind of name is defined.

The Final Steps Are Simple

Initializing the rest of the callee's activation record is very simple. First, consider the instruction part (IP): There is no reason to initialize this field now since it will only be used when (and if) the *callee* becomes caller by calling a procedure.

The dynamic link (DL) field is also simple to initialize; since it points to the activation record of the caller, which is contained in the EP register, the following code suffices:

```
M[callee].DL := EP;          set dynamic link
```

Clearly, this code must be executed before the EP register is altered to refer to the callee's activation record; this is another example of a constraint between the steps.

The next step is to install the callee's activation record as the new active context. Since the EP register always points to the activation record of the active context (the currently active procedure), this is accomplished by

```
EP :=           callee; install new AR
```

The final steps are to allocate space for the activation record on the stack and to enter the callee at its first instruction:

```
SP := SP + size(callee's AR);      allocate callee's AR
goto entry(callee);                enter the callee
```

Both the size of the callee's activation record and the address of the callee's entry point are constants known to the compiler.[2]

The last instruction in the above code sequence is in effect a store into the IP register. That is, '**goto** entry(callee)' is equivalent to 'IP := entry(callee)'. The transfer of the locus of control is effected by the assignments to IP and EP [i.e., 'EP := callee' and 'IP := entry(callee)'].

The steps to call a Pascal procedure are summarized in Figure 6.3. We have improved the code sequence slightly: Since the EP register has already been saved, we can scan down the static chain with *sd* repetitions of 'EP := M[EP]'. Also, since SP points to the next available stack location, it can be used as the base of the callee's activation record, so callee = SP.

EXERCISE 6-4: Draw the state of the stack and registers after each of the steps in Figure 6.3.

EXERCISE 6-5: The instruction sequence of Figure 6.3 is duplicated for every procedure call. If some of these instructions were made part of the code of the callee, they would not have to be duplicated over and over. Rearrange the code of Figure 6.3 to minimize the number of instructions that must be duplicated for each call.

We can estimate the number of memory references in a procedure call by looking at the code sequence in Figure 6.3. There is one reference to save the caller's IP, *sd* references to traverse the static chain, and two references to set the static and dynamic links. (We don't count the time to store the *n* parameters.)

2 This is true for Pascal. Some languages, such as Algol, have dynamic arrays, which means that the size of the activation records can vary at run-time. Compilers for these languages must produce code to compute the activation record size.

```
       M[SP].PAR[1] := eval. par. 1;
                 :                        transmit parameters
       M[SP].PAR[n] := eval. par. n;
       M[EP].IP := resume;                save resume location
       M[SP].DL := EP;                    set dynamic link
sd ×   EP := M[EP];                       scan down static chain
       M[SP].SL := EP;                    set static link
       EP := SP;                          install new AR
       SP := SP + size(callee's AR);      allocate callee's AR
       goto entry(callee);                enter the callee
resume:                                   resume location
```

Figure 6.3 Procedure Call Sequence with Static Chain

Thus, a call costs $sd + 3$ memory references. Notice that the cost of a call (like the cost of a variable access) depends heavily on the static distance to the procedure's declaration. Thus, it will be relatively expensive to call global procedures from inner procedures (a common situation). We investigate solutions to this later (Section 6.3).

Procedure Exit Reverses Procedure Entry

The code for returning from a procedure must reverse the effects of the call. That is, the locus of control must be transferred from the callee back to the caller. In other words, the callee must be *deactivated* and the caller *reactivated*. A return is generally simpler than a call since things are being thrown away rather than created. The two tasks that must be accomplished are:

1. Delete the callee's activation record.
2. Restore the state of the caller.

In practice these two steps must be interleaved since the information required to restore the caller's state (namely, the dynamic link) is in the callee's activation record.

Deleting the callee's activation record is accomplished by subtracting from the stack pointer the size of the callee's activation record:

```
SP := SP - size(callee's AR);            delete callee's AR
```

Reinstalling the caller's context as the active context is accomplished by loading the EP register from the dynamic link of the callee:

```
EP := M[EP].DL;     reactivate caller's AR
```

Since EP now points to the caller's activation record, we can use it to resume execution of the caller:

```
goto M[EP].IP;     resume execution
```

The **goto** is in effect 'IP := M[EP].IP', so these last two steps return the locus of control (EP-IP pair) to the caller. Figure 6.4 summarizes the code for returning from a procedure. This would be compiled either at the end of the procedure body of Pascal procedures, or for each **return**-statement for languages that have **return**-statements. Since memory must be referenced for the dynamic link and the IP field, a return requires two memory references.

EXERCISE 6-6: Draw the state of the stack and registers after each of the instructions in Figure 6.4.

Procedural Parameters Are Represented by Closures

Recall that Algol and Pascal (and many other languages) allow procedures and functions to be passed as parameters to other procedures. For an example of *procedural parameters,* see the program in Figure 6.5. In this case, we have a procedure Q that takes another procedure (corresponding to the formal parameter 'fp') as a parameter. We can see two calls on Q: one in which it is passed the procedure P and another in which it is passed T. There are two problems we must solve: (1) What exactly is it that is passed to Q to represent P or T? (2) How is the indirect call 'fp(5)' in the body of Q implemented?

We will consider the second question first since this will help us to answer the first question. Let's assume for a moment that a call on a formal procedure, such as 'fp(5)', is implemented like any other call, that is, with the code sequence in Figure 6.3. Does this work? The first three steps (transmitting the parameters, saving the resume location, and setting the dynamic link) are all fine. The next step, scanning down the static chain for the environment of definition, can't be

```
SP := SP − size(callee's AR);     delete callee's AR
EP := M[EP].DL;                   reactivate caller's AR
goto M[EP].IP;                    resume execution
```

Figure 6.4 Procedure Return with Static Chain

done, however. This is so because we need to know the static distance from the call to the environment of definition, which requires us to know the static nesting level of the environment of definition. For a normal procedure call this is simple to determine during compilation; it is recorded in the symbol table entry for the procedure. In a call on a formal procedure, such as 'fp(5)', we need to know the static nesting level of the corresponding actual procedure (P or T, in this example). Unfortunately, this can vary at run-time from one call of Q to another. In fact, T's environment of definition isn't even in the active static chain when it is called from Q by 'fp(5)'. Thus, we can see that part of the information that must be passed to Q is the environment of definition of the corresponding actual procedure.

EXERCISE 6-7: Explain why the activation record for T's environment of defi-

```
program A;

  procedure P (x: integer);
  begin
    :
  end {P};

  procedure Q (procedure fp (n: integer));
  begin
    fp(5);
  end {Q};

  procedure R;

    procedure T (x: integer);
    begin
      :
    end {T};

  begin
    Q(P);
    Q(T);
  end {R};

begin
  R;
end.
```

Figure 6.5 Example of Procedural Parameters

nition is not in the active static chain when it is invoked from Q by 'fp(5)'. Draw the stack and all the static and dynamic links at the time of call.

We can take a direct solution to this problem and represent a procedural actual parameter as a two-element record:

1. The *ip* (or *instruction pointer*) field contains the entry address of the actual procedure.
2. The *ep* (or *environment pointer*) field contains a pointer to the environment of definition of the actual procedure.

Such a record is called an *ep-ip pair,* or *closure.*

If 'fp' represents the location in an activation record of the closure passed for a procedural parameter, then 'fp.EP' is the *ep* part of this closure. (Note that 'fp' is a parameter that must be accessed like any other parameter, that is, by using the variable accessing method described in Section 6.1.) Hence, the static link in the callee's activation record can be set by

```
M[SP].SL := fp.EP;        set static link
```

This solves the problem of accessing the callee's environment of definition.

Consider again the code sequence in Figure 6.3. There is another problem. The second to the last step allocates space for the callee's activation record. This requires knowing the size of this activation record, which depends on the number of local variables declared in the corresponding actual procedure. One solution is to pass this information along with the closure; a simpler solution is to make this allocation instruction the first instruction of each procedure. At this point the compiler knows exactly how much space is needed.

The final step, entering the procedure, also requires access to the closure since different procedural actuals have different entry points. Thus the closure specifies the entry address of the argument procedure *(ip)* and the context in which it must execute *(ep).*

The resulting code sequence for calling a formal procedure is shown in Figure 6.6. Five memory references are required (including two for accessing the *ip* and *ep* of the procedure). Procedure exit must be the same as for normal procedures, Figure 6.4, since a procedure may be called both directly and as a parameter.

How is the closure (the *ep-ip* pair) for a procedural actual parameter constructed? The *ip* part is just the entry point to the procedure, which is a constant determined by the compiler. The *ep* part is the environment of definition of the procedure, which is accessed along the static chain using the static nesting level in the procedure's symbol table entry. For example, to construct the *ep-ip* pair for P in the call 'Q(P)', we must follow one link of the static chain. The

```
        M[SP].PAR[1] := eval. par. 1;
                  :                              transmit parameters
        M[SP].PAR[n] := eval. par. n;
        M[EP].IP := resume;                      save resume location
        M[SP].DL := EP;                          set dynamic link
        M[SP].SL := fp.EP;                       set static link
        EP := SP;                                install callee's AR
        goto fp.IP;                              enter the callee
resume:                                          resume location
```

Figure 6.6 Calling a Formal Procedure

code for constructing a closure in 'M[SP] .PAR[1]' is

```
M[SP].PAR[1].IP := entry(P);   build ip part
AP := M[EP].SL;                get environment of definition
M[SP].PAR[1].EP := AP;         build ep part
```

In general, if *sd* is the static distance between the declaration of a procedure P and a call that uses P as the *i*th actual parameter, then the code to build the *ep-ip* pair for this parameter is

```
            M[SP].PAR[i].IP := entry(P);   build ip part
            AP := M[EP].SL;                traverse first static link
(sd-1) ×    AP := M[AP].SL;                traverse remaining static links
            M[SP].PAR[i].EP := AP;         build ep part
```

Notice that $sd + 2$ memory references are required: *sd* to access the environment of definition and 2 to store the *ep* and *ip*.

Pascal, Algol, and many other languages allow procedures and functions to be passed as arguments to other procedures and functions. Considerations of regularity and symmetry may lead us to ask if procedures and functions can be returned as results from other procedures and functions. Allowing functions to accept and return other functions leads to a very powerful style of programming, called *functional programming,* which is discussed in Chapter 10. Unfortunately, most languages do not permit function-valued or procedure-valued functions. The reason is simple. Suppose a function F were to return a procedure P local to F. Observe that the environment of definition of P is that activation of F and that whenever P is called it must execute in that environment. Unfortunately, when F returns, its activation record is deleted from the stack, so the environment of definition of P is destroyed. To implement procedure-valued functions properly, it would be necessary to ensure that the activation record for F were retained so long as P (or any other procedure local to F) could be called. It is not possible to accomplish this with simple stacked activation records of the kind we have described. Functional programming languages must use a different discipline for the allocation and deallocation of activation records.

*EXERCISE 6-8**:* Describe a discipline for the allocation and deallocation of activation records that properly implements function-valued functions (and procedure-valued functions, etc.).

Nonlocal gotos Require Environment Restoration

One other construct found in Algol and Pascal (and most other block structured languages) must manipulate the run-time stack: the **goto**. Why is this? Local **goto**s (i.e., **goto**s to a label local to the block or procedure containing the **goto**) are easy; they are implemented as simple machine jumps. Nonlocal **goto**s (i.e., **goto**s to a label declared in a block or procedure surrounding the block or procedure containing the **goto**) must restore the environment to that of the label, otherwise the stack will not be in the state expected at the destination of the jump. That is, the EP and SP registers must be restored to the values appropriate to the environment of definition of the label. This is analogous to calling a procedure in its environment of definition. Consider the Pascal program in Figure 6.7; the stack and registers just prior to and after the '**goto** 1' are shown in Figure 6.8. We can summarize these observations by saying that a **goto** transfers the locus of control from the **goto** to the label. Both the site (IP) and context (EP) of execution must be altered.

Restoring the context at the destination of the **goto** requires restoring the EP and SP registers. How is this accomplished? Getting to the environment of definition of the label is just like getting to the environment of definition of a procedure: The symbol table entry for the label contains the static nesting level of its definition so the static distance to the environment can be computed at compile-time as the difference of the static nesting levels of the use and definition of the label. Thus, EP can be set (at run-time) to the context of the label by *sd* traversals of the static chain, where *sd* is the static distance between the **goto** and the definition of the label:

```
sd × EP := M[EP];          scan down static chain
    where sd = snl(goto) − snl(label)
```

and 'snl(x)' is the static nesting level of x.

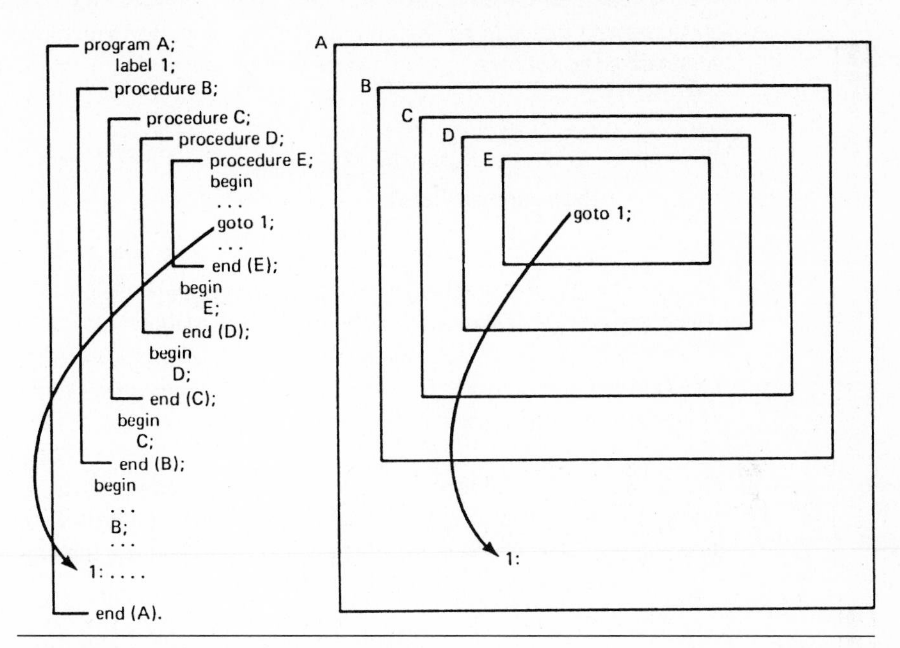

Figure 6.7 Example of a Nonlocal **goto**

The SP register points to the next available stack location above the current activation record, so it can be restored by

SP := SP + size (AR of the label);

The size of the activation record is known to the compiler or can be computed from information in the activation record.

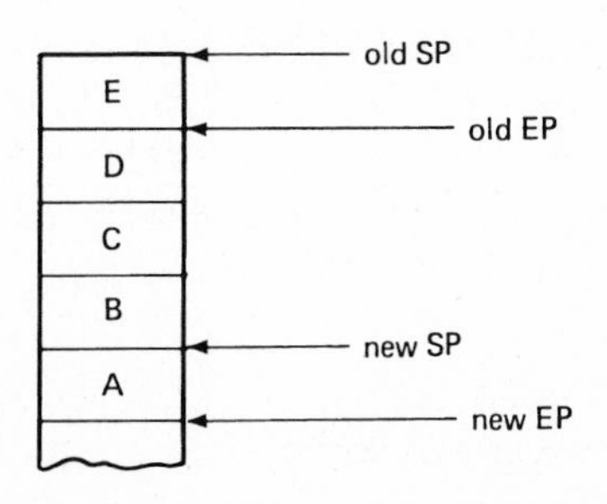

Figure 6.8 Stack and Registers Before and After Nonlocal **goto**

The last step is to transfer to the address corresponding to the label, which is a constant available to the compiler. The steps for a nonlocal **goto** can be summarized as follows:

```
sd  ×   EP := M[EP];
        SP := EP + size (AR of the label);
        goto address (label);
```

We can see that the number of memory references to do a nonlocal **goto** is *sd*, which is the static distance from the **goto** to the label.

EXERCISE 6-9: What is the static distance between '**goto** 1' and the definition of label '1' in the program in Figure 6.7?

EXERCISE 6-10: Some languages (e.g., Algol) allow labels to be passed as parameters to procedures; this is analogous to passing a procedure or function as a parameter. Describe in detail, including code sequences, the implementation of a label actual and a **goto** to a formal label.

Summary of Static Chain Implementation

The memory references required for *static chain* implementation for variables and procedures are summarized in Table 6.1. Do not take the actual numbers in this table too seriously; they may vary from machine to machine depending on the number of available registers, the instructions provided, and the exact format of the activation records. They are indicative of the costs, however, and will enable us to compare the static chain method to other implementation methods.

Table 6.1 Cost of Static Chain Implementation

Operation	Memory References
variable access	$sd+1$
procedure call	$sd+3$
procedure return	2
pass procedural actual	$sd+2$
formal procedure call	5
goto	sd

6.3 DISPLAY METHOD

Displays Allow Random Access to Contexts

We saw in the previous section that accessing a variable requires $sd + 1$ memory references, where *sd* is the static distance from the use of the variable to its declaration. This is fine for local variables but can become quite expensive for global variables in a deeply nested program. The problem results from the sequential organization of the static chain; every access to a nonlocal variable requires scanning down the static chain until its environment of definition is found. Performance could be improved if there were some way of getting *directly* to the environment of definition. This kind of direct access can be achieved by having an array (a *random access* data structure) that contains pointers to all of the accessible contexts. That is, if 'D' is the array, then 'D[*i*]' is a pointer to the activation record for the environment at static nesting level *i*. Such an array is called a *display*. Figure 6.9 shows a stack and its display. Notice that no EP register is required since the compiler knows the level at which each statement will execute. Therefore, if a statement is to execute at level *i*, it can find its activation record through 'D[*i*]'.

How does a display improve variable accesses? Recall that there are two steps in accessing a variable: (1) locating the activation record containing the variable and (2) locating the variable within its activation record. In the static chain implementation, the first step required skipping down the static chain. With the display the activation record is immediately accessible by 'D[*snl*]', where *snl* is the

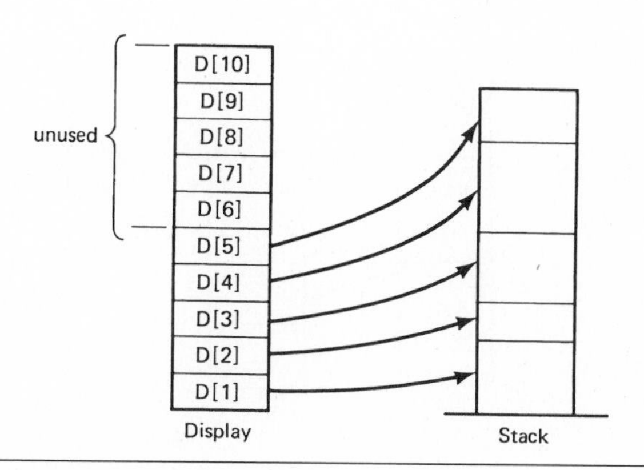

Figure 6.9 Example of a Display

static nesting level of the variable's declaration (recall that this is a constant computed by the compiler and stored in the symbol table entry for the variable). The second step is accomplished by adding the variable's *offset* to the base address given in the first step. Accessing a variable with coordinates (*snl, offset*) is accomplished by

fetch M [D[*snl*] + *offset*]

This requires two memory references: one to get the display entry and one to get the variable itself. In some implementations the display is stored in high-speed registers, which means that only one memory reference is required. In either case, the time required by the display method compares favorably with the $sd + 1$ memory references required by the static chain implementation.

EXERCISE 6-11: In the static chain implementation, access to a *local* variable requires one memory reference (because $sd = 0$). In the display implementation, access to any variable requires two memory references. Suggest a modification to the display implementation that accesses local variables in one memory reference.

Calls Require Saving the Display

Consider a call from static nesting level u to a procedure defined at static nesting level d. If the procedure's name is visible, then it must have been declared at the same or a lower static nesting level than that from which it is being called. In other words, $u \geqslant d$. The stack before and after the call is shown in Figure 6.10.

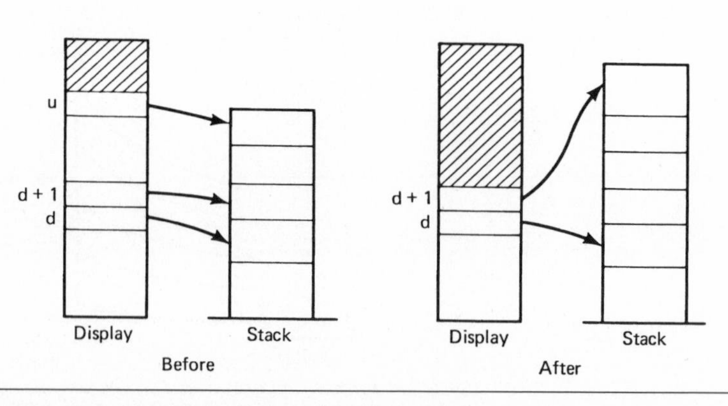

Figure 6.10 Example of Procedure Call with Display

Notice that if the call is from level u, then all of the display entries from D[1] to D[u] must be in use (i.e., contain pointers to activation records). Further, notice that if the environment of definition of the procedure is at level d, then the procedure itself is at level $d+1$, and the pointer to its own activation record must go in D[$d+1$]. This will destroy the previous contents of D[$d+1$], which was in use if $u>d$ (which is often the case). Therefore, the previous contents of D[$d+1$] must be saved. (It is not necessary to save the contents of D[$d+2$] through D[u] at this time; they will be saved if and when a call to the corresponding level takes place.)

To accomplish this we will set aside a field called 'EP' in a procedure activation record to hold the saved element of the display. The parts of an activation record for the display method are

- PAR parameters
- IP resumption address
- EP saved display element
- DL dynamic link

There is no SL (static link) field because the display has taken over its function.

We can get the code sequence for a procedure call with a display by taking the static chain version (Figure 6.3) and replacing the operation to set the static link with an instruction to save the display entry for the level of the callee. The resulting sequence is shown in Figure 6.11. Notice that the number of memory references required (omitting parameter initialization) is 6. This is often cheaper than the $sd+3$ references required in the static chain implementation.

```
        M[SP].PAR[1] := eval. par. 1;
                      ⋮                      transmit parameters
        M[SP].PAR[n] := eval. par. n;
        AP := D[u];                          get caller's AR
        M[AP].IP := resume;                  save resume location
        M[AP].EP := D[d+1];                  save display element
        M[SP].DL := AP;                      set dynamic link
        D[d+1] := SP;                        install new AR
        SP := SP + size (callee's AR);       allocate callee's AR
        goto entry (callee);                 enter the callee
resume:
```

Figure 6.11 Procedure Call Sequence for Displays

```
SP := SP − size (callee's AR);      deallocate callee's AR
AP := M[D[d+1]].DL;                 get caller's AR
D[d+1] := M[AP].EP;                 restore caller's display
goto M[AP].IP;                      resume execution of caller
```

Figure 6.12 Procedure Return with Display

Returning from a procedure just reverses the operations of a procedure call. The IP and the display element must be restored from the caller's activation record, and the callee's activation record must be deleted. The code sequence is shown in Figure 6.12. Notice that restoring the display drives up the cost: It requires five memory references to return with a display but only two with the static chain.

EXERCISE 6-12: Draw the state of the stack, display, and registers after each of the instructions in Figures 6.11 and 6.12.

EXERCISE 6-13: Describe the implementation of procedural parameters with the display method. As with the static chain method, it is necessary to make sure that the callee executes in the correct environment. Develop code sequences for passing procedures as actual parameters and for calling formal procedures (analogous to those in Section 6.2). Compute the memory references required for each of these operations.

*EXERCISE 6-14**:* (Difficult) Discuss the implementation of nonlocal **gotos** with the display method. How will you restore the display so that it correctly reflects the context of the label? Develop the code sequences and compute the number of memory references for a nonlocal **goto**. What conclusions can you draw?

Comparison of Static Chain and Display

Table 6.2 compares the number of references required by various operations using the static chain and display implementations. What conclusions can we draw? Notice that the display implementation accesses nonlocal variables much more efficiently than the static chain implementation. This was the motivation for the display method. On the other hand, the display implementation of procedures is a little *less* efficient than the static chain implementation. Whether the static chain or display implementation is better depends on the relative frequency (at run-time) of procedure calls and variables accesses and on the average static

Table 6.2 Comparison of Static Chain and Display

Operation	Static Chain	Display
local variable	1	2
nonlocal variable	$sd+1$	2
procedure call	$sd+3$	6
procedure return	2	5

distance to each of these. Since most programs do many more variable accesses than procedure invocations, the display is probably preferable.

The static chain and display methods are not the only possible implementation techniques for block-structured languages. In one other method, sometimes called *shallow binding*, each procedure is *statically* allocated one copy of its activation record (cf. FORTRAN activation records, Section 2.3). This static copy always holds the information and local variables for the most recent activation of that procedure. Since these activation records are stored at fixed locations in memory, variable access is always efficient. How is recursion implemented? Whenever a procedure is invoked, the contents of the static activation record area must be pushed onto a stack so that the activation record area can be used by the new activation. When the callee returns, the contents of the activation record will be restored from the stack. Hence, the major cost in the shallow binding method is the cost of saving and restoring these activation records on procedure call and return. Also, since the activation records are allocated statically, their size is fixed so shallow binding cannot be used for Algol and other languages with dynamic arrays.[3]

EXERCISE 6-15: Define and analyze the shallow binding method. Describe the code sequences for variable access, procedure call and return, and nonlocal **goto**s. Analyze the number of memory references required for all of these operations and compare them with the static chain and display methods. What conclusions do you draw?

EXERCISE 6-16:* Some computers have a number of high-speed registers capable of holding display elements. Usually there are not enough of these registers to hold the entire display. Discuss a strategy for making efficient use of the display registers. Show code sequences and estimate the number of memory references required for the various operations (call, return, etc.).

3 This is true so long as the arrays are allocated space in the activation record. If they are allocated space in a separate *heap*, then the activation records may be constant size.

6.4 BLOCKS

Blocks Are Degenerate Procedures

In Pascal, since the procedure is the only scope-defining construct, it is only construct that adds or deletes activation records to the stack. Other languages, including Algol and Ada (which is discussed in Chapters 7 and 8), have another scope-defining construct—the *block.*

Since activation records represent contexts and blocks define contexts, blocks will also have to have activation records. These activation records will have to be created when the block is *activated* (i.e., entered) and destroyed when the block is *deactivated* (i.e., exited). This automatic allocation and deallocation of activation records provide the automatic dynamic storage allocation discussed in Chapter 3 (Section 3.3).

How is block entry-exit implemented? We can solve the problem of implementation of blocks by reducing it to another problem that we have already solved—the implementation of procedures. There is a clear similarity: When a procedure is entered, an activation record is created, just as for a block; when a procedure is exited, its activation record is destroyed, just as for a block. Thus, we can think of entering and exiting a block as calling and returning from a procedure.

To see how this can be, consider the *Algol* program in Figure 6.13; it can be

```
begin
  integer N;
  N := 0;
  begin
    real sum, avg;
    sum := 0.0;
    ⋮
  end;
  N := 1;
  begin
    real val;
    val := 3.14159;
    ⋮
  end;
  N := 2;
end.
```

Figure 6.13 Algol Program with Blocks

translated into the *Pascal* program in Figure 6.14. (We have translated an Algol program into a Pascal program because Algol has blocks but Pascal doesn't and Pascal procedures have local storage but Algol's don't.) Notice that each block has been turned into a procedure that is invoked in exactly one place—where the corresponding block was nested. A perfectly correct implementation of blocks would be to translate them into procedures in exactly this way. We will see next that this is a little inefficient and that a number of improvements can be made by considering the particular characteristics of blocks.

Block Entry-Exit Is a Degenerate Call-Return

We derive the steps for block entry by considering the steps for procedure call (Figure 6.3) one by one. The crucial differences result from the fact that a block corresponds to a procedure that is called from exactly one place in the program. For example, we don't have to perform the first step, saving the resume location, since for a block it is always the same—the instruction immediately following the

```
procedure B1;
  var N: integer;

  procedure B2;
    var sum, avg: real;
  begin
    sum := 0.0;
    :
  end {B2};

  procedure B3;
    var val: real;
  begin
    val := 3.14159;
    :
  end {B3};

begin
  N := 0;
  B2;
  N := 1;
  B3;
  N := 2;
end.
```

Figure 6.14 Pascal Program with Procedures Instead of Blocks

end. Similarly, we don't have to evaluate the parameters because a block is equivalent to a parameterless procedure. Hence, the first step that's relevant to block entry is setting the dynamic link[4]:

```
M[SP].DL := EP;
```

The next step in a procedure call is to find the environment of execution for the procedure and to use this to initialize the static link. The environment of execution for Algol is always the environment of definition, and the environment of definition for a block is always the immediately surrounding block. That is, the static link of a block always points to the immediately surrounding block, which is contained in the EP register. Therefore, the static link of the new block is set by

```
M[SP].SL := EP;
```

Notice that the static and dynamic links are the same; more about this later.

The next steps in a procedure call install the new activation record and allocate its space on the stack. This is also required for a block:

```
EP := SP;
SP := SP + size(AR);
```

The final step of a call, jumping to the beginning of the procedure, is not required for a block since the first instruction of the block immediately follows the block entry code (i.e., the code for **begin**).

Block exit is patterned on procedure return (Figure 6.4). In this case, we omit jumping back to the resume location since this always immediately follows the **end** (i.e., is the next instruction following the exit code).

How can we improve these code sequences? Since the static and dynamic links are always the same for a block, there is no reason to have them both in a block activation record. Therefore, we will eliminate the dynamic link. The result is that a block activation record has a very simple structure:

- LV local variables
- IP resumption address
- SL static link

A resumption address (IP) is required because a block may call a procedure; hence we need a place to save its state of execution.

4 We begin with the static chain method since it is simpler than the display.

The **begin-end** sequence, the code for entering and exiting blocks, is summarized in Figure 6.15. Note that only two memory references are required for entry and exit combined.

Why is it that blocks require only one link but procedures require two? The *static link* leads to the *statically* prior context, and the *dynamic link* leads to the *dynamically* prior context. For a block, the statically and dynamically prior contexts are always the same; hence, only one link is required. To put it another way, a procedure may be activated in a context other than that in which it is defined; hence, we distinguish between the *environment of definition* and the *environment of call.* This *remote activation* potential of the procedure is made possible by the fact that a procedure has a name and hence may be activated anywhere that name is visible.[5] In contrast, a block has no name; it is *anonymous.* The result is that a block can be activated in only one context—the context in which it is textually nested. Therefore, for a block, the environment of definition and the environment of activation are the same—the immediately surrounding block (or procedure). Thus, to be perfectly precise, the link in a block's activation record should be called neither the static link nor the dynamic link for it is in fact both.

EXERCISE 6-17: Draw the state of the stack and registers after each of the steps in Figure 6.15.

EXERCISE 6-18:* Design an activation-record format for some computer with which you are familiar. Write out the instruction sequences for block entry-exit, procedure call-return, and variable access. Design the activation-record format to optimize these operations. Describe the different choices and trade-offs you have to make.

```
M[SP].SL := EP;              set static link
EP := SP;                    install inner AR
SP := SP + size (new AR);    allocate inner AR

          ⋮                  body of inner block

SP := SP − size (new AR);    deallocate inner AR
EP := M[EP].SL;              reinstall outer block
```

Figure 6.15 Block Entry-Exit with Static Chain

5 As we have seen, many languages, including Algol and Pascal, allow a procedure to be passed as a parameter to another procedure, which means that a procedure can even be activated from environments in which its name is not visible.

*EXERCISE 6-19**:* Investigate the call-return sequences used by some computer and language for which you can obtain the appropriate documentation. Relate the instructions and activation-record formats to the models discussed in this chapter. How are the basic functions (save state of caller, etc.) accomplished?

Blocks Require Display Updating

Block entry-exit is also quite simple in the display implementation. First, let's consider block entry. Figure 6.16 shows the display and stack before and after entry to a block at level *snl*. We can see that space for the block's activation record has been allocated on the top of the stack and that the display entry D[*snl*] has been set to point to this activation record. The previous contents of D[*snl*] must be saved in the block's activation record since it may contain a valid activation record pointer. Therefore, the code for block entry is

```
M[SP].EP := D[snl];          save display element
D[snl] := SP;                add inner AR to display
SP := SP + size(locals);     allocate space for inner AR
```

This requires three memory references (for display updating).

Block exit is even simpler: All that is required is to deallocate the block's activation record and restore the display:

```
SP := SP - size(locals);     deallocate inner AR
D[snl] := M[SP].EP;          restore display element
```

This requires two memory references for restoring the display.

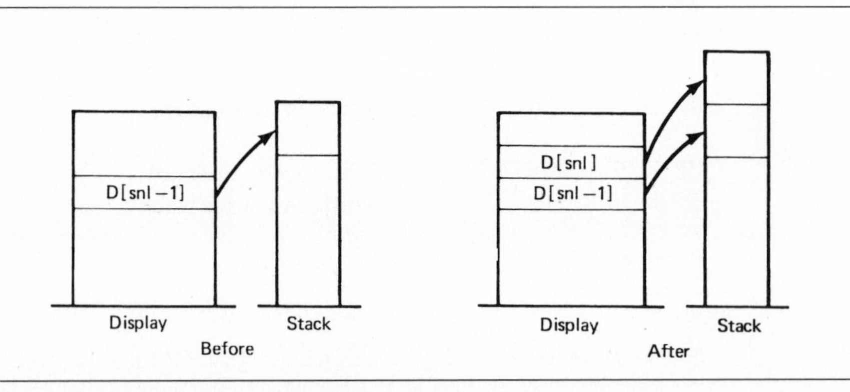

Figure 6.16 Block Entry with Display Method

EXERCISE 6-20:* Explain in detail why it is necessary to save and restore D[*snl*] during block entry-exit. Write in skeleton form a program that would not work correctly if this were not done.

6.5 SUMMARY

In this chapter we have seen one of the most important concepts in the implementation of programming languages—the idea of an activation record. It can be formally defined:

> ***The Activation Record***
>
> An activation record is an object holding all of the information relevant to one activation of an executable unit.

What is an "executable unit"? Most frequently it is a procedure, function, or program, although in later chapters we will see other examples, such as coroutines and tasks. Generally, it is a fragment of a program that includes some code and a name context. Executable units are capable of communicating with other executable units.

We have seen that in languages that provide recursive procedures there can be several *instances* of a procedure in existence at one time. One of these may be active and the others will all be suspended. Each of these instances, or *activations*, has a separate, private naming context (the local and nonlocal variables), although all of the instances of one procedure share the same code. This is so because the variables can be changed but the code cannot. The state of an activation can be completely specified by giving its naming context (the *ep*) and by specifying the place in the code where it is executing (the *ip*).

The state of execution of a computer is also specified by an *ep-ip* pair; this pair is called the *locus of control*. The locus of control specifies the current instruction being executed (the IP register) and the context of its execution (the EP register).

When a procedure is called, a new activation is created, which in turn requires the creation of a new activation record to hold the local context. In many languages (including Algol, Pascal, and Ada), when an activation returns (or exits by a nonlocal **goto**), its activation record is destroyed. This deallocation is possible since these languages do not permit reactivating a deactivated procedure or accessing the local context of a deactivated procedure. There are some languages that do allow these things, and in these the activation records must be preserved after the procedure returns. (This is called a *retention* strategy as opposed to a *deletion* strategy; see Berry, 1971.)

In the languages we have studied, at most one activation can be active at a time; the others are all suspended, awaiting reactivation. Some languages permit more than one activation to be active at a time, which is called *parallel* or *concurrent* programming. In these languages there may be several *loci of control,* one for each (real or virtual) processor. Ada (discussed in Chapters 7 and 8) is an example of such a language. Activations that can execute concurrently with each other are usually called *processes* or *tasks.*

Finally, we have seen that the use of activation records generally leads to a two-coordinate method of addressing things. For example, a variable is addressed by a pair comprising an environment pointer and a relative offset; the environment pointer provides an access path to the activation record containing the variable, and the relative offset locates the variable within that activation record. Similarly, when a procedure is passed as a parameter, it is a closure, an *ep-ip* pair, that is passed; the *ep* specifies the environment of definition of the procedure (an activation record), and the *ip* specifies the code to be executed. Since a thunk (Chapter 3) is essentially a procedural parameter, *name* parameters are also implemented by passing closures. Similarly, label parameters are implemented by *ep-ip* pairs; the *ep* specifies the context of the label, and the *ip* specifies the code to be executed.

In succeeding chapters we will see other language constructs that are implemented with activations records and two-coordinate addressing. Thus, these are important ideas that should be understood thoroughly.

EXERCISES*

1. Describe in detail the implementation of Algol's dynamic arrays. Estimate the number of memory references required to subscript a two-dimensional array and compare with the number of memory references required for a Pascal or FORTRAN array.
2. Describe in detail the implementation of flexible arrays, that is, arrays whose size can change while the array is in existence.

3**. Design a run-time organization that simplifies nonlocal **gotos**.

4**. Pick an existing computer and critique its support for block-structured languages. Suggest changes that would improve its support.

5. Estimate the number of memory references required for procedure call and return in FORTRAN. Compare this with the references required for Pascal procedures and discuss the costs and benefits of the two mechanisms.

6. Estimate the cost of variable accessing if variable names were looked up at run-time rather than being converted to static-distance/offset pairs at compile-time.
7. Describe a run-time organization for *dynamically* scoped block-structured languages. How can you avoid character string comparisons every time a variable is accessed?
8. It is often useful to allow procedures in block-structured languages to call FORTRAN subprograms and vice versa. Describe in detail the implementation of this capability. Discuss run-time organization, information needed by the compilers, required language extensions, and so forth.
9. Produce detailed code sequences for some existing computer for variable accessing and procedure call and return using the static chain method.
10. Do the same for the display method.
11. Do the same for the shallow binding method.

7

MODULARITY AND DATA ABSTRACTION: ADA

7.1 HISTORY AND MOTIVATION

The Software Crisis and Reliable Programming

In the 1970s the recognition of a "software crisis," that is, that the costs of producing software were increasing without bound, led a number of computer scientists to search for a solution. For example, Dijkstra and others observed that the difficulty of producing a program seemed to increase with the square of the program's length, so it seemed that very large programs would be completely infeasible. It thus became necessary to find a means of writing programs that would result in their cost being a *linear* function of their length.

Note: Ada is a registered trademark of the Ada Joint Program Office, U.S. Government.

Parnas's Principles

One of the traditional methods used to control the complexity of a large program was *modularization*, the division of a program into a number of independent *modules*. When this is done, each module is like a small program that can be implemented independently of the other modules. Therefore, the work to implement the entire program is roughly the sum of the work required for each module, that is, linear in the program size. Similarly, each module can be debugged, understood, and maintained individually.

In 1971 and 1972, D. L. Parnas, at Carnegie-Mellon University, developed several principles to guide the decomposition of a program into modules. One of his principles is that there should be one module for each difficult design decision in the program. This means that the results of each decision can be hidden in the corresponding module; if this decision is later changed, only that module has to be modified. This is called *information hiding* and is formalized in the principle already introduced in Chapter 2 (Section 2.5).

Abstract Data Types

A common design decision is the choice of data structure representation. For example, a stack can be represented as an array with a top index or as a linked list; a set can be represented as an array of values or a bit string. Since the choice of data structure representation is a difficult design decision, in a well-modularized program there will be one module for each data structure. Any manipulation of the data structure must then be done through the procedures provided by the module because the representation of the data structure is hidden in the module. To put it another way, users of the module are required to use the *abstract* operations on the data structure (e.g., push and pop for stacks) because they are prohibited from using the *concrete* operations (e.g., subscripting or pointer operations). It is for this reason that a module that provides a set of abstract operations on a data structure (or class of similar data structures) is called an *abstract data type.* This corresponds to our earlier definition of an abstract data type: a set of data values together with a set of operations on those data values. Specific means for designing abstract data types and modules are discussed later.

Experimental Abstract Type Languages

By 1973 a number of programming language researchers had designed languages supporting abstract data types and modules. These languages, which are called *abstract type languages,* include Alphard, CLU, Mesa, Euclid, MODULA, and Tartan. Many of them are based on the idea of a *class,* a construct first included in the language Simula in 1967. The experience gained from using these experimental languages was important in the later development of production abstract type languages, including Ada.

DoD Saw the Need for a New Language

In the mid-1970s the United States Department of Defense (DoD) identified the need for a state-of-the-art programming language to be used by all the military services in *embedded* (or *mission critical*) computer applications. These are applications in which a computer is embedded in and integrated with some larger system, for instance, a weapons system or a command, control, and communication system. At this time DoD was spending about $3 billion annually on software—most of it going for embedded systems. A significant factor in this high cost was limited portability and reuse of software resulting from the fact that over 400 programming languages and dialects were then in use for embedded applications. DoD recognized that its programming needs in the 1980s and 1990s would not be satisfied by the programming languages then in use, and in 1975 it set up the Higher-Order Language Working Group (HOLWG) to study the development of a single language for these applications. It was estimated in 1976 that such a language would save $12–24 billion over the next 17 years.

A Series of Specifications Was Published

In the period 1975 to 1979, HOLWG published a series of specifications that the new language was required to meet. Each specification was more detailed than the previous, as suggested by their names:

- 1975 Strawman
- 1975 Woodenman
- 1976 Tinman
- 1978 Ironman
- 1979 Steelman

Each specification made more specific or froze some of the requirements of the preceding specification.

Information Hiding, Verification, and Concurrency

The specifications placed some general requirements on the design of the language, such as readability and simplicity. More specifically, the specifications required a module facility to support information hiding, mechanisms to allow concurrent programming, and a design amenable to verification of program correctness. There were also many concrete requirements such as the character set and commenting conventions to be used.

There Were Several Competing Designs

In 1977 HOLWG studied 26 existing languages and concluded that none of these met the specifications. This led to a competitive language design effort that lasted from 1977 to 1979 and resulted in the 16 original proposals. Later evaluations resulted in the number being reduced to four, then two, and eventually one.

The Winner Is Named "Ada"

The winning language was designed by a CII-Honeywell-Bull team headed by Jean Ichbiah. In May 1979 HOLWG renamed this language "Ada" in honor of Augusta Ada, Countess of Lovelace, the daughter of the poet Lord Byron. Ada was a mathematician and Charles Babbage's (and, hence, the world's) first programmer. This continued a tradition of naming programming languages after mathematicians (e.g., Pascal, Euler, Euclid). In response to over 7000 comments and suggestions from language design experts in over 15 nations, Ada was revised and reached its final form in September 1980. It become a military and American National Standard in January 1983, and became mandatory for all mission critical (embedded) software in July 1984.

Subsets and Supersets Are Not Permitted

The goal of Ada is to decrease embedded computer software costs by increasing portability and reuse of software. It was clear to the Department of Defense that such a goal could not be achieved if there were a number of mutually incompatible subsets and supersets of Ada in use. Therefore, DoD has taken the unprecedented action of registering the name "Ada" as a trademark. This provides the ability to control the use of this name and to guarantee that anything called "Ada" is the standard language. That is, subsets and supersets of Ada cannot legally be called "Ada." How does DoD decide whether a compiler does in fact implement the Ada language? For this DoD has set up a validation procedure, comprising over 2500 tests, that attempts to ensure that a candidate compiler implements no more and no less than the standard language. Several dozen compilers have been validated so far. We will see later that prohibition of Ada subsets has been the cause of some controversy.

7.2 DESIGN: STRUCTURAL ORGANIZATION

Figure 7.1 displays a small Ada module. We can see that its syntax is quite similar to Pascal's. The convention in Ada programs is to type keywords in lowercase and all other words in uppercase. Ada's constructs can be divided into four categories:

1. Declarations
2. Expressions
3. Statements
4. Types

```
package TABLES is
  type TABLE is array (INTEGER range < >) of FLOAT;
  procedure BINSEARCH (T: TABLE; SOUGHT: FLOAT;
      out LOCATION: INTEGER; out FOUND: BOOLEAN) is
    subtype INDEX is INTEGER range T'FIRST..T'LAST;
    LOWER    : INDEX := T'FIRST;
    UPPER    : INDEX := T'LAST;
    MIDDLE   : INDEX := (T'FIRST + T'LAST)/2;
  begin
    loop
      if T(MIDDLE) = SOUGHT then
        LOCATION := MIDDLE;
        FOUND := TRUE;
        return;
      elsif UPPER < LOWER then
        FOUND := FALSE;
        return;
      elsif T(MIDDLE) > SOUGHT then UPPER := MIDDLE - 1;
      else LOWER := MIDDLE + 1;
      end if;
      MIDDLE := (LOWER + UPPER)/2;
    end loop;
  end BINSEARCH;
end TABLES;
```

Figure 7.1 An Ada Program

Expressions and statements are very similar to their counterparts in Pascal. Types are also similar except that they are more flexible and some of the problems of the Pascal type system have been corrected.

The most significant differences between Pascal and Ada appear in the declarations. The declarations in Ada can be classified:

1. Object
2. Type
3. Subprogram
4. Package
5. Task

The *object declarations* serve the same function as Pascal's constant and variable declarations. Subprogram declarations are similar to Pascal's function and procedure declarations although the name of the procedure is allowed to be one of Ada's built-in operators (+, −, =, >, etc.). This permits *overloading* of additional meanings onto these operators. In previous chapters we have seen that most languages overload the arithmetic operators. For example, '+' normally applies to both integers and reals. In Ada, users can extend this overloading so that '+' applies to their own data types, for example, complex numbers or matrices. We will see an example of this later.

Two of Ada's most important facilities are its *package* and its *task* declarations, both of which declare *modules*. Tasks are distinguished from packages in their ability to execute concurrently (in parallel) with other tasks. Modules (packages and tasks) are the basic components of which Ada programs are constructed.

Each module forms a disjoint environment that can communicate with other modules through well-defined *interfaces*. To accomplish this, the declaration of a module is broken down into two parts: a *specification*, which describes the interface to that module, and a *body* or *definition*, which describes how the module is implemented. Some of the other declarations can also be expressed in this two-part way. The specification of a package contains the specifications of the things (procedures, types, etc.) supplied by the package; the body of the package contains the bodies or definitions of these things. The purpose of this structure is to implement the information-hiding principles you read about earlier and that you will learn more about later in this chapter.

Ada is designed to permit a conventional compiled implementation. Typically, an Ada compiler would be divided into four subsystems:

1. Syntactic analyzer
2. Semantic analyzer
3. Optimizer
4. Code generator

The *syntactic analyzer* (parser) is conventional and only moderately more complicated than an analyzer for Pascal. Some interactive Ada systems replace the syntactic analyzer with a *syntax-directed editor,* which directly generates the parse tree to be used by the semantic analyzer. The *semantic analyzer* performs type checking, as in Pascal, and processes some of Ada's more complicated features, such as generic declarations and overloaded operators (discussed later). The complexity of these features makes Ada's semantic analyzer much larger and more complicated than Pascal's. The result of the semantic analyzer is a program tree that is passed to a conventional *optimizer* and *code generator.*

7.3 DESIGN: DATA STRUCTURES AND TYPING

The Numeric Types Are Generalized

Ada's integer types are essentially like those of Pascal, including the ability to use a *range constraint* to limit the set of permissible values; for example,

```
type COORDINATE is range -100..100;
```

Arithmetic on integers is *exact* and essentially the same as that in FORTRAN, Algol-60, and Pascal.

Ada goes far beyond Pascal's simple provision of a **real** data type: It provides two classes that provide approximate arithmetic on real numbers—the *floating-point types* and the *fixed-point types.* We will investigate the floating-point types first since they are the more conventional.

The declaration

```
type COEFFICIENT is digits 10 range -1.0e10 .. 1.0e10;
```

defines COEFFICIENT to be a floating-point type with at least 10 digits of precision and able to accommodate numbers in the specified range. If the target computer provides arithmetic of several different precisions (such as single and double precision), then the compiler can select the appropriate precision on the basis of the floating-point constraint.

Ada specifies that each implementation must provide a predefined type FLOAT that corresponds to the machine's usual precision. The types SHORT_FLOAT and LONG_FLOAT may also be predefined if they are supported by the implementation, although the use of these types compromises program portability. This also contradicts HOLWG's goal of having no dialects of

Ada.[1] Programmers are encouraged to use the floating-point constraint (i.e., the 'digits' specification) rather than these predefined types so that their programs will be more machine independent. By using a 'digits' specification such as the one above, programmers state the precision they *want* and leave it to the compiler to determine the machine representation that they *need*. This is impossible if programmers use machine-dependent types such as FLOAT and LONG_FLOAT. Unfortunately, programmers frequently do not know the precision they need; further, there is an unfortunate tendency for programmers to write the precision specification that they know will get them a particular representation on a particular implementation. This has been the experience in PL/I, where programmers write 'BINARY FIXED(31)', not because they want numbers of this precision, but because this will be represented as one 32-bit word on an IBM-360. This defeats the entire purpose of these machine-independent specifications.

Floating-point constraints illustrate the Preservation of Information Principle.

> ***The Preservation of Information Principle***
>
> The language should allow the representation of information that the user might know and that the compiler might need.

In other words, if users know their requirements at the more abstract level (number of digits required), they should not be required to state them at the more concrete level (number of words required) since this puts into the program machine-dependent design decisions that are better left to the compiler.

Arithmetic on floating-point numbers is conventional: Operations are effectively performed at the maximum available precision and then rounded to the precision of the operands.

Whereas the floating-point types provide approximate arithmetic with a relative error bound, the fixed-point types provide it with an absolute error bound. Fixed-point arithmetic had been the rule on early computers; it fell into disuse in scientific applications after the introduction of floating-point hardware (see Chapter 1). It is still used in languages for commercial programming (e.g., COBOL), where an absolute bound on the error is required (e.g., one cent). Fixed-point numbers have been included in Ada because they are used by many of the peripheral devices incorporated in embedded computer systems (e.g., analog-to-digital converters). Fixed-point types are specified using a *fixed-point constraint*, for example,

1 The same comments apply to Ada's "optional" types SHORT_INTEGER and LONG_INTEGER.

```
type DOLLARS is delta 0.01 range 0.00 .. 1_000_000.00;
```

The 'delta' specifies the absolute error bound; in this case, values of type DOLLARS will be exact multiples of 0.01. For instance, the number 16.75 would be stored as the binary equivalent of 1675 since $16.75 = 1675 \times 0.01$. The minimum number of bits required to store a fixed-point type is just the logarithm of the number of values to be represented, for example,

$$\log_2 [1+(1000000 - 0)/0.01] \approx \log_2 10^8 \approx 26.6$$

Therefore, 27 bits are required. Converting an integer value to a fixed-point value requires division by the 'delta' value; for example, 'DOLLARS(2.0)' will result in the binary representation of $2/0.01 = 200$. If the 'delta' is a power of 2, then it is a simple optimization to replace this operation by a left shift. For instance, if VOLT is defined

```
type VOLT is delta 0.125 range 0.0 .. 255.0;
```

then the conversion VOLT(20) is accomplished by a left shift of three (since $0.125 = 1/8$. For this reason, the Ada definition permits the compiler to choose an actual 'delta' that is less than the specified 'delta' but a power of 2 to make the conversion more efficient.

The arithmetic rules for fixed-point types are more complicated than those for integers and floating-point types. This is particularly true for multiplication and division. For instance, if VF is a variable of fixed-point type F and VI is an INTEGER variable, then 'VF*VI' and 'VI*VF' are both of type F and the assignment 'VF := VF*VI' is permitted. However, if VG is a variable of any fixed type (including F), then 'VF*VG' is considered to be of type "universal fixed," that is, a fixed-point number of maximum accuracy. It is then illegal to assign 'VF := VF*VG' because the types don't match. An explicit type conversion must be used–'VF := F (VF*VG)'. Division obeys similar rules. These unintuitive rules are an almost unavoidable consequence of fixed-point arithmetic.

EXERCISE 7-1:* Either design a better system of fixed-point arithmetic or show that all of the reasonable alternates are inferior to Ada's system.

EXERCISE 7-2:* We have seen that Ada provides three basic sorts of numbers. Some other languages, such as APL, LISP, and BASIC, provide only one kind (essentially equivalent to floating point) and use it for all purposes. Discuss the relative advantages and disadvantages of these two approaches.

Constructors Are Based on Pascal's

The data structure constructors of Pascal have been carried forward into Ada. These include enumerations, arrays, records, and pointers (called *access* types in Ada). All of these have been varied from the Pascal model in an attempt to eliminate some of their problems. For example, a frequent cause of errors in Pascal programs was changing the discriminant (tag) of a variant record without initializing the corresponding fields. As we saw in Chapter 5, this left a loophole in the Pascal type system. Ada solves this problem by stating that the discriminant can be changed only by assigning a complete record value to the record, that is, by assigning to all of its fields in one operation. In all other situations, the discriminant is treated like a constant. This ensures that the fields that correspond to the discriminant's value are always initialized.

EXERCISE 7-3:* Some languages (e.g., Algol-68) provide a *discriminated union* instead of variant records. A discriminated union type is defined by a declaration such as

```
type PERSON is union (MALE, FEMALE);
```

This means that objects of type PERSON may be either MALEs or FEMALEs, that is, that the set of data values subsumed by the type PERSON is the union of the values subsumed by the types MALE and FEMALE. It is called a *discriminated* union because the language uses a hidden *discriminant* (like Pascal's discriminant in a variant record) to tell whether a particular PERSON is a MALE or a FEMALE. This discriminant is automatically maintained by the system, therefore, it can never be wrong. Compare and contrast these two solutions to the same problem. Are there any security differences? How about readability and efficiency? Suggest how each could be improved or suggest a better alternative to both.

Name Equivalence Is Used

The Ada type system is stronger than Pascal's because of the consistent use of *name equivalence* (which was discussed in Chapter 5). Some of the inconveniences and awkwardness of name equivalence have been mollified through the use of two new concepts—*subtype* and *derived type*—that are discussed later. In its simplest terms' name equivalence states that two objects are taken to have the same type only if they are associated with the same type name. For example, in

```
type PERSON is record ID, AGE: INTEGER; end record;
type AUTO is record ID, AGE: INTEGER; end record;

X: PERSON;
Y: AUTO;
```

the variables X and Y are of different types because the associated type names, PERSON and AUTO, are different. The fact that the structural descriptions of these types are the same is irrelevant. This decision is based on the principle that if programmers restate the same type definition with a different name, it must be because they intend to use the types for different things (as is obvious in this case).

Ada extends the use of name equivalence to types that do not have a name, for instance,

```
X: record ID, AGE: INTEGER; end record;
Y: record ID, AGE: INTEGER; end record;
```

Again, X and Y have different types. The easiest way to understand this is to imagine that the compiler invented names for these two types (such as PERSON and AUTO) and substituted them in the declarations of X and Y. We can see that one effect of name equivalence is to encourage programmers to name their types.

Name equivalence has been used in Ada for a number of reasons. One is the presumption mentioned above that if programmers repeat a type definition, they probably did it because the types are logically different. A second reason is that the alternative, *structural equivalence*, is not well defined. For example, in comparing two record types, is the order of the fields significant? Consider the following:

```
type R is record X: FLOAT; N: INTEGER; end record;
type S is record N: INTEGER; X: FLOAT; end record;
```

Can a variable of type R be assigned to a variable of type S? There are also other questions that must be answered: Are the names of the fields significant? For example, are these compatible types?

```
type R is record X: FLOAT; N: INTEGER; end record;
type S is record A: FLOAT; I: INTEGER; end record;
```

They are represented in the same way.

There is no general agreement on which definition of structural equivalence is best, and almost all of the definitions are difficult for compilers to implement. Thus, name equivalence seems preferable.

EXERCISE 7-4:* Suppose we adopted the version of structural equivalence that ignores the order of fields. Describe the code a compiler would have to generate for a record assignment. Contrast this with the case in which the order of fields is significant.

EXERCISE 7-5:* Do you agree with the preferability of name equivalence? Defend either name or structural equivalence or propose and defend an alternative.

Subtypes Are Clarified

One of the reasons that name equivalence has not been adopted by previous languages is that it is often *too* restrictive. Consider the following declarations:

```
N: INTEGER;
type INDEX is range 1..100;
I: INDEX;
```

Since INDEX and INTEGER have different names, pure name equivalence would consider them different, unrelated types. Hence, the variables I and N have different types, and it is illegal to assign I to N, 'N := I'. This is certainly unintuitive since the type INDEX is just a subset of the type INTEGER. The situation is even worse than this; it is no longer possible to write 'I+1' because the '+' operation is defined on INTEGERs, not INDEXes. This is clearly unacceptable.

Ada solves this problem by stating that a *constraint*, such as 'range 1..100', defines a *subtype* of some *base type*, INTEGER in this case. Subtypes inherit all of the operations defined on the base type, so 'I+1' is still legal. Subtypes are also *compatible* with the base type and other subtypes of the base type, so assignments like 'N:=I' and even 'I:=N' (with a run-time constraint check) are legal.

This implicit definition of subtype is supplemented by an explicit mechanism for declaring subtypes. The declaration

```
subtype INDEX is INTEGER range 1..100;
```

explicitly declares INDEX to be a subtype of INTEGER that inherits all of the operations and properties of the base type. (Notice that we *must* specify INTEGER in the 'subtype' declaration and that we *can't* specify it in the 'type' declaration. Syntactic irregularities like this confuse programmers.)

A subtype can be further constrained:

```
subtype LITTLE_INDEX is INDEX range 1..10;
```

Then any object of type LITTLE_INDEX will also be an INTEGER, an INDEX, and any other subtype of INTEGER (if it is in the appropriate range).

Why are there apparently two methods of introducing subtypes? It seems that the 'subtype' declaration will handle all situations and hence that the subtype interpretation of certain 'type' declarations is superfluous. The only explanation seems to be that these 'type' declarations have no other useful meaning. In this situation Ada supplies a useless duplication of function.

Derived Types

Ada provides yet another facility for declaring types, *derived types*. An example of a derived type declaration is

```
type PERCENT is new INTEGER range 0..100;
```

This defines a new type, PERCENT, that is different from INTEGER, INDEX, and every other type. In particular, it is not possible to assign a PERCENT variable to an INDEX variable or vice versa. This seems useful since we would not want to use PERCENTs and INDEXes interchangeably; they mean different things. What makes a derived type different is that it inherits all of the operations, functions, and other attributes (built-in or user defined) of the type from which it is derived. It is as though every subprogram declaration containing 'INTEGER' or 'INTEGER range 0..100' were copied with these types replaced by 'PERCENT'. Thus, the type PERCENT inherits an entire set of subprograms just like, but distinct from, those defined on INTEGERs. This allows a user to define a new type that is *abstractly* different from the type it's derived from, yet still make use of all of the operations defined on the original type. In fact, it is possible to convert explicitly between derived types and their parent types. For instance, 'PERCENT(N)' converts an INTEGER value N to a PERCENT value.

Constraints Replace Subranges

The Pascal subrange type constructor has been replaced in Ada by a more general facility—the *constraint*. A constraint is a mechanism for restricting the allowable set of data values in a type without restricting the operations applicable to those data types. Thus, a constraint defines a subtype of a given type. The simplest example of a constraint is the *range constraint* that we have already seen. For example, 'INTEGER range 1 .. 100' restricts the integers to numbers in the range 1–100 and 'CHARACTER range 'A' .. 'Z'' restricts the characters to be alphabetic. Range constraints have the same implementation costs and benefits as Pascal subrange types. The Ada constructs are more general because expressions that must be evaluated at run-time are allowed in the constraint. In these cases some checking must be done at run-time that could otherwise be done at compile-time.

We have also seen *accuracy constraints* (e.g., 'FLOAT digits 10 range -1e6 .. 1e6' and 'DOLLARS delta 1 range 1 .. 10') that are applicable to the approximate numeric types. A third type of constraint is the *discriminant constraint*. Suppose PERSON is a variant record whose discriminant can take on two values—MALE and FEMALE. Then 'PERSON(MALE)' is an example of a discriminant constraint; this is the type of PERSON records in which the discriminant has the value MALE. Again, what we have done is restrict the set of possible values; 'PERSON(MALE)' is a subtype of PERSON. If an expression of type PERSON is assigned to a variable of type 'PERSON(MALE)', then a run-time check will be necessary to ensure that the discriminant has the value MALE. This is exactly analogous to the check required by a range constraint.

Index Constraints Solve Pascal's Array Problem

Recall (Chapter 5, Section 5.3) that there was a serious problem resulting from the interaction of Pascal's array types and its strong typing facility. This problem is solved by the fourth type of constraint—the *index constraint.* Suppose we wish to write a general-purpose procedure to sum the elements of a real array. To do this we define a type VECTOR that is an array of FLOAT numbers with the indices unconstrained:

```
type VECTOR is array (INTEGER range < > ) of FLOAT;
```

This declaration means that each VECTOR object is a FLOAT array whose index type is some subrange of INTEGER. Therefore, to declare a VECTOR object, this range must be specified as

```
DATA: VECTOR(1..100);
DAYS: VECTOR(1..366);
```

DATA and DAYS are VECTORS of lengths 100 and 366, respectively. Ada avoids Pascal's problem by allowing programmers to use the unconstrained type in a formal parameter specification, for instance,

```
function SUM (V:VECTOR) return FLOAT is ....
```

The Ada type system will allow both DATA and DAYS to be passed to SUM; i.e., 'SUM(DATA)' and 'SUM(DAYS)' are legal because they are of the same type, VECTOR (remember, a constraint defines a subtype and subtypes are compatible with their parent type). The compiler must pass the actual bounds of the VECTOR as hidden parameters to SUM. Within SUM it is possible to access these hidden parameters by 'V'FIRST' and 'V'LAST'. Therefore, the loop to sum the array could be written:

```
for I in V'FIRST .. V'LAST loop
  TOTAL := TOTAL+V(I);
end loop;
```

It is also possible to declare variables to be of type VECTOR, in which case the actual bounds of the VECTOR have to be stored along with its contents.

EXERCISE 7-6: Discuss how index constraints simplify string manipulation.

Enumerations Can Be Overloaded

Recall that Pascal did not allow an overlap in the elements of enumeration types; for example,

```
type PRIMARY is (RED, BLUE, GREEN);
type STOP_LIGHT is (RED, YELLOW, GREEN);
```

would be illegal in Pascal. Ada does not have this restriction; the above type declarations are legal as they stand. This seems to introduce ambiguities into the program because 'RED' can mean either the PRIMARY 'RED' or the STOP_LIGHT 'RED'; we say that the identifier 'RED' is *overloaded* because it has two or more meanings. Ada uses context to determine which 'RED' is meant. For example, if 'C' has been declared to be a PRIMARY variable, then 'C := RED' is unambiguous; both the compiler and the human reader can see that it is the PRIMARY 'RED' that is meant. There are some circumstances (connected with overloaded procedures discussed later) in which the correct type cannot be determined from context; in these situations programmers are required to specify which they mean—'PRIMARY(RED)' or 'STOP_LIGHT(RED)'. In some cases, even though the use of an enumeration literal is not ambiguous, it may be very difficult for both the human and the compiler to tell what is meant; these will become apparent in Section 8.1. Why do the designers of Ada allow this confusing and potentially ambiguous situation? One reason is convenience; it is normal in natural languages for one word to have several meanings, such as a primary color and the state of a stop light. Another reason results from the fact that in Ada character sets are considered enumeration types. For instance, a character set could be defined by

```
type DISCODE is ('A', 'B', ..., '9', '+', '-', '.');
```

Since the same character, say 'A', will normally appear in several different character sets, overloading of enumeration literals seems to be implied.

EXERCISE 7-7:* Do you agree with the designers of Ada on the issue of overloaded enumerations? Discuss alternates, such as (1) the Pascal solution, (2) other treatments of character sets, and (3) always requiring the type to be specified [e.g., 'PRIMARY(RED)']. Suggest additional solutions to this problem.

7.4 DESIGN: NAME STRUCTURES

The Primitives Are Those of Pascal

The primitive name structures of Ada are based on the Pascal model; there are constant, variable, type, procedure, and function declarations, with improvements in almost all of these. There are also task and package declarations.

One of the simplest declarations is the variable declaration, which, in contrast to Pascal's, allows initialization, for example,

```
APPROXIMATION: FLOAT := 1.0;
```

The consistent use of initialization eliminates a common error: using an uninitialized variable. It also causes a program to be more readable by making the initialization of the variable obvious. The initial value is not restricted to being a constant. It can be an expression of any complexity; it is evaluated when the block or procedure in which it occurs is entered. This is advantageous since it permits the same construct to be used for all initialization, regardless of whether or not the initial value is a constant.

The constant declaration is a modified form of a variable declaration. For instance,

```
FEET_PER_MILE: constant INTEGER := 5280;
PI: constant := 3.14159_2653589;
```

A constant declaration is interpreted exactly like a variable declaration except that its value cannot be changed after its initialization at scope entry-time. It is therefore considerably more general than a Pascal constant because its value can be computed during the execution of the program and may differ in different instances of the scope. This is a useful facility and aids program maintenance. (Recall our discussion of 'MaxData' in Section 5.4, p. 206.)

Notice in the example above that the type of the constant (PI) is not specified in the declaration. Ada allows the type to be omitted if it is a numeric type, and if the expression on the right "involves only literals, names of numeric literals, calls of the predefined function ABS, parenthesized literal expressions, and the predefined arithmetic operators."[2] This unusual feature is included to allow constants of type *universal integer* and *universal real* to be named. These types

2 *Reference Manual for the Ada Programming Language*, July 1980, page 3-3.

have the maximum possible precision and are not normally accessible to programmers. The benefit of this kind of declaration is to permit the programmer to name a type- and precision-independent numerical constant. The cost of this feature is the above-quoted unintuitive and difficult to remember rule.

Specifications and Definitions

In our discussion of the structural organization of Ada, we saw that information hiding was supported by the ability to divide declarations into two parts:

1. One which defines the interface
2. One which provides an implementation

Most of the declarations in Ada can be broken into these two parts. For instance, a constant can be specified by

```
MAX_SIZE: constant INTEGER;
```

This specifies that MAX_SIZE is the name of an INTEGER constant but does not define its value. A "deferred" constant like this would usually be used as part of the specification of a package; this way a package can provide a constant without defining its value to be part of the interface. This constant can be "implemented," that is, given a value, by a conventional constant definition:

```
MAX_SIZE: constant INTEGER := 256;
```

This definition would normally appear in the private part of the package. We will see the way in which these specifications and definitions are used in our discussion of packages below.

Subprograms Can Be Specified

Since subprograms (procedures and functions) form most of the interface to a package, subprogram specifications are very important. For instance, the interface specification

```
procedure BINSEARCH (T: TABLE; SOUGHT: FLOAT;
                     out LOCATION: INTEGER; out FOUND: BOOLEAN);
```

tells the reader and the compiler that BINSEARCH is a procedure with four parameters: The first two are input parameters of type TABLE and FLOAT, respectively, and the third and fourth are output parameters of type INTEGER and

BOOLEAN, respectively. This is the *interface* between the procedure BINSEARCH and its callers, that is, the information that must be known to both the users and the implementer of this procedure. It is essentially a contract between the users and the implementer. A specification such as this would usually appear as part of the interface specification of a package.

A definition of BINSEARCH that meets the above specification appears in Figure 7.1. We can see that the definition repeats the specification; this provides useful redundancy and helps readability. It should be clear that this entire structure supports information hiding by embedding the important design decisions in the body of the procedure.

Global Variables Considered Harmful

In the early 1970s, many programming language researchers were beginning to question the block structure of Algol-60 and other second- and third-generation languages. While it was agreed that such languages had many desirable characteristics, they were also seen to cause problems in large programs. Some of these were described by Wulf and Shaw (at Carnegie-Mellon University) in a paper in *Sigplan Notices* (1973) called "Global Variable Considered Harmful." In this paper they identified four problems with block structure:

- Side effects
- Indiscriminant [sic] access
- Vulnerability
- No overlapping definitions

We describe each of these problems below.

Side Effects

Computer scientists had recognized for many years the danger of *side effects*, a change to a nonlocal variable by a procedure or function. For example, suppose we have the following Algol-60 procedure:

```
integer procedure Max(x,y);   integer x, y;
  begin
    count := count + 1;
    Max := if x>y then x else y;
  end;
```

This procedure computes the maximum of two integers; it also has a side effect of incrementing the variable 'count' (which we assume has been defined in an outer block). We may suppose that the programmer's intention is to determine the number of times the Max procedure is invoked. What is the matter with such a side effect? It makes it very difficult to determine the effects of a procedure from the form of a call of the procedure. For example, if we see

```
length := Max(needed,requested);
```

it is immediately obvious that this call on Max involves the variables 'needed', 'requested', and 'length'. These are clearly part of the *interface* to the Max procedure. We would never guess that this procedure modifies 'count' without looking at an implementation of the procedure. To see the problems this can cause, imagine we were looking through a program to find all the places 'count' was modified because it was connected with a bug. We would very likely overlook the line shown above because it modifies 'count' without ever mentioning it. Furthermore, if the procedure Max is predefined in some library, it may not even be possible to look at its definition. This is a potential maintenance problem. Furthermore, it introduces some semantic problems. Consider the invocation,

```
count := 10;
length := Max(count,10);
```

The procedure Max actually modifies one of its actual parameters. The exact value returned depends on whether Max increments 'count' before or after it tests its parameters. Also, 'length' will be set to 11 if the parameters are passed by name (as in our definition) and to 10 if passed by value. All of these problems arise because the global variable 'count' is a hidden part of the interface to Max. It is really both an input and output parameter but does not appear in the parameter list.

FORTRAN allowed side effects through use of output parameters and COMMON blocks. For the most part, however, they could be avoided by avoiding COMMON. Unfortunately, side effects are a natural consequence of block structure since being nested inside a block implies that all variables declared in that block are visible, and hence alterable. We summarize the problems with side effects as follows:

> *Side effects* result from hidden access to a variable.

EXERCISE 7-8:* Describe some programming situations in which side effects are useful. How could the same thing be accomplished without them? Discuss the trade-offs.

Indiscriminate Access

Closely related to side effects is the problem of *indiscriminate access*, that is, that programmers cannot prevent inadvertent access to variables. We will consider an example of this. Suppose we wanted to provide a stack to be used in an Algol-60 program. We would probably structure our program like this:

```
begin
  integer array S[1:100];
  integer TOP;

  procedure Push(x); integer x;
    begin    TOP := TOP + 1;   S[TOP] := x;   end;

  procedure Pop(x); integer x;
    begin    Pop := S[TOP];   TOP := TOP-1;   end;

  TOP := 0;

  ... uses of Push and Pop ...
end
```

The variable S, which is the stack, must be declared in the same block as Push and Pop so that it is visible from the bodies of Push and Pop. For the Push and Pop procedures to be visible to their users, they must be declared in a block that contains all uses. This means that S is visible to users of Push and Pop and that these users may inadvertently (or intentionally!) use or alter the value of S without going through the Push and Pop procedures. This situation is pictured in Figure 7.2.

There is no way to arrange the declarations in a block-structured language so that indiscriminate access cannot occur. The problem with this kind of direct access is that it creates a maintenance problem. There is no guarantee that all users of the stack go through the Push and Pop procedures, and there may be uses that depend on the details of the way the stack is implemented. Therefore, it will not be possible to change this implementation (e.g., to make it more efficient or correct a bug) without chasing down every reference to S. If we were guaranteed that all users of the stack went through Push and Pop, then we would only have to modify these to change the implementation of the stack; maintenance would be greatly simplified. Unfortunately, there is no way to accomplish this in a block-structured language. We summarize the problem of indiscriminate access:

The problem of *indiscriminate access* is the inability to prevent access to a variable.

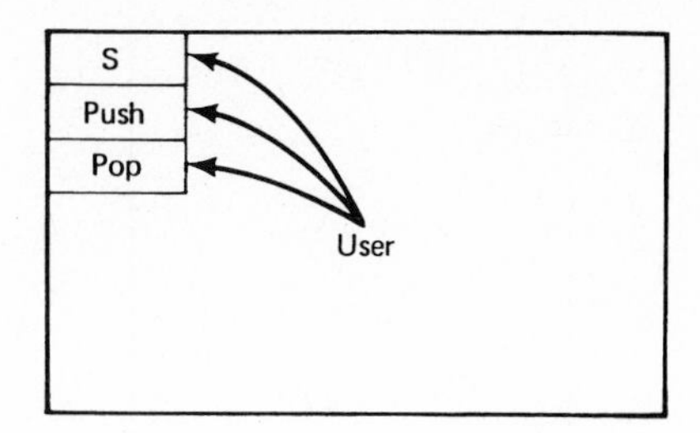

Figure 7.2 Indiscriminate Access

EXERCISE 7-9: Show that indiscriminate access to S cannot be prevented by suitable arrangement of the block structure.

Vulnerability

We saw that the problem of indiscriminate access was that under certain circumstances it was impossible to prevent access to a variable. *Vulnerability* is the dual problem: Under certain circumstances it is impossible to *preserve* access to a variable. The basic problem of vulnerability is that new declarations can be interposed between the definition and use of a variable. Let's see what this means. Suppose we have a very large Algol program that has this structure:

```
begin
  integer x;
  . . . . . many lines of code . . . . .
  begin
    . . . . . many lines of code . . . . .
    ... x := x + 1; ...
    . . . . . . . . . . . . . . . . . . . . . . . . . . . . .
  end;
  . . . . .
end;
```

We will suppose that there are so many lines of code between the definition and use of 'x' that they fill many pages. Let's further suppose that in the process of maintaining this program we decide that we need a new local variable in the inner block; we pick 'x', not realizing that it is already used in that block. This is the result of our modification:

```
begin
  integer x;
```

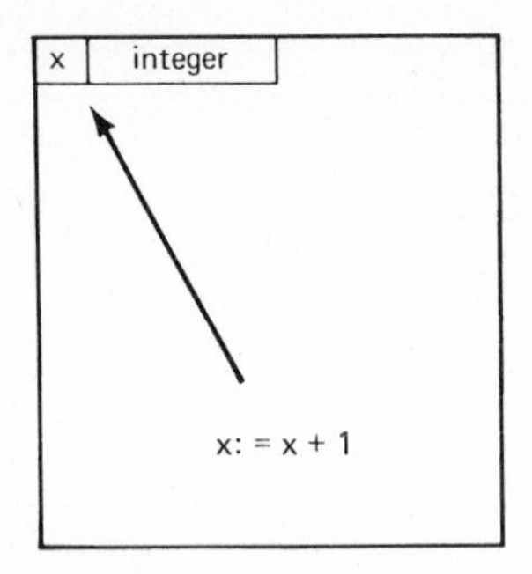

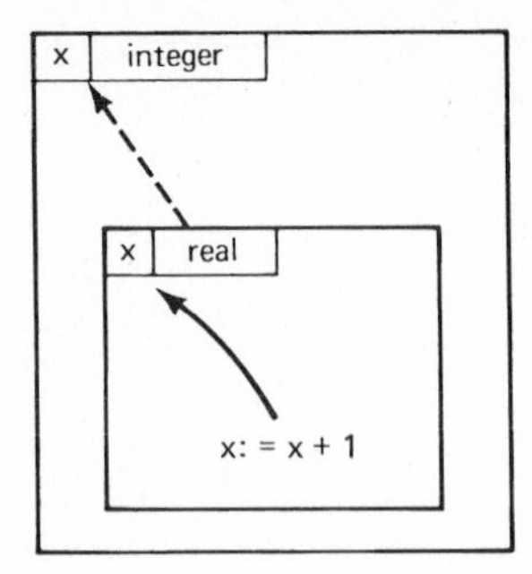

Figure 7.3 Vulnerability

```
   . . . . . many lines of code . . . . .
   begin real x; comment NEW DECLARATION;
     . . . . . many lines of code . . . . .
     . . . x := x+1; . . .
     . . . . . . . . . . . . . . . . . . . . . . . . . . . . .
   end;
   . . . . .
end;
```

We can see what has happened; access to the outer declaration of 'x' has been blocked and the statement 'x := x+1' now refers to the new variable 'x'. The new declaration of 'x' has been interposed between the original definition of 'x' and its use. This is illustrated in Figure 7.3. We can state the problem of vulnerability in the following way: A program segment ('x := x+1' in this case) cannot control the assumptions under which it executes (the integer declaration of 'x', in this case). Summarizing,

> *Vulnerability* means a program segment can't preserve access to a variable.

No Overlapping Definitions

The last problem with block structure that we will discuss is that it does not permit *overlapping definitions*. The need for these arises from attempts to modularize large systems. Suppose we have a large software system composed of four modules P1, P2, P3, P4; these may be procedures or blocks. Also suppose that we want P1 and P2 to communicate through a shared data area (say, an array) DA and that we want P2, P3, and P4 to communicate through a shared data area DB. This situation is illustrated in Figure 7.4.

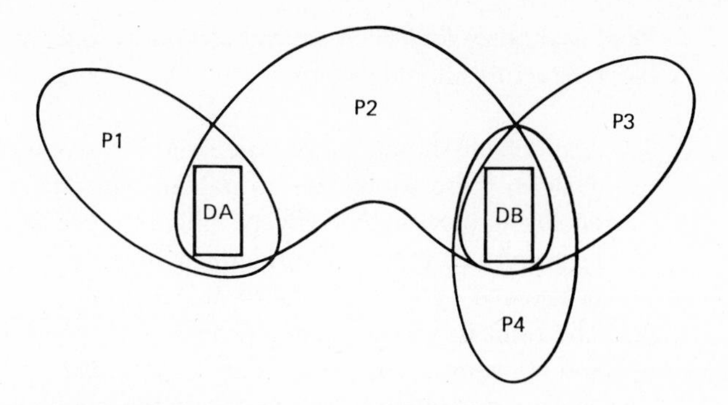

Figure 7.4 Overlapping Definitions

Since DA must be visible to both P1 and P2, it must be declared at the same or surrounding level to these modules. Similarly, DB must be declared at the same or surrounding level to P2, P3, and P4. Therefore, our program must be structured as shown in Figure 7.5. We can see that P1 has access to DB, and P3 and P4 have access to DA. This access is not needed and spreads knowledge of implementation decisions where it is not needed. This can create both a maintenance and a security problem. The problem of no overlapping definitions is summarized as follows:

> *No overlapping definitions* means we can't control shared access to variables.

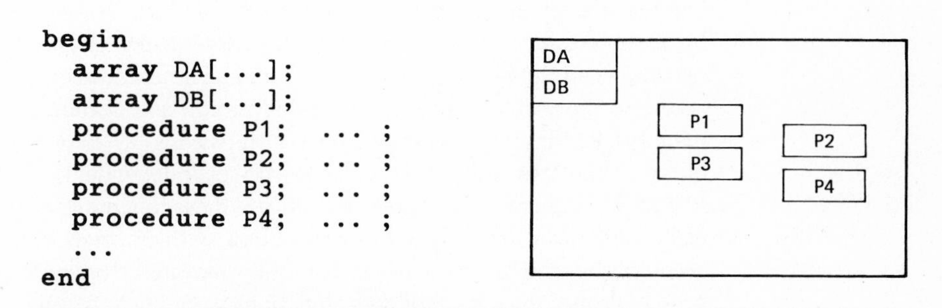

Figure 7.5 No Overlapping Definitions

Attributes of an Alternative

Wulf and Shaw identified several attributes that they thought an alternative to block structure should satisfy:

1. The default should *not* be to extend the scope of a variable to inner blocks. That is, there should be no *implicit inheritance* of access to variables from enclosing blocks. Side effects, indiscriminate access, and vulnerability can all be seen to be results of this implicit inheritance, although these problems are not solved by just eliminating this feature.
2. The right to access a name should be by the mutual consent of the creator and accessor of the name. That is, the creator (definer) of a name should be able to determine who can access the name and who can't, and potential users of the name should never have the name imposed on them if they don't want it. This would solve the problems of indiscriminate access, vulnerability, and no overlapping definitions.
3. Access rights to a structure and its substructures should be decoupled. This means that the ability to access some structure (e.g., a stack) should not imply the ability to access the mechanism that implements it (e.g., the top pointer of the stack or the array containing its elements). This problem, which is related to indiscriminate access, can severely complicate maintenance.
4. It should be possible to distinguish different types of access. For example, it should be possible to give some users read-only access to a data structure and others read-write access. This helps to solve the side-effect and vulnerability problems.
5. Declaration of definition, name access, and allocation should be decoupled. In block-structured languages these functions are usually closely connected. For instance, by declaring a variable in an Algol block (1) the name is defined by its appearance in the declaration, (2) name access is determined by its occurrence in the block since that block and all inner blocks implicitly inherit access to the variable, and (3) storage allocation and deallocation are determined since they will occur simultaneously with entry to and exit from the block. These are really three orthogonal (i.e., independent) functions. In a few cases, languages attempted to decouple these functions. Algol decouples name definition and access from allocation with its **own** variables; Pascal accomplishes the same with its dynamically allocated storage ('new' and 'dispose'). Proper separation of these functions would help to solve most of the problems of block structure. We will see later that although Ada has not abandoned block structure, its packages and other related mechanisms eliminate many of the block's shortcomings.

Parnas's Principles

At about the same time that Wulf and Shaw were doing their work, Parnas enunciated two important principles of information hiding. In the introduction to this chapter, we discussed the general idea of information hiding: Each difficult design decision should be hidden inside a module. This rule determines what should be in each module. The two principles we will see next guide us in designing the interfaces between modules.

> ***Parnas's Principles***
>
> 1. One must provide the intended user with *all* the information needed to use the module correctly *and nothing more.*
> 2. One must provide the implementor with *all* the information needed to complete the module *and nothing more.*

Thus, the user of a module does not know how it is implemented and cannot write programs that depend on the implementation. This makes the module more maintainable since implementors know exactly what they can and cannot change. Similarly, implementors have no knowledge of the context of use of their module, except that provided in the interface. This simplifies maintenance of the module because they know what they can safely change and what they can't. We will see that the Ada package construct directly supports Parnas's principles.

Packages Support Information Hiding

The Ada construct that supports the information-hiding principles and controls access to declarations is the *package.* The declaration of a package is broken down into two parts—an interface specification and a body. The interface specification defines the interface between the inside and the outside of the package; hence, it is that information about the package that must be known to the user, and that information about the way it will be used that must be known to the implementor. The package specification is effectively a contract between the user and the implementor of the package. A package specification has the following form:

```
package COMPLEX_TYPE is
        ... specification of public names ...
end COMPLEX_TYPE;
```

Between the brackets of the package specification ('package'-'end'), all the specifications of the public names (i.e., the names in the interface) are written. A partial specification of a package that provides complex arithmetic is shown in Figure 7.6.

Figure 7.6 shows that the package COMPLEX_TYPE provides a type (COMPLEX), a constant (I), and several functions (RE, IM), and that it overloads the arithmetic operators. The function definitions are specified in the usual way: The types of the parameters and the returned value are specified.

The type COMPLEX is also listed in the interface, but it is defined to be a *private* type. This means that although the name COMPLEX is visible (and hence may be used in object declarations, parameter specifications, etc.), the internal structure of COMPLEX numbers is hidden from users of the package. If this were not done, it would be possible for users to access directly the components of COMPLEX numbers without going through the RE and IM functions. This would interfere with later maintenance if the implementor decided to use a different representation for COMPLEX numbers. Notice that there is an appendage to the package specification introduced by the word 'private'. This private part of the package includes a definition of the COMPLEX type that specifies its representation. What is this information doing in the specification? This is a concession that the Ada designers have been forced to make so that packages will not be too difficult to compile. Users of the COMPLEX_TYPE package will want to declare objects of type COMPLEX, which will require the compiler to allocate storage for these records; thus, the compiler must know the representation of COMPLEX numbers. This is especially necessary if the program using

```
package COMPLEX_TYPE is
  type COMPLEX is private;
  I : constant COMPLEX;
  function +  (X,Y : COMPLEX) return COMPLEX;
  function -  (X,Y : COMPLEX) return COMPLEX;
  function *  (X,Y : COMPLEX) return COMPLEX;
  function /  (X,Y : COMPLEX) return COMPLEX;
  function RE (X : COMPLEX) return FLOAT;
  function IM (X : COMPLEX) return FLOAT;
  function +  (X : FLOAT; Y : COMPLEX) return COMPLEX;
  function *  (X : FLOAT; Y : COMPLEX) return COMPLEX;
private
  type COMPLEX is record RE, IM : FLOAT := 0.0; end record;
  I : constant COMPLEX := (0.0, 1.0);
end COMPLEX_TYPE;
```

Figure 7.6 Specification of Complex Arithmetic Package

COMPLEX_TYPE and the package defining it are compiled separately; under these circumstances only the specification of COMPLEX_TYPE is available to the compiler when it is compiling the program using the package.

We can see that this package also defines a public constant, I, defined as a *deferred* constant. Its value must be deferred because it depends on the representation of COMPLEX numbers, which is private. The actual definition of the constant is given in the private part of the specification along with the type definition.

The package body, which is known only to the implementor, gives the definition of each name mentioned in the specification. It may also declare any local procedures, functions, types, and so on, needed by this implementation; all of these are private. Part of the implementation of COMPLEX_TYPE is shown in Figure 7.7.

EXERCISE 7-10: Complete the definition of the package COMPLEX_TYPE.

```
package body COMPLEX_TYPE is

  function + (X,Y : COMPLEX) return COMPLEX is
  begin
    return (X.RE + Y.RE, X.IM + Y.IM);
  end;

  function * (X,Y : COMPLEX) return COMPLEX is
    RP: constant FLOAT := X.RE*Y.RE - X.IM*Y.IM;
    IP: constant FLOAT := X.RE*Y.IM + X.IM*Y.RE;
  begin
    return (RP,IP);
  end;

  function RE (X : COMPLEX) return FLOAT is
  begin return X.RE; end;

  function IM (X : COMPLEX) return FLOAT is
  begin return X.IM; end;

  function + (X : FLOAT; Y : COMPLEX) return COMPLEX is
  begin
    return (X + Y.RE, Y.IM);
  end;

  -- other definitions
end COMPLEX_TYPE;
```

Figure 7.7 Partial Implementation of a Complex Arithmetic Package

EXERCISE 7-11:* We have seen that the private part of a package specification mixes representation information important only to the implementor with the interface information needed by the user. Describe an alternative that does not mix things up this way but still allows a compiler to allocate storage for objects of private types. You may alter Ada's package declarations or describe an alternative method for the compiler to get the needed information.

Name Access Is by Mutual Consent

We have seen that the implementor of a package can control, by the placement of the declarations in the public part or the private part of the package, which names can be accessed by a user of the package. Anything placed in the specification is public and potentially accessible. A user gains access to the publics of a package with a 'use' declaration, as shown:

```
declare
  use COMPLEX_TYPE;
  X,Y : COMPLEX;
  Z : COMPLEX := 1.5 + 2.5*I;
begin
  X := 2.5+3.5*I;
  Y := X+Z;
  Z := RE(Z)+IM(X)*I;
  if X = Y then X := Y+Z;
  else X := Y*Z; end if;
end;
```

The 'use' declaration makes all of the public names of the package visible throughout the block in which it appears. We can see that this permits using all of the types (COMPLEX), functions (RE, +), constants (I), and so forth, as though they were built in. (In fact, the Ada language is defined as though the "built-in" types are defined in packages that are automatically 'use'd for all programmers.) Thus, name access is by mutual consent: The package implementor determines which attributes are to be public and the package user decides whether to *import* the attributes of a particular package. In fact, Ada provides even more control to package users since, if they don't need all of the names defined by a package, they can select just the ones they want. This is done with a dot notation similar to Pascal's (e.g., 'COMPLEX_TYPE.I') or by a variant of 'use' that we won't discuss here.

Ada also provides control over visibility during separate compilation. Normally only the built-in identifiers are visible to a separately compiled module. However, if a module is preceded by 'with <name list>;' then the public identifiers of the named modules are also made visible.

Packages as Libraries

We have just seen how to use a package to define an *abstract data type*. There are also many other ways that packages can be used to modularize programs; some of these are discussed in the following sections. One of the simplest, which is really a degenerate form of an abstract data type, is a *library*. Suppose we wished to define a PLOT library that provided subprograms for plotting. This can easily be specified as a package:

```
package PLOT is
  type POINT is record X,Y : FLOAT; end record;
  procedure MOVE_TO (LOCATION : POINT);
  procedure LINE (FROM, TO : POINT);
  procedure CIRCLE (CENTER : POINT; RADIUS : FLOAT);
  procedure FIT (DATA : array (INTEGER range < > ) of POINT);
  function WHERE return POINT;
end PLOT;
```

Then, if users wish to do some plotting, they only have to include a 'use PLOT' request in the declaration part of a block or subprogram. Of course, the private part of the package may include the definitions of constants and subprograms that are needed by the implementation but are hidden from users. You can see that a library is just a package that doesn't contain any data structures.

Packages Permit Shared Data Areas

We have just looked at packages that contain procedures but no data structures; we will now look at the opposite—packages that contain data structures but no procedures. For example, suppose we wanted a buffer to be used for communicating characters between two subprograms. This could be done by the declaration:

```
package COMMUNICATION is
  IN_PTR, OUT_PTR : INTEGER range 0..99 := 0;
  BUFFER : array (0..99) of CHARACTER := (0..99 => ' ');
end COMMUNICATION;
```

(The declaration of 'BUFFER' makes it an array initialized to all blanks.) Given this definition of COMMUNICATION, two procedures P and Q can use it for communication by including a 'use' for the package:

```
procedure P is
  use COMMUNICATION;
begin
    :
```

```
  BUFFER(IN_PTR) := NEXT;
  IN_PTR := (IN_PTR + 1) mod 100;
    :
end P;

procedure Q is
  use COMMUNICATION;
begin
    :
  C := BUFFER(OUT_PTR);
    :
end Q;
```

This way of using packages is similar to the way labeled COMMON is used in FORTRAN. It also solves the problem of overlapping definitions discussed in the section on encapsulation; only those subprograms that need access to BUFFER will 'use COMMUNICATION'.

Packages Can Be Data Structure Managers

When we first saw the idea of information hiding, we said that each module should encapsulate one difficult design decision; we also said that the choice of the representation for a data structure was often such a difficult decision. Therefore, a common use of Ada packages is to encapsulate a data structure and provide a representation independent interface for accessing it.

We can take a stack data structure as a common case. When we design a data structure, one of the first questions we must ask is: "What operations are to be available on this data structure?" We will immediately come up with PUSH and POP; there are others, however. What will happen if we try to POP an element from an empty stack? Surely we will generate an error, but it is preferable for the users to have an EMPTY test so that, if they're unsure about whether the stack is empty, they can test it before they do a POP. We may also want a FULL test to determine if there is any room in the stack before we do a PUSH. Finally, we will need an *exception*, STACK_ERROR, which is raised if someone does a POP from an empty stack, and so forth. We also need to know the sort of things that the stack can hold; we will assume they are integers. We now have the information necessary to specify the STACK1 package:

```
package STACK1 is
  procedure PUSH (X : in INTEGER);
  procedure POP (X : out INTEGER);
  function EMPTY return BOOLEAN;
```

```
  function FULL return BOOLEAN;
  STACK_ERROR : exception;
end STACK1;
```

The difficult design decision—whether to represent the stack as an array, linked list, or something else—is hidden in the package.

Once the package has been implemented, it can be used as before. For example, if we intend to use the stack over a large part of the program, we can make its names available with a 'use':

```
declare
  use STACK1;
  I, N : INTEGER;
begin
    :
  PUSH(I);
  POP(N);
    :
  if EMPTY() then PUSH(N); end if;
    :
end;
```

We can also use the "dot" notation to select a public attribute from STACK1 without using the 'use', for example,

```
  STACK1.PUSH(I);
  STACK1.POP(N);
  if STACK1.EMPTY() then STACK1.PUSH(N); end if;
```

This allows users of the package to be as selective as necessary about the names accessed from STACK1; again, name access is by mutual consent.

How would we go about implementing the stack package? For the sake of this example, we will assume that we have decided on an array representation for the stack. The implementation of the stack package is shown in Figure 7.8. We can see that this implementation of a stack has two private names: ST, the array that holds the stack elements, and TOP, the pointer to the top of the stack. These are completely invisible and inaccessible to users of the stack; any attempt to access them, for example, by 'STACK.ST' or 'STACK.TOP', will be diagnosed by the compiler as a program error. The 'raise STACK_ERROR' statement is an example of an *exception*. Exceptions are discussed later (Chapter 8).

EXERCISE 7-12:* Write a package body that implements STACK1 using linked lists. To do this you will need to know a few details about Ada: (1) If T is a type,

```
package body STACK1 is
  ST : array (1..100) of INTEGER;
  TOP : INTEGER range 0..100 := 0;

  procedure PUSH (X : in INTEGER) is
  begin
    if FULL() then raise STACK_ERROR;
    else
      TOP := TOP + 1; ST(TOP) := X;
    end if;
  end PUSH;

  procedure POP (X : out INTEGER) is
  begin
    if EMPTY() then raise STACK_ERROR;
    else
      X := ST(TOP);
      TOP := TOP - 1;
    end if;
  end POP;

  function EMPTY return BOOLEAN is
  begin return TOP=0; end;

  function FULL return BOOLEAN is
  begin return TOP=100; end;

end STACK1;
```

Figure 7.8 Body of Simple Stack Package

then 'access T' is the type of pointers to things of type T. (2) If T is a record type, then 'new T(X1, ..., Xn)' allocates an instance of that record type and returns a pointer to that record. What is the meaning of the FULL function in a linked implementation of stacks?

Generic Packages Allow Multiple Instantiation

Suppose that the program we are writing requires two stacks. To get a second stack, we will have to repeat the entire definition of STACK1 with only its name changed:

```
package STACK2 is
  procedure PUSH (X : in INTEGER);
  procedure POP (X : out INTEGER);
  function FULL return BOOLEAN;
```

```
   function EMPTY return BOOLEAN;
   STACK_ERROR : exception;
end STACK2;

package body STACK2 is
   ... all of the definitions exactly as they
   ... appeared in STACK1.
end STACK2;
```

It is clearly a waste of time to have to copy the entire definition of STACK1 verbatim. Even if this copying is done automatically, say with an editor, it will still create a maintenance problem. Whenever a bug is corrected or the implementation of the package is changed, the modification will have to be repeated for each copy; there is a much greater chance of error. This approach is also inferior from the standpoint of readability since it is not obvious to someone reading the program that the two stacks are really the same; they will have to compare the definitions line by line to determine this. Clearly, what we have here is a failure to modularize; the separate copies of the package should be abstracted out so that they only have to be written and maintained once, which is an example of the Abstraction Principle. This ability is provided by Ada's *generic* facility.

We can see the motivation for this facility by looking at the way that programming languages have solved similar abstraction problems. When we need to repeat the same control sequence several times with different data, we define a procedure that implements the control sequence and then call it with the required data. When we need to repeat the same data structure several times in different storage areas, we define a data type that specifies a *template,* or pattern, for the data structure, and then we use that type in variable declarations so as to create multiple *instances* of the data structure. This is exactly the approach taken with packages. A template for packages, called a *generic package,* is defined. The template can be used to repeat the package by *generic instantiations.* Let's see how this works. A template for a generic stack package would be written:

```
generic
package STACK is
   procedure PUSH (X : in INTEGER);
   procedure POP (X : out INTEGER);
   function EMPTY return BOOLEAN;
   function FULL return BOOLEAN;
   STACK_ERROR : exception;
end STACK;
```

We can see that this looks exactly like our previous specification of the stack package except that the word 'generic' has been appended to its front. This is what informs us that we are defining a template for stacks and not a particular stack. The body for the generic stack package is exactly like that in Figure 7.8 so we won't repeat it.

We have seen how to write a template for a generic package. Next we must investigate the instantiation of these templates. Suppose we want two stacks that we will call STACK1 and STACK2. We can request the creation of two instances, or copies, of the template STACK with the generic instantiations:

```
package STACK1 is new STACK;
package STACK2 is new STACK;
```

These create two copies of the data areas defined by STACK, which are associated with the names STACK1 and STACK2; the procedural code (for PUSH, POP, etc.) can be shared by the instances. The two instances of STACK can be used with the dot notation, for example,

```
STACK1.PUSH(I);
STACK2.POP(N);
if STACK1.EMPTY() then STACK1.PUSH(N); end if;
```

Notice that it is not possible to use the 'use' construct to enter both stacks into the same scope since procedure calls like 'PUSH(I)' would be ambiguous; there would be no way to tell to which stack the PUSH referred.

You have probably already noticed that package instantiation is analogous to the instantiation of procedures, which we discussed in Chapter 3 on Algol-60. In that case, we create a new activation record, or instance, for a procedure, which contains all of its local variable storage but shares the executable code with other instances. When we study object-oriented languages in a later chapter, we will see that these ideas are very closely related. One difference that must be pointed out here is that while procedures may be *dynamically instantiated,* Ada allows only the *static instantiation* of packages; that is, each instance is associated with a declaration and the number of declarations is determined by the structure of the program. (Note, however, that a package declaration may be a local to a procedure that is dynamically instantiated; thus, there can be one instance of the package for each instance of the procedure. This is the only sense in which Ada packages can be dynamically instantiated.) Some other languages, for example, Simula-67 and Smalltalk (Chapter 12), allow the dynamic instantiation of packages in much the same way that records can be dynamically allocated.

EXERCISE 7-13:* Discuss the dynamic instantiation of packages. Is there any need for this facility? Why do you suppose it was left out of Ada? Discuss how such a facility might be included in Ada, and any other mechanisms that would have to be included to support it. Are there any efficiency consequences to dynamic instantiation? How about simplicity or readability consequences?

Instances May Be Parametrically Related

The generic facility has more capabilities than the simple copying of templates. In the generic stack package we have seen defined, the stack was limited to a size of 100. Now suppose that instead of two equal-size stacks we needed STACK1 to be of size 100 and STACK2 to be of size 64. How would we accomplish this? It may seem that we would have to recopy the definition of STACK with all of the occurrences of 100 replaced by 64. Again, this would be a very inefficient thing to do; it would hurt writability, readability, and maintainability. The analogous problem with procedures is solved by parameters; parameters allow the data to vary from one procedure call to another. Ada adapts this approach to packages by allowing parameters on a generic specification. For example, to allow the length of stack to vary from instance to instance, the package is specified:

```
generic
  LENGTH : NATURAL := 100;
package STACK is
  procedure PUSH (X : in INTEGER);
  procedure POP (X : out INTEGER);
  function EMPTY return BOOLEAN;
  function FULL return BOOLEAN;
  STACK_ERROR : exception;
end STACK;
```

Notice that the LENGTH parameter has been given a default value of 100; this is the value it will have if it's not specified. The body of the package is altered by replacing each occurrence of 100 by LENGTH as shown in part here:

```
package body STACK is
  ST : array (1..LENGTH) of INTEGER;
  TOP : INTEGER range 0..LENGTH := 0;
  ... the rest of the definitions,
  ... but with 100 replaced by LENGTH
end STACK;
```

When a stack is instantiated, this parameter must (if not omitted) be bound to a natural number. We can get the 100- and 64-element stacks by

```
package STACK1 is new STACK(100);
package STACK2 is new STACK(64);
```

Since the default stack length is 100, the first instantiation could have been written:

```
package STACK1 is new STACK;
```

Generic packages can have any number of parameters of any types, just as procedures do. They can also have several types of parameters that procedures cannot have. Suppose that we needed to use a stack, STACK3, that contains only characters. Again it would seem that we must copy the entire definition of STACK with every occurrence of INTEGER replaced by CHARACTER. This is undesirable for all of the reasons we have already discussed; instead it is handled by generics. A specification of type-independent stacks is:

```
generic
  LENGTH : NATURAL := 100;
  type ELEMENT is private;
package STACK is
  procedure PUSH (X : in ELEMENT);
  procedure POP (X : out ELEMENT);
  function EMPTY return BOOLEAN;
  function FULL return BOOLEAN;
  STACK_ERROR : exception;
end STACK;
```

The type parameter is defined to be *private* because it acts like a private type: The only operations available on it (within the package) are assignment and equality comparisons. There are other forms of type parameters in generic packages that allow more operations but on a restricted class of objects; this is too detailed to warrant our attention here. The implementation of STACK is shown in Figure 7.9. Given these definitions, the instantiation of general stacks is accomplished as before, for example,

```
package STACK1 is new STACK (100, INTEGER);
package STACK3 is new STACK (256, CHARACTER);
```

These stacks can be used with the dot notation as before, for example, 'STACK1.POP(N)' or 'STACK3.PUSH('A')'. They can also be referred to without the dot notation through the 'use' construct:

```
declare
  use STACK1;
  use STACK3;
  I, N : INTEGER;
```

```
package body STACK is
  ST : array (1..LENGTH) of ELEMENT;
  TOP : INTEGER range 0..LENGTH := 0;

  procedure PUSH (X : in ELEMENT) is
  begin
    .... as before ....
  end PUSH;

  procedure POP (X : out ELEMENT) is
  begin
    .... as before ....
  end POP;

  function EMPTY return BOOLEAN is
  begin return N = 0; end;

  function FULL return BOOLEAN is
  begin return N = LENGTH; end;

end STACK;
```

Figure 7.9 Implementation of a General Stack Package

```
  C, D : CHARACTER;
begin
  PUSH(I);
  PUSH(C);
  POP(N);
  POP(D);
  if STACK1.EMPTY() then ...
  if STACK3.FULL() then ...
end;
```

'Using' both stacks is permitted because context determines which procedure is intended. For example, 'PUSH(I)' is unambiguous because I is an INTEGER and there is only one INTEGER PUSH procedure visible (the other PUSH procedure works on CHARACTERs). In such a situation, the PUSH procedure is said to be *overloaded* since it bears several meanings at once. This is analogous to the overloaded enumeration-type elements previously discussed and to the built-in overloaded operators (e.g., '+' works on INTEGERs, FLOATs, and COMPLEXes). Notice that context cannot be used for the EMPTY and FULL functions because they do not have any arguments (or return values) that depend on the element type; these finctions must still be accessed with the dot notation.

Generic Packages Are Difficult to Compile

All of these convenient facilities are not without cost; efficient generation of code for generic packages can be very complicated. We consider a few of the issues in this section. We saw earlier that generic packages without parameters could be instantiated much as procedures are instantiated: A new data area is created for each instance and the executable code is shared by all of the instances. This case is illustrated by Figure 7.10. This same kind of sharing is possible with most simple kinds of parameterization; for example, the generic STACK package parameterized just by LENGTH can make use of shared code if the differing information, the array length, is stored with the instance. It is also necessary to use the most general representation for TOP (i.e., the largest NATURAL range) since the actual subrange varies from instance to instance. The layout is shown in Figure 7.11. Notice that the variable-length items, ST in this example, have been moved to the end of the package; otherwise it would be necessary to use variable offsets to get to TOP. We can see that it is still possible to share code among instances, although there may be more run-time range checking (e.g., to ensure that assignments to TOP are legal).

Let's consider a case of more general parameterization: type parameters such as we saw in the general stack package. It is possible to instantiate this template with any type for which assignment and equality are defined, which is almost all types. In various instances ELEMENT could be CHARACTER, or INTEGER, or COMPLEX, or personnel records, and so on. We know that it is necessary to know the amount of storage occupied by an array element in order to find the location of any particular element. Therefore, the code to access an element of an array of CHARACTERs differs from the code to access an element of an array of INTEGERs. The apparent consequence of this is that each instance of a type parameterized package must have its own procedures, compiled for the types that appear in that generic instantiation. This is very inefficient since there is no sharing at all, even if the code bodies turn out to be the same. There are several ways to improve on this. For example, the compiler can keep a record of

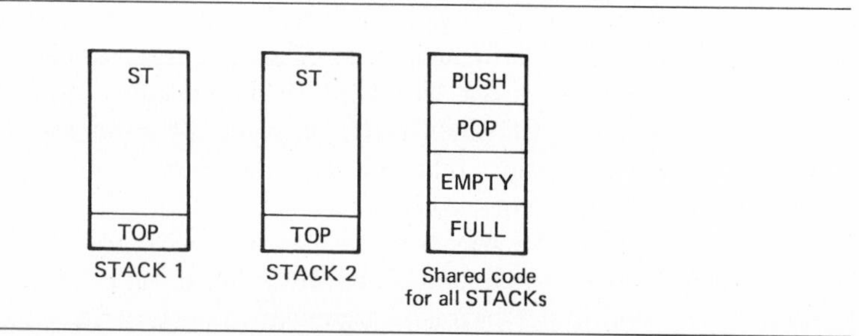

Figure 7.10 Layout of Unparameterized Package Instances

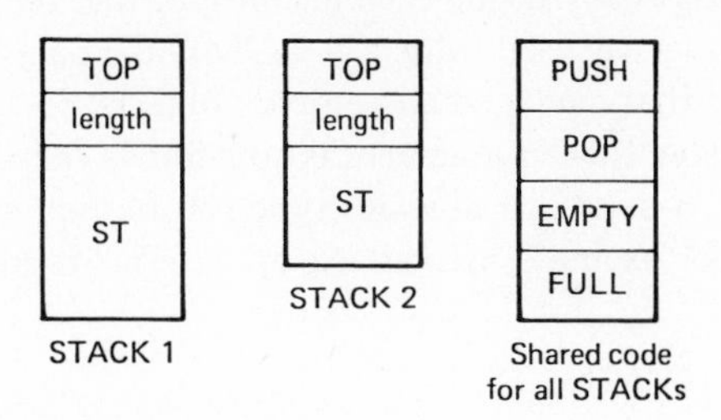

Figure 7.11 Simple Parameterization

every set of generic parameters for which it has generated code, that is, it can remember that it has already encountered a 'STACK(..., INTEGER)', and therefore that it has already generated code for the case ELEMENT = INTEGER. Later, if it encounters another INTEGER stack, it can share this code. This approach can be improved further by sharing code whenever the types are represented in the same amount of storage. For example, if in a particular implementation INTEGERs and FLOATs both occupy one word, then the code bodies for 'STACK(..., INTEGER)' and 'STACK(..., FLOAT)' can be shared. This is possible because the only operations allowed on ELEMENTs are assignment and equality comparison, both of which are usually independent of everything except the size of the value. Since there may be several type parameters to a generic package and there are other more complicated types of parameters, this attempt to find sharable code bodies can be fairly expensive. There is another approach to generic package implementation that simplifies some of the checking at the cost of decreased execution efficiency. This is to record in the instance the length of all parametrically typed objects in the package, much as was done for the length of the array ST. Then this length can be used for computing the position of array elements and similar purposes.

*EXERCISE 7-14**:* Read the discussion of generic packages in the Ada Reference Manual. Criticize this mechanism with regard to its complexity, efficiency, and generality. Suggest improvements to this mechanism or show that most of the apparent improvements are less desirable.

Internal and External Representations

We have handled the representation of data structures in two distinct ways. For example, in our STACK example the procedures for manipulating stacks were "part" of each stack, so we wrote 'STACK1.POP(N)', and so on. This is sometimes called an *internal* representation because the operators on a data structure are conceptually inside each instance of that data structure. The other approach is the one we used with the COMPLEX package: The operators were in one package that managed all complex objects, so we wrote 'RE(Z)', and so on. For this reason, this arrangement is sometimes called an *external* representation. Frequently, a particular abstract type can be represented either externally or internally. For example, we can use an external representation for stacks by:

```
package STACK_TYPE is
  type STACK is private;
  procedure NEW_STACK (out S : STACK);
  procedure PUSH (in out S : STACK; in X : INTEGER);
  procedure POP (in out S : STACK; out X : INTEGER);
  function EMPTY (S : STACK) return BOOLEAN;
  function FULL (S : STACK) return BOOLEAN;
private
  type STACK is record
    ST : array (1..100) of INTEGER;
    TOP : INTEGER range 0..100 := 0;
    end record;
end STACK_TYPE;
```

Then stack objects can be declared and initialized:

```
declare
  use STACK_TYPE;
  STACK1 : STACK;
  STACK2 : STACK;
begin
  NEW_STACK (STACK1);
  NEW_STACK (STACK2);
  PUSH (STACK1, I);
  POP (STACK2, N);
  if EMPTY (STACK1) then PUSH (STACK1, N); end if;
end;
```

(Constant stack objects cannot be declared because of the necessity of initializing them with NEW_STACK.)

EXERCISE 7-15: The STACK_TYPE package only implements integer stacks of length 100. Show how generic packages can be used with an external representation of stacks to provide manipulation of general stacks.

There are several differences between internal and external representations. In Ada, external representations are more general. For example, by using an external representation, it is possible to treat STACKs as bona fide data values; they can be assigned, passed as parameters, and made elements of other data structures. For example, if we don't know exactly how many stacks we will need, we can declare an array or linked list of STACKs and initialize (via NEW_STACK) just as many elements as are required. Thus, for an external representation, the number of instances can be determined dynamically; whereas for an internal representation, the number of instances is limited by the number of generic instantiations the programmer writes. This is not an inherent characteristic of internal representations; for example, Simula and Smalltalk (Chapter 12) use an internal representation for all data abstractions (called *classes*), but allow them to be dynamically instantiated. We will see in Chapter 12 that this is a more *object-oriented* approach to data abstraction.

EXERCISE 7-16:* Compare and contrast Simula's or Smalltalk's *class* facility and Ada's *package* facility. Discuss ease of use, efficiency, security, power, and so forth.

Overloaded Procedures Complicate Operator Identification

We have seen that the members of enumeration types can be overloaded. We have also seen (in COMPLEX_TYPE) that the built-in operators can be overloaded; that is, a particular operator symbol (e.g., '+') can stand for several different procedures, which in turn are selected by the context of the symbol's use. For example, 'Z := X+Y' may invoke the built-in '+' procedures (for INTEGERs and floating-point types) or any user-defined '+' procedure (e.g., one for adding a real number to a complex number), depending on the types of Z, X, and Y. This process is called *operator identification.* In Ada procedures can also be overloaded; this most commonly occurs with generic packages. Suppose INT_STACK_TYPE and CHAR_STACK_TYPE are packages that implement externally represented stacks of integers and characters, respectively. An example of their use is:

```
declare
  S1 : INT_STACK_TYPE.STACK;
  S2 : CHAR_STACK_TYPE.STACK;
begin
  INT_STACK_TYPE.PUSH (S1,5);
  CHAR_STACK_TYPE.PUSH (S2,'A');
end;
```

It is very inconvenient to have to prefix every call of PUSH or POP with INT_STACK_TYPE or CHAR_STACK_TYPE, so we can employ 'use' to avoid this:

```
declare
  S1 : INT_STACK_TYPE.STACK;
  S2 : CHAR_STACK_TYPE.STACK;
  use INT_STACK_TYPE;
  use CHAR_STACK_TYPE;
begin
  PUSH (S1,5);
  PUSH (S2,'A');
end;
```

After the two 'use' declarations have been elaborated, there are two definitions of each of the stack procedures (PUSH, POP, EMPTY, FULL) available, one for integer stacks and one for character stacks. These are distinguished by context, just as for overloaded operators. 'PUSH (S1,5)' must be the PUSH from INT_STACK_TYPE because S1 is an integer stack and 5 is an integer. Because procedures can be overloaded, we can see that an Ada compiler must go through a process of operator identification for procedure names. This process depends on both the arguments of the subprogram and, if it is a function, its context of use. For example, in the expression:

```
Z := F (G (X,Y));
```

the F procedure to be used depends both on the type of Z (i.e., F's context) and on the type returned by G (i.e., F's argument). On the other hand, G itself may be an overloaded procedure so that its meaning depends on its arguments (X and Y) and its context of use (the argument required by F). For the Ada program to be correct, there must be a unique selection for each of F and G that satisfies the above constraints. If there is none, the program is meaningless; if there is more than one, it is ambiguous. We can see that if overloading is used extensively, it may become very difficult for both the human reader and the compiler to determine what an Ada expression means. The operator identification process is further complicated by optional and position-independent parameters, which are discussed in Chapter 8, Section 8.1. Operator identification is usually accomplished by propagating type information up and down an expression tree in several passes, the exact number of passes required being a subject of ongoing research. You may think that overloaded procedures are uncommon, but this is not the case. For example, the Ada input-output package defines over 14 meanings for GET, one for each built-in type (in fact, there are more, since there is one for each enumeration type). Further, programmers are encouraged to overload procedure names by allowing them to declare new meanings for procedures directly.

*EXERCISE 7-17**:* Here are two conflicting goals: (1) Overloaded operators are very convenient for groups of related operations, for example, addition on various kinds of numbers and matrices and PUSH on various kinds of stacks. (2) This extensible overloading introduces complexity into the language for both the reader and the compiler. Discuss various ways of resolving these conflicting goals, and propose and defend a good solution.

EXERCISES*

1. Defend or attack this statement: Strong typing has gotten out of hand; it now gets in the way of programming rather than simplifying it.
2. An Ada constant declaration can bind names to the values of expressions. These expressions are evaluated when the scope of the declaration is entered. Describe in detail the implementation of Ada's constant declarations.
3. Find examples of the interface specification versus implementation distinction in other engineering disciplines, such as electrical engineering, architecture, automobile construction, and stereo systems.
4. Read and critique the discussion of name and structural type equivalence in: Welsh, J., Sneeringer, M. J., and Hoare, C. A. R., "Ambiguities and Insecurities in Pascal," *Software—Practice and Experience* 7, 6, November 1977.
5. Read about at least one other abstract type language (e.g., Alphard, CLU, Euclid, Modula, Tartan) and write a detailed comparison with Ada.
6. Ada provides only a limited amount of control over access to data structures. In "The Narrowing Gap Between Language Systems and Operating Systems" (*Information Processing* 77, North-Holland, 1977), Anita Jones argues that language designers can learn a lot from operating system mechanisms for access control. Read and critique this paper.
7. In "Information Distribution Aspects of Design Methodology" (*Information Processing* 71, North-Holland, 1971), Parnas does not propose any linguistic mechanisms for supporting information hiding. Attack or defend the position that linguistic mechanisms are needed to enforce information hiding.

8. Evaluate the alternatives to global variables discussed in J. E. George and G. R. Sager's "Variables—Binding and Protection" (*SIGPLAN Notices 8*, 12, December 1973).

9**. We have discussed the similarities between generic packages and procedures; they are both parameterized abstraction mechanisms. If procedures were allowed to return packages, then the two would be the same. Develop this idea in detail. What extensions would have to be made to procedures to capture all of the power of generic packages? What implications would this have for the rest of the language? Would implementation of package returning procedures be more or less difficult than implementation of generic packages?

10**. Packages are second-class citizens in Ada. For example, packages can't be passed as parameters, stored in variables, or made elements of arrays. Investigate in detail the design and implementation issues that would result from making packages first-class citizens.

PROCEDURES AND CONCURRENCY: ADA

8.1 DESIGN: CONTROL STRUCTURES

Ada Has a Rich Set of Control Structures

Ada has a much richer set of control structures than Pascal. These include:

1. A conditional
2. An iterator (definite and indefinite)
3. A case-statement
4. Subprograms
5. A goto-statement
6. Facilities for handling exceptions
7. Facilities for concurrent programming

The last two have no corresponding Pascal constructs; the others are generalizations of Pascal.

There Is One, All-Purpose Iterator

Ada provides one iteration statement, the 'loop', which handles definite, indefinite, and even infinite iteration. Although it is quite general and solves some of the problems of previous iterators, it is also quite baroque. The basic loop-statement has the syntax

```
loop <sequence of statements> end loop
```

This is an example of an *infinite* iterator; the sequence of statements is executed forever.

Unending loops are not often needed in programming, so Ada provides an *exit-statement* for terminating a loop. Executing an exit-statement anywhere within the body of the loop will cause the loop to be aborted and control to be resumed after the 'end loop'. For example,[1] this code searches an array A for a key K:

```
I := A'FIRST;
loop
  if I > A'LAST then exit; end if;
  if A(I) = K then exit; end if;
  I := I+1;
end loop;
```

Notice that there can be any number of exits and that they are embedded at any depth within the loop. Thus, Ada's loop-statement provides mid-decision loops and, in fact, multiple mid-decision loops. Furthermore, by using labels, an exit-statement can exit through any number of levels of nested loops and can even exit from blocks (although not from subprograms). The 'exit' has some of the characteristics of a nonlocal **goto**.

Since exit-statements are so often the consequents of if-statements, Ada provides a special abbreviation for this case. Using it, the above loop can be written as follows:

```
I := A'FIRST;
loop
  exit when I > A'LAST;
```

1 'A'FIRST' and 'A'LAST' are automatically bound to the lower and upper index values of the array A.

```
  exit when A(I) = K;
  I := I+1;
end loop;
```

The point of this abbreviation is not the (approximately 10) characters it saves us from typing; rather, it was the designers' goal that loop termination conditions be clearly marked. Unfortunately, the 'exit' can be buried quite deeply in the body of the loop and therefore be hard to spot.

Ada carries this process a step further; since 'exit-whens' so often appear at the beginning of loops, it permits these loops to be written in a form resembling Pascal's **while**-loops:

```
I := A'FIRST;
while I <= A'LAST
loop
  exit when A(I) = K;
  I := I+1;
end loop;
```

Notice that the while-phrase is just a prefix on the basic loop.

Ada provides another abbreviation for cases of definite iteration like that above. This is accomplished by preceding the loop-statement with a for-phrase instead of the while-phrase:

```
for I in A'FIRST .. A'LAST
loop
  exit when A(I) = K;
end loop;
```

Unfortunately, this does not work exactly like the while-loop since the for-phrase automatically declares the controlled variable I, thereby making it local to the loop. This means that outside of the loop it will not be possible to determine where K was found. To correct this problem, we must use a different variable as the controlled variable so that we can save K's location in I:

```
for J in A'FIRST .. A'LAST
loop
  if A(J) = K then
    I := J;
    exit;
  end if;
end loop;
```

Notice that we are back to using a simple exit-statement inside an if-statement.

Finally, observe that the above code does not allow us to determine whether K was actually found or not; this is so because the control flow reaches the 'end loop' in both cases. To solve this problem, we must introduce another variable, as is shown in Figure 8.1.

EXERCISE 8-1:* Discuss Ada's loop-statement. Are the various abbreviations and special cases justified? Are Ada's loops potentially too unstructured? Design a better loop syntax and defend it.

EXERCISE 8-2:* Given that Ada has a goto-statement, discuss the value of also including an exit-statement. Conversely, discuss whether a goto-statement should have been included given that Ada has an exit-statement.

The Exception Mechanism Is Elaborate

Recall that Ada is intended for embedded computer applications. Since Ada programs may be embedded in devices (such as missiles) that must act reasonably under a wide variety of conditions and in the face of failures, it is important that Ada programs be able to respond to exceptional situations. This need is satisfied by Ada's *exception mechanism,* which allows us to define exceptional situations, signal their occurrence, and respond to their occurrence.

```
declare
  FOUND: BOOLEAN := FALSE;
begin

  for J in A'FIRST .. A'LAST
  loop
    if A(J) = K then
      I := J;
      FOUND := TRUE;
      exit;
    end if;
  end loop;

  if FOUND then
    :      -- Handle found case
  else
    :      -- Handle not found case
  end if;
end;
```

Figure 8.1 Example of Ada Loop

For example, suppose that a subprogram in an Ada program, PRODUCER, is responsible for gathering data and storing it in a stack for later processing by another subprogram, CONSUMER. If the data arrives more rapidly than expected, then PRODUCER may attempt to put more data in the stack than will fit. This is an exceptional condition, and it is important that the program handle it appropriately.

Look again at the specification and implementation of the STACK1 package in Chapter 7, Section 7.4; notice that we have specified an exception, STACK_ERROR, and that the PUSH procedure *raises* this exception if we attempt to push onto a full stack. Thus, we have defined a possible exceptional situation (a mistake in using STACK1) and have included code to signal the occurrence of this situation. It remains to define a method of handling this exceptional situation.

In this example, we will suppose that recent data is more important than older data so the proper way to handle stack overflow is to pop a few elements from the stack and then add the new data. This can be accomplished by defining an *exception handler*; see Figure 8.2. If PUSH raises STACK_ERROR, then control proceeds directly to the exception handler for STACK_ERROR, which is at the end of the PRODUCER procedure. The execution of PUSH and of the body of PRODUCER is aborted.

Let's look at this mechanism in more detail. Whenever we see a construct for binding names, we should ask ourselves, "What is the scope of these names?"

```
procedure PRODUCER ( ... );
  use STACK1;
begin
    :
  PUSH (DATA);
    :
exception
  when STACK_ERROR =>
    declare SCRATCH: INTEGER;
    begin
      for I in 1..3 loop
        if not EMPTY() then POP(SCRATCH); end if;
      end loop;
      PUSH(DATA);
    end;
end PRODUCER;
```

Figure 8.2 Definition of an Exception Handler

We can see that if exceptions had the same Algol-like scope rule as other identifiers in Ada, then the definition of STACK__ERROR in PRODUCER would not be visible in PUSH. Thus, exceptions must follow their own rules.

The scope rule that exceptions do follow will be clearer when we discuss the *propagation* of exceptions. Suppose that PRODUCER had not defined a handler for STACK__ERROR. What would happen if PUSH raised STACK__ERROR? Ada says that since PRODUCER does not provide a handler for STACK__ERROR, the exception will be *propagated* to the caller of PRODUCER. If the caller defines a handler for STACK__ERROR, then it will be handled there; otherwise the exception will be propagated to the caller's caller, and so forth. This propagation will continue until a handler is found or until the outermost procedure is reached, in which case the program will be terminated.

Now we can see the essence of the scope rule for exceptions. If the exception is defined in the local environment, we go to its handler; otherwise we look for a handler in the caller's environment. We continue down the dynamic chain, going from each subprogram to its caller, until we find an environment that defines a handler for the exception. Thus, with regard to exceptions, subprograms are *called in the environment of the caller,* although in all other respects they are called in the environment of definition. Although all other names in Ada are bound statically, exceptions are bound dynamically. This makes exceptions something of an exception themselves! It also makes Ada more complex since it violates both the Structure and Regularity Principles.

Exceptions must be implemented almost exactly the way we have described them above. When an exception is raised, a run-time routine must scan down the dynamic chain looking for an environment containing a handler for the exception. During this scan the activation record of any subprogram or block that doesn't define a handler for the exception must be deleted. Thus we can see that an exception is something like a dynamically scoped nonlocal **goto**.

EXERCISE 8-3: Explain why Ada's exceptions violate the Structure Principle.

*EXERCISE 8-4**:* Define and describe a *statically scoped* exception mechanism for Ada. How is it less general than Ada's mechanism?

EXERCISE 8-5:* Evaluate the following argument for a dynamically scoped exception mechanism: A dynamic scope rule is the only useful scope rule for an exception mechanism. It is often the case that different callers of a subprogram will want to handle exceptions arising from that subprogram in different ways. If the handler for an exception were bound in a subprogram's environment of definition, it would be fixed for all time. In that case, it might as well be made part of the subprogram.

Parameters Can Be In, Out, or In Out

In previous chapters, we have seen a number of different *modes* for passing parameters to subprograms, namely, value, reference, name, constant, and value-result. All of these techniques have some advantages and some disadvantages; none of the languages we've studied seem to provide just the right set of modes. Ada, however, provides three parameter passing modes that seem to come close to achieving this. We will discuss why later; first, we will investigate these modes.

Ada's parameter passing modes reflect the ways in which the programmer may intend to use the parameter: input, output, or both input and output. These modes are indicated by the reserved words 'in', 'out', or 'in out' preceding the specification of the formal parameter in the formal parameter list. If the mode is omitted, then 'in' is assumed.

'In' parameters are used to transmit information into a procedure but not out of it; they are essentially the same as the *constant* parameters described in the original Pascal Report (see Chapter 5, Section 5.5). Since these parameters are for input, the language allows only read access to them; assignments to formal 'in' parameters are illegal (i.e., 'in' parameters act like constants within the body of the procedure).

Recall that pass as constant leaves it up to the compiler to determine whether a parameter's value or address is actually passed. Ada doesn't go quite this far; it specifies that scalar parameters will always be copied (i.e., passed by value). For *composite types* (e.g., arrays and records), the compiler may choose either to copy the value (if it's short) or to pass its address.

'Out' parameters are just the opposite of 'in'; they are used for transmitting results out of a subprogram. Hence, these parameters are considered write-only; within the subprogram they can be used as a destination but not as a source. Obviously, the actual parameter corresponding to an 'out' formal must be something into which it is meaningful to store, that is, a variable of some type.

'Out' parameters are quite efficient: Just as for 'in' parameters, scalar 'out' parameters are copied out, and composite parameters may be either passed by reference or copied out. Note that copying out the value of an 'out' parameter is essentially the result half of pass by value-result (Chapter 2, Section 2.3).

The remaining parameter passing mode is 'in out'; this is used for parameters that are to be used as both a source and a destination within the subprogram. Since the actual parameter is potentially a destination, it must be a variable of some sort, just as for 'out' parameters.

The same implementation methods are used for 'in out' parameters: For scalar values the values are copied in on call and out on return, which is essentially pass by value-result. Composite parameters may be passed by reference or value-result, compiler's choice.

Ada seems to have solved the problems that we saw in the parameter passing modes of FORTRAN, Algol-60, and Pascal. The reason is that Ada's solution is more *orthogonal,* that is, it better separates the independent functions. In the case of parameters, there are two issues:

1. How the parameter is to be used (i.e., input, output, or both input and output)
2. How the parameter transmission is to be implemented (i.e., pass by reference, or pass by value and/or result)

The first issue is a *logical* issue, that is, it affects the input-output behavior of the program. The second issue is a *performance* issue, that is, it affects the efficiency of the program. Ada allows the programmer to resolve the first issue (by specifying a parameter as 'in', 'out', or 'in out'). It reserves to the compiler the right to resolve the second issue since requiring the programmer to make this choice would introduce a machine dependency into the programs (and violate the Portability Principle). The other languages we have discussed garbled these two issues; Ada's orthogonal solution can be visualized as follows:

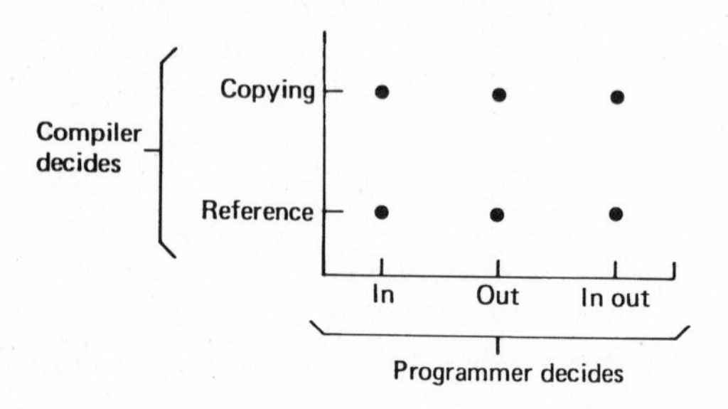

Ada slightly mixes two other issues that should be orthogonal, namely, the reference/copying issue and the parameter's type, since it specifies that scalar parameters are always copied.

How does the compiler decide whether to pass a parameter by reference or by copying? This is easy to analyze. Suppose that a composite parameter occupies s words (or whatever the units of storage may be) and that each component of the parameter occupies one word. This would be the case if, for example, the parameter were an array of integers. Further, suppose that during the execution of the subprogram components of this parameter are accessed n times. We can compute C, the cost of passing the parameter by copying, and R, the cost for reference.

If the parameter is copied, then $2s$ memory references will be required to transmit it and one memory reference will be required for each of the succeeding n accesses to components. Hence,

$$C = 2s + n$$

If the parameter is passed by reference, then one memory reference is required to transmit it (assuming an address fits in one storage unit), and two are required for each of the succeeding n accesses to components. The latter is true because a reference parameter must be accessed indirectly.[2] Hence,

$$R = 2n + 1$$

Now we can determine the conditions under which it is less expensive to pass a parameter by reference than by copying. $R < C$ whenever $2n + 1 < 2s + n$, hence $R < C$ whenever $n < 2s - 1$. We can see the regions where reference or copy is better in the following diagram:

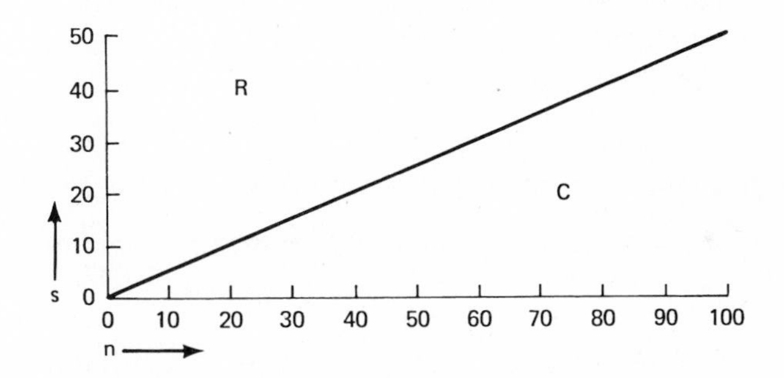

Unfortunately, since n depends on the dynamic behavior of the program, it is usually impossible for a compiler to determine this value. Therefore, the decision of whether to use value or reference parameters must be based on some plausible assumptions. For example, if we assume that the parameter is an array and each array element is referenced once, then $n = s$ (if each element occupies one storage unit), $C = 3n$, and $R < C$; so pass by reference is less expensive. When will copying be less expensive than pass by reference? Note that $R > C$ when $n > 2s - 1$. Therefore, copying is less expensive if on the average each array element is accessed at least twice.

2 We are ignoring the possibility that the compiler might optimize code by keeping the address of the actual parameter in a register across several accesses.

EXERCISE 8-6:* Is it a good or a bad idea that Ada specifies that scalar parameters always be copied (passed by value and/or result)? Discuss the factors involved, including representation independence, efficiency, and predictability.

EXERCISE 8-7: Write a subprogram whose results differ depending on whether a given *composite* parameter is passed by reference or by copying. This permits us to determine the parameter passing methods used by a compiler (and also shows that Ada programs may be implementation sensitive).

EXERCISE 8-8:* A program that depends on the implementation of Ada, such as the one you wrote in the previous exercise, is not considered legal Ada. Unfortunately, it is very difficult for a compiler to check for this situation. Is this a good design decision? Discuss the philosophy of defining errors that can't be practically checked by a compiler. Is there any alternative? Discuss and evaluate the possibilities.

EXERCISE 8-9: The above analysis of the pass by reference/pass by copy trade-off applies to 'in' and 'out' parameters (i.e., parameters that are copied once). Extend this analysis to 'in out' parameters, which must be copied twice. Assume that an address takes two units of storage (e.g., two bytes) rather than one.

Position-Independent and Default Parameters

Suppose we are implementing an Ada package to draw graphs. The package might contain this specification of a routine to draw the axes of the graph:

```
procedure DRAW_AXES (X_ORIGIN, Y_ORIGIN: COORD;
  X_SCALE, Y_SCALE: FLOAT; X_SPACING, Y_SPACING: NATURAL;
  X_LOGARITHMIC, Y_LOGARITHMIC: BOOLEAN;
  X_LABELS, Y_LABELS: BOOLEAN; FULL_GRID: BOOLEAN);
```

Procedures with a large number of parameters, such as this, are not uncommon in subprogram libraries that are trying to achieve generality and flexibility. A call to DRAW_AXES can look like this:

```
DRAW_AXES (500, 500, 1.0, 0.5, 10, 10,
           FALSE, TRUE, TRUE, TRUE, FALSE);
```

It is very difficult to tell the meanings of the parameters from this call; even if programmers know the purpose of DRAW_AXES, they will have to look up its definition to find out the meaning of the parameters.

The problem with the above procedure specification is that the order of the parameters is essentially arbitrary. Although it makes sense that an x-related parameter always precedes the corresponding y-related parameter, there is no particular reason why the scale factors should precede the spacings or the requests for labels follow the requests for logarithmic spacing. People remember things most easily when they are related meaningfully. When there are no meaningful relationships, the only alternate is rote memorization, which is error-prone.

Operating system command languages long ago found a solution to the problem of programs with many parameters: *position-independent parameters.* The basic idea is that the parameters can be listed in any order. Then, in order to tell which is which, a name is associated with each parameter; this names identifies the parameter's function. Our DRAW_AXES example can be written using position-independent parameters in Ada as follows:

```
DRAW_AXES (X_ORIGIN => 500, Y_ORIGIN => 500,
  X_SPACING => 10, Y_SPACING => 10, FULL_GRID => FALSE,
  X_SCALE => 1.0, Y_SCALE => 0.5,
  X_LABEL => TRUE, Y_LABEL => TRUE,
  X_LOGARITHMIC => FALSE, Y_LOGARITHMIC => TRUE );
```

This is more readable and much less prone to mistakes than the position-dependent version.

Position-independent parameters are another illustration of the Labeling Principle.

The Labeling Principle

Avoid arbitrary sequences more than a few items long; do not require the programmer to know the absolute position of an item in a list. Instead, associate a meaningful label with each item, and allow the items to occur in any order.

We have already seen several examples of this principle: All programming languages provide symbolic names for variables rather than requiring the programmer to remember the absolute memory location of the variables. We have also seen (Chapter 5, Section 5.5) the advantages of Pascal's *labeled* case-statement over earlier *unlabeled* case-statements.

Ada provides an additional facility, also suggested by operating system control languages, that can improve the readability of our call on DRAW_AXES; these are *default* parameters. The motivation for these is simple: In an attempt to be general, DRAW_AXES provides many different options. There are several of these that will be rarely used; for example, most users will not want a full grid or logarithmic axes. Unfortunately, all users must specify these options, if only to disable them, in order for them to be available to a small fraction of the users. This is actually a violation of the Localized Cost Principle, which says that users should not have to pay for what they don't use.

Default parameters solve this violation of the Localized Cost Principle by permitting the designer of a subprogram to specify *default values* that are supplied for parameters if the corresponding actuals are omitted. The following is a reasonable set of defaults for DRAW_AXES:

```
procedure DRAW_AXES (X_ORIGIN, Y_ORIGIN: COORD := 0;
  X_SCALE, Y_SCALE: REAL := 1.0;
  X_SPACING, Y_SPACING: NATURAL := 1;
  X_LABEL, Y_LABEL: BOOLEAN := TRUE;
  X_LOGARITHMIC, Y_LOGARITHMIC: BOOLEAN := FALSE;
  FULL_GRID: BOOLEAN := FALSE );
```

This declaration permits us to write the preceding call to DRAW_AXES in a much more compact form:

```
DRAW_AXES(500, 500, Y_SCALE =>0.5, Y_LOGARITHMIC => TRUE,
  X_SPACING => 10, Y_SPACING => 10);
```

Notice that position-dependent and position-independent parameters can be mixed in a single call; the *x* and *y* origins are specified position dependently in the above call.

Position-Independent and Default Parameters Complicate Operator Identification

Of course, all this flexibility does not come without a cost. A major part of the cost is the increased complexity of the language manual and the greater number of constructs that the programmers must learn. In Ada, however, there is a less obvious cost that results from *feature interaction*, in this case, the interaction of overloading with position-independent and default parameters.

Recall that an overloaded subprogram can have several meanings in one context; the compiler determines the meaning intended on the basis of the types of the parameters and the context of use of the subprogram. Consider the following procedure declarations, both occurring in the same scope:

```
procedure P (X: INTEGER; Y: BOOLEAN := FALSE);
procedure P (X: INTEGER; Y: INTEGER := 0);
```

The procedure P is overloaded because it bears two meanings at once. The rules of operator identification tell us that 'P(9, TRUE)' is a call on the first procedure and 'P(5, 8)' is a call on the second. Notice, however, that we have provided a default value for Y in both procedure declarations. What is the meaning of the call 'P(3)'? It could be either one since we have omitted the only parameter that distinguishes the two overloadings. In fact, because the call 'P(3)' is ambiguous, Ada does not allow the two procedure declarations shown above. A set of subprogram declarations is illegal if it introduces the *potential* for ambiguous calls.

These potential ambiguities can arise in many ways. Consider the declarations:

```
type PRIMARY is (RED, BLUE, GREEN);
type STOP_LIGHT is (RED, YELLOW, GREEN);

procedure SWITCH (COLOR: PRIMARY; X: FLOAT; Y: FLOAT);
procedure SWITCH (LIGHT: STOP_LIGHT; Y: FLOAT; X:FLOAT);
```

These look quite different, and there are no defaults. Unfortunately, the call

```
SWITCH (RED, X => 0.0, Y => 0.0);
```

is ambiguous, so the declarations are illegal. Here we can see the interaction of *two overloadings* — an overloaded enumeration and an overloaded procedure.

The rules that specify what overloadings are allowed are actually quite a bit more complicated than we have described. Suffice it to say that both the human reader and the compiler can have difficulty with a program that makes extensive use of overloading and position-independent and default parameters.

EXERCISE 8-10: Explain in detail why the preceding call of SWITCH is illegal.

*EXERCISE 8-11**:* We have seen the benefits both of overloading and of position-independent and default parameters. We have also seen some of the complications that result from the interaction of these features. Has Ada made the right choice? Either propose your own alternative and argue that it is better than Ada's or show that Ada's solution is better than the alternatives.

Ada Permits Concurrent Execution

When people set out to accomplish some task, it is often more efficient and more convenient to do several things at the same time. For example, one person may read a map while the other drives. There would not be much point in finishing the driving before the map reading is started, and it wouldn't be very efficient to do all of the map reading before starting the driving. The same holds true in programming; therefore, Ada provides a *tasking* facility that allows a program to do more than one thing at a time.

Let's consider an example. Suppose we have a small, stand-alone word-processing system that allows users to print one file while they are editing another. This is programmed in Ada by defining two disjoint tasks, say PRINT and EDIT; see Figure 8.3. Here we have a procedure, WORD_PROCESSOR, with two local tasks, EDIT and PRINT. Notice that a task is declared very much like a package, with a separate specification and body. In this case, there are no public names so there is nothing in the specification.

When we call WORD_PROCESSOR, all local tasks are automatically initiated. That is, we do three things at once: We begin executing the bodies of WORD_PROCESSOR, EDIT, and PRINT. We can assume that EDIT does its job of communicating with the user and editing the file while PRINT does its job of listing another file on the printer. What does WORD_PROCESSOR do? In this example, not very much. Since the body of the procedure is empty, we immediately encounter the 'end' and try to return. Ada, however, prevents a procedure from returning as long as it has active local tasks. Hence, WORD_PROCESSOR will wait as long as EDIT and PRINT are executing. When they have both finished (by reaching their end-statements), then WORD_PROCESSOR will be able to return to its caller. This can be visualized as follows:

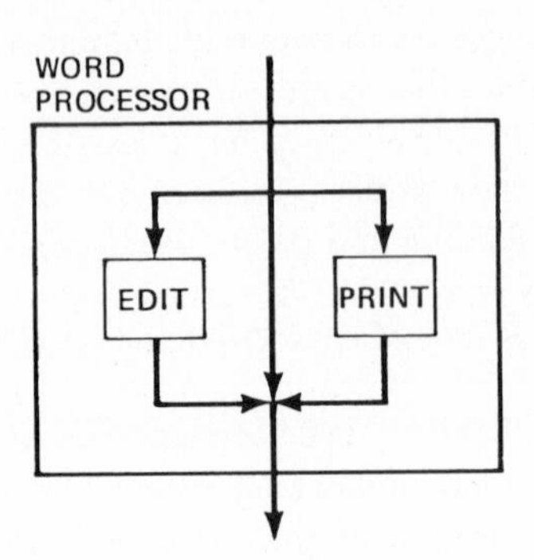

Only when EDIT, PRINT, and the body of WORD_PROCESSOR have all reached their 'end's can WORD_PROCESSOR exit.

Why does Ada require all local tasks to finish before a procedure can exit? Suppose that WORD_PROCESSOR had some local variables; these are visible to EDIT and PRINT because they are declared in the same environment. Consider what happens when WORD_PROCESSOR exits; like all procedures, its activation record is deleted. Any references in EDIT and PRINT to the local variables of WORD_PROCESSOR will now be meaningless; they will be *dangling references.* One alternative is to preserve WORD_PROCESSOR's activation record until EDIT and PRINT have finished. This in turn precludes using a

```
procedure WORD_PROCESSOR is

   task EDIT; end EDIT;

   task body EDIT is
   begin
     :      - - edit the file selected
   end;

   task PRINT; end PRINT;

   task body PRINT is
   begin
     :      - - print the file selected
   end;

begin
   :      - - initiate tasks and wait for their completion
end WORD_PROCESSOR;
```

Figure 8.3 Noncommunicating Tasks

simple stack discipline for activation record allocation and deallocation.[3] The alternative is to delay WORD_PROCESSOR's return until it can be done safely; this is an example of the Security Principle.

EXERCISE 8-12:* Discuss alternative solutions to the dangling reference problem. Either investigate nonstacked activation records, or suggest another approach that prevents dangling references and still permits the use of a stack.

Tasks Communicate by Rendezvous

We have seen an example of two tasks that execute concurrently, but do not communicate. This is not usually the case; consider our driving and map-reading example. If the concurrent map reading is to be useful, it will be necessary for the map reader to communicate directions to the driver. It may even be necessary for the driver to pull off the road and wait for the map reader to decide where they should turn next.

The same is the case in programming. Suppose we have an application that retrieves records from a database, summarizes them, and prints the results. Since

3 This would be an example of a *retention* strategy, such as discussed in Chapter 6, Section 6.2.

the retrieval and summarization processes are fairly independent, we can implement them as tasks that run concurrently. However, they will have to communicate; the SUMMARY task will have to tell the RETRIEVAL task which record it wants, and the RETRIEVAL task will have to transmit the records to the SUMMARY process when they're found. An outline of the program appears in Figure 8.4.

Notice that the specification of RETRIEVAL contains two 'entry' declarations. We can see that these have parameters very much like procedures, and, in fact, they can be called like procedures. For example, the body to SUMMARY might look like this:

```
task body SUMMARY is
begin
  :
  SEEK (ID);
  :
  FETCH (NEW_RECD);
  :
end SUMMARY;
```

```
procedure DB_SYSTEM is
  task SUMMARY; end SUMMARY;
  task body SUMMARY is
  begin
    :     - - generate the summary
  end;
  task RETRIEVAL;
    entry SEEK (K: KEY);
    entry FETCH (out R: RECD);
  end RETRIEVAL;
  task body RETRIEVAL is
  begin
    :     - - seek record and return it
  end;
begin
  :     - - await completion of local tasks
end DB_SYSTEM;
```

Figure 8.4 Communicating Tasks

The SEEK call tells RETRIEVAL to find the record in the database, and the FETCH call puts its value in NEW_ RECD. Although procedures and entries are similar in some ways, there are important differences.

Recall how a normal procedure call works: When one subprogram calls another, the parameters are transmitted from the caller to the callee, the caller is suspended, and the callee is activated. The caller remains suspended until the callee returns; at that time the results are transmitted from the callee back to the caller, the callee is deactivated, and the caller is resumed (i.e., reactivated).

When one task calls an 'entry' in another, it transmits parameters very much like a procedure call. The difference is that once the callee accepts the parameters, the caller continues executing; it is not suspended. The two tasks remain active and continue to execute concurrently. Thus, the call 'SEEK (ID)' is more properly viewed as a *message-sending* operation in which the message (ID) is put into the 'entry SEEK' where it is available to RETRIEVAL. In fact, an 'entry' is often called a *mailbox* or *message port.*

How does a task accept a message? This is accomplished with an *accept-statement*, which has the syntax

```
accept <name> (<formals>) do <statements> end <name>;
```

For example, the body of RETRIEVAL might look like the following:

```
task body RETRIEVAL is
begin
  loop
    accept SEEK (K: KEY) do
      RK := K;
    end SEEK;
    :     -- seek record RK and put in RECD_VALUE
    accept FETCH (out R: RECD) do
      R := RECD_VALUE;
    end FETCH;
  end loop;
end RETRIEVAL;
```

Notice that RETRIEVAL is written as a loop that alternatively seeks a record and returns its value. The first accept-statement accepts a message from the SEEK mailbox and binds the formal parameter K to this message.

What happens if RETRIEVAL reaches this accept-statement before SUMMARY has sent the message? Does RETRIEVAL come away empty handed?

No, just as in our map-reading example, "it pulls over to the side of the road" and waits for a message in SEEK. In other words, it suspends itself awaiting the arrival of a message in the mailbox SEEK. Then, when SUMMARY sends the message, it will be accepted and both tasks will proceed concurrently. Similarly, if SUMMARY attempts to transmit SEEK(ID) before RETRIEVAL is ready to accept it, SUMMARY will be suspended until RETRIEVAL accepts a message from SEEK. Thus, a message is only actually transmitted when the entries to which the sender calls and from which the receiver accepts are the same. This meeting is called a "rendezvous" in the Ada literature. The rendezvous may never take place, so one or both tasks may wait forever, a situation called *dead-lock.*

The structure of the database system is pictured in Figure 8.5. The message ports (mailboxes, entries) are shown as circles. You may be surprised to see that the arrow for FETCH goes from SUMMARY to RETRIEVAL. This is so because SUMMARY places a message in FETCH to request that the value of the record be put in an output parameter (NEW_RECD); RETRIEVAL accepts this message and puts the value in NEW_RECD.

*EXERCISE 8-13**:* We have only touched on the essentials of Ada's task facility. Look up tasking in the Ada Reference Manual and evaluate its other features. Are there too many features? Is the language too complex in this area? Are there too few features? Are there important things that cannot be easily accomplished with Ada's tasks? Explain or defend your answers.

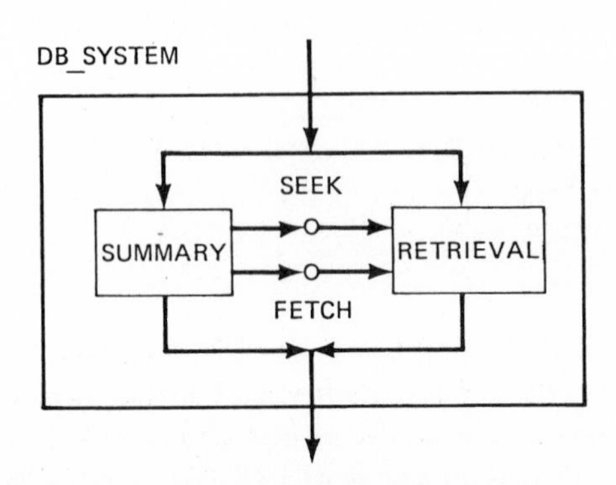

Figure 8.5 Structure of Concurrent Database System

8.2 DESIGN: SYNTACTIC STRUCTURES

Ada Follows Pascal in the Algol Tradition

In most respects Ada's syntactic conventions follow the Pascal tradition (which is in turn in the Algol tradition), although in some cases they have been made more systematic. For example, in Chapter 6 we saw that blocks can be considered degenerate procedures. This similarity is reflected in Ada's syntax for blocks and procedures:

```
declare                           procedure <name> (<formals>) is
   <local declarations>              <local declarations>
begin                             begin
   <statements>                      <statements>
exceptions                        exceptions
   <exception handlers>              <exception handlers>
end;                              end;
```

The difference between procedures and blocks is that procedures have a name and formals (and hence can be called from different contexts with different parameters) whereas blocks do not. We have also seen that functions and task bodies follow a similar pattern.

There are other cases where Ada has made syntactic similarities reflect semantic similarities. For example, Ada's notation for a variant record, which defines several different cases for a record, has been made to look like a case-statement. Also, the notation for position-independent actual parameters is similar to the notation for initializing arrays and other composite data structures. These are examples of the Syntactic Consistency Principle.

> ***The Syntactic Consistency Principle***
>
> Things that look similar should *be* similar; things that *are* different should look different.

Another difference between Pascal and Ada is the use of semicolons. In Pascal, as in Algol, semicolons are *separators*: they come *between* statements. Thus, there is a similarity between infix operators separating their operands:

$(E_1 + E_2 + E_3)$

and semicolons separating statements:

begin S_1 ; S_2 ; S_3 **end**

This convention creates some minor maintenance problems since if we need to insert a new statement before the **end** in a compound statement like the following:

begin
  S_1;
  S_2;
  S_3
end

we must remember to add a semicolon to S_3. Fortunately, both Algol and Pascal allow *empty statements*, so we can write

begin
  S_1;
  S_2;
  S_3;
end

You can't see it, but there's an empty statement between the last semicolon and the **end**. Many Pascal programmers terminate each statement with a semicolon, which simplifies editing.

Ada has adopted a different convention, a *terminating semicolon*, for the reason described above, and also because some studies suggest that a terminating semicolon is less error-prone. Both statements and declarations in Ada end with semicolons, even before 'end's, and there is no need for an empty statement.

Ada Uses a Fully Bracketed Syntax

Recall that one of the contributions of Algol was the *compound statement*, which allows statements to contain other statements. This led to the ability to structure programs hierarchically and spurred interest in structured programming. The compound statement idea had a flaw, however; look at these Pascal constructs:

for i := ... **do begin** ... **end**
if ... **then begin** ... **end else begin** ... **end**
procedure ... **begin** ... **end**
function ... **begin** ... **end**

```
case ... of a: begin ... end; ... end
while ... do begin ... end
with ... do begin ... end
record ... end
```

Notice that all of these compound structures end with the same keyword, **end**. Therefore, if the programmer omits an **end**, it is very likely that the compiler will only discover it at the end of the program and that all the **begins** and **ends** will be matched up incorrectly. Similarly, it can be quite difficult for a human reader looking at an **end** to tell exactly what it is ending.

One solution to this problem is to use a variety of different kinds of brackets. For instance, in mathematics we have (...), {...}, [...]. About the time Pascal was being designed, language designers were experimenting with this solution to the **begin–end** problem, although the ideas go back to at least Algol-58. The result—a *fully bracketed* syntax—arrived too late for Pascal, but was adopted by Ada. This means that each construct has its own kind of brackets; for example, in Ada we have:

```
loop ... end loop
if ... end if
case ... end case
record ... end record
```

For constructs that are named, such as subprograms, packages, entries, and tasks, a unique bracket is made by attaching the name to 'end':

```
function <name> (<formals>) is ... begin ...end <name> ;
procedure <name> (<formals>) is ...begin ... end <name> ;
package <name> is ... end <name> ;
package body <name> is ... end <name> ;
accept <name> (<formals>) do ... end <name> ;
```

This allows the compiler to do better error checking since it can ensure that an 'end' goes with the correct declaration.

The fully bracketed syntax interacts with the if-statement in an interesting way: It is common to break the flow of control into $n+1$ paths P_1, P_2, ..., P_n, P_{n+1} on the basis of conditions C_1, C_2, ..., C_n. This leads to a program that looks like the following (where $n = 3$):

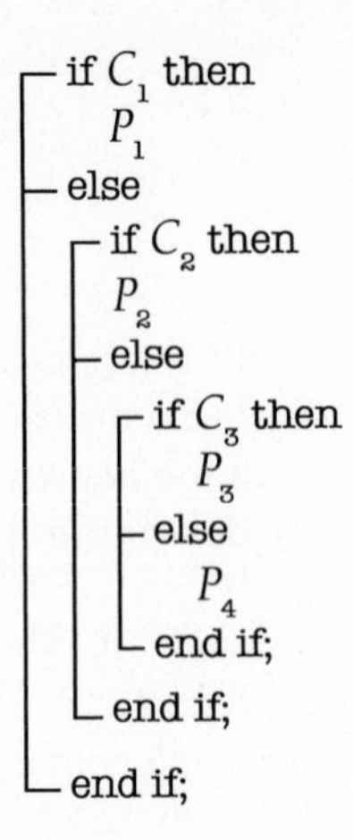

Although the indenting accurately reflects the way in which the if-statements are built up from other if-statements, it does not accurately reflect the intentions of the programmer, which is that there are four similar cases. It actually *violates* the Structure Principle. For this reason Ada provided a case-statement-like syntax for expressing these else-if chains:

```
if C1 then
   P1
elsif C2 then
   P2
elsif C3 then
   P3
else
   P4
end if;
```

This is an idea that originated in the 1960s in LISP (which is discussed in Chapters 9, 10, and 11). It conforms better to both the Structure Principle and the Syntactic Consistency Principle at the cost of some increased syntactic complexity (thus slightly violating the Simplicity Principle). It is typical of the trade-offs that must be made in language design.

8.3 EVALUATION AND EPILOG

Ada Is an Engineering Trade-Off

Ada is certainly not a perfect language. We have seen that in many cases the designers of Ada had to trade off satisfying one principle for satisfying another. In many cases, the trade-off was implicit: providing some facility versus keeping the language simple. Trade-offs of this sort are common in any kind of engineering design, and different designers will make the trade-offs in different ways, depending on the weight they attach to different factors. For example, adding an air conditioner to a car will decrease its fuel efficiency. Whether this is a good trade-off or not depends a great deal on the climate in which the car will be used, the cost of fuel, and the personal preferences (or values) of the occupants.

DoD Has Disallowed Subsets

One solution that has been adopted in many engineering problems is to provide options; this allows customers to make the trade-offs for themselves. For example, air-conditioning on a car is usually an option. Unfortunately, this solution is not permitted for Ada; the Department of Defense has said that there will be no Ada subsets or supersets. In other words, there is only one Ada language; there are no "optional extras."

Why has this been done? The Department of Defense has decided that the existence of language dialects will seriously hamper portability. In other words, if different dialects of Ada provide different subsets of its facilities, then it will only be possible to port a program if the destination Ada compiler provides the facilities used in the program.

Another reason for disallowing subsets is the discipline it imposes on the language designers. Language designers will be less likely to include highly complex, expensive, or hard-to-implement features in a language if they know that such features must be provided in every implementation. It also discourages them from designing in features that they're not sure how to implement.

Ada Has Been Criticized for Its Size

Ada is not a small language. Although there is no accepted way to measure the size of languages, it is significant that while Ada's context-free grammar is some 1600 tokens long, Pascal's is about 500 and Algol-60's is about 600. Of course, Ada provides some important facilities not included in Pascal and Algol-60, such as packages and tasks. But this does not necessarily mean that Ada's size is acceptable.

Some computer scientists, such as C. A. R. Hoare, have suggested that Ada is so big that few programmers will ever master it. In his Turing Award paper, he said, "Do not allow this language in its present state to be used in applications where reliability is critical...." Hoare has suggested that "by careful pruning of the Ada language, it is still possible to select a very powerful subset that would be reliable and efficient in implementation and safe and economic in use." He makes an important observation: "If you want a language with no subsets, you must make it *small*." The size of Ada remains an issue of vigorous debate. These debates are reminiscent of the debates in the late '60s and early '70s about PL/I's size, which were partly responsible for the success of Pascal.

It Is Too Early To Evaluate Ada's Impact

It is still too early to evaluate the eventual impact of Ada. It typically takes about 5–10 years for a language to become established, although the backing of the Department of Defense will speed the acceptance of Ada. Whether it will be Ada as now defined or some subset, it is almost inevitable that Ada will be an important milestone in programming languages.

Characteristics of Fourth-Generation Programming Languages

Some of the characteristics of the fourth generation[4] are simply a consolidation and correction of certain of those of the third generation. In other respects the fourth-generation languages provide important new facilities, such as linguistic support for information hiding and concurrent programming. We consider in turn each of the structural domains.

The most important contribution of the fourth generation lies in the domain of *name structures*. In fact, *fourth-generation programming language* is essentially synonymous with *data abstraction language*, since the primary characteristic of this generation is the provision of an encapsulation facility supporting the separation of specification and definition, information hiding, and name access by mutual consent. Most of these languages allow encapsulated modules to be generic (or polymorphic), thus leading to an operator identification problem such as we saw in Ada. The optimum mix between flexibility and simplicity has yet to be determined (but see Chapter 12).

The second area in which the fourth generation is distinctive is *control structure*, since it is characteristic of this generation to provide for concurrent pro-

4 We are discussing here the characteristics of fourth-generation *programming* languages. The term "fourth-generation language" is sometimes used to refer to application generator programs, which might or might not be programming languages in the technical sense discussed in the first two pages of the Introduction.

gramming. Most fourth-generation languages use some form of message passing as a means of synchronization and communication among concurrent tasks. On the other hand, the basic framework of these languages is still sequential. Fourth-generation languages typically also have a dynamically scoped exception mechanism for handling both system- and user-defined errors.

The data structure *constructors* of this generation are similar to those of the third generation, except that some problems (e.g., array parameters) have been corrected. Name equivalence is the rule in the fourth generation, although there are numerous exceptions to make it secure yet convenient. The primitive data structures tend to be more complicated than in the third generation, because of the desire to control accuracy and precision in numeric types.

Finally, the *syntactic structures* of the fourth generation are largely those of the second and third, that is, they are in the Algol/Pascal tradition. The major exception is a preference for fully bracketed structures.

In summary, the fourth generation can be seen as the culmination and fulfillment of the evolutionary process that began with FORTRAN. Although these languages are far from perfect, it is difficult to see how substantial improvements can be made to them without a radical change of direction. Does this mean that programming language evolution is at an end? Hardly.

Fifth-Generation Programming Languages

We are now entering the *fifth generation* of programming language design. Nobody yet knows what the dominant programming ideas of this generation will be. Many bold experiments are in progress, but their outcome is still uncertain. Therefore, in the remainder of this book we investigate three possible candidates for the programming paradigm of the future. These are *function-oriented programming, object-oriented programming,* and *logic-oriented programming*. The use of the word "oriented" indicates that each of these paradigms is organized around a comprehensive view of the programming process. Each attempts to push its view to the limit. Which, if any, will become dominant it is too early to say. Perhaps it will be some synthesis of them all.

EXERCISES*

1. Attack or defend this statement: Position-independent arguments are worthless; no procedure should have so many parameters that it needs them, since a large number of parameters results in a very wide interface.
2. Ada is unique among programming languages in that the designers have recorded many of the reasons for their design decisions ("Rationale for

the Design of the ADA Programming Language," *SIGPLAN Notices 14*, 6, June 1979). Write a critique of one chapter of the Ada Rationale.

3. Compare the tasking facilities of Ada with those of Concurrent Pascal (Brinch Hansen, P., "The Programming Language Concurrent Pascal," *IEEE Trans. Software Engineering 1*, 2, June 1975).
4. In the Ada Rationale it is asserted that *path expressions* (Campbell, R. H., and Habermann, A. N., "The Specification of Process Synchronization by Path Expressions," *Lecture Notes in Computer Science 16*, Springer, 1974) can be easily expressed in Ada. Show that this is true.
5. Read and critique Hoare's "Communicating Sequential Processes" (*Comm. ACM 21*, 8, August 1978).
6. Read and critique J. B. Goodenough's "Exception Handling: Issues and a Proposed Notation" (*Comm. ACM 18*, 12, December 1975). Compare the proposal in this paper with Ada's mechanism.
7. Ada's use of a semicolon as a terminator rather than a separator is based on research by Gannon and Horning ("Language Design for Programming Reliability," *IEEE Trans. Software Engineering 1*, 2, June 1975). Critique their paper.

8**. Read and critique the revised "IRONMAN" specifications ("Department of Defense Requirements for High Order Computer Programming Languages," *SIGPLAN Notices 12*, 12, December 1977).

9**. Read the revised "IRONMAN" specifications (see Exercise 8) and decide how well Ada has met them.

10. Read and critique Hoare's Turing Award Paper ("The Emperor's Old Clothes," *Comm. ACM 24*, 2, February 1981).

11**. Read and critique a proposal for decreasing Ada's size (e.g., Ledgard, H. F., and Singer, A., "Scaling Down Ada [Or Towards a Standard Ada]," *Comm. ACM 25*, 2, February 1982).

12**. Shaw, Hilfinger, and Wulf designed the language Tartan to "determine whether a 'simple' language could meet substantially all of the Ironman requirement." Read and critique the papers on Tartan ("TARTAN—Language Design for the Ironman Requirement," *SIGPLAN Notices 13*, 9, September 1978).

9

LIST PROCESSING: LISP

9.1 HISTORY AND MOTIVATION

The Desire for an Algebraic List-Processing Language

LISP developed in the late 1950s out of the needs of artificial intelligence programming.[1] In these applications complex interrelationships among data must be represented. The result is that the pointer and, in particular, linked list structures are natural data-structuring methods. In the 1950s Newell, Shaw, and Simon (at Carnegie Institute of Technology and the Rand Corporation) developed many of the ideas of list processing in the IPL family of programming languages. These ideas included the linked representation of list structures and the use of a stack (specifically, a push-down list) to implement recursion.

1 The historical information in this section is from McCarthy (1978).

In the summer of 1956, the first major workshop on artificial intelligence was held at Dartmouth. At this workshop John McCarthy, then at MIT, heard a description of the IPL 2 programming language, which had a low-level pseudo-code, or assembly-language-like syntax. McCarthy realized that an algebraic list-processing language, on the style of the recently announced FORTRAN I system, would be very useful.

FLPL Was Based on FORTRAN

That summer Gerlernter and Gerberich of IBM were working, with the advice of McCarthy, on a geometry program. As a tool they developed FLPL, the FORTRAN List-Processing Language, by writing a set of list-processing subprograms for use with FORTRAN programs. One result of this work was the development of the basic list-processing primitives that were later incorporated into LISP.

McCarthy Developed the Central Ideas of LISP

Use of FLPL resulted in an important contribution to control structures—the conditional *expression.* Recall that FORTRAN I had only one conditional construct—the arithmetic IF-statement. This construct was very inconvenient for list processing, which led McCarthy, in 1957, to write an IF function with three arguments. Here is an example invocation:

```
X = IF (N .EQ. 0, ICAR(Y), ICDR(Y))
```

The value of this function was either the second or third argument, depending on whether the first argument was true or false. In the above case, if N were zero, then X would be assigned the value of 'ICAR(Y)', otherwise it would be assigned the value of 'ICDR(Y)'. An important consequence of this invention was that it made it feasible to *compose* IF functions and list-processing functions to achieve more complicated actions. We have seen the same *combinatorial power* in Algol's *conditional expression,* for example,

```
x := 0.5 × sqrt (if val < 0 then −val else val)
```

Algol's conditional expression was suggested by McCarthy when he was a member of the Algol committee.

In 1958 McCarthy began using recursion in conjunction with conditional expressions in his definition of list-processing functions. This is a very important idea in LISP, as we will see in Chapter 10, Section 10.1. During the summer of 1958, McCarthy became convinced of the power of the combination of these two constructs. Since FORTRAN does not permit recursive definitions, it became apparent that a new language was needed.

The LISP List-Handling Routines Were Developed First

In the fall of 1958, implementation of a LISP system began. One important component of this was a set of primitive list-handling subroutines for the LISP run-time environment. These were the first parts of the system that were implemented. The original intention was to develop a compiler like FORTRAN. Therefore, to gain experience in code generation, a number of LISP programs were hand compiled into assembly language.

A LISP Universal Function Resulted in an Interpreter

McCarthy became convinced that recursive list-processing functions with conditional expressions formed an easier-to-understand basis for the theory of computation than did other formalisms such as Turing machines. In his 1960 paper, "Recursive Functions of Symbolic Expressions and Their Computation by Machine," he presented his ideas.

In the theory of computation, it is often important to investigate *universal functions.* For example, a *universal Turing machine* is a Turing machine that can simulate any other Turing machine when given a description of the latter machine. Given a universal Turing machine, it becomes possible to prove that certain properties hold of all Turing machines by proving that they hold of the universal Turing machine.

McCarthy did just that with LISP. He defined a universal LISP function that could interpret any other LISP function. That is, he wrote a LISP interpreter in LISP. We will see this interpreter in Chapter 11.

Since LISP manipulates only lists, writing a universal function required developing a way of representing LISP programs as list structures. For example, the function call

```
f [x+y; u*z]
```

would be represented by a list whose first element is 'f' and whose second and third elements are the lists representing 'x + y' and 'u*z'. In LISP this list is written:

```
(f (plus x y) (times u z))
```

The Algol-like notation (e.g., 'f[x + y; u*z]') is called *M-expressions* (*M* for meta-language), and the list notation is called *S-expressions* (*S* for symbolic language).

Once the list representation was designed and the universal function was written, one of the project members realized that the group had, in effect, an interpreter. Therefore, he translated the universal function into assembly language and linked it with the list-handling subroutines. The result was the first working LISP system.

This system required programs to be written in the *S*-expression notation, but this was seen as a temporary inconvenience. The Algol-like LISP 2 system then being designed would permit the use of the *M*-expression notation. This system, however, was never completed, and LISP programmers still write their programs in *S*-expressions. Although this was an accident, we will see later that it is now recognized as one of the main advantages of LISP.

LISP Became Widely Used in Artificial Intelligence

The first implementation of LISP was on the IBM 704 (the same machine that hosted the first implementation of FORTRAN). A prototype interactive LISP system was demonstrated in 1960 and was one of the earliest examples of interactive computing. LISP systems rapidly spread to other computers, and they now exist on virtually all machines, including microcomputers. LISP has become the most widely used programming language for artificial intelligence and other symbolic applications. McCarthy claims that LISP is second only to FORTRAN in being the oldest programming language still in widespread use.

9.2 DESIGN: STRUCTURAL ORGANIZATION

An Example LISP Program

Figure 9.1 shows an example LISP program in the *S*-expression notation. The purpose of this program is to generate a "frequency table" that records the number of times a particular word appears in a given list of words. Three functions are defined: 'make-table' and its auxiliary function 'update-entry' construct the frequency table; 'lookup' uses the resulting frequency table to determine the number of occurrences of a given word. The session shown also defines 'text' to be a particular list of words (viz., 'to be or not to be') and 'Freq' to be the frequency table computed from this list.

(Do not expect to be able to read this program unless you have had previous LISP experience. It is included here so that you can see the general appearance of LISP programs.)

```
(defun make-table (text table)
  (cond   ((null text) table)
          (t (make-table  (cdr text)
                          (update-entry table (car text)) )) ))

(defun update-entry (table word)
  (cond   (( null table) (list (list word 1)) )
          ((eq word (caar table))
          (cons (list word (add1 (cadar table)))
                (cdr table)))
          (t (cons  (car table)
                    (update-entry (cdr table) word))) ))

(defun lookup (table word)
  (cond   ((null table) 0)
          ((eq word (caar table)) (cadar table))
          (t (lookup (cdr table) word)) ))

(set 'text '(to be or not to be))

(set 'Freq (make-table text nil))
```

Figure 9.1 Example of LISP Program

Function Application Is the Central Idea

Programming languages are often divided into two classes. *Imperative languages,* which include all of the languages we've discussed so far, depend heavily on an assignment statement and a changeable memory for accomplishing a programming task. In previous chapters we have pointed out that most programming languages are basically collections of mechanisms for routing control from one assignment statement to another.

In an *applicative language,* the central idea is function application, that is, applying a function to its arguments. Previous chapters have shown some of the power of function application. For example, with it we can eliminate the need for control structures, as we did when we defined the 'Sum' procedure using Jensen's device (Chapter 3). Also, in Chapter 8 we saw how even the built-in operators can be considered function applications. LISP takes this approach to the extreme; almost everything is a function application.

To see this, it's necessary to know that a function application in LISP is written as follows:

$$(f\ a_1\ a_2\ \ldots\ a_n)$$

where f is the function and $a_1, a_2, \ldots, a_n$ are the arguments. This notation is called *Cambridge Polish* because it is a particular variety of Polish notation developed at MIT (in Cambridge, Mass.). *Polish notation* is named after the Polish logician Jan Lukasiewicz.

The distinctive characteristic of Polish notation is that it writes an operator before its operands. This is also sometimes called *prefix notation* because the operation is written before the operands (pre = before). For example, to compute 2 + 3 we would type[2]

```
(plus 2 3)
```

to an interactive LISP system, and it would respond

```
5
```

LISP's notation is a little more flexible than the usual infix notation since one 'plus' can sum more than two numbers. We can write

```
(plus 10 8 5 64)
```

for the sum 10 + 8 + 5 + 64. Also, since LISP is *fully parenthesized*, there is no need for the complicated precedence rules found in most programming languages.

Notice that the example in Figure 9.1 consists of all function applications (which is why there are so many parentheses). For example,

```
(set 'Freq (make-table text nil))
```

is a nested function application: 'set' is applied to two arguments: (1) 'Freq' and (2) the result of applying 'make-table' to the arguments 'text' and 'nil'. (The function of the quote before 'Freq' is discussed on p. 338.) In an Algol-like language this would be written:

```
set (Freq, make-table (text, nil))
```

Many constructs that have a special syntax in conventional languages are

2 Some LISP dialects, including Common LISP, permit typing '(+ 2 3)'.

just function applications in LISP. For example, the conditional expression is written as an application of the 'cond' function. That is,

```
(cond
  ((null x) 0)
  ((eq x y) (f x))
  (t (g y)) )
```

evaluates '(null x)'; if it is true, then 0 is returned. Otherwise we test '(eq x y)'; if this is true, then the value of '(f x)' is returned. If neither of the above is true, then the value of '(g y)' is the result. This would be written in an Algol-like language as follows:

```
if     null(x) then 0
elsif  x = y then f(x)
else   g(y) endif
```

We can see that even function definition is accomplished by calling a function, 'defun', with three arguments: the name of the function, its formal parameter list, and its body.

Why is everything a function application in LISP? There are a number of reasons that will be discussed later, but we will mention one, the Simplicity Principle, here. If there is only one basic mechanism in a language, the language is (other things being equal) easier to learn, understand, and implement.

The List Is the Only Data Structure Constructor

We have said that one of LISP's goals was to allow computation with *symbolic data.* This is accomplished by allowing the programmer to manipulate *lists* of data. An example of this is the application:

```
(set 'text '(to be or not to be))
```

The second argument to 'set' is the list:

```
(to be or not to be)
```

(Ignore the quote mark for the time being; it will be explained on p. 338.) LISP manipulates lists just like other languages manipulate numbers; they can be compared, passed to functions, put together, and taken apart. In Section 9.3 (Data Structures), we will discuss in detail the ways that lists can be manipulated.

The list above is composed of four distinct *atoms*:

```
to be or not
```

arranged in the list in the order:

```
(to be or not to be).
```

LISP provides operations for putting atoms together to make a list and for extracting atoms out of a list.

LISP also allows lists to be constructed from other lists. For example, the list

```
( (to be or not to be) (that is the question) )
```

has two *sublists*; the first is '(to be or not to be)' and the second is '(that is the question)'.

The list is the *only* data structure constructor provided by LISP,[3] so again we have an example of the Simplicity Principle. If there is only one data structure in our language, then there is only one about which to learn and only one to choose when programming our application.

Programs Are Represented as Lists

Function applications and lists look the same. That is, the *S*-expression

```
(make-table text nil)
```

could either be a three-element list whose elements are the atoms 'make-table', 'text', and 'nil'; or it could be an application of the function 'make-table' to the arguments named 'text' and 'nil'. Which is it?

The answer is that it is both because a LISP program is itself a list. Under most circumstances an *S*-expression is interpreted as a function application, which means that the arguments are *evaluated* and the function is invoked. However, if the list is *quoted*, then it is treated as data; that is, it is *unevaluated*. The function of the quote mark in

```
(set 'text '(to be or not to be))
```

3 Some dialects of LISP also provide arrays and records (called "structures").

is to indicate that the list '(to be or not to be)' is treated as data, not as a function application. If it had been omitted, as in

```
(set 'text (to be or not to be))
```

then the LISP interpreter would have attempted to call a function named 'to' with the arguments named 'be', 'or', 'not', 'to', and 'be'. This would, of course, be an error if, as in this case, these names were undefined. In any case, it's not what we intended; the list is supposed to represent *data* not *program.*

The fact that LISP represents both programs and data in the same way is of the utmost importance (and almost unique among programming languages). As we will see, it makes it very easy to write a LISP interpreter in LISP. More important, it makes it convenient to have one LISP program generate and call for the execution of another LISP program. It also simplifies writing LISP programs that transform and manipulate other LISP programs. These capabilities are important in artificial intelligence and other advanced program-development environments.

LISP Is Usually Interpreted

Most LISP systems are interactive interpreters; in fact, they were some of the earliest interactive systems. We interact with the LISP interpreter by typing in function applications. The LISP system then interprets them and prints out the result. For example, if we type

```
(plus 2 3)
```

the system will respond

```
5
```

because $2 + 3 = 5$. Similarly, if we type

```
(eq (plus 2 3) (difference 9 4))
```

the system will respond

```
t
```

(meaning *true*) because $2 + 3 = 9 - 4$.

Functions like 'eq' and 'plus' are called *pure functions* (or simply *functions*) because they have no effect other than the computation of a value. Pure functions obey the Manifest Interface Principle because their interfaces (i.e., their inputs and outputs) are apparent (*manifest*).

The Manifest Interface Principle

All interfaces should be apparent (manifest) in the syntax.

Some functions in LISP are *pseudo-functions* (or *procedures*). These are functions that have a *side effect* on the state of the computer in addition to computing a result. A simple example is 'set', which binds a name to a value. The application '(set 'n x)' binds the name (atom) n to the value of x and, almost incidently, returns this value. Thus, if we type

```
(set 'text '(to be or not to be))
```

the LISP system will print the result:

```
(to be or not to be)
```

More important, the name 'text' is bound to this list, which we can see by typing

```
text
```

LISP will then respond

```
(to be or not to be)
```

The atom 'text' can now be used as a name for this list in any expression, for instance:

```
(set 'Freq (make-table text nil))
```

Another important pseudo-function is 'defun', which defines a function. The application

(defun f $(n_1\ n_2 \cdots n_m)$ b)

defines a function (or pseudo-function) with the name f; formal parameters n_1, n_2, ..., n_m; and body b. It is thus analogous to the Algol declaration

procedure f $(n_1, n_2, \ldots, n_m)$; b;

(although in LISP the binding process is dynamic, that is, it takes place at run-time).

This is a good place to mention that LISP dialects differ from each other in many small ways. In particular, the function application used to define functions is different in many dialects, although you should have no trouble relating them to the form used here. (In this book we use the Common LISP dialect; see Steele, 1984.)

Most LISP programs (such as our example in Figure 9.1) take the form of a collection of function definitions and 'set's. Users can then apply the defined functions from their terminals. For example, the application

```
(lookup Freq 'be)
```

results in the value

```
2
```

the number of occurrences of 'be' in the list.

9.3 DESIGN: DATA STRUCTURES

The Primitives Include Numeric Atoms

As we have done on all the languages we've investigated, we classify LISP's data structures into *primitives* and *constructors*. The *constructor* is the list; it permits more complicated structures to be built from simpler structures. The *primitive* data structures are the starting points for this building process. Thus, the primitive data structures are those data structures that are not built from any others; they have no parts. It is for this reason that they are called *atoms* ('atom' in Greek = indivisible thing).

There are at least two types of atoms in all LISP systems. We have already seen examples of *numeric* atoms, which are atoms having the syntax of numbers (i.e., all digits with possibly one decimal point). Various arithmetic operations can be applied to numeric atoms. For example,

```
(plus 2 3)
```

applies the function 'plus' to the atoms '2' and '3' and yields the atom '5'.

LISP provides a very large set of primitive functions for manipulating numeric atoms. These include the arithmetic operations (plus, difference, etc.), predecessor and successor functions (sub1, add1), maximum and minimum functions, relational tests (equal, lessp, greaterp), and predicates (i.e., tests, such as zerop, onep, minusp). All of these functions take both integer and floating-point (and, in some systems, multiple-precision) arguments and return results of the appropriate type.

LISP's use of Cambridge Polish limits its numerical applications. For example, the expression

$$\frac{-b + \sqrt{b^2 - 4ac}}{2a}$$

must be written

```
(quotient   (plus   (minus b)
                    (sqrt (difference    (expt b 2)
                                         (times 4 a c))))
            (times 2 a))
```

Common LISP (and many other dialects) permits symbolic operations, but it's not much of an improvement:

```
(/ (+ (− b) (sqrt (− (expt b 2) (* 4 a c))))
  (* 2 a))
```

On the other hand, it is fairly easy to write a LISP function to translate conventional infix notation into LISP's prefix notation. If we did this, we could write (assuming the function was named 'infix' and special characters are allowed as atoms):

```
(infix '( ( − b + sqrt ( b ↑ 2 − 4 * a * c )) / (2 * a) ))
```

EXERCISE 9-1:* LISP basically provides one numeric type and converts between integer and floating-point (and possibly multiple-precision) representations, as necessary, at run-time. This is very different from the other languages we've discussed, wherein numeric representations are fixed at compile-time. Discuss the advantages and disadvantages of LISP's approach to numbers.

EXERCISE 9-2: Translate the following expressions into LISP:

1. $\frac{1}{2}\sqrt{4r^2 - l^2}$

2. $\dfrac{abc}{4\sqrt{s(s-a)(s-b)(s-c)}}$

3. $\frac{n!}{r!(n-r)!}$, use '(fac n)' for $n!$

4. $\frac{\pi R^2 E}{180}$

Nonnumeric Atoms Are Also Provided

The other kind of primitive data structure in LISP is the *nonnumeric atom.* These atoms are strings of characters that were originally intended to represent words or symbols. We saw nonnumeric atoms in the list '(to be or not to be)'. With few exceptions, the only operations that can be performed on nonnumeric atoms are comparisons for equality and inequality. This is done with the function 'eq':

```
(eq x y)
```

returns 't' (an atom meaning true) if x and y are the same atom, and 'nil' (an atom meaning, among other things, false) if they are not the same.

The atom 'nil' has many functions in LISP; we will see more of them later. One very common operation in LISP is testing something to see if it is 'nil'; this operation is often used as a base for recursive definitions. Although this test can be written

```
(eq x nil)
```

it is so frequent that a special predicate has been provided:

```
(null x)
```

Notice that 'nil' is the noun and 'null' is the corresponding adjective.

Some LISP systems provide additional types of atoms, such as strings. In these cases special operations for manipulating these values are also provided. Recall that an abstract data type is a set of data values together with a set of operations on those values.

EXERCISE 9-3:* Discuss LISP's strategy of dynamic typing and compare it with the statically typed languages discussed in previous chapters. Discuss the advantages and disadvantages of each, paying particular attention to flexibility, security, and efficiency.

The Constructor Is the List

The method of data structuring provided by LISP is called the *list.* Lists are written in the *S*-expression notation by surrounding with parentheses the list's elements, which are separated by blanks. Lists can have none, one, or more elements, so they satisfy the Zero-One-Infinity Principle. The elements of lists can themselves be lists, so the Zero-One-Infinity Principle is also satisfied by the nesting level of lists.

For a historical reason relating to the first LISP implementation, the empty list, '( )', is considered equivalent to the atom 'nil'. That is,

```
(eq '() nil)
(null '() )
```

are both true (i.e., return 't'). For this reason, the empty list is often called the *null list*. Except for the null list, all lists are *nonatomic* (i.e., not atoms); they are sometimes called *composite* data values. We can find out whether or not something is an atom by using the 'atom' predicate; for example,

```
(atom 'to)
  t
(atom 5)
  t
(atom (plus 2 3) )
  t
(atom nil)
  t
(atom '() )
  t
(atom '(to be) )
  nil
(atom '(()) )
  nil
```

(We will indent the responses of the LISP system so we can differentiate them from what the user types.)

Notice that the null list is a definite object and must be distinguished from "nothing." In particular, neither '(( ))' nor '(nil)' is the null list; rather, each is a one-element list containing the null list. If you are familiar with set theory, you will see that this is analogous to the difference between ∅, the null set, and {∅}, a nonnull set containing one element, the null set.

EXERCISE 9-4: Explain the result returned by each of the applications of 'atom' shown above.

Car and Cdr Access the Parts of Lists

We've described the kind of data values that lists are. We've seen in previous chapters, however, that there's much more to a data type than just data values. An *abstract data type* is a set of data values *together with* a set of operations on those data values. What are the primitive list-processing operations?

A complete set of operations for a composite data type, such as lists, requires operations for building the structures and operations for taking them apart. Operations that build a structure are called *constructors*,[4] and those that extract their parts are called *selectors*. LISP has one constructor—*cons*—and two selectors—*car* and *cdr*.

The first element of a list is selected by the 'car' function.[5] For example,

```
(car '(to be or not to be) )
```

returns the atom 'to'. The first element of a list can be either an atom or a list, and 'car' returns it, whichever it is. For example, since Freq is the list

```
( (to 2) (be 2) (or 1) (not 1) )
```

the application

```
(car Freq)
```

returns the list

```
(to 2)
```

Notice that the argument to 'car' is always a nonnull list (otherwise it can't have a first element) and that 'car' may return either an atom or a list, depending on what its argument's first element is.

Since there are only two selector functions and since a list can have any number of elements, any of which we might want to select, it's clear that 'cdr' must provide access to the rest of the elements of the list (after the first).

The 'cdr'[6] function returns all of a list *except* its first element. Therefore,

```
(cdr '(to be or not to be) )
```

4 This is not a new meaning for the term "constructor." We have said that constructors are used to build structures from the primitives or from simpler structures. This applies to structures of all sorts: name structures, data structures, control structures, and now list structures.

5 This is pronounced "cahr." The historical reasons for this name are discussed later in this chapter.

6 'Cdr' is pronounced "could-er."

returns the list

```
(be or not to be)
```

Similarly, '(cdr Freq)' returns

```
( (be 2) (or 1) (not 1) )
```

Notice that, like 'car', 'cdr' requires a nonnull list for its argument (otherwise we can't remove its first element). Unlike 'car', 'cdr' *always* returns a list. This could be the null list; for example, '(cdr '(1))' returns '( )'.

It is important to realize that both 'car' and 'cdr' are *pure functions*, that is, they don't modify their argument list. The easiest way to think of the way they work is that they make a new copy of the list. For example, 'cdr' doesn't delete the first element of its argument; rather, it returns a new list exactly like its argument except without the first element. We will see later when we discuss the implementation of LISP lists that this copying does not actually have to be done.

'Car' and 'cdr' can be used in combination to access the components of a list. Suppose DS is a list representing a personnel record for Don Smith:

```
(set 'DS '( (Don Smith) 45 30000 (August 25 1980) ) )
```

The list DS contains Don Smith's name, age, salary, and hire date. To extract the first component of this list, his name, we can write '(car DS)', which returns '(Don Smith)'. How can we access Don Smith's age? Notice that the 'cdr' operation deletes the first element of the list, so that the second element of the original list is the first element of the result of 'cdr'. That is, '(cdr DS)' returns

```
(45 30000 (August 25 1980))
```

so that '(car (cdr DS))' is 45, Don Smith's age. We can now see the general pattern: To access an element of the list, use 'cdr' to delete all of the preceding elements and then use 'car' to pick out the desired element. Therefore, '(car (cdr (cdr DS)))' is Don Smith's salary, and

```
(car (cdr (cdr (cdr DS))))
```

is his hire date. We can see this from the following (by 'cdr ⇒' we mean "applying 'cdr' returns"):

```
( (Don Smith) 45 30000 (August 25 1980) )
cdr ⇒ (45 30000 (August 25 1980) )
```

```
cdr ⇒ (30000 (August 25 1980) )

cdr ⇒ ( (August 25 1980) )

car ⇒ (August 25 1980)
```

In general, the *n*th element of a list can be accessed by $n-1$ 'cdr's followed by a 'car'. Since '(car DS)' is this person's name '(Don Smith)', his first name is

```
(car (car DS))
  Don
```

and his last name is

```
(car (cdr (car DS)))
  Smith
```

We can see that any part of a list structure, no matter how complicated, can be extracted by appropriate combinations of 'car' and 'cdr'. This is part of the simplicity of LISP; just these two selector functions are adequate for accessing the components of any list structure. This can, of course, lead to some large compositions of 'car's and 'cdr's, so LISP provides an abbreviation. For example, an expression such as

```
(car (cdr (cdr (cdr DS))))
```

can be abbreviated

```
(cadddr DS)
```

The composition of 'car's and 'cdr's is represented by the sequence of 'a's and 'd's between the initial 'c' and the final 'r'. By reading the sequence of 'a's and 'd's in reverse order, we can use them to "walk" through the data structure. For example, 'caddr' accesses the salary:

```
((Don Smith) 45 30000 (August 25 1980))

d ⇒ (45 30000 (August 25 1980))

d ⇒ (30000 (August 25 1980))

a ⇒ 30000
```

Also, 'cadar' accesses the last-name component of the list:

```
((Don Smith) 45 30000 (August 25 1980))
```

```
a ⇒ (Don Smith)

d ⇒ (Smith)

a ⇒ Smith
```

This can be seen more clearly if the list is written as a linked data structure; then a 'd' moves to the right and an 'a' moves down:

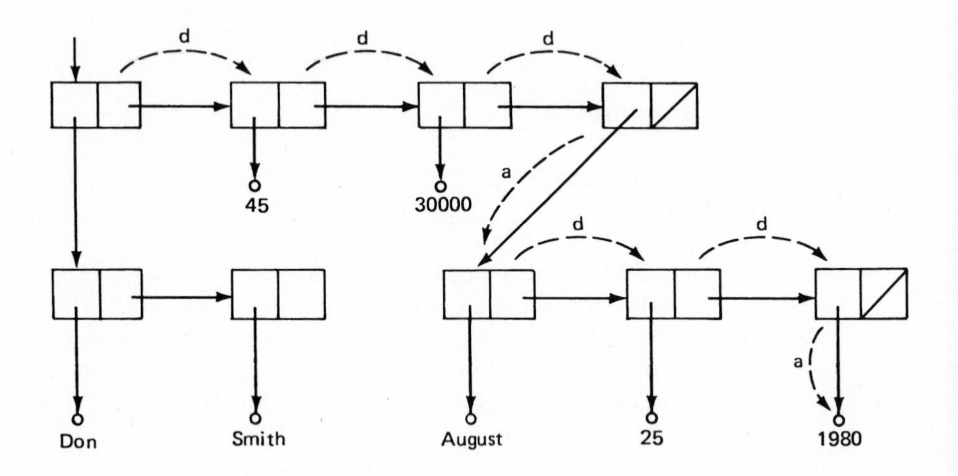

This shows that '(caddadddr DS)' accesses the year Don Smith was hired. Clearly, these sequences of 'a's and 'd's can become quite complicated to read. Writing them is also error-prone. One solution to this is to write a set of special-purpose functions for accessing the parts of a record. For example, a function for accessing the hire date could be defined as:

```
(defun hire-date (r) (cadddr r))
```

Then '(hire-date DS)' returns Don Smith's hire date. Similarly, we could define 'year' to give the year part of a date:

```
(defun year (d) (caddr d))
```

Then Don Smith's year of hire can be written:

```
(year (hire-date DS))
```

which is certainly more readable than '(caddadddr DS)'. It is also more maintainable since if we later change the format of this list (say, by adding a new piece of information), it will only be necessary to change the accessing functions. In other words, we should think of these personnel records as an *abstract data type* that can only be accessed through the provided accessing functions. Unfortunately, LISP does not provide a mechanism analogous to Ada's packages for enforcing *information hiding.*

EXERCISE 9-5: Define the functions 'name', 'age', 'salary', and 'hire-date' for accessing the parts of a personnel record; the functions 'firstn' and 'lastn' for accessing the parts of a name; and the functions 'month', 'day', and 'year' for accessing the parts of a date. Write expressions for accessing Don Smith's last name, salary, and the month in which he was hired.

Information Can Be Represented by Property Lists

A personnel record would probably not be represented in LISP in the way we have just described: It is too inflexible. Since each property of Don Smith is assigned a specific location in the list, it becomes difficult to change the properties associated with a person. A better arrangement is to precede each piece of information with an *indicator* identifying the property. For example,

```
(name (Don Smith) age 45 salary 30000 hire-date (August 25 1980))
```

This method of representing information is called a *property list* or *p-list*. Its general form is

$$(p_1\ v_1\ p_2\ v_2 \ldots p_n\ v_n)$$

in which each p_i is the indicator for a property and each v_i is the corresponding property value.

The advantage of property lists is their flexibility; as long as properties are accessed by their indicators, programs will be independent of the particular arrangement of the data. For example, the *p*-list above represents the same information as this one:

```
(age 45 salary 30000 name (Don Smith) hire-date (August 25 1980))
```

This flexibility is important in an experimental software environment in which all of the relevant properties may not be known at design time.

Information is selected from a simple list by various compositions of 'car' and 'cdr'. How can the properties of a *p*-list be accessed? We can attack this problem by considering how a person might solve it. Asked Don Smith's age, a person would probably begin searching from the left of the list for the indicator 'age'. The following element of the list is Don Smith's age. Let's consider this process in more detail: Exactly how do we search a list from the left? We begin by looking at the first element of the list; if it's 'age', then the second element of the list is Don Smith's age, so we return it and we're done. If the first element of the list is not 'age', then we must skip the first two elements (the first property and its value) and repeat the process by checking the new first element.

Let's begin to express this in LISP notation. Suppose p is the property for which we're looking and x is the object which we're searching. We will write a 'getprop' function such that '(getprop p x)' is the value of the p property in property list x. First, we want to see if the first element of x is p; we can do this by '(eq (car x) p)'. If the first element of x is p, then the value of '(getprop p x)' is the second element of x, that is, '(cadr x)'. If the first element of x isn't p, then we want to skip over the first property of x and its value and continue looking for p. Notice that '(getprop p (cddr x))' will look for p beginning with the third element of x. We can summarize our algorithm as follows:

```
(getprop p x) =
  if (eq (car x) p)
    then return (cadr x)
    else return (getprop p (cddr x))
```

It only remains to translate this into LISP notation. A LISP conditional expression is written:

(cond (c_1 e_1) (c_2 e_2) $\cdots$ (c_n e_n))

The conditions $c_1, c_2, \ldots, c_n$ are evaluated in order until one returns 't'. The value of the conditional is the value of the corresponding e_i. The effect of an "else" clause is accomplished by using 't' for the last condition. The 'getprop' function is:

```
(defun getprop (p x)
  (cond ((eq (car x) p) (cadr x))
        (t (getprop p (cddr x))) ))
```

This definition, like most LISP definitions, is recursive. To find out properties of DS, we can now use 'getprop':

```
(getprop 'name DS)
  (Don Smith)
(getprop 'age DS)
  45
(getprop 'hire-date DS)
  (August 25 1980)
```

```
(year (getprop 'hire-date DS))
  1980
```

Notice that the name of the property is quoted; we want the actual atom 'age', not some value to which this atom might be bound.

What will this function do if we ask for a property that isn't in the property list? By tracing the execution of the function we will see that eventually we will have skipped all the properties and will be asking if the first element of the null list is the indicator we are seeking. Specifically, we will attempt to take the 'car' of 'nil'. Since this is illegal on most LISP systems, we will get an error:

```
(getprop 'weight DS)
  Error: Car of nil.
```

Often we don't know exactly what properties an object has so it would be more convenient if 'getprop' were more forgiving. One way to do this is to have 'getprop' return a distinguished value if the property doesn't exist. An obvious choice is 'nil', but this would not be a good choice since it would then be impossible to distinguish an undefined property from one which is defined but whose value is 'nil'. Nil is too common a value in LISP for this to be a good choice. A better decision is to pick some atom, such as 'undefined-property', which is unlikely to be used for any other purpose. The 'getprop' function can be modified to return this atom when it gets to a null list in its search process:

```
(getprop 'weight DS)
  undefined-property
```

EXERCISE 9-6: Modify the 'getprop' procedure so that it returns 'undefined-property' when the requested property is not defined in the property list.

EXERCISE 9-7: The 'getprop' procedure provided by some LISP systems is not exactly like the one we have described. Rather, it is defined to return all of the property list *after* the indicator. For example,

```
(getprop 'age DS)
  (45 salary 30000 hire-date (August 25 1980))
(getprop 'salary DS)
  (30000 hire-date (August 25 1980))
```

Thus, the value of the property is the 'car' of the result of 'getprop'. This approach permits a different solution to the undefined property problem; the 'getprop' procedure returns 'nil' if the property is not in the list. That is,

```
(getprop 'weight DS)
  nil
```

Define this version of the 'getprop' procedure.

Information Can Be Represented in Association Lists

The property list data structure described on pp. 349–351 works best when exactly one value is to be associated with each property. That is, a property list has the form:

$$(p_1\ v_1\ p_2\ v_2\ \ldots\ p_n\ v_n)$$

This is sometimes inconvenient; for example, some properties are *flags* that have no associated value—their presence or absence on the property lists conveys all of the information. In our personnel record example, this might be the 'retired' flag, whose membership in the property list indicates that the employee has retired. Since property indicators and values must alternate in property lists, it is necessary to associate *some* value with the 'retired' indicator, even though it has no meaning.

An analogous problem arises if a property has several associated values. For example, the 'manages' property might be associated with the names of everyone managed by Don Smith. Because of the required alternation of indicators and values in property lists, it will be necessary to group these names together into a subsidiary list.

These problems are solved by another common LISP data structure—the *association list*, or *a-list*. Just as we can associate two pieces of information in our minds, an association list allows information in list structures to be associated. An *a*-list is a list of pairs,[7] with each pair associating two pieces of information. The *a*-list representation of the properties of Don Smith is:

```
( (name (Don Smith))
  (age 45)
  (salary 30000)
  (hire-date (August 25 1980)) )
```

7 Actually, an *a*-list is normally defined to be a list of *dotted* pairs. We will not address this detail until later.

The general form of an *a*-list is a list of attribute-value pairs:

$((a_1\ v_1)\ (a_2\ v_2)\ \ldots\ (a_n\ v_n))$

As for property lists, the ordering of information in an *a*-list is immaterial. Information is accessed *associatively*; that is, given the indicator 'hire-date', the associated information '(August 25 1980)' can be found. It is also quite easy to go in the other direction: Given the "answer" '(August 25 1980)', find the "question," that is, 'hire-date'. The function that does the forward association is normally called 'assoc'. For example,

```
(set 'DS '((name (Don Smith) (age 45) ...) )
  ((name (Don Smith)) (age 45) ...)
(assoc 'hire-date DS)
  (August 25 1980)
(assoc 'salary DS)
  30000
```

EXERCISE 9-8: Write the 'assoc' function in LISP. You will have to decide how to handle the case where the requested attribute is not associated by the *a*-list. Justify your solution.

EXERCISE 9-9: Write the function 'rassoc' that performs "reverse association"; that is, given the attribute's value it returns the attribute's indicator. For example,

```
(rassoc 45 DS)
  age
(rassoc '(August 25 1980))
  hire-date
```

How will you deal with the fact that several attributes might have the same value? Justify your solution.

EXERCISE 9-10: Write a function 'length' such that '(length *L*)' is the number of (top-level) components in the list *L*. For example,

```
(length '(to be or not to be))
  6
(length Freq)
  4
(length '() )
  0
```

Cons Constructs Lists

We have seen that the 'car' and 'cdr' functions can be used to extract the parts of a list. How are lists constructed? When we design an abstract data type, we should make sure that the constructors and selectors work together smoothly. This is necessary if the data type is to be easy to learn and easy to use. In particular, the data type will be more *regular* if the constructors and selectors are *inverses*; that is, the selectors undo what the constructors do, and vice versa. In the case of lists, notice that the 'car' and 'cdr' functions operate at the *beginnings* of lists; 'car' selects the first element of a list and 'cdr' removes the first element of a list. It is natural then to pick a constructor function that operates at the beginning of a list and reverses the selectors. LISP's only constructor, *cons,*[8] adds a new element to the beginning of a list. For example,

```
(cons 'to '(be or not to be))
```

returns the list '(to be or not to be)'. Notice that 'cons' is the inverse of 'car' and 'cdr':

```
(car '(to be or not to be))        =  to
(cdr '(to be or not to be))        =  (be or not to be)
(cons 'to '(be or not to be))      =  (to be or not to be)
```

Therefore, any list that we can construct we can also take apart, and any list that we can take apart can be reassembled from its parts.

What is the meaning of '(cons '(a b) '(c d))'? One possible answer is '(a b c d)'. But if we consider the inverse relation between 'cons' and the selectors, we can see that the correct answer is '((a b) c d)'. Observe:

```
(car '((a b) c d) ) = (a b)
(cdr '((a b) c d) ) = (c d)
```

because 'car' returns the first element of '((a b) c d)', which is the list '(a b)'. It then follows that

```
(cons '(a b) '(c d) ) = ((a b) c d)
```

These relationships among 'car', 'cdr', and 'cons' can be summarized in the equations in Figure 9.2. Notice that the second argument of 'cons' must be a list, although the first argument can be either an atom or a list.

8 Cons is pronounced "konss," like the first syllable of "construct."

(cons (car L) (cdr L)) = L, for nonnull L

(car (cons x L)) = x

(cdr (cons x L)) = L

where L is a list and x is an atom or list.

Figure 9.2 Equations for the List Data Type

Like 'car' and 'cdr', 'cons' is a *pure function*. That means that it doesn't actually add a new element to the beginning of its second argument. Rather, it acts as though it has constructed a completely new list, whose first element is the first argument to 'cons' and the remainder of whose elements are copied from its second argument. We will see later that the actual implementation of 'cons' is much more efficient than suggested by this description.

Lists Are Usually Constructed Recursively

We saw that the value of '(cons '(a b) '(c d))' was *not* '(a b c d)'. Suppose, however, that we want to concatenate two lists, and that '(a b c d)' is the required result from '(a b)' and '(c d)'. How can this be accomplished? Investigating the programming of a function to do this will furnish a good example of the use of recursion to construct lists. Our goal will be to develop a function 'append' such that

(append '(a b) '(c d)) = (a b c d)

In general, '(append L M)' will return the catenation of the lists L and M.

A good way to start with a problem like this is, first, to identify those cases that are easy to solve, and then to try to reduce the other cases to the easy-to-solve cases. In other words, we should ask ourselves which cases can be solved with the functions already available. In this situation, we can see that if either of the lists to be appended is null, then the result is the other list. That is,

(append '() L) = L
(append L '()) = L

These are the easily solved cases. In LISP the null case is frequently the easy-to-solve case.

We want to proceed by reducing the unsolved cases to the solved cases. That is, we want to work the nonnull lists toward null lists. More specifically, if we can reduce the problem of appending a list of length n to the problem of appending a list of length $n-1$, then we can continue this process until we are appending a list of length 0, which is the null list and already solved. This process is very much like an inductive proof in mathematics.

Let's consider the specific case of appending the three-element list '(a b c)' to the three-element list '(d e f)'. Suppose the problem is already solved for two-element lists, for example,

```
(append '(b c) '(d e f)) = (b c d e f)
```

How can we get from this solution to the solution of the three-element case? The result required is '(a b c d e f)', which is just

```
(cons 'a '(b c d e f))
```

The above can be expressed in terms of the length = 2 solution:

```
(cons 'a (append '(b c) '(d e f)) )
```

Notice, now, that 'a' is the 'car' of the original list '(a b c)' and that '(b c)' is the 'cdr' of this list. This leads us to the general form of the reduction: If L is a list of length $n > 0$, then

```
(append L M) = (cons (car L) (append (cdr L) M) )
```

Notice that '(cdr L)' is of length $n-1$, so we have successfully reduced the length $= n$ problem to the length $= n-1$ problem. As we continue to reduce the length of this list, we are guaranteed to reach the null list eventually, which we know how to solve, so the process *must* terminate. It is now easy to see the program. To compute '(append L M)', if L is null, then return M; otherwise return the result of 'cons'ing '(car L)' onto the result of '(append (cdr L) M)'. In LISP this is:

```
(defun append (L M)
  (cond
    ((null L) M)
    (t (cons (car L) (append (cdr L) M)) )) )
```

Notice that if we had decided to reduce M to the null list, it would have been much more difficult. This is so because the LISP selector functions have been designed to work at the *beginnings* of lists.

*EXERCISE 9-11**: Program the 'append' function so that it reduces its second rather than its first argument to the null list. Accomplishing this will require you to define one or more auxiliary functions.

EXERCISE 9-12: Write a function 'delprop' that removes a property and its value from a property list. For example:

```
DS
  (name (Don Smith) age 45 salary 30000
        hire-date (August 25 1980))
(delprop DS 'age)
  (name (Don Smith) salary 30000 hire-date (August 25 1980))
(delprop DS 'name)
  (age 45 salary 30000 hire-date (August 25 1980))
(delprop DS 'hire-date)
  (name (Don Smith) age 45 salary 30000)
```

EXERCISE 9-13: Write a function 'remassoc' that removes an association from an association list. For example:

```
DS
  ((name (Don Smith)) (age 45) (salary 30000)
    (hire-date (August 25 1980)))
(remassoc 'salary DS)
  ((name (Don Smith)) (age 45) (hire-date (August 25 1980)))
```

EXERCISE 9-14: Write a function 'addprop' that adds a property to a property list if it is not there or alters its value if it is. For example:

```
(addprop DS 'male 'sex)
  (name (Don Smith) age 45 salary 30000
        hire-date (August 25 1980) sex male)
(addprop DS 34500 'salary)
  (name (Don Smith) age 45 salary 34500
        hire-date (August 25 1980))
```

EXERCISE 9-15: Write a function analogous to 'addprop' for *a*-lists.

Atoms Have Properties

LISP was originally developed for artificial intelligence applications. These applications often must deal with the properties of objects and the relationships among objects. Suppose we were writing a LISP program to manipulate European countries. Each country has a number of properties and each is related to a number of other countries. For example, each country has a name, a capital, a population, an area, and various countries on which it borders. How can these be handled in LISP?

In LISP, objects are represented by atoms, and each atom has an associated *p*-list that represents the properties of the atom and the relations in which it participates. We can represent some of the properties of England and France by this diagram:

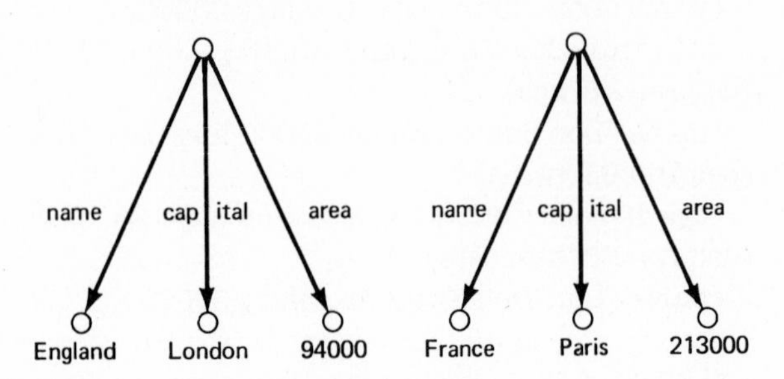

The small circles represent objects (atoms), and the lines show their properties. Notice that the edges are labeled with the *indicators* of the properties and that the values of the properties are often themselves objects (i.e., atoms). How are atoms created and how are they given properties?

Atoms are created in LISP by simply mentioning them. For instance, if we type

```
(England France Spain W-Germany Portugal)
```

then the objects England, France, and so on, will have been created. Each of these objects comes complete with a property, its *print name* or *pname*[9]:

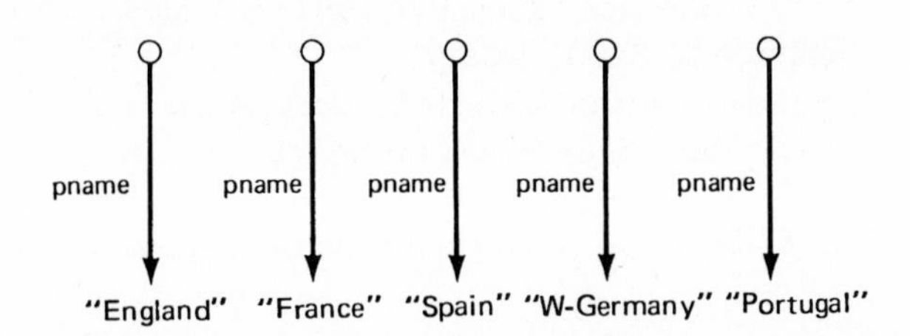

Every atom has a print name; it is the means by which we denote the atom and it is the way the atom is represented when it is displayed.

9 This is the case in the LISP 1.5 system, which is the basis for all later LISP implementations. Other LISP systems may differ in implementation details. For example, several, including Common LISP, use "print-name cells" instead of the 'pname' property.

Suppose that we define 'Europe' to be a list of the European countries:

```
(set 'Europe '(England France Spain W-Germany Portugal ...))
  (England France Spain W-Germany Portugal ...)
```

Now if we request that some atom be displayed, it is its print name that we will see. For example,

```
(car Europe)
  England
```

Similarly, whenever we write a name such as 'England', it will refer to that unique atom whose print name is 'England'. We can see this by using the 'eq' function, which tells us if two atoms are the same:

```
(eq 'England (car Europe))
  t
(eq 'France (car Europe))
  nil
```

Thus, we can see that the print name of an atom is analogous to a proper name in English; it uniquely denotes an object.

We have seen that all atoms come with one property—their print name. How are other properties attached to an atom? Several procedures are provided by LISP for accessing the properties of an atom. For example, to define the capital of France as Paris, we can write

```
(putprop 'France 'Paris 'capital)
  Paris
```

which alters the properties of the object France to:

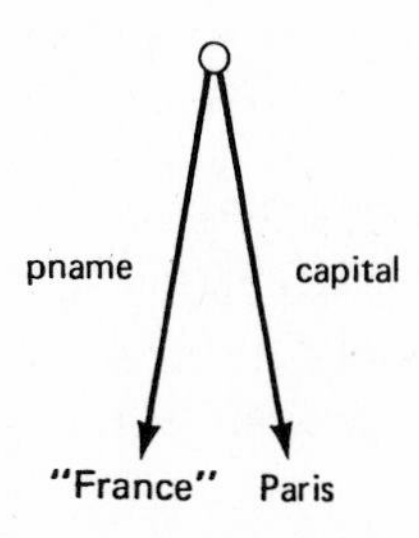

We can find out the value of a property with the 'get' function:

```
(get 'France 'capital)
  Paris
(get 'France 'pname)
  "France"
```

Notice that the 'putprop' and 'get' procedures are reminiscent of the 'addprop' and 'getprop' procedures we saw on pp. 350–357. This is not coincidental, as we will see when we discuss the implementation of atoms.

There are several other important properties that many objects have. One of these is the 'apval' of an atom.[10] When an atom is used in a 'set', it is bound to some value. For example,

```
(set 'Europe '(England France ...))
```

binds the atom 'Europe' to the list '(England France ...)'. The property of being bound to a value is denoted by the 'apval' indicator (which stands for "applied value"). After the above 'set' is executed, the atom 'Europe' will have the properties:

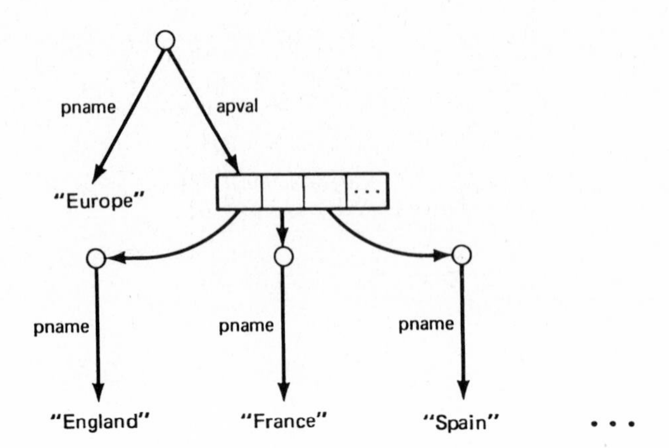

We can see this by typing

```
(get 'Europe 'apval)
  (England France Spain ...)
```

10 Here again we refer to LISP 1.5. Some other LISP dialects use a "value cell" instead of the 'apval' property.

In fact, 'set' is just an abbreviation for a particular application of 'putprop'. '(set 'Europe '(England France ...))' is exactly equivalent[11] to

```
(putprop 'Europe '(England France ...) 'apval)
```

There are several other built-in properties that we will mention briefly. Consider a function definition such as:

```
(defun getprop (p x)
  (cond   ((eq (car x) p) (cadr x))
          (t (getprop p (cddr x))) ))
```

This is another example of binding a name to a value; in this case, the name 'getprop' is bound to a function. Binding of atoms to functions is represented by the 'expr' property.[12] After the above application of 'defun' the value of the 'expr' property of 'getprop' can be found by:

```
(get 'getprop 'expr)
  (lambda (p x)     (cond   ((eq (car x) p) (cadr x))
                            (t (getprop p (cddr x))) ))
```

(The atom 'lambda' indicates a function value, which is discussed in Chapter 10.) Thus, the above 'defun' is equivalent to:

```
(putprop 'getprop
  '(lambda (p x) (cond ((eq (car x) p) (cadr x))
                       (t (getprop p (cddr x))) ))
  'expr)
```

There are a number of other properties used by the LISP system that indicate compiled functions, functions that don't evaluate their arguments, and so forth.

Some LISP systems allow the entire property list of an atom to be accessed.[13] For example,

11 Although, as noted before, some LISP implementations make a special case of 'apval' for the sake of efficiency.

12 In LISP 1.5. Other LISP dialects use "function cells" instead of the 'expr' property.

13 The function to accomplish this is known variously as 'symbol-plist', 'plist', and 'getproplist'.

```
(symbol-plist 'France)
   (pname France capital Paris)
(symbol-plist 'Europe)
   (pname Europe apval (England France Spain ...))
(symbol-plist 'getprop)
   (pname getprop expr (lambda (p x)
                              (cond   ((eq (car x) p) (cadr x))
                                      (t (get p (cddr x))) )) )
```

We can see that the property lists of atoms are just like the property lists we discussed on pp. 349–352.

Lists Have a Simple Representation

Recall that LISP developed out of a desire for an algebraic language for linked list processing. Therefore, although there are many ways that lists can be represented, it is not surprising to learn that LISP lists are usually implemented as linked structures. For instance, the list

```
(to be or not to be)
```

is represented as a sequence of six (not necessarily contiguous) cells in memory, each containing a pointer to the next. Each cell also contains a pointer to the element of the list it represents. This is shown in Figure 9.3. (We have labeled atoms with their print names; their exact representation is described later.) The last cell points to 'nil', representing the end of the list. We will call the two parts of a cell the *left* part and the *right* part. The final null pointer will often be drawn as a slash through the right half of the last cell.

Lists containing other lists are represented in the same way. For example, the list

```
( (to 2) (be 2) (or 1) (not 1) )
```

would be represented in storage as shown in Figure 9.4.

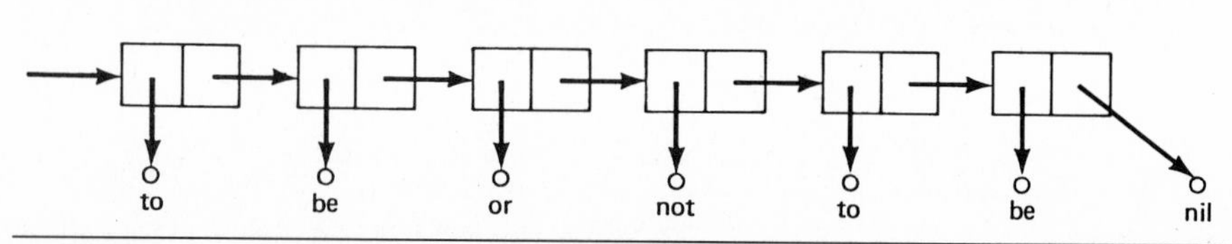

Figure 9.3 Representation of (to be or not to be)

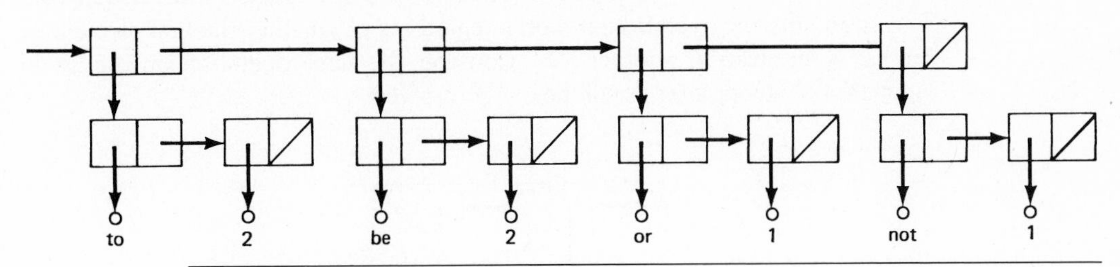

Figure 9.4 Representation of a List of Lists

Since the left part of a cell points to an element of a list, it can point either to an atom or a list (which is in turn represented by a cell). Since the right part of a cell normally points to the rest of the list, it will normally point to another cell or 'nil'. The null list is simply a pointer to the atom 'nil'.

EXERCISE 9-16: Draw the list structures for both the *p*-list and *a*-list representations of the personnel record for Don Smith.

EXERCISE 9-17: Since programs are themselves written as lists, programs can be represented as the same list structures as data. Draw the list structure corresponding to the definition of 'make-table' in Figure 9.1, which is the first four lines of that figure.

EXERCISE 9-18: Draw the list structure corresponding to the following expression:

```
(quotient   (plus   (minus B)
                    (expt (difference (expt b 2)
                                      (times 4 a c))
                          0.5))
            (times 2 a))
```

A structure such as you have drawn is often called an *expression tree.*

The List Primitives Are Simple and Efficient

Let's consider the implementation of the list-processing functions 'car', 'cdr', and 'cons'. Suppose we have a pointer, L, to the beginning of the list in Figure 9.3 and we want to get a pointer A to the 'car' of this list. We can see that this pointer is in the left half of the cell pointed to by L. Therefore, in Pascal notation,

```
A := L↑.left;
```

In other words, follow the L pointer to a cell in memory and return its left half. This is an efficient operation; it works regardless of whether the first element of the list is an atom or another list. Consider the same operation on the list in Figure 9.4. The pointer A will be:

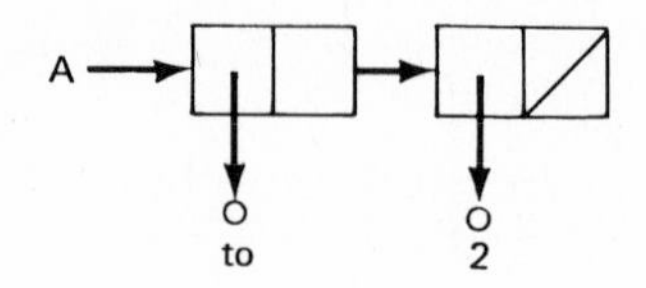

In other words,

```
(car '((to 2) (be 2) (or 1) (not 1)) ) = (to 2)
```

The 'cdr' function is exactly analogous: Follow the pointer and extract the *right* half of the word:

```
D := L↑.right;
```

In the case of the list in Figure 9.3:

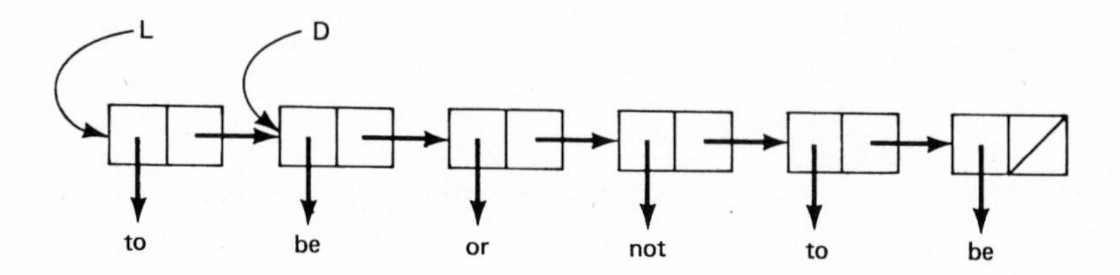

Notice that D actually points to a *sublist* of list L; we will discuss the implications of this on pp. 366–367. Also notice that repeated applications of 'cdr' will "walk" from each element of the list to the next by following its right pointers.

John McCarthy has explained the origin of the cryptic names 'car' and 'cdr'. On the IBM 704 computer, each word had two fields large enough to hold a pointer; these were called the "address" field and the "decrement" field. Thus, if L were a pointer to a list, then '(car L)' would return the "Contents of the Address part of Register L" (memory locations were called "registers"). Similarly, '(cdr L)' meant "Contents of the Decrement part of Register L." Over the years many alternative names for these functions have been proposed, including first/rest, head/tail, first/final, and Hd/Tl. However, none of these have been able to supplant 'car' and 'cdr'. One reason may be that none of these other names are amenable to the construction of compound selectors (such as 'caddar').[14]

Next we will consider the implementation of the 'cons' function. Since 'cons' is the inverse of 'car' and 'cdr', it is already clear what its effect must be; this is shown in Figure 9.5. The result of 'cons'ing two lists pointed to by A and D must be a pointer L to a cell whose left half is A and whose right half is D. In other words, all we have to do is put A and D in the left and right halves of a cell. But which cell? Clearly, it is necessary for L to be a pointer to a cell that is not in use. Therefore, the 'cons' operation requires a *storage allocation* step; a new cell must be allocated from a *heap* or *free storage area.* The mechanism required to do this will be discussed in Chapter 11, Section 11.2; for now we will assume that a procedure 'new' is available that returns a pointer to a freshly allocated cell. This is the case in Pascal: 'new (L)' stores into L a pointer to a new memory cell. Therefore, the steps required to do a 'cons' are:

```
new(L);
L↑.left := A;
L↑.right := D;
```

With the possible exception of memory allocation, which we haven't discussed, we can see that 'cons' is also quite efficient.

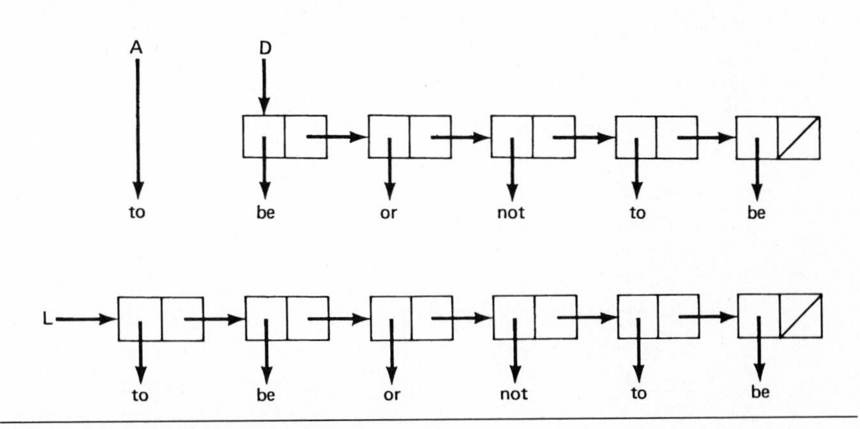

Figure 9.5 Implementation of Cons

14 Common LISP does permit 'first' and 'rest' as synonyms for 'car' and 'cdr'.

Sublists Can Be Shared

Consider the LISP session in Figure 9.6.

The result of these operations is the following list structure:

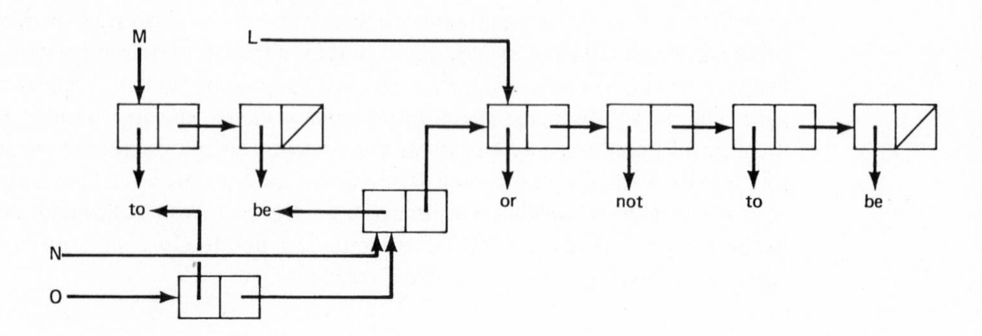

Trace through each of the lists M, L, N, and O to be sure that you see that all the elements are there in the right order. We can see that a lot of the substructure of the lists is shared. This economizes storage. In this case, eight cons-cells are used rather than the 21 that would be required if each list were independent.

In previous chapters we have discussed the danger of *aliasing*, that is, of having more than one path to a memory location. The danger is that a variable can have its value changed without being directly assigned to because it shares its storage with a different variable that has been assigned. This makes programs

```
(set 'L '(or not to be))
  (or not to be)
(set 'M '(to be))
  (to be)
(cadr M)
  be
(set 'N (cons (cadr M) L))
  (be or not to be)
(car M)
  to
(set 'O (cons (car M) N))
  (to be or not to be)
(cons (car M) (cons (cadr M) L))
  (to be or not to be)
```

Figure 9.6 Illustration of Shared Sublists

less predictable and much harder to understand. We might be led to expect that the extensive sharing of sublists in LISP programs makes these exceptionally hard to understand, but this is not the case.

The reason is that aliasing, as well as sharing of data structures, is a problem only when combined with the ability to update data structures. Note that 'car', 'cdr', and 'cons' are all *pure functions*, that is, they have no side effects on lists already created. As we've noted before, 'cdr' does not *delete* an element from a list; the original list still exists with all of its members. Similarly, 'cons' does not *add* an element to a list; rather, it computes a new list with the correct elements. The result is that this sharing of sublists is *invisible* to the user; it increases the efficiency of the program without changing its meaning. We will see below, however, that there are some circumstances in which the programmer can alter list structures. In these cases, it makes a difference as to whether lists are being shared.

List Structures Can Be Modified

In the beginning of this chapter, we contrasted an *applicative* language, which is based on the application of pure functions to their arguments, with an *imperative* language, which is based on assignments to changeable memory locations. Although LISP is predominantly an applicative language, it does have a few imperative features. We have seen the pseudo-functions (or procedures) 'set' and 'defun', which are used for binding names to objects. Now we will discuss two pseudo-functions for altering list structures.

LISP lists are very simple; they are constructed from a number of instances of identical components, cons-cells, all having exactly two parts, their left and right halves. Thus, if we want to alter a LISP list, there are really only two things we can do: alter the left half of a cell or alter the right half of a cell. The two pseudo-functions that LISP provides for this are called 'rplaca' and 'rplacd' (meaning "replace address part" and "replace decrement part").

The implementation of these pseudo-functions is simple—'(rplaca L A)' simply assigns the pointer A to the left part of the cell pointed to by L:

```
L↑.left := A;
```

Similarly, '(rplacd L D)' assigns the pointer D to the right part. This operation is illustrated in Figure 9.7. The dotted lines show the new pointer established by 'rplacd'.

The interaction of sharing and assignment lead to all of the bad effects we have come to expect from aliasing. Consider this example:

```
(set 'text '(to be or not to be))
  (to be or not to be)
```

```
(set 'x (cdr text))
  (be or not to be)
(rplacd x '(is all))
  (be is all)
text
  (to be is all)
```

Notice that the value of 'text' has been changed even though it wasn't even mentioned in the 'rplacd' operation! In real programs (which are much larger than this example), a single 'rplaca' or 'rplacd' can change the values of seemingly unrelated lists throughout the program. It can even change the program since the program itself is represented as a list. Clearly, these operations are a trap for the unwary and must be used with caution!

EXERCISE 9-19: The 'rplaca' and 'rplacd' pseudo-functions are usually used to increase the performance of LISP programs. For example, the 'addprop' function we programmed in a previous exercise changes the value of a property by recopying the entire list up to and including the value to be changed. This could be quite inefficient if the value to be changed were near the end of a long list. Write a new 'addprop' pseudo-function that uses 'rplaca' and 'rplacd' to alter an element of a property list without copying the rest of the list.

EXERCISE 9-20: Write an analogous pseudo-function for *a*-lists.

EXERCISE 9-21: Use the 'symbol-plist' and 'addprop' functions to define 'putprop'.

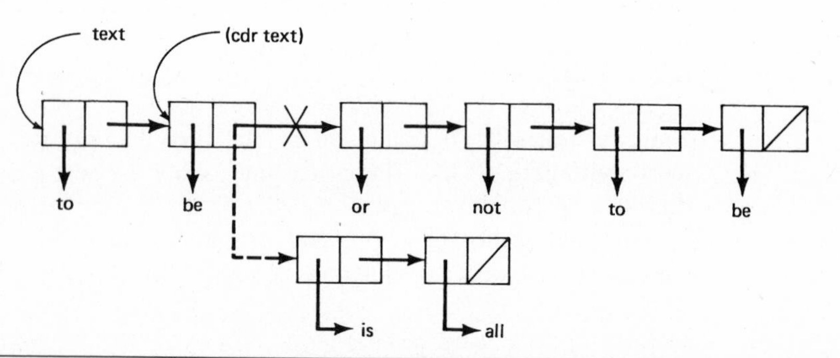

FIGURE 9.7 Execution of '(rplacd (cdr text) '(is all))'

EXERCISE 9-22: Write a pseudo-function 'remprop' that deletes a property's indicator and value from an atom's property list.

EXERCISE 9-23: The following commands will cause many LISP systems to go into an infinite loop printing A's and B's:

```
(set 'x '(A B))
  (A B)
(rplacd (cdr x) x)
  (B A B A B A B A B A B A B A B ....
```

Explain why.

Atoms Are Just Pointers to Their Property Lists

We have seen that the cons-cells from which lists are constructed have two parts, each of which can point to either an atom or a list. In the case of a list, the cons-cell points to another cons-cell, namely, the one containing the 'car' and 'cdr' of the element list. What does the cons-cell point to when it points to an atom? In other words, how are atoms represented in memory?

To answer this question, we can begin by asking what it is that makes one atom different from another. In other words, what constitutes the *identity* of an atom? One obvious answer is the print name; two atoms are different if they have different print names, and they are the same if they have the same print name. This is not the complete solution, however. Recall that atoms, like the real-world objects they are often used to model, have many properties. In the real world, we distinguish different objects by their properties: Two objects are different if they differ in at least one property, and they are the same (i.e., indistinguishable) if they agree in all of their properties. Of course, many different objects agree in *some* of their properties; for example, they might have the same name or the same shape. Computers, however, are finite: It is not possible to model the unlimited number of properties that characterize real-world objects. Rather, a finite subset of these is selected that is relevant to the situation being modeled. Thus, we might find that two distinct atoms, modeling two distinct objects, have exactly the same properties. We know that they are distinct atoms because they participate in different list structures. Since list structures really are just structures of pointers, we find that two atoms are the same if they are represented by the same pointer, and they are different if they are represented by different pointers. In implementation terms, an atom is equivalent to its location in memory; any structure pointing at that location is pointing at the same atom, and any structure pointing at a different location is pointing at a different atom. Hence, the small circles representing atoms in Figures 9.3 and 9.4 are really memory locations.

What is stored in the memory location representing an atom? There needn't be anything since we're really just using the *address* of the location as a tag that uniquely identifies the atom. In fact, it would even be possible to use *illegal addresses*, which don't represent a location in memory at all, to stand for atoms. Some LISP systems make use of these memory locations by using them to hold a pointer to the atom's property list. For example, the original LISP system used regular cons-cells to represent atoms. A special value that was not a legal address (say, -1) was placed in the left field to indicate that the cell represented an atom rather than a regular list. The right field pointed to the property list of the atom. Figure 9.8 gives an example of this.

You will see in the following exercises that the operations on atoms are simple and efficient to implement.

EXERCISE 9-24: Write a Pascal-like expression for determining whether a pointer to a cons-cell is a pointer to a list or a pointer to an atom. This is, in essence, the 'atom' predicate.

EXERCISE 9-25: Write a Pascal-like expression to access the property list of the atom represented by the pointer A. This is, in essence, the 'symbol-plist' function.

EXERCISE 9-26: How is the 'eq' predicate implemented?

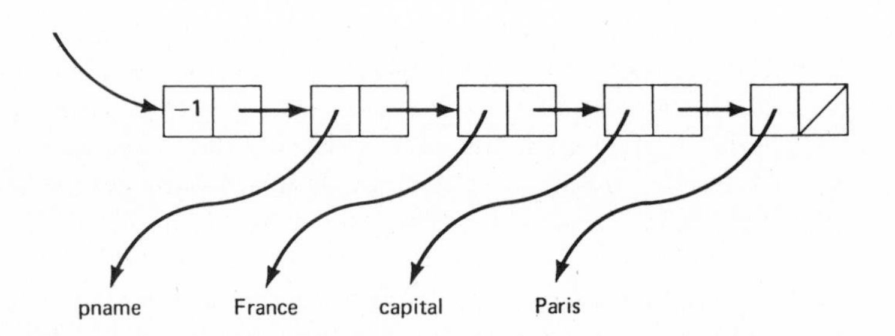

Figure 9.8 Representation of the Atom 'France'

EXERCISES

1. 'Car', 'cdr', and 'cons' all work on the *first* elements of lists. Define the meaning and describe the implementation of the analogous functions 'last', 'butlast', and 'suffix' that work on the last elements of lists. Define 'append' and 'getprop' using these functions.
2. Suppose that arrays are to be represented by linked lists. Write a function '(elt A n)' that returns the nth element of a list A and an "indexed substitution" function '(indsubst x n A)' that returns a list like A except that the nth element has been replaced by x.
3. Write a LISP function to convert a property list into the corresponding association list. Write a LISP function to convert an association list into the corresponding property list.
4. Write a LISP function to reverse a list.

5**. Write the list primitives ('car', 'cdr', 'cons', 'eq', 'atom', 'null') in a conventional programming language such as Pascal or Ada. Write a 'readlist' procedure that reads a list in the *S*-expression notation and constructs the corresponding list structure. Write a 'printlist' procedure that takes a list structure and prints it in the *S*-expression notation. Can you think of a simple way of indenting the list so that it is readable?

6**. It has been observed that many lists occupy contiguous memory locations. Therefore, the right pointers in most of the cells are redundant, since they just point to the following memory location. One alternative representation for lists is called *'cdr' encoding*, in which there are two different kinds of cells. One has left and right halves, as described in this chapter; the other just has a left field, since the right field is assumed to point to the following cell. This halves the storage required for many lists. Develop the method of 'cdr' encoding: Design the formats for list cells; describe the algorithms for performing 'car', 'cdr', and 'cons'; describe what you will do about shared sublists; and estimate the differences in space and time consumed by 'cdr' encoding and the usual representation.

7**. Design a completely different representation for LISP lists. For example, represent all lists in consecutive memory locations in exactly the order in which they are written on paper, including open and close parentheses. Analyze your new list representation, including space and time performance estimates and other advantages and disadvantages.

8. Consider the following LISP commands:

```
(defun message (x) (cons x '(is dull)) )
(message 'That)
(rplacd (cdr (message 'Nothing)) '(a surprise))
(message 'This)
```

The first call of 'message' returns '(That is dull)'; the second call of 'message' (vice 'rplacd') returns '(Nothing is dull)'. What does the third call return? What conclusions can you draw from this example?

9*. Write a LISP function that determines whether a list is circular. To accomplish this you need to know that '(eq x y)' compares the *pointers* to x and to y.

10

FUNCTIONAL PROGRAMMING: LISP

10.1 DESIGN: CONTROL STRUCTURES

Atoms Are the Only Primitives

LISP is remarkable for the simplicity of its control structures. The only primitive control structures are literals and unquoted atoms since these are the only constructs that don't alter the control flow. Literals represent themselves: For example, numbers and quoted atoms and lists are names for themselves. Unquoted atoms are bound to either functions (if they have the 'expr' property) or data values (if they have the 'apval' property). There are only two control-structure constructors: the conditional expression and the recursive application of a function to its arguments.

The Conditional Expression Is a Major Contribution

In the historical discussion of LISP, we mentioned that LISP was the first language to contain a conditional expression. This was an important idea since it meant that everything could be written as an expression. Previous languages, such as FORTRAN, and some newer languages, such as Pascal, require the user to drop from the expression level to the statement level in order to make a choice. Languages that force expressions to be broken up in this way can often make programs less readable. Mathematicians have recognized for many years the value of conditional expressions and have often used them. For example, here is a typical definition of the *signum* (sign) function:

$$\text{sg}(x) = \begin{cases} 1, & \text{if} \quad x > 0 \\ 0, & \text{if} \quad x = 0 \\ -1, & \text{if} \quad x < 0 \end{cases}$$

In LISP this function is defined:

```
(defun sg (x)
  (cond ((plusp x)     1)
        ((zerop x)     0)
        ((minusp x)   -1)) )
```

The LISP conditional has more parentheses than are really necessary; instead of

(cond $(p_1\ e_1) \ldots (p_n\ e_n)$)

it would have been quite adequate if LISP had been designed to use

(cond $p_1\ e_1 \ldots p_n\ e_n$)

However, the latter notation complicates the interpreter slightly and, as we said in the beginning of Chapter 9, nobody imagined that the S-expression notation would become the standard way of writing LISP programs.

The Logical Connectives Are Evaluated Conditionally

McCarthy took the conditional expression as one of the fundamental primitives of LISP. Therefore, it was natural to define the other logical operations in terms of it. For example, the function '(or x y)' has the value 't' (true) if either or both of x and y have the value 't'; in any other case, 'or' has the value 'nil' (false). Another way to say this is if x has the value 't', then the 'or' has the value 't', otherwise the 'or' has the same value as y. Write out a truth table for each of these definitions of 'or' to see that they're equivalent. The latter definition allows 'or' to be defined as a conditional:

(or x y) = (cond (x t) (t y))

EXERCISE 10-1: Define the 'and' function in terms of the conditional.

EXERCISE 10-2: Define the 'not' function in terms of the conditional.

EXERCISE 10-3: Use truth tables to show that the conditional definitions of 'and', 'or', and 'not' give the same results as the usual definitions.

These definitions of the logical connectives have an important property they do not possess in their usual interpretation. That is the fact that their operands are *evaluated sequentially*. To see the importance of this, consider the following example. Suppose we wish to know if a list either has 'key' as its first element or is null. We might write this as

```
(or (eq (car L) 'key) (null L) )
```

This is incorrect, however, since if L is null, it is an error to apply '(car L)'. In most languages (e.g., Algol and Pascal), the only way around this problem is to write a conditional instead of the 'or' (and in Pascal, without a conditional expression, it is quite awkward). In LISP the solution is to write the operands to 'or' in the opposite order:

```
(or (null L) (eq (car L) 'key) )
```

Why does this work? This application is equivalent to

```
(cond ((null L) t) (t (eq (car L) 'key)) )
```

That is, first evaluate '(null L)'; if it is true, then we know the result is true, so we return 't' *without ever having attempted to evaluate* '(eq (car L) 'key)'. The latter expression is evaluated only if '(null L)' is false, in which case the application is valid since L is guaranteed to have at least one element.

This interpretation of the logical connectives is known as the *conditional* or *sequential interpretation*, as opposed to the *strict interpretation*, which always evaluates both arguments. The more "lenient" sequential interpretation of the connectives often simplifies the definition of functions, although it may make it more difficult to prove things about them.

LISP allows both 'and' and 'or' to have more than two arguments. Therefore,

(and $p_1\ p_2 \cdots p_n$)

evaluates the p_i in order. As soon as one returns false (i.e., 'nil'), the 'and' immediately returns false without evaluating the rest of the arguments. Similarly,

(or $p_1\ p_2 \cdots p_n$)

evaluates the arguments until it encounters one that returns true.

Iteration Is Done by Recursion

Except for the conditional, LISP has none of the control structures found in conventional programming languages.[1] In particular, all forms of iteration are performed by recursion. We have seen this in previous examples, such as the 'append' and 'getprop' functions.

Consider the 'getprop' function:

```
(defun getprop (p x)
  (cond ((eq (car x) p) (cadr x))
        (t (getprop p (cddr x)) )) )
```

This is analogous to a **while**-loop in a Pascal-like language; the function continues to call itself recursively until a termination condition is satisfied.

LISP has no exact analog of a **for**-loop, and it generally doesn't need one. In most programming languages, **for**-loops are used to control an index for array subscripting. In LISP it is more common to write a recursive procedure that performs some operation on every element of a list. For example, suppose we need to add all of the elements of a list of numbers, which is the kind of thing we would use a **for**-loop for in Pascal. In LISP we can write a recursive function 'plus-red' that does the *plus reduction* of a list:

```
(defun plus-red (a)
  (cond ((null a) 0)
        (t (plus (car a) (plus-red (cdr a)) )) ))
```

1 This is not entirely true. Most LISPs have a vestigial imperative facility complete with **gotos** and assignment statements. Since this facility is conventional, we will not discuss it further.

Here are two example applications of 'plus-red':

```
(plus-red  '(1 2 3 4 5))
  15
(plus-red  '(3 3 3 3))
  12
```

Trace through the execution of these examples to be sure that you understand them.

Notice that 'plus-red' is quite general: It works on any list of numbers, regardless of its size. There is no "upper-bound" written into the program as there would be in most languages, and there is no explicit indexing that can go wrong. Thus it obeys the Zero-One-Infinity Principle.

The 'plus-red' function is an example of a *reduction*, that is, the use of a binary function to reduce a list to a single value. The next example we will see is an example of *mapping* a function, that is, applying a function to every element of a list and returning a list of the results.

Suppose we want to add one to each element of a list. This can be done by 'add1-map':

```
(defun add1-map (a)
  (cond ((null a) nil)
        (t (cons (add1 (car a)) (add1-map (cdr a)) )) ))
```

For example,

```
(add1-map '(1 9 8 4))
  (2 10 9 5)
```

Again, there are no explicit bounds, no controlled variables, and no indexing.

We have seen an example where we took a list and *reduced* it to one value. We have also seen an example where we took a list and *mapped* it into another list of the same size. Next we will see an example of *filtering* a list, that is, forming a sublist containing all the elements that satisfy some property. In this case, we want to form a list containing all of the negative elements of the given list. That is,

```
(minusp-fil '(2 -3 7 -1 -6 4 8))
  (-3 -1 -6)
```

The function to do this is straightforward; we just make the 'cons'ing of each element conditional on whether it is negative:

```
(defun minusp-fil (a)
  (cond ( (null a) nil)
        ( (minusp (car a))
          (cons (car a) (minusp-fil (cdr a)) ))
        (t (minusp-fil (cdr a)) )) )
```

All of the examples we have seen so far are the equivalent of a single loop; next we will see the equivalent of two **for**-loops, one nested in the other. Suppose we want a function 'all-pairs' that forms all pairs that can be formed from the elements of two lists. For example,

```
(all-pairs '(a b c) '(x y z))
  ((a x) (a y) (a z) (b x) (b y) (b z) (c x) (c y) (c z))
```

You may recognize this as the *Cartesian product* of the two lists. In a conventional language, this would be accomplished with two nested loops, one iterating over the elements of the first list and the other iterating over the elements of the second list. The same is accomplished in LISP with two nested recursive functions: 'all-pairs' will do the outer recursion over the elements of the first list and 'distl' ("distribute from the left") will do the inner iteration over all of the elements of the second list. For example,

```
(distl 'b '(x y z))
  ((b x) (b y) (b z))
```

Here are the definitions:

```
(defun all-pairs (M N)
  (cond ((null M) nil)
        (t (append (distl (car M) N)
                   (all-pairs (cdr M) N)) )) )

(defun distl (x N)
(cond   ((null N) nil)
        (t (cons (list x (car N))
                 (distl x (cdr N)) )) ))
```

(The 'list' function makes a list out of its arguments.)

EXERCISE 10-4: Write a function 'times-red' that computes the times reduction of a list. For example,

```
(times-red '(1 2 3 4))
  24
```

What should be the result of '(times-red '())'?

EXERCISE 10-5: Write an expression that computes the product of adding 1 to each element of a list. For example,

```
(times-add1 '(1 2 3))
  24
```

since $24 = (1+1) \times (2+1) \times (3+1)$. *Note:* You do not have to define any functions beyond those already defined.

EXERCISE 10-6: Write a function 'append-red', for example,

```
(append-red '( (to be) (or not) (to be) ))
  (to be or not to be)
```

EXERCISE 10-7: Write a function 'zerop-map' that returns a Boolean list representing whether the corresponding elements of the argument list are zero (as tested by 'zerop'). For example,

```
(zerop-map '(4 7 0 3 -2 0 1))
  (nil nil t nil nil t nil)
```

EXERCISE 10-8: Write a 'plus-map' function that adds the corresponding elements of two lists and returns a list of the results. For example,

```
(plus-map '(1 2 3 4) '(1 9 8 4))
  (2 11 11 8)
```

Notice that this is different from the other mapping functions because 'plus' is binary whereas 'add1', 'zerop', and so forth are unary. What will you do if the lists are of unequal length? Justify your answer.

EXERCISE 10-9: Trace in detail the following application of 'all-pairs':

```
(all-pairs '(Bob Ted) '(Carol Alice))
  ((Bob Carol) (Bob Alice) (Ted Carol) (Ted Alice))
```

Hierarchical Structures Are Processed Recursively

Most of the uses of recursion we have seen so far could have been written iteratively (e.g., using a **while**-loop) almost as easily. Next, we will discuss the use of recursion to process *hierarchical structures* that would be difficult to handle iteratively.

As an example we will design the 'equal' function, which determines whether two arbitrary values are the same. How is this different from the 'eq' primitive? Recall that the 'eq' primitive only works on atoms; its application to nonatomic values is undefined (in most LISP systems). The 'equal' function will do much more: It will tell us if two arbitrary list structures are the same. For example,

```
(equal  '(a (b c) d (e))  '(a (b c) d (e)) )
  t
(equal  '(to be or not to be)  '((to be) or (not (to be))) )
  nil
(equal  '(1 2 3)  '(3 2 1) )
  nil
(equal  'Paris  (Don Smith) )
  nil
(equal  'Paris  'London )
  nil
(equal  nil  '(be 2) )
  nil
```

The 'equal' function is applicable to *any* two arguments (see, however, p. 382).

We will design the 'equal' function in the same way we have designed other recursive functions: by solving those cases that are easy and then reducing the complicated cases to the easy cases. What are the easy cases? Atoms can be handled immediately since they can be compared with the 'eq' function. Therefore, if both x and y are atoms, then '(equal x y)' reduces to '(eq x y)'. If either x or y is an atom and the other is not, then we know they can't be equal. This can be summarized:

```
if x and y are both atoms, then
  (equal x y) = (eq x y)
if x is an atom and y isn't,
or y is an atom and x isn't,
  then (equal x y) = nil
```

These two can be combined using LISP's sequential 'and':

```
(and (atom x) (atom y) (eq x y))
```

Because of the sequential interpretation, the 'eq' application won't be evaluated unless both *x* and *y* are atoms. If either is not an atom or they're not the same atom, then the above expression returns false. Notice that this also takes care of the case where either *x* or *y* is 'nil' since in LISP 'nil' is considered an atom.

Let's consider the case where neither *x* nor *y* is an atom. Clearly, we want to compare *x* and *y* element by element. That is, we want to compare '(car *x*)' and '(car *y*)' to see that they're equal; if they are, we can eliminate them and call 'equal' recursively:

```
(equal (cdr x) (cdr y))
```

This is guaranteed eventually to reduce at least one of *x* or *y* to the null list, which is the case we've already handled. But how are we to compare '(car *x*)' and '(car *y*)'? We can't use the 'eq' function since it is defined only for atoms and '(car *x*)' or '(car *y*)' might be a list. What is needed is a function that will compare either atoms or lists for equality, and this is the very 'equal' function we are defining. Therefore, we will call 'equal' recursively on the 'car's of *x* and *y*. This solves the problem when *x* and *y* are both lists:

```
if x and y are both lists then,
  (and  (equal (car x) (car y))
        (equal (cdr x) (cdr y)) )
```

In this case, the sequential 'and' increases the efficiency of the program since if the 'car's of the lists are not equal, the program will not bother comparing the 'cdr's of the lists.

We now have two mutually disjoint cases since either at least one of *x* and *y* is an atom or they are both not atoms. Since we have all of the cases covered, we can combine them into a definition of the 'equal' function:

```
(defun equal (x y)
  (or   (and  (atom x) (atom y) (eq x y))
        (and  (not (atom x)) (not (atom y))
              (equal (car x) (car y))
              (equal (cdr x) (cdr y)) )) )
```

This function (which is provided by all LISP systems) is quite complicated to define without recursion. If you don't believe it, try it!

EXERCISE 10-10: Write a recursive function 'count' to count the number of atoms in a list no matter what their level of nesting. For example,

```
(count '(a b (c 4) ((99)) nil t) )
  7
```

EXERCISE 10-11: Explain the behavior of 'equal' when applied to circularly linked lists (i.e., lists pointing to a part of themselves).

Recursion and Iteration Are Theoretically Equivalent

The difficulty of programming a function such as 'equal' without recursion might lead us to suspect that recursion is more powerful than iteration, that is, that there are things that can be done recursively that can't be done iteratively. In fact, this is *not* the case. Consider the stack implementation of recursion that we discussed in Chapter 6. There we saw that all the information relevant to a procedure call, such as its parameters, local storage, and result, could be maintained in a stack of activation records. In theory, any recursive program can be converted into an iterative program by maintaining such a stack. This is effectively what an Algol or Pascal compiler does; it converts recursion into iteration. Although this reduction is a *theoretical* possibility, it is not *practical* to do by hand in most cases, since the resulting program is so much more complicated. From the programmer's viewpoint, recursion *is* more powerful than iteration.

Since recursion can in principle be reduced to iteration, we might wonder if iteration is more powerful than recursion. This is also false. Earlier in this section, we showed how a number of common **while**-loop- and **for**-loop-like structures could be expressed recursively. We will not show how *any* such structure can be so expressed, although you can probably see the general idea. More general structures expressible with **goto**s can also be reduced to recursion, but, like the reduction of recursion to iteration, this is not a result of much practical value.

EXERCISE 10-12: Write the 'equal' procedure iteratively, that is, using **while**-loops. Maintain your own stack of intermediate results.

Functional Arguments Allow Abstraction

Earlier in this section, we saw a definition of the 'add1-map' function, which applies 'add1' to each element of a list. In an exercise you programmed a 'zerop-map' function that applies 'zerop' to each element of a list. Notice that these functions were identical except for the particular function, 'add1' or 'zerop', applied. Mapping any other unary function (e.g., 'not') would also fit the same pattern. We can see here an application of the Abstraction Principle: Since this same pattern keeps recurring, it is to our benefit to *abstract* it out and give it a name. This effectively raises the level at which we are programming and decreases the chances of error. If we repeat essentially the same thing over and over, there is a tendency to become careless and make a mistake. It is much better to do the thing once in a general way that can be used over and over.

Thus, we will define a function 'mapcar' that applies a given function to each element of a list and returns a list of the results. It is not hard to see how to do this since the pattern of the recursion is just an abstraction from the patterns of 'add1-map' and 'zerop-map':

```
(defun mapcar (f x)
  (cond ((null x) nil)
        (t (cons (f (car x)) (mapcar f (cdr x)) )) ))
```

The function is called 'mapcar' because it applies 'f' to the 'car' of the list each time. Most LISP systems provide 'mapcar' for the user, although on some the order of the arguments is reversed. There's not much standardization in the LISP world!

With this definition of 'mapcar' our previous examples can be expressed without having to write a recursive definition:

```
(mapcar 'add1 '(1 9 8 4))
  (2 10 9 5)
(mapcar 'zerop '(4 7 0 3 -2 0 1))
  (nil nil t nil nil t nil)
(mapcar 'not (mapcar 'zerop '(4 7 0 3 -2 0 1)))
  (t t nil t t nil t)
```

EXERCISE 10-13: Notice that as we have defined the 'mapcar' function, it will not work for *binary* functions so we cannot use it to write 'plus-map'. Write a function 'mapcar2' that can be used for this purpose. For example,

```
(mapcar2 'plus '(1 2 3 4) '(1 9 8 4))
  (2 11 11 8)
```

By using certain features of LISP that we will not discuss here, it is possible to define a 'mapcar' function that takes a variable number of arguments so that it will work with any function. The 'mapcar' provided by some LISPs works in this way.

EXERCISE 10-14: Define a function 'filter' such that '(filter *p x*)' is a list composed of just those elements of *x* that satisfy the predicate *p*. For example,

```
(filter 'minusp '(2 -3 7 -1 -6 4 8))
  (-3 -1 -6)
```

EXERCISE 10-15: Define the 'reduce' function that reduces a list by a given binary function.[2] For example,

```
(reduce 'plus 0 '(1 2 3 4 5))
  15
```

In general, '(reduce f a x)' means '(f x_1 (f x_2 ... (f x_n a) ...))'.

EXERCISE 10-16: Show that '(reduce 'cons b a)' is equivalent to '(append a b)'.

Functionals Allow Programs To Be Combined

We have seen that one of the advantages of functional arguments is that they suppress details of loop control and recursion. Next we will see that they also simplify the combination of already implemented programs. The first example we will consider is the *inner product* of two lists.

The *inner product of two lists* is defined to be the sum of the products of the corresponding elements of the two lists:

$$u \cdot v = \sum_{i=1}^{n} u_i v_i$$

The 'mapcar2' function that we defined in the preceding exercises can be used to take the products of the corresponding elements:

```
(mapcar2 'times u v)
  (w1 w2 ... wn)
```

where each $w_i = u_i v_i$. Therefore, the inner product is just the 'plus' reduction of the products:

```
(define ip (u v)
  (reduce 'plus 0 (mapcar2 'times u v)) )
```

For example,

```
(ip '(1 2 3) '(-2 3 4))
  16
```

2 This 'reduce' function is similar, but not identical, to the 'reduce' of Common LISP.

EXERCISE 10-17: Show that 'ip' computes the result above by tracing its execution.

EXERCISE 10-18: Define nonrecursively a function f that computes

$$f(u,v) = \prod_{i=1}^{n} (u_i + v_i)$$

EXERCISE 10-19: Define nonrecursively a function 'pairlis' that computes

(pairlis u v w) =
 ((u_1 v_1) (u_2 v_2) ... (u_m v_m) w_1 w_2 ... w_n)

in which u and v are m element lists and w is an n element list. That is, the function of '(pairlis u v w)' is to pair up corresponding elements of u and v and append them to the front of w. *Hint:* '(list u_i v_i)' returns the pair '(u_i v_i)'.

Lambda Expressions Are Anonymous Functions

Suppose that we need to 'cons' the value bound to 'val' onto all the elements of a list L; this is an obvious application for 'mapcar'. We can do this by writing '(mapcar 'consval L)' but only if we have already defined

```
(defun consval (x) (cons val x))
```

It is inconvenient to give a name to a function every time we want to pass it to 'mapcar' (or to 'reduce', etc.). It clutters up the name space with short function definitions that are only used once. An obvious solution would be just to pass the function's body, '(cons val x)', to 'mapcar':

```
(mapcar '(cons val x) L)
```

The trouble with this is that it's ambiguous; we don't know which names are the parameters to the 'cons' and which are globals. That is, '(cons val x)' could equally well represent any of the following functions:

```
(defun f0 ()         (cons val x))
(defun f1 (x)        (cons val x))
(defun f2 (val)      (cons val x))
(defun f3 (val x)    (cons val x))
(defun f4 (x val)    (cons val x))
```

Notice that they all have exactly the same body—'(cons val x)'. What is required is some way of specifying which of the names in '(cons val x)' are parameters and which are global variables.

A mathematical theory called the "lambda calculus" provides a solution to this problem. It supplies a notation for *anonymous functions,* that is, for functions that have not been bound to names. LISP uses the notation

```
(lambda (x) (cons val x))
```

to mean that function of *x* whose value is '(cons val *x*)'. This is equivalent to the function 'f1'. If 'f2' were the function we wanted, we would write

```
(lambda (val) (cons val x))
```

These *lambda expressions* are values that can be manipulated like any other LISP lists; in particular, they can be passed as parameters.

Now we can solve our original problem. To cons 'val' onto each element of a list L we write

```
(mapcar '(lambda (x) (cons val x)) L)
```

Similarly, to double all of the elements of L, we write

```
(mapcar '(lambda (n) (times n 2)) L)
```

Next we will consider a more complicated example of the use of lambda expressions. Recall that the application '(distl *x N*)' returns a list

$((x\ N_1)\ (x\ N_2)\ \ldots\ (xN_n))$

This is clearly a case of mapping a function on the list *N*, the function being that which takes any *y* into the pair (*x y*). Thus, the function we want to map is

```
(lambda (y) (list x y))
```

(The 'list' function makes a list out of its arguments.) Hence, the definition of 'distl' is

```
(defun distl (x N)
  (mapcar   '(lambda (y) (list x y))
            N))
```

Now let's consider the 'all-pairs' function. First, it is necessary to apply '(distl M_i N)' for each element M_i of M; this will give us a list L of the form

$(L_1\ L_2\ \ldots\ L_m)$

where each L_i is of the form

$((M_i\ N_1)\ (M_i\ N_2)\ \ldots\ (M_i\ N_n))$

The result we want, '(all-pairs M N)', is the result of appending all of the L_i, that is, the append-reduction of L:

(reduce 'append nil L)

The list L results from forming a list of the results of '(distl M_i N)' for each element of M. This can be accomplished with 'mapcar':

L = (mapcar '(lambda (x) (distl x N)) M)

All of these results can be assembled into the following definition of 'all-pairs':

```
(defun all-pairs (M N)
  (reduce  'append nil
           (mapcar '(lambda (x) (distl x N)) M)) )

(defun distl (x N)
  (mapcar '(lambda (y) (list x y))
           N))
```

Actually, the definition of 'distl' is not necessary; it too can be replaced by a lambda expression:

```
(defun all-pairs (M N)
  (reduce  'append nil
           (mapcar '(lambda (x)
                           (mapcar '(lambda (y) (list x y))
                                    N))
                M)) )
```

This is probably carrying things too far, however. Even if the 'distl' function is not used anywhere but in 'all-pairs', it's probably a good idea to give it a name so that the definition of 'all-pairs' does not get too confusing. LISP expressions are like mathematical formulas: They must be kept small to stay readable.

EXERCISE 10-20: Use a lambda expression to write an application to square each element of a list L.

EXERCISE 10-21: Use lambda expressions, 'append', 'cons', and 'reduce' to reverse a list L.

Functionals Can Replace Lambda Expressions

We have seen that in many cases the use of functional arguments allows control-flow patterns to be abstracted out, given names, and used over and over again. We have also seen that the use of lambda expressions can often eliminate otherwise useless function bindings. Recently, programmers have begun using these ideas more systematically, a practice called *functional programming.* A *functional* is defined to be a function that has either (or both) of the following: (1) one or more functions as arguments; (2) a function as its result. We have already seen several examples of functions that have functions as arguments, for example, 'mapcar', 'reduce', and 'filter'.

Let's consider a few examples from earlier discussions. In our discussion of lambda expressions, we wanted to map onto a list a function that consed 'val' onto its argument. We did this by mapping the lambda expression

```
(lambda (x) (cons val x))
```

In the 'all-pairs' example, we performed a similar action—mapping across a list a function that formed a list with x:

```
(lambda (y) (list x y))
```

In each case we turned a *binary* function (e.g., 'cons') into a *unary* function by *binding* one of its parameters to a value. In the first case, the first argument of 'cons' was bound to 'val', and in the second case, the first argument of 'list' was bound to 'x'. Since we have changed one function into another function, we are really doing what a functional does—operating on a function to return another function. We can automate this process (applying the Abstraction Principle again) by defining a functional 'bu' that converts a binary function into a unary function. In other words, instead of

```
(lambda (x) (cons val x))
```

we will write

```
(bu 'cons val)
```

In general, '(bu *f x*)' binds the first argument of *f* to *x*.

To define 'bu' we have to be very clear about its effect. The result of '(bu *f x*)' is a unary function that, when applied to an argument *y*, returns '(*f x y*)'. In other words,

```
((bu f x) y) = (f x y)
```

[Notice that the function being applied to *y* is the function returned by '(bu *f x*)'![3]] That function of *y* whose value is '(*f x y*)' is just

```
(lambda (y) (f x y))
```

The definition of 'bu' then follows immediately (the application of 'function' is discussed in Section 10.2 on Name Structures; for now just interpret it as a sign that a function is being returned):

```
(defun bu (f x) (function (lambda (y) (f x y)) ))
```

The mapping onto L of the function to cons 'val' onto a list can now be written without the use of lambda expressions or auxiliary function definitions:

```
(mapcar (bu 'cons val) L)
```

Similarly, the definition of 'distl' can be simplified:

```
(defun distl (x N) (mapcar (bu 'list x) N) )
```

Notice that the use of the 'bu' functional has eliminated an entire class of errors—mistakes in writing a lambda expression that converts a binary function to a unary function. This is one of the principal values of abstraction.

There's also a lambda expression in the definition of 'all-pairs':

```
(lambda (x) (distl x N))
```

Here again a binary function is made into a unary function by fixing one of its parameters. In this case, however, it is the *second* parameter that is being fixed. The 'bu' functional will not accomplish this since it fixes the *first* parameter. Of course, it would be no trouble to define a new functional, for example 'bu2', that fixes the second argument of a binary function.

Continuing this process would lead to a proliferation of functionals: 'bu2',

3 Some LISP dialects do not permit using a function call as the function in another function call. In these dialects it would be necessary to write '(funcall (bu *f x*) *y*)'.

'bu3', and so on. We wouldn't need this 'bu2' functional if the arguments to 'distl' were reversed; we could then use 'bu'.

In functional programming it is quite common to need to reverse the arguments to a binary function, so the best solution seems to be to define a functional 'rev' such that '(rev f)' is f with its arguments reversed. In other words, '(rev f)' applied to x and y yields '(f y x)'. That is, '(rev f)' is that function of x and y whose value is '(f y x)':

(rev f) = (lambda (x y) (f y x))

The LISP definition follows easily:

```
(defun rev (f) (function (lambda (x y) (f y x)) ))
```

Now, fixing the second argument of 'distl' is the same as fixing the first argument of '(rev 'distl)', so the second argument of 'distl' can be bound to 'N' by

```
(bu (rev 'distl) N)
```

With this information, the definition of 'all-pairs' can be written:

```
(defun all-pairs (M N)
  (reduce 'append nil
          (mapcar (bu (rev 'distl) N) M)) )
```

We can increase the flexibility with which functions can be combined if a uniform style is used for all functionals. We will define functional forms of 'mapcar', 'mapcar2', and 'reduce' that, like 'rev', take a function and return a function. For example, '(map 'add1)' will be a function that adds 1 to each element of a list.[4] In other words:

((map 'add1) L) = (mapcar 'add1 L)

Another way to say the above is that '(map f)' is that function that takes any list L into the result of mapping f onto that list:

```
(defun map (f) (function (lambda (L) (mapcar f L)) ))
```

The value of these functional operators is their *combinatorial power*, and for this reason they are often called *combinators* or *combining forms*. They make it

4 This 'map' is different from the 'map' in most LISP dialects.

simple to combine existing programs to accomplish new tasks. For example, to define a function 'vec-dbl' that doubles all of the elements of a vector, we can use[5] '(map (bu 'times 2))':

```
(set 'vec-dbl (map (bu 'times 2)) )
```

EXERCISE 10-22: Define the functional 'bu2'.

EXERCISE 10-23: Define the functional 'dup' so that '(dup f)' applied to x is '(f x x)':

((dup f) x) = (f x x)

Show that '(dup 'times)' is the squaring function.

EXERCISE 10-24: Use functionals to define a function to square every element of a vector.

EXERCISE 10-25: Define a functional that returns the *composition* of two functions '(comp f g)'. That is,

((comp f g) x) = (f (g x))

EXERCISE 10-26: Define a functional 'map2' that when applied to a binary function f returns the corresponding binary map:

((map2 f) x y) = (mapcar2 f x y)

EXERCISE 10-27: Use functionals to define a function 'vec-sum' that returns the sum of two vectors represented as lists. That is, it returns a list whose elements are the sum of the corresponding elements of the two input vectors.

EXERCISE 10-28: Suppose that matrices are represented by lists of lists (i.e., vectors of vectors as in Pascal). Use functionals to define a function 'mat-sum' that computes the sum of two matrices by adding their corresponding elements.

EXERCISE 10-29: Define a functional 'red' such that '(red f a)' is the f-reduction function starting with an initial value a. For example, '(red 'plus 0)' is the function that adds the elements of a list together.

5 Many LISP systems will not allow a function defined by 'set' to be applied in the normal way. In these cases, the 'expr' property must be defined explicitly by '(putprop 'vec-dbl (map (bu 'times 2)) 'expr)'.

EXERCISE 10-30: Show that the following function computes the sum of the squares of the elements of a list:

```
(comp (red 'plus 0) (map (dup 'times)) )
```

EXERCISE 10-31: In a previous section, we defined an inner product function. Redefine this using functionals.

EXERCISE 10-32: Define a functional 'const' that returns a constant function. That is, '(const *k*)', when applied to any argument, returns *k*. Show that the following function computes (albeit inefficiently) the length of a list:

```
(set 'length (comp (red 'plus 0) (map (const 1)) ))
```

EXERCISE 10-33:* Discuss the readability of programs that make heavy use of functionals. What are the advantages and disadvantages? Suggest guidelines to improve the readability of these programs.

Backus Developed a Functional Programming Style

In 1977 John Backus, the principal designer of FORTRAN (Chapter 2) and of the BNF notation (Chapter 4), received the Association for Computing Machinery's Turing Award.

In his acceptance speech, Backus was highly critical of contemporary programming languages. He said that they "are growing ever more enormous, but not stronger. Inherent defects at the most basic level cause them to be both fat and weak." He proposed "an alternate functional style of programming ... founded on the use of combining forms for creating programs." Backus identified several areas in which programming languages could be improved.

First, he said that conventional languages have a "word-at-a-time" programming style. We have seen this in most of the languages we have studied, where, for example, an array is processed by performing some action on each of its elements individually, with all of the indexing, controlled variables, and loop control this requires. We have seen an alternative style of programming in this section. When we write '(map2 'plus)' to add two vectors, we can think of the vectors as wholes rather than being concerned with the details of iterating over their elements. Operations such as 'mapcar' and 'reduce' deal with *entire data structures* as units (although, of course, the machine will have to process all of the individual elements). Since we do not have to think about the parts of data structures, we are programming at a *higher level of abstraction.* One of the earliest languages to provide facilities like this was APL (early 1960s), which was the source for several of the functionals we've discussed.

A second major goal of Backus's work has been to allow programs to be manipulated, proved, and even derived, by using simple algebraic manipulations.

In other words, it should be about as simple to do things with programs as it is to do high school algebra. In this case, though, instead of adding, subtracting, multiplying, and dividing numbers, we are composing, reversing, mapping, and reducing functions. To make these manipulations clearer, Backus introduced an algebraic notation that makes the structure of a program clearer than Cambridge Polish; we will see examples later. Further, Backus observed that variables (i.e., formal parameters and Algol scope rules) complicate manipulating and reasoning about programs. Therefore, another goal of his notation has been to eliminate the need for variables; thus, his approach has sometimes been called *variable-free programming*. By this he did not mean just the elimination of alterable variables and assignment statements; all applicative languages do this. He meant, in addition, the elimination of formal parameters. We have seen several examples of this, such as eliminating lambda expressions and their associated variables by using the 'bu' and 'rev' functionals.

Many of Backus's functionals correspond closely to the functionals we've discussed; they will serve as an introduction to his notation:

Name	LISP	Backus
application	(f x)	$f{:}x$
mapping	(map f)	αf
reduction	(red f a)	$/f$
composition	(comp f g)	$f \circ g$
binding	(bu f k)	(bu f k)
constant	(const k)	$\overline{k}$
lists	(a b c d)	<a,b,c,d>
built-in functions	plus, times, ...	+, ×, ...
selectors	cdr, car, cadr, ...	tail, **1**, **2**, ...

Notice that there is only one functional, 'α' (meaning "apply to all"), for mapping functions onto lists. Backus has avoided the need for a whole series of functionals 'map2', 'map3', and so on, and followed the Zero-One-Infinity Principle by a simple expedient: All functions are unary. Functions that we normally think of as having several arguments instead have one—a list of the arguments. For example, the '+' function takes a list as an argument—the list of numbers to be added; for example,

```
+:<3,5> = 8
```

Let's work through an example. In a previous exercise, we defined an inner product function using functionals. We will do the same thing now in Backus's notation. The goal is to define a function 'ip' such that 'ip:<u,v>' is the inner product of the two vectors u and v. The first step is to multiply the corresponding elements of the two vectors. But without 'map2' how can we do this? The data structure we are given looks like this:

$$<<u_1, u_2, \ldots, u_n> <v_1, v_2, \ldots, v_n>>$$

that is, a list of two lists. We need to get the corresponding u_i and v_i together, that is,

$$<<u_1, v_1>, <u_2, v_2>, \ldots, <u_n, v_n>>$$

which is a list of two-element lists. In other words, we need to convert a $2 \times n$ matrix into an $n \times 2$ matrix. For this purpose Backus provided a transpose function, 'trans':

$$\text{trans:} <<\ldots u_i \ldots>, <\ldots v_i \ldots>> = <\ldots <u_i v_i> \ldots>$$

The next step is to apply the multiplication operation to each of these pairs; this is accomplished with 'α', which corresponds to 'map':

$$(\alpha \times)\text{:(trans:} <u,v>) = <u_1v_1, \ldots, u_nv_n>$$

To compute the inner product, we just add up all of the products with a plus reduction, '/+' (the initial value 0 is implicit in Backus's notation):

$$\text{ip:} <u,v> = (/+)\text{:(}(\alpha \times)\text{: (trans:} <u,v>))$$

Recall that we want to eliminate variables; this can be done in this case with functional composition. Since

$$(f \circ g)\text{: } x = f\text{:(}g\text{:}x)$$

we can write the definition of the inner product:

$$\text{ip} = (/+) \circ (\alpha \times) \circ \text{trans}$$

Notice the distinctive characteristics of this program: It has no loops, no explicit sequencing, no assignments, and no variables.

For our next example, we will consider the multiplication of two matrices. Suppose M is an $l \times m$ matrix and N is an $m \times n$ matrix, and we want to form the product P, an $l \times n$ matrix. The matrix product is defined as follows:

$$P_{ik} = \sum_{j=1}^{m} M_{ij} N_{jk}$$

The right-hand side of this should look familiar: It is just the inner product of the ith row of M and the kth column of N. Now, the kth column of N is just the kth row of the transpose of N. If we let

$$N' = \text{trans}:N$$

we can see that

$$P_{ik} = \text{ip}:<M_i, N_k'>$$

where M_i is the ith row of M and N_k' is the kth row of N transpose.

How can we build up the product matrix P? Since it is structured as a list of lists, it is reasonable to construct it by two nested mappings, the inner one constructing the individual rows and the outer one combining these rows into the product matrix. The ith row of the product is

$$P_i = <P_{i1}, P_{i2}, \ldots, P_{in}>$$

That is,

$$P_i = <\text{ip}:<M_i, N_1'>, \ldots, \text{ip}:<M_i, N_n'>>$$

It is clear that this can be produced by a map:

$$P_i = (\alpha\ \text{ip}):<<M_i, N_1'>, \ldots, <M_i, N_n'>>$$

Notice that the argument to '(α ip)' is a list of pairs and that the first elements of all of the pairs are the same. They can be factored out by Backus's *distribute left* function, which is defined

$$\text{distl}:<x, <a, b, \ldots, z>> = <<x,a>, <x,b>, \ldots, <x,z>>$$

Therefore,

$$\begin{aligned} P_i &= (\alpha\ \text{ip}):(\text{distl}:<M_i, N'>) \\ &= (\alpha\ \text{ip}) \circ \text{distl}:<M_i, N'> \end{aligned}$$

Let $f = (\alpha\ \text{ip}) \circ \text{distl}$. Notice that the final matrix P is

$$\begin{aligned} P &= <P_1, P_2, \ldots, P_l> \\ &= <f:<M_1, N'>, f:<M_2, N'>, \ldots, <M_l, N'>> \end{aligned}$$

The function f can be factored out by mapping:

$$P = (\alpha f): < <M_1,N'>, <M_2,N'>, \ldots, <M_l,N'> >$$

Since each pair ends in N', each can be factored out with the *distribute right* function:

$$P = (\alpha f) \circ \text{distr}: <M, N'>$$

This gives us the product matrix in terms of M and N.' How can we get it in terms of M and N? For this the *constructor* functional can be used; it uses a sequence of functions to construct a list:

$$[f_1, \ldots, f_n]: x = <f_1 : x, \ldots, f_n : x>$$

In our example,

$$<M,N'> = [\ \mathbf{1}, \text{trans} \circ \mathbf{2}\ ]: <M,N>$$

since $\mathbf{1}: <M,N> = M$ (i.e., '**1**' is Backus's notation for 'car'), and

$$\text{trans} \circ \mathbf{2} : <M,N> = \text{trans}:N = N'$$

since '**2**' is Backus's notation for 'cadr'. Therefore, the product of M and N is

$$P = (\alpha f) \circ \text{distr} \circ [\ \mathbf{1}, \text{trans} \circ \mathbf{2}\ ]: <M,N>$$
$$\text{where } f = (\alpha\ \text{ip}) \circ \text{distl}$$

In other words, a (variable-free) program for computing a matrix product is:

$$\text{mat-prod} = (\alpha f) \circ \text{distr} \circ [\ \mathbf{1}\ , \text{trans} \circ \mathbf{2}\ ]$$
$$\text{where } f = (\alpha\ \text{ip}) \circ \text{distl}$$

One of the goals of Backus's notation is the algebraic manipulation of programs. We can see a simple example of that here. If we substitute the definition of f into 'mat-prod', we get

$$\text{mat-prod} = (\alpha\ ((\alpha\ \text{ip}) \circ \text{distl})) \circ \text{distr} \circ [\ \mathbf{1}\ , \text{trans} \circ \mathbf{2}\ ]$$

Since the doubly nested 'α' s are a little hard to read, we can use the identity

$$\alpha\ (f \circ g) = (\alpha f) \circ (\alpha\ g)$$

to simplify it. The resulting definition of the matrix product is

$$\text{mat-prod} = (\alpha\ \alpha\ \text{ip}) \circ (\alpha\ \text{distl}) \circ \text{distr} \circ [\ \mathbf{1}, \text{trans} \circ \mathbf{2}\ ]$$

We can analyze this program for a matrix product. Some of the operations are inherent in the definition of a matrix product, such as the doubly mapped inner product and the transposition of the second matrix. Others, such as the distribute left and right operations, the selectors ('**1**', etc.), and the constructor, are taking the place of parameters. We can see this by comparing Backus's program with a similar LISP program:

```
(defun mat-prod (M N) (mapcar (bu 'prod-row (trans N)) M))

(defun prod-row (Nt r) (mapcar (bu 'ip r) Nt))
```

The doubly mapped inner product and the transpose both appear here, but the other functions do not. Their purpose has been taken over by the bound variables, which are very powerful mechanisms for rearranging the order of things.

EXERCISE 10-34:* Compare the Backus and LISP programs for the matrix product. What are their relative readability and writability? Which one do you suppose it is easier to prove things about? Separate out detailed issues of the notation (such as whether we write 'map' or 'α') from more fundamental issues (such as the absence of variables).

EXERCISE 10-35: Write a program in Backus's notation to compute the mean of a list. Assume the function 'length', which returns the length of a list, is available.

EXERCISE 10-36: Show that the following identity is true:

$$[\, f \circ 1, g \circ 2] \circ [h, k] = [\, f \circ h, g \circ k]$$

EXERCISE 10-37:* One of the advantages that Backus claims for his approach is that there is a *limited* set of functionals. Since LISP allows programmers to define their own functionals, it provides an *open-ended* set of functionals. Backus claims that a limited set is better because programmers can then master their use. Discuss the advantages and disadvantages between limited and open-ended sets of functionals.

EXERCISE 10-38:* Read Backus's Turing Award Paper (in the August 1978 issue of the *Communications of the ACM*) and discuss it.

10.2 DESIGN: NAME STRUCTURES

The Primitives Bind Atoms to Their Values

As in the other programming languages we have discussed, the primitive name structures are the individual bindings of names to their values. In LISP these bindings are established in two ways—through property lists and through actual-formal correspondence. The former is established by pseudo-functions such as 'set' and 'defun'. For example, the application

```
(set 'text '(to be or not to be))
```

binds 'text' to the list '(to be or not to be)' by placing the 'apval' property with the value '(to be or not to be)' on the property list of 'text'. Similarly, a 'defun' binds a name to a function by placing the 'expr' property on an atom's property list. This property is bound to the lambda expression for the function. For example, the definition of 'getprop' is equivalent to

```
(putprop 'getprop
    '(lambda (p x) (cond  ((eq (car x) p) (cadr x))
                          (t (getprop p (cddr x)) )) )
    'expr)
```

The 'set' and 'defun' pseudo-functions are analogous to the variable and procedure declarations of a conventional programming language.

One important characteristic of bindings established through property lists is that they are *global.* Since there is at most one instance of each distinct atom in existence at a time, any change to the property list of an atom is visible throughout the program. The bindings are somewhat similar to the global subprograms and COMMON variables of FORTRAN (perhaps reflecting that LISP is almost as old as FORTRAN). We will see later that LISP also has a name structure constructor analogous to Algol's blocks.

Application Binds Formals to Actuals

The other primitive binding operation is actual-formal correspondence. This is very similar to other programming languages. For example, if we define:

```
(defun getprop (p x)
   (cond ((eq (car x) p) (cadr x))
         (t (getprop p (cddr x))) ))
```

and then evaluate the application

```
(getprop 'name DS)
```

the formal 'p' will be bound to the atom 'name' and the formal 'x' will be bound to the value of the actual 'DS' (which happens to be a *p*-list representing Don Smith's personnel record).

Temporary Bindings Are a Simple, Syntactic Extension

We have seen two methods of binding names to values—the definition of properties and actual-formal correspondence. What we have not seen is a method of binding names in a local context such as is provided by Algol's blocks. To see the need for this, we will work out a simple example. Suppose we want to write a program to compute both roots of a quadratic equation. They are defined by the well-known equation:

$$r_1, r_2 = \frac{-b \pm \sqrt{b^2 - 4ac}}{2a}$$

We want to define a function 'roots' that returns a list containing the two roots. The general form of this function could be

(defun roots (a b c) (list r_1 r_2))

where r_1 and r_2 are expressions for computing the two roots. When these expressions are substituted in the above formula, we end up with a rather large, unreadable function definition:

```
(defun roots (a b c)
  (list    (quotient (plus (minus b)
                          (sqrt (difference (expt b 2)
                                            (times 4 a c)) ))
                     (times 2 a))
           (quotient (difference (minus b)
                                 (sqrt (difference (expt b 2)
                                                   (times 4 a c)) ))
                     (times 2 a)) ))
```

Using the symbolic operator names provided by Common LISP and some other dialects is little improvement:

```
(defun roots (a b c)
  (list  (/  (+ (- b) (sqrt (- (expt b 2) (* 4 a c)) ))
             (* 2 a))
         (/  (- (- b) (sqrt (- (expt b 2) (* 4 a c)) ))
             (* 2 a)) ))
```

One reason for this unwieldy expression (aside from the Cambridge Polish notation) is that the large expression corresponding to

$$\sqrt{b^2 - 4ac}$$

is repeated in each of the expressions r_1 and r_2. The usual way to avoid writing the same expression several times is to give it a name. For example:

$$\text{Let } d = \sqrt{b^2 - 4ac}$$
$$r_1 = (-b + d)/2a$$
$$r_2 = (-b - d)/2a$$

This obeys the Abstraction Principle, which says that an expression is more readable if the common parts are factored out.

How can we use the Abstraction Principle to improve our 'roots' definition? What we need to do is bind a name (e.g., 'd') to the common subexpression *just long enough* to evaluate the expressions r_1 and r_2 for the two roots. The only mechanism we have seen for temporarily binding a name to a value is actual-formal correspondence. To use this, however, we will have to define an auxiliary function (e.g., 'roots-aux') to bind the formal 'd'. This is what our definitions might look like:

```
(defun roots-aux (d)
  (list (quotient (plus (minus b) d)
                  (times 2 a))
        (quotient (difference (minus b) d)
                  (times 2 a)) ))

(defun roots (a b c)
  (roots-aux (sqrt (difference (expt b 2)
                               (times 4 a c)) )) )
```

Notice that we have not explicitly passed 'a' and 'b' to 'roots-aux'; this is so because LISP functions are *called in the environment of the caller,* the 'roots' function, in this case. This is discussed in more detail later.

The above definition of 'roots' is simpler than our original one. However, it still leaves a lot to be desired because we have really misused a facility. We have used formal-actual correspondence where no parameterization was really involved; we have used it simply to introduce a local name. For this reason a number of LISP systems provide a method of introducing local names analogous to our use of 'let' above. The 'let' function allows a number of local names to be bound to values at one time; the second argument to 'let' is evaluated in the resulting environment. That is,

(let ((n_1 e_1) ... (n_m e_m)) E)

evaluates each of the expressions e_i and binds the name n_i to the corresponding value. The expression E is evaluated in the resulting environment and is returned as the value of the 'let'. For example,

```
(defun roots (a b c)
  (let  ((d (sqrt (difference   (expt b 2)
                                (times 4 a c)) )) )
        (list (quotient  (plus  (minus b) d)
                         (times 2 a))
              (quotient  (difference (minus b) d)
                         (times 2 a)) )) )
```

We can see that the 'let' function is something like an Algol block; it introduces a new scope and declares a set of names in that scope, each with an initial value. It is, in fact, closest to an Ada 'declare' block that contains only constant declarations. That is,

```
declare
  n₁: constant float := e₁;
          :
  nₘ: constant float := eₘ;
begin
  E
end
```

The 'let' function is really just an abbreviation for a function definition and application. That is,

(let ((n_1 e_1) ... (n_m e_m)) E)

is equivalent to the definition

(defun QQQQQ ($n_1 \dots n_m$) E)

(where 'QQQQQ' is a made-up name that does not occur elsewhere) followed by the application

(QQQQQ $e_1 \dots e_m$)

This is an example of *syntactic sugar*: The 'let' construct does not allow us to do anything that could not be done before; rather, it allows us to write the same thing in a much more readable way. One of the important characteristics of LISP is that extensions such as the 'let' function can be defined *within LISP* (although not with the facilities we've discussed). This makes it convenient for LISP programmers to solve their own problems without appealing to systems programmers. It also has the danger of encouraging the proliferation of "personal" LISP dialects.

Dynamic Scoping Is the Constructor

We have already mentioned that LISP uses *dynamic scoping* instead of the static (or lexical) scoping used by the other languages we have studied. Recall (Chapter 3) that dynamic scoping means that a function is *called in the environment of its caller*, whereas static scoping means that it is *called in the environment of its definition.* For example, the 'roots-aux' function had access to the names 'a' and 'b' because it was called from the 'roots' procedure, which declared 'a' and 'b' as formals. In a statically scoped language, these would had to have been passed as parameters. The same is true for the 'let' procedure: It would not be very useful if it didn't *inherit* access to the names bound in the surrounding scope. Since a 'let' is equivalent to a function application, the 'let' must be invoked in the environment of the caller.

The above are some of the advantages of dynamic scoping. In Chapter 3, Section 3.3 (Algol Name Structures), we discussed some of the problems associated with dynamic scoping. We will not repeat that discussion here, but it will be worthwhile to reread it. Here we will discuss those problems peculiar to LISP.

Dynamic Scoping Complicates Functional Arguments

Dynamic scoping can interact with functional arguments in confusing ways. Consider, for example, a function 'twice' defined so that '(twice *f* *x*)' returns the value of '(*f* (*f* *x*))':

```
(defun twice (func val) (func (func val)) )
```

The call '(twice 'add1 5)' returns 7. If we want to double the number 3 twice, we can use a lambda expression

```
(twice '(lambda (x) (times 2 x)) 3)
  12
```

The state of the environment during the first application of 'func' in 'twice' is shown by this *contour diagram* (see Chapter 3):

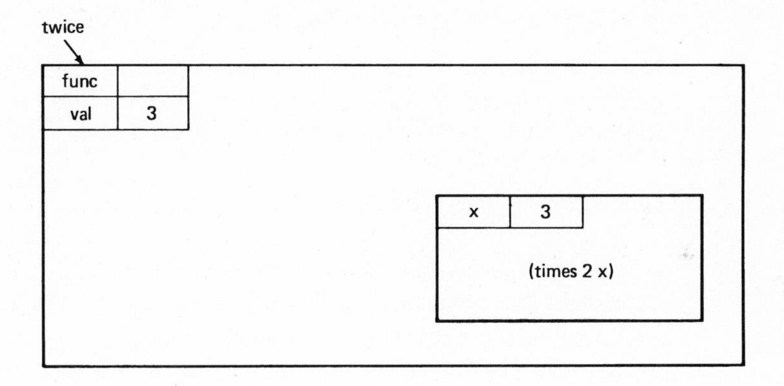

Notice that the lambda expression to which 'func' is bound has been *called in the environment of the caller,* in this case 'twice'. This doesn't cause any problem, however.

Now consider a slightly different example. Instead of multiplying by 2 twice, we want to multiply by some predefined value named 'val'. We have chosen 'val' as the name of this value because it will *collide* with the formal of 'twice'. Here is the example:

```
(set 'val 2)
  2
(twice '(lambda (x) (times val x)) 3)
  27
```

Since 'val' is bound to 2, we should get the same answer as before, 12; but instead we get 27! To see why, we need to look at the following contour diagram:

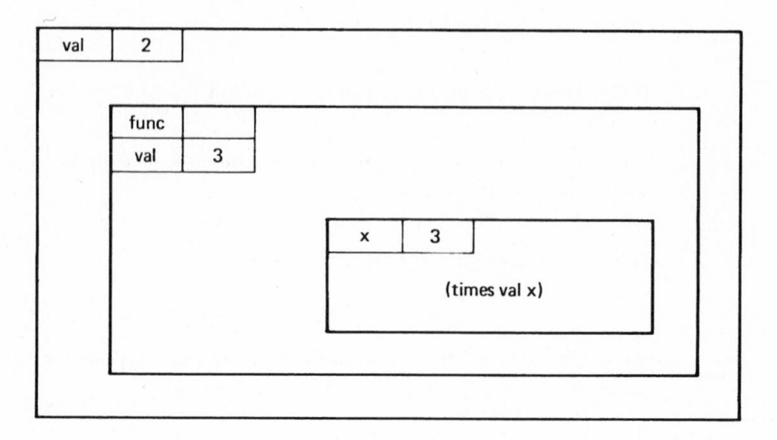

Notice that the use of 'val' in '(times val x)' has been intercepted by the dynamically inner binding of 'val' as a parameter in 'twice'. This is called a *collision of variables.* More specifically, we can see that the lambda expression

```
(lambda (x) (times val x))
```

is *vulnerable* to being called from an environment in which 'val' is bound to something other than what was expected when we wrote it. We might object that we were foolish to use the name 'val' for two different purposes, but in a large program it would be impractical to ensure that all of the names are distinct. Furthermore, we shouldn't have to worry about the names of variables internal to the 'twice' function; knowing these names violates *information hiding.*

This problem was discovered very early in the development of LISP and is known as the "funarg," or "functional argument" problem. It's really just an issue of dynamic versus static scoping. Rather than just using static scoping, however, a more expedient and ad hoc solution was adopted. A special form called 'function' was defined that binds a lambda expression to its *environment of definition.* Therefore, if we typed

```
(twice (function (lambda (x) (times val x)) ) 3)
  12
```

we would get the answer we expect. This is because 'function' has bound the lambda expression to its environment of definition (in which 'val' is bound to 2), so that when it's applied, it's *called in its environment of definition.* We can illustrate this in the following contour diagram:

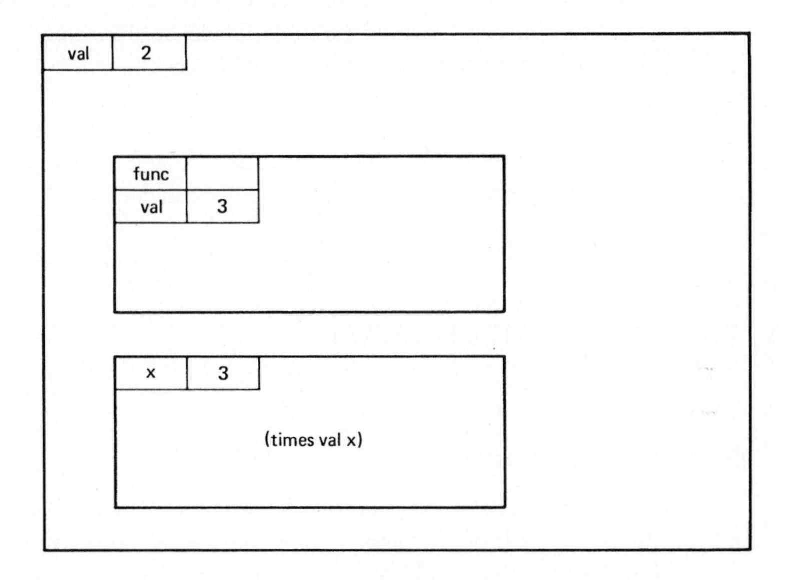

It is for this same reason that we also used 'function' in the definition of all of our functionals. Consider the definition of 'bu':

```
(defun bu (f x) (function (lambda (y) (f x y)) ))
```

The application of 'function' binds the lambda expression to its environment of definition, which in this case includes the bindings of 'f' and 'x'. Without 'function' the definition would be completely wrong since 'bu' would return the lambda expression to the caller's environment, where 'f' and 'x' are either unbound or bound to the wrong values.

The effect of all of this is that LISP has *two* sets of scope rules: (1) it is dynamically scoped by default, and (2) it has static scoping accessible through the 'function' construct. This certainly does not make for a simple, easy-to-understand language. Based on our previous discussions of scope rules, we might wonder why LISP wasn't simply made statically scoped. This probably would have been the simplest solution, but as often happened in LISP (and many other languages), people came to depend on the quirks of this "quick fix" so that it became part of the language. In recent years several statically scoped dialects of LISP have been designed (e.g., Scheme). In addition to solving the problems we have described, they are much easier to compile than the traditional LISP dialects.

*EXERCISE 10-39**: Defend one of the following three positions: (1) LISP should be statically scoped. (2) LISP should be dynamically scoped. (3) LISP should have both static and dynamic scoping.

*EXERCISE 10-40**: One of the goals of Backus's functional programming is to decrease the use of variables, particularly in lambda expressions. Discuss the impact of functionals on the LISP scoping problem.

10.3 DESIGN: SYNTACTIC STRUCTURES

Much of LISP's Syntax Has Evolved

Recall that it was not the original intention of the *S*-expression notation that it be convenient for programming. Rather, this was assumed to be a temporary way of programming that would be replaced by the more conventional LISP 2 language. We discussed in Section 10.1 the unfortunate effect this had on the syntax of 'cond', which is designed more for the convenience of interpreters than of programmers.

Over the years there have been several improvements in LISP's syntax. For example, in the original LISP system the 'define' function was used for establishing global bindings. The application

(define ((n_1 e_1) ... (n_k e_k)))

would define each of the n_i to be e_i. In the case of a function definition, the e_i was a lambda expression. The result is that our definition of 'getprop' from Chapter 9, Section 9.3, would look like this:

```
(define ((getprop
        (lambda (p x)
                (cond ((eq (car x) p) (cadr x))
                      (t (getprop p (cddr x)) )) )) ))
```

In common cases like this, there are many redundant parentheses. It is notation such as this that has led some people to claim that "LISP" stands for "Lots of Idiotic Single Parentheses"! The 'defun' function is clearly an improvement on 'define', although it would be even better if it presented a *template* for application of the function. For example,

```
(defun (getprop p x)
  (cond .... ))
```

Another example of the evolution of LISP (and typical of all programming languages) is the 'set' function. The original LISP system did not have the quote notation; for example,

```
'val
```

had to be written like an application:

```
(quote val)
```

This meant that a binding like '(set 'val 2)' had to be written:

```
(set (quote val) 2)
```

Again, this was convenient for the interpreter but not for the programmer; look back through our examples to see how often quotes appear. Since the first argument to 'set' is almost always quoted, a special form of set was defined, called 'setq', that did this implicitly. This permitted

```
(setq val 2)
```

Later, most LISP systems adopted the abbreviated form of quotation, which makes 'setq' superfluous. Since most LISP programmers still use 'setq', however, most LISP systems still provide it.

*EXERCISE 10-41**: Suggest other improvements to LISP's syntax that are still within the framework of the list notation.

List Representation Facilitates Program Manipulation

The fact that LISP programs are represented as LISP data structures has some important advantages. In particular, it makes it relatively simple to write LISP programs that read, preprocess, transform, and generate other LISP programs.

For example, if A is a list representing an application, then '(car A)' is the function being applied and '(cdr A)' is its actual parameter list:

```
(set 'A '(and (atom x) (atom y) (eq x y)) )
  (and (atom x) (atom y) (eq x y))
(car A)
  and
(cdr A)
  ((atom x) (atom y) (eq x y))
```

To write a Pascal program to separate the parts of a string representing a Pascal function call would be very complicated. The list representation makes it easier to get the important parts of LISP programs. For example, if L is a lambda expression, then '(cadr L)' is its list of bound variables and '(caddr L)' is its body:

```
(set 'L (lambda (x y) (f y x)) )
  (lambda (x y) (f y x))
(cadr L)
  (x y)
(caddr L)
  (f y x)
```

We will see in Chapter 11 that the list representation greatly simplifies writing a LISP interpreter in LISP, which was the original motivation for the list representation. More important, it has allowed LISP programmers to write high-level LISP programming aids and transformation tools easily and conveniently. One result of this is that some of the most advanced programming environments are provided by LISP systems.

EXERCISE 10-42:* Evaluate the representation of LISP programs as lists. Find a way to eliminate its annoying or poorly human-engineered aspects, while retaining its advantages for program manipulation.

EXERCISES

1. Write a LISP function '(bvs f)' that returns the bound variables of a function f. The bound variables are part of the lambda expression that is the value of the 'expr' property of the atom f.

2*. Write the 'mapcar', 'reduce', and 'filter' functionals in a conventional programming language such as Pascal. (You won't be able to write them in Ada because Ada does not permit functional parameters.)

3*. Read about the APL programming language; compare it with the functional programming style discussed in this chapter.

4*. Ken Iverson is the inventor of APL. Read and critique Iverson's Turing Award Paper, "Notation as a Tool of Thought" (*Comm. ACM 23*, 8, August 1980).

5*. One solution to the problem of returning functions from functions (the "upward funarg problem") is described in Bobrow and Wegbreit's "A Model and Stack Implementation of Multiple Environments" (*Comm. ACM 16*, 10, October 1973). Evaluate the implementation described in this paper.

6*. Design a more readable syntax for LISP that still represents LISP programs as LISP lists.

7*. Program in LISP the 'infix' function described in Chapter 9 (Section 9.3).

8**. The "prog feature" in LISP provides an imperative programming facility for LISP (complete with assignment statements and **goto**s). Should this feature be included in LISP? Write a report either attacking or defending the 'prog' feature.

11

IMPLEMENTATION OF RECURSIVE LIST-PROCESSORS: LISP

11.1 RECURSIVE INTERPRETERS

A LISP Interpreter Can Be Written in LISP

In Chapter 9, Section 9.1, we said that the first LISP interpreter resulted from writing a *universal function* for LISP. A universal function is a function that can interpret any other function. In Section 11.1 we develop a universal function for LISP because it is an example of a *recursive interpreter*, one of two major classes of interpreters. In Chapter 1 we saw an example of the other major class, *iterative interpreters*.

The recursive interpreter is written in LISP, although it could be written in any language with recursive procedures and the ability to implement linked lists. Since it is written in LISP, it makes use of the facilities of LISP, such as the list-processing operations 'car', 'cdr', and 'cons'. In particular, these operations are used to interpret 'car', 'cdr', and 'cons' operations in the program that we are interpreting. This might seem circular and pointless. In fact it is exactly analogous to the way floating-point operations were implemented in the pseudo-code interpreter in Chapter 1. There, floating-point operations in the implementation language (say, Pascal) were used to implement floating-point operations in the pseudo-code. Of course, if our implementation language hadn't had a floating-point capability, then these operations would have had to be implemented in terms of more basic operations. Similarly, if the implementation language for a LISP interpreter doesn't have list manipulation operations, it is necessary to implement these in terms of more basic operations. However, since we are using LISP as the implementation language, we can use list manipulation operations directly.

The LISP universal function is conventionally called 'eval' since it evaluates a LISP expression. In addition to the expression to be evaluated, 'eval' must have a second parameter, which is a data structure (a list of some sort) representing the context in which the evaluation is to be done. Recall that it is incomplete just to ask for the value of an expression; it is also necessary to specify the context of the evaluation (see Section 2.5, p. 78, and Section 6.1, p. 225). Hence, if *E* is any LISP expression (written in the *S*-expression notation) and *A* is a list representing a context, then

```
(eval 'E A) = V
```

where *V* is the value of *E* in that context. In other words, the result of evaluating '(eval '*E A*)' is the same as the result of evaluating *E* in the context represented by *A*. Consider the following application (where we have assumed 'nil' represents the empty context):

```
(eval '(cons (quote A) (quote (B C D) )) nil)
  (A B C D)
```

The result agrees with the result of evaluating '(cons 'A '(B C D))' in the empty (or any other) context, which is '(A B C D)'.

The Interpreter Is Arranged by Cases

If we were to evaluate a LISP expression by hand, our first step would be to classify it, that is, to decide the sort of LISP expression with which we are dealing. This is exactly what we will do in 'eval', and the first step is to classify LISP expressions.

First, we have atoms, such as '2' and 'val'. Numeric atoms, such as '2', represent themselves; nonnumeric atoms, such as 'val', represent the value to which they are bound.

All other LISP expressions are represented by nonatoms, that is, lists. These are all some form of *application*. We have *primitive* applications such as '(car x)' and '(cons x y)'. We also have applications of *user-defined* functions such as '(make-table text nil)'. Finally, we have *special* applications, such as '(quote x)' and '(cond (p e) ...)'.[1] The kinds of LISP expressions are summarized in Table 11.1.

The 'eval' function will break its input down into cases as shown in Table 11.1. The LISP mechanism for handling cases is 'cond', so 'eval' will take the form of a large 'cond':

```
(defun eval (e a)
  (cond
    ((atom e)       Handle atoms)
    (t              Handle lists)) )
```

There are two kinds of atoms—numeric and nonnumeric—so the "Handle atoms" procedure is:

```
(cond  ((numberp e)   Handle numeric atoms)
        (t            Handle nonnumeric atoms) )
```

('numberp' is a LISP predicate that returns 't' if its atomic argument is a number.)

Applications fall into two broad categories: (1) the special functions ('quote' and 'cond') that don't evaluate their arguments and (2) the normal applications

Table 11.1 Types of LISP Expressions

Type	Example
Numeric atom	2
Nonnumeric atom	val
Quotation	(quote (B C D))
Conditional	(cond ((null x) nil) (t 1))
Primitive	(cons x y)
User defined	(make-table text nil)

1 Recall that "X' is just an abbreviation for '(quote X)'.

(primitives and user defined) that do. We can distinguish these two cases by looking at the name of the function [given by '(car e)'] to see if it's special:

```
(cond
  ((eq (car e) 'quote)        Handle quotations)
  ((eq (car e) 'cond)         Handle conditionals)
  (t                          Handle normal applications) )
```

By combining all of the above cases, we get the following structure for the 'eval' function:

```
(defun eval (e a)
 (cond
  ((atom e) (cond
             ((numberp e)  Handle numeric atoms)
             (t            Handle nonnumeric atoms)) )
  (t        (cond
             ((eq (car e) 'quote)  Handle quotations)
             ((eq (car e) 'cond)   Handle conditionals)
             (t                    Handle normal applications)) ))
```

With only five distinct cases, it's really unnecessary to have three nested 'cond's; the cases are more obvious if we "flatten" the structure:

```
(defun eval (e a)
  (cond
   ((and (atom e) (numberp e))  Handle numeric atoms)
   ((atom e)                    Handle nonnumeric atoms)
   ((eq (car e) 'quote)         Handle quotations)
   ((eq (car e) 'cond)          Handle conditionals)
   (t                           Handle normal applications)) )
```

We will address each of these cases in the following sections.

The Value of a Numeric Atom Is That Atom

First we will consider the evaluation of numeric atoms. The value of '2' is the atom '2'; therefore,

(eval 2 *a*) = 2

and the case for handling numeric atoms is

```
((and (atom e) (numberp e)) e)
```

Nonnumeric Atoms Must Be Looked Up in the Environment

Next we will consider nonnumeric atoms, such as 'val' or 'text'. These are assumed to be bound to values, and the result of evaluating them is the value to which they are bound. The value to which an atom is bound is determined by the *environment* in which the atom is evaluated. This is the purpose of the second parameter to 'eval'; '(eval *E A*)' calls for the evaluation of expression *E* in environment represented by the list *A*. For example, if the environment *A* binds 'val' to 2 and 'text' to '(to be or not to be)', then

```
(eval 'val A)
  2
(eval 'text A)
  (to be or not to be)
```

There are many ways in which environments can be represented in LISP; one of the simplest is an *association list* (Chapter 9, Section 9.3). An environment that binds 'val' and 'text' as specified above could be represented by this association list:

```
( (val 2) (text (to be or not to be)) )
```

The evaluation of 'val' in this environment is:

```
(eval 'val '((val 2) (text (to be or not to be)) ))
  2
```

We can see now how a nonnumeric atom must be evaluated: We have to look up its value in the association list representing the current environment. Looking something up in an association list is accomplished with the 'assoc' function that we described earlier (Chapter 9, Section 9.3). Thus, if *e* is a nonnumeric atom:

(eval *e a*) = (assoc *e a*)

The first two cases of the 'eval' function are now defined as follows:

```
(defun eval (e a)
  (cond
```

```
((and (atom e) (numberp e)) e)
((atom e) (assoc e a))
... ))
```

A common programming error is to attempt to use an undefined variable. The code above does not check for this error condition; it assumes that the name *e* is bound in the environment *a*. Of course, a good interpreter would check for this error condition; we will omit this and most other checking to keep the presentation simple. Try to identify all the places in the interpreter where error checking should be done.

EXERCISE 11-1: Revise the handling of nonnumeric atoms to issue a diagnostic on an attempt to evaluate an unbound name. Assume a function '(error *m*)' is available that prints the value of *m* and terminates evaluation.

'Quote' Suppresses Evaluation

Next we will consider the evaluation of the various applications, beginning with the special applications 'quote' and 'cond'. The whole purpose of 'quote' is to *suppress* or *prevent* the evaluation of its argument. In other words,

(eval '(quote X) A) = X

no matter what X might be. Therefore, the case for handling 'quote' is trivial:

```
((eq (car e) 'quote) (cadr e))
```

Note that '(cadr e)' is the first (in this case, only) argument of the application 'e'.

The Conditional Delays Evaluation of Its Arguments

The conditional expression is different from other built-in functions in that it delays evaluation of its arguments. That is, an argument (condition or consequent) is not evaluated until its value is needed—in effect it is passed by name. This *lenient* evaluation strategy is necessary, since the conditional may return a value even though some of its arguments are undefined (recall our discussion in Section 10.1 of the conditional interpretation of the logical connectives). Now consider a conditional:

(cond (p_1 e_1) ... (p_n e_n))

Its evaluation proceeds as follows: First evaluate p_1. If it's 't', then evaluate e_1; if it's 'nil', then evaluate p_2. This process continues until one of the p_i is 't'. In that case, the corresponding e_i is evaluated and its value is returned as the value of the 'cond'. (If none of the p_i is true, then we have an error condition for which we won't check.) How can this process be programmed in LISP?

Like most iterative processes, this process is programmed recursively in LISP. Hence, we will develop a function 'evcon' that evaluates the body of a conditional. Since the atom 'cond' has served its function (identifying this expression as a conditional), it can be stripped off before the rest of the conditional is passed to 'evcon':

```
((eq (car e) 'cond) (evcon (cdr e) a))
```

Therefore, the first argument to 'evcon' has the form:

$((p_1\ e_1) \ldots (p_n\ e_n))$

The 'evcon' function must consider each pair in turn until it finds one that evaluates to 't'. If *L* is the list of pairs shown above, then note that '(car *L*)' is the first pair:

(car *L*) = $(p_1\ e_1)$

Therefore, '(caar *L*)' is p_1, the *condition* of the first pair, and '(cadar *L*)' is e_1, the *consequent* of the first pair. Thus, to check the first pair we must evaluate '(caar *L*)' (in the context of the 'cond'); if the result is 't', we evaluate '(cadar *L*)' (in this same context), otherwise we continue checking the rest of *L*. We evaluate '(caar *L*)' by a recursive call to 'eval'. This ensures that any legal LISP expression can be used as either the condition or the consequent of a 'cond', which is one of the sources of LISP's generality.

It is now easy to write the first step of the checking process in LISP:

```
(cond
  ((eval (caar L) a) (eval (cadar L) a))
  (t  Continue checking the rest of L))
```

Note that, as promised at the beginning of Section 11.1, we are using 'cond' to interpret 'cond'.

It remains to determine how to check the rest of the list of pairs *L*. Since we are finished with the first pair, it can be removed by '(cdr *L*)', which yields

$((p_2\ e_2) \ldots (p_n\ e_n))$

Notice that we now have a list of exactly the same form as *L*. Therefore, the rest of the checking process can be accomplished by the recursive application '(evcon (cdr *L*) *a*)'. When we put this all together, we get the following definition of 'evcon':

```
(defun evcon (L a)
  (cond
   ((eval (caar L) a) (eval (cadar L) a))
   (t  (evcon (cdr L) a)) ))
```

This completes the handling of conditionals.

EXERCISE 11-2: How should the situation of a conditional none of whose conditions is true be handled? Justify your answer and make appropriate modifications to 'evcon'.

EXERCISE 11-3: Use pass by name parameters in Algol-60 to program a function 'if' defined so the 'if (*B*, *T*, *F*)' returns the value of *T* if *B* is **true** and the value of *F* if it's **false**. The 'if' function should evaluate a parameter only if it's necessary to do so. Thus, the following invocation is legal:

```
x := if (y = 0, 1, x/y)
```

Arguments Are Recursively Evaluated

The only cases remaining are the applications of primitive and user-defined functions. In both of these cases, the arguments of the application must be evaluated. This will be accomplished by a function called 'evargs', which we must define. Notice that if *e* is the application

$(f\, x_1\, x_2\, \dots\, x_n)$

then '(car *e*)' is *f*, the function to be applied, and '(cdr *e*)' is the list of arguments. Therefore,

(evargs (cdr *e*) *a*)

will be the list of argument values.

How is 'evargs' to be defined? We need to construct a list, the *i*th element of which is the result of evaluating '(eval x_i *a*)'. This is clearly an application for 'mapcar' since we want to perform an operation—evaluation in the environment *a*—on each element of the list. That is, we want to apply to each element of the list the function

```
(bu (rev 'eval) a)
```

since

```
((bu (rev 'eval) a) x_i)
   = ((rev 'eval) a x_i)
   = (eval x_i a)
```

The definition of 'evargs' follows immediately:

```
(defun evargs (x a) (mapcar (bu (rev 'eval) a) x))
```

The function to be applied and the evaluated list of arguments can then be passed to a function 'apply' that performs the application. The 'apply' function has three arguments:

```
(apply f x a)
```

The first, *f*, is the function to be applied, which is computed by '(car *e*)' in this case; the second, *x*, is the list of evaluated actual parameters, which is computed by '(evargs (cdr e) a)' in this case; the third, *a*, is the environment of the caller, which is *a* in this case. Therefore, the case in 'eval' to handle all normal applications is:

```
(t (apply (car e) (evargs (cdr e) a) a) )
```

Primitive Operations Are Performed Directly

There are two types of normal applications: primitive functions and user-defined functions. We will now consider the primitive functions.

Since there are a number of primitive operations, the natural structure for the 'apply' function is a 'cond' that handles the different primitive operations. That is,

```
(defun apply (f x a)
  (cond
   ((eq f 'plus)  Handle a plus)
   ((eq f 'car)   Handle a car)
   ((eq f 'cdr)   Handle a cdr)
   ((eq f 'cons)  Handle a cons)
   and so forth ))
```

We will consider a typical function, 'plus'. Suppose we are evaluating the application

```
(plus 1 (times 2 3))
```

the arguments passed to 'apply' will be

f = plus
x = (1 6)
a = the environment of the caller

Notice that x is a *list* containing the *values* of the actual parameters. What should the result of 'apply' be? In this case, we must add the first argument to the second argument. The first argument is '(car x)' and the second argument is '(cadr x)', so, if f is 'plus', we should return

```
(plus (car x) (cadr x ))
```

In summary, the case for handling 'plus' is:

```
((eq f 'plus) (plus (car x) (cadr x)) )
```

Notice that, as promised at the beginning of this section (p. 412), we are using 'plus' to implement 'plus'. This is correct since we are using LISP as both the implementation language and the interpreted language. Similarly, the list-processing operations ('car', 'cdr', etc.) will be implemented in terms of themselves. If we were using a language such as Pascal as an implementation language, it would be necessary to define these operations in terms of more basic pointer manipulation operations, such as those described in Chapter 9, Section 9.3.

The other primitive functions are similar; we show here an 'apply' function that handles the primitive list manipulation functions. Other primitive operations (arithmetic, predicates, etc.) are implemented in the same way.

```
(defun apply (f x a)
  (cond
   ((eq f 'plus)   (plus (car x) (cadr x)) )
   ((eq f 'car)    (car (car x)) )
   ((eq f 'cdr)    (cdr (car x)) )
   ((eq f 'atom)   (atom (car x)) )
   ((eq f 'null)   (null (car x)) )
   ((eq f 'cons)   (cons (car x) (cadr x)) )
   ((eq f 'eq)     (eq (car x) (cadr x)) )
                      ⋮
              other primitives
                      ⋮
   (t  Handle user-defined functions )) )
```

EXERCISE 11-4: Add the other arithmetic functions ('difference', 'times', 'quotient') and the predicates ('minusp', 'lessp') to the definition of 'apply'.

EXERCISE 11-5:* Add error checking to 'apply'. For example, the arithmetic operations should be applicable only to numbers and the list operators only to lists of the appropriate type (e.g., 'car' only applies to nonnull lists).

Applications Require Four Steps

All that's required to complete our LISP interpreter is to handle the application of user-defined functions. The steps required to do this are very similar to the steps required to invoke a procedure in other languages.

It's easy to see the necessity for these steps. The goal of a function application is the evaluation of the body of the function. However, as we've seen before, an expression only has meaning in some *context* or *environment.* This environment must bind all of the names used in the expression.

Where does this environment come from? It is composed of *locals* and *nonlocals,* the locals being the formal parameters of the function. Since LISP uses dynamic scoping, the nonlocals come from the environment of the caller. Therefore, to construct the environment of evaluation for the function's body, it is necessary to add the formal-actual bindings to the environment of the caller.

We get the formal-actual bindings by binding each formal to the *value* of the corresponding actual. In summary, the four steps required to apply a user-defined function are:

1. Evaluate the actual parameters.
2. Bind the formal parameters to the actual parameters.
3. Add these new bindings to the environment of evaluation.
4. Evaluate the body of the function in this environment.

We have already accomplished the first step; 'evargs' is used to evaluate the actuals before they are passed to 'apply'. Therefore, we will address the remaining three steps.

Constructing the Environment of Evaluation

Suppose that we are evaluating the application

```
(consval text)
```

in an environment that binds 'text' to '(to be or not to be)', binds 'val' to 'whether', and binds the function name 'consval' to

```
(lambda (x) (cons val x))
```

Notice that 'consval' is bound to a lambda expression since this is how a function value is represented.

Since the actual parameters have been evaluated, the arguments to 'apply' are

f = consval
x = ((to be or not to be))
a = (... (val whether) ... (consval (lambda (x) ...)) ...)

Notice that the actual parameter list x is a one-element list containing '(to be or not to be)', the value of the only actual parameter. Before we can do any of the remaining three steps, it is necessary to determine to which function 'consval' is bound. In other words, it is necessary to interpret 'consval' *in context*. This is accomplished by evaluating the function's name since this will cause it to be looked up in the current environment. In this case, '(eval f a)' returns

(lambda (x) (cons val x))

which is the value of 'consval'. Let's call this L, which stands for "lambda expression."

We can now proceed with constructing the environment of evaluation. The first step is to bind the formals to the actuals. In general, L will be a lambda expression:

L = (lambda (v_1 v_2 ... v_n) B)

where the v_i are the formal parameters and B is the body. The actual parameters, x_i, are a corresponding list:

x = (x_1 x_2 ... x_n)

Since environments are represented by association lists, binding the formals to the actuals is accomplished by pairing up the formals and actuals in an association list:

LE = ((v_1 x_1) (v_2 x_2) ... (v_n x_n))

(LE stands for "local environment.") It should now be clear that LE can be constructed by mapping the 'list' function across the list of formals and x. Since the list of formals is just '(cadr L)', we have

LE = (mapcar 'list (cadr L) x)

The next step is to add these new bindings to the environment of the caller, thereby forming the environment of evaluation. Since the 'assoc' function, which is used for variable accessing, searches from the beginning of the association list, if the local environment is appended to the beginning of the nonlocal, the new bindings will supersede any previous bindings of the same names. The environment of evaluation, *EE*, is constructed by:

EE = (append *LE* *a*)

since *a* is the current environment, that is, the environment of the caller.

The last step is to evaluate the body of the lambda expression in *EE*. Since '(caddr *L*)' is the body of the lambda expression, this is accomplished by:

(eval (caddr *L*) *EE*)

These pieces can all be assembled into the following LISP code for applying a user-defined function:

```
(let ((L (eval f a) ))
  (let ((LE (mapcar 'list (cadr L) x) ))
      (eval (caddr L) (append LE a)) ))
```

The complete LISP universal function, or interpreter, is shown in Figure 11.1; it is about 25 lines long.[2] The fact that a LISP interpreter can be written in LISP in so few lines is a testament to LISP's simplicity and power.

EXERCISE 11-6: The LISP universal function is inefficient in one place: The 'append' function copies the entire list *LE*, even though it has just been created by '(mapcar 'list ...)'. Show that this can be avoided by writing a new function 'pairlis' that performs the pairing and appending operations at the same time. That is,

EE = (pairlis (cadr *L*) *x* *a*)

Modify 'eval' to use this new function.

2 We have omitted most of the primitive operations, since they are a routine addition to 'apply'.

```
(defun eval (e a)
  (cond
   ((and (atom e) (numberp e)) e)
   ((atom e) (assoc e a))
   ((eq (car e) 'quote) (cadr e))
   ((eq (car e) 'cond) (evcon (cdr e) a))
   (t  (apply (car e) (evargs (cdr e) a) a) )) )

(defun evcon (L a)
  (cond
   ((eval (caar L) a) (eval (cadar L) a))
   (t  (evcon (cdr L) a)) ))

(defun evargs (x a) (mapcar (bu (rev 'eval) a) x))

(defun apply (f x a)
  (cond
   ((eq f 'car)   (car (car x)) )
   ((eq f 'cdr)   (cdr (car x)) )
   ((eq f 'atom) (atom (car x)) )
   ((eq f 'null)  (null (car x)) )
   ((eq f 'cons) (cons (car x) (cadr x)) )
   ((eq f 'eq)    (eq (car x) (cadr x)) )
   (t (let  (( L  (eval f a) ))
            (let (( LE (mapcar 'list (cadr L) x) ))
                 (eval (caddr L) (append LE a)) )) )) )
```

Figure 11.1 LISP Universal Function in LISP

*EXERCISE 11-7**:* The LISP universal function we have described is not a complete LISP interpreter. In particular, it does not look at the property lists of atoms when evaluating them (i.e., it assumes atoms are bound to values only via association lists). As a consequence, it does not implement property-modifying pseudo-functions such as 'define' and 'set'. Add these facilities to 'eval'.

Closures Implement Static Scoping

In Chapter 10, Section 10.2, we discussed the 'function' construct, which is used to bind a lambda expression to its environment of definition. That is, when we write

```
(function (lambda (x) (times val x)) )
```

we mean that the lambda expression should always be called in the environment in which 'function' is applied. This preserves the context of the lambda expression's body by simulating static scoping.

How is the 'function' construct implemented? Its purpose is to inform the interpreter that the environment of definition of the lambda expression must be remembered so that it can be used when the lambda expression is applied. This is exactly the purpose of a *closure*, which we have discussed many times in the past. A closure has two parts:

1. An *ip*, or *instruction part*, that points to a piece of program
2. An *ep*, or *environment part*, that points to the environment in which that piece of program must be evaluated

In this case, the instruction part is the lambda expression and the environment part is the environment of definition.

Thus, the result of 'function' is a closure containing the lambda expression and its environment. How should a closure be represented? The simplest approach is to use a list, the first element of which is the atom 'closure',[3] to identify the list as a closure. For example,

```
(closure ip ep)
```

This is the data structure that must be constructed by 'function'.

The actual implementation of 'function' is quite simple. Since it is a special function (because it doesn't evaluate its argument), it is handled in the main body of 'eval' in the same way as 'quote' and 'cond'. The modified 'eval' is

```
(defun eval (e a)
  (cond
   ((and (atom e) (numberp e)) e)
   ((atom e) (assoc e a))
   ((eq (car e) 'quote) (cadr e))
   ((eq (car e) 'cond) (evcon (cdr e) a))
   ((eq (car e) 'function) (list 'closure (cadr e) a))
   (t  (apply (car e) (evargs (cdr e) a) a) )) )
```

since '(cadr e)' is the argument of 'e' (i.e., the lambda expression).

The above modification handles just the *construction* of a closure; it does not *use* the closure. The other place where we must deal with closures is 'apply' since

3 In most LISP systems the atom 'funarg', meaning "functional argument," is used instead of 'closure'.

it handles function calls and, hence, must know whether to call in the environment of definition or in the environment of the caller. The result of evaluating the function '(eval *f a*)' may be either a lambda expression or a closure. The case of a lambda expression is the same as in Figure 11.2. Let's consider what must be done if it's a closure:

L = (closure (lambda (x_1 ... x_n) B) ED)

The local environment is constructed just as before, except now it must be appended to the environment of definition, *ED*, rather than the caller's environment, *a*. Hence,

LE = (mapcar 'list (cadadr L) x)
EE = (append LE (caddr L))

since '(caddr *L*)' is *ED*—the environment of definition—and '(cadadr *L*)' is the list of formal parameters.

Since both dynamically scoped lambda expressions and statically scoped closures must be accommodated, the handling of user-defined functions is a little more complicated:

```
(defun apply (f x a)
  (cond
   ((eq f 'car) (car (car x)) )
   ... etc. ...
   (t (let ((L (eval f a) ))
           (cond
            ((eq (car f) 'closure)
             (let (( LE (mapcar 'list (cadadr L) x) ))
                 (eval (caddadr L) (append LE (caddr L)) )) )
            (t
             (let (( LE (mapcar 'list (cadr L) x) ))
                 (eval (caddr L) (append LE a)) )) )) )) )
```

[Note that (caddadr *L*) = (caddr (cadr *L*)) = the body of the lambda expression, which is the *ip* of the closure *L*.]

EXERCISE 11-8: Show that 'caddr' accesses the environment of definition from a closure.

EXERCISE 11-9: Show that 'cadadr' accesses the formal parameter list from a closure.

EXERCISE 11-10: Show that 'caddadr' accesses the function body from a closure.

Lexical Scoping Uses Closures Uniformly

We are now trying to make our interpreter accommodate two incompatible scope rules. As we discussed in Chapter 10, Section 10.2, recent LISP dialects (such as Scheme) have adopted a uniform static scope rule. This simplifies the interpreter. The most obvious simplification is that the 'apply' function only has to handle one kind of function, that represented by closures. Furthermore, since *all* lambda expressions are bound to their environments of definition, there is no longer any point to 'function'. That is,

```
(lambda (x) (cons val x))
```

is considered equivalent to

```
(function (lambda (x) (cons val x)) )
```

A closure is constructed for all lambda expressions. The interpreter that results from these alterations is shown in Figure 11.2; it is as simple as the dynamic scoping interpreter.

Common LISP, in an attempt to gain the advantages of static scoping while remaining reasonably compatible with older LISP dialects, has adopted a combination of static and dynamic scoping. For example, formal parameters and variables (established by 'set's, 'let's, and the like) are normally statically scoped. On the other hand, variables can be given dynamic scope by declaring them "special."[4] Function definitions established by 'defun' are global; therefore, static and dynamic scoping amount to the same thing for them.

11.2 STORAGE RECLAMATION

Explicit Erasure Complicates Programming

In our discussion of the representation of lists (Chapter 9, Section 9.3), we saw that the 'cons' operation calls for the allocation of a new cons-cell. These cons-cells are allocated from a free storage area similar to that used by the 'new' operation in Pascal. Since 'cons's are so frequent in LISP, it is clear that this free storage

4 Certain other constructs, such as "catchers" (analogous to Ada exception handlers) also have dynamic scope. The justification for dynamic scoping of exception handlers was discussed in Section 8.1.

```
(defun eval (e a)
  (cond
   ((and (atom e) (numberp e)) e)
   ((atom e) (assoc e a ))
   ((eq (car e) 'quote) (cadr e))
   ((eq (car e) 'cond) (evcon (cdr e) a))
   ((eq (car e) 'lambda) (list 'closure e a))
   (t  (apply (car e) (evargs (cdr e) a) a) )) )

(defun evcon (L a)
  (cond
   ((eval (caar L) a) (eval (cadar L) a))
   (t  (evcon (cdr L) a)) ))

(defun evargs (x a) (mapcar (bu (rev 'eval) a) x))

(defun apply (f x a)
  (cond
   ((eq f 'car)      (car (car x)) )
   ((eq f 'cdr)      (cdr (car x)) )
   ((eq f 'atom)     (atom (car x)) )
   ((eq f 'null)     (null (car x)) )
   ((eq f 'cons)     (cons (car x) (cadr x)) )
   ((eq f 'eq)       (eq (car x) (cadr x)) )
   (t   (let (( L  (eval f a) ))
             (let  (( LE (mapcar 'list (cadadr L) x) ))
                   (eval (caddadr L) (append LE (caddr L)) )) )) ))
```

Figure 11.2 Statically Scoped LISP Interpreter in LISP

area will be exhausted by most programs. Unless there is some way of returning cells to the free area, the program will have to be aborted.

One solution to this problem—the one adopted by Pascal and many other languages—is *explicit erasure.* This means that when the program no longer needs a certain cell, the programmer must explicitly return it to the free storage area. In Pascal this is accomplished by the 'dispose' procedure. The invocation 'dispose (*p*)' returns to free storage the cell pointed to by *p*. This is normally accomplished by linking the cell onto a *free-list,* where the storage allocator can find it to satisfy a later storage allocation ('new') request.

Explicit erasure has several problems. First, it requires programmers to work harder; they must keep careful track of each cell and of all of the lists in

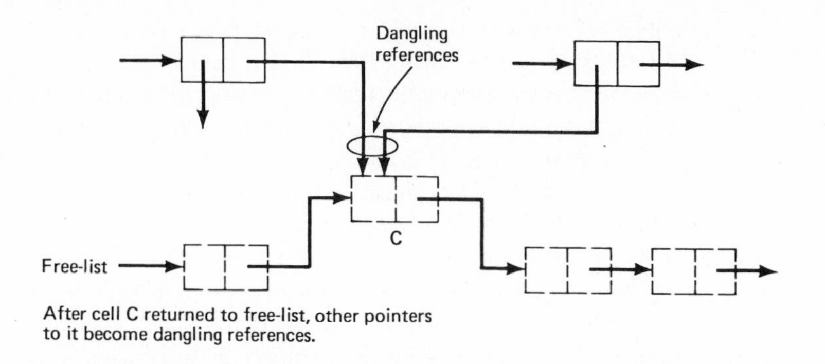

Figure 11.3 Example of Dangling References

which it participates (remember, sublists can be shared) and determine when the cell can be released. Some people have claimed that "good" programmers will understand their programs well enough to be able to do this. You may recognize this as the same argument that was used against early assemblers and compilers (such as FORTRAN): "Good" programmers don't need symbolic names since they know the absolute addresses of all the variables. Now we know that it is much better to have a computer take care of bookkeeping details such as these since it allows programmers to concentrate on more important issues of program structure and organization.

Another problem with explicit erasure is that it violates the *security* of the programming system. Suppose that a cell is returned to free storage but is still referenced by several other lists. These other lists will now have *dangling pointers,* that is, pointers that do not point to an allocated cell. This situation is illustrated in Figure 11.3. When the storage allocator reuses this cell, these dangling references will likely cause mysterious errors. In fact, since unallocated cells may still be accessible from the program (via dangling references), it's even possible to corrupt the storage allocator's data structures (e.g., the free-list).

Reference Counts Identify Inaccessible Lists

We have seen that explicit erasure is low level and error-prone. What is the alternative? The goal is to return a cell to free storage when it is no longer needed, that is, when it is no longer accessible from the program. Therefore, an automatic erasure system must somehow keep track of the accessibility of each cell. In LISP a cell is accessible only if it is *referenced* (i.e., pointed at) by some other accessible cell. The only cells that are *directly accessible* are those used by the interpreter, such as those containing the program being interpreted and the association lists representing environments still in use.

Note that when we are considering whether a cell can be reclaimed, it is not important *which* cells point to this particular cell; all that's relevant is the *number of accessible cells* referencing the cell of concern. This observation leads to a technique of storage reclamation called *reference counts* since it keeps track of the number of accessible references to each cell. One of many[5] ways to do this is to include a *reference count field* in each cell (see Figure 11.4).

Reference counts must be maintained correctly. Whenever an additional reference to a cell is made, that cell's reference count must be incremented. Similarly, whenever a reference to a cell is destroyed, that cell's reference count must be decremented. There are two ways a reference can be destroyed. A pointer can be overwritten (such as happens in a 'rplaca', 'rplacd', or assignment operation) or the cell containing the pointer can itself become inaccessible.

When a cell's reference count becomes zero, it means that the cell is inaccessible and can be returned to the free-list. Notice, however, that each cell contains pointers to two other cells, that is, the pointers in its 'left' and 'right' fields. Therefore, whenever a cell is released, the reference counts of the two cells to which it points must also be decremented since there is now one less *accessible* reference to each. This decrementing may cause the reference counts of either of these cells to go to zero, which means that they also must be freed. Hence, the process of decrementing a reference count may be recursive. Here is the procedure for decrementing the reference count of cell C:

```
decrement (C):
        reference count (C) := reference count (C) − 1;
        if reference count (C) = 0 then
           decrement (C↑.left);
           decrement (C↑.right);
           return C to free-list;
        end if.
```

Notice that this approach reclaims a cell *as soon as* it becomes available. Therefore, if the free-list is ever exhausted, it means that there is *no more* storage available, and the program must be aborted. Further, studies have shown that almost all (95%) reference counts are 1, so at least one cell is usually freed whenever a pointer is destroyed.

5 There are a great many techniques for automatic storage reclamation; in this section we can touch on only the simplest. The interested reader should consult the data structures literature for more information. See especially Cohen (1981).

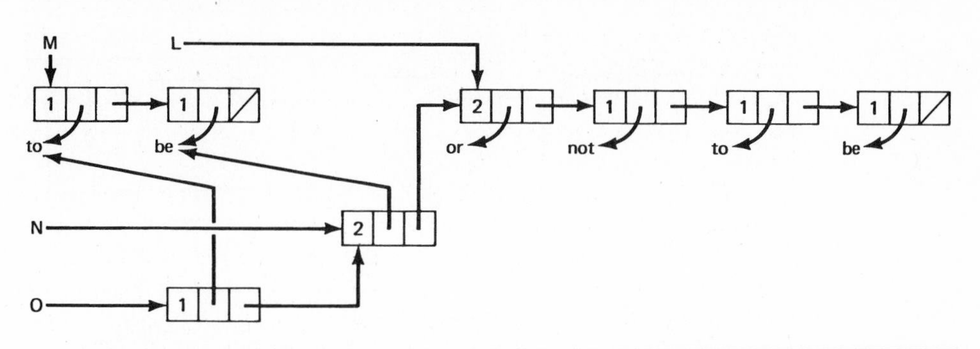

Figure 11.4 Example of Reference Counts

Cyclic Structures Are Not Reclaimed

Consider the list structure shown in Figure 11.5. It is a *cyclic structure* that could have been constructed by using 'rplacd' to make the right field of C point to A. Suppose that the only references to these fields are those shown in the figure; then the reference counts will be as shown. Notice that this structure is only accessible from one place—the pointer entering from the left. Now suppose that this pointer is destroyed, making the structure inaccessible; this will cause A's reference count to be decremented to 1. Since neither A, B, nor C has a zero reference count, no cells will be returned to free storage *even though none of these cells is accessible!* This situation will occur wherever there is a *cycle* in the list structure, that is, wherever there is a path from a cell back to itself. In a reference-counted system, these cells will be lost forever.

Several solutions to this problem have been proposed. One is to disallow cyclic structures altogether. Since they are produced only by using the 'rplaca' and 'rplacd' pseudo-functions, eliminating these will eliminate cycles.[6] Some computer scientists have argued for this solution on the basis that these pseudo-functions have side effects and don't belong in an applicative programming language. They claim that cycles are error-prone and difficult to understand. Other computer scientists have argued that cyclic structures are necessary for some problems. Whether cyclic structures should or should not be a part of LISP or whether they could be included in a tamed form is an open research problem.

EXERCISE 11-11:* Discuss the pros and cons of cyclic list structures. Give at

6 Under some circumstances 'putprop', 'set', 'defun', and similar pseudo-functions can produce cycles through property lists.

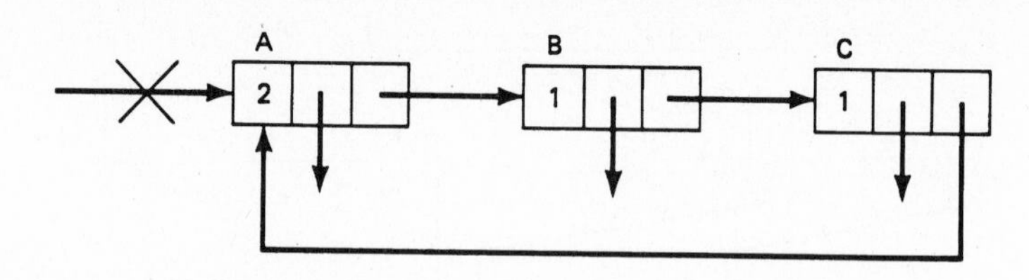

Figure 11.5 Cyclic List Structure

least one example of the usefulness of cyclic structures. Explain how you could do without them in that situation.

*EXERCISE 11-12**:* Develop a reference counting scheme that is not fooled by cycles.

Garbage Collection Reclaims Cyclic Structures

There is an alternative approach to automatic storage reclamation that can handle cyclic structures; it is called *garbage collection.* With reference counts, cells are released as soon as they become inaccessible. Thus, cells that are inaccessible but not available for reuse ("garbage") never accumulate. Garbage collection adopts a different philosophy. Inaccessible cells are simply abandoned; no attempt is made to return them to free storage. When the supply of free cells is exhausted, the system enters a *garbage collection phase* in which it identifies all of the unused cells and returns them to free storage. One way to view garbage collection is that it ignores the storage reclamation problem until a crisis develops, and then it deals with the crisis.

There are many techniques for garbage collection and many analyses of garbage collection under varying circumstances. In this section we will deal briefly with the simplest kind of *mark-sweep* garbage collector, which operates in two phases. In the *mark* phase, the garbage collector identifies all of those cells that are accessible, that is, that are not "garbage." In the *sweep* phase, the garbage collector places all of the inaccessible cells in the free storage area, often by placing them on the free-list.

First, we will investigate the mark phase. We noted earlier that all accessible cells must ultimately be reachable from some number of *roots* known to the interpreter, such as the program structure and the association lists representing the active environments. In the mark phase, the garbage collector starts at the roots and follows the pointers, marking each cell it reaches as accessible. For this purpose each cell requires an associated mark bit that indicates whether or not it is accessible. These mark bits may be part of the cell or may be stored in a separate area of memory; we will draw them as though they are part of the cells.

At the beginning of the garbage collection process, all cells are unmarked. Whenever the marking process encounters a cell that is already marked, it knows that it need not continue down that path (since it has already marked it). In particular, this guarantees that cycles in the lists will not put the garbage collector into an infinite loop. Marking is depicted in Figure 11.6; the dotted arrows indicate the path traced by the garbage collector.

The algorithm for the mark phase is thus

```
mark phase:
        for each root R, mark (R).

mark (R):
        if R is not marked then:
           set mark bit of R;
           mark (R↑.left);
           mark (R↑.right);
        endif.
```

Notice that this is a recursive algorithm, and, like all recursive algorithms, it will require space for the activation records of the recursive procedure. You might

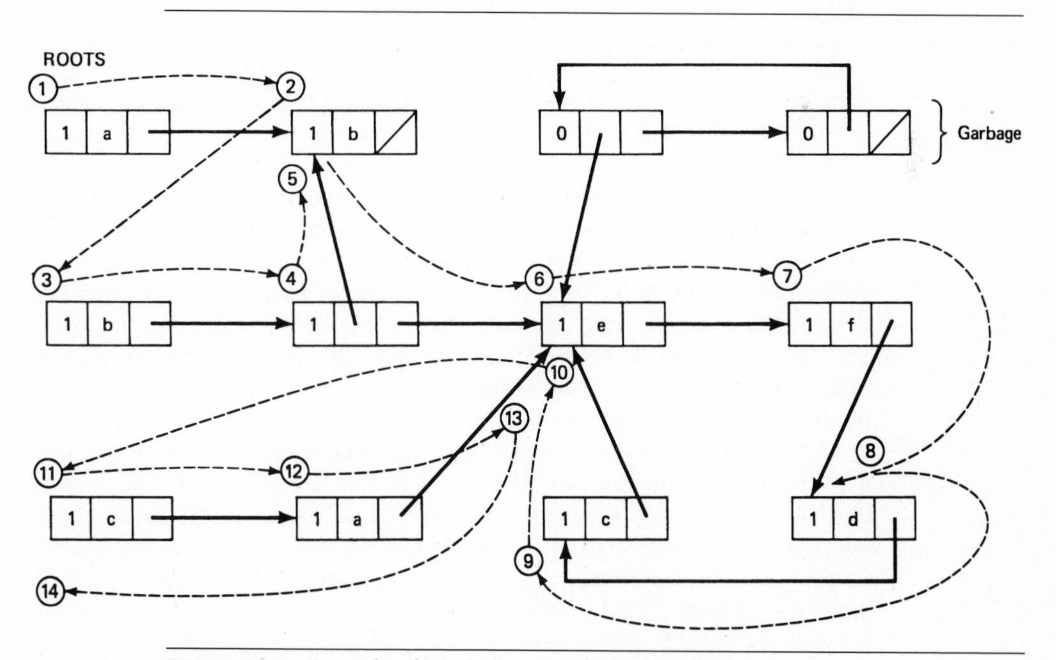

Figure 11.6 Example of Mark Phase of Garbage Collection

wonder how the garbage collector could ever run since it is only called in a storage allocation crisis when no free storage is available. There are many solutions to this problem. One is to invoke the garbage collector before the last cell is allocated and when there is still enough space for the garbage collector's stack. Another solution is to encode the stack in some clever way, such as by reversing the links in the marked nodes. (If you are interested in these issues, consult the literature about garbage collectors.)

The second phase of garbage collection is the sweep, when all of the inaccessible cells are returned to free storage. By the end of the mark phase, all accessible cells have been marked. Therefore, in the sweep phase we can visit each cell in order (that is, *sweeping* through memory). If a cell is unmarked, then it's inaccessible, and it can be linked onto the free-list. If it's marked, then it's accessible; we reset its mark bit (in preparation for the next garbage collection) and go on to the next cell. This procedure can be summarized:

```
sweep phase:
        for each cell C:
          if C is marked then reset C's mark bit,
          else link C onto the free-list.
```

EXERCISE 11-13:* Design a garbage collection algorithm that avoids the necessity for a stack by reversing the links in the list structures.

Garbage Collection Results in Nonuniform Response Time

A serious problem results from garbage collection's crisis approach to storage reclamation. In a large address space, a garbage collection can be quite expensive since it necessitates tracing down all of the lists and visiting every cell in memory. The result is that a program runs along quite nicely until it runs out of storage; then it grinds to a halt for a garbage collection. After the garbage collection (and assuming an adequate amount of storage was reclaimed), it resumes high-speed execution until the next garbage collection. This is quite apparent in an interactive system since, periodically, the system will stop (often for minutes) while a garbage collection is in progress. You can probably imagine how annoying this can be to the users. It is particularly serious in *real time* situations where the program must be guaranteed to respond in a certain amount of time. If a garbage collection happens at the wrong time, it can lead to disaster. (Consider a program responsible for the control surfaces of the Space Shuttle!) This is not as much of a problem with reference counts since the time required for storage reclamation is distributed across the execution of the program. There are also other solutions to this problem, such as parallel garbage collection. With this approach, garbage collection takes place continuously and in parallel with normal program execution. (Once again, see the garbage collection literature if you're interested in these problems.)

11.3 EVALUATION AND EPILOG

LISP Has Been Very Successful in Artificial Intelligence

LISP has become the most commonly used language for artificial intelligence applications. One of the reasons is the same one that motivated its original design: its ability to represent and manipulate complex interrelationships among symbolic data. There are several other reasons that have become apparent through the use of LISP.

LISP Is Suited to Ill-Specified Problems

It is a characteristic of artificial intelligence applications that the problem is not well understood. Indeed, often one goal of the research is to understand the problem better. This characteristic also applies to research and advanced development projects in areas other than artificial intelligence. LISP is very suited to this kind of problem.

One of the characteristics that suits LISP to ill-defined problems is its dynamic type system and flexible data structures. In previous chapters we have seen that one of the recent trends in programming methodology and programming languages has been the specification of *abstract data types.* That is, the programmer first decides what data structures and data types are required and then specifies the necessary operations in terms of their inputs and outputs. Finally, the representation of the data structures and operators is fixed (i.e., the abstract data type is implemented).

On ill-defined problems this methodology doesn't work so well. Often it is not known exactly what operations on a data type will be required. It is difficult to set down ironclad input-output specifications when the ultimate requirements that the data structure must satisfy are not clear. Rather, a more experimental approach is valuable. Just as in a laboratory, where it is necessary to be able to connect equipment together in a wide variety of ways, in an experimental software environment, flexibility of interconnection is also important. A language such as LISP, with few restrictions on invocation of procedures and passing of parameters, is well suited to experimentation.

LISP Is Easy to Extend, Preprocess, and Generate

The representation of LISP programs as LISP lists, although originally an accident, has turned out to be one of LISP's greatest assets. It has meant that it is very convenient to manipulate LISP programs using other LISP programs. We saw an example of this in the 'eval' interpreter. In practice it has meant that LISP programmers have been encouraged to write many programming tools in LISP.

These include programs to transform LISP programs into other LISP programs and to generate LISP programs from other notations. It has simplified writing programs that process LISP programs, such as compilers, cross referencers, and optimizers. It has encouraged special-purpose extensions to LISP for pattern matching, text processing, editing, type checking, and so on. Of course, all of these tools could be (and in some cases, have been) provided for conventional languages such as Pascal. However, they tend to be large and complicated because they must deal with a conventional language's complex, character-oriented syntax. Modifying a Pascal or Ada compiler can be a Herculean undertaking; as a result it is usually only done by systems programmers and only when absolutely necessary. In contrast, it is trivial for one LISP program to access the parts of another because LISP has a *simple, structured* syntax. As a result, programmers are encouraged to experiment with sophisticated programming tools.

LISP Programming Environments Developed

The ease with which LISP programs can manipulate other LISP programs has led to the development of a wide variety of LISP programming tools. From these libraries of tools there developed the idea of a *programming environment.* This is a system that supports all phases of programming, including design, program entry, debugging, documentation, and maintenance. It is significant that the first, and richest, programming environments developed around LISP systems.

LISP's Inefficiency Has Discouraged Its Use

With all that we have said, you might ask, "Why doesn't everyone use LISP?" One reason is that early LISP implementations were quite inefficient. There were several sources of this inefficiency.

First, most LISP systems are interpreted, and interpreters often run two orders of magnitude slower than the code produced by a compiler. This is one reason that many LISP systems now provide compilers and optimizers.

Another reason is that LISP depends heavily on the use of recursion, which (as we saw in Chapter 6) can be fairly complicated to implement. As a result, recursion was inefficient on most machines of the 1960s. More recent machines have included hardware to assist procedure invocation and activation record manipulation for block-structured languages. This improves the performance of implementations of LISP, particularly statically scoped dialects of LISP. In addition, techniques have been discovered that allow many LISP function applications to be replaced by machine branches. Therefore, a loop expressed recursively may be no less efficient than one written using a **goto**.

Certainly, dynamic storage allocation is one of the more expensive aspects of LISP, but it is also one of the most valuable. For this reason, there has been a great deal of work on methods of speeding up both storage allocation and reclamation. One way of doing this has been to include assistance for garbage collection in the hardware. More recently this has led to the development of "LISP machines," that is, computers specially designed for running LISP. Several of these are commercially available.

LISP Shows What Can Be Done with an Applicative Language

LISP is the closest thing to an applicative language in widespread use. Therefore, the experience gained with LISP has been very valuable in evaluating applicative programming languages and applicative programming styles. This experience finds direct application in the development of functional programming languages. We have seen how many ideas, including lists and functionals, have been taken from LISP by functional programming. Again, the LISP experience is evidence in favor of the practicality of functional programming languages. In the future, we can expect the development of new LISP dialects, new functional and applicative languages, and new LISP programming tools and environments.

Characteristics of Function-Oriented Programming Languages

Although LISP is not a purely applicative language, it illustrates many of the characteristics of applicative (function-oriented) programming. We have seen that there is an emphasis on the use of pure functions and minimal use of assignment operations (none in a *purely* applicative language). This leads to the use of recursion as a method of iteration, and Polish (prefix) notation as the basic *syntactic structure.* Applicative languages usually have the list as their principal *data structure.* Use of lists is supported by dynamic (but strong) typing and automatic storage management. The basic *control structures* of applicative programming are the conditional expression and recursion, although many of these languages (especially the specifically *functional* languages) provide higher-level control structures, such as mapping and reduction operators.

Function-oriented languages have many desirable properties. First, their high level of abstraction, especially when functionals are used, suppresses many of the details of programming (in conformance with the Abstraction Principle) and thus removes the possibility of committing many classes of errors. Second, their lack of dependence on assignment operations allows function-oriented programs to be evaluated in many different orders. This evaluation order independence makes function-oriented languages good candidates for programming massively parallel computers. Third, the absence of assignment operations makes function-oriented programs much more amenable to mathematical proof and analysis than are imperative programs. It is difficult to reason about things that change in time. Since function-oriented programming takes place in the timeless realm of mathematics, it avoids the difficulties of temporal reasoning. On the other hand, some applications don't seem to fit easily into this timeless framework. In the next chapter we investigate a very different fifth-generation programming paradigm—one that confronts directly the problem of time by modeling the way objects change in time.

EXERCISES

1*. Implement the 'eval' interpreter in a conventional language such as Pascal or Ada.

2*. Write in LISP a recursive interpreter 'value' for fully parenthesized infix arithmetic expressions. For example,

```
(value '(3 + ((8 - 2) * 4)) )
27
```

3. Write a function '(body *f*)' that returns the body of the lambda expression that is the value of the 'expr' property of the atom *f*.

4. Using the 'body' function defined in the previous exercise, write a LISP program to compile a table giving the frequency of occurrence of each of the functions 'car', 'cdr', and 'cons' in a given function.

5*. In Exercise 6 at the end of Chapter 10 you designed a more readable syntax for LISP. Write an 'eval' function for programs in this form or write a program to translate programs in this form into the usual LISP notation.

6*. (Difficult) Write a list structure editor in LISP. This editor can also be used for editing LISP functions. The editor should comprise the following procedures:

(edit *L*)	- edit list *L*; focuses attention on the top level of *L*
(down *n*)	- focus attention on *n*th element of *CL* (current list)
(up)	- focus attention on list containing *CL*
(delete *n*)	- delete *n*th element of *CL*
(insert *n x*)	- insert *x* after *n*th element of *CL*

Each command should echo *CL* after making the modification. To keep the echoing brief, only the top three levels of *CL* should be echoed (lower-level lists are printed as the atom '<list>'). For example,

```
(set 'GP (body 'append))
  (cond
   ((null L) M)
   (t (cons (car L) (append (cadr L) M)) ))

(edit GP)
  (cond ((null L) M) (t (cons <list> <list>)))

(down 3)
  (t (cons (car L) (append <list> M)))

(down 2)
  (cons (car L) (append (cadr L) M))

(down 3)
  (append (cadr L) M)

(delete 2)
  (append M)

(insert 1 '(cdr L))
  (append (cdr L) M)
```

7*. Extend the 'eval' interpreter to handle 'set' and 'defun'. This will require you to implement property lists.

8. Show how 'set' could lead to a cyclic list structure.

9*. Write a reference counting storage manager in a conventional language such as Pascal or Ada.

10*. Write a garbage collecting storage manager in a conventional language such as Pascal or Ada. *Hint:* To be able to implement garbage collection, you will have to have an array containing all the list cells and use indices into this array instead of list cell pointers.

11*. Based on your experience in the previous exercise, discuss the problems of writing system software such as storage managers in languages like Pascal and Ada. Would writing a garbage collector be easier in FORTRAN?

12*. In the exercises following Chapter 9, you studied 'cdr' encoding. Describe a garbage collector for 'cdr' encoded lists. Compare its performance with the garbage collector for the usual representation of lists.

13*. Obtain the documentation for a commercial "LISP machine." Evaluate it as an environment for program development.

14*. Read and critique "The INTERLISP Programming Environment" by W. Teitelman and L. Masinter (*Computer 14*, 4, April 1981).

15*. Read and critique "Design of a LISP-Based Microprocessor" by G. L. Steele, Jr., and G. J. Sussman (*Comm. ACM 23*, 11, November 1980).

12

OBJECT-ORIENTED PROGRAMMING: SMALLTALK

12.1 HISTORY AND MOTIVATION

Alan Kay Saw the Potential for Personal Computers

The principal person responsible for the Smalltalk language is Alan Kay. When he was a graduate student at the University of Utah in the late 1960s, he became convinced that eventually it would be possible to put the power of what was then a room-sized, million-dollar computer into a package the size of a three-ring notebook. It seemed clear that given the direction in which technology was moving, it would eventually be possible for everyone to own a personal computer of considerable power.

But would most people want a personal computer? They probably would not want to use a personal computer for the scientific and commercial applications that occupy large computers. What language would people use to program their personal computers? Existing programming languages were designed by and for specialists and were oriented to just the sort of applications for which personal computers were not likely to be used. It seemed to Kay that the absence of an adequate programming vehicle might be the main impediment to the success of the personal computer.

Kay Investigated Simulation and Graphics-Oriented Languages

While still at the University of Utah, Kay decided that a simulation and graphics-oriented programming language could make computers accessible to nonspecialists. He already had some experience with a language he had helped design called FLEX. This language took many of its most important ideas (such as *classes* and *objects*, both discussed later) from Simula, a simulation language based on Algol-60 and designed in the 1960s.

FLEX was still too oriented toward specialists, however, so Kay also incorporated ideas from LOGO, a language designed by Seymour Papert and others at MIT. Since the early 1960s, Papert had been using LOGO to teach programming concepts to children 8–12 years old. The LOGO environment taught Kay that nonspecialists require a rich interactive environment making use of graphics and audio communication.

Xerox Supported Dynabook Research

Kay proposed to Xerox Corporation his idea of a personal computer; it was called the *Dynabook*. He anticipated that in the 1980s it would be possible to put into a package the size of a notebook a computer capable of executing millions of instructions per second and of holding the equivalent of thousands of pages of information. To make this information accessible, the Dynabook would have a flat-screen reflective display (like many watches and calculators) that would be sensitive to the touch of a finger. This would allow the user to point at things and would allow a portion of the screen to double as a keyboard. It was also intended that the Dynabook could be connected to a stereo, so that it could be used to generate music, and that it could be connected to communication lines, to provide access to large, shared data banks. Kay believed that the availability of the Dynabook would be as revolutionary as the availability of inexpensive, "personal" books after the Industrial Revolution.

Smalltalk Is the Language for the Dynabook

In 1971 the Xerox Palo Alto Research Center began a research project to develop the Dynabook. Smalltalk-72, the language for the Dynabook, was designed and implemented by 1972, and in 1973 a desk-sized "Interim Dynabook" became available for research. Smalltalk-72 and the Interim Dynabook were used in personal computing experiments involving over 250 children (6–15 years old) and 50 adults. Experience with Smalltalk has led to several revisions of the language, including Smalltalk-74, Smalltalk-76, Smalltalk-78, and Smalltalk-80, which is the dialect described in this chapter.[1]

12.2 DESIGN: STRUCTURAL ORGANIZATION

Smalltalk Is Interactive and Interpreted

Figure 12.1 shows a typical Dynabook display. Notice that the screen is covered by a number of *windows* that are reminiscent of papers scattered about a desk. These windows contain many different kinds of information, including Smalltalk programs, output from programs, mail, documents being edited, debugging information, menus, directories, diagrams, pictures, and status information (e.g., date and time). Users focus their attention on a window by pointing at it with a pointing device (typically, a "mouse"[2] or a finger). This allows users to work on many different things at once since they can suspend their activity in one window and resume a different activity in another window simply by moving the pointing device from the one window to the other.

Smalltalk manages the windows to make their use convenient. For example, if the user "touches" a window (by pressing a button on the pointing device when it is in a window), then that window will be redisplayed on top of any other windows that may have been partially hiding it. Windows can also be moved around the screen by using the pointing device.

To satisfy the requirements of the Dynabook, Smalltalk must be a highly interactive language. Although much of the user's communication with Smalltalk is accomplished by pointing, it is possible to type commands to be executed in a "dialogue" window. This style of programming is similar to that used with LISP: The user types commands to the system that either define things or call for the execution of expressions involving things already defined.

There are two primary ways to define things in Smalltalk. The first *binds* a name to an object. For example,

1 The principal source we have used is Goldberg and Robson (1983).

2 A "mouse" is a pointing device that can be moved across a flat surface such as a desktop. As it's moved, a corresponding cursor moves on the screen.

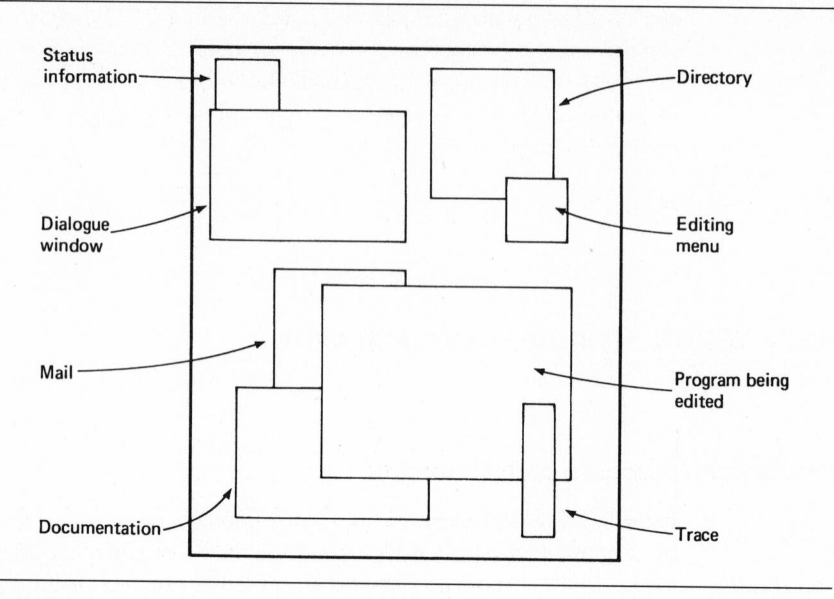

Figure 12.1 Example of a Dynabook Display

```
x ← 3.
y ← x+1
```

binds 'x' to the object '3' and 'y' to the object '4'. This is analogous to an application of 'set' in LISP and to an assignment statement in other languages. The other way to define things is by a *class definition.* Classes are similar to Ada packages; they are discussed later.

The user requests the evaluation of an expression by typing an expression such as 'x*2'. The dialogue looks like this:

```
x*2
  6
```

Smalltalk interprets this action as sending the message '*2' to the object 'x'. This rather unusual view of expressions is explained next.

Objects React to Messages

Since Smalltalk provides a unique programming environment, we will begin by showing a typical Smalltalk session. We have said that Smalltalk is graphics oriented and that it borrowed its interactive style from LOGO. LOGO introduced a style of graphics called "turtle graphics" that is based on objects (called "turtles") that draw as they move around the screen. Smalltalk provides a similar class of objects called *pens.*

In our first example, we will investigate the behavior of a pen named 'Scribe' and see how it can draw on the screen. The display shows us the position of Scribe.

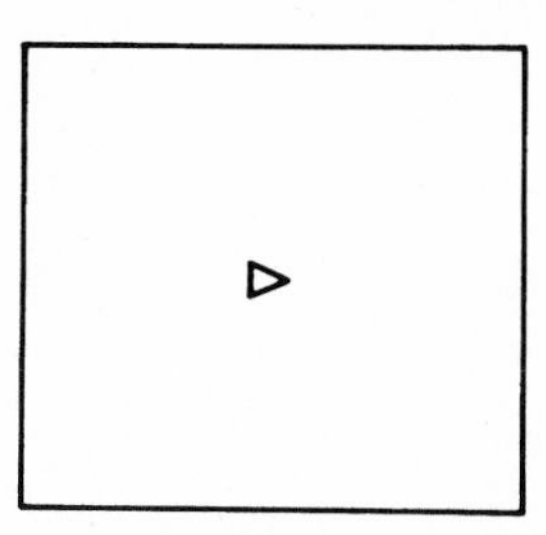

Let's assume that Scribe is at position (500,500), the center of the screen; this is written '500@500' in Smalltalk. To draw a line from coordinates (500,500) to (200,400), we enter

```
Scribe goto: 200@400
```

This is a message to Scribe that tells it to draw a line from where it is to (200,400). The result is

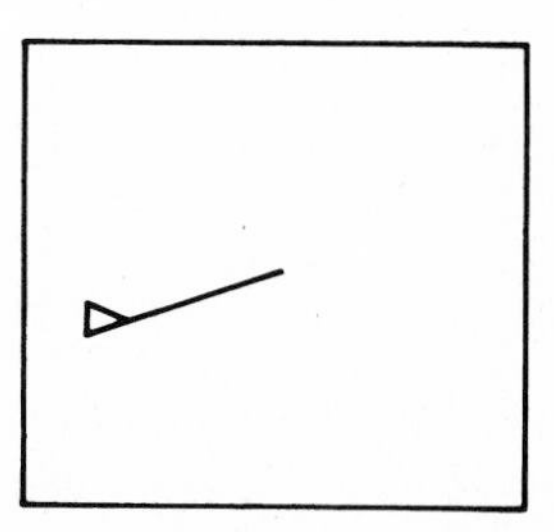

What if we want to move Scribe without drawing a line? We first send the message

```
Scribe penup
```

which tells Scribe to stop drawing. We then move Scribe to the desired point. For example, to draw a vertical line from (500,100) to (500,400), we can enter

```
Scribe penup.
Scribe goto: 500@100.
Scribe pendn.
Scribe goto: 500@400
```

The result is

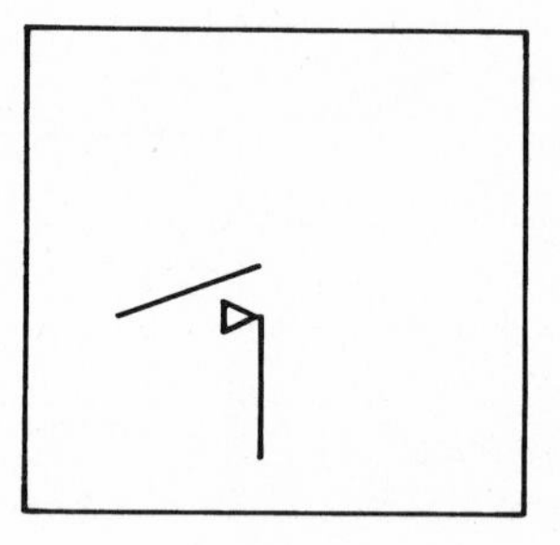

Scribe also has an orientation, so that if we tell it to 'go', it will go a specified distance in that direction. Suppose the direction of Scribe is to the right, then

```
Scribe go: 300
```

has this effect

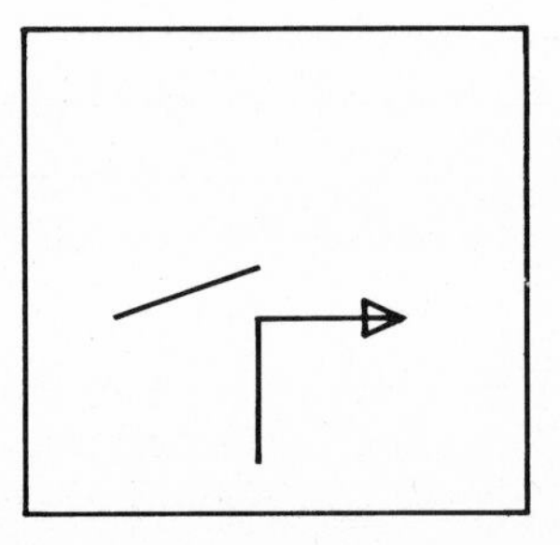

We can complete the square by turning and drawing the remaining lines as follows:

```
Scribe turn: 90.
Scribe go: 300.
Scribe turn: 90.
Scribe go: 300
```

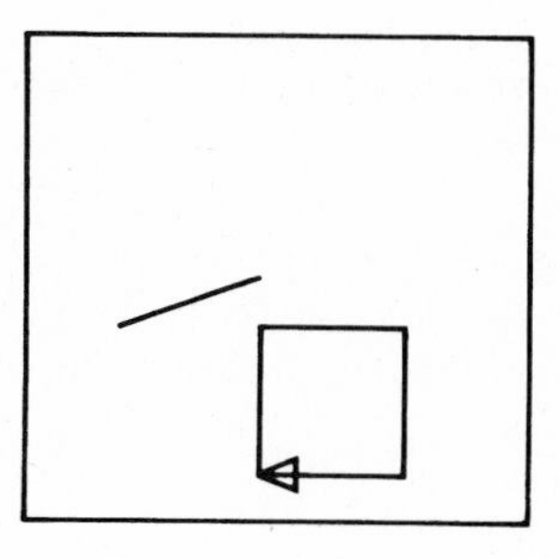

A more convenient way of drawing the square is to use a control structure. To draw a square whose upper-left-hand corner is at (400,800) with a side of length 100, we can write:

```
Scribe penup; goto: 400@800; pendn; turn 180.
4 timesRepeat: [Scribe go: 100. Scribe turn: 90]
```

Notice that in the first line we used an abbreviation, a *cascaded message*, to avoid writing 'Scribe' over and over again. Also notice the extent to which Smalltalk obeys the Regularity Principle: Even control structures are accomplished by sending messages to objects. In this case, the object '4' has been sent the message

```
timesRepeat: [Scribe go: 100. Scribe turn: 90]
```

The object '4' responds to this message by repeating the bracketed expressions four times. The result of these commands is

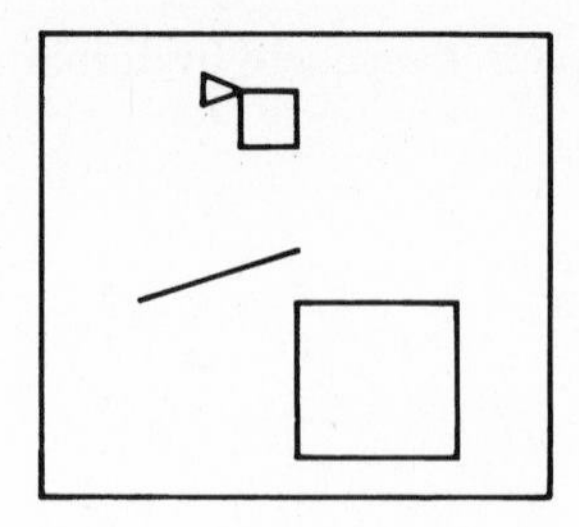

Let's summarize several important ideas in Smalltalk programming:

1. Objects have a behavior.
2. Objects can be made to do things by sending them messages.
3. Repetitive operations can be simplified by using control structures.

Objects Can Be Instantiated

Having learned to use existing objects, the next step for the Smalltalk programmer is to learn to create new objects. Continuing our previous example, suppose that we want another pen and that we want to call it 'anotherScribe'. We can't just ask for a new object; we have to say what kind of object we want. Note that a *class* is just a name for a particular kind of object; for example, the class 'Integer' includes the objects 0, 1, 2, 3, ... Furthermore, every object is an *instance* of some class, so when we create an object, we have to say of which class we want it to be an instance. Thus, the process of creating an object is called *instantiation.*

Recall that every request for action in Smalltalk must be accomplished by sending a message to some object. This includes instantiation. The question is: Which object should be sent the message requesting the instantiation of a new pen? This message could be directed to some universal system object responsible for all instantiations, but we will be more in accord with the Information Hiding Principle if we make the class 'pen' itself responsible for instantiating pens. This is the approach used in Smalltalk. To create a new pen and call it 'anotherScribe', we enter:

```
anotherScribe ← pen newAt: 200@800
```

This sends the message 'newAt: 200@800' to the class 'pen', which creates and returns a new pen located at coordinates (200,800) and pointing to the right.

The name 'anotherScribe' is bound to this new object; hence, we can direct messages to the new object by using this name:

```
anotherScribe pendn.
5 timesRepeat: [anotherScribe go: 50; turn: 72]
```

The result will be:

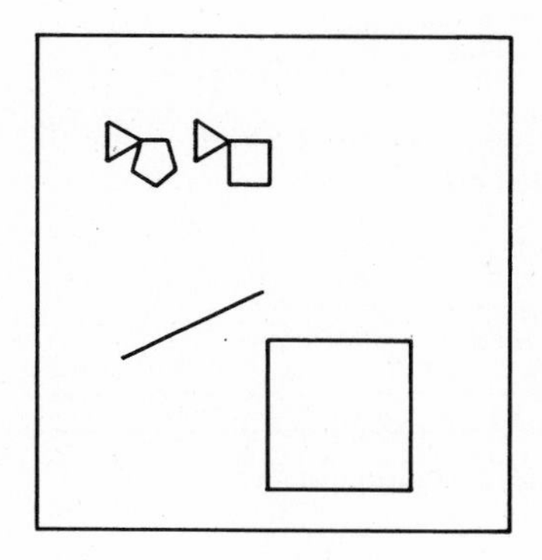

EXERCISE 12-1: What Smalltalk commands will create a new pen called 'Writer' and cause it to draw an equilateral triangle with its apex at (800,800).

Classes Can Be Defined

In our previous example, we sent messages to a pen that caused it to draw a box on the screen. If we wanted to draw another box, we would have to move the pen (or instantiate a new one) and send it the same messages over again. This would violate the Abstraction Principle. A better solution is to define a class 'box' that can be instantiated any number of times. Smalltalk allows us to do this, thus supporting both the Abstraction and Regularity Principles (the latter because user-defined classes are just like built-in classes). To see an example, look at Figure 12.2, which shows a definition of the 'box' class as it would appear on the Dynabook screen.

Notice that a class definition has a two-dimensional arrangement; this is quite different from the one-dimensional syntax associated with the other languages we've studied. Typically, the Smalltalk screen contains a number of overlapping *windows* like those shown in Figure 12.2. Users can type in these windows, move them around, and alter their sizes. Smalltalk obeys the Regularity Principle by adopting the window as a uniform way of interacting with users and organizing the screen.

class name	box
instance variable names	loc tilt size scribe
instance messages and methods	

```
shape | |
   scribe penup; goto: loc; turnTo: tilt; pendn.
   4 timesRepeat: [scribe go: size; turn: 90]

show | |
   scribe color ink.
   self shape

erase | |
   scribe color background.
   self shape

grow: amount | |
   self erase.
   size ← size+amount.
   self show
```

Figure 12.2 Definition of Box Class

Look at the definition of 'box' in Figure 12.2. The first line is self-explanatory: It names the class. The second line lists four *instance variables*. These variables are local to each instance of the class (i.e., to each box) and are instantiated for each box. In other words, each box has its own 'loc', 'tilt', 'size', and 'scribe'. The purpose of these variables is as follows: 'loc' contains the location of the upper-left-hand corner of the box; 'tilt' contains the angle describing the orientation of the box; 'size' is the length of the box's side; and 'scribe' is the pen used by the box to draw its shape.

The rest of the window is devoted to the *instance methods*; these are the methods that describe the behavior of the *instances* when they receive various messages (we will see below that there are also class messages that describe the behavior of *classes* when they receive messages). Suppose B1 is a box; then sending it the message 'shape':

```
B1 shape
```

causes it to (1) lift its pen, (2) go to the specified location, (3) turn to the specified angle, and (4) draw a box of the specified size.

We can see that by changing the color of the pen's 'ink', the 'shape' method can be used either to make the box appear or to make it disappear. This is the purpose of the 'show' and 'erase' messages. Notice that a box responds to each of these messages by changing the pen color and sending itself the 'shape' message. (The instance variable 'self' is implicitly bound to the instance to which it is local.)

Let's look at the 'grow:' method; B1 responds to 'B1 grow: 20' by increasing its size by 20 units. It accomplishes this by erasing itself, increasing its 'size' variable, and redrawing itself. Notice the formal parameter 'amount' to the 'grow:' method. Moving a box would be accomplished in a similar manner.

EXERCISE 12-2: Define the 'move:' method so that 'B1 move: 100@200' moves box B1 to location (100,200).

EXERCISE 12-3: Define the 'turn:' method so that 'B1 turn: 45' causes box B1 to turn 45 degrees.

Classes Can Also Respond to Messages

We have left a very important part of the definition of boxes undone: the method for instantiation. As we said before, the class itself is responsible for creating new instances of itself, so this kind of method is called a *class method.* In Figure 12.3 we have scrolled down the window containing the 'box' class to show its instantiation method. Thus, when we execute

```
B2 ← box newAt: 300@200
```

class name	box
instance variable names	loc tilt size scribe
class messages and methods	

```
newAt: initialLocation | newBox |
   newBox ← self new.
   newBox setLoc: initialLocation tilt: 0 size: 100 scribe: pen new
   newBox show.
   ⇑ newBox
```

instance messages and methods

```
setLoc: newLoc tilt: newTilt size: newSize scribe: newScribe | |
   loc ← newLoc. tilt ← newTilt.
   size ← newSize. scribe ← newScribe

shape | |
   scribe penup; goto: loc; turnTo: tilt; pendn.
```

Figure 12.3 Class Method in Box Class

the message 'newAt: 300@200' will be sent to the class 'box'. This class method begins by sending itself (i.e., the class 'box') the message 'new'. All classes automatically respond to 'new' by creating a new, uninitialized instance of themselves. This new instance is stored in the local temporary variable 'newBox'. The instance variables are initialized with a new instance method that has the template 'setLoc: tilt: size: scribe:'. The 'newAt:' method then orders the instance to 'show' itself and finally returns the instance so that it can be bound to 'B2'.

EXERCISE 12-4: Alter the instantiation method for 'box's so that they are created with a tilt of 45° and a size of 200.

EXERCISE 12-5: Write an additional instantiation method for 'box's, called 'newSize:', that creates a box of the given size, but always at the center of the screen [i.e., (500,500)].

12.3 DESIGN: CLASSES AND SUBCLASSES

Smalltalk Objects Model Real-World Objects

In our discussion of LISP (Chapter 9, Section 9.3), we saw that atoms are often used to model objects in the real world. That is, like real-world objects, atoms in LISP can have properties and be related in various ways. This allows many programs to be viewed as a *model* or *simulation* of some aspects of the real world.

We have mentioned that many of the ideas in Smalltalk derive from Simula, an extension of Algol intended for simulation. These ideas include internally represented objects as instances of classes (internally represented objects are discussed in Chapter 7, Section 7.4). It is thus no surprise that Smalltalk objects are well suited to modeling real-world objects. In particular, the data values inside an object can represent the properties and relations in which that object participates, and the behavior of the Smalltalk object can model the behavior of the corresponding real-world object. Therefore, in Smalltalk, the dominant *paradigm* (or model) of programming is *simulation.*

Classes Group Related Objects

In the real world, all of the objects that we observe are *individuals;* every object differs from every other in a number of ways. However, if we are to be able to deal effectively with the world, we must be able to understand why objects act the way they do so that we will be able to predict their actions in the future. If every object were completely different from every other one and every action and effect were unique, then there would be no possibility of understanding the world or acting effectively. This is not the case, however; objects have many properties in common and we observe broad classes of objects acting similarly. Therefore, we focus on these common properties and behaviors and *abstract* them out. This, of course, is just an application of the Abstraction Principle. The resulting *abstraction*, or *class*, retains the similar properties and behaviors but omits the *particulars* that distinguish one individual from another.

This is exactly the situation we find in Smalltalk. The *class definition* specifies all of the properties and behaviors common to all instances of the class, while the *instance variables* in the object contain all of the particular information that distinguishes one object from another. The behavior of the members of a class, the set of all messages to which the members of that class respond, is called the *protocol of the class*. The protocol is determined by the instance methods in the class definition.

This approach is ideally suited to simulation. When we model some aspect of the real world, we are trying to find out what would happen if certain conditions held. To do this it is necessary to have laws of cause and effect that describe how certain kinds of objects act in certain situations. In other words, it is necessary to know the relevant behavior of certain *classes* of objects. It is exactly this information that is modeled by a Smalltalk *class*: the behavior common to all of the instances of the class.

Subclasses Permit Hierarchical Classification

We have seen how the Abstraction Principle can be applied to individual objects: The properties common to a group of objects are abstracted out and associated with the class of those objects. The Abstraction Principle can also be applied to classes themselves. Consider the class 'pen', which abstracts out the common properties of objects like 'Scribe' and 'anotherScribe'. We have also seen the class 'box', which abstracts the common properties of boxes. Similarly, the class 'window' might include all of the window objects that can be displayed on the screen, such as the window that contains the definition of 'box'. Notice that all of these classes have certain properties in common, for example, coordinates that determine their positions on the screen. We can presume that they also respond to certain common messages, such as to alter their position and to appear and disappear. The Abstraction Principle tells us that we should abstract out these common properties and give them a name such as 'displayObject'. Then, 'pen', 'box', and 'window' will be *subclasses* of the class 'displayObject'. Conversely, 'displayObject' would be called a *superclass* of the classes 'pen', 'box', and 'win-

class name	displayObject
instance variable names	loc
instance messages and methods	

```
goto: newLoc | |
   self erase.
   loc ← newLoc.
   self show
```

Figure 12.4 Example of Superclass DisplayObject

dow'. Figure 12.4 shows part of the definition of 'displayObject' and Figure 12.5 shows how 'box' can be made a subclass of 'displayObject'.

Notice that in the method for 'shape' in the definition of 'box', we make use of the variable 'loc', which is defined in the superclass. That is, the instance variables of the superclass are *inherited* by all of its subclasses. Similarly, any methods defined in the superclass (such as 'goto:') are also inherited.

Smalltalk would violate the Zero-One-Infinity Principle if it allowed only two levels of classes, that is, superclasses and subclasses. In fact, there is no such limitation. Classes can always be *refined* by defining subclasses within them. Conversely, classes can be grouped into more inclusive superclasses. Indeed, there is one grand superclass, called 'object', that includes all other classes as its subclasses. Therefore, all objects in the Smalltalk system are instances (perhaps

class name	box
superclass	displayObject
instance variable names	tilt size scribe
instance messages and methods	

```
shape | |
   scribe penup; goto: loc; turnTo: tilt; pendn.
   4 timesRepeat: [scribe go: size; turn: 90]
```

Figure 12.5 Example of Subclass Box

indirectly) of the class 'object'. The end result of all of this is a unified hierarchical classification of all objects known to Smalltalk. We can visualize this as follows:

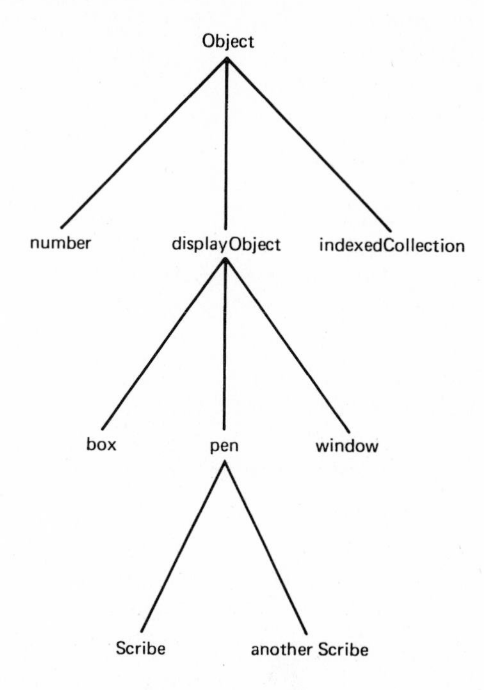

At the lowest level we have individual objects, and at all levels above them we have classes of objects. Each class is a subclass of all of the classes above it, and each class is a superclass of all of the classes below it. The actual Smalltalk class hierarchy is much richer than suggested above; Table 12.1 shows part of the Smalltalk-80 hierarchy of system (i.e., built-in) classes.

Behavior Can Be Extended or Modified

As the previous example indicates, subclasses allow the behavior of a class to be extended. For example, 'box's respond to messages in addition to those to which 'displayObject's respond. Thus, the behavior of 'box's is an *extension* of the behavior of 'displayObject's. The subclass mechanism facilitates building classes on already existing classes. In this case, the 'goto:' method, once written, can be used by any new class that is made a subclass of 'displayObject'; it is never necessary to rewrite this method.

Subclasses can build upon the behavior of their superclasses; they can also modify it. Recall that in block-structured languages, a declaration of an identifier

Table 12.1 Smalltalk-80 System Class Hierarchy (Partial)

Object
- I. Magnitude
  - A. Character
  - B. Date
  - C. Time
  - D. Number
    - 1. Float
    - 2. Fraction
    - 3. Integer
      - a. LargeNegativeInteger
      - b. LargePositiveInteger
      - c. SmallInteger
- II. Collection
  - A. SequenceableCollection
    - 1. LinkedList
    - 2. ArrayedCollection
      - a. Array
      - b. Bitmap
      - c. RunArray
      - d. String
      - e. Text
      - f. ByteArray
    - 3. Interval
    - 4. OrderedCollection
  - B. Bag
  - C. MappedCollection
  - D. Set
- III. DisplayObject
  - A. DisplayMedium
    - 1. Form
      - a. Cursor
      - b. DisplayScreen
  - B. InfiniteForm
  - C. OpaqueForm
  - D. Path
    - 1. Arc
    - 2. Curve
      - a. Circle
    - 3. Line
    - 4. LinearFit

Table 12.1 (Continued)

5. Spline
IV. Behavior
V. BitBlt
A. Pen

overrides any declarations of that same identifier in surrounding environments. The same rule applies to methods: A definition of a method in a subclass overrides any definitions of that method that may exist in its superclasses. Thus, if the standard definition of 'goto:' in 'displayObject' were inappropriate for 'window's, then this method could be redefined in 'window' as shown:

class name	window
superclass	displayObject
instance variable names	size scribe text
instance messages and methods	
goto: loc || ... new definition of goto: ...	

Is the old definition of 'goto:' inaccessible to 'window'? No, it is not. Recall that an object can send a message to itself with an expression like 'self goto: loc'. It is also possible for an object to send a message to itself in its capacity *as a member of its superclass.* For example, if the 'goto:' method in 'window' needed to make use of the 'goto:' method in 'displayObject', we could write:

```
goto: loc | |
   ⋮
  super goto: loc
   ⋮
```

The name 'super' is automatically bound to the same object as 'self', but the object is considered as a member of its superclass. If we had written 'self goto: loc' instead, we would have caused a recursive invocation of the 'goto:' method for 'window's.

Thus, although definitions in a subclass cover up definitions in the superclass, the superclass definitions can be uncovered by an explicit request. This simplifies building new software on already existing software and makes Smalltalk a very extensible system.

Overloading Is Implicit and Inexpensive

Since objects are responsible for responding to messages, there is no reason why objects of different classes can't respond to the same messages. For example, in the expression '3 + 5' the object '3' responds to the message '+ 5' by returning the object '8'. Similarly, in the expression

```
"book" + "keeper"
```

the object

```
"book"
```

responds to the message

```
+ "keeper"
```

by returning the object

```
"bookkeeper"
```

In effect '+' has been overloaded to work on both numbers and strings. Notice, however, that there is no operator identification problem because the system always knows the class to which an object belongs, and this class determines the method that will handle the message. Thus, operators can be automatically extended to handle new data types by including methods for these operators in the class defining the data type.

Classes Allow Multiple Representations of Data Types

Classes also simplify having several concrete representations for one abstract data type. For example, we can define a class 'indexedStack' that implements stacks as arrays. Objects that are instances of 'indexedStack' respond to messages such as 'pop', 'push: *x*', and 'empty'. Similarly, we can define a class 'linkedStack' that implements stacks as linked lists and that responds to the same messages. Each of these classes is a concrete representation of the same abstract type, 'stack'. The key point is that any program that works on 'linkedStack's will also work on 'indexedStack's, because they respond to the same messages.

Thus, in accordance with the Information Hiding Principle, we have hidden the implementation details in the class. Also notice that classes obey the Manifest Interface Principle since the interface to an object is just its *protocol*: the set of messages to which it responds. Therefore, objects with the same protocol (interface) can be used interchangeably.

Objects Can Be Self-Displaying

The problem of displaying objects demonstrates the extensibility and maintenance advantages of the Smalltalk class structure. Suppose that we define a new class 'complex' that represents complex numbers. It is desirable that we be able to print out complex numbers, just as we can print out real numbers and integers. The problem is that in most languages it would be necessary to modify the 'print' procedure to accomplish this; a new case would have to be added to handle complex numbers. This violates the Information Hiding Principle since it forces us to scatter the implementation details of complex numbers around the system.

Smalltalk has a simpler solution: We just require that every displayable object respond to the message 'print' by returning a character string form of itself. For example, we could define complex numbers as shown in Figure 12.6. Then, if 'w' were the object representing $1+2i$ and 'z' were the object representing $2+5i$, sending the message 'print' to the object 'w + z', '(w + z) print', would return the string

```
"3+7i"
```

Similarly, we could define the print method for 'box's to show their location, tilt, and size:

```
print | |
  ⇑ "box at " + loc print
    + ", size= " + size print
    + ", tilt= " + tilt print.
```

Thus, if we entered 'B1 print', we would see

```
box at 100@500, size=100, tilt=0
```

class name	complex
instance variable names	realPt imagPt
instance messages and methods	

```
print | |
  ⇑ realPt print + "+" + imagPt print + "i".

+y | |
```

Figure 12.6 Print Method for Complex Numbers

We are, of course, assuming that 'point's respond to 'print' with a string of the form '*x*@*y*'.

Methods Accept Any Object with the Proper Protocol

The fact that a method will work on any object with the appropriate protocol is one of the factors that make Smalltalk such a flexible, extensible system. It is possible at any time to define a new class and have many existing methods already applicable to it. For example, we might have a number of methods that operate on numbers by using the arithmetic operators. These methods might include expressions such as '(x + y)*x'. If we later defined a class 'polynomial' that responded to messages ' + y', '*y', and so on, then polynomial objects could be passed to these methods. This works because in the expression 'x + y' the object 'x' is responsible for responding to the message ' + y'; if 'x' is a number, it does simple addition; if 'x' is a polynomial, it does polynomial addition. The method containing 'x + y' does not have to know whether 'x' and 'y' are real numbers, polynomials, complex numbers, or any other objects that respond to the arithmetic operators.

Hierarchical Subclasses Preclude Orthogonal Classifications

We will now discuss one of the limitations of a strictly hierarchical subclass–superclass relationship. Consider an application in which Smalltalk is being used for the computer-aided design of cars. We will assume that this system assists in the design in several different ways. For example, it helps in producing engineering drawings by allowing the user to manipulate and combine diagrams of various parts, and it assists in cost and weight estimates by keeping track of the number, cost, and weight of the parts.

Presumably each part that goes into a car is an object with a number of attributes. For example, a bumper might have a weight, a cost, physical dimensions, the name of a manufacturer, a location on the screen, and an indication of its points of connection with other parts. Similarly, an engine might have weight, cost, dimensions, manufacturer, horsepower, and fuel consumption. If we presume that our display shows only the external appearance of the car, then an engine will not have a display location.

The next step is to apply the Abstration Principle and to begin to classify the objects on the basis of their common attributes. For example, we will find that many of the classes (e.g., bumpers, roofs, grills) will have a 'loc' attribute because they will be displayed on the screen. We can also presume that these objects respond to the 'goto:' message so that they can be moved about the screen. This suggests that these classes should be made subclasses of 'displayObject' because this class defines the methods for handling displayed objects. Thus, our class structure might look something like this:

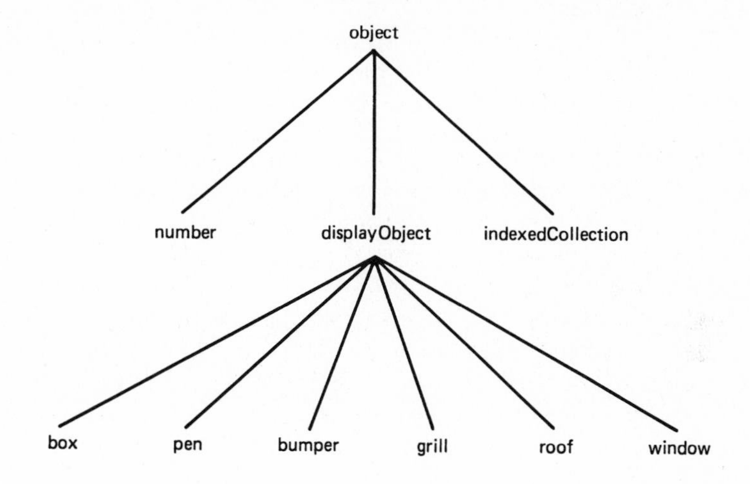

On the other hand, many of the objects that our program manipulates have 'cost', 'weight', and 'manufacturer' attributes. This suggests that we should have a class called, for example, 'inventoryItem' that has these attributes and that responds to messages for inventory control (e.g., 'reportStock', 'reorder'). This leads to the following class structure:

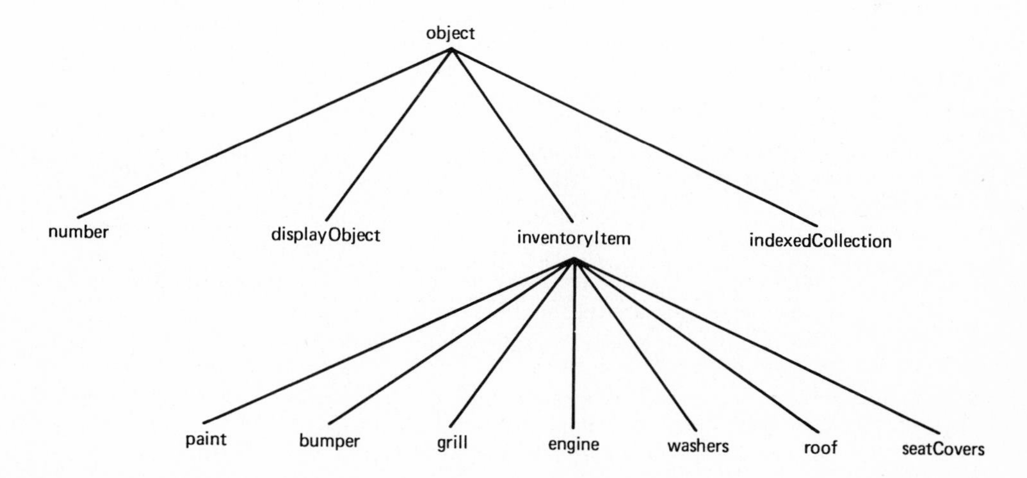

Now we can see the problem. Smalltalk organizes classes into a hierarchy; each class has exactly one immediate superclass. Notice that in our example several of the classes (e.g., 'bumper' and 'grill') are subclasses of two classes: 'displayObject' and 'inventoryItem'. This is not possible in Smalltalk; when a class is defined, it can be specified to be an immediate subclass of exactly *one* other class.

What are the consequences of this? We can choose either 'displayObject' *or* 'inventoryItem' to be the superclass of the other. Suppose we choose 'displayObject'; then our class structure looks like this:

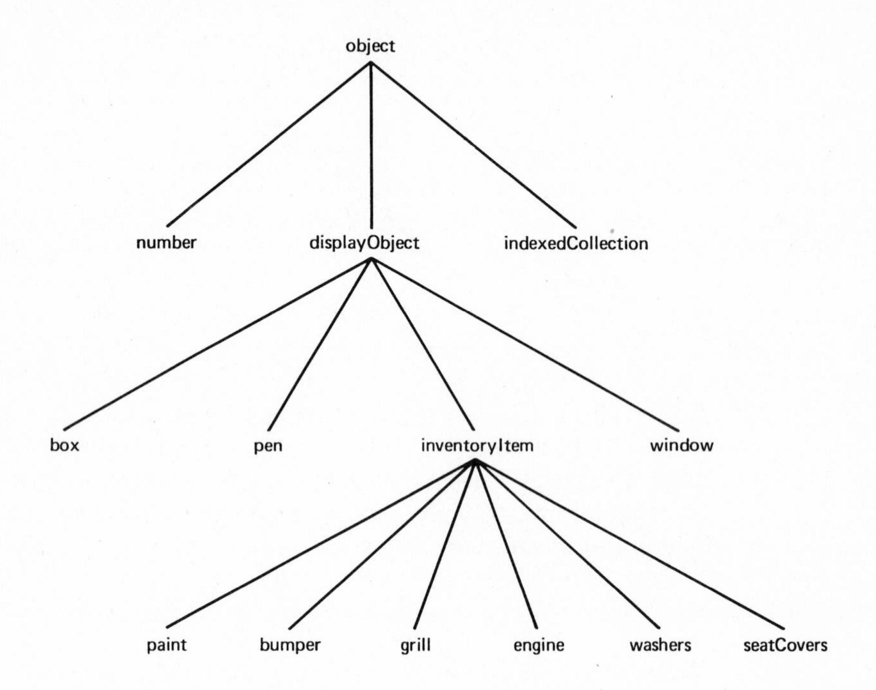

This seems to solve the problem. The display methods occur once—in 'displayObject'—and the inventory control methods occur once—in 'inventoryItem'. Unfortunately, this arrangement of the classes has a side effect: Some objects that are never displayed (e.g., engines and paint) now have the attributes of a displayed object, such as a location. This means that they will respond to messages that are meaningless, which is a violation of the Security Principle. The alternative, placing 'displayObject' under 'inventoryItem', is even worse since it means that objects such as 'pen's and 'box's will have attributes such as 'weight', 'cost', and 'manufacturer'! Thus, we seem to be faced with a choice: either violate the Security Principle by making either 'displayObject' or 'inventoryItem' a subclass of the other or violate the Abstraction Principle by repeating in some of the classes the attributes of the others.

What is the source of this problem? In real life we often find that the same objects must be classified in several different ways. For example, a biologist might classify mammals as primates, rodents, ruminants, and so forth. Someone interested in the uses of mammals might classify them as pets, beasts of burden, sources of food, pests, and so forth. Finally, a zoo might classify them as North American, South American, African, and so forth. These are three *orthogonal* classifications; each of the classes cuts across the others at "right angles":

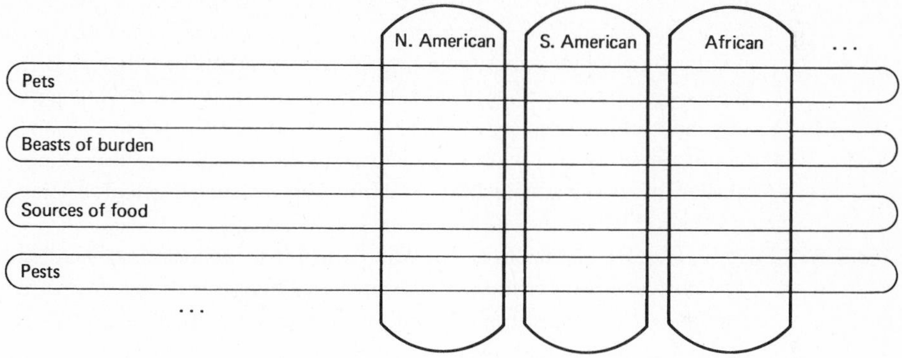

(We have shown only two of the three dimensions.)

In summary, a hierarchical classification system, such as provided by Smalltalk, precludes orthogonal classification. This in turn forces the programmer to violate either the Security Principle or the Abstraction Principle. In essence, Smalltalk ignores the fact that the appropriate classification of a group of objects depends on the context in which those objects are viewed. Some experimental extensions of Smalltalk have attempted to remedy this problem by providing a "multiple inheritance" capability that allows an object to belong to several classes at once.

12.4 DESIGN: OBJECTS AND MESSAGE SENDING

The Primary Concept Is the Object

As we have seen, everything in Smalltalk is an object. This design decision satisfies both the Regularity and Simplicity Principles. In Smalltalk even classes are objects, that is, they are instances of the class named 'class'.

What exactly is an object? Objects have characteristics of both data and programs. For example, objects are the things that represent quantities, properties, and the entities modeled by the program. In Smalltalk numbers, strings, and so on, are all objects. Objects also have some of the characteristics of programs; like programs, they *do* things. For example, Scribe could be made to move, draw lines, change its pen status, and so on. In a conventional language, programs are *active* and data elements are *passive*; the program elements *act on* the data elements. In an object-oriented language like Smalltalk, the data elements are *active*; they respond to messages that cause them to act on themselves, perhaps modifying themselves, perhaps modifying or returning other objects. Another way of saying this is that conventional languages are *function oriented*; things are accomplished by passing objects to functions. In an object-oriented language, things are accomplished by sending messages to objects.

The set of messages to which an object can respond is called its *protocol.* The protocol is determined by the instance methods of the class of which it is an instance. When an object is sent a message, the Smalltalk system produces an error diagnostic if that message is not part of the object's protocol. This run-time checking is necessary to satisfy the Security Principle.

Names Are Not Typed

Most of the programming languages we have studied associate a definite type with each name (variable or formal parameter). Strong typing then ensures that only objects of the same type can be bound to these names. Smalltalk has a different strategy: No names are typed, and any object can be bound to any name. Type checking occurs when a message is sent to the object bound to a name. If the object responds to that message (i.e., the message is in its protocol), then the message is legal; otherwise it's not. Thus, Smalltalk performs *dynamic* type checking, like LISP, as opposed to *static* type checking, like Pascal and Ada.

Notice that dynamic typing does not imply *weak* typing. Strong typing refers to the fact that type abstractions are enforced. This enforcement may be done predominantly at compile-time (static typing) or predominantly at run-time (dynamic typing), so long as it's done. Smalltalk, like LISP, has strong, but dynamic, typing.

In previous chapters we've had a great deal to say about the security advantages of static type checking. Does this mean that Smalltalk violates the Security Principle? No, it doesn't. Since the Smalltalk system will allow a message to be sent to an object only if that object has a method to respond to the message, it is not possible for type violations to cause system crashes. Thus, the system and the user's program are secure.

Another reason for static type checking is that it allows earlier error detection. Specifically, it allows errors to be detected at compile-time, when the compiler can give an intelligible diagnostic, rather than at run-time, when only the machine code is available. This argument does not apply to a system like Smalltalk, however. Since all of the source code is available at run-time, the Smalltalk system can produce run-time diagnostics in terms of the source code of the program.

It might also be argued that early error detection saves both programmer and computer time since in a compiled language the entire program, or at least one module, must be recompiled each time an error is found. In Smalltalk, however, a run-time error causes the program to be suspended so that the programmer can investigate its cause. An offending class can be edited and quickly recompiled, and execution of the program can be resumed. Thus, in the Smalltalk environment, static type checking affords little savings in time.

Another argument for static typing is that it improves the efficiency of storage utilization since a character, for example, occupies less storage than a floating-point number. In Smalltalk, however, every object is accessed through an *object reference*, that is, a pointer. Therefore, all variables and parameters occupy the same amount of storage—one pointer.

A final argument for static typing is documentation. It is easier to understand a program if each variable and parameter has a type associated with it; this declares the use to which the programmer intends to put that variable or parameter. The designers of Smalltalk claim that well-named variables provide just as good documentation. For example, calling a parameter 'anInteger' makes its intended value just as clear as a typed declaration like 'n: integer'.

The last point in favor of Smalltalk's dynamic typing is *flexibility*. We have already seen how any object with the proper protocol can be passed to a method. This makes it much easier to build on existing software in the Smalltalk system. This can be considered a major application of the Abstraction Principle since it allows common algorithms to be factored out of a system without complicated mechanisms like Ada's generics.

EXERCISE 12-6:* Write a short report on the pros and cons of static and dynamic typing. Evaluate each of the above arguments in favor of dynamic typing in Smalltalk. Formulate your own position on typing and defend it.

Messages Are Essentially Procedure Invocations

Recall our discussion of the *internal* and *external* representation of objects in connection with Ada (Chapter 7, Section 7.4). We can see that Smalltalk has *internal* objects since both the fields of the object, such as 'size' and 'loc', and the procedures for manipulating the object, such as 'goto:' and 'show', are part of the object. In other words, there's not much difference between the Smalltalk expression

```
Scribe goto: loc
```

and the Ada statement

```
Scribe.goto(loc);
```

which invokes the 'goto' procedure in the package 'Scribe' with the argument 'loc'.

Let's investigate this similarity in more detail. In Smalltalk, when a class is defined, we specify the variables that are to be duplicated in each instance of the class and the messages to which all instances of the class will respond. Thus, the class definition in Figure 12.2 is similar to the Ada generic package shown in Figure 12.7. Notice that each method has been translated into a public procedure and each instance variable into a private variable (of course, we've had to add type information, so the translation is not exact).

Just as in Smalltalk, in Ada the process of instantiation is separate from the process of class definition. The Smalltalk instantiations

```
B1 ← box newAt 200@500
B2 ← box newAt 800@500
```

are similar to the Ada package declarations

```
package B1 is new BOX (INITIAL_LOC => (200,500));
package B2 is new BOX (INITIAL_LOC => (800,500));
```

A major difference between objects in Ada and Smalltalk is that Smalltalk allows the *dynamic* instantiation of internally represented objects, whereas Ada does not. This can be seen in the above example; the instantiation of the packages B1 and B2 is accomplished by declarations, the number of which is limited by the written form of the program. In Smalltalk, instantiation is done at run-

```
generic
   INITIAL_LOC : POINT;
package BOX is
   procedure SHAPE;
   procedure SHOW;
   procedure ERASE;
   procedure GROW (AMOUNT : INTEGER);
end BOX;

package body BOX is

   LOC : POINT := INITIAL_LOC;
   TILT : FLOAT;
   SIZE : FLOAT;
   SCRIBE : PEN;

   procedure SHAPE is
      :
   end SHAPE;

   :
end BOX;
```

Figure 12.7 Generic Package Similar to a Class

time, by sending an instantiation message to a class. Thus, Smalltalk is more flexible, since it is possible to decide at run-time how many instances of a class are required. In Ada this can only be done with *external* objects (Chapter 7, Section 7.4), which are more limited since they cannot respond directly to messages.

EXERCISE 12-7: Complete the definition of the Ada package 'BOX'.

EXERCISE 12-8:* Discuss the trade-offs between statically and dynamically instantiated objects.

EXERCISE 12-9:* Show that anything that can be accomplished with external objects can also be accomplished with internal objects, and vice versa.

There Are Three Forms of Message Template

You have seen that messages are essentially procedure invocations, although the formats allowed for messages are a little more flexible. In most languages parameters are surrounded by parentheses and separated by commas; in Smalltalk parameters are separated by keywords. For example, the Smalltalk message:

```
newBox setLoc: initialLocation tilt: 0 size: 100 scribe: pen new
```

is equivalent to the Ada procedure call:

```
NEWBOX.SET (INITIAL_LOCATION, 0, 100, PEN.NEW() );
```

although the similarity is more striking if we use position-independent parameters:

```
NEWBOX.SET  (LOC => INITIAL_LOCATION, TILT => 0,
             SIZE => 100, SCRIBE => PEN.NEW() );
```

Note, however, that Smalltalk is not following the Labeling Principle here since the parameters are required to be in the right order even though they are labeled.

The message format, keywords followed by colons, can be used if there are one or more parameters to the method. What if a method has no parameters? In this case, it would be confusing to both the human reader and the system if the keyword were followed by a colon. This leads to the format that we have seen for parameterless messages:

```
B1 show
```

Omitting the colon from a parameterless message is analogous to omitting the empty parentheses '( )' from a parameterless procedure call in Ada.

These message formats are adequate for all purposes since they handle any number of parameters from zero on up. Unfortunately, they would require writing arithmetic expressions in an uncommon way. For example, to compute '$(x+2) \times y$' we would have to write[3]:

```
(x plus: 2) times: y
```

3 The parentheses are necessary, otherwise we would be sending to 'x' a message with the template 'plus:times:'.

To avoid this unusual notation, Smalltalk has made a special exception: the arithmetic operators (and other special symbols) can be followed by exactly one parameter even though there is no colon. For example, in

```
x + 2 * y
```

the object named 'x' is sent the message '+ 2', and the object resulting from this is sent the message '* y'. Thus, this expression computes $(x + 2)y$; notice that Smalltalk does not obey the usual precedence rules.

In summary, there are three formats for messages:

1. Keywords for parameterless messages (e.g., 'B1 show')
2. Operators for one-parameter messages (e.g., 'x + y')
3. Keywords with colons for one- (or more) parameter messages (e.g., 'Scribe grow: 100')

Notice that this format convention fits the Zero-One-Infinity Principle since the only special cases are for zero parameters and one parameter. However, the fact that these cases are handled differently from the general case violates the Regularity Principle. This is a conscious trade-off that the designers of Smalltalk have made so that they can use the usual arithmetic operators. We know this because earlier versions of Smalltalk (e.g., Smalltalk-72) had a uniform method for passing parameters that did not depend on the number of parameters.

EXERCISE 12-10:* Discuss Smalltalk's message formats. Given that Smalltalk's conventions still violate the usual precedence rules for arithmetic operators, was it wise to make a special case of them? Either defend the conventions adopted by Smalltalk, or propose and defend a different set of your own conventions.

Objects Hold the State of a Computation

How an object behaves when it receives a message depends on two things: the method defined for that message (which is part of the object's class and never changes) and the contents of the variables visible to the method. Since it is the instance variables that are different in different instances of a class, it is predominantly the instance variables that determine the individual behavior of objects. For example, the orientation of Scribe after it receives the message 'turn: 90' depends on its orientation before it received that message, which is contained in an instance variable. There is no global table that holds the state of all of the instances of the class 'pen'. Rather, each 'pen' is responsible for keeping track of its own state and responding to messages appropriately.

In general, each object acts as an autonomous entity that is responsible for its own behavior but is not responsible for the behavior of any other objects. All of the information relevant to the individual behavior of an object is contained in that object; all of the information relevant to the similar behavior of a class of objects is contained in the class. Thus, the object-oriented style of programming supports the Information Hiding Principle in an essential way.

The Smalltalk Main Loop Is Written in Smalltalk

Like most interactive systems, Smalltalk is in a loop: Read a command, execute the command, print the result, and loop. This can be written in Smalltalk as follows:

```
true whileTrue: [Display put: user run]
```

This is an infinite loop that repeatedly executes the expression 'Display put: user run'. The variable 'user' contains an object called the 'user task'; this object responds to the message 'run' by reading an expression, evaluating it, and returning a string representing the result. The object Display represents the display screen and responds to the message 'put:' by writing out the argument string.

The simplest user task is an instance of the class 'userTask' shown here:

class name	userTask
instance messages and methods	
run | | Keyboard read eval print	

'Keyboard' is the object responsible for the keyboard on which the user types; it responds to the message 'read' by printing a prompt and returning a string containing the characters typed by the user. For example, if the user types 'x + 2', then the object returned by 'Keyboard read' is the string

```
"x+2"
```

Next, it is necessary that we know that strings respond to the message 'eval' by calling the Smalltalk compiler and interpreter to evaluate themselves. Thus, assuming 'x' is bound to 5, the result of

```
"x+2" eval
```

will be the object 7. We have already seen that objects respond to the message 'print' by returning a character string representation of themselves, so the result of '7 print' is the string

```
"7"
```

This is returned as the value of 'user run' and hence printed on the user's display by the main loop of the Smalltalk system.

Concurrency Is Easy to Implement

Recall that Smalltalk took many ideas from the simulation language Simula-67. Of course, in the real world many things happen simultaneously, or concurrently. Therefore, in a language intended to simulate aspects of the real world, it is important to be able to have several things going on at the same time. We have already seen an example of programming language support for concurrency: Ada's tasks. Message sending in Smalltalk is similar to the "rendezvous" in Ada. We will also see that the autonomous nature of Smalltalk's objects makes them ideal for concurrent programming.

How can we go about doing concurrent programming in Smalltalk? We saw how the main loop of the Smalltalk system ran the user task on every iteration. This suggests that we can do concurrent programming by having the main loop run each of a set of tasks. To do this we will assume that 'sched' is the name of a 'set' that contains all of the objects that are to run concurrently. Therefore, we want to run each object 'Task' in 'sched', that is, for each 'Task' in 'sched' we must evaluate 'Task run'. By a task we mean anything that responds to the message 'run'.

Although we could write a conventional loop for this, it is easier to use a variant of functional programming provided by Smalltalk. Specifically, a set *S* responds to '*S* map: *B*' by applying the block *B* to every element of the set. This is analogous to the LISP expression '(mapcar *B S*)' (see Chapter 10, Section 10.1). Finally, we need *B* to be a block that takes any object 'Task' and sends it the message 'run':

```
[: Task | Task run ]
```

This is analogous to a lambda expression (Chapter 10, Section 10.1) in LISP: '(lambda (Task) (Task run))'. Thus, we can define a class for scheduling concurrent tasks as follows:

class name	scheduler
instance messages and methods	
run | | sched map: [: Task | Task run]	

Every time we send the 'run' message to a 'scheduler' object, that object runs all the tasks in the 'sched' set.

To request that an object T be run concurrently with the other objects, it is only necessary to add it to 'sched':

```
sched add: T
```

Similarly, an object can be terminated (or temporarily suspended) by deleting it from 'sched'. This is just a very simple form of first-in—first-out scheduling; more sophisticated scheduling strategies can be implemented by keeping the objects in an ordered list and reordering the list according to some priority system.

EXERCISE 12-11: Figure 12.8 shows a simple example of concurrency—a class called 'spinner'. Explain what the user would see on the screen after the following two expressions are entered:

```
spinner newAt: 500@200 rate: 1.
spinner newAt: 500@600 rate: 3
```

12.5 IMPLEMENTATION: CLASSES AND OBJECTS

Overview of the Smalltalk-80 System

In this section we will discuss several important issues in the implementation of Smalltalk. The first is portability: Most of the Smalltalk system is written in

class name	spinner
instance variables	theBox rate
class messages and methods	

```
newAt: initLoc rate: R | |
   theBox ← box newAt: initLoc.
   rate ← R.
   theBox show.
   sched add: self
```

instance messages and methods

```
run | |
   theBox tilt: rate
```

Figure 12.8 Example of a Concurrent Class

Smalltalk. This includes the compiler, decompiler, debugger, editors, and file system, which accounts for approximately 97% of the code of the Smalltalk-80 system. A major reason that Smalltalk can be programmed in Smalltalk is that most of the implementation data structures, such as activation records, are Smalltalk objects. This means that they can be manipulated by Smalltalk programs and have the properties of Smalltalk objects (e.g., they are self-displaying).

The part of Smalltalk that is not portable is called the Smalltalk-80 Virtual Machine; its size is between 6 and 12 kilobytes of assembly code. The Smalltalk designers claim that it requires about one man-year to produce a fully debugged version of the Smalltalk Virtual Machine, which makes Smalltalk an excellent example of the Portability Principle.

The Smalltalk Virtual Machine has three major components:

- Storage Manager
- Interpreter
- Primitive Subroutines

The Storage Manager is the abstract data type manager for objects. As required by the Information Hiding Principle, it encapsulates the representation of objects and the organization of memory. The only operations that other modules can perform on objects are those provided by the Storage Manager:

- Fetch the class of an object
- Fetch and store the fields of objects
- Create new objects

Of course, if the Storage Manager is to be able to create new objects, it must be able to get free space in which to put them. Thus, another responsibility of the Storage Manager is collecting and managing free space. For this purpose it uses a reference counting strategy with extensions for cyclic structures (see Chapter 11, Section 11.2).

The Interpreter is the heart of the Smalltalk system. Although it would be possible to interpret the written form of Smalltalk directly, it is more efficient if the interpreter operates on an intermediate form of the program. Recall that we did essentially this with our symbolic pseudo-code interpreter in Chapter 1: We translated a more human-oriented written form into the internal numeric codes required by the interpreter. The operations of this intermediate language are essentially the operations of the Smalltalk Virtual Machine. In other words, the interpreter is essentially the abstract data type manager for methods.

The last component of the Smalltalk Virtual Machine is the Primitive Subroutines package. This is just a collection of the methods that, for performance reasons, are implemented in machine code rather than Smalltalk. They include basic input-output functions, integer arithmetic, subscripting of indexable objects (e.g., arrays), and basic screen graphics operations.

There are three central ideas in Smalltalk: objects, classes, and message sending. We will now investigate the implementation of each of these.

Object Representation

Much of Smalltalk's implementation can be derived by application of the Abstraction and Information Hiding Principles. For example, the representation of an object must contain just that information that varies from object to object; information that is the same over a class of objects is stored in the representation of that class. What is the information that varies between the instances of a class? It is just the *instance variables.* The information stored with the class includes the class methods and instance methods.

Notice, however, that we will not be able to access the information stored with the class of an object unless we know what the class of that object is. Therefore, the representation of an object must contain some indication of the class to which the object belongs. There are many ways to do this, and several have been used by the various Smalltalk implementations. The simplest is to include in the representation of the object a pointer to the data structure representing the class.

Let's consider the example shown in Figure 12.9, which shows the representation of two boxes, B1 and B2. To keep the figure clear, we have abbreviated or omitted some of the component objects. For example, the representation of the object '500@200' is shown, but the representation of '500@600' is abbreviated. Also, we have shown the names of the instance variables, although there is no reason actually to store them in the representation of objects. Finally, the representation of class objects is omitted because this topic is discussed next.

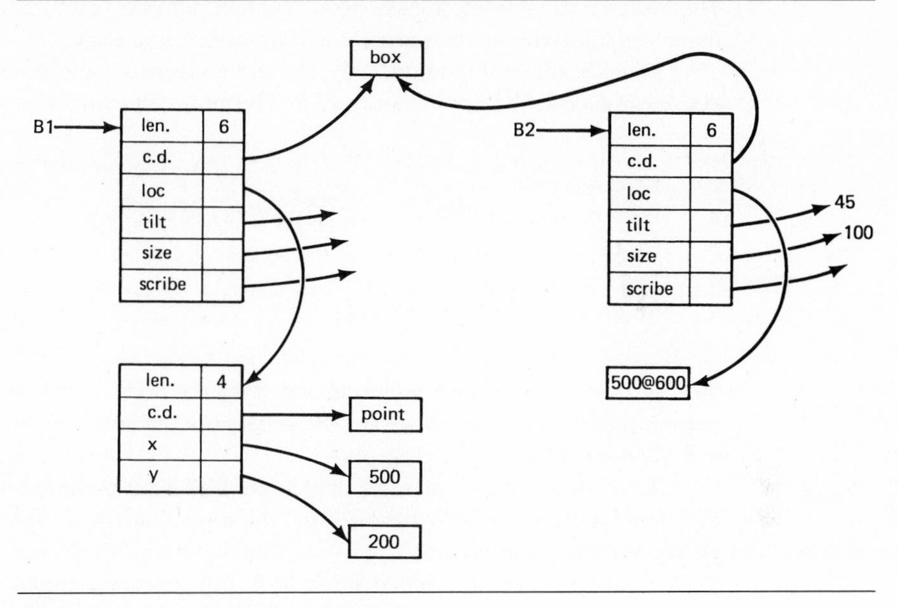

Figure 12.9 Representation of Objects

Notice that in addition to the instance variables and class description ('c.d.'), each object has a length field ('len.'). This is required by the storage manager for allocating, deallocating, and moving objects in storage.

EXERCISE 12-12: Considerable overhead is associated with the class description (c.d.) and length field in the representation of objects. For example, 50% of the space required for a 'point' object is used for the length and class description fields. An alternative to this is to divide memory into a number of *zones* with each zone being dedicated to holding the instances of just one class. Then, from the address of an object the storage manager can tell the zone it's in and, hence, both its class and length. This effectively encodes the class and length information as part of the address of an object. Analyze this implementation technique in detail. Describe the trade-offs between this technique and that described in the text, and discuss the advantages and disadvantages of the two techniques.

Class Representation

We have said that everything in Smalltalk is an object. This rule is true without exception. In particular it includes classes, which are just instances of the class named 'class'. Therefore, classes are represented like the objects just described, with length and class description fields (the latter pointing to the class 'class').

The instance variables of a class object contain pointers to objects representing the information that is the same for all instances of the class.

What is this information? We can get a clear idea by looking at a class definition, such as the one in Figure 12.5. The information includes the following:

1. The class name
2. The superclass (which is 'object' if no other is specified)
3. The instance variable names
4. The class message dictionary
5. The instance message dictionary

(Just as there are instance methods and class methods, Smalltalk allows both *instance variables* and *class variables*. We will ignore the latter, beyond mentioning that they are stored in the class object.)

Thus, observations of class definitions lead to a representation like that shown in Figure 12.10. (We have written the class of an object above the rectangle representing that object.)

Notice that we have added a field 'inst. size' (instance size), which indicates the number of instance variables. The number of instance variables is needed by the storage manager when it instantiates an object since this number determines the amount of storage required. If we did not have this field, it would be necessary to count the names in the string contained in the 'inst. vars.' field to determine this information. This would slow down object instantiation too much.

This leaves the message dictionaries for our consideration. In Smalltalk, a method is identified by the keywords that appear in a message invoking that

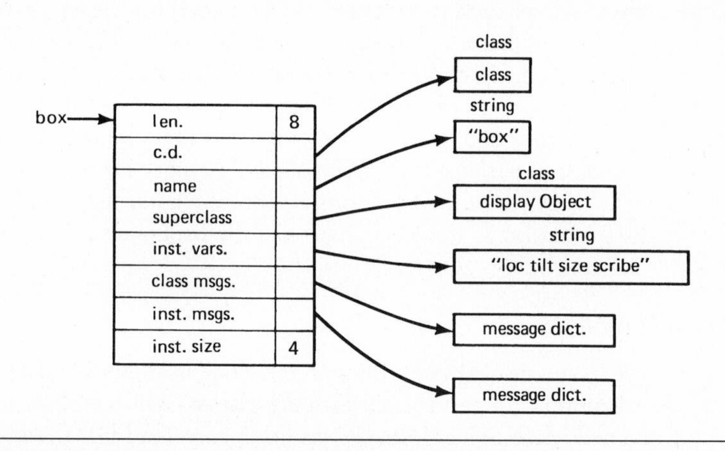

Figure 12.10 Representation of Class Object

method. For example, in 'Scribe go: 100' the keyword 'go:' identifies the method. For multiparameter messages, such as

```
spinner newAt: 500@200 rate: 1
```

the method is determined by the concatenation of the keywords: 'newAt:rate:'. This is called the *message template.* Thus, for each message template acceptable to a class or its instances, one of the message dictionaries must contain an entry specifying a method for that message. The entry can be found in the message dictionary by using hashing techniques.

How should methods be represented? It would be much too slow if the interpreter had to decode the source form of a method every time the method was executed. Therefore, it is a good idea to compile the methods into some form of pseudo-code that can be rapidly interpreted. On the other hand, the source form of methods is needed for editing and displaying class definitions. Therefore, the message dictionaries contain two entries for each message template: one containing the source form of the method and one containing a compiled form. Figure 12.11 shows the representation of a message dictionary.

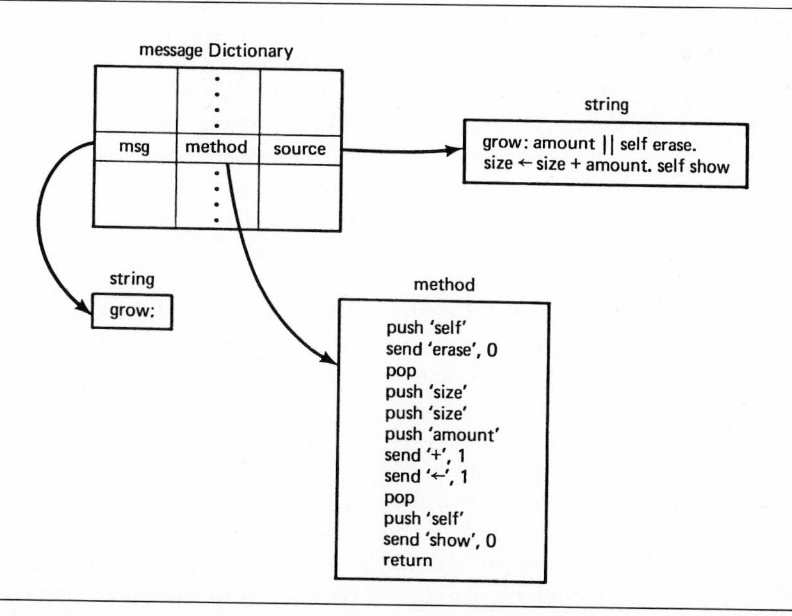

Figure 12.11 Example of a Message Dictionary and Compiled Code

Activation Record Representation

We will now investigate the implementation of message sending, the last of the three central ideas in Smalltalk. We have seen that there is a strong resemblance between message sending in Smalltalk and procedure calls in other languages. Thus, it should not be surprising that very similar implementation techniques are used, although there are some important differences.

In Chapters 2 and 6, we saw that *activation records* are the primary vehicle for procedure implementation. Since an activation record holds all of the information that pertains to one activation of a procedure, the processes of procedure call and return can be understood as the manipulation of activation records. The same is the case in Smalltalk: We will use activation records to hold all of the information relevant to one activation of a method.

What is the structure of an activation record? In Chapter 6 (Section 6.2), we saw that activation records for block-structured languages have three major parts. Smalltalk activation records follow the same pattern:

- *Environment part*: The context to be used for execution of the method
- *Instruction part*: The instruction to be executed when this method is resumed
- *Sender part*: The activation record of the method that sent the message invoking this method

We will consider these parts in reverse order.

The *sender part* is just the *dynamic link*, that is, a pointer from the receiver's activation record back to the sender's activation record. It is just an object reference since activation records, like everything else in Smalltalk, are objects.

The *instruction part* must designate a particular instruction in a particular method. Since methods are themselves objects (instances of class 'method'), a two-coordinate system is used for identifying instructions:

- An *object pointer* identifies the method-object containing all of the instructions of a method.
- A *relative offset* identifies the particular instruction within the method-object.

This two-coordinate addressing is necessary because instruction addressing goes through the storage manager (thus adhering to the Information Hiding Principle).

The final part of the activation record is the *environment part*, which must provide access to both the local and nonlocal environments. The local environment includes space for the parameters to the method and the temporary variables. This part of the activation record also must provide space for hidden temporary variables such as the intermediate results of expressions. For example, the local environment area for the method

```
newAt: initialLocation |newBox|
  newBox ← box new.
    ⋮
```

must contain space for the parameter 'initialLocation', the temporary variable 'newBox', and intermediate results:

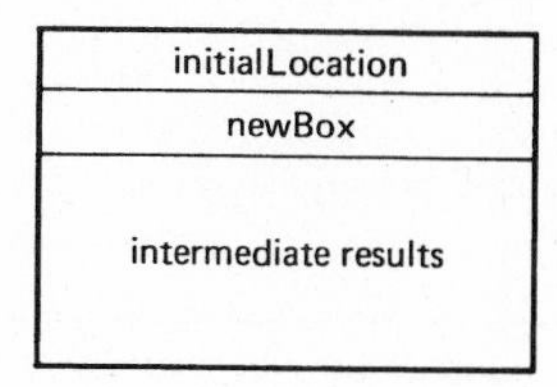

The nonlocal environment includes all other visible variables, namely, the instance variables and the class variables. The instance variables are stored in the representation of the object that received the message, therefore, a simple pointer to this object makes them accessible. The object representation contains a pointer to the class of which the object is an instance, therefore, the class variables are also accessible via the object reference. Finally, since the class representation contains a pointer to its superclass, the superclass variables are also accessible. The parts of an activation record are shown in Figure 12.12.

Notice that this approach to accessing nonlocals is very similar to the static chain of environments that we encountered in block-structured languages. There, the static chain led from the innermost active environment to the outermost environment. Here, the static chain leads from the active method to the object that received the message, and from there up through the class hierarchy, to terminate at the class 'object'. Just as in block-structured languages, variable accessing requires knowing the static distance to the variable and skipping that many links of the static chain to get to the environment that defines the variable. (If you are unclear about this, review Chapter 6, Section 6.1.)

EXERCISE 12-13: Show the code for accessing a Smalltalk variable, given its coordinates. Assume the environment coordinate is given as a static distance.

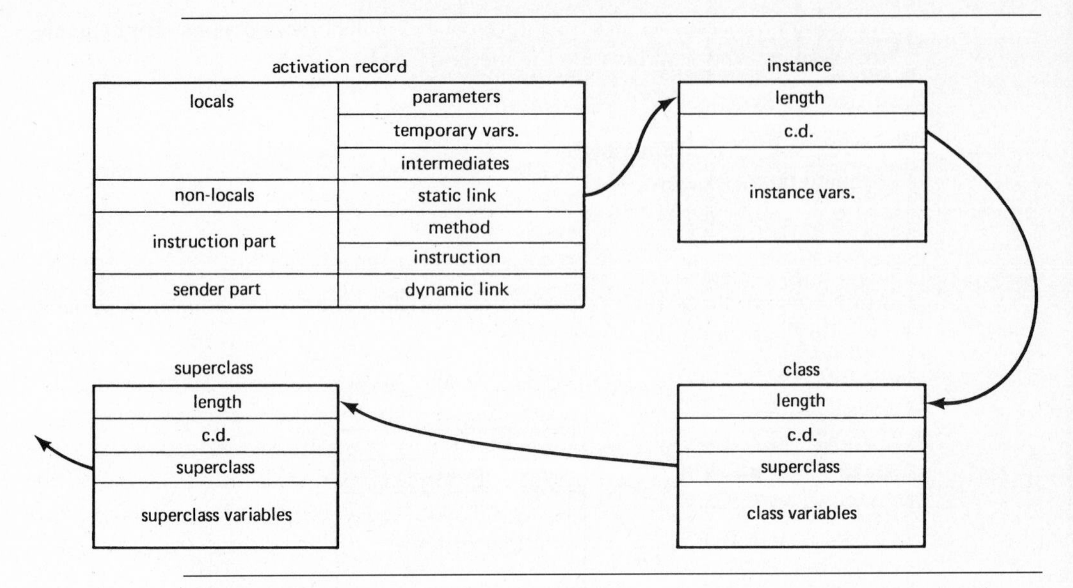

Figure 12.12 Parts of an Activation Record

Message Sending and Returning

We will now list and analyze the steps that must take place when a message is sent to an object:

1. Create an activation record for the receiver (callee).
2. Identify the method being invoked by extracting the template from the message and then looking it up in the message dictionary for the receiving object's class or superclasses. That is, if it's not defined in the class, we must look in the superclass; if it's not defined in the superclass, we must look in its superclass, and so on.
3. Transmit the parameters to the receiver's activation record.
4. Suspend the sender (caller) by saving its state in its activation record.
5. Establish a path (dynamic link) from the receiver back to the sender, and establish the receiver's activation record as the active one.

As we would expect, returning from a method must reverse this process:

1. Transmit the returned object (if any) from the receiver back to the sender.
2. Resume execution of the sender by restoring its state from its activation record.

We have omitted deallocation of the activation record as part of returning; we explain this next.

In accordance with the Information Hiding Principle, the Storage Manager handles allocation and deallocation of *all* objects; this includes activation record objects. The effect of this is that activation records are created from free storage and reclaimed by reference counting, just like other objects. This is the reason we don't explicitly deallocate activation records. This approach is quite different from the implementation of the other languages we've studied in which activation records occupy contiguous locations on a stack. The Smalltalk approach is a little less efficient, although this is compensated for by its greater simplicity and regularity.

There is another reason that Smalltalk does not allocate its activation records on a stack. The implementation of concurrency we discussed in Section 12.4 has an important limitation: The scheduler must wait for each task to return from its 'run' message before it can schedule the next task. In fact, if one of the tasks went into an infinite loop, the entire system might halt. Therefore, real Smalltalk systems provide an interrupt facility that automatically interrupts the executing task after it has run for a certain amount of time. This ensures that all of the active tasks get serviced regularly. It also means that a runaway task can be deactivated (removed from the 'sched' set) by another task.

What does this have to do with activation records? Consider what must occur when a task is interrupted. Since its execution is being suspended, its state must be stored in its activation record. Now, suppose that Smalltalk's activation records were held on a stack. Further, suppose that in a task *A*, the method *M* is activated; an activation record for *M* will be placed on the top of the stack. Suppose that before *M* returns, task *A* is interrupted and task *B* is resumed. Assume that task *B* activates method *N* , which causes an activation record for *N* to be stacked. The stack now looks like this:

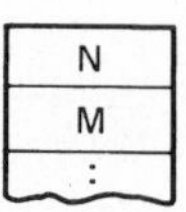

Next, suppose that task *B* is interrupted before *N* returns and that task *A* is resumed. Finally, suppose that task *M* returns and deletes its activation record from the stack. We are faced with two possibilities: Either (1) popping *M* will also pop off *N*'s activation record, which is incorrect since *N* has not returned; or (2) *M* is popped out of the middle of the stack leaving a hole, which means that we're not using a stack after all. The point is that a stack is the appropriate data structure only if we are dealing with something that follows a LIFO (last-in–first-out) discipline. Procedures in a sequential (i.e., nonconcurrent) language follow a LIFO discipline; procedures in a concurrent language do not.

EXERCISE 12-14: Write the instruction sequences for sending a message and returning from a method in Smalltalk. These are simple adaptations of the static chain call and return sequences discussed in Chapter 6, Section 6.2. Assume that the Storage Manager functions listed on p. 473 of the present section are available.

12.6 EVALUATION AND EPILOG

Smalltalk Is Small, Flexible, and Extensible

Smalltalk demonstrates what can be accomplished with a small, simple, regular language. The small number of independent concepts in Smalltalk makes it an easy language to learn. Its ideas are orthogonal—they can be understood independently—and are individually quite simple. Even concurrency is quite manageable since the object orientation of Smalltalk means that individual objects can be treated as autonomous actors.

Smalltalk has demonstrated its flexibility by being used in a number of applications, including simulations, games, office automation, graphics, computer-assisted instruction, and artificial intelligence. It has even been used in systems programming; recall that most of the Smalltalk system is written in Smalltalk.

The design of Smalltalk has been dictated by several powerful principles: Simplicity, Regularity, Abstraction, Security, and Information Hiding.

Smalltalk Is an Example of a Programming Environment

Smalltalk has introduced several important ideas other than the language itself. One of these is the idea of windows as a uniform interactive interface. The importance of windows is that they allow a large amount of information to be organized on a display screen and that they allow a programmer to keep track of several different activities at a time. Window-like systems have been adopted by many newer programming systems, including LISP machines, office automation systems, and even personal computers. As bit-mapped raster-scan display devices decrease in cost, windows can be expected to become very common.

Smalltalk is also an excellent example of an advanced programming environment (or integrated programming system). Although it was not the first programming environment, its integration of graphics, windows, and an advanced language demonstrate what can now be accomplished. The experience acquired in Smalltalk's design and use will be valuable to future programming environments, including those for conventional languages such as Ada.

Smalltalk Introduces a New Programming Paradigm

Smalltalk's most important contribution may be its distinctive view of programming. Although most of its ideas have appeared in other languages, Smalltalk's integration of these ideas is novel.

The essence of the Smalltalk view is that programming is simulation. Smalltalk incorporates into the language the idea that programs model, sometimes in a very abstract form, some aspects of the real world. Since the real world is populated by objects, Smalltalk provides an object-oriented method of programming. These programming objects have properties just like real-world objects.

Science develops models of the real world by classifying objects according to similarities in their behavior. Smalltalk does the same thing with its class structure. Classification is an essential part of organizing knowledge, although the strictly hierarchical classification provided by Smalltalk is inferior to a system that permits orthogonal classification.

We understand the interactions of objects by causal laws, in particular, by laws that determine how objects act when acted upon by other objects. Smalltalk permits causal interactions among objects by message sending: One object may cause another to do something by sending it a message. Just as in the real world, an object responds to a situation according to its nature, that is, according to its particular properties (its instance variables) and its general properties (its class).

Object-oriented programming—the systematic treatment of programming as simulation—provides a fundamentally different model of programming from those we've seen before. It is our second example of a *fifth-generation* programming paradigm. Whereas functional programming concentrates on timeless mathematical relationships, object-oriented programming addresses directly the behavior of objects in time. Which is better? The answer probably depends on the nature of the problem, on whether time is an essential aspect of the problem to be solved. It may very well be the case the function-oriented programming and object-oriented programming are *complementary*, rather than *competing*, fifth-generation programming language technologies.

EXERCISES

1*. For what purposes would you (or do you) use a very inexpensive, powerful personal computer. Would Smalltalk be a good language for these purposes? Would another language be better?

2. Define a class 'cell' that implements LISP-like list structures.

3*. Read about the Simula *class* mechanism (e.g., in Dahl, Dijkstra, and Hoare, *Structured Programming*, Academic Press, 1972) and compare it with Smalltalk's classes.

4**. Modify Smalltalk to permit nonhierarchical and orthogonal classification. Briefly discuss the implementation issues.

5*. Smalltalk has been used to implement several experimental software systems. Critique Alan Borning's article, "The Programming Language Aspects of ThingLab, a Constraint-Oriented Simulation Laboratory" (*ACM Trans. on Programming Languages and Systems 3*, 4, October 1981).

6*. Design a better message sending syntax for Smalltalk.

7*. Discuss Smalltalk's two-dimensional syntax.

8*. Show how to do object-oriented programming in LISP. That is, if B1 is an object of class 'box', then '(B1 grow: 10)' will send the message 'grow: 10' to B1.

9*. Discuss the problems of compiling Smalltalk into conventional object code. Pay particular attention to the matter of type checking.

10**. (Difficult) Write a Smalltalk Virtual Machine in some conventional language such as Pascal or Ada.

11*. The August 1981 issue of *Byte Magazine* (Vol. 6, No. 8) is devoted to Smalltalk. Critique one of the articles in this issue.

12*. Discuss the Smalltalk programming environment. Is this a good environment in which to develop software? What improvements can you suggest?

13*. Write an essay on the topic "Computer Programming Is Just Simulation."

13

LOGIC PROGRAMMING: PROLOG

13.1 HISTORY AND MOTIVATION

Nonprocedural Programming: Saying 'What' Instead of 'How'

Whenever things can be arranged in a series, it is natural to ask if there is a first or last element in the series. For example, once we know that one program can be *smaller* than another and perform the same function, it is natural to ask if there is a *smallest* program to do this function. Similarly, the notion of a faster program leads us to seek a fastest program, and the notion of a *better* program (by any criterion) leads us to ask if there is a *best* program.

One of the ways in which we judge a programming language is whether it is a *higher-level* language than another language. The general idea is that a language is higher level than another if we can express the same program with less detail. That is, a higher-level language does more automatically. This is valuable because if less is done manually, there is less chance of human error. An alternative way of expressing this is that a higher-level language is *less procedural* than a lower-level language. In other words, in a higher-level language we can concentrate more on *what* is to be done, and less on *how* to do it.

The notion of higher level immediately suggests the notion of highest level. Can there be a highest-level language? Similarly, the notion of a less-procedural language suggests the notion of a least-procedural language or even a *nonprocedural* language. What would this be? It would be a language in which the programmer stated only what was to be accomplished and left it to the computer to determine how it was to be accomplished.

Consider the following example. Suppose we wished to sort an array. How would we express this problem in a nonprocedural language? We would have to describe what we meant by sorting an array. For example, we might say that B is a sorting of A if and only if B is a permutation of A and B is ordered. We might also have to describe what we meant by a permutation and what we meant by an array being ordered. For the latter we might say that B is ordered if $B[i] \leqslant B[j]$ whenever $i<j$.

It would be the responsibility of the nonprocedural programming system to determine how to create an array B that is an ordered permutation of a given array A. Conceivably it might use any sorting algorithm, including a bubble sort, Shell-sort, or quick-sort. This selection is part of the procedural part of the programming process, which we are assuming is performed automatically.

Logic Programming and Automatic Deduction

Nonprocedural programming turns out to be related to an active research area in artificial intelligence: automated theorem proving. The goal of automated theorem proving is the development of programs that can construct formal proofs of propositions stated in a symbolic language. How is this connected with nonprocedural programming? Suppose that for a given array A we wanted to prove the proposition:

> There is an array B that is a sorting of A.

One way to prove this proposition is to exhibit the array B, thus proving that such an array exists. This is exactly the strategy that would be chosen by many automated theorem-proving systems. Thus, a side effect of proving that the array A *can* be sorted is *construction* of the sorted array.

Logic programming makes explicit use of the observation, made in the early 1970s by Pay Hayes, Robert Kowalski, Cordell Green, and others, that applying standard deduction methods often has the same effects as executing a program. Programs are expressed in the form of propositions that assert the existence of the desired result. The theorem prover then must construct the desired result to prove its existence.

In this chapter we investigate logic programming as the third example of a fifth-generation programming technology. We illustrate logic programming by means of the logic-oriented language *Prolog.*

Prolog Uses Symbolic Logic as a Programming Language

In the early 1970s, Alain Colmerauer, Philippe Roussel, and their colleagues of the Groupe d'Intelligence Artificielle of the University of Marseilles developed a programming language based on these ideas. It is called Prolog, which stands for "programming in logic." The GIA group developed a Prolog interpreter in Algol-W in 1972, in FORTRAN in 1973, and in Pascal in 1976. Since then Prolog interpreters and compilers have been developed for a number of computer systems, including personal computers.

Prolog has been growing in popularity as a language for artificial intelligence work since the mid-1970s; its proponents have suggested it as the successor to LISP for these applications. Although there are now many variants of logic programming, we will investigate Prolog since it is typical.[1]

13.2 DESIGN: STRUCTURAL ORGANIZATION

A Program Is Structured Like the Statement of a Theorem

Consider the Prolog program in Figure 13.1. It is divided into three major parts, much like the statement of a mathematical theorem. First, we have a series of *clauses* that define the problem domain, which in this case is kinship relations. For example, the first line can be read "*X* is a parent of *Y* if *X* is the father of *Y*." Thus, the first two lines express the idea that *X* is a parent of *Y* if either *X* is the father of *Y* or *X* is the mother of *Y*. The third line can be read, "*X* is a grandparent of *Z* if, for some *Y*, *X* is a parent of *Y* and *Y* is a parent of *Z*." The next two lines are a recursive definition of the ancestor relation: "*X* is an ancestor of *Z* if either *X* is a parent of *Z* or, for some *Y*, *X* is a parent of *Y* and *Y* is an ancestor of *Z*." You can see that it is fairly easy to translate our definitions of kinship ideas into Prolog.

The first part of this Prolog program states a number of general principles; the second part states a number of particular facts. Thus, we see that Albert is the

1 Prolog has not been standardized. In this chapter we follow the Edinburgh dialect described in Clocksin and Mellish (1984).

```
parent(X,Y) :- father(X,Y).
parent(X,Y) :- mother(X,Y).
grandparent(X,Z) :- parent(X,Y), parent (Y,Z).
ancestor(X,Z) :- parent(X,Z).
ancestor(X,Z) :- parent(X,Y), ancestor(Y,Z).
sibling(X,Y) :-  mother(M,X), mother(M,Y),
                 father(F,X),father (F,Y), X \= Y.
cousin(X,Y) :- parent(U,X), parent(V,Y), sibling(U,V).

father(albert, jeffrey).
mother(alice, jeffrey).
father(albert, george).
mother(alice, george).
father(john, mary).
mother(sue, mary).
father(george, cindy).
mother(mary, cindy).
father(george, victor).
mother(mary, victor).

:- ancestor(X, cindy), sibling(X, jeffrey).
```

Figure 13.1 Example Prolog Program

father of Jeffrey and that Alice is the mother of Jeffrey. This part of the Prolog program can be thought of as a *database* that defines interrelationships among the atomic individuals (people, in this example).

The parts of the Prolog program discussed so far all make *assertions.* To get the program to compute something, we must ask a *question.* This is the purpose of *goals,* which are usually typed interactively to a Prolog system. We can see an example of a goal in the last line of the Prolog program in Figure 13.1:

```
:- ancestor(X, cindy), sibling(X, jeffrey).
```

This goal asks if there is an individual who is an ancestor of Cindy and a sibling of Jeffrey. In this case, there is such an individual satisfying the goal, so the Prolog system responds:

```
X = george
```

We can find out if there are other individuals satisfying the goal by typing a semicolon after the previous answer.[2] In this case, there are no more, so the system responds 'no'.

Some goals merely ask if a fact is provable on the basis of the assertions. For example, a Prolog system will respond as shown to these goals:

```
:- grandparent(albert, victor).
yes
:- cousin(alice, john).
no
```

Note that when the Prolog system responds 'no' it does not necessarily mean that the goal is false; it means only that it could not be proved on the basis of the general rules and particular facts provided.

Some goals may require several individuals for their satisfaction and may be satisfiable in several ways. For example, if we type the goal

```
:- sibling(A,B).
```

we will receive the answer

```
A = jeffrey, B = george
```

There may be more solutions, so we type a semicolon after each, which yields the answers:

```
A = jeffrey, B = george;
A = george, B = jeffrey;
A = cindy, B = victor;
A = victor, B = cindy;
no
```

Notice that the system responds 'no' when there are no more solutions. Also notice that the system produces all possible ways of satisfying the goal, even if some of them are uninteresting.

EXERCISE 13-1: Show in detail how each of the above pairs satisfies the goal ':- sibling(A,B)'.

EXERCISE 13-2: Show in detail that X = 'george' satisfies the goal

```
:-ancestor(X, cindy), sibling(X, jeffrey).
```

2 This is the convention on many Prolog systems, but it is far from standard.

EXERCISE 13-3: Show in detail that the goal ':− grandparent (albert,victor)' is satisfiable.

EXERCISE 13-4: Show in detail that the goal ':− cousin(alice,john)' is unsatisfiable.

EXERCISE 13-5: Recall the personnel file example of Chapter 9 (Section 9.1). How might the facts about Don Smith be represented in Prolog?

Proving the Theorem Generates the Answer

The Prolog system may arrive at the answer 'X = george' by generating a proof such as the following: The goal is to find an X such that 'ancestor (X, cindy)' and 'sibling (X, jeffrey)'. Now, 'sibling (X, jeffrey)' is true if there are individuals M and F such that 'mother (M, jeffrey)', 'father (F, jeffrey)', 'mother (M, X)', and 'father (F, X)'. Now we see that if we set M = 'alice' and F = 'albert', we will have 'mother (M, jeffrey)' and 'father (F, jeffrey)'. But it's now necessary to find an X such that 'mother (alice, X)' and 'father (albert, X)'; this X is 'george'.

This is not our answer though since there may be other X's that are siblings of Jeffrey; we must also determine if 'ancestor (george, cindy)' is true. Now 'ancestor (george, cindy)' is true if either 'parent (george, cindy)' or there is a Y such that 'parent (george, Y)' and 'ancestor (Y, cindy)'. Further, 'parent (george, cindy)' is true if either 'father (george, cindy)' or 'mother (george, cindy)' is true. But we are given 'father (george, cindy)', so the theorem is true with X = 'george'.

EXERCISE 13-6: Determine if the following goals can be satisfied, and if so, exhibit the individuals that satisfy them:

```
:- sibling(X, cindy).
:- ancestor(albert, victor).
:- ancestor(john, X).
:- ancestor(jeffrey, mary).
:- grandparent(john, X), parent(Y, X), sibling(Y, jeffrey).
:- cousin(X,Y).
```

Clauses Are Constructed from Relationships

A Prolog program is constructed from a number of *clauses.* These clauses have three forms: *hypotheses* (or *facts*) such as

```
mother(mary, cindy).
```

goals, such as

```
:- ancestor(john,X).
```

and *conditions* (or *rules*) such as

```
grandparent(X,Z) :- parent(X,Y), parent(Y,Z).
```

In *pure* logic programming, the order of these clauses is irrelevant to the logic of the program, although it may be very important in Prolog (which is only *logic-oriented*). Issues relating to the ordering of clauses are discussed in Section 13.4.

The general form of a clause is:

```
<head> :- <body>.
```

If '<head>' is omitted, the clause is considered a goal; if ':- <body>' is omitted, it is considered a hypothesis. Both the <head> and the <body> are composed of *relationships* (also called *predications* or *literals*), which are applications of a *predicate* (such as 'parent') to one or more *terms* (such as 'john' and 'X'):

```
parent(john,X)
```

Relationships are intended to represent properties of and relations among the individuals of the problem domain. Terms may be (1) atoms, such as 'john' or '25'; (2) variables, such as 'X'; or (3) compound terms, which are described below. Note that many Prolog systems require variables to begin with an uppercase letter, and other terms to begin with a lowercase letter (or a nonletter). This is the convention adopted in this chapter, although there is little standardization among Prolog systems.[3]

Prolog, like many logic programming languages, allows at most one relationship in the <head> of a clause but any number in the <body>. This restriction is called the *Horn clause form*; it permits an especially efficient kind of automatic deduction.

EXERCISE 13-7: To define 'brother', 'sister', 'son', and 'daughter', we need to know the sex of individuals. Add rules and facts to the program of Figure 13.1 to define these predicates. *Hint:* Define 'male' and 'female'.

Terms Can Be Compound

In all of the examples we've seen so far, the terms have been names—either constants such as 'cindy' or variables such as 'X'. Since terms represent individuals in

3 Also, some Prolog systems use '←', 'if' or other symbols instead of ':-'.

the problem domain, constant terms represent specific individuals and variable names represent indefinite individuals. Although it is easy to show that any proposition can be expressed by using just constant and variable terms, it is often convenient to allow expressions as terms, which are called *compound terms.* These give us the ability to describe individuals without giving them individual names.

The value of compound terms will be clearer if we look at an example. Suppose that we wanted to write a Prolog program to do symbolic differentiation. We must express the idea that the derivative of $U + V$ with respect to X is $DU + DV$, where DU is the derivative with respect to X of U and DV is the derivative with respect to X of V. These ideas are easy to write using compound terms:

```
d(X, plus(U,V), plus(DU,DV)) :- d(X,U,DU), d(X,V,DV).
```

The name 'plus' is called a *functor* because it acts in many ways like a function. Notice, however, that in the compound term 'plus(U,V)' no function is being called; rather this term is a data structure similar to the LISP list '(plus U V)'. A functor is just a *tag* that can be used on data structures (i.e., compound terms).

The above differentiation rule can be made even clearer if we allow (as some Prologs do) the use of infix functors:

```
d(X, U+V, DU+DV) :- d(X,U,DU), d(X,V,DV).
```

Here 'DU + DV' does not mean arithmetic addition; it is simply an alternate notation for the compound term 'plus(DU,DV)'.

To express this clause without the use of compound terms requires us to introduce a predicate 'sum(X ,Y,Z)', which means $X + Y = Z$. The resulting clause for the derivative of a sum is

```
d(X,W,Z) :- sum(U,V,W), d(X,U,DU), d(X,V,DV), sum(DU,DV,Z).
```

This is considerably more difficult to read and also has some subtle difficulties that are discussed later (p. 500). We will see further applications of compound terms in Section 13.3, Data Structures. (See Figure 13.2 for a more complete symbolic differentiation program.)

13.3 DESIGN: DATA STRUCTURES

There Are Few Primitives and No Constructors

We will see in the following section that there are essentially no data structure constructors in Prolog. Rather, data structures are defined implicitly by their properties. The same approach could be used to define all data types, including traditionally primitive types such as the integers. For example, the natural numbers and natural number arithmetic could be defined by clauses such as these:

```
sum(succ(X),Y,succ(Z)) :- sum(X,Y,Z).
sum(0,X,X).
dif(X,Y,Z) :- sum(Z,Y,X).
```

The first clause says that the sum of the successor of X plus Y is the successor of Z, *if* the sum of X and Y is Z. The second clause says that the sum of zero and X is X. The third clause says that the difference of X and Y is Z, *if* the sum of Z and Y is X. In effect, this is a recursive definition of arithmetic. If we type the goal

```
:- sum(succ(succ(0)), succ(succ(succ(0))), A).
```

(meaning '$2+3=A$'), we will get the answer

```
A = succ(succ(succ(succ(succ(0)))))
```

(meaning '5').

Although this definition of addition and subtraction is correct, it would be very inefficient to use since all computers implement integer arithmetic directly. Hence, all Prolog systems build in certain predicates and functions for basic arithmetic. Unfortunately, as usually implemented, the logical properties are compromised. For example, addition cannot be done "backwards" as is done in the above definition of 'dif'. This is discussed further in Section 13.4, p. 511.

The small number of built-in data types and operations in Prolog is an example of the Simplicity Principle. The uniform treatment of all data types as predicates and terms is an example of the Regularity Principle.

EXERCISE 13-8: Explain in detail the satisfaction of the goal corresponding to '$2+3=A$'.

EXERCISE 13-9: Write a goal corresponding to '$4-2=D$' and show its satisfaction.

Compound Terms Can Represent Data Structures

Prolog doesn't have a fixed set of data structure constructors as Pascal and Ada do. Rather, Prolog can operate directly with a logical description of the properties of a data structure. LISP-style lists form a good example of this.

Recall that in Chapter 9, Section 9.3, we saw these equations, which form an abstract definition of LISP lists:

```
(car (cons X L)) = X
(cdr (cons X L)) = L
(cons (car L) (cdr L)) = L, for nonnull L
where L is a list and X is an atom or list.
```

It turns out that only the first two of these are necessary, since we can prove the third if we assume that every list is either 'nil' or the result of a 'cons' call (you will prove this in an exercise).

We take the first two equations as a basis for a Prolog definition of lists:

```
car( cons(X,L), X).
cdr( cons(X,L), L).
```

This means that if we take the 'car' of 'cons(*X*,*L*)', we'll get *X*, and if we take the 'cdr' of 'cons(*X*,*L*)', we'll get *L*. Notice that 'car' and 'cdr' are predicates; for example, 'car(*L*,*A*)' means that the 'car' of *L* is *A*. On the other hand, 'cons' is a functor; thus, 'cons(a,nil)' is a compound term with components 'a' and 'nil'.

To complete this implementation of lists, we need to define the predicates 'null' and 'list'. When is something a list? There are two ways to get a list in LISP: (1) take the *primitive* list, 'nil', or (2) *construct* a list by applying 'cons' to an arbitrary value and a list. In other words, *X* is a list if either it is 'nil' or it is a result of 'cons':

```
list(nil).
list(cons(X,L)) :- list(L).
```

Since the only way to get a null list is as a result of 'nil', we write:

```
null(nil).
```

Notice that we have not written a rule for 'null(*L*)' for the case when *L* is nonnull: Prolog will take a list to be nonnull when it cannot prove that it's null (via the fact stated above).

There is something rather unusual going on here: There is no separate representation for lists; lists are represented by the expressions that construct them. Thus, we might type into a LISP system:

```
(car (cons '(A B) '(C D)))
  (A B)
```

To accomplish the same thing in Prolog, we would enter the goal:

```
:- car( cons( cons(a, cons(b,nil)),
              cons(c, cons(d,nil)) ), X).
X = cons(a,cons(b,nil))
```

We can see that the answers are equivalent although the LISP notation for constant lists is much clearer. To solve this readability problem, some Prolog systems allow infix operators in compound terms. For example, if '.' were used for 'cons', the above goal and its solution would be[4]:

```
:- car( (a.b.nil).(c.d.nil), X )
X = a.b.nil
```

Indeed, most Prolog systems make a special case of the dot operator and allow the abbreviation:

$[X_1, X_2, \ldots X_n] = X_1.X_2. \cdots .X_n.\mathrm{nil}$

In addition, 'nil' is usually written '[]'. Thus, we could write:

```
:- car( [[a,b],c,d], X).
X = [a,b]
```

as expected. Don't let the syntactic sugar fool you, though: Lists are just compound terms.

EXERCISE 13-10: Given that every list L is either 'nil' or the result of a 'cons', prove

(cons (car L) (cdr L)) = L, for nonnull L

from the other two list equations.

Components Are Accessed Implicitly

Let's consider an example using these definitions of lists: the 'append' function described in Chapter 9 (Section 9.3). We will define this function as a predicate 'append' such that 'append(X, Y, Z)' means that Z is the result of appending X and Y. The approach is the same as we used in Chapter 9: First handle the primitive (null) list and then handle constructed lists. The clauses are

4 Note that '.' is right-associative: 'a.b.nil' means 'a.(b.nil)'.

```
append( [], L, L).
append( X.L, M, X.N) :- append(L,M,N).
```

(We use the '.' abbreviation for 'cons'.) The last clause can be read: "The result of appending the 'cons' of *X* and *L* to *M* is the 'cons' of *X* and *N*, where *N* results from appending *L* and *M*."

Let's consider a few steps in the execution of the goal

```
:- append( [a, b], [c, d], Ans).
```

When stripped of syntactic sugar, this is equivalent to:

```
:- append( a.b.[], c.d.[], Ans).
```

The Prolog system will attempt to match this goal to the clauses for 'append'. It does this by a process called *unification,* which means finding an assignment of values to the variables that makes the goal identical to the head of one of the clauses. In this case, the match will succeed on the second clause with X = 'a', L = 'b.[]', M = 'c.d.[]', and Ans = 'a.*N*'. Hence, these variables are bound to these values (*instantiated,* in Prolog terminology), which leads to the subgoal

```
:- append( b.[], c.d.[], N).
```

This will eventually result in *N* being bound to 'b.c.d.[]' (you will fill in the steps in an exercise). Then, since Ans = 'a.*N*', Ans will be bound to 'a.b.c.d.[]'. The latter, when sugared on output, will be printed as

```
Ans = [a, b, c, d]
```

Compare the Prolog with the LISP definition of 'append':

```
(defun append (L M)
  (cond
    ((null L) M)
    (t (cons (car L) (append (cdr L) M)) )) )
```

They are similar in that they are both recursive definitions based on the null list. They are different in that the LISP definition uses 'car' and 'cdr' explicitly to break L into its components, whereas the Prolog definition doesn't use 'car' and 'cdr' at all. Instead, by matching a pattern such as 'X.L' against a list such as 'a.b.[]', it implicitly breaks the list into its components X = 'a' and L = 'b.[]'.[5]

Frequently in Prolog selector functions are not needed to access the components of composite data structures; instead, the data structures can be matched against the appropriate constructor expressions. This is essentially asking the question: "What two things would I have to 'cons' together to get 'a.b.[]'?" Thus, "taking apart" is explained in terms of "putting together." Inverse operations are often thought of in this way. For example, we might explain $5-3$ to a child by asking: "What number do I add to 3 to get 5?" This is the basis for the definition of 'dif' that we showed on p. 493.

Although matching is a very simple way to select components of structures, it is not necessarily a very efficient way. Recall that LISP's 'car' and 'cdr' functions are implemented as simple pointer-following operations and thus are very efficient. In Prolog, component selection is accomplished by pattern matching, which is usually much less efficient. Some Prolog implementors have developed optimizations that make component selection in Prolog almost as fast as in LISP.

EXERCISE 13-11: Fill in the rest of the steps of the 'append' example above.

EXERCISE 13-12: Define the 'assoc' function (Chapter 9, Section 9.3) in Prolog.

EXERCISE 13-13: Write a predicate 'equal' analogous to the LISP 'equal' function. That is, it determines if two lists are equal in all their elements and to arbitrary depth. *Hint:* This is *very* simple in Prolog.

EXERCISE 13-14: Write clauses for a predicate 'sum_red(*L*,*S*)' such that *S* is the sum-reduction of the list *L*. (Use the 'sum' predicate already defined and assume numbers are represented in unary.)

EXERCISE 13-15: Write clauses for a predicate 'succ_map(*L*,*M*)' such that the list *M* is the result of taking the successor of every element of the list *L*.

Complex Structures Can Be Defined Directly

We have seen in the previous sections how compound terms can be used to represent data structures. In particular, we have used terms of the form 'cons(*X*, *Y*)' (or '*X*. *Y*') to represent lists. This is such a common use of compound terms that many Prolog programmers think of compound terms as records, similar to the records in Pascal and Ada. Thus, 'cons(*X*, *Y*)' is not thought of as a function

5 Many Prologs allow '[X|L]' as an alternate notation for a list whose head is X and whose tail is L.

application; rather, it is considered a record of type 'cons' with the fields X and Y. And, in fact, this is essentially the way many Prolog systems implement compound terms.

We know from our investigation of LISP that any structure we want can be defined with lists. In Prolog it is not necessary to do this since more complicated structures can be defined directly as terms or predicates. For example, suppose we want to write a program for performing symbolic differentiation. In most programming languages, it would be necessary to define data structures representing algebraic expression trees. In Prolog we can simply use compound terms. For example, the expression '$x^2 + bx + c$' could be represented by

```
plus( plus( sup(x,2), times(b,x) ), c)
```

Since many Prolog dialects interpret the arithmetic operators as functors for constructing compound terms, in these dialects we could write

```
x↑2 + b*x + c
```

Again, we must emphasize that this is just syntactic sugar for a compound term similar to the one shown previously in prefix notation.[6]

Given the infix notation for compound terms, the symbolic differentiation program is easy to write and read (see Figure 13.2). Here, the terms represent themselves; there is no need for a separate data structure for the program to manipulate. The Prolog system essentially generates records of the form 'plus (X, Y)', 'times(X, Y)', and so on, but this is not a concern of the programmer. Thus, the Automation Principle is being obeyed.

EXERCISE 13-16: Trace the execution of the following goal:

```
:- d(x, x↑2 + b*x + c, Ans).
Ans = 2 * x↑(2-1) * 1 + (0 * x + b * 1) + 0
```

Notice that the expression is not simplified by these rules.

EXERCISE 13-17: Trace the execution of the goal: ':- d(x, x+y, A)'.

EXERCISE 13-18: Trace the execution of the goal:

```
:- d(t, 2*t + x, Rate).
```

6 Some Prolog dialects permit programmers to define their own prefix, infix, and postfix functor symbols.

```
d(X, U+V, DU+DV) :- d(X,U,DU), d(X,V,DV).
d(X, U-V, DU-DV) :- d(X,U,DU), d(X,V,DV).
d(X, U*V, DU*V + U*DV) :- d(X,U,DU), d(X,V,DV).
d(X, U/V, (DU*V-U*DV)/V↑2) :- d(X,U,DU), d(X,V,DV).
d(X, U↑C, C * U↑(C-1) * DU) :- d(X,U,DU), atomic(C), C \= X.
d(X, X, 1).
d(X, C, 0) :- atomic(C), C \= X.
```

Figure 13.2 Symbolic Differentiation in Prolog

EXERCISE 13-19: Trace the execution of the goal:

```
:- d(y, y↑n / (x+y), Dy).
```

EXERCISE 13-20: Write a differentiation rule for negations. Assume "negative U" is written '~U'.

EXERCISE 13-21: Write a differentiation rule for the special case 'C*U', where C is atomic and C≠X.

Predicates Can Represent Structures Directly

We have said before that compound terms can often be replaced by predicates. For example, instead of having terms 'plus(X,Y)', 'times(X,Y)', etc. representing arithmetic expressions, we could have predicates 'sum(X,Y,Z)', 'prod(X,Y,Z)', etc. Let's consider the consequences of this in more detail.

Consider the compound term '(x + y) * (y + 1)' representing an arithmetic expression. This is a description of a data structure—a tree—as can be seen by writing it in prefix notation:

```
times(plus(x,y),plus(y,1))
```

Thus, it is exactly analogous to a LISP structure such as:

```
(times (plus x y) (plus y 1))
```

How can we express these same relationships in terms of predicates? In effect we need to describe a tree in terms of relationships among its nodes. We can get a hint of how to do this by recalling the kinship program in Figure 13.1. There we used the predicates 'father' and 'mother' to describe a *family tree.* We can describe the relationships in an *arithmetic expression tree* by predicates such as 'sum' and 'prod'.[7] For example, let 'sum(X, Y,Z)' mean that the sum of X and Y is Z. Then the expression '(x + y) * (y + 1)' is described by the three facts:

```
sum(x,y,t1).
sum(y,1,t2).
prod(t1,t2,t3).
```

since they say that the sum of 'x' and 'y' is 't1', the sum of 'y' and '1' is 't2', and the product of 't1' and 't2' is 't3'. We can see the first difficulty with representing data structures as predicates: the loss of readability.

Suppose we write our differentiation program (Figure 13.2) so that it works with expressions represented as predicates. The sum and product rules would look like this:

```
d(X,W,Z) :- sum(U,V,W), d(X,U,DU), d(X,V,DV), sum(DU,DV,Z).
d(X,W,Z) :- prod(U,V,W), d(X,U,DU), d(X,V,DV),
            prod(DU,V,A), prod(U,DV,B), sum(A,B,Z).
d(X,X,1).
d(X,C,0) :- atomic(C), C \= X.
```

The sum rule doesn't look bad; it's quite readable: "The derivative with respect to X of W is Z if: W is the sum of U and V, and the derivative with respect to X of U is DU, and . . . ." The product rule is not so good though. The variables 'A' and 'B' get in the way; the only reason they are there is that we have to be able to name the intermediate nodes in the expression tree. So the predicate representation also makes the *rules* less readable. There are more subtle problems, however.

Suppose we have the following fact in our database:

```
sum(x,1,z).
```

This says that the sum of 'x' and 1 is 'z'. Now suppose we enter the goal

```
:- d(x,z,D).
```

This asks the system to find a 'D' such that the derivative with respect to 'x' of 'z' is 'D'. Since 'z' is the sum of 'x' and 1, we expect 'D' to be the sum of 1 and 0.

7 Here we use 'sum' to represent an algebraic relationship between terms. There is no relationship between this use of the predicate 'sum' and its use to perform unary addition shown earlier.

Will the goal be satisfied? It unifies with the head of the sum rule by the assignments X = x, W = z, Z = D, which leads to the subgoals:

```
:- sum(U,V,z), d(x,U,DU), d(x,V,DV), sum(DU,DV,D).
```

The first subgoal is satisfied by U = x and V = 1, since we have in our database the fact 'sum(x,1,z)'. Hence, we get the subgoals:

```
:- d(x,x,DU), d(x,1,DV), sum(DU,DV,D).
```

Now the first two subgoals here are satisfied by DU = 1 and DV = 0, so only one subgoal is left:

```
:- sum(1,0,D).
```

It seems that our program is done, but in fact this subgoal will *fail*, since there is no fact (or rule) of the form 'sum(1,0,*D*)' in the database! Of course, if we had had the foresight to make an assertion such as

```
sum(1,0,a).
```

then the system would report the correct[8] answer 'D = a', but it is unreasonable to expect such foresight. Had the answer been more complicated, the situation would be even worse, since we would have had to anticipate the entire expression tree of the answer, else the system wouldn't find it.

Prolog Models a Closed World

What is the source of this unintuitive behavior? The deductive rules of Prolog are based on a "closed world" assumption. This means that, so far as Prolog is concerned, all that's true about the world is what can be proved on the basis of the facts and rules in its database. In many applications this is a reasonable assumption. For example, in our kinship program it is reasonable to assume that there are no people and no relationships among people other than those represented (explicitly or implicitly) in the database. It makes sense to assume that there is no object having a given property if one cannot be found in the database. The closed-world assumption is very reasonable in *object-oriented* kinds of applications, that is, in applications in which the objects and relationships in the computer model those in a real or imagined world.

Where the closed-world assumption does not work well is in mathematical problems. In mathematics an object is generally taken to exist if its existence

8 The answer is correct because the fact 'sum(1,0,a)' asserts that 'a' is the sum of 1 and 0.

does not contradict the axioms. Mathematically, it's natural to assume that an expression of the form '1 + 0' exists whenever one is needed. Its existence does not have to be explicitly asserted or provable from the hypotheses. Of course, we could explicitly axiomatize the existence of all arithmetic expressions we might need, but this seems unnatural and more trouble than it's worth.

In summary, it's possible to replace compound terms with predicates connecting their parts, but the closed-world assumption makes it hard to guarantee the right objects are there when we need them. Perhaps the conclusion we should draw is that predicates should be used for expressing object-oriented relationships and compound terms should be used for mathematical relationships.

Data Structures Are Inherently Abstract

We have discussed *abstract data types* in many places in this book: An abstract data type is a set of data values together with the operations defined on those data values. The primary value of abstract data types is that they are implementation independent, which makes them easier to maintain and more portable. Notice that in Prolog *all data types are inherently abstract.* This is so because the only way to describe a data type in Prolog is to give an abstract, algebraic description of the properties of its operations. The Prolog system decides on the proper representation of the data. We can view this as a nonprocedural approach to data structures.

A result of Prolog's approach to data types is a strict adherence to the Security Principle since the only operations defined on data values are those that the programmer has specifically described.

Should Infinite Terms Be Permitted?

Suppose we have the fact 'equal(X,X)' in the database and that we type in the goal ':− equal(f(Y),Y)'. What will happen? The only way to satisfy this goal is to unify 'equal(f(Y),Y)' with 'equal(X,X)'. That is, we have to find bindings of 'X' and 'Y' that make these two relationships equal. The only way to do this is to bind Y = 'f(Y)', which makes the goal ':− equal(f(Y),f(Y))', which obviously unifies with the fact 'equal(X,X)' by the assignment X = 'f(Y)'. Since the goal has been successfully satisfied, the Prolog system will print out the resulting bindings. We will see something like this:

```
Y =  f(f(f(f(f(f(f(f(f(f(f(f(f(f(f(f(f(f(f(f(f(f(f(f(f(f(f(f(f(f(f(f(f(f(f(f(f(f(f(f(f(f(f(f(f(f(f(f(f
     f(f(f(f(f(f(f(f(f(f(f(f(f(f(f(f(f(f(f(f(f(f(f(f(f(f(f(f(f(f(f(f(f(f(f(f(f(f(f(f(f(f(f(f(f(f(f(f(f
     ....
```

The system will continue printing 'f(' until we stop it. What's happened?

The system is attempting to print out the value of 'Y'. But the value of 'Y' is 'f(Y)'. So to print this it must print 'f(', followed by the value of 'Y', followed by ')'. But the value of 'Y' is 'f(Y)', and so on and so on. The variable 'Y' is in effect bound to an infinite term, which we can see by substituting 'f(Y)' for 'Y' every time it occurs:

```
Y  =  f(Y)
   =  f(f(Y))
   =  f(f(f(Y)))
   ⋮
   =  f(f(f(f(f(f(f(f(f(f(f( ··· )))))))))))
```

What are we to make of infinite terms? In the context of logic they are illegitimate, and if Prolog implemented the resolution algorithm correctly, it would not permit them. However, to prevent them would require checking to make sure that a variable is not bound to a term containing itself. This "occurs check" is relatively expensive; it takes quadratic time. Since unification is otherwise linear, implementing the check could significantly slow down the execution of Prolog programs. Hence, most Prologs do not make the "occurs check" and thus will behave as illustrated above.

Can this liability be turned into an asset? Or, as some would say, can this bug be turned into a feature? A self-embedding term is not necessarily meaningless. If f is a function, then the equation $Y = f(Y)$ asserts that Y is a *fixed point* of the function f. Now, some functions have fixed points and some don't. For example, the sine function has a fixed point at zero ($0 = \sin 0$); the logarithm function does not have a fixed point. Hence, in some contexts, the equation $Y = f(Y)$ may be perfectly meaningful.

But, you may object, an infinite term is an infinite data structure. Even if it makes sense mathematically, it can't have any use in a program. As the example shows, the computer can't even print it out. In fact, infinite terms such as these *are* representable on computers—by circularly linked lists. If we take a list $Y = (f\ X)$ and store into the left ('car') component of its second cell a pointer back to the head of the list, then we will have a list satisfying the equation $Y = (f\ Y)$. If we traverse this list by following the pointers, it will look for all the world like an infinite data structure, but it is represented in a finite amount of memory. In the case of the Prolog binding Y = 'f(Y)', the circular link is through the symbol table that binds 'Y' to its value.

We have previously noted (Chapter 11, Section 11.2) that there isn't agreement on whether circular structures should be permitted. There are certainly difficulties, both theoretical and practical (e.g., how do you print them?). On the other hand, Colmerauer and other computer scientists have argued that circular structures are the natural way to represent information in a variety of domains, including language processing and optimization.

*EXERCISE 13-22**: Discuss the usefulness of infinite terms. Show some situations in which they would be convenient. How would you handle these situations if infinite terms were prohibited? Should Prolog permit them or prohibit them?

13.4 DESIGN: CONTROL STRUCTURES

Logic Programming Separates Logic and Control

Logic programs do not have control structures in the usual sense.[9] In a conventional programming language control structures determine the order in which the actions comprising a program take place. This order is essential to the correctness of the program; indeed, it is unusual when the order of statements can be changed without altering the meaning of the program. Thus, the *logic* of a program is intimately related to its *control.*

Logic programming effects a much greater separation of logic and control. The order in which the clauses of a program are written has no effect on the meaning of the program. In other words, the logic of the program is determined by the logical interrelationships of the clauses, not by their physical relationship.

Control affects the order in which actions occur in time. The only actions that occur in the execution of a logic program are the generation and unification of subgoals. As we will see, this order can have a major effect on the efficiency of the program. Hence, in logic programming, issues of control affect only the performance of programs, not their meaning or correctness.

The separation of logic and control is an important application of the Orthogonality Principle. It means that a program can be developed in two distinct phases: logical analysis and control analysis. *Logical analysis* is entirely concerned with the correctness of the program, in other words, with producing the correct clauses to characterize the answer. *Control analysis* is entirely concerned with the efficiency of the program. It may be performed entirely by the logic programming system, or it may be partially under the control of the programmer. For example, the order in which the programmer writes clauses may affect the order in which subgoals are generated and hence the program's performance. Other systems allow the programmer to give the interpreter hints, such as that

9 Note that in this section the term "logic program" refers to *pure* logic programs. We will see later that Prolog programs are not *pure* logic programs. Material in this section is based on the work of Robert Kowalski (1979).

certain predicates are functions. In every case, there is a clear separation of logic—what the program does—from control—how it does it.

Top-Down Control Is Like Recursion

There are two principal ways in which subgoals can be generated: top-down and bottom-up. In top-down control, we start from the goal and attempt to reach the hypotheses; in bottom-up control, we start with the hypotheses and attempt to reach the goal.

To illustrate the difference between these, we will use a simple example: the generation of Fibonacci numbers. The Fibonacci numbers are the series

1, 1, 2, 3, 5, 8, 13, 21, ...

in which each number is the sum of the two previous numbers. Hence, if F_n represents the nth Fibonacci number, then

$$
\begin{aligned}
F_0 &= 1 \\
F_1 &= 1 \\
F_n &= F_{n-1} + F_{n-2}, \qquad \text{for } n>1
\end{aligned}
$$

This can easily be expressed in a logic program in which the relationship 'fib(*N*, *F*)' means that the *N*th Fibonacci number is *F*[10]:

```
fib(0,1).
fib(1,1).
fib(N,F) :- N = M+1, M = K+1, fib(M,G), fib(K,H),
            F = G+H, N > 1.
```

That is, the *N*th Fibonacci number is *F* if there are natural numbers *K* and *M*, with $N = M+1 > 1$, $M = K+1$, such that the *M*th Fibonacci number is *G*, the *K*th Fibonacci number is *H*, and $F = G+H$.

Let's trace the top-down execution of the goal

```
:- fib(2,F).
```

To satisfy this goal, we must find a clause with which it can be *unified*, that is, a clause that can be made identical to the goal by some assignment of values to the

10 Throughout the discussion of the 'fib' program, we use equations of the form '$Z = X + Y$' as abbreviations for relationships of the form 'sum(*X*, *Y*, *Z*)'. The 'sum' predicate was defined on p. 493.

variables of each. No assignment of values to 'F' will make 'fib(2,F)' equal to either of the first two clauses, so the only candidate for unification is the third clause. Clearly, the assignment N = 2 will make 'fib(N,F)' equal to 'fib(2,F)'. Hence, to achieve the goal 'fib(2,F)', we must satisfy the subgoals

```
:- 2 = M+1, M = K+1, fib(M,G), fib(K,H), F = G+H, 2 > 1.
```

The subgoal '2 > 1' is satisfied, so it can be discarded, leaving

```
:- 2 = M+1, M = K+1, fib(M,G), fib(K,H), F = G+H.
```

The assignment M = 1 allows the satisfaction of the subgoal '2 = M + 1', so we get a new set of subgoals:

```
:- 1 = K+1, fib(1,G), fib(K,H), F = G+H.
```

(Notice that the assignment 'M = 1' has been made in all the subgoals.) Similarly, the assignment K = 0 leads to the subgoals

```
:- fib(1,G), fib(0,H), F = G+H.
```

We have now reached the hypotheses since the assignments G = 1 and H = 1 allow 'fib(1,G)' to unify with 'fib(1,1)' and 'fib(0,H)' to unify with 'fib(0,1)'. This leaves a single subgoal:

```
:- F = 1 + 1.
```

which is satisfied by the assignment F = 2, which is the answer sought.

Notice that the top-down execution of a logic program is very similar to the execution of a recursive procedure. The order in which the steps are taken is essentially the same as in this Pascal function:

```
function fib (N: integer): integer;
begin
  if N = 0 or N = 1 then fib := 1;
  else fib := fib(N - 1) + fib(N - 2)
end;
```

Notice that simple recursion is not a very efficient way of computing Fibonacci numbers. Suppose our goal had been

```
:- fib(10,F).
```

The top-down execution of this program would involve setting up the subgoals 'fib(9,G)' and 'fib(8,H)'. Suppose we began by attempting to satisfy 'fib(8,H)'; this would require computing the eighth Fibonacci number. After this is accomplished, we would attempt to satisfy 'fib(9,G)', which would lead to the subgoals 'fib(8,G')' and 'fib(7,H')'. Now, if we followed the top-down discipline naively, satisfying the goal 'fib(8,G')' would require us to recompute the eighth Fibonacci number again! This recomputation would take place at each stage of the recursion, which results in a very inefficient algorithm (an algorithm whose execution time is an exponential function of *N*). For this reason, some logic programming systems remember subgoals they have already satisfied so that they will not duplicate their satisfaction.

EXERCISE 13-23: Prove that the naive top-down computation of 'fib' has exponential time complexity.

EXERCISE 13-24: Trace (by hand) the top-down execution of the goal ':− fib(3,A)'.

EXERCISE 13-25: Show the top-down satisfaction of the goal

```
:- grandparent(albert,victor).
```

EXERCISE 13-26: Show the top-down satisfaction of the goal

```
:- ancestor(X,cindy), sibling(X,jeffrey).
```

Bottom-Up Control Is Like Iteration

A different strategy for controlling the generation of subgoals is bottom-up, in which we attempt to reach the goal from the hypotheses. Consider the bottom-up satisfaction of the goal

```
:- fib(3,F).
```

We begin with the hypotheses, which are

```
fib(0,1), fib(1,1).
```

(For clarity, we will omit the hypotheses about integer arithmetic, which are built into the system.) These two hypotheses can be unified with the right-hand side of

```
fib(N,F) :- N = M+1, M = K+1, fib(M,G), fib(K,H),
            F = G+H, N > 1.
```

by the value assignments K = 0, M = 1, N = 2, G = H = 1, and F = 2. This allows us to conclude 'fib(2,2)', which, combined with the existing hypotheses, yields:

```
fib(0,1), fib(1,1), fib(2,2).
```

The last two of these can again be unified with the right-hand side of the abovementioned clause by the assignments K = 1, M = 2, N = 3, G = 2, H = 1, F = 3 to yield the hypotheses:

```
fib(0,1), fib(1,1), fib(2,2), fib(3,3).
```

The last of these hypotheses can be unified with the goal 'fib(3,F)' by the assignment F = 3, which is the answer sought.

Notice that the order of operations resulting from a bottom-up execution is the same as in an iterative program. The bottom-up execution of this program is analogous to that of the Pascal function:

```
function fib (N: integer): integer;
  var n, Fn, Fm, Fk: integer;
begin
  Fn := Fm := Fk := 1;
  n := 1;
  while n<N do
    begin
      Fn  := Fm + Fk;
      Fk  := Fm;
      Fm  := Fn;
      n   := n + 1
    end;
  fib := Fn;
end;
```

Notice that the bottom-up execution of the logic program is much more efficient than its naive top-down execution since the bottom-up execution does not recompute Fibonacci numbers needlessly. In fact, the time required for the bottom-up execution of this program is a linear function of its input (N).

Pure top-down and pure bottom-up are not the only ways of executing logic programs. We have already indicated a modification of top-down that remembers already satisfied subgoals. There are also various mixtures of top-down and bottom-up that work from both the goals and the hypotheses and attempt to meet in the middle. The details of these approaches go beyond the scope of this book; the interested reader can find them discussed in books and courses that deal with artificial intelligence and logic programming.

EXERCISE 13-27: Show a bottom-up satisfaction of the goal

```
:- grandparent(albert,victor).
```

EXERCISE 13-28: Show a bottom-up satisfaction of the goal

```
:- ancestor(X,cindy), sibling(X,jeffrey).
```

Logic Programs Can Be Interpreted Procedurally

There is another way of looking at logic programs that makes them easier to compare with programs in conventional languages. In this interpretation, clauses are viewed as procedure definitions and relationships are viewed as procedure invocations. Consider a clause such as

```
fib(N,F) :- N = M+1, M = K+1, fib(M,G), fib(K,H),
            F = G+H, N > 1.
```

The head (left-hand side) of the clause is analogous to the head of a procedure declaration; it defines a template for invoking the procedure. The body (right-hand side) of the clause is analogous to the body of a procedure declaration; it is composed of a series of procedure calls. Multiple clauses that define the same procedure are analogous to the branches of a conditional in a conventional definition of a procedure (for example, compare the LISP and Prolog programs for 'append' on p. 496). A goal is just the procedure call that starts a program going, and a hypothesis is just a procedure that returns without invoking any other procedures.

Consider the procedural interpretation of the goal

```
:- fib(3,F).
```

We are invoking the procedure 'fib' with the input parameter N = 3 and the output parameter 'F' unbound. The first subgoal in the body of 'fib', 'N = M+1', unifies 'N' with 'M+1', which results in 'M' being bound to 2. The second subgoal, 'M = K+1', binds 'K' to 1. Next we have two recursive invocations of 'fib': 'fib(2, G)' and 'fib(1,H)'. The second of these is an invocation of the hypothesis

```
fib(1,1).
```

which is really just an abbreviation for

```
fib(1,1) :- .
```

Since this has no procedure invocations on the right, it immediately returns H = 1. When 'fib(2, G)' returns its result G = 2, we will be able to return the result of the program, which is F = 3.

Procedure Invocations Can Be Executed in Any Order

One difference between the procedural interpretation of logic programs and procedures in other languages is immediately apparent: The statements in the body of a logic procedure need not be executed in any particular order. That is, 'fib(2, G)' can be executed before 'fib(1,H)', or vice versa. As we've noted before, this is very different from conventional languages in which the order in which things are done is essential to the meaning of the program. In a logic program, the procedure calls can be executed in any order or even concurrently. This makes logic programming languages a potential way to program multiprocessing and highly parallel computers.[11]

Backtracking Is Necessary and Frequent

In the examples that we have discussed, we have assumed that when there were several clauses defining a procedure, the correct clause was always selected by a procedure invocation. For example, the invocation 'fib(1, G)' matches the head of both of these clauses:

```
fib(N,F) :- N = M+1, M = K+1, fib(M,G), fib(K,H),
            F = G+H, N > 1.
fib(1,1).
```

Suppose that we select the first clause for execution; this will set up the subgoals

```
:- 1 = M+1, M = K+1, fib(M,G), fib(K,H), F = G+H, 1 > 1.
```

Notice that the last subgoal, '1 > 1', cannot be satisfied; therefore, there is no way to satisfy this set of subgoals. In other words, the invocation 'fib(1, G)' fails when we select the first clause. Hence, the interpreter must *backtrack* to the last point where it made a choice [in this case, selecting the first of the two clauses

11 Again, note that we are talking about *pure* logic programs; we discuss later the extent to which these observations apply to Prolog.

that match 'fib(1,G)'] and make a different choice. In this example, the only other choice is the hypothesis 'fib(1,1)', which will allow the goal to be satisfied.

It may be that the system tries all of the alternatives available for a procedure call and that it can't satisfy the subgoal with any of them. If this occurs, the system must backtrack further, to an earlier choice, and try additional alternatives there. If the system runs out of all alternatives, the goal is unsatisfiable, which must be reported to the user.

The result of this process is that a logic programming system spends a lot of its time backtracking. In most languages and systems, backtracking is considered an unusual event that is usually connected with error recovery. Therefore, backtracking is commonly considered expensive. Since in logic programs backtracking is the rule rather than the exception, much of the challenge of the implementation of logic programming languages is the development of more efficient backtracking mechanisms. These mechanisms are beyond the scope of this book.

Input-Output Parameters Are Not Distinguished

There is another major difference between procedures in logic programming languages and those in other languages. We have seen that a goal such as

```
:- fib(3,F).
```

will result in binding F = 3; this tells us that the third Fibonacci number is 3. The system proves constructively that there is an 'F' such that 'fib(3,F)'. Consider instead this goal:

```
:- fib(N,3).
```

which asks the system to prove constructively that there is a number 'N' such that 'fib(N,3)'. This seems to be a request for the number *N* such that the *N*th Fibonacci number is 3. Will this work? Let's trace its execution.

The goal 'fib(N, 3)' sets up these subgoals:

```
:- N = M+1, M = K+1, fib(M,G), fib(K,H), 3 = G+H, N > 1.
```

To determine if these subgoals can be satisfied, the interpreter must try various value assignments to the variables. For example, it might try in order

```
G = 0, H = 0
G = 0, H = 1
G = 1, H = 0
G = 1, H = 1
G = 0, H = 2
    ⋮
```

and so on, until it reaches G = 1 and H = 2, since this is the first assignment that satisfies '3 = G+H'. This value assignment leads to the subgoals

```
:- N = M+1, M = K+1, fib(M,1), fib(K,2), N > 1.
```

The subgoal 'fib(M,1)' unifies with the hypothesis 'fib(1, 1)' by the assignment M = 1, which leads to

```
:- N = 1+1, 1 = K+1, fib(K,2), N > 1.
```

Only the assignments N = 2, K = 0 will allow satisfaction of 'N = 1 + 1' and '1 = K + 1', so we get the subgoal

```
:- fib(0,2).
```

This unifies with the head of

```
fib(N,F) :- N = M+1, M = K+1, fib(M,G), fib(K,H),
            F = G+H, N > 1.
```

yielding the subgoals:

```
:- 0 = M+1, M = K+1, fib(M,G), fib(K,H), 2 = G+H, 0 > 1.
```

Since the last subgoal ('0 > 1') is not satisfiable, we must backtrack to the last choice and seek a new alternative.

In this case, the only choice was the selection of the values G = 1, H = 2 to satisfy F = G+H. Suppose instead we continue enumerating values until we reach G = 2, H = 1; this yields the subgoals

```
:- N = M+1, M = K+1, fib(M,2), fib(K,1), N > 1.
```

'fib(K, 1)' unifies with the fact 'fib(1, 1)' by the assignment K = 1, so we get the subgoals

```
:- N = M+1, M = 1+1, fib(M,2), N > 1.
```

This leads to the value assignments M = 2, N = 3 and the subgoal

```
:- fib(2,2).
```

Since the second Fibonacci number is in fact 2, we can see that this subgoal is satisfiable (you will provide the details in an exercise). Therefore, the value assignment N = 3 will be returned as the answer to

```
:- fib(N,3).
N = 3
```

Notice the remarkable thing that logic programming permits: Neither parameter of 'fib' is inherently an input or an output. If either is supplied as an input, then the other can be computed as an output. It is the use of 'fib' in each particular context that determines the function of its parameters in that context. One way of looking at this is that a logic program can be run either forward or backward as needed!

We summarize: In the goal ':- fib(*N*,*F*)', if *N* is supplied as an input, then *F* can be computed as an output; if *F* is supplied as an input, then *N* can be computed as an output. Also, we've seen in the satisfaction of goals such as 'fib(2,2)' that *both* *F* and *N* can be supplied as inputs. What happens if *neither* *N* nor *F* is supplied as an input? In this case, we are asking the system to prove constructively that there are *N* and *F* such that 'fib(*N*,*F*)' is true. Of course, there are, and the system immediately finds N = 0, F = 1:

```
:- fib(N,F).
N = 0, F = 1
```

As usual we can type a semicolon to request the system to search for other solutions, and it finds them:

```
:- fib(N,F).
N = 0, F = 1;
N = 1, F = 1;
N = 2, F = 2;
N = 3, F = 3;
N = 4, F = 5;
N = 5, F = 8
yes
```

The response 'yes' indicates that there may be additional solutions. Hence, our logic program 'fib' can be used as a way of enumerating the Fibonacci numbers.

Such enumeration could be required, for example, during backtracking. Suppose we wanted to search for an N such that $N + F_N = 13$. We could enter the goal

```
:- fib(N,F), N+F = 13.
N = 5, F = 8
```

The subgoal 'fib(N,F)' is initially satisfied by N = 0, F = 1, but this assignment does not satisfy 'N+F = 13'. Therefore, we backtrack to 'fib(N,F)' to find another (N,F) pair satisfying this relationship. Eventually this backtracking produces the pair N = 5, F = 8, which satisfies the goal.

EXERCISE 13-29: Show that the goal ':– fib(2,2)' can be satisfied.

EXERCISE 13-30: Trace in detail the satisfaction of the goal ':– fib(N,F)' from N = 0 through N = 3.

EXERCISE 13-31: Trace in detail the satisfaction of

```
:- fib(N,F), N+F = 9.
```

EXERCISE 13-32: Explain what happens when we enter the goal

```
:- fib(N,F), N+F = 10.
```

Suggest ways of avoiding the difficulty.

Prolog Uses Depth-First Search

In the preceding pages, we have discussed logic programming's separation of logic and control. With this separation the programmer worries about the logical relationships in the program, while the system worries about implementing a proper control strategy to execute the program. Recall that avoiding the procedural "how to" issues is the whole point of nonprocedural programming. We will see that this separation holds only for *pure* logic programming languages, that is, for logic programming languages that implement some complete deductive algorithm (such as J. Alan Robinson's *resolution algorithm*). Unfortunately, it does *not* hold for Prolog.

Prolog abandons the separation of logic and control by *specifying* the control regime to be used, rather than leaving it up to the Prolog system. The Prolog language is *defined* to use a depth-first search strategy. This design decision has many consequences, both good and bad, that we discuss in the remainder of this section. Before investigating these, however, we must say exactly what we mean by *depth-first search.*

The easiest way to understand Prolog's control strategy is to remember that it does everything in a specific order: first to last (i.e., top to bottom, left to right). Thus, if we have the subgoals

```
:- ancestor(X,cindy), sibling(X,jeffrey).
```

Prolog will attempt to satisfy them in the order written. Hence, the first subgoal is 'ancestor(X,cindy)'. To satisfy this it will try the clauses for 'ancestor' *in the order in which they were entered into the database.* Thus, it starts with

```
ancestor(X,Z) :- parent(X,Z).
```

Replacing 'ancestor(X,cindy)' by 'parent(X,cindy)' leads to the subgoals:

```
:- parent(X,cindy), sibling(X,jeffrey).
```

Notice that the new subgoal, 'parent(X,cindy)' is put at the *beginning* of the list of subgoals; this leads to a *depth-first* search order.

Again, Prolog starts with the first subgoal on the list of subgoals; in this case, it is 'parent(X,cindy)'. There are two clauses for 'parent' and the first, 'parent(X,Y) :- father(X,Y)', leads to the subgoals:

```
:- father(X,cindy), sibling(X,jeffrey).
```

The subgoal 'father(X,cindy)' unifies with the fact 'father(george,cindy)' by the assignment X = 'george', so we get the subgoal:

```
:- sibling(george,jeffrey).
```

And so on. A complete trace (such as produced by a Prolog system) is shown in Figure 13-3. (Note that 'Exit' means successful satisfaction of a goal and 'Fail' means unsuccessful satisfaction of a goal. This is common Prolog terminology.)

If there had been a failure in the satisfaction of 'ancestor(X,cindy)', the system would have backtracked, trying additional alternatives in order. It would not move on to the subgoal 'sibling(X,jeffrey)' until an 'X' satisfying the first subgoal had been found. Furthermore, if this 'X' hadn't satisfied 'sibling(X,jeffrey)', then the system would have been forced to backtrack to find other 'X's satisfying 'ancestor(X,cindy)'. The search for these other 'X's would pick up where it had left off when it found X = 'george'.

EXERCISE 13-33: Given the definition of 'sum' on p. 493, trace the Prolog execution of the goal

```
:- sum(succ(succ(0)), succ(succ(succ(0))), A).
```

EXERCISE 13-34: Given the same definition of 'sum' and the definition of 'dif' in the same place, trace the Prolog execution of:

```
:- dif(succ(succ(succ(0))), What, succ(0)).
```

```
:- ancestor(X,cindy), sibling(X,jeffrey).
```

Invocation	Depth	Event	Subgoal
(1)	1	Call:	ancestor(X,cindy)
(2)	2	Call:	parent(X,cindy)
(3)	3	Call:	father(X,cindy)
(3)	3	Exit:	father(george,cindy)
(2)	2	Exit:	parent(george,cindy)
(1)	1	Exit:	ancestor(george,cindy)
(4)	1	Call:	sibling(george,jeffrey)
(5)	2	Call:	mother(M,george)
(5)	2	Exit:	mother(alice,george)
(6)	2	Call:	mother(alice,jeffrey)
(6)	2	Exit:	mother(alice,jeffrey)
(7)	2	Call:	father(F,george)
(7)	2	Exit:	father(albert,george)
(8)	2	Call:	father(albert,jeffrey)
(8)	2	Exit:	father(albert,jeffrey)
(9)	2	Call:	not george=jeffrey
(10)	3	Call:	george=jeffrey
(10)	3	Fail:	george=jeffrey
(9)	2	Exit:	not george=jeffrey
(4)	1	Exit:	sibling(george,jeffrey)

```
X = george
yes
```

Figure 13.3 Trace of Prolog Program Execution

EXERCISE 13-35: Trace the Prolog execution of the goal

```
:- d(x, (2 * x) * (x + 1), Deriv).
```

EXERCISE 13-36: Describe algorithmically a breadth-first search strategy for logic programs.

Prolog Loses Many of the Advantages of Logic Programming

Consider again our Fibonacci program; it is not legal Prolog as it stands, but it is close. The difficulty is with the arithmetic equations such as 'N = M+1' and 'F = G+H'. Recall that in most Prolog dialects an expression such as 'M+1' denotes a compound term equivalent to 'plus(M,1)'; it does not call for addition to be performed. Furthermore, the '=' sign denotes a pattern-matching (unification) operation. Thus, 'N = M+1' is a request to unify 'N' and the compound term 'M+1'. Now this was not our intention; for 'fib' to work correctly, 'N = M+1' must be interpreted as the assertion that 'N' and 'M+1' are *numerically* equal.

There is a simple (but inefficient) way out of this difficulty. Recall our definition of unary addition:

```
sum(M,0,M).
sum(M,succ(N),succ(S)) :- sum(M,N,S).
```

Thus, if M, N, and S are compound terms representing (natural) numbers in unary notation (i.e., applications of 'succ' to 0), then 'sum(M,N,S)' asserts that S is *numerically* equal to $M+N$. Given this definition of 'sum', our Fibonacci program can be written in Prolog:

```
fib(0,succ(0)).
fib(succ(0),succ(0)).
fib(N,F) :- sum(M,succ(0),N), sum(K,succ(0),M),
            fib(M,G), fib(K,H), sum(G,H,F).
```

Notice that we have had to write '1' as 'succ(0)'. As far as Prolog is concerned, '1' and 'succ(0)' are just terms; there is no inherent connection between them. When these changes have been made, our definition of 'fib' becomes a legal Prolog program that will behave just as discussed earlier in this section (i.e., any combination of its arguments may be bound or unbound).

There are several difficulties with this. First of all, it is very inconvenient to express numbers in unary notation. Finding out the fifth Fibonacci number looks like this:

```
:- fib(succ(succ(succ(succ(succ(0))))), A).
A = succ(succ(succ(succ(succ(succ(succ(succ(0))))))))
```

There are ways we can get around this in Prolog (such as writing a converter between unary and regular numbers), but there is a more fundamental problem.

Doing arithmetic by unification on terms representing numbers in unary notation is an extremely inefficient way of doing precisely what computers are built to do efficiently: arithmetic. As noted earlier, all Prologs provide some means for making use of the computer's built-in arithmetic capabilities. In many Prologs this takes the form of the built-in predicate 'is'. Suppose N is a variable and E is an arithmetic expression all of whose variables are bound (*instantiated*, in Prolog terminology). Then the subgoal 'N is E' has the following effect: The expression E is evaluated to yield a numeric value V. If N is unbound, then N

becomes bound to *V*; if *N* is already bound, then its bound value is compared with *V*. Thus, if *N* is unbound, then '*N* is *E*' behaves much like an assignment, '*N* := *E*'. If *N* is bound, it behaves more like a comparison, '*N* = *E*'. In either case, however, the expression *E* is evaluated using the arithmetic capabilities of the computer.

The obvious way to improve the efficiency of our Fibonacci program is to translate the 'sum' relations into 'is' relations:

```
fib(N,F) :- N is M+1, M is K+1, fib(M,G), fib(K,H),
            F is G+H, N > 1.
```

This looks very much like our original formulation. Unfortunately, it will not work.

Consider the goal ':- fib(2,A)'. In evaluating the subgoals from left to right, we begin with 'N is M+1'. However, 'M' is unbound, so the arithmetic expression cannot be evaluated, and the program aborts. Taking our clue from imperative languages, we might try to solve this problem by rearranging the subgoals like this:

```
fib(N,F) :- M is N-1, K is M-1, fib(M,G), fib(K,H),
            F is G+H, N > 1.
```

This will in fact satisfy the goal ':- fib(2,A)' correctly.

EXERCISE 13-37: Trace in detail the depth-first satisfaction of this goal.

Now, however, suppose that we try the goal ':- fib(A,3)'. In this case, 'N' is unbound, so the subgoal 'M is N-1' fails. We have lost the ability to execute 'fib' "backward." Perhaps another order will work. Perhaps we can make use of backtracking's ability to enumerate (*N*,*F*) pairs satisfying 'fib(*N*,*F*)' in order to avoid the ordering dependencies inherent in 'is'. For example, we can program:

```
fib(N,F) :- fib(K,H), M is K+1, fib(M,G),
            N is M+1, F is G+H, N > 1.
```

Suppose now we execute the goal ':- fib(3,A)'. The first subgoal is 'fib(K,H)'. Since 'K' and 'H' are not bound, this subgoal will be satisfied by K = 0, H = 1. This in turn leads to 'M' being bound to 1 and the subgoal 'fib(1,G)', which is satisfied with G = 1 and the fact 'fib(1,1)'. Now, however, the subgoal 'N is M+1' compares 3 (the value of N) with 2 (the value of M+1), and so fails. This causes a backtrack to seek another value of G satisfying 'fib(1,G)'. Since both the facts have been tried, we now take N = 1 in the rule headed 'fib(N,F)'. As before 'fib(K,H)' is satisfied by K = 0, H = 1, so we set up the subgoal 'fib(1,G)'. But this is precisely the subgoal we were already trying to satisfy. The 'fib' predicate has been called recursively with precisely the same arguments as a call already active; we are in an infinite loop! (A trace is shown in Figure 13-4.) Once again we've failed to produce a correct version of 'fib' (one that works with every possible combination of arguments).

We will not continue this exercise; the point has been made. Suffice it to say that we have come a long way from the goal of nonprocedural programming: telling the computer *what* you want, not *how* to get it. In Prolog, not only do we have to specify in the correct order the steps that must be taken to reach the goal, but we also have to cope with a complicated, expensive, and unintuitive control strategy.

Notice that all our versions of 'fib' were *logically* the same; reordering the subgoals affects only the control properties. Unfortunately, in Prolog, as

:- fib(3,A).

Invocation	Depth	Event	Subgoal
(1)	1	Call:	fib(3,F)
(2)	2	Call:	fib(K,H)
(2)	2	Exit:	fib(0,1)
(3)	2	Call:	M is 0+1
(3)	2	Exit:	1 is 0+1
(4)	2	Call:	fib(1,G)
(4)	2	Exit:	fib(1,1)
(5)	2	Call:	3 is 1+1
(5)	2	Fail:	3 is 1+1
(4)	2	Redo:	fib(1,G)
(6)	3	Call:	fib(K',H')
(6)	3	Exit:	fib(0,1)
(7)	3	Call:	M' is 0+1
(7)	3	Exit:	1 is 0+1
(8)	3	Call:	fib(1,G')
(8)	3	Exit:	fib(1,1)
(9)	3	Call:	1 is 1+1
(9)	3	Fail:	1 is 1+1
(8)	3	Redo:	fib(1,G')
(10)	4	Call:	fib(K'',H'')
⋮	⋮	⋮	⋮

Figure 13.4 Trace of Incorrect Definition of 'fib'

opposed to *pure* logic programming, the control properties can determine the correctness of the program. In pure logic programming, on the other hand, the correctness of the program depends only on the logic of the algorithm. Control is an issue of efficiency, which can be dealt with after the program is correct.

Concern for Efficiency Has Motivated Prolog's Search Strategy

Given the unintuitive consequences of Prolog's control regime, we should ask ourselves why the designers have decided to specify a specific strategy at all, let alone the specific one they chose. The first reason is that a depth-first search may be considerably more efficient than other search strategies, such as a breadth-first search. Since the search goes *deep* through the search tree, the information that must be stored is that gathered along a single path down the tree. On the other hand, a breadth-first search is in effect pursuing all search paths in parallel (this is why it's guaranteed to find a solution if there is one), so it must retain the information for all these paths. For this reason, a breadth-first search tends to need exponentially more space than a depth-first search. That's certainly a good reason for going depth-first.

The trouble with depth-first is that the search tree may be infinitely deep. That is, although some branches may lead to a solution in a finite number of steps, others are infinitely long and never reach a solution. If the search has the bad luck to stumble into one of these "black holes" before it finds a solution, then it will never come out.

Since there's no general procedure by which the Prolog system can determine whether or not it has started off on an endless search, the burden has been put on the programmer. The language specifies the precise order in which the search is done. The programmer then has the responsibility of arranging the clauses and subgoals in the program so that it will terminate when used in the intended way (but not necessarily in unintended ways, as we saw above).

There is another reason that Prolog specifies its search order, which comes from the fact that Prolog is used for programming that is not, strictly speaking, logical. For example, most Prologs have "special" predicates for performing input and output. Thus, a subgoal involving the predicate 'write' succeeds exactly once but causes the arguments to be written out as a side effect. Conversely, a subgoal involving 'read' has the side effect of reading a term from a file, which is then unified with the argument. A new term is read every time the system backtracks to the 'read'.

Predicates such as these allow programmers to use conventional programming idioms in their Prolog programs. Obviously, however, they would be of little value if they weren't executed at predictable times. Hence, the desire to do things such as input-output dictates a defined search order.

EXERCISE 13-38: Explain the consequence of the following Prolog definition of 'ancestor':

```
ancestor(X,Z) :- parent(X,Z).
ancestor(X,Z) :- ancestor(X,Y), parent(Y,Z).
```

EXERCISE 13-39: Write Prolog clauses for a predicate 'unary' that relates natural numbers to their unary representations. For example,

```
:- unary(N,U).
N = 0, U = 0;
N = 1, U = succ(0);
N = 2, U = succ(succ(0));
N = 3, U = succ(succ(succ(0)))
```

EXERCISE 13-40: Why can't a Prolog (or any other) system decide in general whether a particular search path will terminate?

EXERCISE 13-41:* Can you suggest a way of handling input-output in logic programs that does not depend on a specific search order? *Hint:* How can the organization of information on the input-output media be specified *logically*?

Assert and Retract Permit Nonmonotonic Reasoning

One facility that depends crucially on Prolog having a defined search order is the ability to *assert* and *retract* facts and rules. Satisfying a subgoal of the form 'retract(*C*)' causes the first clause matching the term *C* to be removed from the database. Resatisfaction (e.g., during backtracking) may cause additional matching clauses to be removed.[12] Satisfying a subgoal of the form 'asserta(*C*)' or 'assertz(*C*)' causes the term *C*, interpreted as a clause, to be inserted into the database (at its beginning for 'asserta' or end for 'assertz'). Thus, the Prolog database is an *updatable* database.

While it seems perfectly reasonable for a database to be updatable, it is not so obvious what assertions and retractions mean in the context of *logic* programming. In predicate logic (on which Prolog is based), a proposition is either true or false; it cannot be true now and false later, or vice versa. We say that predicate logic is *monotonic* (mono = single, tonos = tone), that is, the set of known truths

12 Some Prolog systems do not permit resatisfaction of 'retract's.

never decreases. Applying the deductive rules of a monotonic logic can increase the set of propositions known to be true, but never decrease it. Deduction never causes things known to be true to cease being true (or things known to be false to cease being false).

It certainly seems reasonable for logic to be monotonic: If we could prove something yesterday, it seems we ought to be able to prove it today. Yet there are situations in which a *nonmonotonic* logic is just what's needed. Consider a robot vehicle planning its path across a terrain. It will decide which path is best on the basis of a variety of information sources, including general rules and particular facts. Some of these facts may turn out to be false. For example, a road which was "known" to connect two points is now found to be closed. Or what looked like solid ground from afar is found to be a swamp on closer inspection. In other words, things that were thought to be true turn out to be false, and vice versa. Therefore, conclusions that were drawn on the basis of these hypotheses (such as the best route) are found not to hold. The robot vehicle must be able to revise its conclusions on the basis of this new information.

In an application such as this, propositions are not simply true or false; they are true or false *at a particular time* in the program's execution. Thus, it becomes important for programmers to know the order in which things are done in their program. They must pay attention to the *temporal* as well as the *logical* relationships.

EXERCISE 13-42:* Suggest a way in which nonmonotonic reasoning could be handled in a *pure* monotonic logic programming language. *Hint:* How can you express logically the temporality of facts?

Cuts Are Used to Guarantee Termination

Consider the following straightforward Prolog definition of factorial:

```
fac(0,1).
fac(N,F) :- N1 is N-1, fac(N1,R1), R is R1*N.
```

The following goal gives the expected answer:

```
:- fac(4,A).
A = 24
```

Unfortunately, this (obvious) definition of 'fac' has a hidden trap. Let's consider what happens if we try to satisfy the following (unsatisfiable) goal:

```
:- fac(4,A), A = 10.
```

As before, the subgoal 'fac(4,A)' succeeds with the instantiation 'A = 24'. If we number the 'fac' clauses (1) and (2), then we can represent the series of choices by which this solution was reached:

```
(2), (2), (2), (2), (1)
```

That is, we had to take the second clause for N = 4, 3, 2, 1, but for N = 0 we took the first clause.

Now consider what happens when we try to satisfy the subgoal 'A = 10'. Since 'A' is bound to 24, this subgoal fails, which causes Prolog to backtrack to the last choice it made. In effect, it will try to find another 'A' for which 'fac(4,A)' is true. Of course, the Prolog system has no way of knowing that each number has only one factorial, so it will search for another one even though it doesn't exist. It does this by trying to find another clause to unify with the last subgoal it satisfied. In this case, that subgoal was 'fib(0,R)', which was satisfied by clause (1) of the definition of 'fac'. Hence, Prolog searches for another clause to unify with 'fib(0,R)' and it finds clause (2), which unifies by the assignment N = 0. This sets up the subgoals

```
:- N1 is 0-1, fac(N1,R1), R is R1*1.
```

Execution of the 'is' immediately leads to the subgoals

```
:- fac(-1,R1), R is R1*1.
```

The system is now off looking for a factorial for −1, and, of course, it won't find one. The system is in an infinite loop, although a simple 'no' is the answer we expect.

What was the cause of this difficulty? We can see that once the system had found A = 24 as a solution of 'fib(4,A)', it never should have looked for another solution; a number has at most one factorial. It would be useful if there were some way to say to Prolog, "You've found all the solutions there are; don't bother trying to find any others."

Prolog provides just such a mechanism; it is called a *cut* (presumably because it "cuts off" the search for alternatives). In this case, we would like to say, "Once you've found the solution A = 1 for 'fib(0,A)', don't look for any others." This is expressed in Prolog:

```
fac(0,1) :- !.
fac(N,R) :- N1 is N-1, fac(N1,R1), R is R1*N.
```

The symbol '!' is the "cut." It is a predicate that always succeeds, but past which you can never backtrack. Hence, having once found the solution A = 1 for 'fib(0,A)' we will not attempt to find another solution. Now we get the expected response if we execute

```
:- fac(4,A), A = 10.
no
```

This example illustrates one of the common uses of a "cut": signaling that the right solution has been found.

Unfortunately, our problems with 'fac' are still not solved. Suppose we enter the goal

```
:- fac(0,0).
```

(asking if the factorial of zero is zero). The system will again go into an infinite loop. Since 'fib(0,0)' does not unify with 'fib(0,1)', the head of the first clause, the system will go on to the second clause, and we are off on the same goose chase. There are several solutions to this problem. Since our definition only works if 'N' is instantiated, perhaps the simplest is to add conditions on 'N':

```
fac(0,1) :- !.
fac(N,F) :- N > 0, N1 is N-1, fac(N1,R1), R is R1*N.
```

EXERCISE 13-43: Rewrite the above definition of 'fac' so that the factorial of negative numbers is 'infinity'. (Of course, 'infinity' is just an atom like 'nil' or 'albert'.)

Cuts Are Used to Control Execution Order

Prolog's defined search order, in addition to "impure" features such as the "cut," have encouraged many programmers to adopt a very procedural Prolog programming style. Here is an example:

```
squares_to(N) :- asserta(current(1)),
                 repeat,
                 one_step,
                 current(N).
```

```
one_step :-   current(K),
              Sq is K*K,
              write(Sq), nl,
              NewK is K+1,
              retract(current(K)),
              asserta(current(NewK)),
              !.
```

The predicate 'repeat', which is built into most Prologs, is defined by the clauses:

```
repeat.
repeat :- repeat.
```

Viewed logically, these clauses are curious indeed. They mean something like "repeat is true; also repeat is true *if* repeat is true." To understand their significance it is necessary to *trace* the execution of 'squares_to'. Suppose we enter the goal ':- squares_to(5)'. We will see this:

```
:- squares_to(5).
1
4
9
16
yes
```

These are the squares of the numbers from 1 up to but not including 5. Consider how the Prolog system goes about trying to satisfy this goal.

To satisfy ':- squares_to(5)', the system must satisfy *in order* the subgoals:

```
:- asserta(current(1)), repeat, one_step, current(5).
```

The 'asserta' enters the fact 'current(1)' in the database and succeeds. The 'repeat' subgoal also succeeds because the fact 'repeat' is in the database. Next we come to the subgoal 'one_step'; to satisfy this we must satisfy the subgoals given by the clause for 'one_step'. The first of these simply binds 'K' to 1 (since we just put 'current(1)' in the database). The second binds 'Sq' to 'K' squared, which is 1 in this case. The following 'write' prints the value 1, which is followed by 'nl', a built-in predicate to go to a new line. The next three subgoals retract 'current(1)' and assert 'current(2)'. The "cut" means that we will not try to resatisfy 'one_step'. Since 'one_step' has been satisfied, we return to 'squares_to' and attempt to satisfy 'current(5)', but since 'current(2)' is the only relevant fact in the database, this attempt fails.

Now we must backtrack. Since 'one_step' has been "cut," we cannot try it again, so we go back to 'repeat' and attempt to resatisfy it. There is another clause for 'repeat', namely, the rule 'repeat :— repeat', so 'repeat' can be satisfied if we can satisfy —'repeat'! Since 'repeat' is a fact, the rule can be applied, and 'repeat' can be satisfied *in a different way* from the first time. Hence, we can return to the 'squares_to' rule and satisfy again 'one_step'. This time satisfaction of 'one_step' prints '4', which is 2 squared. In the process it retracts 'current(2)' and asserts 'current(3)'. However, since 'current(5)' still fails, we backtrack again to the 'repeat'. And so we continue, repeating 'one_step' until finally 'current(5)' has been asserted, at which point 'squares_to(5)' is satisfied and our program stops. See Figure 13-5.

How far we've come from logic programming! And how far we've come from *nonprocedural* programming! This program is certainly as procedural as any we might write in Pascal or LISP. The predicate 'current' is in effect a variable, and the asserts and retracts just implement assignments to this variable. The 'repeat' predicate, as its name implies, has the effect of beginning a loop, which is returned to by the backtracking mechanism. The Pascal equivalent is simply:

```
procedure SquaresTo (N: integer);
  var current: integer;
begin
  current := 1;
  repeat
    writeln(current*current);
    current := current + 1;
  until current = N;
end;
```

It can be argued that the programmer's intent is more clearly expressed in the Pascal program. Certainly, we will be very confused if we attempt to attach any logical significance to the clauses in the Prolog program.

EXERCISE 13-44:* Do you prefer the Pascal or Prolog program? Explain why.

EXERCISE 13-45:* Discuss procedural programming in Prolog. Should it be encouraged or discouraged? What benefits does it have over procedural programming in conventional languages? How could it be discouraged, given Prolog's depth-first search order?

```
:- squares_to(5).
```

Invocation	Depth	Event	Subgoal
(1)	1	Call:	squares_to(5)
(2)	2	Call:	asserta(current(1))
(2)	2	Exit:	asserta(current(1))
(3)	2	Call:	repeat
(3)	2	Exit:	repeat
(4)	2	Call:	one_step
(5)	3	Call:	current(K)
(5)	3	Exit:	current(1)
(6)	3	Call:	Sq is 1*1
(6)	3	Exit:	1 is 1*1
(7)	3	Call:	write(1)
(7)	3	Exit:	write(1)
(8)	3	Call:	nl
(8)	3	Exit:	nl
(9)	3	Call:	NewK is 1+1
(9)	3	Exit:	2 is 1+1
(10)	3	Call:	retract(current(1))
(10)	3	Exit:	retract(current(1))
(11)	3	Call:	asserta(current(2))
(11)	3	Exit:	asserta(current(2))
(4)	2	Exit:	one_step
(12)	2	Call:	current(5)
(12)	2	Fail:	current(5)
(3)	2	Redo:	repeat
(3)	2	Exit:	repeat
(13)	2	Call:	one_step
⋮	⋮	⋮	⋮

Figure 13.5 Trace of Procedural Prolog Program

Prolog Indirectly Supports Higher-Order Rules

If we wanted to add all the elements of a list, we could use clauses such as these:

```
sum_red([],0).
sum_red(X.L,S) :- sum_red(L,T), S is X+T.
```

This is a "sum reduction" such as we studied in Chapter 10. Other reductions would follow a similar pattern. This should lead us to ask if there is a way in Prolog of defining a general reduction operation such as we defined in LISP.

Let P be a predicate corresponding to a binary operation F. Thus, $P(X,Y,Z)$ if and only if $Z = F(X,Y)$. We would like to define a predicate 'red' such that 'red(P,I,L,S)' means that S is the result of doing an F reduction (starting from the initial value I) of the list L. That is,

$$S = F(L_1, F(L_2, \ldots, F(L_{n-1}, F(L_n, I)) \ldots))$$

The natural way to do this is simply to make 'P' and 'I' parameters to the predicate:

```
red(P,I,[ ],I).
red(P,I,X.L,S) :- red(P,I,L,T), P(X,T,S).
```

Unfortunately, this rule would not be legal in most logic programming languages. The reason is that the 'P' parameter refers to a predicate, which makes it a *higher-order rule.* In general, logic programming is restricted to *first-order logic,* that is, to logic in which the variables may be bound to individuals (terms), but not higher-order objects (predicates).

Although most Prolog systems do not permit higher-order rules, some do allow the same effect to be achieved in a more roundabout way. In these systems 'red' could be defined:

```
red(P,I,[ ],I).
red(P,I,X.L,S) :- red(P,I,L,T), Q =.. [P,X,T,S], call(Q).
```

The strange looking predicate '=..' binds 'Q' to the result of converting the list '[P,X,T,S]' into the internal representation of the subgoal 'P(X,T,S)'. The subgoal 'call(Q)' then causes the system to attempt to satisfy the subgoal represented by the structure 'Q'. In effect 'call' passes its argument to the Prolog interpreter (in this sense it's like LISP 'eval').

The '=..' predicate depends on the fact that the internal representation of subgoals (code) is very similar to the internal representation of compound terms (data). We saw an analogous situation in LISP, where the program structures and data structures are represented the same way: *S*-expressions. This is especially clear if we write the list '[P,X,T,S]' in *S*-expression notation: '(P X T S)'.

In LISP both code and data are represented as first-order objects. In Prolog, on the other hand, we need an operator to convert a first-order object, such as the term '[P,X,T,S]', into a higher-order object, such as the relationship 'P(X,T,S)'. Hence, Prolog provides limited access to higher-order clauses by way of their representation as first-order terms.

Why doesn't Prolog simply permit higher-order clauses, rather than requiring this detour through first-order representations? The answer is simple, but fundamental. Robinson's resolution algorithm is *refutation complete* for *first-order* predicate logic. This means that if the goal is derivable from the clauses in the database, then the resolution algorithm will find a derivation.[13] Unfortunately, Gödel's incompleteness theorem tells us that neither resolution nor any other algorithm is refutation complete for *higher-order* predicate logic.

EXERCISE 13-46: Write a predicate 'map' that maps a function across a list. That is, if $P(X,Y)$ if and only if $Y = F(X)$, then 'map(P,L,M)' returns a list M that is the result of applying F to each element of L.

EXERCISE 13-47:* Discuss the following language design issue: Is it better to permit higher-order clauses, knowing that a complete deductive procedure doesn't exist, or to restrict programs to first-order clauses, which in effect prevents people from writing nonterminating programs?

Negation Is Interpreted as Unsatisfiability

The problem of negation in logic programming languages illustrates some further applications of higher-order rules. What is the problem of negation? Suppose we want to define a predicate 'can_marry(X,Y)' that means that X can legally marry Y. For the sake of the example, we assume that X can marry Y provided that they are not more closely related than (first) cousins.[14] Thus, X can marry Y if (1) X and Y are not the same individual, (2) X and Y are not siblings, and (3) X and Y are not cousins. How can we express this in Prolog?

Expressing that X and Y are not the same is easy since most Prologs have a built-in not-equal predicate '\=' (but see below). Thus, we might begin

```
can_marry(X,Y) :- X \= Y, nonsibling(X,Y), noncousin(X,Y).
```

We face difficulties, however, when we try to define 'nonsibling'. Our rule for 'sibling' says that two individuals are siblings when they are not the same and they have the same mother and father. Hence, we can negate this to find out the ways in which two individuals could be *non*siblings. Thus, X and Y are not sib-

13 Note that we are talking about the resolution algorithm. Since Prolog implements only a subset of resolution, it may not find a solution even if one exists. We've seen several examples of this.

14 Since the sexes of individuals are not represented in the database, we cannot add the condition that X and Y must be of opposite sex. See Exercise 13-7 regarding this extension.

lings if (1) they are the same, or (2) they have different mothers, or (3) they have different fathers:

```
nonsibling(X,Y) :- X = Y.
nonsibling(X,Y) :- mother(M1,X), mother(M2,Y), M1 \= M2.
nonsibling(X,Y) :- father(F1,X), father(F2,Y), F1 \= F2.
```

It would seem that this does it, but suppose we try:

```
:- nonsibling(albert,alice).
no
```

The system tells us that it is *not* the case that Albert and Alice are nonsiblings, that is, that Albert *is* a sibling of Alice. Yet if we look at Figure 13.1 we can see that Albert and Alice do not have common parents. We can also see the cause of the problem: So far as the program is concerned, Albert and Alice do not have parents at all! Of course, this doesn't mean that they don't *in fact* have parents, but only that our database must stop somewhere: You can't record the entire state of the world in a computer. Yet the "closed-world" semantics of Prolog acts as though anything not recorded in the database is not true. As far as our program is concerned, Albert and Alice are parentless. Hence, to complete our definition of 'nonsibling' we must take care of the possibility that either X or Y doesn't have a parent:

```
nonsibling(X,Y) :- no_parent(X).
nonsibling(X,Y) :- no_parent(Y).
```

Now we face another difficulty: How do we express the fact that X doesn't have a parent? The trouble is that there is no positive fact that expresses the *absence* of a parent. Of course, we could add facts such as 'no_parent(albert)' to the database, but that doesn't solve the fundamental problem, to which we now turn.

We have seen that the predicate 'nonsibling' is definable if we are willing to put in enough negative facts of the form 'no_parent(X)'. A similar approach works for 'noncousin'. The trouble is that this general approach to defining negative predicates—considering all the possible ways the corresponding positive predicate could fail to hold—is tedious at best and error-prone at worst. We would like to take a more direct approach: define 'nonsibling(X, Y)' to hold in exactly those cases in which 'sibling(X, Y)' does not hold. Unfortunately, with Horn clauses such as this:

$$C :- P_1, P_2, \ldots, P_n$$

we can say only that C holds if the premises $P_1, P_2, \ldots, P_n$ *do* hold; we can conclude nothing from the fact that they *don't* hold.

The problem may be summarized as follows. The facts in a Horn clause program state a number of relationships that hold among a number of individuals. The rules allow a number of additional facts to be deduced from the given facts. Thus, from the fact that certain relationships hold, we can conclude that further relationships hold, and these are the *only* conclusions we can draw. So we can conclude that relationships *do* hold, but there is no way to conclude that they *don't* hold. From positive relationships we can deduce only positive relationships. Unfortunately, in the case of 'nonsibling' and 'noncousin' we need to deduce negative relationships. The only way to conclude negative relationships is to put in facts with negative import, as we did with 'no_parent'. Unfortunately, this approach often leads to a knowledge explosion, since the number of ways something can fail to be true is often much greater than the number of ways it can succeed at being true.

Solving these difficulties with negative predicates requires going beyond pure Horn clauses. One way to do this is with the "cut-fail" combination. This is a Prolog idiom that combines the "cut" with a predicate 'fail', which always fails. Although it is built into most Prologs, the 'fail' predicate is easy to define: We simply avoid putting the fact 'fail' into the database!

To illustrate this idiom we define 'nonsibling'. We want to guarantee that 'nonsibling(*X*, *Y*)' fails when 'sibling(*X*, *Y*)' succeeds, but allow it to succeed otherwise. The rules are:

```
nonsibling(X,Y) :- sibling(X,Y), !, fail.
nonsibling(X,Y).
```

Logically, these rules are absolute hash, but they work given Prolog's procedural interpretation.

To see this, observe that in attempting to satisfy 'nonsibling(jeffrey,george)' we must first satisfy 'sibling(jeffrey,george)'. Since this succeeds we execute the "cut" (which always succeeds) and then move on to the 'fail' (which always fails). Since the "cut" has prevented backtracking, the entire clause fails. The resulting nonsatisfiability of 'nonsibling(jeffrey,george)' correctly reflects the fact that Jeffrey and George are siblings.

Now consider the goal 'nonsibling(albert,alice)'. The system attempts to satisfy the first clause for 'nonsibling', but this requires satisfying the subgoal 'sibling(albert,alice)'. Since this subgoal cannot be satisfied the system backtracks (which is allowed since we haven't reached the "cut"), and tries the second 'nonsibling' clause. This immediately succeeds, so the system correctly deduces that Alice and Albert are not siblings.

This situation is common enough that most Prolog dialects provide a 'not' predicate defined so that 'not(*C*)' succeeds if *C* fails, and vice versa. It can be defined within Prolog by means of the "cut-fail" combination and higher-order features:

```
not(C) :- call(C), !, fail.
not(C).
```

Given 'not' it is easy to define 'nonsibling':

```
nonsibling(X,Y) :- not(sibling(X,Y)).
```

That is, 'nonsibling(X,Y)' is satisfiable if 'sibling(X,Y)' is not satisfiable, and vice versa. In fact, the simplest solution is probably to dispense with the negative predicates altogether, and simply define 'can_marry' using 'not':

```
can_marry(X,Y) :- X \= Y, not(sibling(X,Y)), not(cousin(X,Y)).
```

This is certainly much more readable than our original definition. Unfortunately, 'not' contains some hidden traps.

EXERCISE 13-48: Trace the execution of the goal

```
:- can_marry(george,mary).
```

EXERCISE 13-49: Explain in detail the operation of the above definition of 'not', both when it succeeds and when it fails.

Difficulties with Negation as Unsatisfiability

Although the preceding definition of 'not' seems straightforward enough, it has some dark corners that we now explore. Consider the following goal, which enumerates all of the ways of appending two lists to get '[a,b,c,d]':

```
:- append(X,Y,[a,b,c,d]).
X = [], Y = [a,b,c,d];
X = [a], Y = [b,c,d];
X = [a,b], Y = [c,d];
X = [a,b,c], Y = [d];
X = [a,b,c,d], Y = [];
no
```

Each semicolon causes the system to backtrack and find additional variable instantiations that satisfy the goal. Now, consider the following goal:

```
:- not(not(append(X,Y,[a,b,c,d]))).
```

In logic two 'not's cancel each other, so we would expect this goal to mean the same as the original goal. This is not the case, however, as we can see by tracing the execution: The outer 'not' sets up the subgoal 'not(append(X,Y,[a,b,c,d]))', which in turn sets up the subgoal 'append(X,Y,[a,b,c,d])'. The latter we know is satisfiable by X = [] and Y = [a,b,c,d]. Since the 'append' succeeds, it causes, through the "cut-fail" combination, the failure of the inner 'not'. Now, we know that whenever a subgoal fails, we must backtrack, so any bindings made in the attempt to satisfy that subgoal are unbound. Hence, 'X' and 'Y' return to their unbound state. Finally, since the inner 'not' failed, the outer 'not' succeeds, and so the goal is satisfied, but with 'X' and 'Y' unbound! We will see something like this:

```
:- not(not(append(X,Y,[a,b,c,d]))).
X = _0, Y = _1;
no
```

Here '_0' and '_1' are symbols used by the Prolog system to indicate that the variables 'X' and 'Y' are unbound. Thus, although a double negation has no effect logically, it may have a major effect on the solutions found by a Prolog program. Once again logic has been inadequate to explain the outcome of a Prolog program. Rather, we have had to appeal to a *procedural* understanding of its execution.

What is the cause of this unintuitive behavior? We have been fooled by the name 'not' into expecting this operation to behave like logical negation. In fact, 'not' in Prolog does not mean the same thing as 'not' in logic. In Prolog 'not' means "not satisfiable." In logic there is an important difference between proving that something is false and not being able to prove that it is true. Yet, in effect, the Prolog 'not' predicate identifies these two concepts. This illustrates again how far Prolog is from logic programming.

Prolog Provides Term Equality

Notice that in the kinship program (Figure 13.1), if it weren't for the condition 'X \= Y' in the definition of 'sibling', people would be considered siblings of themselves. In fact, they would be considered their own cousins! In common usage, we say that X is a sibling of Y if X and Y have the same parents *and* X is not the same person as Y. Hence, it is our intention that 'X \= Y' mean that 'X' and 'Y' are not the same person.

What, exactly, does the predicate '\=' mean? By investigating this question we will discover some interesting issues in logic programming. Formally, not-equals can be defined in terms of equals:

```
X \= Y :- not(X = Y).
```

Thus '$X \backslash = Y$' is satisfiable just when '$X = Y$' is not satisfiable. This reduces the question of the meaning of '\=' to the meaning of '='.

There are many notions of equality. With all of these we would expect 'albert = albert' to be true, but some of the other consequences are not so obvious. For example, Leibniz' *Principle of the Identity of Indiscernibles* says that two things are identical if all of their properties are the same. This seems plausible enough: If there's no property by which the two things can be discerned, then what basis is there for the claim that there are two things? On the other hand, the principle has some surprising consequences when applied to logic programs. For example, since in our database in Figure 13.1 'cindy' and 'victor' participate in exactly the same relationships, Leibniz' principle tells us that they are identical. Similarly, 'jeffrey' and 'george' are identical.

This is clearly unsatisfactory. It is our intention that 'cindy' and 'victor' correspond to distinct persons (Cindy and Victor), who no doubt differ in many of their properties, although they happen to coincide in those properties represented in our database. Thus, Leibniz' principle, no matter what its virtues in the real world, cannot be applied in the simulated world of the computer. We need a stronger notion of equality.

There is another notion of equality, *term equality*, that is implicit in the Prolog system. We can define this equality predicate by a single fact:

```
X = X.
```

By the usual rules of unification, the above clause will be satisfied only if both its arguments are the same term. Thus, 'cindy = cindy' will unify with the above fact. On the other hand, two different terms cannot both be unified with 'X'. Hence, 'cindy = victor' will not be satisfiable. In effect, two atomic terms are equal if and only if they are denoted by the same string of characters.[15] This seems to be just what we expect. Every object mentioned in our program is distinct; each has its own identity. This is a reasonable expectation whenever we are doing *object-oriented* programming, that is, whenever the objects in the computer are simulating objects in the real world. In these situation it is natural to consider two objects to be distinct *unless* they are specified to be the same.

What about equality of compound terms? This is just a recursive extension of atomic equality. That is, two compound terms are equal if they have the same functor and the same number of arguments, and if the corresponding arguments are equal. This is in effect the 'equal' function of LISP (see Chapter 10, Section 10.1). It is a very intuitive notion of equality since terms are equal just when they're written the same way.

15 This is essentially the notion of equality of atoms used in LISP (see Section 9.3).

Other Equivalence Relations Cannot Be Defined

Term equality is not always the kind of equality that's needed. Suppose we were defining finite sets, including various operations such as membership, intersection, and union. A straightforward approach is to represent the null set by the atomic term 'empty' and nonnull sets by compound terms of the form 'adjoin(*X*,*S*)'. The intended interpretation of 'adjoin(*X*,*S*)' is $\{X\} \cup S$. Thus, the set {a,b,c} is represented by the term

```
adjoin(a,adjoin(b,adjoin(c,empty)))
```

Many of the set operations are now easy to define; for example, membership:

```
member(X,adjoin(X,S)).
member(X,adjoin(Y,S)) :- member(X,S).
```

We have to be careful, however, when we come to equality between sets.

Suppose we are implementing an inventory control program and we have a predicate 'parts(*X*,*S*)' that means that *S* is the set of parts required to build product *X*. Further suppose we need a predicate 'same_parts(*X*, *Y*)' that means that *X* and *Y* require the same set of parts. An obvious (but incorrect) way of defining 'same_parts' is:

```
same_parts(X,Y) :- parts(X,S), parts(Y,S).
```

The problem will be clearer if we write this rule in the equivalent form:

```
same_parts(X,Y) :- parts(X,S), parts(Y,T), S = T.
```

We are using *term equality* to compare the sets of parts required for *X* and *Y*. What's wrong with that?

You know that sets are considered identical if they have the same elements—regardless of the number of times elements appear or the order in which they're listed. Thus, these all are descriptions of the same set:

```
{a,b,c}, {c,a,b}, {a, b, b, c, a}
```

Analogously the following compound terms all represent the same set:

```
adjoin(a,adjoin(b,adjoin(c,empty)))
adjoin(c,adjoin(a,adjoin(b,empty)))
adjoin(a,adjoin(b,adjoin(b,adjoin(c,adjoin(a,empty)))))
```

Clearly, though, they are different terms, and so will not be considered the same under term equality. Thus, our definition of 'same_parts' will not work because it requires the sets of parts to be written in the same way; the sets of parts will be considered different if they happen to be written in a different order. Hence, the term equality test is too strong.

The obvious solution is to define a 'set_equal' predicate that explicitly axiomatizes the fact that the order of set elements doesn't matter. We use a typical axiomatization of set equality.[16] First we state that all null sets are equal:

```
set_equal(empty, empty).
```

To express the fact that element multiplicities don't matter we write:

```
set_equal(adjoin(X,adjoin(X,S)), adjoin(X,S))).
```

To express the fact that element order doesn't matter we write:

```
set_equal(adjoin(X,adjoin(Y,S)), adjoin(Y,adjoin(X,S))).
```

These are all facts; we also need rules that specify the standard properties of equivalence relations:

```
set_equal(X,X).
set_equal(X,Y) :- set_equal(Y,X).
set_equal(X,Z) :- set_equal(X,Y), set_equal(Y,Z).
```

Unfortunately, although these are perfectly correct logically, they will throw Prolog into an infinite loop. The reason is Prolog's depth-first search order; a breadth-first search, though expensive, would terminate.

In the case of sets, there is an alternative, more procedural way of defining equality (you will work it out in an exercise), but the fact remains that in Prolog one cannot generally define equivalence relations in terms of their logical properties. Again, Prolog forces us to program procedurally rather than logically.

EXERCISE 13-50: Show an example goal involving 'set_equal' that leads to an infinite loop.

EXERCISE 13-51:* If we wish to allow sets as members of sets, then the above definition of 'set_equal' is not even *logically* correct. Identify the logical problem and solve it.

16 Our set equality axioms are based on Manna and Waldinger (1985).

EXERCISE 13-52: Trace the goal

```
:- member(c,adjoin(a,adjoin(b,adjoin(c,empty)))).
```

EXERCISE 13-53: Trace the goal

```
:- member(z,adjoin(a,adjoin(b,adjoin(c,empty)))).
```

EXERCISE 13-54: Explain why we do not need a clause beginning 'member(X,empty) :- ...'.

EXERCISE 13-55: Define set intersection.

EXERCISE 13-56: Define set union.

EXERCISE 13-57: Define set difference.

EXERCISE 13-58: Define the (improper) subset predicate.

EXERCISE 13-59: Define set equality in terms of the subset predicate.

EXERCISE 13-60: Define the proper subset predicate in terms of the subset predicate and the equality predicate.

EXERCISE 13-61:* Recall our discussion of the Name and Structural Type Equivalence Rules (Chapter 5, Section 5.3). Define each in Prolog.

Difficulties with Inequality

Even term inequality is not without its difficulties. Suppose we have defined the following predicate for determining if two different individuals have the same father:

```
same_father(X,Y) :- X \= Y, father(F,X), father(F,Y).
```

Now suppose we enter the goal:

```
:- same_father(cindy,A).
no
```

The correct answer is 'A = victor'. What went wrong? To understand we have to trace our program. In this case, the goal unifies with the 'same_father' clause by the assignments X = cindy, Y = A. This sets up the subgoal 'cindy \= A'. Now recall that in most Prologs '\=' behaves as though it were defined:

```
X \= Y :- not(X = Y).
```

Thus, to satisfy 'cindy \= A' we set up the subgoal 'cindy = A'. The latter is satisfiable since 'A' is an unbound variable, and an unbound variable unifies with anything. Since 'cindy = A' succeeds, 'cindy \= A' must fail. Hence, our goal, 'same_father(cindy,A)', also must fail.

The problem is that '\=' is defined in terms of 'not' and, as we saw before, 'not' is unsatisfiability, not logical negation. Hence, we must continually remind ourselves that '\=' doesn't mean "not equal"; rather, it means "not unifiable with," which is quite a different thing.

Is there any solution to these difficulties? Some dialects of Prolog (e.g., the Marseilles Prolog II system) have attempted to solve this problem by building in a much more sophisticated notion of inequality. In effect 'cindy \= A' is retained as a *constraint* (sort of a negative variable binding) until such time as 'A' becomes bound.[17] When this occurs the term bound to 'A' can be compared with 'cindy' by term equality: If they're different terms, we continue, else we backtrack. This interpretation of inequality seems to have more intuitive behavior than that found in most Prolog systems.

EXERCISE 13-62: The necessity of having to trace one's program in order to understand it is a violation of one of our principles. Name the principle and explain the nature of the violation.

13.5 EVALUATION AND EPILOG

Logic Programs Are Self-Documenting

It is too soon to be able to evaluate logic programming; there is too little experience in its use. However, it has many promising characteristics, at least in its pure form. In this section we review these characteristics, both in the case of *pure* (Horn clause) logic programming, and in the case of the logic-oriented language Prolog.

One of the benefits of logic programming is its high level and application orientation. Since programs are described in terms of predicates and individuals

17 The actual Prolog II semantics is more complicated than this.

of the problem domain, programs are almost self-documenting. This is apparent in the kinship (Figure 13.1) and symbolic differentiation (Figure 13.2) programs. This characteristic promotes clear, rapid, accurate programming.

Pure Logic Programming Separates Logic and Control

Pure logic programming's separation of logic and control issues simplifies program development by permitting the correctness and performance of a program to be addressed as separate problems. One important result of this separation is that correctness proofs are greatly simplified because they only have to deal with the logic component of a program. It also means that programs can be optimized with confidence since changes in the control discipline cannot affect the correctness of a program.

This separation is an important application of the Orthogonality Principle. The knowledge that is used in solving a problem (the logic) is clearly separated from the way it's used (the control).

Prolog Falls Short of Logic Programming

Prolog wears its control strategy on its sleeve. Prolog programmers must be intimately aware of it in every clause they write. Indeed, many Prolog programmers go far beyond mere awareness of Prolog's control strategy, and make explicit use of its idiosyncrasies. The resulting programs have little to do with logic. On the contrary, the necessity of reasoning about the order of events as Prolog works its way forward and backward through the program rivals in difficulty the temporal reasoning required with the most imperative of programming languages.

Researchers in logic programming are well aware of the problems described above. As Clocksin and Mellish (1984) say, "Among the highest priorities of workers in this area is to develop a practical system that does not need the 'cut' and has a version of **not** that exactly corresponds to the logical notion of negation." Hence, we may hope that future logic-oriented languages will retain the efficiency of Prolog while preserving the benefits of pure logic programming.

Implementation Techniques Are Improving

Even though Prolog's deviation from pure logic programming is motivated by performance considerations, it is still far from being an efficient programming language. This characteristic limits its use to two kinds of applications: (1) those in which performance is not important and (2) those that are so complicated that they might have been unimplementable in a conventional language. Prolog is often unacceptable for the vast middle ground of moderate-sized programs with moderate performance requirements.

However, new methods of interpreting and compiling Prolog programs are being invented. Some current compilers produce code comparable in efficiency to LISP. While this still leaves a lot to be desired, it does point the way to Prolog systems whose performance will compete with conventional languages.

Prolog Is a Step Toward Nonprocedural Programming

Perhaps the most important characteristic of pure logic programs is that they are examples of nonprocedural programming. People have discussed the possibility of nonprocedural programming for many years, but pure logic programs are the first that can really lay claim to the title. Thus, they prove the possibility of nonprocedural programming.

Unfortunately Prolog falls short of this standard. Its depth-first search strategy requires programmers to think in terms of the operations that must be performed and their proper ordering in time. It can be argued that this is more difficult than in conventional languages due to Prolog's more complicated control regime. Perhaps the conclusion we may draw is that, while Prolog was a step in the right direction, there is still much important work to be done before nonprocedural programming will be practical.

EXERCISES

1*. Read and critique at least one paper from the "Proceedings of a Symposium on Very High Level Languages" (*SIGPLAN Notices* 9, 4, April 1974).
2. Implement association lists in Prolog.
3*. Define a Prolog data structure for representing Prolog programs. Write an editor for these data structures in Prolog.
4*. Does Prolog have data types? Discuss the notion of typing in Prolog.
5*. Read and critique Kowalski's "Algorithm = Logic + Control" (Kowalski, 1979).
6*. Discuss how the procedural interpretation of Prolog could be used as the basis of a Prolog implementation.
7*. Describe how pure logic programs could be executed in parallel to increase their performance. How could Prolog be modified to permit parallel execution?
8*. Suggest architectural features that could improve the performance of Prolog programs.

9*. Evaluate Prolog's syntax.

10*. Compare and contrast function-oriented programming (e.g., LISP), object-oriented programming (e.g., Smalltalk), and logic-oriented programming (e.g., Prolog).

11*. Attack or defend this statement: Prolog makes all other programming languages obsolete.

14

PRINCIPLES OF LANGUAGE DESIGN

14.1 GENERAL REMARKS

The Perfect Programming Language

It is natural to ask if there is a perfect programming language. If there is such a language, then we should strive to identify its characteristics so that we don't waste more time on imperfect languages. In this section we argue that there is not, and cannot be, such a thing as a perfect language.

What would a perfect language be? Presumably it would be a language ideally suited to all situations—for all users, for all applications, and for all computers. This seems highly unlikely; almost every artifact or tool exists in a variety of forms designed for different situations. Consider cameras. We have cameras for novices, cameras for professionals, black-and-white cameras, color cameras, high-speed cameras, manual cameras, automatic cameras, inexpensive cameras, expensive cameras, and so on. Even an artifact as simple as a shoe exists in many different designs for the various situations in which it might be used.

What leads to this diversity in all things? We can make the following general observations about the situations in which programming languages occur:

- There are many different classes of *uses* of programming languages.
- There are many different classes of *users* of programming languages.
- There are many different classes of *computers* on which programming languages can be implemented.

Each of these classes has different characteristics that dictate different designs.

Consider this analogy with aircraft: A training plane must be more tolerant than other planes of pilot error, even if this results in lower performance. A cargo plane must be able to carry a very large load, even if this requires it to fly slower. On the other hand, a fighter will have a lower cargo capacity but greater speed and maneuverability. Transcontinental planes must have a high ceiling to enable them to cross mountain ranges, and so forth.

Each class of uses, users, and computers leads to design decisions that are often inappropriate for the other classes. The diversity of situations in which programming languages are used is so great that any language that tried to accommodate all of these situations would be a poor compromise. A much better solution is to identify broad classes of similar uses, users, and computers and to create languages whose design decisions are optimized for these classes. This is depicted in the following diagram:

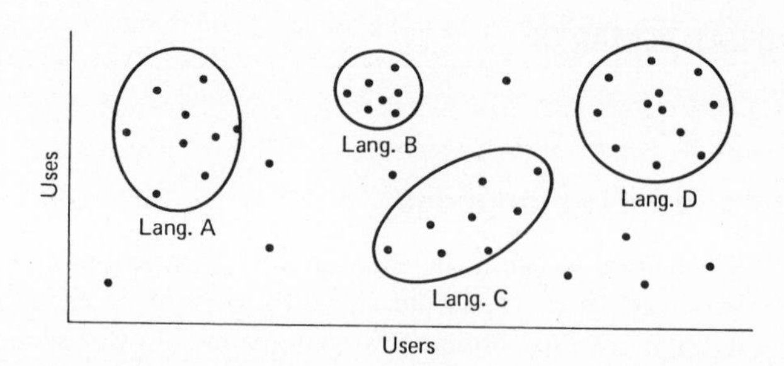

We show just two of the axes—uses and users. The points represent combinations of uses and users that frequently occur. We have drawn circles around clusters of points representing languages oriented to particular combinations of the classes. This is a better engineering approach than either extreme: designing one language to cover all points or designing a different language for each point. Of course, it is a difficult engineering problem to determine the optimal number of languages. This is particularly true since points are appearing and disappearing as computer technology evolves.

The Perfect Language Framework

The arguments we have given against the possibility of a perfect language do not preclude a perfect *language framework.* The idea of a language framework is based on the observation that although languages may differ in their details, they are often similar in their general structures. For example, a scientific programming language might have real, integer, and complex data types, extensive array handling, and many mathematical operations. A language for string processing might have character and string data types, a record data type, and pattern-matching operations. Thus, each language has sets of application-oriented data types, functions, and operators that optimize it for a particular class of uses. The choice of these application-oriented parts also affects the class of users and computers for which the language is appropriate.

Notice that the application-oriented features are embedded in a matrix of application-independent facilities, such as definite and indefinite iterators, selectors (**case**- and **if**-statements), function and procedure declarations, and blocks. These are the same in many languages regardless of the application-oriented facilities provided. They are also relatively independent of the particular characteristics of the different classes of uses, users, and computers. Such a collection of application-independent facilities is called a *language framework.*

Can there be a perfect language framework? Our previous argument does not rule this out since the framework is independent of most of the situation-specific details. Therefore, there is some hope that a small number of simple, broadly applicable facilities can be combined into a language framework that can be used as the basis for a number of more specialized languages. Some computer scientists believe that function-oriented languages similar to LISP may provide this framework. Others think that object- or logic-oriented programming is a better choice. This question remains an important research area.

EXERCISE 14-1:* Write a report defending function-, object- or logic-oriented programming as a basis for a universal language framework. As an alternative, write a report defending the thesis that there can be no universal language framework.

14.2 PRINCIPLES

"Knowing how to apply maxims cannot be reduced to, or derived from, the acceptance of those or any other maxims."

—Gilbert Ryle

In this section we collect the language design principles that have been illustrated throughout this book. Before presenting them, however, it is well to consider how they should be interpreted. For example: Are they ironclad laws, never to be violated? Do they form a mutually consistent set of language design *axioms*? Do they constitute an algorithm, or at least a set of formal constraints, for language design? The answer to all these questions is, sadly, *no*.

First, observe that these principles are not independent; some of them are corollaries of the others. For example, the Zero-One-Infinity Principle is a corollary of the Regularity Principle since one way to make a language more regular is by limiting the numbers in its design to zero, one, and infinity. Similarly, the Orthogonality Principle is a corollary of the Simplicity Principle since an orthogonal design is usually a simpler design. We have included these derivative principles because they focus on important special cases of the other principles.

These principles are sometimes contradictory; if one is satisfied, it may mean that another one or more cannot be satisfied. For example, strong typing satisfies the Security Principle but at the cost of adding to the complexity of the language (thus violating the Simplicity Principle) and adding to the overall cost of the implementation (thus violating the Localized Cost Principle). Combinations of facilities that are not very useful may result from obeying the Orthogonality Principle, but it would be a violation of the Simplicity Principle to exclude them.

How are we supposed to use a collection of nonindependent, sometimes contradictory, design principles? This is the difficult part of language design. It is also the difficult part of any engineering design process. For example, one principle of airplane design might be to minimize weight; another might be to maximize safety. Yet we must sometimes increase weight to increase safety. The trade-offs among the various goals of design, as embodied in these principles, require great sensitivity to the intended use of the artifact.

In many engineering disciplines, at least some of these trade-offs can be made *quantitatively*. In other words, we can compute how much a certain safety feature will weigh and perhaps make up for the extra weight by leaving something else out (say, a few passengers). For the most part, there are (as yet) no quantitative measures of the properties of languages. A number of computer scientists are working in this area, so we can hope that eventually at least some parts of the language design process will be quantifiable. In the meantime we must make our trade-offs on the basis of qualitative judgments according to principles such as these:

1. **Abstraction**: Avoid requiring something to be stated more than once; factor out the recurring pattern.
2. **Automation**: Automate mechanical, tedious, or error-prone activities.
3. **Defense in Depth**: Have a series of defenses so that if an error isn't caught by one, it will probably be caught by another.
4. **Information Hiding**: The language should permit modules designed so that (1) the user has all of the information needed to use the module correctly, and nothing more; and (2) the implementor has all of the information needed to implement the module correctly, and nothing more.
5. **Labeling**: Avoid arbitrary sequences more than a few items long. Do not require the user to know the absolute position of an item in a list. Instead, associate a meaningful label with each item and allow the items to occur in any order.
6. **Localized Cost**: Users should only pay for what they use; avoid distributed costs.
7. **Manifest Interface**: All interfaces should be apparent (manifest) in the syntax.
8. **Orthogonality**: Independent functions should be controlled by independent mechanisms.
9. **Portability**: Avoid features or facilities that are dependent on a particular machine or a small class of machines.
10. **Preservation of Information**: The language should allow the representation of information that the user might know and that the compiler might need.
11. **Regularity**: Regular rules, without exceptions, are easier to learn, use, describe, and implement.
12. **Security**: No program that violates the definition of the language, or its own intended structure, should escape detection.
13. **Simplicity**: A language should be as simple as possible. There should be a minimum number of concepts, with simple rules for their combination.
14. **Structure**: The static structure of the program should correspond in a simple way to the dynamic structure of the corresponding computations.
15. **Syntactic Consistency**: Similar things should look similar; different things different.
16. **Zero-One-Infinity**: The only reasonable numbers are zero, one, and infinity.

EXERCISE 14-2:* State and illustrate at least three language design principles other than those listed above. Describe a situation under which it would be desirable to violate each of your principles.

EXERCISES*

1. We have shown that certain of the principles are corollaries of certain of the other principles and that certain principles contradict other principles. Explore in detail the interrelationships of the principles, explaining which are corollaries and which are contradictories.
2. Write a report on "Beyond Programming Languages" by Terry Winograd (*Comm. ACM 22*, 7, July 1979).
3. Write a report on "The Future of Programming" by Anthony Wasserman and Steven Gutz (*Comm. ACM 25*, 3, March 1982).

4**. Design a programming language.

BIBLIOGRAPHY

American National Standards Institute (1983). *Military Standard Ada Programming Language.* ANSI/MIL-STD-1815A-1983.

Backus, J. (1978a). "The History of FORTRAN I, II, and III." *SIGPLAN Notices,* vol. 13, no. 8 (August 1978), pp. 165–180.

Backus, J. (1978b). "Can Programming be Liberated from the von Neumann Style? A Functional Style and its Algebra of Programs." *Communications of the ACM,* vol. 21, no. 8 (August 1978), pp. 613–641.

Berry, D. M. (1971). "Introduction to Oregano." *SIGPLAN Notices,* vol. 6, no. 2 (February 1971), pp. 171–190.

Clocksin, W.F., and Mellish, C.S. (1984). *Programming in Prolog,* Second Edition. Springer-Verlag, 1984.

Cohen, J. (1981). "Garbage Collection of Linked Data Structures." *ACM Computing Surveys,* vol. 13, no. 3 (September 1981), pp. 341–367.

DeRemer, F. and Kron, H. (1976). "Programming-in-the-Large Versus Programming-in-the-Small." *IEEE Trans. on Software Eng. SE-2* (June 1975), pp. 80–86.

Dijkstra, E.W. (1968). "Go To Statement Considered Harmful." *Communications of the ACM,* vol. 11, no. 3 (March 1968), pp. 147–148.

Goldberg, A. (1984). *Smalltalk-80: The Interactive Programming Environment.* Addison-Wesley, 1984.

Goldberg, A., and Robson, D. (1983). *Smalltalk-80: The Language and its Implementation.* Addison-Wesley, 1983.

International Standards Organization (1982). *Specification for Computer Programming Language Pascal.* ISO 7185-1982, 1982.

Jensen, K., Wirth, N., Mickel, A.B., and Miner, J.F. (1985). *Pascal User Manual and Report.* third edition, Springer-Verlag, 1985.

Johnston, J.B. (1971). "The Contour Model of Block Structured Processes." *SIGPLAN Notices,* vol. 6, no. 2 (June 1971), pp. 55–82.

Kowalski, R. (1979). "Algorithm = Logic + Control." *Communications of the ACM,* vol. 22, no. 7 (July 1979), pp. 424–436.

Manna, Z., and Waldinger, R. (1985). *The Logical Basis for Computer Programming.* Addison-Wesley, 1985.

McCarthy, J. (1960). "Recursive Functions of Symbolic Expressions and Their Computation by Machine." *Communications of the ACM,* vol. 3, no. 4 (April 1960), pp. 184–195.

McCarthy, J. (1978). "History of LISP." *SIGPLAN Notices,* vol. 13, no. 8 (August 1978), pp. 217–223.

Naur, P. (1978). "The European Side of the Last Phase of the Development of Algol 60." *SIGPLAN Notices,* vol. 13, no. 8 (August 1978), pp. 15–44.

Perlis, A.J. (1978). "The American Side of the Development of Algol." *SIGPLAN Notices,* vol. 13, no. 8 (August 1978), pp. 3–14.

Steele, G. L., Jr. (1984). *Common LISP: The Language.* Digital Press, 1984.

United States Department of Defense (1980). *Reference Manual for the Ada Programming Language,* July 1980.

Wirth, N. (1971). "The Programming Language Pascal." *Acta Informatica,* vol. 1 (1971), pp. 35–63.

Wirth, N. (1975). "An Assessment of the Programming Language Pascal." *SIGPLAN Notices,* vol. 10, no. 6 (June 1975), pp. 23–30.

Wulf, W., and Shaw, M. (1973). "Global Variable Considered Harmful." *SIGPLAN Notices,* vol. 8, no. 2 (February 1973), pp. 28–34.

INDEX